D1144445

SEVENTEENTH-CENTURY POLITICAL AND FINANCIAL PAPERS

CAMDEN MISCELLANY
XXXIII

SEVENTEENTH-CENTURY POLITICAL AND FINANCIAL PAPERS

CAMDEN MISCELLANY XXXIII

CAMDEN FIFTH SERIES
Volume 7

CAMBRIDGE
UNIVERSITY PRESS

FOR THE ROYAL HISTORICAL SOCIETY
University College London, Gower Street, London WC1E 6BT

Published by the Press Syndicate of the University of Cambridge
The Pitt Building, Trumpington Street, Cambridge CB2 1RP
40 West 20th Street, New York, NY 10011–4211, USA
10 Stamford Road, Oakleigh, Melbourne 3166, Australia

First published 1996

A catalogue record for this book is available from the British Library

Library of Congress cataloguing in publication data applied for

ISBN 0 521 57395 5 hardback

SUBSCRIPTIONS. The serial publications of the Royal Historical Society, *Royal Historical Society Transactions* (ISSN 0080–4401), Camden Fifth Series (ISSN 0960–1163) volumes and volumes of the Guides and Handbooks (ISSN 0080–4398) may be purchased together on annual subscription. The 1996 subscription price (which includes postage but not VAT) is £35 (US$56 in the USA, Canada and Mexico) and includes Camden Fifth Series, volumes 7 and 8 (published in July and December) and Transactions Sixth Series, volume 6 (published in December). There is no volume in the Guides and Handbooks series in 1996. Japanese prices (including ASP delivery) are available from Kinokuniya Company Ltd, P.O. Box 55, Chitose, Tokyo 156, Japan, EU subscribers (outside the UK) who are not registered for VAT should add VAT at their country's rate. VAT registered subscribers should provide their VAT registration number.

Subscription orders, which must be accompanied by payment, may be sent to a bookseller, subscription agent or direct to the publisher: Cambridge University Press, The Edinburgh Building, Shaftesbury Road, Cambridge CB2 2RU, UK; or in the USA, Canada and Mexico: Cambridge University Press, 40 West 20th Street, New York, NY 10011–4211, USA. Copies of the publications for subscribers in the USA, Canada and Mexico are sent by air to New York to arrive with minimum delay.

SINGLE VOLUMES AND BACK VOLUMES. A list of Royal Historical Society volumes available from Cambridge University Press may be obtained from the Humanities Marketing Department at the address above.

Printed and bound in Great Britain by Butler & Tanner Ltd, Frome and London

CONTENTS

I
The Parliamentary Papers of Nicholas Ferrar 1624

Edited by David R. Ransome

CONTENTS

ACKNOWLEDGEMENTS

The parliamentary papers of Nicholas Ferrar are here reproduced by permission of the Librarian of the University of Sheffield and by permission of the Master and Fellows of Magdalene College, Cambridge. At Sheffield the editor gratefully received help from Tim Raylor, now of Carleton College, Minnesota, and Mark Greengrass; at Magdalene he benefited from the advice and help of Richard Luckett, Mary Coleman, and Aude FitzSimon. For the right to consult typescripts of other diaries of the parliament of 1624 and for her advice and comments, he thanks Maija Jansson, the Executive Editor at the Yale Center for Parliamentary History. He is also grateful to Andrew Thrush and his colleagues at the History of Parliament Trust for their welcome counsel, information, and access to unpublished materials. As always, the staffs of the British Library and the Public Record Office at Chancery Lane have cheerfully given their assistance. Alison and David Quinn, Joel and Karen Ordahl Kupperman, and especially Joyce Olson Ransome, have provided suggestions and encouragement; the editor thanks them all.

INTRODUCTION

Nicholas Ferrar's fame in the twentieth century rests largely upon religious foundations – as a saint of the Church of England and as one of the moving spirits at Little Gidding – but in fact his historical importance is more than merely religious, and indeed religion did not dominate his life before 1625. Born in London in February 1593, the youngest but one of a family of six,[1] Nicholas was named for his father, a highly successful Merchant Adventurer who was also a Master of the Skinners Company. Small, fair-haired, precocious and frail, Nicholas was always his mother's favourite, and it was she who largely influenced his development. At the age of seventeen he was a Fellow of Clare College, Cambridge, but soon after his twentieth birthday he left Cambridge for the sake of his health, spending the years 1613–17 on the continent, chiefly at Padua, where he studied medicine. On his return to England he did not resume his fellowship at Clare,[2] but remained in London with his parents, attending to his now elderly father's business affairs – which included membership of the East India and Virginia Companies – and acting as his executor upon his death in 1620.

The Virginia Company of London, which had been chartered in 1606 and re-chartered in 1609 and 1612, was controlled until 1619 by its first Treasurer, that is to say Governor, Sir Thomas Smith. He was, however, displaced in April of that year by his Assistant, Sir Edwin Sandys, at the same time as Smith's son-in-law, Alderman Robert Johnson, was replaced as Deputy by Nicholas Ferrar's elder brother John. Under these new managers, with Sandys devising policy and John Ferrar responsible for its daily implementation, Nicholas took an increasing part in the administration of the company. In June 1619 he sat on an ad hoc committee, a year later he joined the permanent committee which advised the company's London council, on 2 May 1621 he was named to the council itself, and on 22 May 1622 he succeeded his brother John as Deputy.[3] This last advancement resulted from the terms of the company's charter, which permitted the Deputy to hold office for three years but without possibility of re-election. The

---

[1] In all there were nine children, but three died before Nicholas's birth. A daughter followed by five sons survived to reach the age of 21.

[2] He did not, however, resign it until 1631.

[3] S. M. Kingsbury, *The Records of the Virginia Company of London*, 1906–35, i. 222–3, 386, 467, 473; ii. 29.

Treasurer, on the other hand, was elected annually with no limitation on his terms of office. In 1620 nevertheless Sandys found his re-election blocked by the king. The company, perforce, accepted the king's veto but in retaliation rejected all the king's nominees for the office and chose instead someone in sympathy with Sir Edwin's policies. This person was the earl of Southampton, who was re-elected three times and held office until the dissolution of the company. In furtherance of the company's interests the earl twice provided his deputy with a parliamentary seat at Lymington, Hampshire. In 1621 John Ferrar chose to sit for Tamworth, where he had also been chosen,[4] but in 1624 Nicholas accepted the seat at Lymington, taking a more active part in parliamentary affairs than his brother had apparently done in 1621.

Nicholas's parliamentary papers – a diary, the text of two speeches, and the drafts of several petitions – have hitherto lain unnoticed among the Ferrar Papers which the family accumulated over five generations.[5] The earliest items belonged to old Nicholas and passed to his sons John and Nicholas, who added to them the archive of the Virginia Company of London, and in 1625 took them to Huntingdonshire when they moved to Little Gidding. For a century and a quarter the collection grew – somewhat haphazardly and not without losses – as it passed, after Nicholas's and John's deaths in 1637 and 1657, to John's son, grandsons, and great-grandchildren, but with the death of Judith (Ferrar) Horne in 1749 the direct descent ended. Strictly the papers should have gone to her cousin, a penniless army pensioner, and indeed they may have done so briefly, but by the end of the 1750s they were in the hands of another cousin, Edward Ferrar, a lawyer of Huntingdon. Having no sons, Edward bequeathed the papers in 1769 to his son-in-law, the Reverend Peter Peckard, who in 1781 became the Master of Magdalene College, Cambridge. Peckard died in 1797, and his wife in 1805. Since they were childless, the papers, with other property, were left to the college, where they remain, and it is by permission of the Master and Fellows of Magdalene College that items from the collection are reproduced below.[6]

Although the papers were used by nineteenth-century historians, chiefly to illumine the life of Nicholas Ferrar at Little Gidding, they were not fully sorted and described until the twentieth century: by Alan

---

[4] His patron at Tamworth was Lord Paget, another member of the Virginia Company's London council.

[5] In addition another item, annotated by Sir Nathaniel Rich, passed into the possession of the Mandeville Commission, and thus into the Manchester Papers. For this item, see below.

[6] A microfilm edition of the Ferrar Papers, with an introduction and handlist by D. R. Ransome, was published by Microfilm Academic Publishers of Wakefield in 1992.

Maycock in the 1930s, by Noel Malcolm in 1979, and by David Ransome in 1989–90. It was on the last occasion that the three fragments of Nicholas Ferrar's parliamentary diary for 1624 were re-united and identified. Had the diary survived in its entirety, it would have equalled in scale any other which we have for that parliament. Even in its truncated condition it is of an unmatched narrative vividness. Comprising 43 unnumbered folios, it now provides only a list of the members of parliament originally returned and an incomplete account of events for the first month of the parliament, ending on 8 March 1624.[7]

The diary is a fair copy of Ferrar's original notes, written by Tristram Conyam, a clerk often employed by the Ferrars on Virginia Company business. At times he could not read Ferrar's hand and left blanks, which Ferrar sometimes filled later. (Ferrar's insertions are indicated by the use of bold type). But since Ferrar's original notes for the morning of 5 March have also survived,[8] Conyam's accuracy can be checked. As will be seen below, he was remarkably successful in reading Ferrar's dashingly fluid hand. Proper names, especially foreign proper names, sometimes defeated him, but instead of guessing Conyam was usually content to leave honest blanks.[9] Furthermore it is also possible to test the accuracy of Ferrar's memory. In reporting the progress of the Spanish Match as related by the Duke of Buckingham and others, Ferrar gives the gist of various diplomatic letters which were cited by the speakers. These documents are now in the Public Record Office and they reveal not only that they were annotated for use in the debates of 1624 but that Ferrar's reporting of them was all but word-perfect.

After an initial concern with the collapse of the Spanish marriage, the 1624 Parliament in April turned its attention to the woes of the Virginia Company and an attack on Lionel Cranfield, earl of Middlesex

---

[7] Ferrar Papers 1433 is entitled [f.1r] 'Passages in the Parliament/1623'. It then lists [ff.1v–5v], by English counties alphabetically followed by the Welsh constituencies, the members of the House of Commons as originally returned. Since this list, amended to take account of later returns, is available in *Return of Members* (1878), pp. 456–62, it is not reproduced below.

The first of the diary's three fragments [ff.1–6] opens with the list of members, continues with the events of 12–19 February 1623/4, and ends while the king is making his opening speech. The second fragment [ff.7–22] begins on Saturday 21 February with the presentation of the Speaker to the king and continues until the afternoon of Tuesday 24 February. The third [ff.23–43] recounts events on Monday and Tuesday 1 and 2 March, and after three blank pages in the manuscript [ff.30v–31v] runs from Thursday 4 March to the morning of Monday 8 March, breaking off in mid-sentence. The final pages [ff.42–43] record King James's reply at Theobalds on 5 March to a parliamentary delegation of both houses.

[8] Ferrar Papers 1584c.

[9] When possible these blanks have been filled from other parliamentary diaries, a list of which appears as Appendix 1.

and Lord Treasurer. The latter was unleashed on the afternoon of 28 April 1624 before a Committee meeting in the Star Chamber, and was inaugurated by a quartet of speeches made by Nicholas Ferrar, Lord Cavendish, Sir Edwin Sandys, and Sir John Danvers, all four of whom were, not uncoincidentally, members of the London council of the Virginia Company. That very morning the Quarter Court of the company had authorised the four men to speak on the company's behalf.[10] Two copies of Ferrar's speech survive: one, time-damaged, is in the Ferrar Papers;[11] the other, unmutilated and all but identical, is among the Hartlib Papers in the University of Sheffield.[12] Nothing indicates how it came to Hartlib, but he and John Ferrar were corresponding in the 1650s,[13] and in all probability Ferrar sent this Virginia Company document to Hartlib. In addition, the Ferrar Papers contain part of Lord Cavendish's speech, perhaps – from their format – the very notes from which he spoke.[14]

The last component of Ferrar's parliamentary papers are six petitions[15] deriving from the Committee for Trade, of which Sir Edwin Sandys was chairman. Edward Nicholas noted in his parliamentary diary on 19 May 1624 that at Sir Edwin's request the House ordered Nicholas Ferrar to aid Sandys in drawing up the petitions to the king concerning trade. Indeed Sandys, who was still in de facto control of the Virginia company, employed not only Ferrar, the company's Deputy, but Edward Collingwood, the company's Secretary. The draft petitions were written by one or other of the two men, and indeed in one petition the two men alternate in copying paragraphs.[16] Some of the petitions, moreover, are endorsed by Tristram Conyam, the clerk whom Ferrar used not only to fair copy his diary but also to make the Ferrar Papers copy of his speech against Cranfield.

Nor are these clerical efforts the whole extent of the Virginia Company's involvement in the Parliament of 1624. Sandys, Ferrar, Lord Cavendish, and Danvers, all councillors of the Virginia Company, spoke against Cranfield in the Star Chamber on 28 April; and the Treasurer, Southampton, not only brought about the Deputy's election at Lymington, but secured the election of three other members of the

[10] Kingsbury, ii. 537–8.
[11] Ferrar Papers 1589.
[12] Sheffield University, Hartlib MS 61/2. The version given below appears by permission of the Librarian of Sheffield University. The photographic copy of the original was obtained with the aid of the university's Hartlib Papers Project; the editor is particularly grateful to Mark Greengrass and Tim Raylor for their help.
[13] See, for example, John Ferrar's letter of 28 November 1653 to Hartlib, printed in *The Reformed Virginia Silkworm* of 1655.
[14] Ferrar Papers 1576b.
[15] Ferrar Papers 1397a; 1397c; 484d; 484e; 484a & b & c: 1628a & b.
[16] Ferrar Papers 484c.

company's London council as well as two freemen of the company (and two Wriothesleys): at Newport, Newtown and Yarmouth on the Isle of Wight, and at Lymington, Southampton and Winchester on the mainland, all very much within his Hampshire sphere of influence.[17]

Finally, there is item 371 of the Manchester Papers.[18] Compiled by Nicholas Ferrar, it is usually described, following the endorsement, as a list of MPs who were also freemen of the Virginia Company. In fact it is more accurately described by the heading Ferrar gave it: 'The names of divers Knights Cittizens and Burgesses of the Lower house of Commons that are Adventurers and free of the Virginia Compagny and yett have not had [any parte *erased*] nor followde the buissines for sundry yeares'. Miss Kingsbury hesitantly dated this document 'May(?), 1623', but it belongs rather to April, or perhaps May, 1624. Ferrar listed 52 MPs in all.[19] Of the 52, company records confirm that 41 were freemen; one (James Lord Wriothesley) was the son of the Treasurer, Lord Southampton; the membership of five cannot be confirmed, but three were probably the heirs of men known to have been freemen. On second thoughts Ferrar crossed out two of the 52, apparently crossing out one of them,[20] who was certainly a freeman, because he took an active part in company affairs. At the end of the list Ferrar admitted that it was incomplete, adding the saving phrase: 'with divers others which wee cannot upon a sudden set doune.' He was right to signal the partial nature of the list of freemen, together with one who was the son of a freeman, and seven others whose names are those of freemen but not distinctive enough to be sure that they were both MPs and freemen. In addition another 50 or so MPs may well have been heirs or close kinsmen of freemen of the company. The existence of so many in the Commons of 1624 offers one reason why the attack on Cranfield developed as it did. It also throws into greater prominence the role of Virginia Company affairs in this parliament, and suggests the need for a more complex assessment of alignments in this parliament than hitherto.[21]

[17] The other councillors besides Ferrar were Christopher Brooke (Newport, IoW), Sir John Danvers (Newport, IoW), John More (Lymington); the freemen, Thomas Bond (Southampton) and George Garrett or Gerard (Newtown, IoW); the kinsmen, his son and heir, James Lord Wriothesley (Winchester) and Thomas Wriothesley (Yarmouth, IoW).

[18] Kingsbury, iv. 157. Before their sale in New York city, the Manchester Papers were microfilmed and a copy of the film was deposited in the British Library: B.L. microfilm RP 420. It is this microfilm that the editor consulted.

[19] And began a 53rd but crossed out after writing only 'Mr Art'.

[20] Sir Arthur Harris.

[21] See, for example, Thomas Cogswell, *The Blessed Revolution: English Politics and the Coming of War, 1621–1624* (1989), which all but ignores the Virginian dimension in the politics of 1624.

EDITORIAL CONVENTIONS

Abbreviations:
Conventional abbreviations with the exception of 'ye' for 'the', have been silently extended. Precedents are however, cited in the original form.

Spelling:
Original spelling has been retained save that initial 'ff' appears as 'F'. For ease of reading, letters have occasionally been added to words in square brackets.

Punctuation:
The punctuation and paragraphing created by Ferrar's clerk Conyam has been retained. It has, however, been supplemented by editorial additions in square brackets.

Italicisation
Conyam indicated by a change of handwriting where italics were desired. Such words and phrases are here indicated by italics.

Quotations:
No attempt has been made to identify biblical quotations or to translate those in other languages.

Pagination:
The manuscript has no seventeenth-century pagination or foliation. The modern foliation, added when the fragments of the manuscript were reassembled, is indicated in the text. Catchwords are given only where they differ from the first word on the next page.

Editorial insertions:
Ferrar and Conyam both left gaps in the manuscript. Wherever possible these have been filled, the additions appearing within square brackets. The source is usually one or other of the 1624 parliamentary diaries which are listed in Appendix I. Where no source for the insertion is offered, the reader should understand that the editor has supplied the missing word from the context.

In many cases Conyam reinforced the final full stop of a paragraph with a slash. In this transcription such slashes have been deleted.

i

Nicholas Ferrar's Diary, 12 February–8 March
1623/4

[F.6r] Concerning the Passadges in the Parliament Anno 1623

The Parliament was Summoned against the 12th of February beinge Thursdaie which fell out to be a bitter morninge Snowinge continually.

I was sworne before Secretarie Calvert & the Lord Cavendish.

On Thursday the Lords prorouged the Parliament till munday the 16th of February.

On Munday morninge divers of the Lords being com to Whitehall to ride with the Kinge. the suddaine death of ye Duke of Lennox[1] hindred, soe itt was prorouged againe till ye Thursday followinge.

Upon Twesdaie the Kinge heard the Sommer Islands buisines, & ordered that Sir Thomas Smith should be Governor, & mr Edwards Deputy till next Quarter Court when hee promised wee should have a Free Eleccion.

On Wednesday the Kinge gave Marques Hambleton[2] ye Staffe of Stewardshipp not onely for this present necessitie of Parliament for the better Goverment of his house, soe that itt is supposed his Comission is as the former was during his life, he added withall that hee thought noe man soe fitt or able to performe ye place, as the Marques was but onely hee that was dead.

The Lord Steward gave a Comission to 14: to give the Oath to the Burgesses whereof the Lord Cavendish was the First.

On Thursday the Kinge rid to the Parliament in a Chariott drawne with Six black horses; The Prince on horseback –

The weather was faire –

Whilste hee was in the Abby hearinge the Sermon, ther was by the fall of a little plaister in the paynted Chamber such a feare as some cryed Treason. and Traytours and a great confusion grew theron, as some lost cloaks and Hatts, and one of the Guard lefte his Holbert and went away.

The [Bishop of Exeter[3]] made the Sermon in ye Abby Church

The Kings speech was to this purpose.

---

[1] The Lord Steward.
[2] James Hamilton, 2nd Marquis of Hamilton.
[3] Valentine Cary: *Letters of John Chamberlain* (Philadelphia, 1939), ii.546.

That hee was like the Husband and his people ye wife and as Christ loved this Church, soe a Husband ought to love his wife, And if there were any matter of discontent to seeke reconciliacon.

The love of a Kinge to his people could not be shewed butt by two waies:

The Constant Goverment of them &

The Love and respect unto ye representative body ye Parliament.

[f.6v]   For the first, hee could answere itt to God and ye worlde that all his endeavours and desires were for their good; although perhapps some errors had passed in Actions, butt against his will.

For the Second poynte a Kinge shews his love in every Parliament butt hee would now shew itt in an extraordinary manner by the especiall trust that he would committ unto them uppon the most weightie Affayres that ever were treated of; For accordinge to the writt that Summons them to consult of the weightie affayres of the Kingdome hee would give them a Free consultacion uppon all his treaties, and concerninge ye settlinge of his Childrens estate, wheruppon all ye peoples welfare & safety depended.

Hee had for divers years treated with a single Intencion for ye Common good of Christendome and the particularities of this King-dome, hopinge the same affeccions had been in others, and soe their words were, butt the success was allwaies contrary.

Now because delay was daungerous the Prince made request unto him that hee might goe that great Voyadge to see how his owne presence might worke, hee yeilded, and comaunded Buckenham the man whome he most trusted to goe along with him and not to leave him till hee brought him back againe.

Although this was a hard matter for him to graunt being a Father yett he did itt and the good effects therof hee saw had taught him a poynte of wisedome, that **Dolus versatur in universalibus** [NF] they have great good words but when they should com to ye particulars all is as farr off as at the begininge, and although hee had very lately had greater and more certaine Offers then formerlie yett he ment to referr all to them and from his Secretarie they should shortlie understand the wholl passadges according to ye Prince & Buckenhams Relation, And soe they should consider & deliberate *Super totam materiam* assuringe them that itt was and should be brought unto them as *Res integra*.

But hee was to be not onely a good Husband butt a good Hus-bandman, who doth not onely plante good Plantes butt weede upp ye weedes that would else destroy the good Plantes, and ye only ill weede was Jealousy, for as for his Actions he coulde answer them with the face of a Christian Prince before God and his Angells, but for iudginge of his intenciones hee would have them to iudge of them, protestinge that the cheife of all his cares and intencions was *Religion* and *Salus Populi*, & although some might suspect him to have been of late Colde on the matter of Religion, yett itt was nothinge soe hee did indeed thinke fitt like a good horseman not allwaies to use the Spurr butt sometimes the brydle, and some times to holde itt hard and sometimes slack, the execucion of the penall Statute.

[catchword: good][4]

[f.7r]   Satterday in the afternoone the 21th of February 1623

The Kinge beinge sett in ye Upper house mr Speaker[5] was admitted and goinge to the Barr after some pause hee spake to this effect.

Most Sacred Majestie

The Knights, Cittizens and Burgesses assembled by your Majesties Writts in the Lower house of Parliament the representative Body of your Commons beinge accordinge to their Custome to make choyse of a Speaker neglectinge many tall Coedars in their house have made choyse of mee the lowest Shrubb, And although I sought earnestly to avoyde itt, alleadginge both my personall weaknes, and other insuffi-tienties best knowne to my selfe, and yett not unknowne to them, yett not beinge able to prevaile; I com now an humble Supplyant appealing[6] unto the Throne of your Sacred Majestie beseechinge you to release mee and to direct them to make a new choyce of some more worthy personn, able and meet to performe soe great a service:

The Lord Keeper[7] haveing first spoken with the Kinge made Answere to this Effect.

What Plato said of Gorgius That in his declayminge against Rhet-oricians, hee had shewed himselfe to be the greatest of Retoricians his Majestie now saide of him that in seekeinge soe to avoyde the Office of Speaker hee had shewed himselfe most worthy to be Speaker, and did exceedinglie comend and approve the choyce of the house takinge itt for a good [omen[8]] that in ye begininge they had done soe well,

---

[4] For the rest of this speech see, e.g., *Nicholas* or BL, Harleian MS 159 ff.11v–12v. For the Lord Keeper's charge to the Commons to choose a Speaker: ibid., ff.12v–13.
[5] Sir Thomas Crew.
[6] First written as 'according'.
[7] John Williams, Bishop of Lincoln.
[8] BL, Harl.MS 159 f.13v.

wherfore hee said ther was noe reply her[e]in farther to be made, *Exivit verbum ex ore Regis* the old Parliament word *Le Roy Vivit*.[9]

Then Mr Speaker beganne a[10] longe speech to this effect

Most Sacred Majestie

Since I can present noe Olive branches of intersession that may be avayleable to decline this Office I must with patience sett my selfe to performe itt; This is noe small comforte that I never sought itt, butt itt beinge by the Free choyce of the House putt uppon mee & now confirmed by your Majestie I cannot butt acknowledge itt to be the worke of God, that hath the heartes of Kings in his handes, and *impellit quoqunque Vult*: Wherfore I doe [f.7v]   most humbly submitt my selfe haveinge learned in ye best booke *Obedience is better then Sacrifice* and with an Ancient fatherly *Domine da quod iubes, et iube quod Vis*, beseechinge you to stretch forth the Scepter of your grace in a continuall good acceptance of my endeavours in this service

Then he spake of the Kinge callinge him *Princeps hereditarius*. The ofspringe of those famous Princes that had united the Two Roses, butt hee by a farr more admirable coniunction had united both Kingdomes; And wheruppon the death of Queene Elizabeth ther hunge such a cloude of daunger over our heads, as all other Nations stood expectinge our utter Ruyne, his happy and blessed Cominge in preserved all, beinge received by us with such ioy as could not be expressed, they spread their garments to entertaine him and received him not soe much into the Gates of their Citties as of their heartes, and of his blessed cominge to the Crowne hee might truely say what the Poet did [*Mira cano, sol occubuit nox nulla sequuta est*[11]]

And then he made prayer for the Kings longe and prosperous Raigne and the Princes after him.

Then he comended his good Government especiallie his mayntenance of Religion, for which God had soe blessed him protectinge him from his enimies both abrode and att home, as from divers wicked con-spiracies soe especially from the Exicrable Powder Plott, which was to have been his execucion in that place; Besides hee remembred the great peace and happiness in these times of his Raigne, which thinges hee saide hee did remember to give thankes to God from whence those greate mercies came: *For it is a good thinge to give thanks unto the Lord and*

---

[9] Conyam has here misinterpreted Ferrar's hand. Ferrar no doubt wrote *Le Roy le Veut*.
[10] 'lardge' erased; according to J. Hacket, *Scrinia Reserata...*, 1693, Pt I p. 176, the speech lasted 'about the time of half an Hour'.
[11] BL, Harl. MS 159 f.14.

declare his wonders in the Congregatione. And added farther that the thankfull acknowledgment to God of a benifitt received is a[sic] invitacion of a new.

Next hee saide concerninge the present Occasion, ye Parliament, hee thought fitt to remember Three severall Parliaments, one in the latter end of Kinge Henry ye 8th called *Parliamentum Doctum*, because of the many good Lawes and Orders made therin especially for idle personnes And the Second in the 30: of Eliz: called *Pium* by a grave Bishop because itt provided soe especially for charitable works wherof, one principall was that itt might be lawfull for any man without a [licence[12]] to endow any Hospitall to ye Rent of 200 li per Annum.

[f.8r] Butt these thinges were not absolutely enacted for ever but uppon probacion, which beinge now passed soe longe & found soe good, and proffitable hee desyred they might now & together with them those other good matters which the last Parliament (which hee called [?*gratiosum*][13]) endeavour the providinge against *Promoters and Informers*, the abolishinge of divers *Monopolies*; And Lastlie the Bill of grace & Pardon by which meanes itt would com to passe thatt *Mercie* and *Trueth* would com together, and *Righteousnes* and *Peace* kisse each other; Soe that this might have the name of *Parliamentum Felix*, and make amendes for those other unhappy meetinges of late, To which intent hee prayed God that the Greatness and Waightiness of the present Occasiones might inclyne their myndes to the settlinge of them, and that all former passadges might be forgotten, and a Law of Oblivion of all discontents and jealousies, This clause hee ended with *Quam bonum et iucundum est Regem et Populum Convenire in Unum*.

Then hee spake in the comendacion of the excellencie & benefitt of ye Common Law, and for the Kings Prerogative hee saide itt was in his hand [a septer of gould[14]] butt beinge putt in others, it was *Virga ferrea*, to ruyne & breake all.

Next touchinge supply of monney, which Princes extraordinary occasions doe require, hee saide that all other wayes butt that of Parliament was grievous, and those given by Parliament however hard and high yett cheerfully paide, because that everie man hadd his voyce in the bestowinge of them, and every mans purse helps ther unto in an equall proporcion, all other contribucions though small in them selves yett very greevous to the people, and little or nothinge beneficiall to the Prince, especially in regard of the great damadge in their affeccions, for howsoever they were called they were nothinge lesse then *Benevolencies* –

---

[12] See 39 Eliz. I c. 5: An Act for erecting of Hospitals...; Conyam has misread Ferrar's '39' as '30'.
[13] See BL, Harl. MS 159 f.16v: the Lord Keeper's speech.
[14] Ibid., f.14v.

Next he commended the Kinge for his care of Religion ye greatest of all blessings, and he said God had likewise extraordinarilie blessed him, therfore as in all other thinges soe especially in the perfect obedience of his Subiects [f.8v] For those Princes which teach their Subiects to obey God God teaches their Subiects to obey them, Butt of late that accursed Generation of Preists and Jesuites that w[ere w]ont formerlie to live in darknes now came openlie into the light, Soe as like the Frogs in Egipt they had allmost covered the face of the Earth and heere he intimated the suppression of them.

Next hee spake touchinge the miserable estate of the Lady Elizabeth and her children whose dowrie and Inheritance ought of althings First to be recovered from ye hands of theire cruell enymies who with soe much vyolence & crueltie had dispossessed them, And this cause was to be tender unto us, not onely for their allyance & affinitie sake butt even for the remembrance of those Antient kindenesses which our Nation had received in the cruell time of persecution heere in England; That country haveinge beene not onely a saffe Harbour for them but where they received many kindenesses, and this poynte hee concluded, That as Cato was wont to say when hee gave his vote in Senate *Sic Censeo et Carthaginem esse evertendam*, soe hee for his parte to everie Act of Parliament would say *Sic Censeo et Palatinatum esse redimendum*.

Next hee spake concerninge the Navy which was the Tower and Bullwark of this kingdome wherof the Sea was the Walls and therin hee comended ye Kings extraordinary care and provisions –

Then hee spake touchinge the late reformacion of Ireland *Quorum pars* [*?impar fui(t)*] and therin hee shewed his Majesties great wis[?dome an]d care in settlinge Justice removeall of greev[?ances &c] He allsoe declared his exceedinge Pyetie in the liberall Endowment of the Bishopricks and other Church lyvings out of his owne proper demaynes.

Lastly hee concluded that the Knights Cittizens & Burgesses did humbly desire his Majestie for his gracious confirmacion of their Antient Pryveledges; First that their personnes goods and servants might be Free from Arest, [f.9r] Secondly, That they might have libertie of speech in ye house which hee doubted not they would use with all due modestie and obedience; Thirdly and that uppon their urgent Occasions they might have free access unto his Royall presence as hee shoulde thinke fitt; And Lastly a favourable interpretacion both duringe the sittinge, And after of all their Actions, And soe ended his speech.

Which done the Lord Keeper and ye Kinge spake together allmost a quarter of an hower;

And then the Lord Keeper spake to this effect.[15]

---

[15] For this speech, see also Hacket Pt I pp. 176–79.

His Majestie Mr Speaker hath not onely with great Patience butt approbacion heard your long speech and comaundeth mee to give answer which I shall doe, not accordinge to ye severall braunches of your speech which beinge soe longe & continued were difficult, and besides I doubt[,] if I should take in sunder the Frame of your speech[,] I should not soe concinly sett itt together againe, Butt haveing observed certaine generall heads whereunto your speech may be reduced –

First of your selfe

Next of his Majestie:

Then touching some Parliaments and some late abortions of Parliament.

Then you have spoke in comendacions of ye Common Lawe

Of the nature of Benevolencies

Of the Care of Religion

The recoverie of ye Palatinate.

The Provisions of ye Navy. & ye

Reformation of Ireland.

And lastly you have made 4 severall Peticions.

[f.9v]   1: That your person and your servants may be free to come to the house

2   That you may have libertie of speech in ye House –

3   That you may have access to his Majestie uppon ye important occasions of ye house –

4   And Lastly that you may have a benigne Interpretacion out of the house –

These beinge the heads of your speech I shall make answer therunto –

For the First your selfe his Majestie doth not only stretch forth his Scepter of grace but with Ashuerus[16] maketh answere *fiat tibi secundum tuam Petitione[m]* – Assuringe you most graciously that his Royall favour and good acceptacion of your faythfull services shall goe alonge duringe the wholl time of your imployment & afterwards.

For the acknowledgment of his Majesties Royall generacion and the great blessings wee enioy under him, together with ye greate & miraculous preservacions.

For the Parliament which you have remembred. His Majesties Intencion is not onely to confirme these butt what ever other thinges shalbe found for ye publique good, And particularly for matter of grace in Bills of Pardon His Royall intencion is that itt shalbe like himselfe, Soe that itt shall deserve the names of *Parliamentum Manificum.*[17]

As for those late Aborcions of Parliament, *Quamquam animus meminisse horet laetuque refugit,* They have made the name of a Parlyament to be

---

[16] King Ahasuerus, in *The Book of Esther.*

[17] Did Ferrar write 'magnificum' or 'munificum'?

the significacion of a Monster. or Chimera haveinge brought forth nothinge but that which itt least should *Discontent and Jealousi*, butt a Parliament ought to be ye cause of good effects; The first Parliament that ever was betweene God the Father Sonne and Holy Ghost brought forth all Entities *Fiat et factum est*, But these Parlyaments of late have brought forth [f.10r] nothinge butt Nullities; And I wish the memorie of them att least of those thinges that caused this aborcion might be forever forgotten, accordinge as you Mr Speaker did in the close of this poynte desire keepinge the best Wine for the last, That a Law of oblivion should be made, and as the Spartans did complayne to the [Comon Councell of the Amphirtions[18]] ye Supreme Magistrate of Greece, that the Athenians[19] had sett upp a Monument of their Victory against them sayinge That itt became not the Greacians to erect Trophes of Tryumph over the Greacians, soe I may say itt doth not become Prince and People Kinge and Subiect to renew the memorie or to preserve any way the memoriall of their discontents;

For your comendacion of the excellencie of ye Common Lawe itt is soe true as nothinge can be too much spoken in prayse therof haveinge respect unto the Meridian, for which itt was framed and such is the kinges high esteeme and opynion therof as Tully saide.[20] soe I may saie nothinge pleaseth him that is not conformable and grounded on the comon Lawe.

As for Supply you spake of itt is true that although all the famous Princes of this Land have made at some one or other time use of *Benevolences*, yett itt was never a Course soe pleasinge nor well liked of as that of Parlyament, for those good reasons you spake of and declared; And in deed those other they have found called out of good will yett to be neither good nor willinge; Butt for ye last contribucion in this kinde how unwillingly his Majestie was drawen unto, wee that have the happiness to stand neer him best know, and if itt were displeasinge to any man most of all to him, butt the necessitie of occasions abroade enforced, and the many invitacions here att home drew itt on, and if itt be well Considered how and where itt was bestowed, for the supply of that most Noble and sweet Lady, some time the Subiect of Majestie when shee was Queene of Bohemiah and now ye patterne of Heroyicall patience, I hope ther wilbe noe man found soe malevolent as to speake against this *Benevolence* –

[f.10v] As for your comendacion and exhortacion of his Majestie for the mayntenance of Religion, his Majestie giveth you most hearty

---

[18] BL, Harl. MS 159 f.16v.
[19] In fact the Thebans: ibid.
[20] Cf. Hacket Pt I p. 177.

thanks and wee all exceedingly reioyce itt beinge the foundacion of all good to understand the exceedinge greate zeale of the particular members of your house in this matter soe that as Tully saide of [the town of Enna[21]] That[22] *Quot Cives tot Sacerdotes*, soe I may say of you, for soe your extraordinary fervencie doth merrite, As many *Burgesses* soe many *Churchmen*

As for his Majesties late Accions in the Suspencion of some Penall Statutes againste Papists, his Majestie wishes as [Alphonsus the great[,] king[23]] of Aragon did *Utinam omnes* [?*subditi*][24] *reges fuissent*, then would they be able to conceive the necessitie and wisdome of his proceedinges, and herein I cannot say better, then what his Majestie last did deliver; That a Kinge is like a horseman, for God himselfe compares itt his people to the horse, The Lawe the Spurr, Raynes, and Brydle which are all in their due times to be used, now with slacknes, now with streightnes, and truely his Majestie doth protest, which wee that have knowne more particularlie of his Counsells must all testifie, that hee never remitted nor abated the execucion of any Lawe in this kinde but for the performance of a greater, nay the highest of all Lawes *Salutem Respublice*, and not onely for the temporall good hath hee done itt, butt even for ye better propagacion of true Religion itt selfe –

Next mr Speaker his Majestie giveth you most harty thanks for the exceedinge tender care & love which you have declared to the distressed estate of his Royall children the Releevinge of whome and the deliverance from the oppression of their Cruell enymie, wee hope will not be soe difficult, if itt have not onely your Counsells butt your helpes that are the reprsentative body of the Commons, True itt is that by treatie [GAP][25]

As for the mayntenance and provisions of the Navy the strength of this Kingdome and terrour of other Nations, although this great and excellent worke [f.11r] have been wholly and onely done att the cost and charges of his most Sacred Majestie and especially dyrected and ordered by his wisedome, yett as the Assirrians did allow [the carver[26]] to ingrave his name in divers partes of the Temple although nothinge therof was done att his cost, Soe itt is his Majesties gracious pleasure, that I should give a due acknowledgment of the great deserts in this

---

[21] Ibid., p. 178.

[22] Hacket ibid. gives the full quotation: '*Non domum sed fanum. ubi quot cives tot sacerdotes*'.

[23] BL, Harl. MS 159 f.17; Hacket Pt I p. 178 calls him 'Aphonso the Wise'.

[24] Cf. BL, Harl MS 159 f.17: '... that all his subjects were kinges'.

[25] Ferrar appears to have here misunderstood the Lord Keeper: ibid., f.17v.

[26] Hacket Pt I p. 179: 'And yet as that Carver that beautified the Temple of Diana, although he wrought upon other Mens Charges, was suffered notwithstanding to engrave his own Name in some eminent Places of the Building:' Did Ferrar really write 'Assirrians' or has Conyam misread Ferrar's 'Ephesians'?

buisines of the most excellent personage that hath the Supreame Office whose paines care and providence hath soe much forwarded itt in this Seaven yeares time of experience, And next his Majestie is due to him the prayse and thanks *proximus illi, sed longo proximus intervallo.*[27]
ffor ye Reformacion of Ireland.[28]

Now lastlie for your 4 Peticions his Majestie doth most amply graunt them, and doth most graciously confirme unto you all the pryveledges and liberties that doe truely belonge unto you, not doubtinge butt you will use them all especially that of the libertie of speech, with that modestie and dutie which becomes you and in this poynte his Majestie doth graciously promise that hee will not be nice nor scrupalous except (which God forbid) you force him butt hee doth now graunt unto you all your pryveledges without reservacion, Quallification or Suspension of any oath whatsoever onely one thinge I have to add That as when itt was saide *Quid est Cato sine libertate* itt was well answered *Quid est Libertas sine Catone* Soe I now say what is wisedome without libertie, when itt cannott be manyfested, soe libertie without wisedome is intollerable libertie –
Thus hee ended and after a small pause hee said the house was adiourned till Munday Nyne of the clocke
Then wee delivered to the house where was read a bill touchinge providinge for [An act concerning probate of suggestions in cases of prohibition[29]]
which beinge done mr Speaker adiourned the house till munday att eight of the clocke.

[f.11v]   Munday the 23th of February 1623

The house beinge sett the clerke reade the Confession afterwards the Collects for the Kinge, And then mr Speaker a prayer for the Parliament with a thanks giveinge from the Powder deliverance
Next was read the bill for keepinge the Saboth, which Sir James Berrat[30] commendinge alleadginge [the last two parliaments[31]] moved the receavinge of the Communion as had been hertofore used for the good effects belonginge to that Holy Sacrament & now a particular commemoracion and thanksgivinge to God for the Princes saffe deliverance from the daunger of body life and State. And that noe man should be admitted to com into the house till hee brought certificate of haveinge received the communion.

[27] The Lord Keeper is here referring to George Villiers, Duke of Buckingham.
[28] For the missing details, see BL, Harl. MS 159 f.18, or Hacket Pt I p. 179.
[29] *Nicholas.*
[30] i.e. Perrot.
[31] *Nicholas.*

Sir Edward Cecill by the example of Netherlands moved for a Fast day to be appoynted, which Sir William Stroude saide hee liked butt desyred his Majesties pleasure might be first knowne by some of the Honorable personages neer the chayre which because itt was to be a g[e]nerall thinge throughout England was thought fitt, and Sir Edward Cecell, mr Secretary Calvert and Sir [Richard Weston, Chancellor of the Exchequer[32]] were desyred to goe instantlie before the Kings deperture which they did and after allmost an hower returninge Sir Edward Cecill saide they had good hope[33] of their desire from his Majestie who patientlie heard them and answered hee would conferr with his Bishopps therabout;

In the meane while the celebracion of the Communion was ordered to be att Stt Margaretts on Sunday next (divers undertakinge the parish should give way to the House) and Doctor Bargrave was chosen to preach the Sermon recomended by Sir [William 'Bowser' i.e. Bulstrode[34]] and other although Sr [John Jephson[35]] moved for Bishopp [Ussher[36] who was pre]sent att this time and haveinge done itt soe much to the sattisfaccion of ye House the last time, hee conceived itt would be some disreputacion to him to be neglected now, butt the reason was not approved

And Sir Nathaniell Rich undertooke to know Doctor [Ussher's[37]] mynde to be against [?his being chosen] & some others were appoynted to receive the Ticketts.

Sir Thomas Hobby moved to that entent that buisines might be dispatched & they might be begunn, and that a reviewe might be taken of all the passadges of the late Parliment which came to the perfeccions of Bills, wherin hee moved

That those that were then fully past might be now first read and confirmed –

Next those that were sent upp ready drawne –

And thirdlie they that were redie prepared

[f.12r] And that till these in their severall order had received perfection noe other might be read, which mr Pym would have with two reservacions, that itt should not exclude their publique Bills, that some [BLANK] occasion might require to have [BLANK]. Soe that itt should be [BLANK]

That noe bills of course,

---

[32] *Holles.*
[33] A gap in the ms here appears to be of no significance.
[34] *Nicholas*
[35] Yale footnote to *Nicholas*.
[36] Ibid.
[37] Ibid.

And the second was that itt should not exclude ye reading of pryvate Bills in the morninge before the house were full for the benifitt of Mr Speaker.

Sir John Straunge[38] moved the nominatinge of a Committee touchinge of Eleccions that might be controversed, which Sir Jo[39] [Perrot[40]] desyred might be of the Auntientest of the House, and Sir Thomas Hobby, that everie member of the House that would com might have a voyce in that Committee, which although divers seconded att sundry times yett was not in ye end allowed because itt had noe former presydent, although divers alleadged how in many other cases itt was done, butt [BLANK] and others spake against itt as a new thinge and daungerous affirminge that if they once broke the custome they should not know where they were, instanceinge how last Parliament contrary to all former use all those spoke in a buisines were made of the Committee although itt was formerlie observed that none that spake against the bodie of a bill should be of ye Committee

Sir Edward Cooke for ye experience of the Knights of ye Sheire which hee conceived should best know the severall Eleccion moved that they might be added to the Committee nominated which were a great many, butt mr Alforde disliked soe great a number, affirminge that auntientlie 12 were a great number for a Committee and now they had made allmost 40: For the ioyninge of ye Knights of the Sheirs itt was answered a great part of them were new men that were never formerlie of the House

In the end the particular Committee was appoynted & mr Pym moved they might have authoritie from ye house: The Cheaker[41] chamber was the place they should sett Twesdaies and Frydaies –

[f.12v]   Mr Bradkin presented a complainte of ye Freholders of Cambridgsheire for a wronge in their Eleccion And divers[42] that were chosen att two places declared for which they would serve, Wheruppon itt was ordered Mr Speaker should take order that new writts should be sent downe –

Then the wholl house was appoynted to sitt Committee for Greevances

After this was read an Act against Swearinge

An Act [for the general quiet of the subject and against all pretences of concealments whatsoever[43]]

---

[38] i.e. Strangways: e.g. *Hawarde.*
[39] *Recte* James.
[40] *Pym.*
[41] i.e. Exchequer.
[42] 'signified' erased.
[43] *Nicholas*

And then a Cattalogue of all the bills passed and redy drawne to be passed the last Parlyament.

After which the Bill read on Satterdaie for [probate[44]] of Suggestions which beinge twise read and noe excepcions beinge taken mr Speaker saide itt ought to be deemed fully passed, Butt mr Glanvilde moved that for order sake itt might be committed though to a Committee that might instantly returne with itt, if they found noe iust cause of alteracion.

Sir [George More[45]] saide a Bill ought not to be committed without some excepcion taken against itt Wheruppon some thought itt did not fully provide for [the ease of such as live in the counties of Cumberland. Durham. Northumberland and Westmorland where the judges of assize come but once a year[46]] Wheruppon Sr Edward Cooke and some others were entreated to withdraw into the Committee Chamber and in the doinge therof came the two Lord Cheife Justices[47] who made most humble reverence to the house, and particularly to mr Speaker who with much gravitie resaluted them, [?he] haveinge ended [?they] declared that the Lords desire was to expedite the weightie buisiness mencioned by his Majestie concerninge the Relacion of his treaties and those other passadges [?that] had moved them therin Wheruppon they had appoynted itt to be reported to them by the Lord Admirall and the two Secretaries which they outt of their Affeccions[48] with the Lower house, desyred might be done ioyntly with them and wheruppon requested a meetinge of the wholl house to morrow att Two of the clocke in the [f. 13r]   paynted Chamber for a conference wher if any man should move any Question hee should receive sattisfaccion

Then they were dismissed, mr Alforde, Sir Edward Cook and divers others thinkinge itt unfitt that any Questions should be asked without particularr warrant from ye house, Although Sir George More, Sir William Stroude & others thought itt not unfitt that particular men might receive sattisfaccion, and the buisnes be expedited yett itt was resolved to goe onely with ears which yett they would not by an order forbidd esteeming everie mans discrecion sufficient to refrayne.

As for ye Secretaries they were admitted to speake not as members of the house butt his Majesties Secretaries

The Speaker was not to goe for the house could not give any meetinge to the upper house and to Committees the Speaker never ment,[49] The Judges were called in and the message delivered in these termes

---

[44] Ibid.

[45] Ibid

[46] Ibid.

[47] Ley and Hobart: Ibid.

[48] A gap here appears to be of no significance.

[49] *Sic*, but ?*recte* went.

The house did give great thanks for their Lordships desire of good Correspondencie which they would allwaies studdy to [?preserve] and did Embrace to give a meetinge as a Committee att the time and place appoynted

And to make the report besides the Secretaries were chosen mr Chauncellor of the Exchequor[50] and Sir Frauncis Collington[51]

After a verie long argument Sir Robert Phillips, Sir Dudley Diggs, Sir Edward Cooke [BLANK] haveing all ernestly excused themselves.[52]

[ff.13v & 14 r: BLANK]

[f.14v] **Vppon**[NF] Twesday in the afternoone the 24th of February – 1623

Wee went to Whitehall the Lord Steward himselfe kept the dore with much trouble and paine to doe us service as hee said yett was hee not sent to[53] by the house as hee ought to have beene, butt onely the Treasuror[54] and Comptroler[55] of ye house were entreated therfore his Noble courtesie was the greater because itt was freelie of himselfe.

About 3. of the clock the Prince came in and sitting downe in a Chaire att the upper end of the Table att which sate ye greate Officers and Earles, and on 3 severall benches on each side the Bishops and other Barrons, they beinge covered, all others continuinge bare headed.

The Duke of Buckhenham standinge by the Prince soe as hee leaned on his chayre and the two Secretaries standing behinde on each side, began.—excusinge himselfe if hee should not performe the buisines as might be expected consideringe his inhabillitie and that hee had never spoken in such an Audience before, That hee could not hope to make the Relacion in any reasonable manner without the Assistance of his highnes, noe more than hee had been able to have gone through ye Negotiacion itt selfe without the help of his excellent wisedome & iudgment

That itt was such a kinde of Narration as hee could no waie gaine honour by, for if they that heard him were well affected they must not onely be troubled butt blush for shame. If ill affected they would esteeme him Mallicious, thinkinge itt impossible the Actions themselves should have passed in that manner as hee should relate them, Butt hee

---

[50] Sir Richard Weston.

[51] *Sic*, but *recte* Cottington.

[52] Conyam has written this sentence as a separate paragraph, but sense requires that it be read as a continuation of the preceding sentence.

[53] 'as' erased.

[54] Sir Thomas Edmondes.

[55] Sir John Suckling.

would accordinge to his Majesties comaund declare the passadges and buisinesses truely and playnely without refleccion on the persons of the Mynisters of either of the Kings, hee of Spaine[56] or his Majestie of England.

Now for the buisines itt selfe hee needed not begin higher then the Ambassadge performed by the Chauncellour of ye Exchequor 1621, who in his Negotiacion att Brussells made ye first discoverie of their Intentions, and the first cause of suspicion and Jealousie here att home, by writinge that hee did beginn to doubt that. Which intelligence was the ground and cause of a Dispatch from Hampton Courte the 3th of October – 1622 from the Kinge to the Earle of Bristoll.[57]

To this effect.

Cosen and Councellour you know best how notwithstandinge all opposicions to the contrary by a longe patience grounded uppon the Kinge of Spaines promises and assurances, Wee have desyred to merritt of that Kinge & of ye house of Austria[.] [f.15r] Wee have acquainted you from time to time with ye occasions of the proceedings dyrectly contrarylie to the promises in words, the fruite of all which have been nothing but dishonour and scorne, whilest wee are confidently assured of ye restitucion of all[,] that which remayned is taken away[: namely,] *Heldiberge*[58]

The Infanta[59] to whome wee are referred to treate for all her Comission pretends want of power soe that uppon the consideracion of these perticulars wee are forced to call home *Chichester*[60] and *Weston*.

And whilest wee have been over confident uppon ye promises of that Kinge wee have neglected all those meanes that might otherwise have probably secured if not regayned the Pallatinate.

For the Garrisons that wee kept in *Heldeberge* & [?Frankenthal] were not that wee did rely any thinge uppon their strength butt onely to keepe a footinge till by Compos[it]ion an Honorable end might be made and a redelivery of the wholl

But all those promises and confidence in both parts have not [?led to] any other effect then to an abuse of both of us though in a different degree.

Wherfore you shall repayre to that kinge & acquainte him with the premises and desyre of him an assurance under his hand and Seale by Letter or otherwise, That Heildeberg shalbe intirely restored within 70 daies with all that was taken in itt, That ther shalbe a Sessation of

---

[56] Aged sixteen, Philip IV had succeeded his father on 31 March 1621.

[57] John Digby, 1st Earl of Bristol, ambassador to the court of Spain.

[58] Heidelberg, whose English garrison surrendered on 19 September 1622.

[59] Isabella Clara Eugenia, 'sovereign prince' of the southern Netherlands, together with her husband the Archduke Albert.

[60] Arthur Lord Chichester of Belfast, sent as envoy to the Palatinate in 1622.

Armes, And that ther shalbe a generall treaty sett on foote for the
accomodacion of thinges accordinge to a letter formerly written unto
you. And if this may prevail[61] [?not, …] that Kinge shall promise to
ioyne his forces with ours against the Emperour or any other for ye
recovery of that which hat been lost onely through over much trust
and confidence on his word; And if hee will not doe this that yett att
least hee shall graunt a Free passadge through all his dominions to our
Forces and Armes of all which Proposicons – (vizt)

> Restitution
> Cessation –
> Proceedinge in Treaty

Joyninge in Armes or at least giveinge a free Passage, you shall
disiunctively require and returne us an answere within 10 days, else
you shall immediately returne home;

This was the substance of the Kings letter thus playnly because that
hee might truely know what hee was to trust to, And if hee could not
by these meanes then hee might have time otherwise to provide for
the Recoverie –

[f.15v]   Now concerninge the Earle of Bristolls returne – although that
were directly charged in this publique lettre yett there went a longe a
pryvate letter to will him to stay although hee should make couller of
cominge awaie to draw the better answer from them, butt howsoever
hee was charged to press these demaunds earnestlie which hee did not
with that dilligence that hee ought to have done, butt proceedinge
therin with remissness, was the cause of an other despatch sent by
Indimean[62] Porter who had order within 10 daies to bring dyrect
answere butt not beinge able to obteyne any seeinge ye time past hee
himselfe stepped to *Count Olivares*[63] whose [?acquaintance] hee was[,]
haveinge been brought upp in his house from his childhood, and
besought him in that regard that hee would soe much favour him as
hee might carry back unto the King a good Answere concerninge the
Proposicions; Count Olivares demaunded what they were, Porter
answered, no other then those that had been soe often promised by
the Kinge of Spaine. (vizt) His ioyninge in Armes against the Emperour
in case hee could not otherwise procure the restitucion of ye Palatinate
And the speedy accomplishinge of the Marriage;[64]

For the first Olivares grew into a greate rage swearinge itt was a

---

[61] Sense requires the insertion of a 'not'. The size of the gap here suggests that
additional words are missing.

[62] Endymion.

[63] Gaspar de Guzman, conde-duque de Olivares.

[64] To the sister of Philip IV, the Infanta Maria, who in 1629 married her first cousin,
the future Emperor Ferdinand III.

preposterous demaund, What[?] should the King of Spaine take Armes against his uncle[65] the cheife of his house, The head of the Catholique[s.] hee willed him never to speake more of itt.

For the second poynte Count Olivares answered hee neither understood the Marriage nor any word of itt

Porter was much amazed at this, went to the Earle of Bristoll and told him of itt who grew in greate Choller swearinge that if Olivares held that language hee should give him sattisfaccion, [(]as though hee ment to fight with him) addinge hee would make him know that an English Earle was as good as a Spanish Count.

This was overnight butt the next morninge hee[66] had chaunged his mynde and was growen more colde thinking itt fitt to proceed with more temper and discrecion and therfore would speake with Olivares in pryvate, which haveing done hee afterward told Porter that Olivares had soe used him[67] because hee was not a publique mynister [f.16r]   and therfore would not reveale himselfe to him – Porter tooke this displeasingly, stept againe to Olivares expostulated itt as a greate unkindeness that hee should use such strangnes with him consideringe hee had been brought up in his house from his childehood, and was trusted[,] as hee knew[,] from hence with the knowledg of all thinges; Olivares replyed with sharpnes chardging him with great breach of trust in revealing to Bristoll what hee had delivered to him with such confidence esteeminge him as hee termed him in ye nature of his owne childe, which should have caused him to have kept itt to himselfe

Porter made answeare that hee was the Kings servant, and bound in his duty to doe as hee did –

This matter Olivares tooke soe haynously as hee afterward told him [**Vz the D of Buckingham**:NF] that hee hated the ground that Porter went on. Soe I conceaved[68] the Duke. Butt Sir Richard Weston related itt not as though Olivares had himselfe told itt [**to the Duke**:NF] butt as Bristoll from Olivares.

And here the Duke of Buckenham observed that allwaies the Spanyards had treated uppon generallyties & would never com to the particulars.

The Prince understandinge these thinges & seeinge therby; how his Fathers honour was dayly impayred how his *Sisters Inheritance* was cleane gone & lost And how they daylie gayned divers matters in Religion which otherwise they could never have done, How our frends and Alyes abroad were weakned, and all by the meanes of this treatie of

---

[65] The Emperor Ferdinand II, who was brother to Philip's mother.

[66] i.e. Digby/Bristol.

[67] i.e. Porter.

[68] This word comes at the end of a line. Conyam's eye seems to have skipped over the next line or lines of Ferrar's draft, and thus written nonsense.

the Marriadge, Resolved,[69] although itt were a daungerous attempt, Butt desperate diseases must have desperate remedies[,] to goe himselfe into Spaine, and by his owne presence to negotiate the buisines & to bringe them to a head one way or other [wishing[70]] him to acquainte the Kinge who in the end gave way therunto they Three onely knowinge of itt; soe they went and arryvinge in Spaine first manifested themselves to the *Earle of Bristoll* att Madrill, & the next morninge the *Prince* sent him to Olivares to acquainte him of his Arivall, who was soe civell as hee would not be visited in his house by him [f.16v]   butt in a garden wher after the first complements hee begann to magnifie the Princes iourney for which the Kinge of Spaine could never be able to make sattisfaccion, And in the end concluded that itt should be a Match and they would be frends & devide the Worlde betweene them –

Heere the *Prince* spake pleasantly sayinge That hee had allwaies heard that their appetite was greate to swallow the wholl world, soe now hee saw their liberallytie was not lesse, that would at once parte with halfe to us, The Duke went on, At this meeting the Embassadours were present who immediatelie theron beinge very ioyfull desyred him to signifie to the Kinge how true their Informacions had beene concerninge the real intentions of ye Marriage

Hee replyd that these were generallyties, if hee found the same good sattisfaccion when they came to the particularities that hee would doe itt to the full –

After this the Prince and the Kinge of Spaine mett together in the Pradoe, after which Olivares takinge them together saide lett us make itt a match without callinge the Pope to give any Assistance –

Hee answered hee liked itt well butt knew not how itt could be done; Olivares replyed if the Prince will be converted, which hee hoped well of by reason of his Journey –

Heere the Prince spake and saide That hee replide That hee was com settled in his Religion which was dearer unto him then all other thinges whatsoever, and rather then hee would doe the least towards any such thinge, hee would breake match and frendshipp and all. The Duke went on.

Olivares replyed ther was then no other meanes left then to hasten the Dispensacion and theruppon hee writt a letter to Cardinall [Ludoviso Ludovisi] the Popes Nephew[71] which hee shewed him and hee found itt to be verie [insufficient and[72]] desyred him by way of Postcript [*sic*] to press itt more earnestly Olivares asked him how, Hee said that hee

---

[69] 'with him' deleted.
[70] *Nicholas.*
[71] Alessandro Ludovisi, as Gregory XV, was Pope 1621–23.
[72] Cf. *Nicholas*: 'which being not so effectuall as he wished'.

should signify ye greatnes of the Obligacion, the Princes cominge had
putt uppon them the disreputacion and discontent that would be to
him to returne without his wife, That therfore ye Dispensacion should
be sent free and cleere without cloggs of condicions, and that speedilie
for delay would be interpreted denyall;

[f.17r]   Count Olivares grew verie angrie sayinge itt could not be done
as hee desyred, more then hee had writt hee might not.

The Prince hee was much troubled hereat ye Embassadours encouraged him and counselled not to press itt – Aston[73] spake some what
doubtfully, Digby made a more favourable Interpretacion – The Duke
himselfe saide that hee then tolde the Prince, his iudgment was that
they neither ment Marriage nor Palatinate, & hardlie their Returne to
England –

The Messenger was dispatched to Rome, in ye meane while the
Prince had a sight of the Infanta his Mistris as shee went to divers
Churches purposely that hee might see her, hee pressed to visit her
Olivares promised him day after day, for fower or five days together
and yett hee could not see her; Att the last the Duke understood the
resolucion was taken in the Counsell that the Prince should not see her
till the Dispensation was com, and demaunded of Olivares whether itt
wer soe or noe hee confessed itt sayinge hee had ventured too farr
alredy to lett him see her as hee did in the streets wherat the Spanyards
were much scandalized, esteeminge her dishonored to be soe carryed
upp and downe to be seene.

Then hee replyed Olivares you should have done well to have told
the Prince soe att the first that hee might have settled his mynde. Butt
after much adoe and long time the Prince was allowed to visite ye
Infanta which hee did in a certaine distance by an Interpreter and was
not to speake butt in sett words dictated to him –

Heer the Prince spake sayinge hee would tell the reason which they
gave, That because they did not know whether shee should be his wife
they would not have him speake to her as his Spouse but as a *Princes* –

The Duke of Buckenham went on, sayinge after this Olivares told
him itt must needs a Match and if the Dispensacion were com hee
should ly with her the selfe same night, And att another time hee tolde
the Prince that if the Pope should hinder ye Marriage if hee might not
have the Infanta as his wife hee should have her as his Mistris –

[f.17v]   Now to entertaine time they carry the Prince to a County[sic]
house called Araniuez,[74] and there they dealt hotlie with him to convert

---

[73] Sir Walter Aston.
[74] Aranjuez, a royal palace south of Madrid.

him and att the last that att least hee would not be an enemie to their Religion; Heer the Prince saide, hee made Answere hee was not an enemie to the persons of them that professed that Religion, And whereas they desyred him to give leave to a Lady to trie whither shee could doe any good uppon him, hee answered verie willinglie, for hee held himselfe likelyer to convert ye Lady then shee him ... The Duke went on.

They then pressed him to give a meetinge to certaine Devines touchinge Religion which the Prince refused, The Prince spake[:] for these Reasons I refused.

First I had no manner of [scruple[75]] and therfore ther was noe reason to admitt any dispute and itt would be of perpetuall blemish to mee − If I should any whit alter[.] besides I ought not to be soe used nor pressed to any thinge against myne owne likinge haveinge com over and putt my selfe soe freely into their hands, I was likewise sure they would not prevaile, and then they would thinke themselves much dishonoured that they could not prevaile uppon a younge man, and the Infanta would perhapps be ye more unwillinge to goe with him because shee would conceive itt impossible to convert him afterward, which if hee were not tryed heere shee would goe with ye better hope of itt.

The Duke went forwards.
Olivares saide hee would treate of the termes and ende of Frindship, which the Prince refused till the marriadge were concluded; Heer the Prince spake saying hee was not willinge to treate of the Restitucion of the Palatinate before because hee hoped after the marriadge itt would goe forward much better, and besides hee did feare that they were soe desyrous to treate of that because they would theruppon finde some occasion and collour of delayinge the Match

The Duke went forwarde
At last came the Dispensation which was kept 4: or 5 daies which at last they understoode of, then were certaine Comissioners appoynted to treate of itt, with [w]home the Prince was divers times himselfe, And heere Olivares was sent to schoole to learne, for by the treatie they perceaved that hee indeed never understood soe much as one particularr either touching marriadge or *Palatinate.*

Now the Prince understood butt underhand that ye Dispensacion was [?come] with [?several] lymitations, and theruppon demaunded of Olivares whether itt were soe or noe, and whether amongst the rest one Clause, That the Kinge of Spaine [f.18r] should take good securitie of the Kinge and Prince of England to performe all thinges

[75] *Rich.*

and otherwise hee should sweare to take upp Armes against them, which the Prince said hee observed to be a straunge condicion in a treatie of soe neere Alliance and tolde them if there were any farther necessitie of sendinge to Roome hee would proceed no further, And did himselfe demaund of the Kinge of Spaine whither hee would take that oath or noe before he read the Dispensacion; The Kinge of Spaine made answere hee did not know what hee should doe.

Then they begann to treate of the Articles, the Prince hee would have nothinge added to those sent from England, and if there were any thinge added itt neither was the Princes, nor his fault, true itt is there was one particularr requyred by the Pope touchinge matter of Religion, which the Prince and hee refused as new: Butt the Earle of Bristoll did strongly maynteyne that itt was a poynte included in the treatie betweene the Two Kinges and agreed on formerlie, concerning which the Prince writt unto the Kinge, and had likewise told him of itt since, And the Kinge said Bristoll was in the wronge & they were in the right.

Well the treaties went forward and the Prince sattisfied ye Committee in althinges save onely in Three particulars (vizt)

1 The Nurse.
2 The bringing up of the Childe
3 And the Church. –

Which three thinges hee did reserve to give the Kinge of Spaine himselfe sattisfaccion in, and did soe and gave Olivares the noates of them in writinge which hee tooke and saide hee could not desire more, and theruppon swore shee was his wife. Butt the next morninge came the Earle of Monteclaros[76] and the Earle of Gondamarr[77] in an other tune, and they made protestacion, that except the Prince would yeild to all thinges as they came from Rome without leavinge out any they could not proceed, for they had not power soe much as to change a word, though itt were to mend false lattine

The Prince said heere hee grew discontented & nowe made a full Resolucion to himselfe of their intentions And when they were urdged by him that these were not accordinge [GAP of three lines]

The best answere they made was they were Beasts & blinde and could not read their owne language.

The Duke went forward.

[f.18v] Count Olivares then made two Proposicions to the Prince

Either to send to Rome to obteyne sattisfaccion there accordinge to his desires –

---

[76] Juan Manuel de Mendoza y Manrique, marques de Montesclaros.
[77] Diego Sarmiento de Acuna, conde de Gondomar, the former Spanish ambassador to the court of England.

Or else to send to the Kinge of England and to make him iudge of the differences.

The Prince spake and said hee liked them both well they should immeadiatelie send to Roome and he would returne to his [?father the conduct of] the Negotiacion.

The Duke went on Olivares tooke this for a breach and ther uppon made another proposicion that the Prince would stay 20 daies till his Fathers answeare might be returned.

The Prince would not yeilde butt he said hee woulde instantlie be gone

Olivares desyred him to make some other ye messenger of that newes to the Kinge.

Bristoll hee earnestly perswaded him to stay telling him itt was but a *Puntillio*.[78] hee might promise boldlie for hee understood from good hands they ment not to hold him to his words;

Heere the *Prince* [spake] sayinge when hee had once yeilded hee never heard more of the Pantillio

The Duke went on.

Olivares hee made excuse to him touchinge his the Princes stay, hee replyed hee need not doubt any thinge the Prince was verie well sattisfied.

Then they said they would drawe upp ye Articles to send to the Kinge of England which should be readie in two daies.

The Prince said because the wether was hott hee would send Cottington before that hee might goe [BLANK] & hee would send the Articles after him by another that should overtake him, They pressed much that Cottington might stay to carry them himselfe, The Prince would not yeild butt sent him before, after whose departure 2. and 10. and 20 daies run out before they brought the Articles And then they had inserted some new ones thinkinge belike that the overmuch desire of sendinge them awaie would have made them negligent to peruse[79] them and soe pass them from the prince,[80] [?but the Prince] beinge carefull found itt and soe tooke excepcions against them, and produced ye [f.19r]   Oath betweene Queen Mary and Kinge Phillip desyringe they would follow that president; They perceivinge their dealinges discovered snatched the *Articles* out of his hand sayinge they would mend them, Butt the Prince caused *Bristoll* to drawe them upp which hee did in the space of 6 howers and soe they were sent awaie.

Now the [Junta[81]] of *Devines* that had been assembled to consider of

---

[78] Puntillio, Pantillio, i.e. Punctilio: a petty formality.
[79] Written over 'pursue' erased.
[80] Sense requires the insertion of the following words.
[81] *Nicholas.*

the marriage made their Relation that the Infanta might not goe till the Springe;

The *Prince* heere spake. Sayinge that at the verie first appearinge of those Devines hee was much troubled and demaundinge of Olivares what the meaninge of itt was, hee answered itt was a matter onely of forme, but should not hinder the buisines not an hower;

The Duke went on.

Olivares after this opynion of the *Devines* given, begun to iudge and presse that the *Prince* would at least stay till they might understand out of England that the Kinge had performed the *Articles* sent unto him.

The Prince made answere this proposicion was worse then any of the former, for perhaps the Ambassadours might be ill affected, and would either delay itt longe or doe itt unperfectlie, besides what if itt should happen that ther should be any [?trouble] in the farther partes of England or Ireland as might perchance be stirred, although noe doubt itt would be most easily repressed.

Olivares hereuppon beinge much pressed to expedite the matter soe that the *Prince* might carry the Infanta with him bid the *Duke* goe himselfe to the *Devines* where they were assembled, and they would give him sattisfaccion, and as hee was goinge[,] said the Duke[,] hee called mee backe againe tellinge mee I should putt the Question to them in these words: *What is the most that the Kinge of Spaine may doe by way of gratitude for soe greate a favour as the Prince of wales had done him by soe putting himselfe into his hands.*

I answered that was not the Question yett because hee was verie earnest I went and asked him[82] in ye same wordes they wondred much to see mee com in amongst them, and more to heare the Question, and lookinge wisely [f.19v] one uppon an other for a long while[.] att last one of them answered that I should aske Olivares, with this answere I returned to him who seeinge mee smilinge asked mee whither I had receaved a good answere, I told him a very good one and such a one as[,] had they given mee any other, I should not have reputed them to be that wise and grave Counsell which they were, and theruppon told itt him, att which hee in greate rage rapped his staffe against the wall, and said hee would goe to them himselfe which hee did takinge mee alonge with him and ther talked with them a greate while as though they should understand more then I perceived they did butt in vaine, wheruppon I prayde him to spare any further labour I was well sattisfied.

Then one of them the *Bishop of* [Segovia[83]] saide that itt were not fitt to send the Infanta till they saw thinges a little settled for that which

---

[82] *Sic*, but ?*recte* 'them'.
[83] *Nicholas.*

the Kinge of England was to performe must needs cause a Rebellion; I asked him what[;] hee saide if the Kinge of Spaine should doe as much in Spaine they would rebell, And the Kinge of England was not more powerfull in his Dominions then the Kinge of Spaine

That which hee had and was to doe was as much as a Tolleracion Heere the *Prince* saide hee observed that their desire was to putt his Father uppon such thinges as might cause a Rebellion.

The Duke went on:

I answered that itt was onely a connivence at ye execucion of some Penall Statutes which was in the Kings power not a Tolleracion which could not be performed but in and by a *Parliament.*

Heere uppon they all looked straunge uppon *Gondemarr* as if hee had made some other reporte of thinges, Wheruppon after some whole silence hee begann to commende the Kinge, sayinge that hee was a wise Kinge, a learned kinge and much in the hearts of his people, butt for all that it was allwaies understood and purposed and you my Lords best knowe, That the Infanta should never com till all thinges were fully settled as there need be no more feare, Nay then replyde I: you move mee, I never knew any such thinge butt the cleane contrarie, That when you first came to mocion this Match you did not onely entreate butt begg itt, vowinge itt should be without any preiudice either to matter of State or Religion And when the Kinge my Maister made answere that hee could not treate with you on equall termes, for when [f.20r] you had drawen him to what was for your owne turne you had a back dore to slipp away your selves from all that you had promised.

The Popes authoritie and comaund to which you know what Oathes and protestacions you made that althinges should be really and punctually performed; *Gondemar* was exceedingly vexed with this reply, and did not cease all the time of my beinge in Spaine to requite mee with ill Offices which I valew not.

Heere the Prince spake – Sayinge that after this Olivares told him that [?if] hee would be content to accept her in ye Springe he should have a blanke given him wherein hee might write what condicions hee would touchinge ye Palatinate.

The Duke: went on.

That shortly after the Prince sent him and Aston[84] to solicite the dispatch of the marriage;

Olivares replyed that hee must take her accordinge to the condicion of the Dispensacion and otherwise hee must gaine the Palatinate by Armes, This message the Duke said hee caused the Interpreters to deliver unto ye Prince; sayinge allwaies after hee had treated with them hee brought his Interpreter to make Relacion.

---

[84] Sir Walter Aston.

Att last the Prince yeilded to stay till the newes were returnd from England, wheratt the Spanyard soe much reioyced as I never saw greater shews of alacritie especially in Olivares Wheruppon thinkinge to take the opertunytie I pressed him to expedite the match soe as the Prince might have her a long with him, alleadginge sundry reasons how ye King was striken in yeares, and therfore the Princes presence not onely to comforte butt a thing of necessitie, how ye Princes desyres were soe longinge as could not otherwise be sattisifed, and that itt would be a great blemish to him to returne without her, besides I added, if the rather by my sollycitacion hee should effect itt, I should take itt for an infinite favour and obligacion.

Olivares answered mee I had bewitched him itt should be done, butt the Prince must not know hee would make preparations, and a day was appoynted, but shortly after came newes that the Infanta tooke itt wondrous ill, and the Countess of Olivares[85] came to the Prince to tell him soe much[,] how that she tooke itt for an argument of his coldness in love not to be willinge to stay soe longe for him[sic], and theruppon perswaded

(him:catchword)

[f.20v] that hee would stay seaven yeares butt hee would carry her with him, which shee said hee should noe waies be bound unto butt itt would give the Infanta greate sattisfaccion as noe doubt shee would be willinge to goe with him The Prince was content, and I then pressed Olivares to [BLANK] with his promise, hee made answere in some choller, whether I thought the Kinge of Spaine had nothinge to doe with his monney, but to cast itt outt att a windowe,

Heer the Prince spake. sayinge I made answere I would be att the cost of all, Shortly after came letters from the Secretaries and Ambassadours of very good sattisfaccion declaringe that all thinges had beene performed in England to the full, And that the Kings comaund was the Prince should com away within one monneth att the farthest Uppon these lettres I never saw men more deiected then they then were.

    Heer the Prince spake sayinge
hee would not say they had an Intention to raise Rebellion butt haveinge dealt with him a new to be a Catholique hee prayed them to forbeare, tellinge them that the least suspicion of any such thinge in England would raise a Rebellion; To which Olivares made answere, wee will send an Army with you, And I[,] said the Prince[,] replyed The remedy was worse then the disease.

Now said the Duke they began to press the Prince againe to stay till

---

[85] Ines de Zuniga had married her first cousin Olivares in 1607.

the Springe, The Prince offered to stay .6. weekes soe as hee might have the Lady with him –

When Sir Fra: Cottington reported this hee said, That ye Prince had here forgotten one thinge which hee had comaunded him to relate, That the Earle of Bristoll would needs lay a Ringe of 1000 *li* with the Prince that hee would keepe his Christmas in Spaine which Ringe att the Princes cominge away was paide

The Duke went on.

Then Olivares would know What the Princes expectacion was touchinge the matter of the Palatinate – whoe made answere restitucion of all – Olivares replyde that the Emperour would be content to restore the Landes to ye Palatines sonne butt never to the Father, As for the Electorate itt was a thinge in the Ayre and was desyrous that his Nephew (soe hee called the Prince Pallatines sonne) might marry the Emperours second daughter, That I liked well said the Prince and farther that hee should be brought upp in ye Emperours Court, That I disliked said the Prince –

[f.21r] The Duke went on.

One time I demaunded of Olivares what the Kinge of Spaine would doe in case the Emperour were refractorie and would not be brought to such conditions as they promised, whether the Kinge of Spaine would then take upp Armes against him or noe, hee replyed hee was his Uncle &c and soe ought him soe much reverence & dutie as hee might not beare Armes against him though hee buffited him.

Heere the Prince saide that hee protested without a full Restitution there should follow neither marriage nor frendship.

The Duke went on.

One day I challenged Olivares that these delayes were his fault remembring him what hee had said att the begininge that ye Dispensation would come iust as they should request itt, and that hee could doe what hee list with the Pope, And that uppon the first Assemblinge of the [Junta] of Devines, hee had affirmed itt was a matter onely of forme, which now proved ye onely lett, Hee [re]plyed That the Devill had putt itt into his head to call that [Junta]. And said there were now lefte onely Three waies to make the Match; Two wherof were good, & ye Third a bad one.

The First was the *Princes Conversion* wherof hee now sawe little hope.

The second was that as hee had putt his person soe alsoe he should putt all thinges absolutely into the Kinge of Spaines [hands] without capitulacion who noe doubt would theruppon require lesse

The third was to bind him hand and foote soe fast as hee could not goe backe.

The Prince replyde they had chosen the worst of the Three and

when hee [**Olivares**:NF] was farther urdged to shew his power which
hee had soe magnified sayinge **often formerly**[86] itt was in his power
to conclude itt hee replyed soe itt was notwithstandinge all these
obstacles, And if either hee were a private Counseller or the Kinge 30
yeares old or hee himselfe Kinge hee would doe itt butt now consideringe the Kings mynoritie & that the burden of all should be layde
on him hee durst not butt in such sure manner as noe blame should
followe
[**The Duke went on Olivares one day tolde him it was a
match**:NF], hee answered hee hoped soe itt could not be otherwise
haveinge been 7 yeares amaking Olivares replyed noe nor seaven
monneths which because itt seemed straunge beyound beleife Olivares
said hee would make itt good by acquaintinge him with two letters the
one from the kinge of Spaine to him, and the other his answere

[f.21v]   These letters hee brought to the Prince and Duke and lefte
them with them to read butt uppon solemne promise not to take a
Coppie. Heere the Prince spake; To observe this promise wee did not
indeed take the Coppies of them butt myselfe, Buckenham and Aston
read them and soe often as wee had allmost learned them without
booke and soe sendinge them backe againe did afterwardes out of our
memories sett downe the substance of them soe truely as they are not
lesse true then the Coppies would have bene.

The First was from the Kinge to Olivares bearinge date ye 5th of
November 1622. the same yeare the Prince came and the selfe same
time that Porter was there as was mentioned in the begininge –

The letter was to this Effect.
The kinge my Father declared att his death that itt was never intended
to marry the Infanta Dona Maria my Sister to the Prince of Wales,
and therfore the mynisters imployed theraboute did allwaies treat the
buisines with intention of delay as your Uncle Don Baltazar[87] well knew
itt beinge onely sett on foote for the advancement of our designe
on Germany and Flaunders; Now because itt soe pressed as some
proceedinges must follow [**and the averseness**:NF] of the Infanta
[**soe greate**:NF] who is resolved the same day itt shalbe concluded
to enter into the [**Discalze**:[88]NF] I would have you finde some meanes
to breake itt, and I will make itt good, butt soe as may stand with the
sattisfaccion of ye kinge of *Greate Brittaine* whoe hath deserved verie well
of us in these buisinesses and I desire his satisfaccion in all thinges
except the Match.

---

[86] By NF, over 'after' erased.
[87] Baltasar de Zuniga, uncle to both Olivares and his countess, directed Spanish foreign
policy from 1617 until his death in 1622.
[88] i.e. the Discalced Carmelites.

Olivares at the same time shewed likewise his answere to the demaundes which was to this effect [The rest of the page is BLANK]

[f.22r]   Sir Walter Aston seemed much troubled and confounded uppon the readinge of those Letters in regard that hee said that uppon the death of Phillip the Third hee went to the now kinge, desyring to understand his Majesties resolution touchinge the Match whether hee ment to proceed therin as his Father had begunn, whose Reply was, that wheras itt **went**[89] before itt should now runn.

The Duke of Buckenham here observed that in all the proceedings hitherto there was nothing promised but generallities and that after such a manner [**(hee sayde)**:NF] as if any certainetie could be grounded theron himself was the [**weakest**:NF] man alive. [The rest of the page & f.22v are BLANK]

f.23r   [NF: **Munday the first of March 1623**,] in ye forenoone. [NF: **I came somewhat late and before I came Sir Beniamin Ruddier had spoke a speech much aplauded by the house**]

Next stood upp Sir Georg More who made a long speech cheiflie in comendacion of the *Princes* wisedome and constancy of Religion in Spaine; And ended[;] his advise was The Treaty should goe noe farther Sir Robert Phillips moved that wee might at last leave these talkinge Treaties wherby wee had allwaies lost and by manly English waies seek to regaine what was lost, and comendinge the speech of [Sir Ben Rudyard[90]] hee saide with a lardg and Eloquent comparrison: The last English Prince that returned from Spaine returned thence laden with Honour and Triumph for haveinge restored a rightfull, though a Tyrant Kinge, butt our *Prince* returned with much more Honour bringinge with him the saffetie and securitie of this State[.] hee gloried in the Captivitie of a French Kinge, this had much more cause in the recoveringe of a ruyned kingdome and as that Prince in the *Parlyament* sawe & redressed the evill growne by the misgoverment of Favorits under his Father, soe hee hoped noe lesse happilie and successively this *Prince* would by the meanes of this *Parlyament* be a cheife instrument to free the kingdome of these unsupportable greivances wherunder itt groaned –

Concerninge ye marriadge hee devided his speech into Three poynts.
1. Whither the Treaties should proceed
2. Whither ther were any hope of Success.
3. Whither if there were, itt were good.

---

[89] Correction by NF, over 'were'.
[90] *Nicholas, Holles*.

For the first hee thought itt was butt to procure our selves too be abused –

For the rest he did not thinke any thinge really ment on that parte; hee said this Treaty was the best Armie that ever the Kinge of Spaine raysed, Itt had gayned more to the house of *Austria* then Charles the 5th did with all his Warlike proceedings, more than Phillip with all his Jesuite Counsell, Wee by itt had lost our frends abroade[,] our selves [f.23v] at home; almost God Almightie with whome wee hadd broken truce, In this way wee coulde finde nothinge butt a base, butt obnoxious-ness –

Concerninge the recoverie of the *Pallatinate* hee declared his greife &c. Hee said the [Q. of Bohemia[91]] was a *Princess* borne under an Infortunate Planett, that not soe much for want of power as will in Three great kingdomes was not onely not maynteyned in her [?former/?temporary] greatnes of *Bohemia* butt depryved of her lawfull Inheritance the *Pallatinate*[,] which negligence hee prayed God not to lay to our charge[;] hee was sure posteritie would, and summinge upp the evill Consequence of this Treatie, the routinge of all our party in Germany[,] the gaining of his in matter of Religion &c Hee saide that this Treatie had lost more Protestant Blood then Charles the Fifte ever shedd, had lefte us a people without reputacion hee concluded That the Spanish Armes had gott the Pallatinate possession & would defend itt –

That the Match and itt were inseparable –

The Counsell of Roome and Court of Spaine each in other.

The Kinge of Spaine the enemy –

The match never intended for they were wise men and could not meane itt.

That a diversive Warr was to be undertaken for no possibilitie of recovering the Pallatinate –

And in the end they desyred a conference with the Lords

Sir Miles Fleetwood made a longe speech with like sattisfaccion

After him Sir Fraunces Seymour in a grave & vehement manner declared the practizes and intents of this Treatie to have been the alteracion of Religion instanceinge the frequenting of the Spanish Ambassadours house[,] the great number of Protestants converted, their attempt uppon the Prince himselfe. Next the amplyfyinge and increase of their owne powers haveinge turned out the Kings Children &c –

[f.24r] Their contempts of us not esteeminge us worthie of Christian buriall; In the end hee wished the Ambassadours might be sent home to report their good services, and for the rest that a diversive warr

<hr>

[91] *Pym*.

might be enterprized not doubtinge spite of ye Kinge of Spaines teeth
that wee should therby make exchaunge for as good or better then the
Pallatinate.

And Lastlie that the Lawes might be putt in execucion against the
Papists

Sir John Eliott interpretinge his Majesties referringe this matter to
our Councell not to be as if hee had any doubt what himselfe meant
to doe, butt onely to declare his gracious favour to us to make us
partakers in this Relation; moved that since the Imbargo was certaine,
and the preparacions extraordinary of a Navy, that our owne estates
might be secured by all good meanes, and to that intent the Fleete
immeadiatlie made redy att the charges of the *Papists* who haveinge
runn into divers preminyres[92] by receivinge *Preists* &c. hadd a great
favour shewed them if they might com off with soe easy a matter:

Mr Pym and Serieant [NF: **Hichen**] spake touchinge ye clearness
of the resolucion, which mr Pym saide no mans reason could add
evydence unto nor perswasion [NF: **earnestness**] and ye other
amongst other thinges, that *Gondamar* himselfe yf hee were now present
would not for the falsitie of this buisiness putt himselfe uppon the tryall
either of God or the Countrie, butt uppon a *Nihil dicit*; & soe seemed
to conclude an absolute necessitie of breakinge off ye Treatie of
Marriage.

Then came a message from the Lordes, by Seiriant Crue[93] and mr
Atturney[94] who signified the Lords were desyrous that since the Relation
was made equally to both houses the Representation of the Duke of
Buckenhams cleeringe might be likewise by both, and therfore our
House Committee to ioyne with their, which mr Alforde although in
ye [?beginning] hee professed himselfe to have beene of another mynde
moved might be agreed unto.

Mr Recorder[95] added that the number of Committees, Time and
Place, were to be requyred of the Lords by a messadge sent upp from
our house which in the end was agreed unto [f.24v] mr Solliciter[96]
haveinge first delivered the Committees preparacion in this buisines
which was a paper drawne upp by way of direction to mr Speaker:

1. First That the Duke of Buckenham did not say any thinge, but
   that which the necessitie of the matter lead unto him –
2. That hee lett nothinge fall that might reflect uppon the personn
   of the Kinge of Spaine to his dishonour –
3. That all which hee saide was avowed by the Prince

---

[92] i.e. praemunires.
[93] Sir Ranulph Crew, King's Serjeant.
[94] Sir Thomas Coventry.
[95] Heneage Finch.
[96] Sir Robert Heath.

4 And that they conceived for whatsoever had passed in that Relation hee deserved not onely noe blame butt honour and thanks –

5 That they esteemed itt a great wronge to the house, for if soe emynent a person in soe worthy a matter should be soe highlie questioned noe particular member of their house durst with any saffety speake;

Wherfore they besought his Majestie not to give eare to any pryvate Informacions in this kinde; Sir James *Perratt* thought the word Reflectinge too generall, Mr Alforde would have the Comittee have power of themselves to drawe upp perfectlie this Report with the Lords, butt this last was not approved, The first not thought materiall.

Before this was concluded. The Mr of the Rolls[97] and ye Lord Cheife Barron[98] brought an other message that ye Lords desyrous to give expedition to soe weighty & important buisines, did desire if our convenyencies would allowe itt to have a conferrence with us to morrow att Whitehall at two of the clocke with divers called uppon[;] and Sir Edward Cecill spake much for, sayinge delay was daungerous, and that hee would venture his head wee should have an enterprize on us if wee did not speedily begin, besides many other passadges, that all *Parlyament* men might heare their reasons. Butt Sir Dudley Diggs and others thought itt much too soone, wee haveinge had noe time to deliberate –

Wheruppon Sir Robert Phillips seconded by mr Glandveild[99] after some interrupcion in allmost the selfe same Tearmes moved that the messengers might be returned with answere [f.25r] that if possiblie wee could prepare our selves wee would attend their Lordships as they requyred[,] otherwise they should understand from us that wee could not to morrow morninge, & with this message the Lords messengers were dispatched and ours sent uppon the former message touchinge the clearinge of the Duke of Buckenham.

Secretarie Calvert saide the kinge had willed him, to signify to the house understandinge that complaintes were come against the Lord *Keeper*, His Majesties desire was ye House should not meddle with any except they challenge him for corruption, for the particular orders made by him were many, and a hard case to call him to accompt for everie one not fitt except therin were allegation of Corruption, from which hee hoped the Lord Keeper would be found Free, As for those allredy putt in hee was ready to make his Justification –

Mr Secretary demaunded the Answere. Which was. No [BLANK]

[97] Sir Julius Caesar.
[98] Sir Lawrence Tanfield.
[99] i.e. Glanville.

att that present consideringe that there were presidents of [BLANK] by Acts of *Parlyament* besides those which were given outt of [BLANK] butt att the breakinge upp of the house, itt was resolved after the dispatch of this great buisines to take this message into more especiall consideracion and to returne his Majestie an answere therin –

The the great buisines comminge afoote againe Sir Henry Mildmay and mr Covington[100] moved that ye wholl house might sitt this afternoone as a Committee, and mr Speaker be present if occasion were to make itt a house. Sir John Straunguage made a longe speech tendinge to these fower poyntes –

1. The confyninge of the Papists to men well grounded in Religion to the intent ther might be noe daunger of Insurrection –
2. The securinge of the Portes by dispersinge of Forces which hee said were in England trayned men not lesse the[n] One hundred and threeskore thousand. [f.25v]
3. Reunitinge the dispersed Forces of the Princes of Germany –
4. And the securinge of Ireland.

Sir Dudley Diggs moved that the House might be made a Committee wherin men might speake freely Consideringe that the nature of the buisiness requyred the advise of severall professions –

Sir Edwin Sandis desyred our deliberacions might be bounded in the termes propounded *Continuance* or *Dissolvinge* of Treaty[;] for the poynte of Warr however itt might be a necessarie consequence uppon ye discharge of the Treaties yett itt was none of ye poynts now propounded

As for ye continuinge of Treaties hee said hee had in Italy heard Ambassages and Treaties called ye Spanyards owne weopon att which hee would ever foyle us –

Hee added likewise that wee were not singly to deliver our opynions, butt to deliver likewise reasons to fortyfie itt, for our opynion was nothinge with the Kinge nor ought to be, butt reasons would sway & prevaile in the whole world;

Sir Peeter Haymond seconded by mr Mallory moved against the clarks setting downe mens names to their mocions which hee said was a ferrular that divers men had beene payd with, and could instance of some men that had beene tolde, you spake soe many times in Parlyament to such & such purpose, and therfore moved that the specifyinge of names might be lefte; Mr Speaker and Mr Pym and some others affirmed that divers that they knew had received benifitt by the Clarks entry uppon some questyoninge of these speeches afterwards –

Commendinge his greate care and discrecion to have been such as hee never sett downe what might preiudice any man, in the end this

---

[100] i.e. Coryton.

was thought fitt to be considered of by a Committee –

Mr Alforde presented a paper conteyninge 17 reasons which together with a Peticion was the last Parlyament 1621 delivered to the Kinge att Greenwich in the [f.26r] name of the whole house which hee conceived would help expedite the present business –

One[101] moved to stay the East India Ships nowe bound outward .5. in nomber wherin hee alleadged went 1500 Marriners which was too greate a number to spare consideringe the great want that was of them, now by reason of the [W. country mariners being at Newfoundland and would not be back until Michaelmas[102]] wheron they were imployd, hee affirmed that on Satterday ther hadd been 800 musketts carryed aboard and great quantitie of Powder besides other Provisions –

Sr Robert Mansell seconded this motion. Mr Abbott made answere the Ships sent butt fower nor above 600 men well provided, and as hee conceived bound on an enterprize as much for the honour and benefitt of the Kingdome as any other, ye Spanyards haveinge given Comission to cease [seize] on all our Ships in those partes uppon pretence of wronge offered att Ormuse;[103] This matter was deferred.

Sir Edward Cooke reported that the Committee of our house had mett with the Lords and their words for cleering the Duke were allmost ye very same as theirs soe that as wee conceive God must be acknowledged to have putt itt into their mouthes.

[The rest of the page is blank, as are ff.26v,27r]

[f.27v] Tuesday morninge the 2th of March – 1623.

Mr Burlamach and [Mr Giles Bandyputt[104]] naturalyzinge were propounded[;] betweene the first and second readinge they tooke the Oathes of Alleigance and Supremacy –

Sir Arthur Ingram and mr Bateman moved that great Circumspection might be had in this kinde for the grauntinge of this Priveledge promisiail onely[105] would both preiudice the Kings Custome which are greater from Straungers then Free denizons, and be a meanes of clokinge the goods of Marchants in forraigne partes whose Factors onely the most of these here in London were, and for their advantage sought this greatly to the detryment of ye English Subiects.

Mr Glandveilde that had the chaire of the Committee for Pryveledges

---

[101] Sir Edward Seymour: *Nicholas.*
[102] Ibid.
[103] In the Persian Gulf, taken by the English from the Portuguese in April 1622.
[104] *Nicholas;* 'Van de Putte': *Hawarde.*
[105] Here Conyam has not understood Ferrar, who probably wrote 'promiscuously'.

reported that Sir William Gray beinge knight for *Northumberland* and since made a Barron they conceived a new *Writt* to be sent downe, which mr Speaker signified was done –

Next whereas the Sherrife had returned Two Writs for Southwarke in both which mr Yarwood was, itt was resolved his choyse was good and hee should be allowed to sitt in the house, butt for Bromfeilde and Mynguy, the opinyon was of the wholl Committee that the returne was naught butt for ye Election itt selfe the Committee was equally devyded in opynion whether itt were on Bromfeilds parte or a new Writt to be sent which the house in ye end ordered[,] not fyndinge ye Election of either of them certaine.

Sir Edward Cooke in this *Argument* delivered if a Letter of Atturney be made to Three severall personns ioyntlie and severally, all Three or any one of them hath power butt not two of them because their Act is neither ioyntlie nor severally.

The Bill against Usury was read the first time, beinge to prohibite the takinge of above 8 per centum.

Next ye Bill for libertie of buyinge and sellinge Wooles and Yearne, which was ordered should be referred to a sett time taken, together with itt should be read all the Bills of the same nature.

[f.28r]   The Report of the Select Committee was delivered by Sir Edwin Sandys as beinge as followeth[106]

Sir Robert Phillips observed divers Acts of the Spanyards playnly declaringe their Intentions were never to performe either Match or Restitucion of the Pallatinate –

That Spinola[107] raysed his Forces under Colour to assist ye *Emperour* in *Bohemia* butt did in deed take in ye Palatinate and that att the same time the Kinge of Spaine had drawne our Kinge to send his Navy to ioyne with his against the *Pirates* and *Turkes*. –

That whilste the Chauncellour of the Chequor[108] att their Invitation treated they tooke in *Heildeberge* & [Frankenthal] &c. although the English Collours were hunge out on the Walls –

That the Electorate was given to [Maximilian I, Duke of Bavaria] duringe the Princes beinge in Spaine, and Letters of Congratulation came with the newes from Bruzells –

Hee moved the Conferrence might be given ye Lords in ye after-noone. Sir Henry Mildemay to send messengers to them instantly which was done.

Sir Dudley Diggs moved that by way of addition to ye reasons in

---

[106] A gap of two or three lines follows.
[107] Ambrogio Spinola, the Genoese general of the Spanish troops in the Netherlands.
[108] Sir Richard Weston.

writinge, There might be especiall thanks given ye Lords for their good correspondencie –

Next they should be desyred to ioyne with us to give the Prince comon thanks for his openinge our eyes & admirable care of Religion and the Comon good. And that hee should be humbly entreated in the name of both houses & consequently of the wholl kingdome to present publique thanks to his Majesty for his singular favour in assembling us and comittinge matters of such weight and trust to our consideracions – And farther beseech him uppon the approbacion of our ioynt advise to declare his owne pleasure by giveinge an end to all these fruitless Treaties. And that Lastly a day of publique thanks might be ordered through the wholl kingdome for all these reasons, and for the prayinge for good successe.

Sir Edward Giles seconded him and thought fitt that the Inveterate malice of the Spanyards against us uppon the opynion of soe many and dishonourable iniuries received from us might be touched, itt beinge a sure argument they would never forgive us and all the while they had kept fayre quarter with us, itt was onely to bring us more into daunger.

[f.28v]   Sir Edward Cooke moved the Penultime clause of Sir Dudley Diggs his motion att which hee was absent. beinge gone upp to carry the messadge to the Lords –

Sir Nath: Rich would have the Kinge desyred to doe itt[109] speedilie. –

And wheras divers had moved that if the Lords should have [BLANK] uppon our reasons wee should not then mencion them

Mr Treasurour[110] moved that wee might proceed *gradatim* with them as they signified their opinion soe not to declare our – And as they should give reasons soe wee to declare ours although they should be ye same; –

Which course was approved and the deliverie of these and the mannadginge of the Conferrence referred to Sir Edwin Sandys, Sir Edward Cooke, Sir Robert Phillips, mr Solliciter, mr Recorder and Sir Dudley Diggs besides whome none else might speake, The reasons were approved by the house butt ordered they should not be delivered in writinge but the substance of them by word of mouth.

[The rest of the page is BLANK.]

[f.29r]   Tuesday in the afternoone ye 2. of March 1623:

---

[109] 'prespeden' erased.
[110] Sir Thomas Edmondes, Treasurer of the Household.

Beinge assembled att Whitehall in the Hall, The Lord Keeper began.[111]

First signifyinge the Lords good exceptance of our ready correspondencie which they earnestly desyred might be continued until the end.

Next hee declared their Lordships[,] desyrous to give expedicion to the mayne buisines, had desyred this Conferrence for two poyntes to deliver unto us, by way of Suplement[:] An Accompt of certaine particularities omitted in the Princes and Dukes late Relation, And to acquainte us with their opynion touchinge the buisinesses propounded.

The First Consisted in three particularrs –

1. Touchinge the Marriadge
2 Touchinge ye Pallatinate. and
3 Touchinge a Heroyicall Act and resolution of ye Prince-

Which Three thinges the Lords desires were should be delivered unto us the representative bodie of the Commons that soe itt might after pass to all

1   For the first itt was that the Match did not move from hence butt was first begunn and moved 1614 by ye Duke of [Lerma[112]] to the Earle of Bristoll

2   Touchinge ye Second that the Earle of Bristoll had from ye Kinge particuler and certaine assurances by promise of ye Restitucion of ye Pallatinate as should by certaine dispatches be manyfested in due time.

3   Third Suplement was to the eternall honour of ye Prince and unspeakable comforte of us all who about July last understood that ther was a rumour spread in Spaine that they would steale away, wheruppon great preparacions & sure were made to intercept them, and uppon their soe intercepting a resolucion to keepe them as Prisoners, The Prince understanding this sent ye Duke to ye Comittee to acquainte them that although out of love hee had without their knowledge putt himselfe into their handes yett hee would never out of feare steall from them adding *Mala mens mala animus* and that[,] howsoever[,] they should finde him free from such base thoughts, butt understandinge that the Rumor still Continued hee begann [f.29v] to give himselfe for a lost man and ther uppon haveinge sent away Grymes[113] with a dispatch hee gave him in comaund that if hee heard nothinge of any detension hee should not say any thinge, Butt if soe be hee should heare that hee was any way restrayned, hee should[114] then

---

[111] For this speech, see also Hacket Pt I pp. 185–86.
[112] *Nicholas*
[113] Richard Grimes or Greames, gentleman of the horse to the Duke of Buckingham.
[114] A repetition of 'heare that hee was any way' cancelled.

in his name intreate his Father not to thinke any more of him butt as a lost man, and without any remembrance of him reflect all his Royall thoughts uppon his Sister (whom hee desyred him presently to send for) and uppon her Childern and uppon the safety of his owne estate –

These were ye Suplements, now touchinge their Lordships opynion Itt was this that haveinge advised *Super totam materiam*, their Resolucion was, That his Majesty cannott remayne nor rely any farther uppon either of both Treaties, that of the *Marriadge*, or that of the Palatinate with any convenyencie for the preservacion of Religion nor safety of his owne honour nor safety of his estate, nor good of his *GrandChildren*, nor generall good of this Kingdome –

This was the Lords opynion, And now their desire was, to know what ours was in these poyntes –

Who made answere that the Knights Cittizens and Burgesses &c. had comaunded him to make answere that haveing duly considered, deliberately consulted, They had maturely resolved *nullo contradicente*, That his Majesty should absolutely dissolve both Treaties and give an end. haveinge in this followed the Precept in Judges, *Consider, Consult*, and then give sentence soe that hee had nothinge to say butt onely to treade in ye same stepps their Lordships did; Butt farther hee was to beseech them they would ioyne with them in humble Peticion to his Majesty who never had denyed what was in the name of both houses peticioned, that hee would att his convenyencie (and their humble desire was itt might be with expedicion) deliver his Royall determination and Resolution, for breakinge upp of these Treaties and after his resolucion soe made that hee would be graciously pleased to make a publique & manyfest declaration of itt, to be a guide unto us in our subsequent proceedings, and to inable us with more allacritie to goe on to the comforte of all good people both att home and abroade –

This was ye substance of his speech much short of what the house ordered [f.30r] The *Lord Archbishop of Canterbury*[115] spoke sayinge hee was comaunded by the Lords, first to signifie their thanks to God that had brought thinges open to light.

Next to his Majestie that was so graciously pleased to ask advise

And to you the Commons for haveinge concurred in ye same. [BLANK] as itt came from one Fountaine, ye Kinge soe itt was Received with one heart, for they were butt one heart although they might be compared to the two eyes concludinge that they conceived this Match would not stand either with Incorporacion of Religion, or ye safety of ye Kinge or the preservation of the *Prince*, or the honour or good of this Kingdome.

---

[115] George Abbot.

And to the intent the buisines might not coole, they had chosen from amongst themselves a Committee of 24 to meete with a Committee of our house, to conferr together touchinge the speedy settinge downe of reasons, that they might goe to his Majesty not onely with opynion butt with ground of reason for this their Resolucion, such as might give his Majesty and the wholl Christian world sattisfaction.

The Prince added that after this was performed a Convenient number of both houses should goe with their reasons to ye Kinge –

And soe itt beinge answered to morrow morninge ye house would take order for these thinges.

The meetinge dissolved.

The Lord Keeper at ye close sayinge that ye Lords had againe comaunded him to iterate their ioy for ye good Correspondencie from our house –

[Ff.30v,31r,31v are blank.]

[f.32r]   Thursday morninge the 4th of March – 1623

[About a third of the page is blank.]

Next followed ye Relacion of Sir Robert Cotten who declared how in January – 1614, That Gondamar haveinge sent twise or thrice to him came att last to visite him att his house in Black Fryers under pretence of comunicatinge with him the Coppie of Certaine Articles

[Three lines are blank.]

27. hee moved him to sett [BLANK] with the Earle of Somersett the Proposicions of a Match with the Prince and the second daughter of Spaine.

10 February beinge againe pressed by Gondamarr hee acquainted his Majestie who gave him warrant to goe on to sound their Intentions Wheruppon hee desyred Gondamarr to declare if hee had any power concerninge any such thinge who then shewed him a letter to such purpose signed.

All this while Sir Robert Cotten never went to Gondamar butt hee came home to him, att last hee tould him hee had acquainted the Earle of Somersett, who was unwillinge in regard of the straunge answere soe lately received from the Kinge [of] Spaine touchinge the other Match &c. And that itt was a fatall thinge to begin such a Treatie.

Butt the 9th of Aprill hee saide his Proposicion would be harkned unto soe that the Kinge of Spaine would give securytie *Verbo Regi[s]* that hee intended itt sincerely *Fide Christiano* that hee conceived that itt might stand with his Religion. [f.32v] And Thirdlie that hee would be content with reasonable conditions touchinge matter of Religion, in which poynt hee shewed him ye demaunds of [?the Emperor Charles V] and of Mounser[116] when hee was suter to the Queene to be content with [The rest of this line and the next two are blank.]

For the first hee tould him Charles the Fifte under pretence of Two Marriadges [to] Mary ye daughter & Sister[117] abused Henry ye 8th Fifteene yeares togeather by this meanes and with the *Expence* of *Three hundred Thousand pounds* of his as himselfe acknowledged obteyned in ye meane while the *Empire*; yeat for all this att ye intersession of the *Parliament* in Tolledo, although their had been bookes sett forth of the Espousall with the latter Mary hee marryed Issabella of Spaine.[118] and therfore hee requyred good security in these poyntes.

The 10th of June ye Spanish Ambassadour sent for him where duringe his beinge [there, there] arryved a packett from Spaine which hee opened in his presence, & ther was a letter of the Kings owne hand writinge with two lines att the bottome blurred, wherin hee writt that because itt had not yeat beene comunicated farther then to ye Earle of Somersett and Cavaliro[119] Cotten itt was not decent in him to appeare butt hee had given full Authoritie and Credence to the Duke of Lerma, who writt lardglie that the Kinge of Spaine ment itt in all good fayth and sinceritie for ye good of both kingdomes[;] That hee was resolved by his Confessor who promised to write a Booke in defence therof that itt might be lawfully done. And that for matters of Religion hee would desire nothinge to our preiudice, and desyred expedition that itt might not be **no** [?NF; thereafter BLANK, as is the next line]

The Kinge of England haveinge then a Treaty with Fraunce on foote, replyed hee would not like a Marchaunt have Two comissions a foote att once, hee would first ende one before he begann an other.

These letters were belike Counterfeyted by Gondamar [f.33r] For afterward the Kinge tould Sir Robert Cotten that hee[120] was a Juglinge Jack and not long after this by reason of some troubles that befell him, knowne to a honorable personne in our house his Treaties Concerninge this matter broke off.

---

[116] The Duke of Alençon.

[117] Plans for the marriage of Henry VIII's sister to the future Emperor Charles V occupied the years 1506–14, and for Charles V's marriage to Henry's daughter the years 1520–25.

[118] *Recte* Portugal, in 1526.

[119] Cavaliero or Caballero: i.e. Sir (Robert).

[120] i.e. Gondamar; cf. BL, Harl. MS 159 f.25v.

Sir Edward Cooke after the endinge of this Relation tooke notice that hee understood himselfe to be designed by these wordes of Sir Robert Cottens whome hee confessed about 1615 to have had in examination for divers matters for which hee had the Kings Free Pardon, butt amongst the rest his Correspondency with the Spanish Embassadours was one, which hee questioned him of in regard that itt is a Maxim, *Subditis omnia iura hospitalitatis et familiaritatis Cum Legatis prohi[bita sunt?]* Butt when hee sawe the warrant which Sir Robert Cotten shewed him hee was content.

Heere Sir Robert Phillips tooke the Narration and said how that the ArchBishop said that hee tould Sir Richard Weston uppon his returne and plaine discovery, that hee should ever love honour and pray for him.

And the Prince added that the Relation of his proceedinges beinge longe were not yeat fynished butt should be for the sattisfaccion of his Majestie and the wholl Christian world

The Archbishop tolde them hee had charge to remember three Suplements.

　1: First touchinge the first begininge of the Match from ye Spanyards.
　2 Next touchinge the assured promises of Restitution.
　3 The Third Concerninge the fickleness of their Continuall Res-
　　olutions –

1.　Concerninge the First a letter[121] was read from Sir John Digby to ye Kinge of the 3th of January 1614 beinge verie long wherin was sett downe, how the Duke of Lerma haveinge formerly moved a Match which by reason of the French Treaty was neglected, did with strong ernestness press itt, att his returne into Spaine, cominge on purpose pryvately to his house in a morninge swearinge hee desyred nothing more in the world then to see this match effected And how that occasions and Circumstances of time had changed [f.33v] the state of buisinesses, soe that the Kinge of England was not to be discouraged by the former refusall in *Prince Henries* propounded Match; And therfore motioninge if ther were any possibillitie of divertinge the French Marriadge that itt might be sett on foote[;] That the Cardinall of Tolledo the Confessor and one *Padro Frederico* a Jesuite butt a moderate man were appoynted Comissioners for the buisiness because the Dukes leasure would not serve; Wheruppon ye Kinge gave Sir John Digby a warrant to treate of this buisines.

2.　Concerninge the Second pointe the Restitucion of ye Palatinate was read a letter[122] from Sir John Digby dated the 9th of August 1622 To the Kinge confidentlie promisinge that althinges should be restored,

[121] Now PRO, SP 94/21 f.33.
[122] Now PRO, SP 94/25 Pt I f.182.

And att the same time an other[123] from him to Secretary Calvert att
large, declaringe how that the Counsell of Spaine had playnlie resolved
to sattisfie ye Kinge of Great Brittaine by intercession or by ye King
takinge Armes against the Emperour that the King of Spaine had
written letters to that purpose to the Emperour in verie playne termes
although for the Emperours honour they were not willinge to give
Coppies of them desyringe rather to have reall authoritie with the
Emperour then to bragg of itt and his Secretary Seliza[124] did by a
formall message deliver unto him uppon the 4th of that August – That
Gondemar had besturred himselfe bravely in this buisines and did
speake the most honorably that was possible both of the Kinge and
Nation –

Another letter[125] was allsoe read of the 24th of October 1622 wherin
Digby writt, that haveinge followed the Kinge of Spaine to the
[Escoriall] uppon a dispatch from England that unless he had there
red[y?] assurance first from Olivares that the Palsgrave[126] performinge
the Conditions promised the Kinge of Spaine would either by fayre
meanes with the Emperour see him restored or else assist the Kinge of
England with his Armes to doe itt by force, and next from the Kings
owne mouth, that if the Kinge of England had not entire sattisfaccion
from the Emperour, hee himselfe would take Armes against him, soe
that hee writt except they were falser then the Devills in Hell ther was
noe doubt of a good end to ye kinges owne heartes desire.

[f.34r]   Ther was likewise read another letter[127] of the 10th of December
162[2] from the Earle of Bristoll to Secretary Calverte wherin hee writt
how that although uppon new accasions[sic] there had beene some in
the Counsell that had given their Votes that the Kinge of Spain should
by noe meanes take Armes against the Emperour yett the greatest parte
had overrulde itt in performance of their former promises – And therin
he writes that the Kinge of England had not soe many great men and
Counsellours in all Christendom hartely affected to him as in that
Court, Farther that the vulgar did with incredible ioy and allacritie
entertaine the rumor purposely spread to trie their affections of ye
conclusion of the Match, That mr [Gage[128]] had extraordinarily performed his parte, testifyinge that ye Catholiques in England did not
require further securitie then ye Kings and Princes word, And concluded

---

[123] Ibid., ff.169–70.
[124] Juan de Ciriza.
[125] Now PRO, SP 94/25 Pt II ff.263–66, *recte* of 21 October 1622.
[126] The Elector Palatine or *Pfalzgraf*, Frederick V, husband of James I's daughter
Elizabeth, and briefly in 1620 King of Bohemia.
[127] Ibid., ff.342–26.
[128] Ibid., f.325.

that for ye Emperour and Bavier[129] hee had little hope in them further then they should be constrayned; –

And here Secretary Calvert observed that although ye Earle of Bristoll had Instructions to Treate of both Match and Restitution ioyntly, yett not soe as to make the first dependant on the last, and said hee was not his advocate and therfore would not take uppon him ye defence of his negligence, and observed farther how Contrarie the Spanish proceedings were in the Papists, that though the Match seemed to goe forward, yett ye restitucion went att the same time backward.

3. The Third Suplement propounded by ye Lord Archbishop was that they never from the begininge intended any Match

And ye Prince here observed that Gondemar did in ye first propositions of Treatie make offer of the Title of ye united Provinces to be Cast into the Dowry, but after the Match was interteyned itt was never mentioned soe that itt was butt a bayte onely to entice & allure us.

And here was recounted a passage between Digbie and Spinola who uppon his returne 1621 uppon Digbys reporte what answere the Kinge of Spaine had given touchinge Restitucion of the Palatinate, replyed noe doub[t] Soe wee by the Kinge of Englands assistance may have our [f.34v] Rebells reduced to their due obedience, The like answere did Gondemar make unto him that ther was little hope of itt, And ye Lord Chamberlayne[130] reported how Diego De Metza[131] uppon the like occasion made him the [132] same answere, which the Earle of Carlill likewise attested And soe confident they grew in this Resolucion that it was propounded to ye Kinge himselfe, whoe as the Prince reported made a Noble Answere, That hee had found them a Free estate and would soe leave them –

Next Sir *Robert Phillips* reported how Sir Edwin Sandis delivered the Reasons of the House with exceeding Comendacion and applause of the Lords haveinge by way of Introduccion (which Sir Edwin Sandys afterwards affirmed to have been onely by way of explanation) shewed how the Kinge of Spaine did seeke to diminish the Soveraigntie of his Majestie by causinge the Papists to have a dependance on him for the use of their Religion obteyned at [BLANK] intercession and to be maynteyned by his meanes, & if itt were interrupted, to be restored by his Armes for soe ye Pope requyred that hee should by his oath bynde himselfe unto.

Mr *Treasurour*[133] tolde how Gondemar comminge by *Paris* when hee was Ambassadour they tould him how the cheife motive of the Match

---

[129] i.e. Bavaria.
[130] William Herbert, 3rd Earl of Pembroke.
[131] Diego de Mexia, marques de Leganes, ambassador from the Archdukes in 1623.
[132] 'like' erased.
[133] Sir Thomas Edmondes.

was desire of advanceinge the Catholique Cause in England, and
without good successe therin nothinge could be done for itt was
impossible that the Kinge of Spaine could agree to bestowe his daughter
wher the [**Saynts of god**:NF] (soe hee called them) wer martyrd.
That itt was not to preferr their house which was the best blood in the
world, nor any other respect then this which made them parte with a
Lady and such a huge portion; Butt if there was good success in the
matter of Religion, not only the portion butt the whole [**Indies**:NF]
should be at our [?disposal]

And yett att the same time hee told another gentleman that negotiated
with him, that all thinges were concluded and the Kinge of England
should not be prest to any more such straunge contradiction of
[BLANK][.] hee challengeth him, & demaundinge in which hee should
beleive him *Gondemar* blushinge replied hee spake accordinge to ye
occasion.

[f.35r] Sir Edwin Sandis saide the *Protestants* in Fraunce have no
manner of dependence in the world in any other Prince then their
owne Kinge [**nor that king any truer subiects then they[;] that
the exercise**:NF] of their Religion is by Lawe &c

Sir *James Perrat* moved that ye Reasons might not be delivered in
writinge butt the Lords should first deliver theirs[.] This was well liked
but quallyfied by mr *Recorder*[134] that a *Coppie* might be given to the
Prince onely for his sattisfaccion not any way as an Act of the house,
but they were onely by word of mouth to be reported –

Sir Isack [**Wake**:NF] was called uppon to repeate what hee did
deliver yeasterday to the Prince and Lords which hee did to this
purpose.

That the Duke of Savoy being young an offer was made him of the
Infanta Katherina[135] (although [**Rodolph**:NF] the then Emperour
sought her butt the State of Spayne conceived [**his**:NF[136]] allyance
more beneficiall to them) that her portion should be *Eight hundred
Thousand Crownes*[,] the recoverie of [**Suchazella, Finall** – – – – – – – –
And Savona:NF] and other[137] [**places in the possession of Geno-
va**:NF] and to ye heire male by her[,] the Investiture of the Duchy of
Millan[.] these [**offers**:NF[138]] drew him against his Counsells will to
Spaine – wher the [**Duke of Infantado** –:NF] mett him received
him with all respect as his Maisters sonne in Lawe & theruppon

---

[134] Heneage Finch.
[135] The Infanta Catalina Micaela (1567–97) married Charles Emmanuel, Duke of Savoy
in 1585.
[136] over 'haveinge'.
[137] 'possessions' deleted by NF.
[138] deleting a word now illegible.

perswaded him not to stand uppon Articles with the Kinge of Spaine, which Counsell (although otherwise advised by his owne Counsell) hee followed beinge assured that the first night of their marriage hee should under ye Infantaes pillow finde whatsoever hee wished, and with such fayr wordes was hee sent againe into Italy, tellinge him with the person of the Infanta hee carryed with him whatsoever hee desyred, portion hee should finde ready in Italy, and all the kinges mynisters there ready to performe ye other promises to the full, but his portion was turned into a pension after ye rate of 8 per centum, and that paide butt for a verie fewe yeares and former assignements that hee had in the Duchy of Millane and a revennue uppon ye Silke [f.35v]   in [**Messina**:NF] were taken from him and hee thrust into a warr against the Kinge of Fraunce, which Whilst hee was buisied about neer Marcellis[139] the Kinge of Spaine sent his daughter (who in the Dukes absence governed his affayres beyound ye Mountaines) a letter charginge her in Vertue of her obedience to deliver the Cittadell of [**Turin**:NF] to a Spanish Garrison which hee appoynted under pretence of securinge itt, butt in deed to depose the Duke of his Inheritance[.] the letter shee sent to her husband who absolutely forbiddinge her shee refused to obey her Fathers Comaund Wheruppon the Kinge would not give her his blessinge till her dyinge day although shee instantly sought itt

Uppon Sir Edwin Sandis his report of ye Committees for Trade [**desyre**:NF] Tuesday was likewise appoynted for that buisines, & mr Chauncellour of the Chequour[140] desyred to desyre the Lord Treasurour[141] to send all ye papers and proceedinges in this buisines which passed through his hands ye last Parlyament when hee sate in the Chayre for this particular —

Sir Dudley Diggs reported how ye Lords desyred a SubCommittee of 16: to ioyne with 8 of theirs to draw upp ye reasons in writing[,] divers Lords and his highness haveinge delivered sundry particularrs of the Spanyards undue proceedinges in their treaties, which are ye same that were drawne upp as ye [**proofes and Instances**:NF] of the last Article —

Mr Chauncellour of ye Chequour related some of ye passadges of his Ambasage. That although they had accepted our treaty with ye Kinge of England & had allowed him to be answerable for all the [**incapacitys** – :NF] of ye Pallatine that stood [**proscribed** – :NF] yett they first quarrelled with his Comission, because the Palsgraves hand was not to itt and when in this they were sattisfied, yett every day they found new defects, and although they att first assured that

---

[139] Marseille.
[140] Sir Richard Weston.
[141] Lionel Cranfield, Earl of Middlesex.

the Infanta[142] had full power, in the end they denyed shee had any to conclude on the Emperours behalfe. That within 3: or 4 daies, that hee had received most Confident letters from ye Earle of Bristoll [f.36r]   hee had the worst answere from the Infanta that possibly could be; That when ye cessation of Armes was urdged they alleadginge Mansfeilds[143] comminge into Flaunders, made answere that none could be except the Kinge would declare himselfe a defendour of their Provinces. –

The bill for transportinge wollen cloth was read.

[The rest of the page is blank.]

[f.36v]   [144]Fryday morning the 5th of March 1623

Sir Edwin Sandis[145] made reporte that the Duke of Buckenham[146] delivered itt to be his Majesties pleasure,[147] that the Committees of both houses should attend this afternoone; That hee had presented the Reasons of the house in writinge to his highnes as of especiall confidence whose pleasure and of ye whole Committee was there should be noe Coppies[148] given of them to any whosoever, That the SubCommittee of the Lords had approved their reasons without any alteracion except an addition in the [149] end, beinge matter of Instance of the insinceritie of the Spanish Intentions in their proceedinges which was by five particularrs demonstrated

[The ensuing gap, of about a third of the page, can be filled by FP 1584b, in the hands of John Ferrar and Tristram Conyam. It is endorsed by Conyam: 'Reasons Conceived by ye SElect[*sic*] Committee touchinge The/Dissolvinge of the Treatie/March ye 1623.' and headed:

Reasons Conceived by the [150] house of Commons to fortify the Resolution[151] to advyce his Majesty to proceede noe further in the treatys with Spayne

[142] The Archduchess Isabella Clara Eugenia.

[143] Count Ernst von Mansfeld, then in the service of the Elector Palatine.

[144] Here begins FP 1584c, the only original notes made by Nicholas Ferrar to have survived. Since Conyam reproduced them with a high degree of accuracy, they are not here given in full. NF's variations, are, where legible, given in subsequent footnotes.

[145] 'Sandys'.

[146] 'D of Buckingham'.

[147] 'pleasur', over 'commaunde' erased.

[148] 'Coppye'

[149] 'last' erased.

[150] 'Selecte Committee' erased.

[151] 'of the House' erased.

First it is observed that the State of Spayne not Content with those ordinary provissions for the exercisse of the Romane Religion by the[152] Infanta and her family which[153] other princes in like case would have[154] demaunded and [155] which his Majesty with greate reasonne might at the beginning of this treaty have Conceived they would have binne Contented with, have with greate Vehemence upon advantadg of having the Princes personne in there possession pressed a Generall Connivence for all his Majestys Subiectes of the Romane Religion to the Greate dishonour of Almighty god in the sincerity of his Service in this Realme and to the[156] *apparent deminution of his Majestys soverainty by establishinge an nessary dependence for protection upon a Forraine king and State and to the great derogation of the*[157] of the lawes of this kingdome and lastly the Greife and discouradgment of all his Majestys well affected Subiectes from whose generall discontents they expected as well appeareth a Consequence of no small Mischeyfe

Secondly It is observed that during the Continuance of this treaty and by[158] reasone of the same the Popish faction have exceedingly increased in this Realmes booth in[159] Multitude and[160] bouldnes And when as heeretofore they have binne devided a mongst them Selfves in to the Partie of the Jesuits depending upon Spayne and the Secular Priest otherwise: They are generally now[161] stronglie united togeather dependinge noe lesse uppon Spaine for temporall respects then uppon Rome for Spirituall, which consideringe the house of Spaine hath been allwaies Capitall enemies to our Religion to encrease their owne greatness by Exterpatinge ye Protestant party in all places where they can prevaile, cannott be butt of most daungerous Consequence to ye saffty of the Kinge and this Realme, unlesse a remedy be provided with speed, for the abatinge of that Party hiere at home, which cannott be duringe the time that[162] these Treaties are on foote

3   Thirdly itt is observed that by advantage of these Treaties and therby keepinge of his Majesty in hope of generall Peace They have contraryly under pretence of assistinge ye Emperour, oppressed the Protestant Party in most parts of Christendome beinge the Auntient

[152] 'Lady' erased.

[153] 'would' erased.

[154] 'demanded' erased.

[155] 'with' erased.

[156] 'greate derogatione' erased.

[157] John Ferrar has interpolated the words between the two asterisks.

[158] 'occatione' erased.

[159] 'multitue' erased.

[160] 'Couradg' erased.

[161] 'be all' erased. At this point John Ferrar ceases to write, and Tristram Conyam takes over.

[162] 'that of' erased.

Allyes and confederates of this Crowne to the endaungeringe not only of the whole State of the Reformed Religion, but allsoe of ye Common saffety of all the Professors of the same –

Fourthly during the time of these Treaties of Love with his Majesty they have with all kinde of hostillytie sett uppon his Majesties sonne in Lawe the husband of his onely and most Royall daughter invaded[163] his Townes & Territories in all places,[164] and in fine disinherited him with all that Royall Ofspringe of all his Auntient Patrimoniall Honours and Possessions, to the great dishonour of his Majestie and extreame greife of all his well affected Subiects And now allso at the last,[165] when they should have come to make good the hope of Restitution[,] they have layde new grounds for endless delays, and turned pretended difficulties into apparent Impossibillities not forbearinge allsoe now to annex as a condition to the weake hope of their uncertaine and unperfect Restitucion. That the Eldest sonne of ye Count Pallatine[166] should be brought upp in ye Emperours Courte Soe restless are their desires to worke the overthrowe of our Religion by all possible devises.

Lastlie itt is too apparant how manyfoldly from time to time they have deluded and abused his Majesty with their Treaties, how small respect they have showed to the Princes greatness and Worth What Indignitys[167] the *oferred againe and againe to His Highnes by impor-tuning him, upon all advantages to forsake his religione contrary to the coustome of all princes and contrary to the antient lawes of Honour and hospitallity: whoe ought to have binne used there with all Princely frendlynes and pressed to nothing unto which he was indisposed Considering with what Confidence being soe great a Prince he had put him selfe within their power although it pleased god to fortifie his Princely harte that he Constantly withstoude all there attempts and Machinations to his own[168] immortall Honour and to the unspeakeable Comforte of all the good peopull of his Fathers kingdome where unto may be ceded the Infinite advantagiousnes and endles delays in there Treateys inviting still to new Treaties*[169] invitinge still to new Treaties and turning all to the advantadge of their owne particular ends, being true to nothinge but their owne grounded Maxims with which neither the Match nor Restitucion of ye Palatynate can possibly consist butt

---

[163] Interpolated by John Ferrar.
[164] Here John Ferrar has erased 'invaded'.
[165] 'cast' erased.
[166] Frederick Henry (1614–29).
[167] Inserted by Ferrar, after erasing Conyam's 'Dishonours'.
[168] 'imp-' erased.
[169] John Ferrar has added the words between the asterisks in place of Conyam's few words: 'have obtruded uppon our Nation and Religion'. Ferrar's clause 'inviting still to new Treaties' repeats Conyam's.

uppon such termes as threaten to our State an incurable mischeife[170]

And for a further Justification of the Charge of insinceritie in all their proceedings these particulars insuing a mongst many other may be produced

First in that Treaty Conserning Prince Henry[171] after many Spetious Motions on there parte it was folowed with disadvowing their owne Ambassadors and a Scornefull propositione to the king of that Princes altering his Religion

Secondly in the Treaty of Brussells where in Sir Richard Weston was employed[172] he found nothing but delayes and deceipts: And after divers peremptorie Commands from Spayne for his Majestys satisfactione they wrought noe other effect then the Seige and takinge of Heidelberge: Soe that he was forced to returne with a Protestation

Thirdly when the Baron Boscott[173] came hether to continew the former treaty: the first news we heard was the Translatione of the Electorate to the Duke of Bavaria: Of which the both the Baron and Don Carloe[174] protested Ignorance and that the King of Spayne would make the World see how much he resented such an affront

Yeat it playnely appeareth by the letter of the Conde Olivares given to the Prince that the State of Spayne booth had intelligence of it before and expected it to be effected at that Dyet.

Fourthly when his Highnes was in Spayne the Conde Olivares shewed him tow letters by which it playnely appeared that till his Comming thether there was nothing really intended: which they were not asshamed directly to avow to the Prince him selfe And that After for the requitall of soe hazardous a iourny and Such an extreordinary trust when all Articles were a gaine Concluded they found a new sheft upon A Junta of Devines to lett the Prince come home with out the Lady for whose personne his Highnes had Cheifely put him selfe to that hazard.

Lastly when upon his Highnes happy returne hether we had iust cause to expect the uttermost they would doe in Restoring the Pallitinat (the faithfull promises of which was the only cause that the Prince yealded to the Junta of Devines) the Despossories being presently to follow. The Borgstratt[175] was delivered to the Elector of Mentz[176]: being

---

[170] Here Conyam yields to Ferrar again, who writes the rest of the document.

[171] Henry Frederick, Prince of Wales (d.1612).

[172] In 1622.

[173] Ferdinand de Boiscot, ambassador of the Archdukes in February 1623.

[174] Don Carlo Coloma, the Spanish ambassador.

[175] ?Burgstadt (today in Saxony) 8 miles NW of Chemnitz, or (more likely) ?Burstadt (today in Rhenish Hesse), 5 miles E of Worms & 7 miles N of Mannheim.

[176] i.e. Mainz.

wonne by the king of Spaynes[177] Armes and parte of it then in possession of his owne Ministers: Contrary to an expresse Article in the Treaty Concluded by Don Carlo and Baron Boscott where in it was particularly provided that noe alteratione should be made in these Teritoryes till the Generall treaty were at an End.]

Which was by the Lord Chamberlaine[178] and himselfe[179] drawne upp[.] The house approved this addition to be added to their former reasons. Next hee related how Sir Isack Wake produced 2 letters[180] within his imployment in Savoy which hee had intercepted[181] from Cardinall [Ludovisi[182]] to Fryer Jacyntho[183] then in Spaine both many-festinge there was noe intent of Restitucion of the Palatinate butt a dyrect Resolucion to translate the Electorate.

[184]After this hee saide the Archbishop was appoynted by word of mouth to deliver the resolucion of both houses to this effect. The substance wherof was comprised in writing beinge.[185] [f.37r]   That the Lords and Commons &c [Two lines are then blank.][186] did first give God thanks for dispellinge those cloudes & mistes that had soe long time dazelled the eyes of allmost all Christendome touchinge these buisinesses of the Treaties –

And next unto his Majestie all humble thanks for his great grace in vouchsaffinge to require our advise and Counsell which with all humble manner wee ioyntlie offer not one discentinge in either house uppon mature deliberation & after exact consideracion of all the par-ticularities[187] of ye want of sinceritie in these Treaties, haveinge delib-erated *super totam materiam*. That[188] these Treaties cannot any longer be continued[189] with the honour of your Majestie the safetie of your people the welfaire of your Posteritie or assurance of your Allyes.[190]

This paper was by the generall vote of the house allowed to be the

[177] 'owne' erased.
[178] William Herbert, Earl of Pembroke.
[179] Sir Edwin Sandys.
[180] Now PRO, SP 92/9 Pt I ff.140–43: Abstract of letters of Card. Ludovisi to Pere Hyacinth of 22 May/1 June, & 1/11 June 1622.
[181] NF's original reads: 'which in his imployment in Savoy hee had intercepted'.
[182] *Nicholas*.
[183] Hyacinthe: *Nicholas*.
[184] 'Then hee' erased.
[185] 'being to this effect'.
[186] As in NF's notes.
[187] 'with all sitt' erased; 'of ye want ... Treaties' interpolated.
[188] 'his ma.t may not' erased.
[189] 'then but immediately discharge them with' erased.
[190] 'wch mixed kynde of repone was' erased.

messadge, although Sir *Robert Harly* and some others requyred the reason of the preservation of *Religion* which was here [BLANK][191] should be added, butt itt was replyed by Sir Edwin Sandis and others that the Committees had well weighed that and consideringe ye kinges exceedinge Cautelousness not[192] to make any breach uppon matter of *Religion,* itt was thought fitt to omitt itt in this messadg and that the rather because itt was att lardge expressed in the reasons of both houses, wherof uppon further occasion use might be made –

Sir James Perrat moved that as the Prince had a Coppie of our reasons soe wee might have one of this draught of the Lord of Canterburies which was thought reasonable.

Lastlie[193] Sir Edwin Sandis[194] delivered that they fell uppon a knottie poynte (which as hee afterwards interpreted itt was not because of the[195] Substance of the thinge itt selfe butt because they conceived itt would be controverted in the house which the shortnes of time did not permitt)[196] In the expeditinge of which hee did highly comend the Princes great wisedome and iudgment touchinge allsoe by waie his singuler industry wherwith hee followeth these buisinesses –

[f.37v]   The matter was this, The Earle of Southampton[197] saide that many in the Upper house made an obiection, what if uppon our soe resolute[198] advise his Majestie shall[199] reply the dissolvinge of these Treaties doth necessarilie breed a breach, uppon that a Warr, this cannott be mannaged without monneys[.] Of myne owne I have not, what supply shall I expect from you, This obiection was conceived[200] would most probably[201] be made, and an answere therto to be pre-pared[202] thought soe necessarie, as the Earle of Southampton was desyred to frame one which hee did and the whole house approved of[,] digested in these words –

In pursuinge of this advise wee will assist his Majestie with our persons and[203] our fortunes accordinge to our abillities as becommeth good & well affected Subiects

---

[191] 2want[in]g.
[192] 'to seeme to make it a' erased.
[193] 'hee delivered the' erased.
[194] 'Sandys'.
[195] 'dif' erased.
[196] 'That was the pr' erased.
[197] 'that morn[in]g/had in the upper house made' erased; 'saide ... Upper' interpolated.
[198] 'soe resolute' interpolated over an illegible erasure.
[199] 'demaunde' erased.
[200] 'not onely soe moast probably' erased.
[201] 'most probably' interpolated.
[202] 'therto to be p'pared' interpolated.
[203] 'and' interpolated.

Mr Alforde spake first against this Proposition sayinge itt was a kinde of engagment of all our Estates, That the Committees had noe authoritie to[204] Treate of any such buisines; That though wee ment[205] to doe as much, yett wee should not thus doe itt upon ye Lords Motion for therby wee lost our thanks and herin[206] they wronged us. That the Custome of the house was not to passe any bills under 3 daies consideration,[207] it was therfore too little time to doe this soe suddenly, wherby wee passed away all our estates, That itt was untimely till wee had obteyned some releife for the Kingdome by easinge it of those great burdens wherunder itt groaneth, especially haveinge the last Parlyament graunted Two Subsidies for nothinge, besides the *Benevolence* given to the *Queene* of *Bohemia* –

Sir *Robert Phillips* answered the house with saffety might make this generall promise since they[208] allwaies intend[209] to performe what the Common wealth should be enabled by riddinge itt of the greivances,[210] till then wee should not have power, butt now wee ought to shew our will.

That for engagement itt was a needles feare, the advise wee gave did really binde us by necessity of Consequence our owne hearts to more, For wronge from ye Lords sure there was none in their Intention[211] nor in the [f.38r] thinge beinge a motion[212] in generall terms uppon Conditions The exceptions taken against the Upper house in some former Kings times was because they tooke uppon them to dyrect particularly the way and the proportion of Contribucions.

Sir William Stroud and mr Corrington[213] thought it untimely to make this Proposicion and Sir John Savell ioyned with them sayinge itt was a greate engagement, and that haveinge once passed itt was not[214] in our power to revoke itt nor moderate itt,[215] butt the Kinge would be iudge what wee are able that ye Kinge might remayne[216] confident, and beyond all doubt secure Then[217] wee would not faile to the uttermost of our powers consideringe that everie mans life, Religion &

[204] 'speake' erased.
[205] NF perhaps wrote 'were'.
[206] NF wrote 'therin'; 'and therin they wronged us' interpolated.
[207] An illegible erasure precedes 'consideration'.
[208] 'never' erased.
[209] 'with intent to bee performed when' erased; 'intend ... what' interpolated.
[210] 'till' erased & replaced.
[211] 'they inf' erased.
[212] 'uppon' erased.
[213] i.e. Coryton.
[214] NF wrote: 'haveinge once passed itt it was not...'.
[215] 'nor moderate itt' interpolated.
[216] 'fully' erased.
[217] NF perhaps wrote 'that'.

libertie lay uppon the Consequence therof; That wee should first provide for the remedies of this Kingdome; Next the saffety of Ireland Then the Provisions of the Navy, that[218] itt was a shame for Forraigne Nations[219] to thinke that the Kinge of England could not be able to goe through with a warr without his peoples ayde, Hee was a mighty Kinge able to doe ye greatest in *Christendome* one good turne for another, and Two ill turnes for one.

Sir Robert Hayly[220] was contrarie, that haveinge begunn with such zeale if wee[221] should be found in the least to stagger, wee could[222] not expect butt the Kinge would be more slowe in his Resolucion
[At this point a line and a half are BLANK.]
[   ][223] to avoyde the feare of unlymited engagements would have itt added. In a Parlyamentary way.

Mr Recorder saide the Committee were sorry when they heard itt propounded, because itt was not yett a seasonable time to enter into soe greate engagements; That ye Kinge could expect noe more then an answere to his proposition which was onely touchinge the Treaties proceedinge or ceasinge.

That hee would by noe meanes have itt a Question, least if itt past against itt the[224] Correspondencie in all thinges with the Lords which was [BLANK][225] onely in the same desyres, butt in the selfe same words might[226] seeme any thinge infrynged. That therfore if the Kinge made the Question itt might be answered wee had not taken itt[227] into Consideration. That itt was a great Dishonour to the Kinge that wee should imagine hee was not confident [f.38v] of our Loves, and the performance of all what were fitt That such kinde of Ayde and Supplys ought to proceed from this house Voluntarily not by motion of ye Lords

Heer mr Atturney[228] and Serieant Davys[229] brought a messadg from the Lords that they had appoynted Twelve to goe to the Kinge and desyred 24 to be appoynted by us to meete at Tenn of the Clocke with them in the paynted Chamber who were returned with this answere

---

[218] 'there was noe' erased.
[219] 'for fforraigne Nations' interpolated.
[220] NF wrote 'Harly'.
[221] NF wrote 'if wee now should …'.
[222] 'should' erased.
[223] NF wrote 'Mr Wandesford'; Christopher, not John: Ruigh, *Parliament of 1624*, p. 194.
[224] 'Lords' erased.
[225] 'hitherto not' are the words Conyam failed to read.
[226] 'bee' erased.
[227] Conyam has added this word which is not in NF's original notes.
[228] Sir Thomas Coventry.
[229] Sir John Davies, serjeant-at-law.

That wee would immeadiately send messengers unto them of our owne, for this new dispute made the house uncertaine what answere to returne –

Mr Mallory thought since this Proposition came butt accidentally wheither the obiection would be made, wee should not trouble our selves to make answere, and seemed to impute some blame to ye Committees for intertayninge itt beyond their Comission to which if hee thought they had given any furtherance hee would move to have them thrust out of ye houses –

Sr Humfry May spake [GAP] and passionately that after soe greate a flame kindeled, hee was sorry to see so much water powerd on itt, that Rome & Spaine would Tryumph att this days worke, and worke out their owne advantages, that wee should as good as tell the Kinge that wee had as far as in us lay engaged him in [a] Warr hee was to hazard not onely his owne person butt his posteritie, his Crowne ittselfe and would not tell him how farr wee would assist him, that hee was not afrayde of Cuttinge throats in this house[,] he was by marring all by this straunge Coldnes and allmost going backe[.] what[?] should wee feare to say what wee ment to doe.

Sir *Dudley Diggs* made answere first to Mr Mallory, that itt was in their Comission to here the Lords and to make report and farther assent they had not given and less then itt they could [f.39r] not; butt hee did esteeme ye Lords might[,] as neer to the Kinge[,] know more then wee could, of ye necessitie of providinge some answere, that the nobleness of the first propounder did assure him that noe wronge was ment to this house any way, that although hee was sorry as mr Recorder had reported what hee first heard itt, yett now hee did Counsell itt should be assented unto, that they that had spoken against itt, had all of them professed much more, and engaged themselves, more then the paper did which hee would not care what became of itt by any other meanes, the affectionate zeale of ye house which every one had declared could be manyfested that therefore itt should be delivered with the addition in a Parlyamentary manner –

Sir *Fraunces Seamour* thought not fitt butt iust & reasonable and consonant to the Kings honour to rely uppon us without any such timely Declaration –

Sir *William Beecher* saide Modesty in this case was Treachery since itt must com to itt at last, itt were good to save soe much time which was now soe precious, That being all engaged in the highest degree itt was straungness to the [?delaying[230]] of itt; The last Parlyament ther was a Protestation of a farr greater and larger extent then this

<hr>

[230] Cf. *Rich.*

Sir *Edward Giles* and Sir *Thomas Bellart*²³¹ would have itt respited till a more seasonable time, the Question was not yett propounded to us.

Sir Edwin Sandis said the Relatinge of this was necessary through the Comaundement of reportinge, That laste Parlyament the Protestation was drawne upp in 2. or three howers, to which hee confessed hee gave not his assent for ye generallytie and continuance they therby byndinge themselves to continue supplies till ye Recovery of the Pallatinate which hee thought impossible.

That this irresolution would all disadvantage of Circumstances be caryed to Rome and Spaine *Vellem vobis placere sed magis prodesse* –

[f.39v]   That itt was not reasonable to engage his Majestie by our advise in a Warr and not to give him soe much encouragment as this was that a middle way was the worst, That for preventinge all Jealousie and removeinge all doubts itt might be putt with Two Additions

1. In a Parlyamentary way to avoyde ye imposinge of *Benevolences* and other kinde of Contribucions
2. And to the intent wee should not charge ye Subiects without inablyng him, that itt might be closed upp to this effect not doubtinge of his Majesties grace that this Parlyament by ye releiving of *Greivances* and taking off burdens, shall enable the *Subiects* to performe itt in some good manner and wished that as in some other Companies of London they were on their Oathes inioyned to keepe togeather the thinges propounded by the Governour and Counsell soe now such Courses might be provided in this house and that after this particularr they might have charge on their consciences to doe itt –

Sir Edward Cooke found this difference between this Proposition and ye last Protestation that this moved from the Lords[,] that sprange immediatly outt of this house, that the Lords did intrench into the liberties and pryveledges of the house if they seemed any way to dyrect or lead us and soe itt was adiudged by the kinge in a case 9th Henry 4, that all Supplies and *Contributions* ought freely to move and proceed freely from us in regard the Commons beare ye wholl burden the Lords verie little, And heere hee declared that a Subsedy was about *seaventy Thousand pounds* and a Fifteenth about *Thirty thousand pound* and therfore would not have the paper passe

Mr Pym would have itt [BLANK] fullie cleered by the annexinge of those Two clauses by Sir Edwin Sandys, and in particuler that doubt of Sir Edward Cookes for since itt was not the Parlyamentary waie that the Lords should propound to us any thinge of this nature, that Addition would provide against the feare or designe sufficiently.

²³¹ *Recte* Belasyse: *Holland.*

[f.40r]   Butt mr *Glandvilde* would by noe meanes allowe itt with any
Quallyfication whatsoever. The Committees that had spoke for itt, yett
wished itt had not beene moved at all, soe that nowe their yeildinge to
itt was butt for feare of giveinge discontent to ye Lords, if this reason
were admitted any straunge Proposition might be obtruded uppon us
whiles wee could not refuse itt because itt moved from the Lords or
perhapps other higher powers, that hee was not afrayd the advantage
would be soe greate to Spaine or Rome that this refusall should give
by puttinge them in hope of raysinge Jealousy between the Kinge and
us at the [BLANK] of Discretion and Wisedome in the house would
affrighten them which had been in this kinde wantinge in former
Assemblies: And therfore hee would have itt answered in case the
Kinge demaunded the Question.

That wee had not presumed to take this into our considerations not
haveinge received express warrant from his Majestie

Butt Sir John Jepson replyed that were noe true answere since wee
had soe long debated of it, and wee must not tell him untrueths which
hee could soe easily discover

Sr R. [BLANK] would have word sent upp to the Lords wee could
not conclude any thinge att present beinge soe much devyded, butt
this motion was utterlie disliked & soe was²³² moved that wee might
send the Lords an answere that as pryvate men wee would make the
promise butt not as ye Parlyament, this was thought an impossible
[BLANK]

In the end the Speaker beinge much troubled Sir Edward Sandys
moved that the Two former writinges might be sent upp and this last
sylenced without giveinge any answere on[e] way or other to itt, which
course was well liked of and agreed unto; yett mr Mallory putt a doubt
that since the Lords had resolved itt, if ye Speaker beinge of their
house did say itt wee should be bound therby

[f.40v]   The Election of Sir Symond Stuard, and Sir Edward Payton
was adiudged voyde, in regard the Sherrife beinge requyred did not
putt it to the Poll, and that hee did not pronounce his Choyce in the
place butt afterwards, for which as allsoe that hee had taken bound to
be saved harmeless, and divers other disorders hee was ordered to be
sent for by the house and itt was concluded lastly that noe affidavits
touchinge Elections or any thinge of them should be accepted hereafter
in the Trialls of Elections –
[The next third of the page is blank.]²³³

[Saterday morning the 6 of March: NF]

²³² The appearance of a missing line here seems to have no significance.
²³³ Ferrar's original notes end at this point.

Sir *Dudley Diggs* acquainted the house of Sir Robert Mansell [who] in regard his Patent was questioned as *Greivance*, did out of modestie forbeare to enter into the house except first knowinge their pleasure, the house willed hee should com in.

There were seven bills besides engrossed carryed upp to the Lords by Sir Edward Cooke beinge such as had passed the last Session.
The Lords by message desyred the SubCommittee of both houses might be to drawe upp the Kings answere soe as the Reporte might be uniforme.

[f.41r]   Sr *Thomas Escott* moved the stay of the East India Ships in regard of the great quantitie of money in them to be exported –
Mr *Morrice Abbot* made answere they were under ye Lord Admiralls arest,
mr *Bateman*[:] noe monney in them yett
Butt mr Abbott delivered the sum intended to be putt aboard to be under Fortie Thousand pound,
mr Bateman beinge requyred by the house to deliver the Summ –
Captaine *Bond* speakinge in his eare was by mr Alforde challenged sayinge hee had seene one called to the Barr for the like Carriadge –
The buisinesses past thus over[,] divers publique bills were read and Committed
[The rest of the page is blank]

[f.41v]   Munday morning the 8:th of March. 1623

A Petition was presented from Sir *Thomas Gerrard* chosen Burgess for L[iv]erpoole in Lancasheire that in regard of incurable sicknes which would not give him leave to doe the house service hee might be freed and a new Writ chosen

But wee beinge informed that hee was a knowne Recusant great exceptions was taken that hee should presume to procure himselfe to be chosen, and although Sir John Stanhopp affirmed on his knowledge that hee was in course of Phisique, hee was comaunded to attend the house the next morninge –

Mr Recorder made the Report of the passadges at Theobalds [and] the kings answere[.] hee read itt accordinge to the Committees agreement beinge that which after followeth [*]

Then itt was moved that because the buisines was exceedinge weightie therfor time might be taken to deliberate theron and Coppies given to whosoever of the house should require itt which Sir[234] Baptist Hicks moved might be done att Reasonable Rates.

---

[234] 'Dudley Diggs' erased.

The Chauncellour of the Chequer signified that ye Report concerninge his Majesties   pryvate State which the Kinge had formerly
said

[The rest of the page is blank.]

[f.42r]   [*] *My Lords and Gentleman all.*
I have cause first to thanke God with my heart & all the faculties of
my mynde that my speech which I delivered in Parlyament hath taken
soe good effect amongst you as that with an unanime consent you have
freely and speedilie given mee your advise in this great buisines; For
which I allsoe thanke you all as hartilie as I can.

I allsoe give my particuler thanks to the gentlemen of the Lower
house for that I heard when some amongst you would have Cast
Jealousies and *Doubts* betweene mee and my people you presentlie
qualled those Motions which otherwise might have hindred the happy
agreement I hope to finde in this Parlyament, you give mee your advise
to breake of both the treaties aswell concerning the Match as the
Palatinate –

And now give mee leave as an olde Kinge to propound my doubts,
and hearafter to give you my answere.

First itt is true that I whoe have beene all the daies of my life a
peaceable kinge and have had the honour in my Tytles and Impresses
to be styled *Rex Pacificis* [*sic*] should without necessity imbroyle my selfe
with warr farr from my nature, and[235] from the Honour which I have
had att home and abroade in endeavoringe to avoyde the effusion of
Christian Bloode of which too much hath beene shedd is soe much against
my hearte that unless itt be uppon such a necessitie that I may call itt
as some merrilie say of weomen *Malum necessarium* I should be loath to
enter into itt. And I must likewise acquainte you that I have hadd noe
small hopes given mee of obteyninge better conditions for the Restitution
of the *Palatinate*, and that even since the sittinge downe of the *Parlyament.*
Butt be not jealous nor thinke mee such a Kinge that would under
pretence of askinge your advise putt a scorne uppon you by disdayninge
and reiectinge it

For you remember that in my first speech unto you for proofe of
my love to my people, I craved your advise in these great and weightie
affaires. Butt in a matter of this weight I must first consider how this
Course may agree with my conscience and honour, And next accordinge
to the parrable uttered by our Savyour; After I have resolved of ye
necessitie & Justnes of ye Cause to Consider how I shalbe enabled to
rayse Forces for this purpose.

[235] 'and' erased.

[f.42v] As Concerninge the Case of my Children, I ame now[236] old and would be glad as Moyses saw the Land of *Promise* from a high Mountaine though hee had not beene to sett his Foote in itt, Soe would itt be a great Comforte to mee that God would butt soe prolonge my daies as[,] if I might not see the Restitution[,] yett att least to be assured that itt would be. That then I might with old Symion say, *Nunc dimittis servum tuum Domine &c* otherwise itt would be greate Regreet unto mee and I should dy with a heavie and discomforted heart.

I have often saide and particularlie in ye last Parlyament and I shall ever be of that mynde, that as I ame not Ambicious of any other mens goods of Lands soe I desire not to breake a furrowe of Land in *England, Scotland* or *Ireland*, without Restitucion of ye Palatinate, & in this mynde I will live and dye Butt lett mee acquainte you a little with ye difficulties of this Case.

Hee is an unhappie man that shall advise a Kinge and itt is an unChristian thinge to seeke that by bloode which may be hadd with peace; Besides I thinke your Intentions are not to ingage mee in Warr but withall you will consider how many thinges are requisite therunto.

I omitt to speake of my owne necessities, they are too well knowne, sure I ame I have had the least helps in Parlyament of any kinge that Raygned over you these many yeares, I must lett you know that my dissabillyties are encreased by the Charge of my Sonnes goinge into Spaine which I was att for his Honour and the honour of this Nation, by sendinge of *Ambassadours*, By mayntenance of my Children And by assistinge of the Palatinate, I have encurred great debt to the Kinge of *Denmark* which I ame not yett able to pay.

The Low Countries who in regard of their nearnes are fittest to help for ye Recovery of the Palatinate, are att soe Lowe an Ebb as if I assist them not they are scarse able to subsist

[f.43r] The Princes of Germany that should doe mee any good are all poore wracked and dishartned and doe expect assistance from hence –

For Ireland I leave itt to you if that itt be not a backe dore fitt to be secured –

For the Navy I thanke God itt is now in a better Case then ever itt was, yett more must be done and before itt can be prepared as itt ought to be itt will require a new Charge as well for its owne strength as for ye securinge my Coasts.

My *Children* I vow to God eate noe Bread butt by my meanes[.] I must maynteyne them and not see them want in ye meane time till the Palatinate be Recovered.

---

[236] 'very' erased.

My Customes be the best part of my Revennues and in effect the substance of all I have to live on[;] all which are farmed out uppon condition that if ther be Warr those *Bargaines* are to be disanulled which will enforce a great *Defaulcation* –

Subsidies aske a greate time to bringe them in[.] Now if you assist mee that way I must take them upp before hand uppon credite which will eate upp a great part of them

This beinge my Case to enter into Warr without sufficient meanes to support itt, were to shew my teeth and doe no more –

In the meane time I hartelie thanke you for your advise and I will seriously thinke uppon itt as I pray you to consider of these other partes.

My Treasuror to whose Office itt apperteynes shall more att large enforme you of these things that Concerne my estate

Thus freely I doe open my heart unto you & haveinge your hearts I cannot want your helps for itt is the heart that opens the Purse and not the purse the heart, I will deale Francklie with you[.] shewe me butt the meanes, how I may doe what you would have mee, and if I take a resolution uppon your advise to enter into a Warr. [f.43v]   Then your selves by your owne Deputies shall have the disposinge of the monneys I will not meddle with itt, butt you shall appoynt your owne Treasurours[.] I say not this with a purpose to invite you to open your purses and then to slight you soe much as[237] not to follow your Counsell, nor engage you before I ame engaged[238] my selfe, Give mee what you will for my owne meanes; Butt I protest none of the monneys which you shall give for those uses shalbe issued butt for those ends and by men elected by your selves –

If uppon your offer I shoulde finde the meanes to make the warr honorable and saffe, and that I resolve to embrace your advise, Then I promise you in the word of a Kinge that although *Warr* and *Peace* be ye peculyer Perogatives[*sic*] of Kings, yett as I have advised with you in the Treaties on which Warrs may ensue Soe I will not Treate nor Accept of Peace without first acquaintinge you with itt and hearinge your advise and therin goe the proper way of *Parlyament* in conferringe and consultinge with you in such great and weightie affaires. And happilie the Conditions of Peace[239] will then be the better when wee be prepared for Warr accordinge to the old Proverb That weapons bourd Peace.

Your kind carriage gives mee much content & that Comfortes mee (which my lord of Canterbury said) That there was not a contrarie

[237] 'to' erased.
[238] 'your' erased.
[239] 'wilbe' erased.

voyce amongst you, all like the 70 Interpreters which were ledd by the trueth of God.

I ame soe desyrous to forgett all rends in former Parlyaments that itt shall not be in my default if I be not in love with Parlyaments and call them often & desire to end my life in that entercourse betweene mee & my people for the makinge of good Lawes reforminge of such abuses as I cannot be well informed of butt in Parlyament & maynteyninge ye good Goverment of ye Common wealth The[r]fore goe on cheerfully and advise of these poynts and my resolucion shall then be declared

[END of ms]

Speeches in Committee

A. Speech by Nicholas Ferrar 28 April 1624.

FP 1589 and Sheffield U., Hartlib MS 61/2 are two copies of the same item. FP 1589 is written by the Ferrars' clerk Tristram Conyam and annotated by Nicholas Ferrar (1593–1637) and Edward Ferrar II (d.1769); the Hartlib ms is in a hand unknown to the editor. FP 1589 has lost the bottom right hand corner of all its pages. The following transcript is therefore taken from the Hartlib MS; alternative readings from FP 1589 are supplied in the footnotes. Catchwords are usually omitted, as are the two original systems of page and folio numeration.

FP 1589 Cover: 'a Speech' [Edward Ferrar II, d.1769]

The Declaration of Nicholas Farrar Deputy of the Compagny of Virginia made before the Committe appoynted by the Parliament uppon Wednesday the [BLANK][1] of Aprill in the Starr Chamber touching the Oppressions in matter of Tobacko [Nicholas Ferrar]

'Tobacco Speech by NF' [Edward Ferrar II]

Hartlib MS 61/2

[f.2A]   I will not mispend any of your tyme (every minet whereof is so precious) in going about to commende the worke, wherof I suppose and hope every member of this honorable Committee that knowes itt to be aswell opinioned as my self, and though not somuch yet as truly affected in hart to it with in its owne nature and at all tymes did deserve the favour of the Parliament, for it self but now I conceave much more yf so be our strongest desires and hopes shall succeed, That a iust warr shall folowe a deceyptfull peace, wherunto how much this plantacion of Virginia and that of the somer Ilands may conduce, I will use no other argument, then the presente example of our wise frends and neighbours the Hollanders, who have within this two yeares, with thexpenc[e] of above One hundred thowsand poundes attempted

---

[1] The missing day is 28 April; for which see S. M. Kingsbury, *Records of the Virginia Company of London*, ii.539, and *Journal of the House of Commons*, i.691 col. 1.

to gayne a litle footing in those parts, knowing well that a few forces there will much more harme their enemy and benefitt them selves, then ten tymes as many and greate here att home, So that what they make a principall care of their state to begin, I hope we shall conceive ought to be a publique care of ours to preserve, and that with asmuch spedy care and tendernes as it may certeinly be expected, the Enemy will with violent endeavour to deprive us of it, For considering the incredible vigilancy and sollicitousnes that the Spanyards have alwaies used to prevent even the knowledg of those partes and the great cruelty and inhumanity that they [f.2B] Have practized to the rooting out of some fewe plantacions begun by other nations in the parties nere adioyning to Virginia I meane the French in Florida there is no reason to ymagine but they will indeavour to apply the same remedies at the last for the defenc[e] of their owne safety, which that they have not hitherto don we can conceive no other reason but that they hoped & expected it should by other meanes have ben effected for otherwise it cannot be but the self same feares and dangers which this plantacion of Virginia threatneth to them should have drawne from them the self same executions upon itt, but they hoped it wolde have been don here att home by our selves, And surely since the plantacion being in the yere 1619 recovered out of those negligent hands (to say no worse of them) wherein it had well nigh pined 14 yeares, began like a withered plant refreshed with a gentle showre to lift up its head & seeme to promis a speedy and prosperous growth it is almoste incredible how variously it hath been contynually interrupted, and distressed by so many calamities and oppressions as when this honorable Comittee shall have understood the Relacion but of some parts for all neither can be nor are perhapps fitt to be related, wee doubt not but you will rather marvaile that there is any thing att all remayning of the plantacion then that it is no forwarder; and surely for our selves wee attribute it only to the mercy of god, That there hath ben either branche or Roote remayning of this plantacion, so many & grevous [f.3A] Have the interrupcions been, Of one whereof being in matt[er] of proffitt I am to give you first an accompt of; The subiect is Tobacco a comodity first fallen upon by the Planters, because easy and very beneficiall and hitherto the only, for the prosecuting of all others hath been by them hitherto neglected through the discouragement receaved contynually in the oppressions of this, In which oppressions for they have not been as we conceave lighter then to merite such a heavy name, I shall present unto you not only the overthrowe and distruccion of the Plantacion commingly Woven into the whole cariadge, but the great deceipte and wronge of his Majestie in his Revennues and exceeding damage of this kingdome in matter of trade besides grevanc[e] of unparraleld Monopolies,

But before I enter into the particulars I am commaunded by the company to make their humble protestacion aswell toching this matter. I am to deliver as what you shall after heare from my Lord and thother gentlemen[2] That although his Majesty's name and aucthority, and the Lords of his Majesty's most honorable privie councell their consent & commaund have ben used in most of theis severall passadges of which wee complaine, yet for his Majestie as our sufferinges have been not only to the damage of the plantacion but much to the preiudice of his Majesty's revennues and honour: So we doe acknowledg they have been most contrary to his gracious Invencions for the administring of equall Justice and the advancement of the plantacion, in both which particulars we must and do acknowledg to have receaved most gracious remonstracions of his roiall Justice and favour to the plantacions by especiall recomendacion and particular charges and direccions uppon the severall occasions [f.3B] And for that most honorable Board of the privie councell as they are most of them Noble and lardge adventurers in the Accion, so we have alwaies founde them most zealous[ly] affected to itt so that wee owe much thanckes unto them and no complaint of any but of the Lord highe Treasurer whose most greatnes of place and office in theis latter tymes and formerly the reputacion which his particular knowledg and experienc in theis kynde of bussinesses bred [?in] him didd contynnually frustrate and deprive us of those iust releifs and favours which otherwise, that most honorably disposed Board had certenly afforded us.

And so I comme unto the buissines wherein I most humbly crave your honorable attencion and patience, thought I do itt with some more largenes then perhapps you shall att first conceive necessary for in thend you shall finde every circumstance to beare great weight and to have a particul[ar] Intencion of wronge and oppression[s *erased*] in the Actours of them

First therfore itt pleased his Majestie out of his princ[e][l][y] grace by his second lettres pattentes (for three severall lettres Pattentes the company have had) To free the company of Virginia for payeng any

---

[2] At a Virginia Company Quarter Court held that same morning, 'The Court taking into Consideracion that the matters to be delivered to the Parlyament did fall under fower generall heads (vizt) the Matter of Tobacco and all the greivances therin: The buisines of the Contract. The proceedings of the Comissioners and the passadges since, and conceivinge that neither Counsell att Lawe could be soe fully informed as were requisite, and perhapps would not be soe well heard, did therefore thinke fitt to beseech the Lord Cavendish Sir Edwin Sandis and Sir John Da[n]vers to take uppon them the delivery of the three last partes, (vizt) The Lord Cavendish the buissines of the Comission, Sir Edwin Sandys that of the Contract, and Sir John Da[n]vers the last: And for ye matter of Tobacco they imposed itt uppon mr Deputy. His Lordship very Nobly vouchsaffed to promise his performance of their desires, and the like did the other of their partes.' [Kingsbury, ii.538]

customes or chardges whatsoev[er] during the space of seaven yeares for any comodities which they should bring from the plantacions, which though itt was of his Roiall grace intended for their good, yett was itt to them of little or no benefitt, in regard they had not in[3] all the tyme raised any comodity or att least any quantety butt the yeare after that this priviledg was determyned, there came aboute thend of May 1619 from Virginia nere upon twenty thowsand weight of Tobacco being a comodity newly fallen [f.4A] uppon by them in Virginia and of good esteeeme here in England being then worth fyve shillings the pound

The company gave order to their officers ymediatly to cause this Tobacco to be soulde, that there might be supplies of apparell Armes and other necessaries retorned to the colony in Virginia which then stood in great neede thereof, wherupon the companyes officers going downe to the customehouse, and tendring the custome that the customers demaunded although it was duble what was due to them; One mr Abraham Jacobs whome you well knowe came whilest the tobacco was weighing out and commaunded the customers not to deliver out the Tobacco to the company except the company would pay him six pence upon each pound for ympost, which he challenged by vertue of his Majesty's Lettres Pattentes dated the 22th of March going before wherein was graunted unto him the saide Abraham Jacobs for the terme of fyve yeares and for the rent of fyve thowsand pound yerly to be paid the king, that he shold have one shilling six penc[e] upon each pound of spanish Tobacco, and six pence the pound upon Virginia and Somer Ilands Tobacco The company shewed him their lettres pattentes of the sixt of his Majest's raigne being ten yeares before his, wherein they were directly freed from all Imposicions whatsoever, saving only the payment of five per centum upon their goods for custome wch they were redy to performe, But notwithstanding all this mr Jacobs caused the companyes tobacco to be violently deteyned; wherupon the company peticioned the comissioners for the Treasury the 16th of July 1619 [f.4B] who referred the matter to the now Lord Treasurer the[n] Sir Lyonell Cranfeild and mr of the wardrobe and to Sir Henry Yelverton then his Majesty's atturney generall, bu[t] Mr Attorney declaring his opinion in private to mr Jacobs that he was in the wronge in keping the companies goods which ought to be free, the matter wa[s] so handled as no report could be procured, Werupon the company solliciting the Lords of the councell and acquainting them with the great damage that grew to their Tobacco being a perishinge comodity and also the great danger that the colony would be [in] in case they were not supplied, The Lords writt their Lettres to Jacobs willing him to deliver the company their goods, they entring into bond

---

[3] Interpolated over 'at' which has been erased.

to pay him whatsoe[ver] should appeare to be his due by their Lordships Judgment upon certificate from his Majesty's learned councell and within one moneth after it should be determyned which the company did offer to mr Jacobs to performe

But mr Jacobs refused except they woulde enter into bond to pay him his demaund at a certen day unles in the meane tyme they procured a defalcacion for so much of the rent which he was to pay, which the company not being able to performe durst not undertak[e] but very earnestly desired him that he would for the supply of the colony lett them have half their Tobacco to sell, and they would leave thother half in his hands till the matter were decided but he woulde by no meanes yeald therunto, And shortly after[,] it being thend of Sommer[,] their Lordships brake upp [f.5A] their sitting in councell and mr Jacobs kept their Tobacco by violenc[e] till December folowing, When the company againe peticioned their Lordships, who appointed a day to heare both parties, and commaunded mr Attorney to attend: mr Jacobs was summoned but would not appere, because the mr of the Warderobe through other busines could not comme with hym, Wherupon their Lordship comytted the said Jacobs for his contempt, And after they had seene and heard the companyes lettres Pattentes read they demaunded of Mr Atturney generall what hee said, who ymediatly then declared in presenc[e] of the whole board, that the company were not lyable to that ymposicion, and that Jacobs could not by his Lettres pattentes exact it of them

Wherupon their Lordships gave the company almost assurance of releif, and the Lord Verulam the chauncellour delivered it as a clere case in the companies behalf: yet they appointed a second day to heare Jacobs personally who came accordingly And the mr of the Warderobe with him, and first the Mr of the Warderobe demaunded right of the Lords against the Attorney generall, For that he had saide, that it was one of Cranfeldes Trickes, And then he pleaded the kinges latter graunt to Jacobs with great violenc[e] urging it and still pressing his Majesty's proffitt which he said yf the Virginia company were freed should be much preiudiced, For the king must make defalcacions for somuch out of the rent of fyve hundred[4] Poundes which he was to receave of Jacobs as their Tobacco at vjd a pound came to, And when the Lords shewed him the plaine expres wordes in the lettres pattentes (viz) "And for their further Incouragement of our especiall grace and favour, wee do by theis presentes for us our heires and successours yelde and graunt to and with the said Threasurer and company and their successours [f.5B] And every of them their Factours and assignes, That they and

---

[4] FP 1589: a hand that is probably Nicholas Ferrar's has corrected 'hundred' to 'thousand'.

every of them shalbe free and quitt of all subsedies and customes in
Virginia For the space of one and twenty yeares, and from all Taxes
and ymposicions for ever upo[n] any goods or merchandizes att any
tyme or tymes hereaf[ter] either upon ymportacion thither or export-
acion from thenc[e] into our Realme of England or into any other of
our domynions by the said Threasurer and company and their successours their deputies Factours and assignes or any of them, except
only the fyve poundes per centum due for custom upon all such goods
and merchandizes as shalbe brought or ymported into our Realme of
england or any other of thei[s] our domynions, according to the
auncient trade of merchan[dize] which fyve poundes per centum only
being paid; itt shalbe then Lawfull and free for the said Adventurers
the same goods and merchandizes to export and cary out of our said
dominions into Forraigne partes without any custome taxe or other
duty to be paid to us our heires or successours, or to any other our
officers or deputies["],

And then demaunded of hym what he coulde say to so expres words,
Hee the said mr of the warderobe now Lord Treasurer Replyed, That
it was the Auncient trade and custome of Merchantes to pay what the
king would laye upon them, and so should the Virginia company now
do

In thend by the now Lord Treasurers meanes, Notwithstand[ing] mr
Atturneys Judgment so plainly and openly delivered the company were
forced to pay for that present three pence of the six penc[e] which
Jacobs demaunded and shortly after (though under an other colour)
they were constrayned to yealde to the whole six pence

But not only in this poynte was his Lordship so oppressiv[e] to the
company, but also in another matter for the company [f.6A] being to
pay according to their Chartre only 5 per centum, and their Tobacco
was not soulde for above five shillinges att the most they ought to have
paid but 3d custome, but the customers demaunded and exacted of
them vj^{d} which was the double of what they ought to pay, and [t
erased]herupon they together with the former buisines complayned of
this and had such faire and Noble answer from the Lordships as they
were in good hope to have been releived, but the same man (viz) The
now Lord Treasurer opposed them with such violenc[e] as they could
not obteyne itt, So that even for that wronge they were beholding to
hym, Now by this deteyning of their Tobacco uniustly and against
Lawe with such violence the company by the dryeng and waste and
fall of price lost above Two thowsand fyve hundred poundes besides
this 3d that they paid Jacobs,

Theise are the Three oppressions in poynt of comodity that the
company complaine of in the yeare – 1619:

1 The great losse by deteyning their goods by mr Jacobs

2 The having an ymposicion putt upon them against Lawe by the meanes of the now Lord Treasurer and mr Jacobs,

3 The holding and forcing them to pay six penc[e] custome whereas they ought to have paid but 3d[5]

What the effectes of theis courses were and how they wrought to the hinderanc[e] and stop of the Plantacion is not to be conceaved but by them that then observed itt I assure you it was like the powring of a greate deale of colde water upon a litle hott: And had not the Treasurer and councell with other members of the company by divers wise and prudent addresses made repaire aswell by extenuating theis blowes as presenting other fairer hopes added new courage, there had been litle more to have been hoped for, for to fynde them selves so wronged by Jacobs in deteyning their goods and not able to Right them selves, To fynde by the enhauncement of custome, and this new ymposicion against lawe [f.6B] To have all hope of proffitt in the first budding of it cutt of[,] To see the lettres patents the Basis and foundacion whereo[n] their adventures were grounded not weakned but derided wer[e] such discouragements as made very many that were before resolve[d] to adventure larg[e]ly to fall quite of, but itt kept out many mo[re] from coming into so regardles a buissines. But this grevance and oppression is so much the more grevous and oppressive because it was not to the kinges benefi[tt] but only to mr Jacobs and his partiners.

For do not thinck that they that so wronged the company and hindered the Plantacion did intend his Majesty's gayne or proffitt or honour, For what greater losse or damage coulde they do him then the strangling of this childe which shall I hope to the worlds end be a memoriall of his honour, No No itt was thei[r] owne private Lucre their uniust gayne they aymed att which I shall thus discover and proove

May it please you therfore to understand that the now Lord Treasurer then a private man had for some yeares together with other partiners the Farme of the ympost of Tobacco from his Majestie For which they paid only Foure hundred poundes per annum And made therof Foure thowsand fyve hundred poundes as b[y] some of the partiners I have been enformed, which great and excess[ive] gayne of above tenn for one being discovered to his Majestie itt pleased him to resume the buissines into his owne hands and the yeare 1618: at Michaelmas mr Abraham Jacobs was apoin[ted] and sworne his Majesty's collectour for the gathering of the ympo[st] which was one shilling six penc[e] the pound on Spanish Tobacco And for the encoradging him to a faithfull performanc[e] of his chardge his Majestie was graciously pleased to give unto hi[m] a Fee of one hundred and fifty poundes per annum during his lyfe and his sonns

---

[5] FP1589 p. 8: at the foot of the page, after '... to have paid butt 3d', Nicholas Ferrar has added: '. ... ... according [MISSING]ation yt: there Tobacko was sold at [MISSING].

who was to succeede him in the office[.] being thus beforehand rewarded
and thus bound by duty and oath hee enters upon the performanc[e] of
this place at Michaelma[s] [f.7A] 1618. and so contynues until the xxijth
of March – 1618 by which day he had receaved for his Majesty's accompt
upon the ympost of Tobacco the somme of Five thowsand pound att the
least[6] was receaved by him before the first of March, Now he having this
greate summe in his hands upon the first half yeres accompt and well
knowing that there was asmuch more Tobacco to comme in upon the
second half yere as upon the first, so that the ympost of the whole yere
wolde come att least to ten thowsand pound: Hee by meanes of the now
Lord Treasurer then mr of the warderobe makes offer to his Majestie of
Farming the ympost of Tobacco at fyve thowsand Pound the yeare, which
the now Lord Treasurer propounded to his Majestie as a very beneficiall
and advantagable bargaine to him And so upon a sudden the bargaine is
concluded, And the 22th of March there is a Lease made to Jacobs of the
Farme of the ympost for the terme of fyve yeres to begin at Michaelmas
going before, and his Lease as appeareth by the dockett passed the great
seale by ymediate warrant, all thother seales being omitted, which mr
Attorney generall signifieth to be done by order of the Lords comissioners
of the treasury one of the which was the now Lord Treasurer the cheif
and indeade sole meadiatour of this buissines, and the reason alleadged
is because Jacobs being to pay for his half yeres rent att our Lady day
Two thowsand fyve hundred pound itt was fitt hee should have the graunt
before:

   This is the reason alleadged by mr Attorney of this undue omission
and expedicion which no doubt him self and the Lords comissioners
beleaved all of them except the now Lord Treasurer who coulde not
but knowe the true ground and reason of this sudden expedicion to be
the purpose and desire of mr Jacobs in defrawding his Majestie not
only of the presente summe in his hands, but in the whole bargaine it
self to both which endes itt was necessary for him to use both such
Arte to conceale what he had then received, and such expedicion to
finish the [f.7B] Bargayne, For if it had proceeded the ordinary course
of all the seales passing through so many hands and offices itt could
hardly be caried with that secrecy but notice thereof coming abroade
intelligenc[e] would have been given to the Lords comissioners or his
Majestie what great quanteties were alredy comme in, and consequently
how frawdulent that offer was, Wherfore to prevent this discovery
which was thus likely to happen, Although there was tyme enough to
have gon the ordinary way, For about the 6th of March att which tyme
he had receaved above Fyve thowsand pound, they hadd procured a
warrant to mr Attorney generall to drawe up the bookes soe they had

---

[6] Sense would seem to require a repetition: 'This Five thowsand pound...'.

almost twenty dayes, yett they studiously and purposely deferr the proceedinges in the buissines till the 20th of March and then pretending the necessity of dispatching itt in two or three dayes, they procure itt to passe the greate seale ymediatly, Only because there should be no notice taken of itt abroade, which yf there had been they coulde not possibly have effected itt And as this was the cause of deferring the thinge so longe till the very last, so the speedy passing of itt then was as absolute necessary, For had it not been concluded and finished before our Lady day Jacobs must then have paid into thexchequier the Fyve Thowsand Six hundred seaventy fyve poundes receaved by him, itt being truly hi[s] Majesty's mony and coulde not have avoyded itt by any meanes or cullour whatsoever, Which being once done, itt woulde have been ympossible for him to obteyne the Lease on those condicio[ns] which he then did, but now having gott thus concluded, Hee payes the kyng Two thowsand fyve hundred poundes for his hal[f] yeres rent and deteynes to him self the rest of the kinges money which was Three thowsand one hundred seaventy fyve [catchword: Poundes] [f.8a] This was the bargayne and the manner that mr Jacobs used in procuring itt, with what honesty or conscience I leave it to your [conscienc *erased*] Judgments but certenly with good successe, for he gayned almost eighteene hundred pound more that yeare, for the ympost of Tobacco that yeare came to att the least, Nyne Thowsand seaven hundred and seaventy eight poundes [and his Fee of one hundred and fifty poundes being deducted *erased*] So that his rent being only Five Thowsand poundes and his Fee of one hundred and fifty poundes being deducted he paid the king only Foure Thowsand eight hundred and fifty poundes, and the rest him self and partners devided being fowre thowsand nyne hundred twenty eight poundes att the least

This ymmoderate and unduly obteyned gayne was made upon his Majestie by mr Jacobs his sworne officer and by my Lord Treasurer, on whose fidelity hee so especially relyed, and yett after all this did they force and vyolent the company of Virginia to those former payments which I have declared For they had made this excessive gayne before the Virginia Tobacco came in which surely had they not been unreasonable in their desires and appetite, they might well have spare for who woulde not have been contented with the gayne of allmost fyve thowsand pound in the rent of fyve thowsand pound but they were not but with violence and against Lawe exact the extremity of their unduely procured bargayne to the destruccion of the plantacion And yett though his Majestie was thus haynously abused the pretence and alleagacio[n] made by the now Lord Treasurer was his tender and faithfull regarde of his Majesty's proffitt which by no meanes he might not suffer to be deminished, and diminished itt must have been by a defalcacion of soe much rent yearly as the [f.8B] Virginia tobacco

should comme to att vjd a pound, for mr Jacob[s] was resolved not to
loose any thing that he might clayme and my Lord Treasurer thought it
fitt and iust that the kyng shoulde make good his bargaine with mr Jacobs
to the ful[l] having promised itt under his greate seale, and yett his
Roiall promise and assurance under his greate seale to the company, on
confidence whereof, they had spent one hundred thowsand poundes, a
farr more valuable consideracion then mr Jacobs his payeng him a rent
of Fyve thowsand poundes, for that which yelded tenn, This promise I
saide and the performance thereof, the Lord Treasurer did not conceave
his Majestie obliged unto, And what might be the reason of this, Not
different but contrary Judgm[ent] and opinion of my Lord Treasurer in
the self same matter and subiect, Nott the kings honour and proffitt but
his owne gayne and commodity, For you may be pleased to understa[nd]
which I shall by report of testimony farr above all excepcio[n] make good

The Lord Treasurer was not only the mover the ymediat[e] the sole
efficient of this bargaine, but he was a partiner in a greate share with mr
Jacobs even from the very begynning besides whatsoever in thend and
upshott of the buissines hee did further gayne, which there is no reason
to conceave was a small matter, but was no doubt proportionable to his
worth and dignity that was far[r] above the rest and answerable to his
desert and merri[tt] which was ten tymes double to Jacobs in catching
this prey and riche booty

What[?] shall I use many Words[?] in breif this itt was[:] the first
yeare from Michaelmas 1618 till Michaelmas 16[19] mr Jacobs by his
bargaine cleered neere Five thowsand [f.9A]   Pounde more then his
rent, And from Michaelmas 1619 [mr Jacobs *erased*] till Midsomer 1620
at which tyme it was taken from hym hee cleered more then his rent
above foure thowsande pound, And then there being a greater offer
made to his Majestie and of another nature, which you shall hereafter
heare of Jacobs being of necessity to quitt this bargayne, there was
given him in lewe and satisfaccion of his losse Three thowsand pound,
so that in les then the space of Two [*over* seaven *erased*] yeares hee
cleerly gayned betwene Eleaven and twelve thowsand pound, and the
Kynge lost soe much, and that not by a faire bargayne made in the
begynning nor by good Luck in thend but by the meanes you have
formerly heard, concealement of what was receaved, Omission of due
and ordinary proceedinges concluding thinges in an instant and all this
from those persons whose experienc[e] skill and knowledg in theis
particulars bred in his Majestie and the honorable comissioners of the
Treasury to whome he intrusted[7] the mannadging of those buissines,
an opinion that he could not be deceived nor wronged, and their

---

[7] FP 1589 p. 15: Tristam Conyam at first wrote 'interested', which Nicholas Ferrar
corrected to 'entrusted'.

obligacions of duty gratefulnes and oathe did bynde them they should not deceive, So that their fault and his Majestie's wronge is somuch the more by how much of all others it ought least to have proceeded from them, For surely had a stranger not interressed gon aboute to procure this bargaine from his Majestie (viz) To have the ymposicion att Fyve thousand pounds per annum, no doubt but the Lord Treasurer and especially mr Jacobs wolde have by all meanes opposed itt and alleadged that by their duties oaths and consciences they were bounde to give a true information of the state and condicion of that buissines, that by want of knowledg of the particulars his Majestie were not wrong[e]d [f.9B] And therfore not doing itt, now being them selves interress[ed] doth add much to the heynousnes of the offenc[e] in regard they did deceive the trust ymposed in them, which is a breache of the highest obligacion that is amongs men in the intercourse of civill accions, I am forced to Runn out thus a little in the expression of this matter because upon the due consideracion thereof I suppose the mynds of this honorable comittee will the more easily be perswaded to the beleife of that opinion and Judgmen[t] which the company did long agoe conclude even att tha[t] very tyme of their sufferinges, and have ever since retayned that the very destruccion of the plantacion was directly intended by mr Jacobs, I tell you howe aunctient itt is, that you may not esteeme it a thinge newly forged by me, and you will not thinck itt to[o] grea[t] an ymputacion to be laid to them who you see were guil[ty] of greater, for they that wronged the kynge in this manner for their owne gayne, what cryme or synne could be of so highe a nature as to breede any scruple in their myndes if itt might turne to their particuler gayne, you see the overburdenning and oppressing [of] the comodity they stuck not att, for the first yeare having gayned almost Fyve thowsand pound, yett they woulde not spare the Virginia[,] but for a litle advantage under five hundred pound*e*s they brought a dammadge upon the company and Tobacco of above half as many thousands

And the second yere they did establish and confirme this heavy and undue ymposicion so longe to indure as their Lease and benefitt, But this is but small parte of that crime which wee lay to their [f.10A] chardge they intended the very overthrowe of the commodity [it] self, For else why should Jacobs so obstinately opposing the Lords lettres Refuse to deliver the Tobacco, why would he not accept of such an indifferent offer as was made hym to leave half the comodity in deposito for satsfieng what he demaunded,

If he only had sought the payment of vjd upon a pound either of theis condicions as they did amply secure him so they would sufficiently have contended him, Butt his violent deteyning the Tobacco did and do ymply a direct intencion to abase ruyne and destroye the comodity,

For having the Lease now for Fyve yeares and receaving upon spanish tobacco one shilling six penc[e] and upon the Virginia only six pence, the venting every pound of Virginia was to their damage and losse one shilling Wherfore concluding the plantacions and this comodity to be an enemy of their proffitt, they resolve to be an Enemy to both, and seeke all meanes to ruyne and overthrowe them, and to the accomplishment of this intent and purpose was the vyolent and longe deteyning of their Tobacco which I formerly acquainted you, (viz) from July till thende of December, when by the yll keeping and usage of itt, itt was not soulde for Two shillinges the pound, whereas the company might have had fyve shillings for itt, upon the first coming home, Now by this meanes they effected what they desired, for this being the first greate quantety proving very bad not of itts owne nature and condicion but by the yll keeping of itt, there grewe an yll esteeme and reputation [f.10B] of Virginia Tobacco as a base and unwholsome sorte whereby the taking thereof that began formerly to growe in greate use, was almoste utterly neglected and this accidentall evill which they had caused with greate Arte and conyng by them selves and divers their Instruments purposely spreading the discommendacions and disprayses of the Virginia tobac[co] They did constantly maynteine and increase only by breeding a dislike and disesteeme of the Virginia to keepe the spanishe in a contynuall and increasi[ng] Vent

And as by thus spoiling of the comodity they brought itt into disreputacion, soe by the Lowenes and basenes of the price, the[y] prevented the repairing of the esteeme thereof, For the planters there fynding the charge att least fyfteene pence and the comodity not to yelde above thre shillings and knowing the price being once this sett, itt was very harde to rayse itt, They afterwardes bent their cares only to make a greate deale rather then good, that so the quantety might produce the gayne which their goodnes and worth did not,

Theise were the passadges endes and yssues of this buissines from July 1619 till July 1620, And now I doubt not butt this honorable committee is fully satisfied in this poynte toching the conclusion which I first sett downe, that the Plantacions overthrowe and ruyne was directly intended in thi[s] [f.11A] Accion of mr Jacobs and his partiners, and that the kinge was exceedingly wronged and deceyved by them in his honour and his proffitt And so I comme to the next particuler of oppression in this commodity that followed in the begynnings of the yeare − 1620[8]

---

[8] Neither copy of the speech goes any further. At this point Ferrar would have handed over the attack on the Lord Treasurer to 'my Lord and thother gentlemen', namely Lord Cavendish, Sir Edwin Sandys and Sir John Danvers [See above p. 73 n. 2, citing Kingsbury, ii.538].

B. Fragment of a speech by Lord Cavendish, 28 April 1624 [Ferrar Papers 1576b]

1 They procure by misinformation a lettre from his Majestie of ye 18 May[9]

   .1. to forbid all from Courts that had not men on their shares. so no Court could be kept

   .2. to forbid Complaynts to be brought in ye Companies name though but in particular names subscribed for generall wronges.

And ye limitations of this lettre are expressed to be of force till ye end of ye Commission which shewes the drift of ye procurers, for so noe Courts could be kept, nor complaynts exhibited, and yet a Commission ex parte

2. But ye King being truely informed, wee are set free by a lettre of ye 4th of June[10] .7. weekes since ye Commission was ordred, a month since under ye seale, but from ye 18 of May till this time all Courts were forborne.

3. now ye faction that prepare accusations against us, though to ye king and before ye Lords, they were [?sent] under .20. yet in subscribing but .3. Arg.[11] Johns[12] Wrot[13] all .3. etc.

6 Lastly, seeing all these wayes could not drive us from our resolution besides disgracing us they endeavour to take from us all such helpes and defences as were absolutely necessary in this case, and by ye Power and art of my Lord Treasurer

1. All our letters returned from Virginia brought to the Commissioners unopened by their order, and by vertue of ye words ["]by all wayes and meanes["] and here out of private and discontented [letters *erased*] persons letters they labour to find out supplementall proofe for Capt. Butler to our disgrace

2. Not finding any thing for that purpose in the publique lettres from ye Counsell there, they examine whether it be not by practise etc. so ye publique lettres must not excuse us and ye private must condemne us now unequall iudging a [private *erased*] publique for a private enformer.

3. These long kept and unseene by us but to the [xxx][14]

4. Though all our Court bookes & Evidences were before with the Clarks of ye Councell yet ye Commissioners themselves (a strange

---

[9] Cf. Kingsbury ii.434-5.
[10] Cf. Kingsbury ii.437.
[11] ?Sir Samuel Argall.
[12] ?Alderman Robert Johnson.
[13] ?Samuel Wrote.
[14] Three illegible letters.

partiality) procure an order to have from us all rough draughts blurred bookes transcripts or Coppyes nay even the very minutes of Courts taken in loose papers were exacted so as no memoriall of our businesse might remayne

5. But this alone served not to take away our armes, but they must remove our principall exemplify by ye businesse of Trade so he in this that endevored etc. Though he had of late forborne the Courts, yet because they thought his advise and direction might ayd the company my lord Treasurer told him, as he sayd in frendship that it was etc. but promising to[,] and forgot. He denyed. and their divers Complaynts Comming against him the king without my lord Treasurers knowledge recalled him

And thus I have run over these strange discouragements and Interruptions after ye Commission issued, and before we Come to charge others or defend our selves[.] now I come to represent unto you the execution of ye Commission it selfe.

2. Now my last part is this, to make you acquainted with the uniust and partiall proceedinges of ye Commissioners [it selfe *erased*] them selves or of such from whom they receaved instructions, contrary to the commission it selfe under the Great Seale.

And this I devide into 2 parts
1. their partiall and uniust proceedings in favour of the opposite party
2. theyr partiall and uniust proceedinges in disfavour to the Company and particular members thereof,

1. For their partiall proceedinges [erasure now illegible] in favour of ye opposite party.

The company being now at liberty by his Majesties lettres of ye 4th of June to make their complayntes against those that had wronged them and ye Colony, they first exhibited their Complaynts against Sir Thomas Smithes accounts and his goverment which was thus proceeded in,

1. My Lord Delaware, Sir Edward Sackevile and my selfe[15] with others comming to the Commissioners house, finde Sir Thomas Smith and that party locked [erasure] in, with the commissioners who litle expected[,] now Sir Edwin Sands was absent[,] that any preparation was made for his charge, so one comes out and gives knowledge that if there be any that have any charge against Sir Thomas Smyth in

[15] Cf. Kingsbury ii.437.

respect of his accounts he may now be admitted to present them.

2. So unlooked for by him, we came in and presented 12 Articles against his accounts, and from that day to the end of the Commission he never after appeared before them.

3. That day being the 10th of June the Commissioners alledged that our exceptions were generall. And yet one of our exceptions was that he charged himselfe with 80 and odde thousand pounds, whereof for above halfe he neyther shewed warrants for the disbursements, nor receipts from those to whom he had disbursed it. And besides, wee knew not what to prove till wee knew what he would deny, but for all this they pressed us to expresse particularly how much Sir Thomas Smith was indebted to the Company.

4. They being desired by us that wee might have Sir Thomas Smithes bookes of accounts to make our proofes by them they refused, and so they cast upon us as it were an Impossibility of our farther proceeding therein.

5. Friday after[,] being the 13th of June, wee againe desired Sir Thomas Smithes answer in writinge to our exceptions, and that as they had commanded the Company to bring in all their bookes, so they would also be pleased to command him to bring in his originall Cash booke, alleadging that the sight thereof would conduce much to ye cleering of ye businesse.

6. To this his frend Alderman Johnson and others replyed that other Cash bookes he had none then what was delivered. But this was disproved for the bookes delivered to the Company were but Coppies, and Sir Thomas Smith before confessed so much to the Commissioners.

7. I now speake by relation, for being desired to retire, they stayed our Deputy and demanded of him whether this was all wee had to say against Sir Thomas Smithes accounts adding that if wee said no more by Wednesday next then wee had done yet they would cleere him, and that they would be his Commissioners though the Lords were theirs.

8. This order the Deputy would have had in writinge, which at first they said he should, but after changing their minde, which he pressing they after commanded him to signify this unto the Company without more adoe.

9. Tuesday after wee againe pressed the bringing in of Sir Thomas Smithes originall Cash bookes, and Sir Thomas Smithes answer in writinge to our formal exceptions against his accounts

10. The Commissioners instead of giving us an answer to this, demanded if wee had any thing to say against his goverment, willing us to bring it in ye next day, or else intimating that they would cleere him in that point also.

11. Wee saying that for that point wee could not be prepared so soone, they pressed it the more, but indeed it was knowne, that by the kings

favour Sir Edwin Sands was agayne comming to towne and much desiring to despatch this businesse ere he came, commanded us to bring this in, and refused to go on with the accounts saying they would first begin with his goverment, and yet the day before they would needes have cleered his accounts.

12. Accordingly the next day of meeting wee brought a charge of great length against his goverment and consisting of many Articles which were reduced to 4 generall heades.

13. 1. of such strange neglect and unorderlinesse in his goverment, as implyed an intent rather utterly to ruine and destroy the Plantatin then to advance it.

  2. An usurpation of strange and unlawfull [?rool, i.e. rule]
    1. in suppressing the kings majesties instructions
    2. neglecting the assistance of his Majesties Councell for Virginia and
    3dly by his owne authority sending a booke of Martiall Lawes into Virginia for ye goverment of [Virg *erased*] the Plantation, whereby many were cruelly and tirannously executed.

  3dly wee complayned of him not only for great wast and ill husbandry in ye expending the Companies mony, but also for much deceipt and fraud in ye keeping of his accounts whereby the Company conceave them selves wronged many thousand pounds.

  4. The first sending over and after supporting of Sir Samuel Argall who had robbed and spoyled the Plantation, and turned the whole stocke of ye Company to his owne use.

14. This charge as it was unlooked for, so it was very unwelcome to them, who had not the cleeringe of this in their secret Instructions [?that] [?great] [?now] [?questioned] [?how] might give them

15. To this charge and that formerly concerning his accounts Sir Thomas Smith brought in his answer the 5 of July, the most poore and generall reply to so heavy a charge that I yet ever saw, which was then given to us, and instead of directing us to reply upon it, they told us that a charge should shortly be brought in against us, and advised us to prepare for an answer and that instantly because very shortly the Commission should breake up.

16. Against ye next meeting and upon view of his answer wee drew proofes of our 2 first exceptions against his accounts, whereby we playnely proved out of his bookes and billes under his hand that he had receaved 800 *l* more then in his receipts were acknowledged, and these proofes under friday the 11 of July were pressed before the Commissioners, desiring a sufficient answer or else that this 800 *l* might be presently payd.

17. And for his disbursements himselfe confessed that he had neyther warrants nor acquittances for almost 40000 *l* disbursed.

18. wee then also acquaynted the Commissioners that his true originall Cash bookes were not brought in whatsoever he pretended to the Contrary, which we know by ye breaking open of seales and unsowing some leaves of ye booke which he sent us for which Sir William Jones was Angry that wee presumed to breake open these seales.

19. Besides wee acquainted them that by perusall wee had found his servants kept double Cashes, not one agreeing with another, which is the greatest falsehood that can possibly be in accountants, and we further shewed that there had bene use made of those double Cash bookes to avoyd the Companies exceptions.

20. Notwithstanding all this the businesse slept and wee could get no manner of redresse.

21. for the matter of his accounts it thus dyed in the Commissioners hands and wee heard no more neyther did they make any report of it to the Lords [of the Privy Council], as by the Commission they are directed.

22. And for ye other chardge of his misgoverment short warninge being given us to attend, upon the .16. of July, having viewed his answer wee exhibited proofes of 3 principall branches of that charge, and proffered upon reasonable time to do so to the [next *erased*] rest, which they were shortly after and now ready to make good, but the Commissioners though they sate all Michaelmas terme against us never called us unto it.

23. And the Company conceave that in these particular points of accounts and misgoverment being principalply recommended to their examination by this Commission, the Commissioners have violated their duty to his Majestie and done good wrong to the Company.

I shall be shorter in the other particulars.

2. Another Partiality in favor of the opposite party appeared in ye proceeding touching Capt. Butlers unmasking of Virginia

1. This paper of his with another was delivered by them first to his Majestie[,] by his Majestie referred to the Councell Table, and [so] was it that [which] there begat ye Commission, and because it was matter of discouragment to Adventurers it was specially to have bene examined.

2. Upon the evil report of Virginia, diverse that knew ye place well, came unto ye Virginia Court and proffered their testimony, which they also set downe under their hands voluntarily, and to the Contrary of what C. Butler had affirmed

3. And forasmuch as Capt. Butler had [?therein *interlined*] chardged some persons with private ends The Company had made an Answer unto that part also of the same paper

4. And now the Company had cause to expect that witnesses should have bene examined concerning the truth both on ye one side and ye other and to that end May .17. delivered to ye Commissioners a Copie of ye Unmasquing delivered unto them by the Lords of ye Counsell, and with it the Answer of these that voluntaryly had set downe their testimony before, together with [*erasure*] the Companies answer to so much of it as concerned the aspersion of private ends.

5. The .10. of June, They pressed [?on them] the truth hereof examined; but ye Commissioners answer that Capt Butler had not offred it and that if wee will make it a complaynt of ours, wee must have it under his hand and one said that it may be C. Butler is now of another minde, and another said, it may be that Lettres now come from Virginia will make it good.

6. The .13th. of June, C. Butler avowed his Vnmasquinge, and for confutation wee presented the said voluntary testimonyes which they refused to read. Alledging that it was not ye Answer of ye Company as if ye Company could give answer touching the quality of ye ayre, water and soyle of Virginia otherwise then by the testimony of such as had bene there. And Sir William Jones said their testimony was disabled by havyng bene preexamined by ye Company[.][16]

---

[16] Here the notes end.

iii
Petitions, May 1624

1. FP 1628b: in the hand of Nicholas Ferrar[1]

[f.1r]   [Heading missing]   May 1624

Your Majesties moast[2] humble Commons, taking into carefull consideration, the greate wante of mony in this your Realm at this day;
wherby Rents are unpayde, Contracts broken, Bonds forfeited, Marketts
and Fayres much deserted, or unfrequented, the better sort impoverished, and the meaner (for want of meanes in the better) not sett
on worke; extending, not onely to a generall Distemper amongst your
subiects at home, but to the hinderance alsoe of Trade, and Traffique
abroade; (mony being as well the Mother as Daughter therof) And
doubting, [the *erased*] least the same wante, may in fyne alsoe redounde
to the preiudice of your Majesty in Subsidie and other dutys, Graunted,
or to be graunted for the service of your Majesty; and necessary defence
of your kingdomes, they have thought fitt, to present [one princi *erased*]
to your Majestys princely regard, one principall cause of this want,
amongst divers others, which the streightnes of tyme, doth exclude
from exact (and full *interpolated*) consideration.

It is generally knowen, that the West Indies are at this day almoast
the onely Fountayne, and Spayne as it were the Cesterne, from whence
Silver is derived into all parts of Christendom.

The cause of the greate Importation of Silver from thence into this
Realme, hath beene for that Spayne having soe greate need of many
English Commodities [f.1v] [GAP[3]] to [C]ounterballance them with
theire owne they have beene forced to make the accompt eeven with
Mony.

But since this weede of Tobacko hath growen into request, they have
payde, (as *erased*) (as their Proverb is) for all our Commodities with
Their Smoake: And the rayne of there silver to us ward, hath beene
in a manner dried upp, to the loss of a Million and a halfe in mony in
theese fifteene yeares last past. For uppon very full and exact examination, it hath very playnely and undeniably appeared, that [, *erased*]
what by undersale of our Native Commodities to make ready mony

---

[1] There are two copies of this petition: FP 1628b, in the hand of Nicholas Ferrar, and
FP 1628a, in the hand of Edward Collingwood.

[2] FP 1628a: most.

[3] FP 1628a: and being not able.

for [*replacing* of *erased*] their Tobacko, what by the mony it selfe payde unto them for that weede, there hath beene [lost *erased*] losse to this Kingdome of one hundred Thousand pounds every yeare, which else would have returned in mony from thence. And a miserable kynde of Trade hath beene driven with that Nation, our Native Commodities being undersolde, and the foreigne overbought; and the Treasure[4] of mony transformed into a Smoaking weed.

Your humble Commons therfore, moast instantly crave of your Majesty, that the Importation of Tobacko, may bee prohibited from all (other *interpolated*) parts (other then *erased*) save your Majestys (owne *interpolated*) Dominions, according to the Practize in like Cases of all other Nations, in favour of there[5] native Commodities, and of their Natural people: [f.2r]   (and in part perished *erased*)

The rest of the page is blank, as is f.2v.

2.   FP 484a: in the hand of Nicholas Ferrar[6]

[f.1r]   May 1624   *Turky Merchants*   1[7]

The Merchants[8] trading to the Levant, commonly called the Turky merchants, complayne of the excessive Burthens, Lately layde uppon Currans,[9] being a Commodity in many cases of necessary use. They alleadge, that to the subsidy of eighteene pence uppon[10] the hundred weight (of Currans *erased*), there hath been addition made, in the yeare 1608, of three shilling foure pence; and of two shillinges twopence more, in anno 1620.[11] Which additions of five shilling sixpence, make[12] (upp *erased*) the whole burthen (upp *interpolated*) seven shillings, which is neere a full fourth parte of the entyre price of the[13] Currans, and too greate a Burthen for any Commodity to beare.

And, wheras it hath been sayde that this addition of five[14] shilling

---

[4] FP 1628a: Treasury.

[5] FP 1628a: there *abridged to* the.

[6] Three copies of the Turkey Merchants petition survive: FP 484a and FP 484b are entirely in Nicholas Ferrar's hand; FP 484c is in the hands of Nicholas Ferrar and Edward Collingwood. The text above is FP 484a; variants taken from FP 484b are given in the footnotes which follow. Cf. BL, Harl. MS 159 f.44.

[7] FP 484b does not italicise Turky Merchants, and is numbered '2'.

[8] FP 484b names them 'Turky merchants'.

[9] FP 484b: corrans.

[10] This word has been added in the left hand margin.

[11] FP 484b: twopence now in Anno 1620.

[12] FP 484b: maketh.

[13] 'Commodity' *erased*.

[14] The five is first erased and then put back.

sixpence, is noe more, then the merchants themselves have formerly
layde; your Majesty may bee graciously pleased, to receive this true
Information, that the first Imposition uppon Currans was in Anno 1575
(at the then Earle of Leicesters suite and *interpolated*) uppon a graunte
of the sole Importation, of Currans, Zant Oyle, and Greek Wynes, to
one Acerbo Velutelli[15] which Imposition lay wholly uppon the stranger[16]
merchaunt, the English[17] not trading then in that commodity.

The Venetians, to be quitt with us for that Imposition, forthwith
layde lardge Impositions uppon all our English Commodities as likewyse
uppon their owne yf solde to the English: thirty seven shillings [f.1v]
uppon a broade Cloath: ten shilling uppon an hundred weight of
Wolle[18]: as much uppon Tyn: five shilling six pence uppon an hundred
of Currans: (30s *erased*) thirty shillings uppon a Butt of[19] sweet wyne[20]:
and soe uppon others; which Impositions, raysed uppon that unfortunate
occasion, continue['s' *erased*] there uppon our Nation to[21] this (very
interpolated) day; notwithstanding the greate Indeavour of Q. Eliz.[22] to
gett them off, with like offer to lay down her owne. [Paragraph sign]
But fynding her selfe frustrated of all hope by her Treaties, in Anno
1590 she graunted (to the Merchants *interpolated*) a Patent for Trade to
Venice and Turks,[23] to continue for 12 yeares, with power to rayse
Impost uppon the Straunger Merchants,[24] (soe *interpolated*) to make
themselves (a *erased*) recompence for those Venetian Impositions. And
then was the Imposition of five shilling sixpence layde by[25] our Turky
merchants: wherby they levied to their own use five thousand poundes;
the Dammadge by the Venetian Impositions, amounting as they
compute, to (six score *erased*) one hundred and twenty thousand pounds
(as they compute *erased*) since it first was layd.

Aboute eight yeares after, this Patent being avoyded, uppon some
defect discovered, they had a new Patent offered of sole Trade to
Turky and Venice, uppon condition, that this 5s-6d (layde formerly on
Straungeres for[26] use of the Merchants) might bee transported to the

---

[15] Interpolated over 'Velbatelli' erased.
[16] FP 484b: straunger.
[17] FP 484b: Englishmen.
[18] FP 484b: wooll.
[19] 'muskadyne' *erased*.
[20] FP 484b: wynes.
[21] *Originally* 'unto', *the* 'un-' *being erased*.
[22] 'the late' is added in the left hand margin, then erased. FP 484b has 'Elizabeth' in full.
[23] FP 484b: Turky.
[24] FP 484b: Merchant.
[25] 'the' *erased*.
[26] FP 484b: and for.

Queene, and extended to all Currans imported by whomsoever[27] which offer being refused by the merchants, they in fyne to procure that Pattent for sole trade, assented to pay her foure thousand pound (yearlie *interpolated*) rent: for raysing wherof, they imposed on there currans, sometymes more, sometymes less, but three shillinges at the moast

[f.2r]   The[28] Pattent, at the comming in of your Majesty, was forfeited and avoyded, for Non-Payment of Rent. And anno 1605, they obtayned of your Majesty there present Pattent in Perpetuity.[29] And then[30] five shillings six pence (was *erased*) levied uppon them by some other, till finally in anno 1608 your Majesty[31] determined the same by[32] resuming it into your owne handes, and[33] made that[34] addition (forementioned *interpolated*) of three shilling foure pence: which was entered into the Booke of rates by order from your Majesty.

The Turky Merchants complayne of bothe Additions but cheifely of this later;[35] not yet entred[36] in the book of rates as beinge layde uppon an erroneous grounde, themselves having never levied[37] that five shillings sixpence, save uppon the Venetians onely.

They alleadge, that this buthen is insupportable; and that it eateth away the whole proffitt of their[38] Trade, being mayntayned with greate chardge, and through much hazard and daunger.

Your Commons therfore, moast humbly beseech your Majesty, of your Justice, and Grace, to yeeld a favorable eare to this necessary complaynte, and to releive them, at least of this greivous surchardge, the same alsoe setling uppon your people:, conceiving (alsoe *interpolated*) that this greate overchardging of that trade, may tende to the utter impoverishing, and dishartening of those merchants, who mantayne a greate navy of good shipps, and marriers: and vent a greate quantity of died, and dressed cloaths: besides a multitud of new manifactures, to the[39] advancement of your Majesty's customs, and to (the *interpolated*) greate benifitt of this your Realme.

[27] 'wch' *erased*.
[28] FP 484b: This.
[29] The full stop replaces a comma, which has been erased.
[30] NF's 'then' is erased, and 'then was' added in another hand.
[31] 'resumed' *erased*.
[32] 'pr' *erased*.
[33] 'that' *erased*.
[34] 'former' *erased*.
[35] 'being layde upon a false (*changed by NF to* an erronious)' is all erased. In their place another hand has interpolated 'not yet entred ... erroneous'.
[36] FP 484b: entered.
[37] 'it saving uppon t' *erased*.
[38] FP 484b: the.
[39] 'gre' *erased*.

[f.2v] [endorsement by Tristram Conyam:] Concerninge the Turkie Merchants Trade.-

In FP 484c the date at the head of the document, May 1624, has a line through it, and the number '3' which follows has been altered to '2'. The first three paragraphs are written by Edward Collingwood, the next three by Nicholas Ferrar, and the last four by Collingwood

3. FP 484d[40]: in Nicholas Ferrar's hand

2. Eastland Companie

Your Commons, in their(e *erased*) former Declaration and Petition to your Majesty having expressed, to the best of theire Understanding and Judgement, the true state of the Cloathing of this Kingdom, wherin consisteth the greatest parte of the wealth of your people; Have in the next place, taken into Consideration, the shipping and Marriners, in which, standeth noe small parte of the strenght of this your Realme (and by *interpolated*) which the Merchant also improveth the wealth therof. And fynding that the Eastland Compagny have ["obtayned by Pattent the sole Importatio[n]" *erased*] partly by theyre Pattent and partly by your Majestys late Proclamation obtayned the sole Importation of the cheife materialls for shipping, as Masts, Deals, Hempe, Cordage, Pich, Tarr and other[41] have thought it their[42] duty, to represent unto your Majesty's princely consideration,[43] and wisedome, certayne necessary considerations, as well for support, and increase of the shipping of this Realme; as alsoe for the more generall content of the Merchants of the same.

first, wheras your Majesty by your late Proclamations the one in favour of the Eastland, and the other of the Turky Compagny, hath commaunded that no man[44] excercise those[45] Trades, either into the places respectively[46] of their(e *erased*) Priviledges, or homewards from thence, save in English Bottoms, which hath beene to the greate Increase of the shipping

[Catchwords: of this your Realme,:]

---

[40] Contrast BL, Harl. MS 159 f.46v.
[41] This word is interpolated above 'the like from the / p' *erased*.
[42] NF at first wrote 'there duty'.
[43] Another hand has changed this word to 'iudgement'.
[44] NF at first wrote 'none' in place of 'no man'.
[45] Interpolated by NF over the original 'either of theire' *erased*.
[46] Interpolated by the other hand.

[f.1v] (this yr Realme' *erased*) Your Commons, (though)[47] having taken into due consideration, that the freight[48] of Duch ships being much cheaper then our owne, the restrayning to English bottoms must needs be a chardge to the Merchant, and likewise[49] endearing of theire ware to the subiect: Yet in regard, that encrease of chardge is wholly amongst your people, so that your Kingdom is noe whit the poorer by it, and the publique benifitt by encrease of shipping is incomparably greater; they humbly thanking your Majesty for this your provident care, only pray, that there may bee some dispensation for a while for the bringing in of greate masts in straunger Bottoms till such tyme as the Merchants may provide English[50] shipping for the same.

Secondly they humbly pray (for sundry Important reasons, and principally *interpolated*) in favour of the greate shipping of this your Realme (and for preserving the honnour of the English Navigation *interpolated*), that the Merchants trading for those Eastland and Norway Commodities, may fech them at the wellheade onely, where they (originally *interpolated*) grow, or are made, and not at other places   at the second hand, which would bee a greate meanes to diminish the greate shipping of this your Realme.

[f.2r]   Thirdly, for that it[51] is founde by dayly experience, that this restraynte of (trade for *interpolated*) the materialls of shipping, to one place onely, is inconvenient to the Merchants of the outports of this (your *interpolated*) Realme, being there(by)[52] disfurnished, of those necessary provisions for the building, rigging, and setting forth of their[e *erased*] shipps;* they humbly pray, that your Majesty will bee pleased, to take such order, that the rest of the Merchants of this Realme, may bee admitted into this (Eastland *interpolated*) Compagny, at the fyne of five markes;[53] (But for the trade of Norway alone, that they may bee admitted without fyne.) And that the Merchants of the outports may once a yeare, sende there deputys to (the Courts of *interpolated*) this Compagny, to treate, and agree uppon such orders as may bee for the better [ar *erased*] menadging of that (trade *interpolated*) and directing the Goverment therof to the Publique benifitt of this your Realme

---

*They humbly pray that your Majesty will bee pleased soe to enlardge this trade, that the merchants of the outports may freely

[47] Interpolated by the other hand.
[48] Interpolated by NF over 'chardge' *erased*.
[49] Interpolated by the other hand.
[50] Interpolated by the other hand over Nf's 'fitt'.
[51] 'hat' *erased*.
[52] Added by the other hand, NF's separated 'by' being erased.
[53] 'which liberty onel' *erased*.

excercise the same, paying onely a fyne of five markes to the Compagny, and not to bee farther subiect to the Goverment of the same: [f.2v] which by reason of the remoteness of theire dwellings, would be troublesom unto them, and otherwyse inconvenient for the speed of theire Voyadges.

4. FP 1397c in Edward Collingwood's hand

[May 1624 *erased*] *Patent for Ginny and Binny*

3

[Ginny *erased*]

Your Commons most humblie complaine, in behalf of the Merchaunts, Clothiers, Dyers and other good subiects of this your Realme, of a Patent graunted in the 16th yeare of your Majesty's raigne, for sole Trade to the partes of Africa, called Ginny, and Binny. Which Patent, having been graunted upon untrue suggestions to your Majestie, that some of the Patentees had been the first discoverers of that Trade: (Whereas it is apparant, that those partes have been traded to about fifty yeares since by Sir John Hawkins deceased, and since from tyme to tyme by divers other Merchants): Tending also to the great wrong, and impoverishing[54] of your subiects by depryving them of their lawfull Trade; and raising the price of those Merchandizes, to a most extreeme rate, being of necessarie use for Dyers and Clothiers.

They most humblie beseach your Majestie, that the said (surreptitious *erased*) Patent, may be avoyded, and cancelled; [as being repugnant to the Lawes, and liberties of this your Realme; iniurious to your Majestie, by misinformacion; as also to your subiects by manifold wrong and oppression *all erased*]

FP 1397b: Nicholas Ferrar, with variant spellings, fair copies the preceding.

5. FP 484e[55]

[May 1624 *erased*] 5[56] *Serdges & Perpetuanas*

The merchaunts of the Western Ports, of your Countys of Devon, Sommersett, Dorsett, and Cornewall, complayne of the Farmers of

---

[54] Interpolated over first 'depop' *erased*, then 'privation' *erased*.
[55] Cf. BL, Harl. MS 159 ff.45v–46r.
[56] '6' has been erased.

your majesty's Customs; that, wheras the first Invention of those new
Draperys, called [Pe *erased*] Perpetuanas, and Serges, was in those
Westerne Partes, to the benifitt of your Majesty in your Customs, and
subsidies, and to the comfort of your (poore *interpolated*) people by
stoare of worke: And, wheras at the very first, there were 2 sorts of
Perpetuan[a]s, one better, of the valew of 3 ll and upwards: and one
worse, of the valew of 40 shillinges and under: bothe which are rated
in the booke of Rates, (sett oute by your Majesty) as by a midle
valuation, of -50^s shillings[57]: the sayde Farmers, of there owne Authority
have increased the valuation, of the one to three poundes fifteen
shillings, without any diminution of ye[58] rate for the other: [Paragraph
sign] Wheras alsoe the narrow serges, are rated in the sayde booke, at
30^s, though in truth at this day, by reason of the slight making, (with
erased) the true valew runneth betweene fifteene and five and twenty
shillings (the Merchants directing to have them made at[59] soe lowe a
price, because otherwise they would not vente to the poorer sorte in
forreigne partes) the sayde Farmers, uppon there owne like unlawfull
Authority, have of late yeares drawen them up to three tymes there
valew, namely fifty shillings; under a colorable[60] pretence, that theese
Serges are Perpetuanoes. and that they would punish the slight and
base[61] making of there stuffs: there being not (any *interpolated*) statute
concerning the making of them

[f.1v]   And, whereas your Majesty in your sayde booke of Rates, hath
given Directions[62] that in case of such Question, concerning the nature
of the Wares, the triall of the Valuation should bee by the Merchants
Oath; the sayde triall having beene offered, hath been refused, notwithstanding your Majesty['s] order soe direct and just.

Your Commons having taken this cause[63] into serious consideration,
and having heard the Allegations on bothe parts, at lardge, with the
Proofs and Witnesses; and fynding it (very *interpolated*) straunge, and
fearfull in Precedent, that the sayde Farmers, uppon their[64] owne wills,
should presume to alter the Rates in the sayde booke, being the Act of
your Majesty; and to transgress your Majesty's Just Order and Direction;
and contrarily to make themselves both Parties and Judges, and as it
were to fyne your Majesty's subiects, for there owne private benifitt,
have conceived the same to bee an offence of greate presumption and

---

[57] NF has written both the superscript 's' and the full word.
[58] The superscript 'e' has been added by another hand.
[59] Interpolated by the other hand over NF's 'of' *erased*.
[60] Interpolated by the other hand over NF's 'an untrue' *erased*.
[61] NF has interpolated 'slight and base' for 'faulty' *erased*.
[62] Interpolated by the other hand over NF's 'a proper and just direction' *erased*.
[63] Interpolated by the other hand over NF's 'case' *erased*.
[64] Corrected by the other hand from NF's 'there'.

unlawfulness towards[65] your Majesty, and of greivous Extorsion and oppression of[66] your sayde subiects. And they moast humbly desyre of your Royall Majesty, that the aforesayde Rates and Directions may [bee *erased*] bee observed: and the sayde Farmers make restitution for the summons so unduly levied. –

6. FP 1397a[67]: in the hand of Nicholas Ferrar

7[68]   Cloathworkers   I

[May 1624 *erased*]

The Cloathworkers, being (one of the first o *erased*) an Auntient Compagny in the Citty of London, and one of the first Twelve sett upp by your famous progenitor K. Ed: the 3., for advancement of the Cloathing of this Realm (brought in by him to his immortall Fame and Honnour) Complayne of their[69] greate Poverty, wherinto, (being twelve thousand soules at this present) they are brought, for wante of worke, and by being deprived of those Laws, which the wisdom of this state hath (provided *erased*) ordeined for providing worke for the poorer sort: (T *erased*)

They Compleyne therfore in particular, That they are bereaved of the fruite of a stat: made 8° Eliz.[70] which provided, that every person transporting nine cloaths unwrought, should[71] carry the tenth wrought, that is Rowed, Barbed, First Coursed, and shorne from one ende to the other, by which worke the Cloathworker is mantayned.

This statute not longe after was disused, whence Complaynt grew of the Clothworkers[72] agaynst the merchant Adventurers, which was referred to the award of Sir William Cordall, and the late Queenes Sollicitour Broomeley, whoe by their[73] Order[74] in writing under there handes and seales, dated 7° Jun[e] 18° Eliz. awarded that the Statute shoulde bee observed: which award was alsoe confirmed by the Merchants. Aventurers, (them selves *erased*) under the seale of there Compagny. (but *erased*)

But the gayne of the White Cloaths, quickening the witts and desyres

[65] Adapted by the other hand from NF's 'undutifulness to / wards'.

[66] Interpolated by the other hand over NF's 'to' *erased*.

[67] Cf. BL, Harl. MS 159 f.46v for variations in the wording.

[68] '8' has been erased.

[69] Corrected by another hand from NF's 'there'.

[70] *Statutes of the Realm* iv.i.489: 8 Eliz.I c.6.

[71] Interpolated by the other hand over NF's 'shall' *erased*.

[72] Adapted by the other hand from NF's 'Clothiers'.

[73] Corrected by the other hand from NF's 'there'.

[74] Interpolated by the other hand over NF's 'Hand' *erased*.

of the Merchant. Adventurers[,] meanes were[75] founde to give a stopp, both to the statute, and to the award: And[76] other order hath since beene taken for[77] some releife to the Cloathworkers (by setting them to woork in[78] *interpolated*) wetting some of the white Cloaths, and searching the rest, which order notwithstanding hath not been performed unto them.

[f1v] 2 Your Commons therfore (in commiseration *interpolated*) of this greate and Distressed Compagny, craving onely the Inheritance of there Labors, and your Majesty's Laws, [moast *erased*] humbly beseech your Majesty that the sayde statute by your Majesty's royall commaund may be henceforth observed., [paragraph sign] wherby the Compagny also of Diers, now complayning of like wante of worke, and (increase of *interpolated*) poverty, may bee alsoe comforted and releived; their[79] state having a dependency uppon the good estate of the Cloathworker.

7. [f2r]   8 Tobacko[80]

The Importation of Tobacko which is not of the groweth of your majesty's owne Dominions, is founde to bee one of the greatest occasions of the disordering of Trade and want of mony within this kingdom Therfore we humbly pray that your Majesty will give order that noe tobacko bee from henceforth imported but such as is the proper groweth of your own Dominions

8.   Eastland Compagny[81]

9 Although the E[astland] Compagny bee founde now to bee very proffitable to this your Majesty's Realme yett theire Pattent with the Proclamation of restraynte pursuing it, is for the present burthensom to divers parts therof Wee therfore humbly pray, that though forraigne shipping bee forbidden to bring in commodities which are not of theire owne groweth yett till a good Law may bee made in Parliament for the setling of it, that forreigne shipps may bee allowed to bring Mast Rafts and Deales on any English ships all other necessary commodit[ie]s for shippings and Mynes[82] into any of the outports of this your Realme

[f2v]   Blank

[75] Interpolated by the other hand over NF's 'was' *erased*.
[76] Adapted by the other hand from NF's 'and'.
[77] Interpolated by the other hand over NF's 'of' *erased*.
[78] Interpolated by the other hand after erasing NF's 'by'.
[79] Corrected by the other hand from NF's 'there'.
[80] Cf. BL, Harl. MS 159 f.46v.
[81] Cf. ibid.
[82] Harl. MS 159 f.46v here reads 'Wynes'.

APPENDIX I

Other Diaries of Proceedings in the House of Commons, 1624

The details of the documents listed below derive chiefly from Appendix B in Robert E. Ruigh, *The Parliament of 1624: Politics and Foreign Policy* (Harvard Historical Studies, 87) Cambridge, Mass, 1971, pp. 405–6.

1. D'Ewes, Sir Simonds, Diary of 12 February–29 May 1624 from the manuscript Journals of the House of Commons and unidentified private diaries and separates: British Library, Harleian MS 159 ff.59–136v.
2. Dyott, Richard, MP for Stafford, Staffordshire. Diary of 5–15 March, & 20 April–29 May 1624: Staffordshire Record Office, MS D 661/11/2.
3. Earle, Sir Walter, MP for Poole, Dorset, Diary of 19 February–29 May 1624: BL, Add. MS 18597.
4. Hawarde, John, MP for Bletchingly, Surrey. Diary of 12 February–29 May 1624: Wiltshire Record Office, unnumbered manuscript deposited by the Marquess of Ailesbury, pp. 143–307.
5. Holland, Sir Thomas, MP for Norfolk. Diary of 25 February–9 April 1624: Bodleian Library, Tanner MS 392; diary of 10 April–15 May 1624: Bodl., Rawlinson MS D 1100.
6. Holles, John, MP for East Retford, Nottinghamshire. Diary of 23 February–19 May 1624: BL, Harleian MS 6383. ii 80v–141.
7. Horne, Robert, Synopsis of proceedings of 19 February–29 May 1624, compiled from separates and newsletters: Bodl., Rawlinson MS B 151 ff.58–70 & 103v.
8. Jervoise, Sir Thomas, MP for Whitchurch, Hampshire. Diary of 23 February–28 April 1624: Jervoise family manuscript, Herriard Park, Hants.
9. Nethersole, Sir Francis, MP for Corfe Castle, Dorset, parliamentary newsletters to Sir Dudley Carleton: Public Record Office, SP 81/30 (German) and SP 14/161–165 & 167 *passim*.
10. Nicholas, Edward, MP for Winchelsea, Cinque Ports, diary of 19 February–29 May 1624: PRO, SP 14/166.
11. Pym, John, MP for Tavistock, Devon. Diary of 19 February–7 May 1624 Northamptonshire Record Office, Finch-Hatton MS 50; diary of 13 April–10 May 1624: BL, Add. MS 26639, ff.1–37v, a fragment

of a diary, 23–26 February 1624: BL, Harleian MS 6799 ff. 131–133.

12. Rich, Sir Nathaniel, MP for Harwich, Essex. Diary of 23 February–6 March 1624: BL, Add. Ms 46191; of 2 April 1624 formerly PRO. 30/15/Box I/Part II, 168 (Manchester MSS) available in BL, as BL microfilm RP 420.

13. Spring, Sir William, MP for Suffolk. Diary of 19 February–27 May 1624: Harvard University, Houghton Library, MS English 980.

14. Wright, John, Clerk of the House of Commons. Third version of the Commons Journal, 12–25 February. House of Lords Record Office, Braye MS 73; proceedings in the Committee of Grievances, 21 & 24 May 1624: House of Lords Record Office, Commons Journal MS., first version, vol. II ff.49–50v

15. Anonymous diary of 19–24 February 1624: Bodl., Rawlinson MS D 723, ff.84–90v.

APPENDIX II

Parliament Men
mentioned in Nicholas Ferrar's Diary

KING JAMES I: ff.6, 6v, 9, 25, 36v, 42–43
CHARLES Prince of Wales: ff.6, 6v, 14v–21v, 30, 33, 34

HOUSE OF LORDS:

BRISTOL, John Digby, Earl of: ff.14v, 15v, 16, 17, 18, 19, 20v, 29, 33, 33v, 34, 35v
BUCKINGHAM, George Villiers, Duke of: ff.6v, 14v–22, 36v
CAESAR, Sir Julius, Master of the Rolls: f.24v
CANTERBURY, Goerge Abbot, Archbishop of: ff.30, 33, 34, 36v, 37
CHICHESTER of Belfast, Arthur Chichester, Lord: f.15
COVENTRY, Sir Thomas, Attorney-General: ff.24, 38v
CREW, Sir Ranulph, King's Serjeant: f.24
DAVIES, Sir John, Serjeant at law: f.38v
EXETER, Valentine Cary, Bishop of: f.6
HAMILTON, James Hamilton, Marquis of: ff.6, 14v
HOBART, Sir Henry, Lord Chief Justice of the Common Pleas, Chancellor to the Prince of Wales: f.12v
LENNOX, Ludovic Stuart, Duke of Richmond &, Lord Steward of the Household: f.6
LEY, Sir James, Lord Chief Justice of the King's Bench: f.12v
LINCOLN, John Williams, Bishop of, Lord Keeper of the Great Seal: ff.7, 9–10v, 29–29v, 30
Lord Admiral: *see* Buckingham, Duke of
Lord Chamberlain: *see* Pembroke, Earl of
Lord Chief Baron (of the Exchequer) *see* Tanfield, Sir Lawrence
Lord Chief Justice: *see* Hobart, Sir Henry, *and* Ley, Sir James
Lord Keeper (of the Great Seal): *see* Lincoln, Bishop of
Lord Steward (of the Household): *see* Lennox, Duke of; *and* Hamilton, Marquis of
Lord Treasurer: *see* Middlesex, Earl of
PEMBROKE, William Herbert, Earl of, Lord Chamberlain: ff.34, 36v

SOMERSET, Robert Carr, Earl of: f.32
SOUTHAMPTON, Henry Wriothesley, Earl of: f.37
TANFIELD, Sir Lawrence, Lord Chief Baron of the Exchequer: f.24v

HOUSE OF COMMONS

—— Sir R: f.40
ABBOT, Maurice (Kingston-upon-Hull, Yorks): ff.26, 41
ALFORD, Edward (Colchester, Essex), ff.13, 24v, 25v, 37v, 41
BATEMAN, Robert (London): ff.27v, 41
BEECHER, Sir William (Leominster, Herefs): f.39
BELASYSE, Sir Thomas (Thirsk, Yorks): f.39
BRAKYN, Francis (Cambridge, Cambs): f.12v
BROMFIELD, Robert (Southwark, Surrey): f.27v
BULSTRODE, Sir William (Rutland): f.11v
CALVERT, Sir George (Oxford U.) Secretary of State: ff.6, 11v, 12v,
    25, 33v, 34
CAVENDISH, William, Lord Cavendish (Derbyshire): f.6
CECIL, Sir Edward (Dover, Kent): ff.11v, 24v
COKE, Sir Edward (Coventry, Warks): ff.12, 12v, 13, 26, 27v, 28v, 33,
    39v, 40v
CONWAY, Sir Edward (Evesham, Worcs) Secretary of State: f.12v
CORYTON, William (Cornwall): ff.28, 38
COTTINGTON, Sir Francis (Camelford, Cornwall) Secretary to the
    Prince of Wales: ff.13, 18v, 20v
COTTON, Sir Robert (Old Sarum, Wilts): ff.32–33
CREW, Sir Thomas (Aylesbury, Bucks) Serjeant at law, Speaker: ff.7–
    9, 11v, 25v, 27v, 40
DIGGES, Sir Dudley (Tewkesbury, Glos): ff.13, 24v, 28, 28v, 35v, 38v,
    40v
EDMONDES, Sir Thomas (Chichester, Sussex) Treasurer of the
    Household: ff.14v, 28v, 34v
ELIOT, Sir John (Newport, Cornwall): f.24
ESTCOURT, Sir Thomas (Gloucestershire): f.41
FINCH, Sir Heneage (London) Recorder of London: ff.24, 28v, 35,
    38, 39, 41v
FLEETWOOD, Sir Miles (Launceston, Cornwall): f.23v
GERRARD, Sir Thomas (Liverpool, Lancs): f.41v
GILES, Sir Edward (Totnes, Devon): ff.28, 39
GLANVILLE, John (Plymouth, Devon): ff.12v, 24v, 27v, 39v
GREY, Sir William (Northumberland): f.27v
HARLEY, Sir Robert (Herefordshire): ff.37, 38
HEATH, Sir Robert (East Grinstead, Sussex) Solicitor-General: ff.24,
    28v

HEYMAN, Sir Peter (Hythe, Kent): f.25v
HICKS, Sir Baptist (Tewkesbury, Glos): f.41v
HITCHAM, Sir Robert (Orford, Suffolk) Serjeant at law: f. 24
HOBY, Sir Thomas Posthumus (Ripon, Yorks): ff.11v, 12
INGRAM, Sir Arthur (?Appleby, Westmorland, or ?York, Yorks): f.27v
JEPHSON, Sir John (Petersfield, Hants): ff.11v, 40
MALLORY, William (Ripon, Yorks): ff.25v, 38v, 40
MANSELL, Sir Robert (Glamorganshire): ff.26, 40v
Mr Attorney, *see* House of Lords, Coventry, Sir Thomas
Mr Chancellor of the Exchequer, *see* Weston, Sir Richard
Mr Comptroller (of the Household), *see* Suckling, Sir John
Master of the Rolls, *see* House of Lords, Caesar, Sir Julius
Mr Recorder (of London), *see* Finch, Sir Heneage
Mr Secretary (of State), *see* Calvert, Sir George, *and* Conway, Sir Edward
Mr Solicitor, *see* Heath, Sir Robert
Mr Speaker, *see* Crew, Sir Thomas
Mr Treasurer (of the Household), *see* Edmondes, Sir Thomas
MAY, Sir Humphrey (Leicester, Leics): f.38v
MILDMAY, Sir Henry (Westbury, Wilts): f.28
MINGAY, Francis (Southwark, Surrey): f.27v
MORE, Sir George (Guildford, Surrey): ff.12v, 13, 23
PERROT, Sir James (Pembrokeshire): ff.11v, 12, 24v, 35, 37
PEYTON, Sir Edward (Cambridgeshire): f.40v
PHELIPS, Sir Robert (Somerset): ff.13, 23–23v, 24v, 28, 33, 34v, 37v
PYM, John (Tavistock, Devon): ff.12, 24, 25v, 39v
RICH, Sir Nathaniel (Harwich, Essex): ff.11v, 28v
RUDYARD, Sir Benjamin (Portsmouth, Hants): f.23
SANDYS, Sir Edwin (Kent): ff.25v, 28, 28v, 29v, 34v, 35, 35v, 36v, 37, 37v, 39, 40
SAVILE, Sir John (Yorkshire): f.38
SEYMOUR, Sir Edward (Callington, Cornwall): f.26
SEYMOUR, Sir Francis (Marlborough, Wilts): ff.23v–24, 39
STANHOPE, Sir John (Derbyshire): f.41v
STEWARD, Sir Simeon (Cambridgeshire): f.40v
STRANGWAYS, Sir John (Dorset): f.12
STRODE, Sir William (Devonshire): ff.11v, 13, 38
SUCKLING, Sir John (Middlesex) Comptroller of the Household: f.14v
WAKE, Sir Isaac (Oxford U.): ff.35, 36v
WANDESFORD, Christopher (Aldborough, Yorks): f.38
WESTON, Sir Richard (Bossiney, Cornwall) Chancellor of the Exchequer: ff.11v, 13, 14v, 15, 16, 33, 35v, 41v

YARWOOD, Richard (Southwark, Surrey): f.27v

Preachers

BARGRAVE, Dr Isaac: f.11v
USSHER, James, Bishop of Meath: f.11v

II
The Letters of Sir Cheney Culpeper (1641–1657)

Edited by
M.J. Braddick and M. Greengrass

CONTENTS

PREFACE

This volume has been, for its editors, a work of collaborative endeavour which draws considerably upon the efforts of others. The materials on which it is based form a small fraction of the papers of Samuel Hartlib, located in Sheffield University Library. In 1987, a substantial grant was awarded by the British Academy and the Leverhulme Trust to transcribe and edit in electronic form the totality of this archive. The Hartlib Papers Project was established under the direction of Michael Leslie, Mark Greengrass and the University Librarian, Michael Hannon. A team of transcribers worked with the Project over the following five years and this volume is one of the results of their labours. The project research associate from 1988 until 1992 was Timothy Raylor, now at Carleton College, Minnesota. He was responsible for first conceiving of this edition and a good deal of the initial editing of the Culpeper materials. Two project assistants also played an important part in making sense of various aspects of these letters. Julie Macdonald, now Archivist of the Cutlers' Company of Hallamshire, undertook research on the Culpeper family history whilst Stephen Clucas, now at Birkbeck College, London, worked on the alchemical references. Some assistance was also given towards interpreting the political context by Alison Gill. The final research and preparation of the edition for publication has been in the very capable hands of Sue Wallace and Jonathan Sanderson. The latter has been indefatigable in ensuring the integrity of the final edition. Mr W.J. Hitchens, Hartlib Research Fellow, kindly translated the Comenius letter and checked the other Latin translations in the edition. David Cleggett, historical advisor and archivist to the Leeds Castle Foundation, has assisted us with materials from Kent County Record Office. Antonio Clericuzio of the University of Cassino, Italy, helped with the identification of several alchemical references. Dr Joan Thirsk kindly saved the editors from some blushes in the orthography of Kentish names; and John Young was a careful proof-reader. The editors warmly acknowledge the financial support both of the British Academy and the Leverhulme Trust through their initial grants to the Project. The assistance of various members of Sheffield University Library has been of significance to the Project throughout its life-cycle. More recently, the Scouloudi Foundation and the Department of History of the University of Sheffield have provided grants towards the costs of final preparations for this edition, for the errors and shortcomings of which, in accordance with Victorian tradition, the editors remain entirely responsible.

MJB/MG
December 1994

ABBREVIATIONS

The following abbreviations have been used throughout this volume:

Batten   J. M. Batten, *John Dury: Advocate of Christian Reunion* (Chicago, 1944)

BL   British Library

CSPD   *Calendar of State Papers, Domestic Series*

CDPR   *Constitutional Documents of the Puritan Revolution 1625–1660*, ed. S. R. Gardiner, 3rd edition (Oxford, 1906)

Clarendon   Edward Hyde, Earl of Clarendon, *The History of the Rebellion*, ed. W. D. Macray (Oxford, 1888)

Clucas   Stephen Clucas, 'The Correspondence of a seventeenth-century 'Chymicall Gentleman': Sir Cheney Culpeper and the chemical interests of the Hartlib circle', *Ambix*, 40 (1993), pp. 147–70

CJ   *Journals of the House of Commons*

DNB   *Dictionary of National Biography*

DSB   *Dictionary of Scientific Biography*, ed. C. C. Gillespie, XVI vols (New York, 1970–80)

F&R   *Acts and Ordinances of the Interregnum*, eds. C. H. Firth and R. S. Rait (1911)

Gardiner   S. R. Gardiner, *History of the Great Civil War 1642–1649*, IV vols (1897–8)

Gardiner, *CW*   S. R. Gardiner, *History of the Commonwealth and Protectorate, 1649–1660*, IV vols (1903)

GI   Charles Webster, *The Great Instuaration: science, medicine and reform, 1626–1660* (1975)

HDC   G. H. Turnbull, *Hartlib, Dury and Comenius: Gleanings from Hartlib's Papers* (Liverpool and London, 1947)

Legacy   R. Child *et. al.*, *Samuel Hartlib his Legacy of Husbandry* (Wing H991), 3rd edn. (1655).

LJ   *Journals of the House of Lords*

N&S   *British Newspapers 1641–1700, A Short-Title Catalogue of Serials Printed in England, Scotland, Ireland, and British America*, eds. C. Nelson and M. Seccombe, (New York, 1987).

OED   *Oxford English Dictionary*

Partington   J. R. Partington, *A History of Chemistry*, III vols (1961)

PRO   Public Record Office

SHAL   Charles Webster, *Samuel Hartlib and the Advancement of*
                Learning (Cambridge, 1970)
SRP   *Stuart Royal Proclamations*, ed. James F. Larkin and Paul
                L. Hughes, II vols (Oxford, 1974–83)
STC   A. W. Pollard and G. R. Redgrave, *A Short-Title*
                Catalogue of Books Printed in England, Scotland & Ireland
                ... *1475–1640*, 2nd edn, rev. W. A. Jackson, F. S.
                Ferguson and Katharine F. Pantzer, II vols (1976,
                1986)
Thomason   British Library, Thomason Tracts
UR   *Samuel Hartlib and Universal Reformation: Studies in intel-*
                lectual communication, eds. M. Greengrass, M. Leslie,
                and T. Raylor, (Cambridge, 1994)
Wing   Donald F. Wing, *Short-Title Catalogue of Books Printed in*
                England, Scotland, & Ireland ... *1641–1700*, 2nd edn, 3
                vols (New York, 1972–1988)

EDITORIAL NOTE

In the transcriptions from the original documentation, common abbreviations have been silently expanded: *viz* – whch, wth, wt, concern., bec., fro, Sr, ye. yt, yn, ym. Other words where there has been editorial expansion have been placed in square brackets and the expansion indicated in italics. Minor alterations and deletions have not been retained; however, Hartlib's alterations and annotations are noted in square brackets preceded by the initial <H. The letters are placed overall in chronological order – although in some instances the dating of particular letters is conjectural with the result that the order of the letters may not be strictly observed. Dates are generally in the Old Style with the exception of some from the Continent where both New Style and Old Style dates are indicated in accordance with contemporary seventeenth-century practice. All years are treated as beginning on 1 January.

All manuscript references are to the Hartlib Papers (50H) in Sheffield University Library unless otherwise indicated. Facsimiles of the letters will be available in due course on the CD-ROM edition to be published by University Microfilms Inc., Ann Arbor, Michigan.

Cross-references to other letters in this edition are indicated in footnotes by the number of the letter in bold, followed by the date of the letter in brackets.

Genealogical Table of the immediate family of Sir Cheney Culpeper

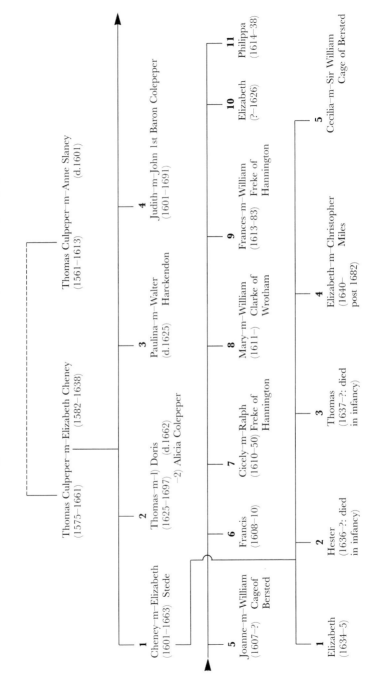

Thomas Culpeper–m–Elizabeth Cheney
(1575–1661)   (1582–1638)

Thomas Culpeper–m–Anne Slaney
(1561–1613)   (d.1601)

1
Cheney–m–Elizabeth
(1601–1663)   Stede

2
Thomas–m–1) Doris
(1625–1697)   (d.1662)
         –2) Alicia Colepeper

3
Paulina–m–Walter
(d.1625)   Harckendon

4
Judith–m–John 1st Baron Coleper
        (1601–1691)

5
Joanne–m–William
(1607–?)   Cageof
           Bersted

6
Francis
(1608–10)

7
Cicely–m–Ralph
(1610–50) Freke of
          Hannington

8
Mary–m–William
(1611–) Clarke of
         Wrotham

9
Frances–m–William
(1613–83) Freke of
           Hannington

10
Elizabeth
(?–1626)

11
Philippa
(1614–38)

1
Elizabeth
(1634–5)

2
Hester
(1636–?: died
in infancy)

3
Thomas
(1637–?: died
in infancy)

4
Elizabeth–m–Christopher
(1640–   Miles
post 1682)

5
Cecilia–m–Sir William
          Cage of Bersted

INTRODUCTION

Sir Cheney Culpeper (1611–1663) was a lawyer and gentleman from the north Kentish Weald. Yet he never rose to prominence in the legal profession. Nor did he take up public office either as an MP or as a diplomat – although he occasionally entertained the possibilities of both. Such aspirations would not have been surprising in someone who was the eldest son of a family which enjoyed connections to the wheels of power in Stuart England. He expected to inherit a considerable portion of the family's not inconsiderable estates – which included Leeds Castle. Yet he was, at a critical juncture, in effect disinherited by his father. Although a committed Parliamentarian, Culpeper did not play a major part either in county or national politics during the Civil War and the Interregnum. His career was, in worldly terms, hardly a success: if success alone were the criterion to justify the publication of his letters over three hundred years later, this volume would not see the light of day.

Yet Culpeper has been taken as the voice of the naturally 'voiceless' – 'the dim squires, men who, more often than not, never raised their voices to speak publicly across the centuries, who did not publish theories, or make set speeches in Parliament, but who were nevertheless the angry men in Parliament and behind Parliament, the men who, from behind, struck down their lukewarm, politic, legalistic, aristocratic and clerical leaders and pushed on, over their bodies, to destruction'.[1] So Culpeper's letters – surviving exclusively (so far as we can determine) amongst the Papers of Samuel Hartlib in Sheffield University Library – are of considerable significance because they illuminate the context and contacts which engaged and informed one 'honest radical' in the 1640s and 50s.

Family background and fortunes

Cheney Culpeper's letters are as informative of his intellectual constituency and his approach to politics as they are taciturn about his background. The latter must be reconstructed from other sources. The Culpepers were a respectable gentry family from mid-Kent with its

[1] H. R. Trevor Roper, 'Three Foreigners: The Philosophers of the Puritan Revolution' in *Religion, the Reformation, and Social Change* (1967), p. 239.

seat at Greenway Court, Hollingbourne.[2] Thomas Culpeper, Cheney's
father, had been educated at Hart Hall, Oxford and the Middle
Temple.[3] He was MP for Winchelsea in the Parliament of 1601, the
year of Cheney's birth, having already served as the MP for Rye in
the Parliament of 1597. Following his knighthood in 1619, Sir Thomas
Culpeper began cautiously to cut more than just a county figure. He
published (anonymously) an influential pamphlet against usury to
coincide with the debates in the Parliament of 1621 on the 'decay of
trade'. Whether it was true or not, as contemporaries and the later
editions claimed, that it was instrumental in reducing rates of interest
that year from 10% to 8%, it continued to be of significance, being
reproduced in the light of similar debates in the Parliaments of 1624
and again during the Long Parliament.[4] In the early 1630s, Sir Thomas
added to his various properties in London, Kent and Sussex with the
distinctly grandiose estate and house at Leeds Castle which he purchased
from the executors of Sir Thomas Smythe. When his wife Elizabeth
died in 1638, he added a chapel to Hollingbourne church and commissioned an exquisite marble effigy in her honour from the distinguished sculptor, Edward Marshall.[5] Standing in the centre of the
chapel still today, its inscription describes Elizabeth as 'Optima Fæmina,
Optima Coniunx, Optima Mater'.

Thomas' eldest son, Cheney Culpeper, was given his mother's maiden
name at his baptism on 15 April 1601 in the Parish Church of All
Saints, Hollingbourne.[6] He followed his father to Hart Hall, Oxford,
where he matriculated on 6 November 1618, and gained his BA on 7
February 1620.[7] A year later, on 7 May 1621, he was admitted to the
Middle Temple and entered chambers with William Hyde on the
following 15 June. The heady and convivial climate of politics, mixed
with religion and business, often made the Inns of Court of early Stuart
London the nurseries for the men of affairs of the next generation. It
certainly seems to have left its mark on Cheney Culpeper. The sociable

---

[2] Edward Hasted, *The History and topographical survey of the county of Kent*, 4 vols (1778–99),
ii. 466. D. A. H. Cleggett, *Hollingbourne and the Culpepers* (privately published, Hollingbourne,
1988).

[3] Joseph Foster, *Alumni Oxonienses; the members of the University of Oxford, 1500–1714 . . .*, 4
vols (1891–2), i. 303. H. A. C. Sturgess, *Register of Admissions to the Honourable Society of the
Middle Temple*, 3 vols (1949), i. 66 (admitted 15 May 1594).

[4] [Sir Thomas Culpeper], *A tract against usurie. Presented to the high court of Parliament* (1621),
STC 6108. The treatise went through a further reprinting in 1621, a second edition in
1624, a third in 1641 and a fourth in 1668. It is reprinted in J. Thirsk and J. P. Cooper
(eds.), *Seventeenth-Century Economic Documents* (Oxford, Clarendon Press, 1972), pp. 6–12.

[5] Rupert Gunnis, *Dictionary of British Sculptors* (1964), p. 213, describes it as one of the
finest surviving examples of Marshall's work.

[6] Parish records of All Saints, Hollingbourne, Kent County Record Office.

[7] Foster, i. 303.

connections (and where would any would-be gentleman in Stuart England have been without such a network?) he made at the Middle Temple seem to have stayed with him for the rest of his life. Some of them are echoed in his letters: Edward Parteridge, Robert Honywood, Anthony and Francis Rous, and his future brother-in-law, William Freke.[8] Others, like William Weston, Henry Lyde and even Thomas Hobbes, we may map onto the networks which engaged Culpeper's attention later on.[9]

Cheney left chambers in the Middle Temple on 10 February 1625 and, doubtless thanks to his father's influence, was knighted by Charles I at Farnham on 8 September 1628 – the potential beginnings of court service.[10] Yet it was a county, not a court, match which followed on 24 October 1632 at St Martin's, Ludgate.[11] Sir Cheney married Elizabeth Stede, the grandaughter of William Stede of Harrietsham, Kent. William Stede was the half-brother of Sir Cheney's uncle, Francis Culpeper. At the time of the marriage, both her parents were dead and she was under the guardianship of her uncle, Dr William Stede, a judge in the ecclesiastical courts and a friend of Sir Cheney. Reinforcing kinship and county links became part of a familiar pattern in the other marriages of Thomas' offspring. In due course, Cheney's sisters would marry into the Colepeper cousinage from the Sussex Weald and buttress the family's standing in mid-Kent through marriages to the Frekes of Hannington, the Cages of Bearsted and the Clarkes of Wrotham.[12]

At the time of his marriage, Sir Cheney was the eldest of the two surviving male offspring of the family. By what was intended as a

[8] Robert Honywood was from a neighbouring gentry family to the Culpepers at Charing; he was admitted on 31 June 1620 (Sturgess, i. 111). Edward Partridge (var: Partheridge) was a family friend, possibly even a distant family relative, of the Culpepers and gave 'Greenewaye Court', the Culpeper seat, as his residence when he was admitted on 17 January 1621 (ibid., 113). William Freke [var: Freake] was admitted on 12 October 1622 (ibid, 124). Sir Edward Partridge was involved much later on with the drainage of the Bedford Level and moved to live in Ely where he had an experimental farm. See L. E. Harris, *Vermuiden and the Fens* (London, 1953), pp. 97–9; 109–112 and H. C. Darby, *Drainage of the Fens* (Cambridge, 1958, reprinted 1968), p. 70. The editors are very grateful to Joan Thirsk for providing these references.

[9] William Weston was the son of Richard Weston, the Surrey gentleman whose 'Discourse of Husbandrie used in Brabant and Flanders' would be published by Hartlib in 1652. The preface from Sir Richard, dated 1645, explains that he left it as a 'Legacie' to his sons. (*A Discours of Husbandrie used in Brabant and Flanders* (1652), Wing 1483, sig B (1r).) Henry Lyde was one of the partners in a saltpetre production company in whose affairs Hartlib and Worsley were interested.

[10] C. H. Hopwood, ed., *Middle Temple Records*, 2 vols (1904), ii. 96. W. C. Metcalfe, *A Book of Knights* (1885), p. 189.

[11] *Allegations for Marriage Licences issued by the Bishop of London (1611–1828)*, ed. G. J. Armytage, *Harleian Society*, vol 26, (1887), p. 208.

[12] F. W. T. Attree and J. H. L. Booker, 'The Sussex Colepepers', *Sussex Archaeological Collections*, 2 parts, especially part II, 48 (1905), 65–98.

jointure (though apparently the document did not make it explicit), his father settled the Leeds Castle estate on Sir Cheney and his wife.[13] This complemented other miscellaneous properties which Sir Cheney had acquired in Kent and Sussex. In 1623, for example, he had purchased the manor of Wigsell in Sussex from his distant cousin Sir John Culpeper.[14] He also had a £500 a year interest in the manor of Appledore on Romney Marsh from his father, a farm at Icklesham and various other parcels of land and titles to property around Hollingbourne itself.[15] Some of this may have been inherited through his wife since the Stedes had a large holding on Romney Marsh. Parts of the estate were leased, it seems, from an Oxford college since he was concerned about payment of the rents during the latter period of the civil wars.[16] According to the estimates of the Committee of Sequestration, prepared on 22 September 1646, Culpeper's father had been worth before the troubles, and after the annual payment due to his son, but before other charges, of about £730.[17] After deductions for leases and charges allowable for the costs of maintaining sea banks and ditches on the Romsey levels, his fine was set at £1,318. There is no comparable estimate available for Sir Cheney's estates; but he spoke of himself in 1644 as worth £500 per annum before the troubles and having a marriage portion worth, (presumably in capital terms) some £3,000.[18] All the signs are that he anticipated a comfortable income from his estates, and borrowed and leased accordingly.[19]

From 1641 onwards, however, actuality did not follow anticipation. At some point in the late spring or summer of 1641, Sir Cheney Culpeper became gravely ill and was not expected to live.[20] Whatever effects the illness may have had on his sense of purpose and future

---

[13] Cleggett, p. 4.

[14] PRO, Chancery, Close Rolls, C54/2538 No 30.

[15] The charges are mentioned in PRO SP 23/188 – pp. 82–5.

[16] Below **73** (1 April 1645); **111** (1 October 1646); **114** (21 October 1646).

[17] Calculated from the properties listed as belonging to Sir Thomas Culpeper of Hollingbourne in the County of Kent in PRO SP 23/188 pp. 82–5.

[18] *Calendar of the Proceedings of the Committee for Compounding*, ed. M. A. E. Green, 5 vols (1889–92), ii. 1,235; **40** (n.d. – 1643–4); **59** (18 December 1644).

[19] **59** (18 December 1644). On 6 December 1638, for example, Sir Cheney Culpeper was one of several who was cited by Anne, Viscountess Dorchester, the widow of Sir Dudley Carleton, whom he had met during his time at The Hague, for money which had been lent to him – CSPD (Addenda 1625–January 1649), p. 744. In 1639 he became embroiled in a dispute in Chancery over a deed he had signed in 1631. The other principal parties were his cousin, Sir Alexander Culpeper and Anthony St. Leger (PRO, C2/Chas 1/C52/70). On 10 August 1639, he joined with his father and Edward Parteridge in the lease of some land in Shoreditch to Richard Briggenshawe, a cutler – Kent County Record Office, U23T63.

[20] He was well again by September 1641 as the letter from John Dury (**2** (27 September 1641)) makes clear.

direction, its consequences for his livelihood were serious and prejudicial to his future financial security. Three years later he explained to Hartlib what had happened.[21] During his illness he resigned the control of his estates to his father, on the condition that he would regain them when he recovered. During the winter of 1641–2, however, Sir Cheney's support for the Parliamentarian cause became more pronounced, just as his father's royalism was reinforced by the appointment of his son-in-law, John Culpeper, as Charles I's undertreasurer, Chancellor of the Exchequer and Privy Councillor.[22] Their political disagreements were of the kind which fuelled the famous 'Kentish Petition', proposed by Sir Edward Dering to the Maidstone assizes in March 1642, and the strong reactions both nationally and locally which greeted it.[23] So Sir Thomas chose not to relinquish the estates of his son when the latter had recovered his health and continued to frustrate his enjoyment of them for a decade thereafter.

Sir Cheney Culpeper's financial difficulties were already apparent in the early summer of 1642 when his rents failed to materialise and he was forced to delay a payment due to Hartlib.[24] The following year, he wrote that he was 'much trowbled' by his 'priuate pressures' and that 'all is questioned'.[25] 'I hope by the equity of my case & my faythe & constancy to my Country I shall not finally suffer' he wrote; but his underlying doubts were to prove entirely justifiable.[26] In the early months of 1644, his hopes for a settlement of his dispute with his father rose; but, within months, his 'estate stoode yet questioned' and he was obliged to borrow from others in order to raise even the modest sums he owed Hartlib.[27] A year later, he was reduced to pawning the contents of a box which we may plausibly imagine were some of the jewels or effects of his wife: 'you see' (he wrote to Hartlib) 'howe my poverty makes me trowblesome to my frindes'.[28] A month later he complained of being 'very muche in debte' with 'heavy pressures on my broken estate'.[29] A few months thereafter, there was 'a generall assaulte on all hands vpon our small estate' such that 'it too much robbes me of my quiet & reposed thowghts'.[30]

By this date, he was barely able to maintain the standing of a

---

[21] **40** (1643/4).
[22] CSPD (1641–3) p. 239.
[23] See Tom Woods, *Prelude to Civil War 1642. Mr Justice Malet and the Kentish Petitions* (Wilton, Salisbury, 1980).
[24] **10** (September 1641–June 1642?) and **18** (19 April 1642).
[25] **29** (Autumn 1643) and **40** (1643–4).
[26] **40** (1643/4).
[27] **43** (24 January 1644); **46** (21 February 1644); **50** (4 April 1644).
[28] **67** (4 February 1645) [summarised in this edition].
[29] **70** (7 March 1645) [summarised in this edition].
[30] **80** (17 July 1645).

gentleman. He could not contemplate entertaining Benjamin Worsley at his house, feeling himself unable to offer hospitality appropriate to the occasion.[31] His 'presente poore and lowe condition' allowed him to retain a slender household of only two maids ('this was not my former condition').[32] One of the latter had been secured through the good offices of Hartlib; having served a merchant family in London she took ill to the church-mouse frugality of her new country master.[33] The device on Culpeper's seal, that of a snail carrying all the burdens of its household upon its back had become, he mused, 'an emblem fitting my presente condition'.[34]

By the close of the first civil war, Sir Cheney Culpeper's difficulties in recovering his estates from his father had become enmeshed in wider problems. Because of his father's antipathy to the Parliamentarian cause and his cousin (and son-in-law) Thomas's known royalism his estates (including those which had been made over to Sir Cheney but had reverted to him in 1641) lay subject to sequestration. On 30 April 1646, Sir Cheney's father was investigated for his royalism before the Parliamentary Committee for Compounding and, on 16 May, Sir Cheney asked leave to compound on his behalf on the grounds that his father was too old and frail to do so himself.[35] At the same time as pursuing the recovery of his property, Sir Cheney had to fend off his father's creditors (and his own) whilst suing for relief from Parliamentary forced loans, levied from him on the basis of estates which he did not possess and whose revenues he did not enjoy.[36] On 4 November 1646 the delinquency fine was set at £1,318 and Culpeper, perhaps with that fact fresh in his mind, wrote the same day that his 'domestique affaires doe howerly rise into such a storme as (I feare) my anchor, & cable will hardly holde'. He actively contemplated following in his brother-in-law, John Culpeper's, footsteps (albeit for different reasons) and fleeing abroad to escape his creditors.[37]

These darker thoughts were doubtless also prompted by one of several periodic visitations from his father. Sir Thomas's return to Hollingbourne almost invariably opened up old wounds. In October 1646, Sir Cheney remarked tersely: he 'neglectes his owne busines & hinders me in myne'.[38] A week later, the tone was more exasperated as he reflected on his 'vnhappy condition in a Father whose actions

---

[31] **94** (31 October 1645).
[32] **100** (12 January 1646).
[33] **123** (23 February 1647?).
[34] **117** (11 November 1646).
[35] *Calendar of the ... Committee for Compounding*, ii. 1,289.
[36] **100** (12 January 1646).
[37] **116** (4 November 1646).
[38] **114** (21 October 1646).

driue wholy to my prejudice, it takes away that contente & joy which I myght take in the Fortunes which God & nature had caste vpon me'.[39] He found himself driven to despair by 'my [Fathers] debtes & bitternes'.[40] The subsequent visit in the Spring of 1647 evoked similar tensions and resentments.[41] Even as late as 1654, Hartlib reported to Robert Boyle that 'Sir Cheney complains more than ever, that his father hath utterly undone him'.[42]

Sustaining what was left of the family fortune through this difficult period required the continuous application of Sir Cheney's time and resourcefulness. He negotiated in due course a reduction in the delinquency fine – first to £1,044 5s 0d on 16 January 1647 and then to £844 1s 0d on 27 November 1647.[43] Leeds Castle itself had been commandeered as an arsenal during the Civil War. Sir Cheney lodged complaints before the Council of State at the depredations in the property and requested its return to him.[44] On 21 October 1651, his Parliamentary loyalties and persistence were finally rewarded and the County Committee ordered the removal of all the arms and munitions stored at Leeds to Upnor Castle, seat of his brother-in-law and exiled royalist Sir John Culpeper, and the return of Leeds Castle to its rightful owner.[45] Meanwhile, Sir Cheney had lodged a Bill of Complaint in Chancery, along with his wife and his wife's sister, Cicely, and her husband, William Sandys.[46] The case was brought against Sir Thomas and Dame Cicely Peyton, Ralph Weldon and William Swann and it concerned a contested will of Cromer Stede, the brother of Cheney's mother.[47] Whether it succeeded or not is unknown, but Culpeper had his eyes on the Isle of Elmley which belonged to the Stede estate.[48]

With property once more in his possession, Culpeper was in a position to mortgage his way out of his more immediate difficulties and

---

[39] **115** (29 October 1646).

[40] **116** (4 November 1646).

[41] **124** (1 March 1647).

[42] *The works of the Honourable Robert Boyle*, ed. T. Birch, 6 vols (1772), vi. 83 (Hartlib to Boyle, 28 Feb. 1653/4).

[43] *Calendar of the ... Committee for Compounding*, i. 102; ii. 1235; 1289.

[44] CSPD (1650), p. 290 (16 August 1650); CSPD (1651), pp. 197–8 (13 May 1651); p. 454 (30 September 1651).

[45] Ibid., p. 487.

[46] PRO Chancery Proceedings C6/102/31.

[47] According to the Bill of Complaint the disputed will, in which Cromer Stede left all his property to his widow, Cicely (who had subsequently married Sir Thomas Peyton), her son William Swan (she had previously been married to Sir Thomas Swann) and to Ralph Weldon, was a forgery.

[48] Hence the reference in Hartlib's diary, or *Ephemerides*, for 1649: 'Sir [Che*ney*] [*Culpeper*] is like to have the whole Island to him*self* which amounts to 18 [hund*red*] [*acres?*] of excellent Chalky Lands for keeping of Conies, or a Warren' – 28/1/22A. Elmley is an island in the middle of the river Swale on the Isle of Sheppey.

to buy himself more time. Already anticipating the likely recovery of
Leeds Castle, he had used it as security in a loan for £3,500 in March
1651.[49] On 24 May 1654, he remortgaged the Castle for a much larger
amount – £15,000 at a peppercorn rent.[50] Finally, by an indenture
dated 1 August 1659, he once more mortgaged the Castle, this time to
his brother-in-law, Ralph Freke, who undertook to repay all the
preceeding mortgages.[51] This was by no means the only obligation
which Sir Cheney had entered into with the Freke family and with
others. In a surviving indenture of 29 September 1659, Ralph Freke is
also recorded as leasing land, described as being in the tenure of Sir
Cheney Culpeper, from John Peck of Ulcombe.[52]

Every mortgage, however, compromised both Sir Cheney's future
financial stability and his potential legal title to his estates. This
underlying weakness was easily exploited when the restoration of the
monarchy in 1660 brought with it the exultant return of the royalist
Culpepers – in particular his brother-in-law, Lord John Colepeper. The
latter died in 1662 and was succeeded by his son, named Thomas after
his father-in-law. Charles II had made Lord John Colepeper's loyalty
well worth his while by granting him a large stretch of land in Virginia
and brokering a rich second marriage to Margaret van Hesse. His son
wasted little time in making use of that fortune to acquire, by various
means, much of the land and property that had at one time belonged
to Sir Cheney Culpeper and his father (who died shortly after the
Restoration in 1661), and especially the Leeds Castle estate. Sir Cheney
himself died intestate and in considerable debt in London, probably
towards the end of March 1663. He was buried at the entrance into
the north aisle of the Middle Temple on 2 April 1663.[53] At least two
individuals filed as his unassigned creditors amongst the administration
entries in probate records.[54] Only the manor of Appledore seems to
have escaped unscathed. It was the two annuities on this property, one
of £100 and the other of £400, which Sir Cheney's widow, Elizabeth,
bequeathed to her daughter Elizabeth by her will of 29 June 1674.[55]

Sir Cheney Culpeper's fortunes certainly did not flourish. But

---

[49] The loan was made by Edward Atkins, A Justice of the Court of Common Pleas,
Sir Thomas Dacres, Sir Anthony Aucher and Edward Wright.
[50] The mortgage was entered into by a nominee, Dudley Palmer of Grays Inn, London.
[51] Kent County Record Office U23T11.
[52] Ibid., U23T9. A further series of indentures from 1654 identify the same John Peck
as having acquired the lease of a water-mill and the rights to a water course from Sir
Cheney Culpeper – U23T53.
[53] F. A. Inderwick, *A Calendar of the Inner Temple Records* (1896), iii. 445.
[54] There is an entry in December 1666 which names John Colvert as a creditor; a
further entry in March 1691 names William Smith – PRO PCC Administration Act
Books, Prob 6/41 fol 203; Prob 6/67 fol 40ʳ.
[55] PRO Probate 11/345, fols 249ᵛ–250ʳ.

although it is tempting to ascribe his radicalism directly to his disappointed expectations, or to imagine that his practical interest in
agricultural innovation grew out of his misfortunes, he made no such
connections himself. The relationship between his domestic 'lowe
condition' on the one hand and his intellectual interests and political
concerns on the other was a complex one in which a providential
stoicism played a prominent part: 'I thank God that as He hathe taken
away my wealthe Frinds & other [worldly] comfortes, He hathe in lieu
of them giuen me greater comforts & a minde that wants lesse ...'.[56]

Commitments and endeavours

Culpeper's commitments grew out of, and around, his social networks.
This was notably the case in respect of his residence at the Middle
Temple where there was a further continental aspect to such connections. The invasion of the Palatinate by Habsburg forces in 1621
and the exile of the Elector Palatine, Frederick V, and his wife Elizabeth,
evoked strong reactions in England. James I shrewdly exploited for his
own diplomatic purposes (and, at the same time, contained) those which
surfaced in the Parliament of 1621.[57] Others were less easily predicted
and trammelled; and it was apparently to the annoyance of James I
that 30 young men of the Middle Temple elected to swear an oath to
live and die in the service and protection of Elizabeth of Bohemia, the
Winter Queen, at this juncture.[58] Although there is no direct proof that
Cheney Culpeper was amongst this group, there is every sign that,
alongside his friends and kinsman William Freke and Robert Honywood, he was. This act of commitment, from a gentleman who took
such things seriously, would provide the background to a
Palatine/Bohemian axis to his intellectual contacts and his politics.
These contacts already surfaced in the later 1620s. In 1629, Culpeper
was sent with the official letter of condolence from Charles I to his
sister on the death of her eldest son. He may have spent some time at
The Hague thereafter.[59] He was certainly still there in early 1631 and
hoping to be given a place as a gentleman in her service.[60] He returned

[56] **100** (12 January 1646).

[57] C. Russell, *Parliament and English Politics, 1621–1629* (Oxford, 1979), ch. 2.

[58] The affair is referred to in a letter from Joseph Mede to Sir Martin Stuteville of 25
January 1622. Cf. J. Bruce Williamson, *The History of the Temple, London* (1924), p. 275.

[59] In a letter dated 9 July 1629, Abraham Williams reminded the secretary of state,
Viscount Dorchester, that Sir Robert Carr had received a diamond worth £200 for a
similar errand and that a similar gift for 'this honest gentleman' would also be
appropriate – PRO SP16/46, fol 51.

[60] PRO SP 16/185, fol 5 (Sir Thomas Culpeper to Sir Francis Nethersole, The Hague,
15 February 1631); ibid., 18/36, fol 191 (the same, 20 February 1631).

with various letters in early July 1631.[61] He must have eventually been granted the place as gentleman since, on 21 December 1631, he was awarded an annuity of £400 per annum for a period of 35 years for his services to Elizabeth.[62] The portrait of Elizabeth of Bohemia as a young girl which now forms part of the Leeds Castle estate, and a set of hairbrushes reputedly belonging to her, may well constitute gifts which she made to him at some stage in return for his service. Thereafter Culpeper had a continuing involvement and interest in the affairs of the Palatine princess which surfaces in his letters. '[T]hat relation I bothe had & still have towards her and hers ... ' is evident when, for example, Dury was provided with a chaplaincy by Elizabeth, or when her son the Prince Elector arrived in England, to whom Culpeper naturally paid court.[63] There are occasions, too, when one suspects that Culpeper was in London about her affairs, pressing Charles I and Parliament for the payment of a pension to the Palatine cause. He retained good contacts with the court at The Hague. Robert Honywood would become Elizabeth of Bohemia's steward, occasionally pursuing her affairs in England on her behalf. His relative, possibly an uncle, Sir Thomas Culpeper was resident there, a long-suffered retainer.[64] William Freke, too, may have been her servant, and certainly lived in the Low Countries.[65] When Culpeper contemplated fleeing the country in 1646 it was doubtless to The Hague that he would have gone, that discreet retirement home for country royalists, unrewarded Parliamentarians and doubting Thomases in retreat following the English civil war.[66]

There were others in London, however, who supported the Palatine cause and who wished to help the plight of the Palatine exiles in the Netherlands and elsewhere. Amongst the most prominent and persistent of them was the recipient of the majority of Culpeper's letters in this volume, Samuel Hartlib (c.1600–2). Born into a merchant family from Elbing around 1600 of an English mother and a German father,

[61] PRO SP 84/144, fols 5–8; 'the bearer hereof Sr Cheney Culpeper, whose affection to your Lordships person and service is well knowne unto me ...'. See also Mary Hervey, *The Life, Correspondence and Collections of Thomas Howard* (Cambridge, 1921), p. 309.

[62] *Calendar of Treasury Books, i (1660–1667)*, ed. William A. Shaw (1904), p. 445.

[63] **42** (9 January 1644); for Culpeper's subsequent solicitude for the Prince Palatine, see **132** (August 1647) and **147** (18 January 1648).

[64] Elizabeth of Bohemia referred to him in later life as 'a little high flowen, and in his old humour ...' – L. M. Baker, *The letters of Elizabeth of Bohemia* (1953), p. 239.

[65] Culpeper forwarded money to him there through Hartlib – **92** (21 October 1645). In the *Ephemerides* for 1650, Hartlib recorded: 'The 9 of February Sir Cheney Culpeper brought Mr Freck [Freke?] to my house the first time. Hee lived at Vtrecht and much commended for a good and excellent man' – 28/1/45B.

[66] **116** (4 November 1646).

Hartlib's life and career is now relatively well-known.[67] He took up permanent residence in England in the late 1620s, a casualty of the political and religious crisis in Germany of the Thirty Years War and a member of London's 'stranger communities'. Thereafter Hartlib lived off his wits like other Calvinist refugees from Germany of his generation and increasingly found himself drawn to the promotion of educational change and scientific advancement, charitable endeavour and protestant evangelization of the temper which had characterised the smaller Calvinist states of Germany on the eve of the Thirty Years War.[68]

That an indigent Kentish squire should have found an enticing world of movement, reformation and change through his contacts with a refugee from central Europe caused Culpeper some reflection. He had no occasion, however, to regret the serendipity which had led their paths to cross: 'I shall allwayes rejoyce in conversinge with the spirits of good men & I can truly say that I often rejoyce in that hower in which (by a meere occasionall readinge of Dr Gaudens sermon) Gods prouidence brought me to your acquaintance, & hath synce & dothe still by it bringe me to the acquaintance of others'.[69] Parliament ordered Gawden's sermon, preached before the Long Parliament at St Margaret's Westminster on Sunday 29 November 1640, to be published. It contained an enthusiastic endorsement of Hartlib's dreams for peaceful but profound change through cooperative and educational endeavour. In particular, Gawden commended the works of the Moravian educationalist and exile, Jan Amos Comenius (Komensky), who 'hath laide a faire designe and foundation for the raising up of a Structure of Truth, Human and Divine, of excellent use to all mankinde, for the easiness and exquisitness of attaining the true knowledge of things'.[70] He also welcomed the peace-making activities of John Dury (1596–1680) who 'hath long studied, and with greate pains endeavured and wel advanced the peace and unity of the reformed churches ...'. According to Hartlib's diary, or *Ephemerides*, Culpeper and Hartlib first met on 13 April 1641 at the house of Dr Smith, a physician in Shoe lane, Holborn.[71] At that meeting, Culpeper contributed £5 to Hartlib's endeavours – by this date he was probably raising money for the

---

[67] See G. Turnbull, *Samuel Hartlib. A sketch of his life and his relations to J.A. Comenius* (Oxford and London, 1920); HDC; GI.

[68] Evoked in M. Greengrass, 'Samuel Hartlib and International Calvinism', *Proceedings of the Huguenot Society*, 25 (1993), pp. 464–475.

[69] **99** (December 1645).

[70] John Gawden, *The Love of Truth and Peace. A sermon before the House of Commons by John Gauden*, (1641) Thomason, E.204 (10), p. 41. The text of the sermon was Zechariah 8:19 – 'I will turn your fasts into feasts; therefore love the truth and peace'.

[71] 'The 13. of April acquainted with Sir Cheney Culpeper at one Dr Smith's house a Dr of Phyisick in Shoe Lane at that part of the lane towards Holborne'.

forthcoming visit to London by Comenius.[72] This was followed by further sums of £5 and £15 in May 1641, making Culpeper second only to the Surrey gentleman Nicholas Stoughton in the value of his contributions that month to Hartlib's cause.[73] Culpeper's enthusiasms for Hartlib's endeavours might have remained short-lived but for his illness and subsequent recovery in the summer of 1641 which seems to have strengthened his commitment. John Dury's letter to him of 27 September 1641 urged him to be 'henceforth as a new Man' and to 'ruminate with your selfe what vse yow should make of the life, which he hath restored vnto yow; & of the Talents which yow possesse therein committed to your trust, to profitt withall.'[74] Dury's desire that 'we should dive into the particular intencion of God towards vs' was written six months before the pact which he made with Comenius and Hartlib on 3 March 1642 to work together for the edification of the common weal.[75] Although Culpeper was not a party to any such formal covenant, he clearly saw his involvement as more than the charitable endeavours of a gentleman with means.

In the Autumn of 1641, Hartlib's plans concentrated on the establishment of a reformed Chelsea College to become a kind of 'Solomon's House' for the new age.[76] Many years later, Comenius remembered Culpeper as being instructed by Parliament to tell Comenius to hold himself ready to direct the new institution.[77] If Culpeper was closely involved with political activities in the Long Parliament at this time, then it would probably have been through the agency of his brother-in-law and cousin John Culpeper, who was an MP there. John Culpeper had made his mark in the opening session through a famous speech which introduced the grievances of Kent and he was a rising star in the political firmament.[78] If Culpeper had been as instrumental as Comenius remembered, it would be in line with the pattern which

---

[72] According to Hartlib's accounts – 23/2/13B.

[73] 23/12/3B; 23/10A.

[74] **2** (27 September 1641).

[75] HDC, pp. 458–60.

[76] For the background to Chelsea College see **10** (n.d., 1641).

[77] *Comenius' självbiografi [Comenius about himself]*, eds. Stig G. Nordström and Wilhelm Sjöstrand, (Stockholm, 1975), pp. 154 (trans); 236 (Latin facsimile) – 'Parliament also more than once admonished us (for the most part through the most noble gentleman, Cheneus Culpeper) to hold ourselves in readiness; a commission of prudent men from Parliament were to be appointed, who would take cognizance of the whole matter on either side and dispose thereof.'

[78] A copy of the speech of 9 November 1640, famous for its passage against monopolists, survives amongst Hartlib's papers: 'It is a Neast of Waspes, a swarme of Vermin which have overcrept the land I meane the Monopolers, the Polers of the [people?], These like the froggs of Egipt have gotten possession of our dwellings, we have scarce a roome free from them, They sip in our Cupp, they dipp in our dish, they sitt by our fire ...' – 55/5/3A.

would evolve in the future. Culpeper became a figure who offered Hartlib an intelligent, sometimes critical, appraisal of what was proposed, coupled with useful behind-the-scenes commendation of particular prospectuses to people whose voices might count in the politics of the nation.

Through Culpeper's correspondence, we can plot and accurately date the evolution of Hartlib's endeavours in the 1640s. His plans for Chelsea College vanished like the morning dew with the arrest of the Five Members and the approach of civil war in the winter of 1641/2. During the civil war, Culpeper's contact with Hartlib turned more towards news, politics and military experiment, in particular leather guns and 'Felton's engine', a mobile tank-like device for protecting infantry from artillery attack.[79] In the Autumn of 1645 and towards the close of the civil war, Hartlib's plans for a reformed Chelsea College were given a further airing, this time on a private rather than a public foundation.[80] Once more, Culpeper's reactions were positive but pragmatic. He set a high store by educational welfare provision, continuing to support individuals in their studies despite his straitened circumstances.[81] But he had never been attracted to the term 'pansophy' and, by this date, he sounds a distinctly sceptical note towards Comenius' grander designs: 'he calls lowde for attention & hathe (methinckes too many sowndings or prodromusses before he enters the stage'. Progress on a private footing would be slow but in the end it was 'like to set vp suche Herculean pillars & ne plus vltra-s' as would support a true and profound reformation of state and society.[82]

By the close of the civil war, however, the possibilities for a more localised, more ambitious and more fundamental reformation were opened up. Individuals and groups who had not been part of the pre-civil war ruling estalishment came to the fore and began to see the possibilities for change created by the fractures of old institutions and the sequestration of ecclesiastical and royalist property. The pattern was set by Sir Cheney Culpeper's distant Sussex kinsman, Sir William Waller. His ambitious schemes for a reformation of the schooling and welfare provisions of Sussex were promoted by Hartlib and earned

[79] For Felton's engines, see the articles by Timothy Raylor, cited in notes to **31** (22 November 1643).

[80] **88** (late Autumn/December 1645).

[81] The letters refer to his financial assistance to a scholar who lodged with Hartlib, a 'mechanicall Glawberus' who was impoverished by the expenses of his studies – **141** (10 November 1647). He approved of John Milton's treatise *On Education* and wondered if he could be persuaded to become a tutor in his household – **96** (12 November 1645). He almost certainly supported the Bohemian exile Georg Ritschel as a student at Oxford – **111** (24 May 1646).

[82] **100** (12 January 1646), **87** (late autumn/December 1645).

Culpeper's approval. He could 'wishe wee may be soe happy in Kent'.[83]
Culpeper himself had already envisaged the possibilities of a scheme in
which each parish would have its educational instructor, responsible to
overseers, who would teach the young to read and write. Those parishes
with 'dirty wayes' which did not cooperate would be required to send
someone to a kind of Comenian seminary to teach them how to instruct
the youth of their locality. There needed to be more free schools and
more university places for those of modest means.[84] Yet, in Culpeper's
mind, such local reformations never replaced or were a substitute for,
the overturning of the 'great monopolies' of state, aristocracy, church
and monopolistic merchant corporations, upon the achievement of
which alone such local reformations might take root and flourish.

    In any case, by the Autumn of 1645, Culpeper found himself
commenting on Hartlib's response to a localised reformation of learning.
This was an ambitious and exciting proposal for a distributive agency of
knowledge and information, his famous 'Office of Address'. Culpeper's
reactions were favourable and supportive. He was attracted by its
possibilities, especially if it could be combined with the indexing system
of Thomas Harrison, of which he had been informed through Hartlib
himself.[85] By March 1646, its possibilities would 'hardly let me sleep, I
professe I apprehende greate things of them'.[86]

    At the end of the Civil War, Hartlib sought Parliamentary backing
and funds for the Office of Address. He found himself by turns
encouraged at the favourable reactions he received towards his proposal
and disillusioned at the lack of financial support for it.[87] The choice
was once more between public and private sponsorship of the proposal.
If the former were to be the sponsor, then Hartlib's Office would
undoubtedly become a matter of politics and chance; if the latter then,
as Culpeper said, 'I feare ... that it will come but slowly on'.[88] Culpeper
was prepared to offer up to £20 a year to maintain a clerk in the
Office on condition that others such as Dury and Robert Boyle also
provide similar contributions.[89] The proposals remained in suspended
animation until after the conclusion of the second civil war. In due
course thereafter it became clear that it would be on a private and ad
hoc basis that the Office of Address would function, with Hartlib
enjoying occasional remuneration from Parliament for his endeavours.
It is highly likely (although we do not have Hartlib's accounts for any

[83] **98** (27 November 1645).
[84] **66** (28 January 1645).
[85] **102** (17 February 1646).
[86] **106** (11 March 1646).
[87] **133** (7 September 1647).
[88] **152** (24 March 1648).
[89] **141** (10 November 1647).

years after the civil war) that Culpeper helped sustain the Office financially and became one of its regular correspondents.

Before its establishment, Culpeper had already acquired an engaging fascination with technical change. In a gentleman who had less to worry about in his financial affairs this might be accounted a wealthy man's fancy for mechanical toys. In Culpeper's case, however, it was an abiding interest in the processes of technical development, sustained by the elements of a specialist library in the subject.[90] He understood the significance of prototypes ('modules' as he calls them). He wanted to evaluate new developments as scientifically as possible. Utility was an important criterion in assessing the significance of a particular innovation. During the civil war, he experimented with wooden-barrelled and leathern guns.[91] He supported the development of the infantry-protection device of Edmund Felton – in reality a padded mobile troop carrier which utilised bales of wool to absorb the impact of artillery. Culpeper contributed (along with others, including John Milton) to the public subscription for it.[92] He sought information on different designs of pumps which he had heard about and kept his eye open for all kinds of interesting new mechanica.[93] He had a prototype pantograph built to Petty's specifications to experiment with 'double-writing'.[94] He took more than a passing interest in new carriages.[95] It is easy to dismiss his enthusiasm to find out (for example) more about a new river-boat on the Thames powered by dog-paddles as no more than the naive enthusiasm of an amateur virtuoso. Yet this would be to ignore both Culpeper's commitment to change through technical innovation and also his altruism. For he was one of those 'whose spirits God hathe raysed out of this mudde of custom' and who 'muste indeavor (at the leaste) to improve theire talents towards others'.[96] These are distinctive features which distinguish him from the successor

[90] Culpeper had his own copies of the works of Giovanni Battista della Porta, Hugh Plats and Gabriel Plattes.

[91] **30** (4 October 1643).

[92] 8/40/10A (November 1643) for the subscription; **30** (4 October 1643) and **33** (3 December 1643); also **50** (4 April 1644).

[93] **16** (5 April [1642]) and the various letters concerning Wheeler's snail-wheel pump – **94** (31 October 1645) etc. He made the acquaintance of Lord Goring, known for his mechanical ingenuities. Hartlib's *Ephemerides* notes information from Culpeper on new clock-designs from the Netherlands (1658; 29/7/9B), new machinery for making gear-wheels from Northampton or Warwickshire (1649; 28/1/29A) as well as numerous references on new seed-drills and irrigation techniques.

[94] **148** (25 Jan 1647[?8]).

[95] He was interested in the practicalities of the new design of coach by the projector John Lanyon (*Ephemerides*, 1653 – 28/2/69B). In 1658, Hartlib noted: 'Mr Palmer is making one of the travelling charrets with some additions, and then Sir Cheney Culpeper will have one also adding his contrivances to make it the more perfect' (29/7/9B).

[96] **118** (1646?).

English virtuosi of the period after the Restoration, whose agenda, in other respects, he helped to shape.[97]

Such commitments led to social encounters which Culpeper felt to be of an unusual kind. He rubbed shoulders with the unlettered, the self-taught, and self-made who, in their various ways, had found unique opportunities coming their way during the civil war. Those who figure in his correspondence are a distinctly rum bunch. Cressy Dymock was an agronome from near Doncaster of humble estate but lavish promises. 'Captain' John Shaw was 'the Adeling Hill man', apparently of equally ordinary origins and similarly high hopes for his designs of water meadows. Edmund Felton was the son of the assassin of the duke of Buckingham who appeared to have inherited some of his father's unstable personality. William Petty was the super-confident and intelligent son of a Hampshire clothier who seemed to be able to turn his hand to anything and solve any problem. Mr Joyner was a would-be saltpetre-man whose mistress apparently drove a hard bargain for her share of the profits of whatever innovation he hoped to bring to the business of saltpetre manufacture. Mr Wheeler, the drainage engineer, was a frustrated innovator, well-known for his 'shortwitted craftiness, jealousy & instability' according to the habitually courteous Culpeper.[98] Coping with their exalted estimations of their own abilities and the possible benefits of their innovations drove Culpeper to distraction; 'I have so little good fortune in the company of these ingenuous men' he complained to Hartlib in the wake of a peremptory note from William Petty, 'that I shall not ouer fondly, shut vp with any more, where my plaine meaninge proues ill matched'.[99] Three weeks later, he declared 'a resolution, not to trowble my thowghts any farther with these kinde of people'.[100]

'These kinde of people' were not the company to be ordinarily expected of a Kentish country gentleman. Yet, as Culpeper reminded Hartlib: 'I doe of late religiously condiscend to things & men of lowe degree, at leaste soe farre as to examine & knowe them.'[101] 'I have learn'd of you not to vndervalewe a whole man for one disproportion'.[102] Hartlib and Dury provided the buttress for such 'religious' condescension and Culpeper's fundamental social convictions reflect theirs. The talents given to every individual human being were entrusted to them by God not as a private estate or monopoly of gifts but for use

[97] M. Hunter, *Science and Society in Restoration England* (Cambridge, 1981), ch. 3.
[98] **149** (11 March 1647[?8]).
[99] **168** (11 October 1648).
[100] **169** (1 November 1648).
[101] **103** (24 February 1646).
[102] **102** (17 February 1646).

in the common cause.[103] Such talents were not to be 'buried in a napkin'.[104] God would decide the outcome of this pooling of human resources: 'The issues of our thoughts and indeavours, as well as the firste preparations of our hearts, are from the Lord'.[105] Capital investment in human endeavour was thus a matter of faith, of casting bread upon waters. Culpeper himself used more specifically agrarian analogies – 'to plante to posterity though our selues may not perhaps hope to injoy any other part or frwite of the action then to haue done it'.[106] The resulting 'subterraneal treasures' (as Gabriel Plattes would have described them) would help to build Solomon's House, or at least to 'prepare some materialls'.[107] Initially we would be aware only of the unpredictable and powerful changes, the 'via' or 'fluxu' of motion, which the 'complications of ingenuities, managed & improved by ingenuous persons, may produce'.[108] Such gradual upheavals would only occur in a collaborative environment where we 'stirre up one another'.[109] We should not always act in accordance with 'the wishes of the Hoghens moghens'.[110] Rather, we would find that it is 'the People or middle rancke muste do it in all places'.[111]

How should the 'middle men' be rewarded for their endeavours? In default of a proper public system of recompense, along the lines adopted in the Netherlands and advocated by Culpeper, he favoured a limited return to the system of patents to individuals for a fixed number of years in order to reward adequately their initial capital investments ('disbursements') and willingness to develop prototypes. But how to determine what proportion of benefit from any particular innovation should be returned to the 'private adventurer' was not evident; 'time and experience' would be the guide.[112] Culpeper was convinced that it was insufficient guarantee for an individual projector to base his investment on Parliamentary ordinances. These were easily overturned or infringed by a subsequent ordinance and gave no redress to the projector. Yet there was an inevitable contradiction between his rooted opposition to monopolies of all kinds and his willingness to contemplate the granting of selected patents for economic endeavours and scientific improvement.

Culpeper's opportunity to change the system of patents came when

---

[103] **150** (15 March 1648).
[104] **31** (22 November 1643).
[105] **88** (Late autumn/December 1645?).
[106] **58** (20 November 1644).
[107] **97** (n.d., November 1645?).
[108] **88** (Late autumn/December 1645?).
[109] **99** (December 1645).
[110] **71** (18 March 1645).
[111] **60** (Autumn 1644).
[112] **166** (25 September 1648).

he was appointed one of the fifteen Commissioners for the Advancing and Regulating of Trade by the Rump Parliament on 1 August 1650.[113] The secretary of the committee was Benjamin Worsley, whose scientific research trip to the Netherlands in the late 1640s had been encouraged, even putatively sponsored, by Culpeper. Other commissioners included Culpeper's old Middle Temple companion, Robert Honywood. The Council of Trade lasted until the end of 1651, producing some fifteen reports on a wide range of detailed issues, including patents. Little detailed evidence exists relating to its deliberations so the role which Culpeper was able to play in its affairs is impossible to determine and there is an unfortunate gap in his surviving correspondence for those years.[114] However, it is not difficult to imagine that his appreciation of Le Pruvost's ambitious scheme for economic regeneration, or his views of how the state should enable technical change to take place, had some effect on the direction of its reports. It is perhaps from this period, however, that what may be Culpeper's only publication can be held to have derived. The publication in question is *An Essay upon Master W. Potters Designe: Concerning a* Bank *of* Lands *to be erected throughout this* Common-wealth which was published by Hartlib through his established printer, Richard Wodenothe in 1653 both separately and as the last five pages of a larger pamphlet on *A discoverie for division or setting out of Land*, a scheme for the laying out of newly reclaimed or colonized land drafted by Cressy Dymock. The *Essay* was, in reality, (as so often with Hartlib's publications), little more than the published version of a thoughtful and supportive commentary on a scheme proposed by the inventor William Potter to establish a Public Bank after the fashion of the Dutch. The key novelty of the scheme was that the Bank was to function not on the security of a specie deposit, but on the basis of land. The former was recessionary and held by Potter and the author of the *Essay* to make England vulnerable to those (especially Spain) who could intervene in the supply of precious metals (notably silver) to the European market. The latter, however, provided an indigenous security, and one which (with prudent management) could only increase its worth. The author of the *Essay* was represented as 'A Person of singular *Zeal* and *Integrity* to all PUBLIKE INTEREST' and has never been more precisely identified than that. Late in 1994, however, a copy of the work appeared for sale in the United Kingdom in which, in a contemporary manuscript hand, the author is clearly identified as 'Sr Cheney Culpeper' in a marginal note on the title-page.[115] This

[113] F&R, ii, 403.

[114] For an appreciation of the role of Benjamin Worsley in the council of trade, see UR, pp. 230–2.

[115] The item was listed in catalogue No. 270 of E. M. Lawson & Co of Kingsholm, East Hagbourne, Oxfordshire. The editors are very grateful to Professor Timothy Raylor

ascription is strengthened to the point of near-certainty by a set of notes in Culpeper's hand amongst Hartlib's papers which make no sense unless read as a comment on Potter's proposal.[116] The notes compare 'these banckes' (i.e. Potter's proposed land banks) with 'that of Amsterdam'. As Culpeper notes, the public bank at Amsterdam allows credit purely in accordance 'to the moneye it receiues' whereas the land banks would extend the credit basis immeasurably. Culpeper shrewdly notes that the Amsterdam Bank is purely a commercial 'exchange betweene persons' whereas a national land bank 'is a kinde of political constitution with which all persones contractes are made'. The Culpeper who had been alert to the infringement of private property implied in the L'Amy/Le Pruvost plantation proposals of the 1640s could hardly help but be aware of the constitutional implications for a state where its landed base became harnessed to public interest by reins of credit. Thirdly, he noted that the Amsterdam Bank only provided money or credit to those who presented themselves in person before the Bank whereas the Land Bank proposal 'giues such bills of credit as will ... commande mony, credit or commodity in any of the place <bancke> or with any privat person, I mean, when the busines is once settled with confidence in mens mindes' Culpeper briefly entertained the notion of a paper-credit based economy and found it as intoxicating as he would the indexing system of Thomas Harrison. For, whereas the Amsterdam Bank extended private credit no further than the money deposit it received from private individuals, in the Potter Land Bank scheme 'the credite of priuate persons, is made fully currente to the vtmoste extente of his theire wealthe or credit with theire frindes, & therefore rayse the credit as much above that of Amsterdam, as the wealthe in all kindes, is more then the mony of a nation, for there is nothinge that a man hathe eyther in mony commodity, lande, or frinds but may commande mony or credit in the bancke'. So pervasive would be the credit of the Land Bank that Culpeper conceived (and with his own estate encumbrances in mind, it must have pleased him to speculate on the matter) that it would not even need necessarily to charge interest on the loans which it made on the basis of landed security.

With the dissolution of the Council of Trade, Culpeper's interests seem to have concentrated more specifically on agricultural experimentation and innovation, mainly along Dutch lines. In this respect, Culpeper was probably building on something of a family tradition, in turn reinforced by his links with the Netherlands through the exiled

---

for drawing it to their attention, and to Messrs W. J. and K. M. Lawson for kindly providing a photocopy of the title-page of the pamphlet.

[116] 30/2/15A–16A.

Palatine court. One of his relatives, possibly his father, gained a patent in 1636 to make turf from English marshes 'after the manner used in Holland'.[117] It was certainly his father of whom Hartlib wrote in the *Ephemerides* on 19 March 1656:

> Sir Thomas Culpeper hath most seriously studied this Husbandry [*sainfoin*] and hath sewen with it of late 10. Acres intending to sow with it afterward 40 more. Hee admires that it hath beene not more practised, but it is for wante of knowing how to order it rightly ... Sir Thomas hath given to his son in writing the <true> Husbandry of St-Foyne as he hath observed it these many years in case he should dye...'[118]

The son in question, however, was 'Mr Culpeper', Cheney's younger brother Thomas. The family rift went on, even to the extent of mutual rivalry over the adoption of agricultural innovations: Thomas against Cheney, sainfoin versus clover.

By the 1650s, Culpeper's credentials as an agricultural reformer were well-established. Already in 1645, he conjectured a 'squinte upon the improvement of landes'.[119] The newly drained Romney marshes were ideal testing-grounds for many of the Dutch methods of intensive husbandry. There is no doubt that Culpeper experimented systematically with new nitrogenous crops, particularly clover.[120] By 1654, he planned to experiment with convertible husbandry on his Romney marsh estates by grazing sheep on the clover rather than cropping it.[121] At the same time, he did not ignore cereal husbandry, concentrating on improved methods of sowing corn by means of a mechanical seed drill as well as exploring the possibilities for a mechanical thresher.[122] In 1649, he put up £10 as one of the co-sponsors of Cressy Dymock's proposal to measure the yield increases of new methods of crop cultivation by means of a controlled experiment over two similar farms in the same area.[123] His interests in irrigation machinery and chemistry derived naturally from his agronomical involvement.

Culpeper was far from being alone in his interest in agricultural improvements; others were ploughing similar furrows including Cul-

---

[117] CSPD (1635–1636), p. 349 (Grant to James Vandebrooke, Sir Thomas Culpeper and Nicholas Scandalarius of a patent for 14 years, 2 April 1636).

[118] 29/5/64A.

[119] **80** (17 July 1645). See, too, Culpeper's interests in compost for cereal cultivation and compost 'barrows' as well as rabbit breeding in various letters, references which are set in context by Joan Thirsk in *The Agrarian History of England and Wales* (Cambridge, 1985), vol V.ii (1640–1750: Agrarian Change), ch. 19, esp. pp. 551–2.

[120] **156** (6 July 1648) and **159** (19 July 1648).

[121] **187** (post 16 May 1654).

[122] **156** (6 July 1648); **158** (12 July 1648); **165** (30 August 1648).

[123] 62/48/1A–2B (22 May 1649).

peper's neighbours, friends and acquaintances – Sir Thomas Payton from the Kentish Weald, Mr Stoughton from Norfolk, Sir Richard Weston from Surrey and others who feature (if only by their initials) in *Samuel Hartlib his Legacie.*[124] Sharing practically-minded and modest 'hints' on agricultural improvement amongst a horticultural elect in the end best suited Culpeper's temperament and condition. This was his way of fulfilling the talents with which he had been endowed. To agricultural historians, however, Culpeper provides an important example of the slow, empirical fashion by which agricultural improvement took root in the English countryside in the seventeenth century.

To stress the utilitarian and practical aspects of Culpeper's concerns would be to forget the literary, bookish characteristics of his culture. He was far from being the 'dim squire'. He read widely and with the attentive and not uncritical eye of a lawyer.[125] He had a good working knowledge of several languages, especially Latin and French.[126] He attempted a translation of Part One of Glauber's *Furni Novi.* He was keen to keep abreast of the latest developments, whether in the confused politics of the civil war or the *arcana* of chemical philosophy. Hartlib, who had run a newsletter service in the 1630s for a variety of committed English gentry, was a natural source of news-books as well as printed and manuscript materials of all kinds. But his knowledge and reading were inevitably constrained by his location and by the time at his disposal. In his scientific endeavours, he never quite engaged with the experimental method, preferring to reflect on what he had read. As Stephen Clucas says, 'For Culpeper, chemistry seems largely to have been a literary experience'.[127] That literary experience consisted principally of grafting what he learnt from his reading onto a common stock of first principles, derived from his protestant Biblicism and an energetic application of what he saw as equity and reason.

His interests in chemistry went back to his years at the Middle Temple which is probably where he first encountered the works of the French neo-platonist chemists of the sixteenth century whom he quotes most frequently from in his letters – Nuysement and Vigenère.[128] As

---

[124] *Samuel Hartlib his Legacy* (1655), pp. 245–7.

[125] He was particularly keen to find out more about Dury's method of analysing a text, developed for use in scriptural analysis. He hoped it would assist him in the critical appraisal of written material – see **41** (3 January 1643[?4]) where he applies it to the text of the letters sent by Charles I from Madrid and **65** (21 January 1645).

[126] The letter to him from Dury in German in the **Appendix** (**197**) suggests that Dury thought he was reasonably fluent in German. However, whilst referring to his translation of Glauber, he mentions that he had no knowledge of the language, **133** (7 September 1647).

[127] Clucas, p. 154.

[128] **99** (December 1645).

Clucas says, it was largely in their words that Culpeper described his own chemistry and the natural philosophy which underlay it.[129] The purpose of natural philosophy, as Culpeper saw it, was to discover that 'hidden & inwarde motion which nature makes within herselfe'.[130] Within nature there was an agent or *agens*, an active and motivating principle, and a patient or *patiens*, a constraining and limiting grossness in matter. The former was the means by which 'nature, or the spirite of nature, is put into motion, in all those circulations which wee see nature to make & by the reiterated apposition of which, the true Artiste may put nature into those reiterated motions which nature cannot give herself'.[131] The main natural agent of this motion was the sun and it was by heat and cold that the motions in nature were determined. Hence Culpeper's interest in preservation of meat by artificial refrigeration or chemical injection and his desire to discover the 'vegetative principles' within metals which might help to explain the processes of metallic decay. These were crucial aspects of the process of organic change in nature, its 'motions'; and 'motion' is as fundamental to understanding Culpeper's view of the political universe as it is of his view of the natural world.[132]

Against this active spirit of nature stood the 'ignis non materia', the 'sulpher externa' and 'feces grossières' which constrained the powerful spirits of nature. The tasks of the chemist and metallurgist were to release the latter from the former. The art was 'the reiterated putting of nature into a fitting motion' to liberate the powerful spirits of nature from the bondage of gross matter. The most powerful spirit of nature imaginable would be a 'menstruum universale' or Alkahest of the kind claimed by Helmont or the secretive Scottish alchemist Carmichael. Culpeper accepted the possibilities of an Alkahest and may even have tentatively identified saltpetre as having some of the constituency of this 'spirit of nature'.

Like Nuysement, Vigenère and the Polish chemist Sendivogius, Culpeper sought support for his natural philosophy in a chemical reading of the Scriptures. This was initially why he had been so concerned to have a full exposition of Dury's 'analytical method'. He remained concerned, however, that the role of a natural philosopher, metallurgist or chemist was limited to helping nature 'with some gentle ripening'. Nature could not be forced or brutalised. Excessive, artificial heating of elements in elaborate stills would turn chemistry into a

---

[129] Clucas, p. 153.

[130] **148** (25 January 1647[?8]).

[131] **150** (15 March 1648).

[132] For the important part played by motion in the chemical texts on which Culpeper relied, see Alien Debus, 'Motion in the Chemical Texts of the Renaissance' in *Chemistry, Alchemy and the New Philosophy, 1550–1700* (1987), ch. 5.

monopolising force, not a releasing and liberating power. The true chemist should 'make vse of the elements, not be [*sic*] changing their natures but by soe adopting [*leg:* adapting] theire severall motions as may best fit our endes'.[133] Culpeper was therefore cautious in his reactions to Glauber's chemical methods and claims. An unnatural chemistry was as potentially damaging to the Great Instauration as the constraint of civil society by a political, ecclesiastical or commercial monopoly; and against these latter, Culpeper was equally vocal.

Political and ecclesiastical concerns

According to Lord Dacre, Culpeper was an apolitical animal, one of those who was 'interested not in politics but in practical improvements and their estates – or in the Apocalypse and Armageddon'.[134] The generalisation needs substantial qualification in the light of this correspondence. In this volume he emerges as a committed Parliamentarian with a developed and radical political agenda, aware of the European as well as English context of events, and inspired at every turn by his fundamental eschatology.

Following the death of Richelieu in 1642, Culpeper foresaw the formation of a Catholic alliance against Protestant Europe, a realignment that would make fundamental questions clear: 'then the vniversal question will be between Protestancy and liberty on the one side & Popery & tiranny on the other; for certeinly Babylon or confusion muste fall as well in Ciuill as Ecclesiasticall gouermente when in bothe (by a dayly greater shining forthe of truthe into the harte of all nations) Reuel: 19: c: 17: & 18: v: shall be fulfilld'.[135] This response was characteristic of Culpeper's politics during the 1640s. At its heart lay a religious vision of imminent reformation, and the passage from Revelation was to recur with renewed urgency in the late 1640s. Throughout the decade he interpreted its political instability as the consequence of religious differences and sought political progress through greater religious freedom. His identification of tyranny in the state with popery in the church was consistent and central to his views. He regarded both as encroachments on fundamental, primitive freedoms. These freedoms had been engrossed by monopolisers who defended their private interests by appeal to 'custome' and 'knowne laws'. The attack on these things in church and state he identified with an attack on received wisdom more generally. As greater light and understanding unlocked the secrets of nature, so it would dispel the gloom from the 'dark corners of prescription'. Political instability, or 'motion', became

---

[133] **88** (Late Autumn/December 1645).
[134] Trevor-Roper, p. 257.
[135] **34** (5 December 1643).

increasingly exhilarating for Culpeper – as exciting as the processes of chemical change. His vision was a compelling mixture of Baconian millenarianism and it fuelled his desire for religious and social reformation. The rhetoric which he adopts is, at times, bracingly radical; but it was held within a legal-constitutionalist view of the English polity which clearly bore the stamp of his background and training. But Culpeper's legalism was of a creative, fluid kind, his concern being to recover fundamental rights encroached upon by custom. Human reason, properly applied, could retrieve a lost state of primitive purity and understanding.

Peace, for Culpeper, could only come through a pacification of the churches. This in turn would only be achieved through toleration and freedom of conscience. With a letter to Hartlib in 1642 he enclosed a copy of another which stated that 'the Conscience is Gods peculiar', a place beyond episcopal jurisdiction. To try to tempt or force another against his conscience was a sin and the fundamental error of popery: 'I am sorry to see that in matters of Conscience, you send mee to Authority; my reason & will are myne owne though not to Consent yett to be submitted by me to Authority; but the Conscience is Gods peculiar, which to offend (though Erroneous) is a sinne, & if a sinne in me to doe it I <*H*: can>not Conceave it (else in them, that by any kind or degree of Persecution) tempt or force me'.[136] When Dury encouraged Culpeper to discover God's particular purpose for him in the wake of his serious illness in 1641, he assumed a necessary freedom of conscience in order to be able to follow God's direction and to be pliant to His purpose.[137] Any settlement in Church or state which obstructed tender consciences would be inadequate and insecure to Culpeper. The principal obstacle lay within popery but, in keeping with the Independency which he manifested through the 1640s, ecclesiastical monopoly could be established in a variety of ways – by bishops or presbyters. By contrast, a communion of the saints could be created 'out of this presente Chaos of opinions … by pressinge a Scripturall necessity of charity & communion amonge those who soe holde the fowndation, as they may (all vnsober & furiously zealous thowghts caste aside) hope well of one anothers saluation'. He could not see 'why, (yf there be any consolation in Christe, any comforte of loue, any fellowship of the Spirit, any bowells & mercies) <philipp: 2: 1: 3:>[138] suche as sufficiently holde the fowndation & nothinge destructiue of it, showlde not be like minded hauinge the same loue till it shall please God (by

---

[136] **20** (n.d. July–August 1642).

[137] **2** (27 September 1641).

[138] Philippians 2:1 – 'If there be therefore any consolation in Christ, if any comfort of love, if any fellowship of the Spirit, if any bowels and mercies'.

the spirit of prophecy to reveale the reste)'.[139] This stands well alongside his broader altruism. Throughout the correspondence he expresses concern that individuals, by accident or through selfishness, bury their talents rather than making them fructify to the public good.

The secular counterpart to ecclesiastical monopoly, and the immediate obstruction to settlement in England in the 1640s, lay in the tyranny of Kings and the aristocratical interest. Between them, these had engrossed freedoms to themselves and encroached on the primitive freedoms of the people. In January 1647 he castigated the Scots 'for th'ingrossinge that very tyrany to them selues which they formerly condemned, in others'.[140] By 1646, Culpeper pictured a common redemption from this double tyranny: 'I cannot but hope & joy to see howe that true effluxe of supreme power hauinge firste freed the people from there Ciuill & Ecclesiasticall Babilons, will afterwards restore Christe to his Spirituall & the People to its Ciuill supremacy'.[141] Not only were these issues interconnected but the remedy, or so it seemed, was near at hand.

[*M*onopolizinge] Corporations of Merchantes, may perhaps finde (ere longe) imploymente inought to defende theire paste incroachements vpon the liberty of the subjectes & truly the monopoly of trade will proue as greate a greeuance (when rightly vnderstoode) as any in this kingdome whatsoeuer, nexte vnto that monopoly of Power which the [K*ing*] claimes; & beleue it, nowe wee are pullinge downe of suche monopolies wee shall starte a greate many which yet ly hid in the bushes but the great monopoly muste firste downe; & then the monopoly of trade the monopoly of Equity, (a thinge which nowe begins to be lookt into), & the monopoly of matters of conscience & scripture (a very notable monopoly), all these & many more wee shall haue in chace & what one hownde misses another will happen in the sente of & thus will Babilon tumble, tumble, tumble tumble.

This made Culpeper contemplate the difficulty of settlement in 1646 with a degree of equanimity – the stones of Babylon had not yet been laid sufficiently low.[142]

The origins of these great monopolies were historic and human. They had no divine sanction. The remedy similarly lay in the application of human reason. Rational examination would illuminate the injustice which they caused and the people would overthrow custom. Just as talents could be lost due to lack of attention from their bearer, the

[139] **75** (6 May 1645).
[140] **146** (12 January 1647 [?48]).
[141] **108** (30 April 1646).
[142] **105** (4 March 1646).

persistence of monopolies was greatly aided by the unreformed spirits of individuals. Thus,

> The primitiue Christians lazines in spirituall concernements, was punnished in the tiranny of theire shepeards, whoe at once, ingrossed bothe dominion & prophecyinge; This tiranny of the elders was punnished by that thinge wee call a Bishop; whilste tiranny thus crepte into the Churche the Emperors were not lesse tirannous in the State, & theire tiranny (in Constantine the firste Christian Emperor) was againe punished by the tiranny of that mungrell synce called Ecclesiasticall; The supreme Ciuill power thus inslaued in the Emperors, hathe (since the dissolution of the Empire) continued soe in the 10: Kings & thus did the [K*ing*] & Bishops loose bothe of them theire vsurped powers to the pope.

Reformation had begun eighty years previously with the accession of Elizabeth. Now the process was accelerating.[143] For reformation to continue, however, a questioning spirit had to be inculcated in the people. For 'this present age haue soe muche reuerence to our owne or ancestors wisdome as euery thinge (in churche or state or any other kinde) yf newe to vs (thowgh not in itselfe or the principles of scripture or reason) findes as yet a difficulte passage in mens thowghts'. By 1644, however, the progress was tangible as a result of the 'three yeeres liberty which men haue taken of ransackinge & touzinge those starched vp & vnjointed postures whereine our ancestors lefte vs like soe many images without motion but from without'. By seeking motion within, Culpeper was confident, 'wee can ... redeeme ourselues into this liberty' and open up the prospect of a universal and enduring reformation.[144]

Motion, change and growth were, as we have seen, fundamental to Culpeper's understanding of nature and the processes of generation and decay. In the civil firmament, too, there was an active principle which could be frustrated by gross matter − by an artificial reverence for the past. '[A*ll*] the Royalistes are alltogether fownded on that Roman Catholik principle of doinge as theire Fathers did, euen to a continuance in grosse degree of slauery'.[145] He was sure, however, that 'the Knowne Lawes of priuate fancy or a mouldy custome cannot destroy that higheste right of a people to dispose of themselues'.[146] The 'stone is rollinge, & (I am confidente) will not ly still any where but in the peoples true Intereste of an equall, frequente, & powerfull Parliamente, where newe Lawes & (yf necessity or the Peoples will incline

---

[143] **108** (30 April 1646).
[144] **58** (20 November 1644).
[145] **118** (n.d. [1646?]).
[146] **65** (21 January 1645).

that way) newe Gouernments may be orderly settled'.[147] Through free
parliaments, responding to the motions of free people, civil government
could be set in motion. This was the secular counterpart of the
aspiration to 'restore to the Spirite of Nature its naturall motion'.[148]

Culpeper's political declarations also bore the imprint of his legal
training. Thus, in September 1647, he deduced the supremacy of the
House of Commons from legal principles. This went beyond the
acknowledged particular power to grant money, but to 'judge of suche
prerogatiues & priuiledges as the [King] & [Lords] eyther haue noe
right to or muste acknowledge themselues to haue receiued from the
Peoples consente'. This consent could only be granted through the
House of Commons. If it were not so, then it must have derived from
the sword – in which case it could be withdrawn. The third possibility,
that the king and lords enjoyed powers by prescription, was discounted
on common law grounds. Prescription 'is a right which a man claimes
to some thinge which can belonge to noe particular man by the Lawe
of nature, & this plea is that the thing he claimes is suche as can
appropriately belonge to noe man by the Lawe of nature, & that
himselfe & his Ancestors haue beene soe longe posseste of it as that
noe memory of man or record can shewe the contrary'. Culpeper's
objection to this argument when applied to royal prerogatives was
fundamental: 'euery man is wholy free by nature, & soe noe right to
this his freedome but by his owne consente'. This consent could only
be expressed in the House of Commons.[149]

For Culpeper, as for many of his contemporaries, law and politics were
interrelated; rights to property were also political freedoms. In Culpeper's
thought this connected his politics once more with his wider aspirations
for reformation. '[P]rescription (that greate bull warke of the Royallistes)
cannot ly or be pleaded to take away that of which euery sonne of Adam
is a proprietor & possessor by the Lawe of nature, I meane, an exemption
from politicall power'.[150] The later encroachments on this freedom are
akin to the tyranny of popery ('this dark dungeon of theire owne
invention'[151]) and will give way before reformation. The light of reason
should, Culpeper hoped, achieve what Worsley had failed to do and 'dazle
(thowgh not converte) those birdes of darkenes whose greatest shelter &
refuge is to loose themselves & those whome they argue with, in the darcke
corners of . . . prescription & custome, as thowgh that custome of doinge

---

[147] **153** (5 April 1648).
[148] **76** (6 May 1645).
[149] **134** (15 September 1647). He also pointed out that the powers enjoyed by the
monarchs had been interrupted by the depositions of Richard II and Edward II. See
also his views on the meaning of the coronation oath in **75** (16 April 1645).
[150] **135** (22 September 1647).
[151] **134** (15 September 1647).

wronge, (even in the face of the originall Lawe of nature) did not soe muche increase the wronge as create a right'.[152] Here, as elsewhere in the surviving correspondence, 'custom' has a strict legal sense, and one to which Culpeper the lawyer, hostile also to the monopoly of equity, is opposed. This vision of legal reform is congruent with, and part of, the larger programme of reformation pursued by the Hartlib circle. In political terms, the consequence was that the primitive and fundamental freedoms of the House of Commons had to be defended against 'the knowne lawes of private fancy'.[153] The rights of the monarch to create aristocrats could be questioned,[154] negatives in the supreme council of a nation were 'a true Babylonishe intrusion'.[155]

In the 1640s, Culpeper perceived the 'aristocraticall interest' as a persistent obstacle to settlement. It was a private interest standing in the way of public good. Yet he was not a republican any more than he was in favour of completely unrestricted freedom of worship. He cautiously offered some support in early 1644 for a plan to depose Charles I and elect as his successor Charles Louis, the prince elector palatine.[156] In November 1648 he continued to hope for a settlement which included the King; and in January 1649 he had reservations about the legality of parliament as it was then constituted.[157] This was despite the fact that he had likened the king and the aristocracy to Lucifer. They had denied their creator, the people, and they thus, by rights, should be cast out of heaven.[158] An enforced settlement, Presbyterian or Independent, gave Culpeper 'little hope to see the signe of the Sonne of man'. Instead, 'Gods glory [will] be seene in bringinge peace, order & harmony out of Warre, confusion, & discorde, & in the Lambes victory vpon the Lyon by turning not destroyinge him, & that by its example of Christian patience & suffering; not by warre & bloode'.[159] Diversity of religious practice was inevitable until the full truth of God's word was accepted in this world. Hence, in matters of church government: '[c]ongregational Churches & a residence of the power of personall excommunication in them' were to be the preferred solution.[160] The power to excommunicate whole congregations had no justification either in Biblical injunction or right reason. Separatism

---

[152] **141** (10 November 1647).

[153] **59** (18 December 1644).

[154] **65** (21 January 1645). He also hoped for the extinction of the aristocracy (or at least its atrophy) by natural wastage and attainder, if new creations were halted: **54** (16 May 1644).

[155] **159** (19 July 1648).

[156] **42** (9 January 1644).

[157] **169** (1 November 1648), **170** (31 January 1648[?9]).

[158] **135** (22 September 1647).

[159] **171** (28 February 1649).

[160] **42** (9 January 1644).

was to be deplored. Those who perceive themselves as the elect should not stand apart from the rest of the worshipping congregation, 'standinge single in theire severall darke corners'.[161] They should seek to place their spiritual talents at the disposal of the common good. The power of ostracisation of a recalcitrant individual remained, however, an important moral authority vested in the congregation: 'there restes in euery assembly of Christian professors a duty of not soe muche as eatinge with one whoe (being called a brother) liues yet inordinately, & I conceiue the Ciuill swoorde ordained to cut [off] suche whoe (thowgh for conscience sake) shall robbe or murder theire neyghbor'.[162] Toleration could only be extended to 'suche as sufficiently holde the fowndation & nothinge destructiue of it'.[163] Culpeper's priority then, was to resist 'the swellinge of Monarchy' and the 'Aristocraticall negatiue or of any suche Churche Gouernmente as shall eyther be imposed on vs by another nation or soe settled as not to leaue a Doore open for suche future reformation as God shall invite vs to'.[164] Impediments to the motions which God intends for us should be progressively removed; and '[un]till the nations of the earthe can thus render themselues free from all selfe interested negatiues there will be but a slowe motion towards the happines of a nation whether in religion or liberty'.[165]

Although Culpeper associated the second coming with confusion, he set a high value on civil order in church and state in the meantime. In secular affairs he allowed only for lawful resistance.[166] Toleration was not available to those who threatened it; and, until the revelation of ultimate truth, Christians must learn 'with patience to submitte where they cannot consente or approue'.[167] Lions must learn to lie down with Lambs – a difficult and implausible message for the confused domestic politics of England in the 1640s. Yet Culpeper was not the only contemporary who grappled with the problem of how to secure order from the contradictory motions of individuals in society. Thomas Hobbes, Culpeper's contemporary in the Middle Temple back in the early 1620s, also pictured a world of perpetual restless motion 'which ceaseth only in death'.[168] But he went on to argue that it was individual

---

[161] **127** (21 April 1647). This letter suggests unease about the use of any coercion except that of the spirit.

[162] **20** (n.d. July–August 1642).

[163] **76** (6 May 1645).

[164] **78** (13 June 1645).

[165] **71** (18 March 1645).

[166] **40** (n.d. [1643–4]). He also suggested that resistance would not be necessary if parliament were properly reformed: **47** (n.d. [February 1644?]).

[167] **76** (6 May 1645).

[168] Hobbes, *Leviathan*, ed. A. D. Lindsay (Everyman edition, 1914), p. 49. See also p. 30: 'For there is no such thing as perpetuall Tranquillity of mind, while we live here;

self-interest which should incline these individuals to choose to submit
to order. Whereas Hobbes was influenced by a mechanistic universe,
Culpeper's views reflected those of his animist chemical universe. Such
order would derive from the true reflection of God's purposes for
individuals in the same way that nature held the active and passive
principles of matter in a delicate balance. Discord would give way not
to uniformity but to a harmony of the spirit of individuals pursuing
their various godly callings free from man-made constraints. In seeking
to achieve practical ends in this world, it was better to 'deale with &
expecte from euerry man according to his principles, thus doe we make
vse of the elements not by soe adapting theire seuerall motions as may
best fit our endes'. In other words, 'wee muste not expecte that water
showlde goe vpwards or the ayre downwards but apply to eache such
a mill or other engine as beste fits eyther'.[169]

These general principles were clarified and confirmed through Culpeper's responses to political events during the 1640s, notably in his
changing attitude towards the Scots. Initially Culpeper had high hopes
of the Covenant made between the English Parliamentarians and the
Scots: 'For to the Couenante lately made for the vniting of ourselues &
to another which I hope shortly to see for the stronger vnion of the 2:
[Kingd*oms*] in theire [Com*mon*] intereste of Religion & liberty; a
Confession of Faythe wowlde be necessary to beget a better vnion &
correspondency between all the reformed Churches & States, against
the Ciuill & Eclesiasticall Babylon which God will certeinly bringe to
judgemente'.[170] In November 1644 he professed to 'haue noe hope (to
speake as a man) but in our geud brethren the Scottes'.[171] The dry
irony of 'our geud brethren' was given more emphasis as Culpeper
became, first suspicious of, and then openly hostile towards, the
Presbyterian interest. By February 1646 he could write to Hartlib that:
'yf our geud Brethren shall impose theire judgemente on vs eyther in
what they thincke beste policy or what they conceiue accordinge to the
woorde of God I shall make noe difference between a [K*ing*] & a
Scotte; I haue been a moste hearty Scottsman, (none beyonde me); but
truly I nowe feare them'.[172] He increasingly suspected the Scots of an
'Extranationall interpretation'[173] of the Covenant, and of seeking to
impose their presbytery on England. It was nothing more than 'Presbiterian Popery, (I meane that persecutinge Spirite which they haue

because Life it selfe is but Motion, and can never be without Desire, nor without Feare,
no more than without Sense'.
[169] **88** (Late autumn/December 1645?).
[170] **26** (16 June 1643).
[171] **58** (20 November 1644).
[172] **102** (17 February 1646).
[173] **108** (30 April 1646).

pulled downe in others that themselues myght get in the saddle)'.[174]
Since popery meant the coercion of conscience, Presbyterians were
seeking to recreate another Babylon: 'the Scottishe Aristocraticall
Intereste bothe in Churche & State whoe hauinge (for theire owne
endes of greatnes & power) joined in pullinge downe the Power of
Monarchy & Episcopacy, doe begin to finde themselues to be parte
allsoe of that Babilonishe rubbishe which muste downe'. By this date
his hopes lay elsewhere with the 'Lilburnistes' whose 'time is not yet'
but who might further their ends by 'with drawinge & reseruinge theire
strenght'. This may serve them 'well whilste the other rubbishe pulls
downe one another'.[175] As early as the autumn of 1645 he had written
that 'i neuer shall make any difference betweene an imperiall, nationall,
prouinciall, prebiteriall parochiall or congregationall Pope'.[176] Clearly
all forms of Church government had the potential for coercion of
conscience and Culpeper was nothing if not an emphatic Independent.

Two other issues of direct contemporary relevance recur throughout
the correspondence of the 1640s. On the one hand there is the threat
that the King or Lords might emerge with a continuing power to veto
legislation passed by the Commons. On the other is the issue of the
control of the militia. Given his views on the supremacy of the Commons,
Culpeper's views on the former are predictable. '[T]he [King's] negatiue
in parliamente wowlde be more sowndly handled, for Quis sit Iudex[177] is
the vniversall question bothe in Eccesiasticall & Ciuill gouernemente'.[178]
Similarly, and in relation to the latter: '[t]he sworde is all, & but one, &
they that haue it not, will not thincke them selues safe, in beinge at the
mercy of others, eyther for their happines, or tenets'.[179] Without control
of these matters the Commons, the supreme efflux of power, would be
trammelled. On this issue Culpeper was steadfast.

There are occasions in the later 1640s when Culpeper's letters reveal
his excitement at the accelerating political changes which he witnessed.
His references to the Book of Revelation become more frequent and
have a greater sense of immediacy. In April 1646, he writes that political
change would accelerate, 'Babilon beinge nowe in the precipice of her
fall'.[180] In March of the following year, the imagery is heightened: 'I
haue still a super confidence that God will finally breake those linsy
woolsy packinges vp of thinges, which our ecclesiasticall & ciuill
Aristocracies muste make for theire owne defence, & that the stone

[174] **145** (5 January 1648).
[175] **152** (24 March 1648).
[176] **90** (n.d. [Autumn 1645]).
[177] 'Who should be the judge'.
[178] **23** (9 April [1643]).
[179] **147** (18 January 1647[?8]).
[180] **108** (30 April 1646).

(nowe in full motion) will not ly still, till it come to the bottome of the hill'.[181] In March 1648, he is ecstatic:

> [f]or (me thincks) I see howe the Lords, in joininge to pull downe the [King], as the Bishops in pullinge downe the Pope, & the Presbiterian in outinge the Bishops, doe nowe finde themselves all deceiued, not foreseeinge that them selues alsoe are but Babylon – cut into sippits & soe, onerly the better fitted, for that time, when the fowles of the ayre shall be called to supper, & you knowe, our meate muste be cut & fitted (by euery one, for the mowthe) Before wee can chewe & swallowe it, & truly, this quarteringe of the Popes in Bishops, & Iointinge of the Bishops into presbiters, in that which wee call Ecclesiasticall, & of the Emperor into [Kings], & of [Kings] into the nobility & noblesse in the Civill Gouermentr it is, but a fittinge them, firste for the spitt, & then for the trencher, thence to the mouthe & soe to the guttes, & from thence, you knowe what will become of all these our benefactors; Amen.[182]

Culpeper's certainty about the imminence of the arrival of the fowls of the air is, once more, congruent with his views on the workings of the natural world. '[E]uery thing being drawne from its center falls naturally into motion[183] and as things approach their proper centre that motion accelerates. Thus in July 1648 he could see that 'the Lords beginne nowe to moue to their proper center, Let them goe'.[184] His history of ecclesiastical and civil Babylon carried a sense of accelerating change. The

> imperiall AntyChriste was (throwgh Gods prouidence) pulled downe heere 8o: yeeres synce & the spoyle diuided between the [King] & Bishopps; They hauinge fullfilled the Cowncell of God vpon the pope; are themselues bothe of them lately called to accownt by a kinde of Aritocracy in Churche & state; & these againe (Babilon beinge nowe in the precipice of her fall), are (in a quicker motion) called to accownte againe by another generation which thowgh standinge somewhat neerer the truer intereste of the People, hath yet that kinde of dominion in it which was at firste vsurped ouer the People by those whoe are bid to be examples to, not lords ouer Gods heritage; & truly this laste diuell as it had its firste rise in the lazines & voluntary blindenes of the people, soe (throwgh Gods blessinge) is it not like to be caste out but by rowzing all Christians to that noblenes

---

[181] **124** (1 March 1647).
[182] **150** (15 March 1648).
[183] **90** (n.d. [Autumn 1645]).
[184] **160** (25 July 1648).

of spirit for which the Bereans were commended.[185]

So the fluidity of events in the late 1640s encouraged Culpeper to believe that the sky was thick with the fowls of the air called to feast and that the millennium was at hand.

But what active role did Culpeper take in this? He was active in politics in minor ways but not an uncritical supporter of any party.[186] His letters contain, for example, a draft county petition, a letter to his royalist brother-in-law encouraging him to reconsider his royalist affiliations, thoughts and suggestions on the organisation of the militia and on the raising of taxes. He was, evidently, a commissioner for the subsidies granted by the Long Parliament.[187] Although he never became an MP, his views and approach to politics are in line with those identified by David Underdown as common to the 'honest radicals' who were elected to the Long Parliament in the recruiter elections of 1645.[188] So it is not surprising to find that his name was apparently being canvassed to stand for Kent. However his own enthusiasm for being elected was brief and may have rested, at least in part, on his desire to avoid being prosecuted for debt. He continued to follow events closely in the later 1640s. He remained ambivalent towards the Scots, regretting their dealings with the King but hoping for an anti-monarchical alliance with them.[189] He favoured a union of the kingdoms as a practical solution to the problems of that relationship.[190] He continued to hope for a settlement but he had few illusions in 1648 that it could be easily achieved.[191] By the end of the decade he was evidently an observer of the unfolding of God's design rather than a direct participator.

How should we explain his passivity? In part we can attribute it to his pursuit of the victory of the Lamb, his concern for legality and his consequent suspicion of all the parties to the conflict. We have already seen how, in seeking to achieve practical ends, Culpeper thought it prudent to 'deale with & expecte from euerry man according to his principles' and so 'make vse of the elements'.[192] Another important part

[185] **108** (30 April 1646).

[186] He frequently noted, for example, how corruption in the supply of the parliamentary war effort cost support for the cause: **65** (21 January 1645), **76** (6 May 1645).

[187] **18** (19 April 1642).

[188] David Underdown, '"Honest Radicals" in the Counties, 1642–1649' in D. H. Pennington and K. Thomas, eds., *Puritans and Revolutionaries. Essays in Seventeenth-Century History presented to Christopher Hill* (Oxford, 1975), pp. 186–205.

[189] **116** (4 November 1646) **117** (11 November 1646), **130** ([5?] August 1647), **131** (11 August 1647), **144** (n.d. [March 1647?]), **145** (5 January 1648), **151** (22 March 1648), **152** (24 March 1648).

[190] **143** (22 December 1647), **159** (19 July 1648), **163** (16 August 1648).

[191] **169** (1 November 1648).

[192] **88** (Late autumn/December 1645?). See above, p. 130.

of the explanation was his confident expectation that the millennium was at hand. In his letter to Hartlib of December 1645, Culpeper quoted a well-known passage from the treatise ascribed by Culpeper to Paracelsus, the 'De tinctura physicorum'.[193] It is one in which Paracelsus lent his support to the myth, to be found in other alchemical writings in the sixteenth and early seventeenth centuries including van Helmont's, of the return of the prophet-artificer Elijah – Elias Artista.[194] The return of Elias was generally seen as ushering in a new age of enlightenment. Although the myth was well known, however, authors differed on the anticipated moment of return, the events which would occur alongside it, and the expectations which it should arouse. Paracelsus was distinctive because he had predicted a specific date, contending (partly in the passage cited by Culpeper) that the age of Elias would begin in the 58th year following the first sixteen centuries of the Christian era, and that it would be accompanied by the destruction of two thirds of the world by war and pestilence. Culpeper concluded, along with others, that the onset of the new age would specifically fall in the fifty-eighth year following the year 1600, i.e. in 1658. Part of his expectant passivity in the late 1640s and 1650s is perhaps attributable to his anticipation of what was to transpire in that year.

Sadly, the surviving correspondence stops in 1657 and so we do not have Culpeper's reflections on the death of Oliver Cromwell in September 1658 and the political chasm which opened up thereafter for the Protectorate. From passing references in other sources, it would seem that he was still pursuing his agricultural endeavours as well as spending time in London.[195] He was eager to set his hand to the new plough which John Wilkins, the Master of Wadham College had promised to perfect – 'I know no ploughman can be so greedy of his meath, as he is after that invention. He begged not so much a scheme as a mechanical model of it, or the thing itself, promising most willingly to pay for it.'[196] There are also, however, signs that he was taking a renewed and more active interest in the political choices facing the nation after the dissolution of Richard Cromwell's Parliament in April 1659 and the recall of the Rump on 7 May. In a pamphlet entitled *A Proposition in Order to the Proposing of a Commonwealth or Democracy*, published

[193] **99** (December 1645).

[194] The myth was supported by, for example, the late sixteenth-century alchemist, Alexander von Suchten, many of whose writings were circulated by Hartlib around his acquaintances. See Walter Pagel, 'The Paracelsian Elias Artista and the Alchemical Tradition' in *Medizinhistoriches Jahrbuch*, xvi (1981), 6–19.

[195] In a letter from Edward Parteridge to Clodius of 18 November 1658, he says that he is staying at Sir Cheney Culpeper's lodgings at the 'Sign of the Black Boy' in the Old Bailey, a lodging house often used by lawyers.

[196] Boyle, *Works*, vi. 99 (Hartlib – Boyle, 7 January 1658). See also the earlier letter of 8 December 1657 – vi. 97.

with the consent of James Harrington and in support of his 'Proposition for setling the Government of this Commonwealth', it was suggested that a grand Committee be established with the blessing of the Rump.[197] It was proposed that it should meet every Tuesday and Friday afternoon in the Banqueting House and elsewhere in Whitehall as a kind of Committee of Safety. In due course it would determine the constitution of the nation. The 102 names proposed for its composition were as wide and bizarre a mixture of the talents as could be imagined. Included on the list, however, were the names of Sir Cheney Culpeper, Sir Robert Honywood, Sir William Waller, William Petty, and others who were familiar to him. Some contemporaries even saw it as a deliberate device to foster ill-will between the army and the Rump.[198] Others said that it had emanated from a Harringtonian Club meeting in Bow St, Covent Garden.[199] If so, it may tell us something of the composition of that club. Certainly, it is not too surprising to find Culpeper attracted to support Harrington, whose views on elective government, aristocracy, and the problem of how to create order from the motions of individuals, came close to his own.[200] At the end of June 1659, Culpeper was appointed as one of the Commissioners for the Westminster Militia, a post which he presumably held through to the Restoration.[201] It is tempting to suggest that this was someone for whom the Good Old Cause was one whose time was only just nigh.

Culpeper's surviving correspondence is fascinating not because there was anything greatly original in Culpeper's thinking, but because he reflects the ideas and aspirations of Hartlib's 'Great Instauration'. He does so with a slightly naive coherence and symmetry, despite the breadth of his interests and concerns. Civil and ecclesiastical Babylon would fall as primitive knowledge and purity were recovered. This fall was imminent, but it was to be worked for, and waited for, with Christian patience. The letters as a whole present something of a paradox, of an eschatalogical political vision pursued with an almost quietist pragmatism. The victory Culpeper sought was the victory of the Lamb, and the excitement he felt at accelerating motion was the excitement of a witness, not an activist. Although he was exceptional among Hartlib's correspondents for the detail in which we can represent

---

[197] The pamphlet was reproduced by Thomas Birch in his edition of *The Oceana of James Harrington; and his other works* (Dublin. 1737). It was published, along with a hostile response in *An Answer to a Proposition* ... (1659) Thomason, E.986 (24) – dated by George Thomason to 17 June 1659.

[198] J. Ashley, *John Wildman* (1957), p. 121.

[199] J. G. A. Pocock, *The Political Works of James Harrington* (Cambridge, 1977), p. 111.

[200] See Jonathan Scott, 'The rapture of motion: James Harrington's political thought' in N. Philippson and Q. Skinner (eds), *Political Discourse in Early Modern Britain* (Cambridge, 1993), pp. 139–163.

[201] F&R, ii. 1290.

his views, this paradox of a quietist, submissive, tolerant, utilitarian and yet apocalyptic vision was far from unique. To Culpeper the collapse of the ecclesiastical and political orders of Europe which he thought he saw occurring about him was a sign of the imminence of enlightenment and an opportunity to play his part in the 'Great Instauration'.

THE LETTERS OF SIR CHENEY
CULPEPER (1641–1657)

1641

1 *John Dury to Culpeper, 25 [NS?] June 1641 [from Hamburg].* (2/4/2)

Grace & Peace bee to yow

Sir Cheney
　　　gladly would I haue bidde yow farewell by word of mouth; but
Mr Hartlieb can testifie how suddain my departure must bee by reason
of the Conveniencie to passe into Holland,[1] where I purpose not to
staye aboue a moneth or sixe weekes Godwilling, & then at my returne
hoping to find yow confirmed in health I shall haue occasion to
recompense this default with larger conversation then hitherto I haue
beene able to haue with yow; that the thinges wherof yow haue hadde
but a taste till now may bee largely sette before your understanding to
feed theron by the grace & illumination of Gods spirit. keep your heart
in a cheerfull frame under the good will of God; & lette it not bee
troubled for priuat euills or public distractions, yow know that God
can bring light out of darknesse & will also doe it to such as feare his
name, I remember my respects unto yowr Ladie & rest.

2 *Copy letter, John Dury to Culpeper, 27 September 1641.* (6/4/113–114)

[*Hartlib's hand*: To Sir Cheney Culpeper.]

Right [wor*shipfull*],
being returned into these partes,[2] I have vnderstood, with great Ioy,
that yow are restored fully to your former health; for which, as I praise
God with yow; so I thought it my Duty to congratulate the same vnto
yow, beseeching the Father of Mercies, who killeth & maketh alive,

---

[1] At this date, John Dury was resident in Hamburg. He alluded to the delicacy of his
proposed short visit to the Netherlands in a letter to Sir William Pelham of 25 June 1641
(2/4/1A). He had arrived in Rotterdam, by 5 July [NS] – see 2/5/1A–2B.
[2] Dury returned to England in August 1641 – Batten, p. 90.

who bringeth downe to the grave & bringeth vp, that he would, with the restitucion of your bodily health & strength multiply all the Goodnes & Graces of his Spirit vpon yow, to enable yow to returne the life; which so vnexpectedly yow have received from him; backe againe vnto him, by all dutifullnes in his service with cheerefullnes; that from henceforth as a new Man, having once renounced this world & received within your selfe the sentence of Death, yow may not live any more vnto your selfe the life of the world; but the life of the Spirit of him, who hath in a manner raised yow from your Grave. When I consider that God hath a speciall end in all his workes, which he doth towards his Children, & cheifely in such things, as concerne their life in this world, or in the world to come, their being, or not being in the one or the other; then I conceive it would be our greatest wisedome, that in this life we can aime at or attaine vnto, to learne this end & to observe his purpose, that we may compley with him in it, & do not disappoint him of it now we know that his generall purpose in all things is his owne glory; but the bare notion or conception of a generality cannot make vs truly wise, except it be particularized & determined vnto vs. Therefore we ought not to content our selves with an indefinite notion of the glory of God, to be made manifest by vs; but we should dive into the particular intencion of God towards vs, to know what part & what property of his glory, how & where he will have it made knowne by vs. & this we should learne by prayer vnto him for illuminacion herein; & by a serious consideracion of the Talents which he hath given vnto vs, & of their vsefullnes to advance his Kingdome amongst Men. The ground of our prayer in this particular request of Illumniacion to this effect should be a resolucion to resigne our selves, as a living Sacrifice vnto God, that entering into a speciall Covenant with him, as Iacob did, Gen: 28 to take him to be our God;[3] he may find a fitt disposicion of heart in vs to apprehend the Revelacion of his will; that by his Grace (which will never be wanting to such as seeke his face) we may gett experience, & prove what is good, that acceptable, & perfect will of God towards vs, wherein he doth intend to make vse of vs, as vessells of Honour in his Howse: for every one that doth sett himself apart vnto God, with an vpright heart, will be made vse of by him to some good purpose or other, & God will let a man, that is desirous to know wherein he should be vsefull, see the purpose & end to which he will make vse of him; if he take into serious Consideracion the Talents which he hath received of God & looke upon the profitt

---

[3] Genesis 28: 20–21 – 'And Jacob vowed a vow, saying, If God will be with me, and will keep me in this way that I go, and will give me bread to eat, and raiment to put on, So that I may come again to my father's house in peace; then shall the Lord be my God'.

which may redound vnto Gods Kingdome by the same, if they be fittly employed. This is then the Counsell which I would give yow as a friend vnto your soule, that yow would pray to God for this manifestacion of his will & ruminate with your selfe what vse yow should make of the life, which he hath restored vnto yow; & of the Talents which yow possesse therein committed to your trust, to profitt with-withall. This will be a true meanes to continue & confirme your health & strength; till your time come, when yow shall be fully dismissed & licensed from labours, to receive the reward of eternall rest in the Kingdome prepared for all his faithfull Servants. Pray for me that I maybe diligent to follow the Counsell which I do give yow; and as I give it yow with a hearty desire, that it may be most effectuall vnto yow through Gods Blessing; so I shall not be wanting according to the ability which *the* Lord shall supply from time to time to me, to second it with my prayers vnto him for yow, & with farther advice & encouragements to further yow in the race, which we are to runne, wherein as I study to be your Companion; so I shall approve my selfe allwaies in the presence of God

3 *Culpeper to Hartlib, 29 September [1641]. (13/342‑3)*

Mr Hartlib,
        I haue receiude your letter of 7:ber 21th whereby I vnderstande of Mr Commenius his arriuall at London;[4] I intend God willinge shortly to be in towne & shall then be very glad to be knowen to him, and acquainted with him; & shall doe what I haue formerly promised; In the meane time I pray presente my kindeste respects vnto him
        Yf you see Mr. Pell; I pray commend me to him; & intreate him in my name for a transcripte of that paper by which he tawght me And (yf when I come to London) I finde him better prepared in that kinde as he vndertakes in his printed paper which I receiued from you;[5] hee will finde [me?] ready to joine issue with him; I heartily wishe you well and reste

[4] Jan Amos Comenius arrived in London from Leszno on 21 September 1641 – HDC, p. 354. For an account of Comenius's visit to England see R.F. Young, *Comenius in England* (Oxford, 1932), passim; HDC, pp. 349‑70.
[5] The mathematician John Pell (1611‑85) wrote an early version of his 'Idea of Mathematics' and sent it to Hartlib in 1634. It was subsequently printed and published in a single folio sheet in 1638 ([*An Idea of Mathematics*] STC 19564.5). Culpeper is referring either to this printed tract or to a manuscript copy which Hartlib had despatched to him. A title-page copy of such a copy, written in Hartlib's hand, is to be found amongst his papers in 14/1/6A. In 1650, Pell's 'Idea' was published as an appendix to John Dury's Reformed *Library Keeper* (1650), Wing D2882, pp. 33‑46. See also P.J. Wallis, 'An Early Mathematical Manifesto – John Pell's *Idea of Mathematics*', *Durham Research Review*, 18 (1967), 139‑48; HDC, p. 88.

[*PS.*] My seruice I pray to Mr Dury

[*PPS.*] This letter missed the Carrier laste weeke; & that was the reason you receiue it soe late :8:ber 6:xt

4 *Culpeper to Hartlib, 28 October [1641].* *(13/344–5)*

Mr Hartlib;

   I am very sorry I receiued not Mr Dury his propositions in your laste packet; For I had (at the beste) rather a happy oportunity of presentinge what might recommende it selfe, then any intereste of pressinge or recommendinge any thinge vpon my owne judgemente; & I nowe feare that euen that oportunity is loste;

  I muste still thanke you for your newes but wowlde not haue you trowble your selfe to sende the printed papers except it bee some speciall ones & for those I shall be youre debtor till I see you: In the meane time I pray commende me very kindly to bothe your woorthy guesse [*guests*]; For Mr Pell I was very glad when you firste mentioned him to me as beinge (accordinge to his owne pretence) a man fitte for my turne but my knowledge of the man & my late reviewe of his paper makes me rather wishe then hope for soe great a jewell from him; which beinge (at firste) beste tried & perfected in the mathematickes wowlde (I conceiue) become an example eyther of serche or discussion or of demonstratiue proofe in other occasions thowgh more circumstantiall; my paper is done; I reste

[*Hartlib adds:*]
I confesse j expect not an exact book of Analyticks till you perfect yours. Sir Charl*es* Cavendish the 18 Decem*ber* 1641.

5 *Culpeper to Hartlib, 15 November [1641].* *(13/340–1 [summary only])*

Culpeper hopes to be in London very shortly and sends respects to Comenius and to Dury, if he is still in London and not yet departed for Ireland.

6 *Culpeper to Hartlib, 18 December [1641?].* *(13/346–7 [summary only])*

Culpeper refers to the arrangements for the direction of money which he had promised to provide for John Dury's endeavours. Such arrangements were to be 'not at all hortatory for the layinge out of the mony is allready resolued on'. Culpeper wants

several possible projects short-listed and ranked by order and value. Their success lies in God's hands.

7 *Copy letter, John Dury to Culpeper, 20 December 1641. (6/4/117–120)*

Worthy S*i*r Cheney
Thankes is due vnto yow in all respects; but cheifly for these occasions which yow afoard vnto me towards the improveme*n*t of spirituall thoughts, which is a great kindnes from yow to me. would to God many were thus affected; for then o*u*r life would be a great deale more happy then now it is: in the midst of this contentious generation. only let vs pray to God that o*u*r Conferences may tend to his glory & o*u*r mutuall edificac*io*n & then we both shall haue Cause to praise his name together. Concerning my first discourse I haue noe need of it in haste, yow may therefore keepe it as long as yow please:[6] I am sorry it doth not give that satisfaccion which yow wish; & it is not wel possible to give full satisfaccion to men discontented in p*ar*ticulars at such a distance, & when their scruples & grounds of exception are [<*H:* not>] distinctly knowne, nor did I intend in my discourse to give any satisfac*io*n to p*ar*ticular matters so much as to shew how men of vnderstanding vpon occasion should proceed to give satisfaccion to such as are doubtfull either through weakenesse & simplicity or through stubbornesse & craft of hypocrisie. if either they thems*elves* that receive noe satisfacc*io*n, or yow would be pleased for them, to sett downe what is excepted [aga*inst*], or that wherin I am defective in the matter, perhaps God might put a word in my mouth fitter for their vnderstanding when I should perceive where their scrupules doe lye.

The matter of publick prayer which yow menc*io*n againe I am very willing more fully to discusse, when yow shall haue weighed what I haue said in my last, which then I wrote in some hast & haue not kept a Coppy. in the meane tyme for our better discussing of the matter we may order o*u*r thoughts vpon these heads. first let vs agree what prayer & what publick prayer is; which I call the drawing neere of the heart off a whole Congregation, either by the voice of one leading the rest, which follow either audiblely or silently his expressions; or by the voice of eu*er*y one joyned together in one expression, as in singing of psalmes or in the responsories of the Letany &c. Secondly because our doubt is Cheifly concerning him that leadeth the rest, the question concerning his acc*io*n & the Relac*io*n which it hath to the mind of his auditory must be estated distinctly as thus.

---

[6] At least nine works were published by Dury in 1641. This may perhaps refer to his *Summary Discourse concerning the work of Peace Ecclesiasticall* (Cambridge, 1641), Wing D2889.

1. whether the reading of a prayer out of a booke; be ordinarily as effectuall & fervent a meanes to raise the affections either of ones selfe or of those that heare vs pray, as the præmeditate vttering of the motions which Gods spirit doth [<*H?:* indite>] vnto vs? 2. whether when a prayer is read in a booke he that doth read it must not be devided in his thoughts as well as they which heare him? that is whether he must not first thinke vpon the thing which he readeth to vnderstand it, before he can raise it vp as an affectionat request to God? & if yea, whether then he is not obliged to doe two Acts at once; aswell as they which heare him in an extemporary prayer? 3. whether any prayer ought to be extemporary? that is conceived without all premeditacion of the matter to be vttered? I conceive noe; for I suppose it is not beseeming the Reverence due vnto Almighty God to come rashly before him & the place of Eccles. 5. 2. doth expressly forbid it both in the mouth & heart.[7] 4. whether any words can be conceived fitt enough to a perpetuall & constant vse of a Congregacion, soe [soe] that vnalterably they may be applyed to all circumstances & occasions of the State thereof with the more fruite of edificacion then other words which a faythfull minister may vtter. 5. whether in the vttering of publick prayers when one goeth before & the [<*H:* rest>] follow, it be necessary that all that pray should haue an equall share in the Harmoney, so, as at one instant of tyme, all should jointly vtter the same words & thinke the same thoughts? & whether the harmony of affections cannot aswell stand in a different space of tyme, when the followers vnderstanding him that goeth before them distinctly & slowly, shall say to euery period of his request affectionatly – Amen? or else when they repeate secretly all his words in their heart imediatly when he doth vtter them, & put them vp to God after him with the raising of their desires towards him. 6. whether the attencion of the mind is not greater & consequently more devout, & fit to be more affectionate; when it is somewhat suspense & not fully acquainted with the matter or words which the Minister is about to vtter; then when it hath gotten a prayer by Rote & custome, to be altogether familiar? for it seemes that the customarinesse of a prayer, cheifly are set words doth lessen the attention; because the soule wilbe wandring of tymes to other matters; when the mouth by helpe of the memory is vttering words which are very familiar vnto vs. 7. whether to frame publick prayers or a booke of publick prayers fitted for a whole Congregacion, it may not suffice to reckon vp the heads of matters to be mencioned & insisted vpon at all occasions leaving the particular expressions thereof vnto the vnderstanding zeale & affection

---

[7] Ecclesiastes 5:2 – 'Be not rash with thy mouth, and let not thine heart be hasty to utter any thing before God: for God is in heaven, and thou upon earth: therefore let thy words be few'.

of the Minister? or if the bare, nameing of matters be not thought a sufficient helpe to fixe all mens spirits one way & to [<*H:*præinforme>] them enough for a conjonction of motions in *the* spirit; the question may be, whether (if also the words which may be thought expedient to be vttered should be added); it ought not to be left free never the lesse vnto the Prudent Preacher to vse other words & arguments belonging vnto the same matter which he shall thinke either Equivolent or more emphaticall according to the seuerall circumstances of tymes & dispositions of his particular congregation? 8. if it be not fitt to leaue it altogether free vnto the Minister to haue the Sole choise of the matter to be vsed in publick prayer (as I thinke it not fit) then the question will be how the matter & by whom, & how farre it should be determined? & what restraint should be laid vpon ministers lest they bring in matters in their prayers which are not to be allowed & wherevnto their auditory cannot say Amen. 9. But if the matter should be in Cases left free vnto the minister to propose, whether he ought not, before he put forth his prayers in particular requests, to acquaint his auditory, either by way of exortation, or by the way of instruccion in a breife discourse premised to his prayer, with the heads whereof he is to pray that so they may be in some sort better prepared to joyne when he cometh to particulars? These are the cheife heads which at this tyme seeme to be most considerable in this matter. the last thing which yow mencion in your letter concerning the Analising of the Scriptures; I acknowledge my selfe a debter therein vnto yow more then vnto many others because I see a greater love of knowledge in yow then in many which I hope will proue beneficiall to your owne Soule & the good of many others; therefore I am reddy to give yow all satisfaction as it shall please God to inable me for your Sake: only I must haue tyme to learne of Mr. Hartlib what the papers are which yow received from him that I may Judge what the grounds of your demand is; that soe according to the principles which yow are by that write [<*H:* initiated>] into I may be able to adde something to your light. my tyme is short & my paper at an end, & the matter at this tyme fitte to be vttered, spent; therefore I will Commend yow to the Grace of God; & desire yow to joyne to all your prayers premeditations and examinacions of your state; and to remember me therein when yow mention the peace of Jerusalem & the Reformacion of abuses.[8] beseech *the* Lord [<*H:* also>] to give vs more light in these doubts & to send forth vpon vs as he hath promised by the Prophet Zachary the Spirit of prayer & supplicacion, to which I shall not cease to recommend yow

---

[8] This and succeeding correspondence with Culpeper resulted in Dury's published treatise *A Motion Tending to the Publick Good of This Age, And of Posteritie* (1642), Wing D2874.

8   *Culpeper to John Dury, n.d. [October 1641?].   (13/325–6)*

Mr Dury

I assure you I expecte noe thankes from you, & yf by your meanes it may please God to rayse my vnderstanding & will to a right way of dedicatinge myselfe, & those talents with me, to his seruice & glory, the prayses shall be his, the kindenes yours, & the thanks onely mine.

I haue viewed & receiued your firste discourse about the difficulties in these times, which (thowgh in itselfe rationall) yet (partly in respecte of the persons it is intended for, whose tenets are soe deere & precious in theire owne eyes as they are afrayde to be made to see any ill of them, & partly throwgh my owne weakenes betweene which & the engine, there is yet a greate disproportion) I finde not alltogether soe vsefull as I cowlde wishe; I haue not yet returned it; intendinge to make a reviewe of it, but yf by this posts returne I may vnderstande your wante of it, you shall not fayle of it the nexte weeke[9]

I haue allsoe reade ouer your laste of publike prayer, which (by accident) I haue nowe to shorte time to answere Onely for a touche; I conceiue one necessary requisite to publique prayer is that euery presente member showld haue a gauelkinde share bothe withe duty & good of it; And (perhaps throwgh my owne weakenes) I cannot yet see howe the sowle can at one pointe of time, bothe, sufficiently & in equall proportion with the minister sende up to God what it hathe receiued & yet reserue one whole sence & parte of it selfe for somewhat else which the minister is then teachinge; where neyther the matter nor forme is fore knowne; for where the whole is due & (by the minister) payed, there I conceiue (that the truste may beare an equall share in the harmony) they allsoe muste pay the whole, & leaue noe parte of the soule loose or at liberty eyther in the eare or any other sence; and as I remember Acontius obserues that in the Jewes time the Temple was indeed a publike place but not of publike prayer but where euery soule presented its owner, & yf in these times wee will haue the prayers publike as well as the place, I cannot yet see but where euery muste haue an equall share, there muste they allsoe haue an equall share of foreknowledge and premeditation; which euen to closet prayers is in a greater or lesse degree nesessary; muche allsoe migh be sayde againste the ministers sole choyce of the matter, leaste he sometimes impose suche as the reste consente not to, & for example of this I will goe noe farther then the prayer againste the Scotts in which (thowgh from another kinde of hande) the analogy of reason holdes, & to which my owne eares hearde very fewe Amens; And in truthe it seemes to me

---

[9] It is not clear to which of Dury's numerous treatises from 1641 Culpeper here refers.

that as closet prayers are therefor lefte at liberty because priuate, soe on the contrary publike prayers, because publike, owght to be conformed to a plublike intereste eyther by way of inlargement or stinte, & not to the largenes or narrowenes of one mans faculties or judgemente, the ende of publicke prayer beinge a publike worship, not the ventinge of priuate thowghts; but enowght for the presente of this & more then I thowght when I began

I haue two or three little tractes of yours concerninge the analisinge of the scriptures or other authors; whereby to comprehende all the wisdome of the writer in one of the tracts you are pleased to confesse your selfe a debtor in Gods behalfe to any one whoe without obtrusion is ready to receiue it; I doe heereby as farre as I may claime my parte of the debte & doe heartily desire you that yf you can by your selfe or any other author directe my thowghts to a comprehension of it that I may haue your helpe

For I thus conceiue that beste examples whether diuine or humane are the neereste way to wisdome, & the way to these beste examples muste be by anilizinge of them; this you vndertake may be done & in this (yf I may) I claime my parte from you whereby I may be able firste vnderstande the breadthe lenght & depthe of the beste authors & from the Idea of theire wisdome better to directe my owne words & actions; Mr Commenius in his pansophia for thinges & his Janua for words,[10] & Mr Pell in the mathematicks doe bothe of them driue at this scope, but because they are yet in fieri I showlde be glad for the presente to stay my appetite with somethinge from you, which may thowgh not teache me to [compose] yet be a key in my hande to the beste composed authors; my times endes with my paper; I pray let me heare from you

9   *Copy letter, John Dury? to Culpeper, n.d.   (6/4/121–122)*[11]

Sir Cheney.

If my discourse hath given yow any satisfaccion, or some   overture towards a satisfaccion, which in tyme to come yow may receive, I am very glad of it. I desire therefore that yow would propose any doubts

---

[10] Comenius' *Pansophiae Prodromus* had been published in London in 1639 with a preface by Samuel Hartlib. His *Janua linguarum reseratae vestibulum*, a grammar book arranged as a small encyclopaedia of useful knowledge, had been first published at Leszno in 1631, and had been popularised in England by a pirated edition, published in London in 1632 – see HDC, pp. 88–9.

[11] Although the copy is undated it is clearly by John Dury and follows the preceeding letter in subject-matter and should be assigned to the last months of 1641 – see HDC, p. 224.

or scruples that may come into your mind further, that thereby the matter may be more fully discussed: for although I have not been able to satisfy my selfe in what I have declared at this tyme, yet I hope to find leasure hereafter to insist more at large vpon that subject: for it is very worthy of a full disquisicion. As concerning the doubt which yow propose vpon the words of my [*letter*] to Sir J. Tempell[12] touching the prayers to be conceived in a family (for I speake of the duty of a Chaplain in a family, & not of a private devotion in a closett) whether they ought to be stinted to a precise forme or no? I would have yow to observe, first, that I speake not simplily of the conceiving & vttering of prayers extemporalily by the Chaplaine; as if therein any great matter did stand that it should be done ex tempore: no I do not thinke soe: for I suppose all things are better don in the way of premeditacion, then without it; & the word of precept is cleere for a premeditate manner of prayer against extemporality. Ecclesiastes 5. 2.[13] Be not rash with thy mouth, & lett not thy heart be hasty to vtter anything before God: for here is a prohibicion as I conceive of that extemporality, which some seeme to affect: but my meaning & speech also in that place is concerning the exercising & teaching of the Members of the family to pray in spirit & truth: to which teaching & exercising I oppose the binding of the Chaplain to certayne precisely stinted formes & the binding of the Members of the family also to the same: as if they should content themselves with the saying over of the same at morning & Evening prayers: for if either he or they thinke themselves bound to certayne formes & stinted thereby; then the exercise of the duty & the endevours to teach them how to performe it in spirit & truth will be quite lost. This is then the first thing to be observed that I speake rather of the Chaplaines intention to teach & exercise others in prayer, then to conceive the same himselfe; yet I do not exclude him from practising that (as the mouth of the society) which he is to teach the Members thereof to do in private: but I leave him at his owne liberty & would not have him precisely stinted. Secondly I would have yow to consider that it is another thing to vse a constant sett forme at certayne times & certayne Actions, & another thing to be stinted to certayne formes so precisely, that it is not lawfull without offence to vse any other. The first may be don freely according to the discrecion of him

---

[12] Sir John Temple (1600–1674) was created master of the rolls in Ireland in 1641. He had been instrumental in the offer to Dury of a post as household chaplain to the Earl of Leicester, Lord Lieutenant in Ireland in May 1641. Dury explained to Hartlib that his principal duties were 'that I am called to order & have an inspection over the family in matters concerning Religion & Gods private worship therein', which was doubtless the issue of the letter relating to household religion which had been sent to Culpeper for comment – 9/1/147A–150B.

[13] See above, p. 156 note 7.

that is to be the mouth of the family towards God, & according to their capacity, that are to follow him in praying: but the second doth imply an expresse limitacion of the Spirit: from which I would have the leader of others vnto spirituall devotion to be freed.

Thirdly he that is to be the mouth of a society vnto God which is committed to his charge, & whereever he is to watch as one that must give an accompt, will certainly have at many tymes seuerall things to represent vnto God which in a stinted forme cannot be contayned: therefore I would not have him tyed to a precise forme, but left to himself to vse or not to vse a certaine forme constantly, as he shall thinke expedient for the vse of edificacion: for yow must know that I do not discommend a sett forme of publicke prayers to be vsed either in the Church or in a family; but I thinke it both vsefull & expedient that for the most parte a constant forme should be vsed; yet I would not have the forme so strictly imposed vpon the Minister that it should be accounted a fault in him not to vse att all tymes one & the same forme of words, or not to vse the words prescribed.

Thus being preconceived concerning my meaning I come now to answer your doubt, which is that prayers that best admitt of an equality suite best to Gods end in publicke worship, & that euery one who should beare a part in the duty of prayer, should also have some fore knowledge of the part they are to beare lest in the concurrence of two principall Actions at once the Soule be distracted from both, & do neither as it ought to doe: for these Reasons yow conceive that extemporary prayers are not so vsefull for a publicke meeting as sett formes which euery one doth know before hand.

To this I answer that Gods end in publick worship is to be found of vs by drawing neere vnto him according to his will: now his will is that we should serve him with the vnderstanding, & the more vnderstandingly the Requests are putt forth, the better service is don to him; & the more our affeccions are raysed in neerenes towards him, he accepteth the better of our service: Here then it is to be considerred, whether or no (seeing one must be the leader of the Action of worship in a society) those that follow him that goeth before them vnto God: can be said to have an equall parte with him, whether he vseth his owne words & conceptions which he thinketh most fitt for the occasion: or some prescribed words which may be suitable to all occasions? I conceive that neither way they can be said to have an equall parte in the action with him because they both wayes are but followers & he is alway their Leader. But yow say that they follow him more easily when they foreknow the words which he is to vtter & so are the better able to performe their duty vnderstandingly & affectionatly: whereas if they have no foreknowledge of the parte which they are to beare in the harmony of spirituall mocions, that then they shall not be able to joyne so effectually neither in vnderstanding nor affection. All this I will not deny to be soe in some whose sences are not exercised to spirituall mocions: but in such whose spirits are often raysed to God vpon all occasions incident, this will not prove to be soe: for these men will be able both to conceive vnderstandingly at an instant whatsoeu*er* is distinctly vttered, & to joyne their affections fervently vnto that which they conceive: the first are to be supported and drawne by degrees to a more ready & vigorous mocion of the spiritt: the second being already co*m*me to some measure of the same are made dull & heavy by a stinted forme Thus yow see that I approve of both wayes & would have them vsed according to the Capacity of the Congregacion; which is to be discerned by their Leader, who should teach them towards the perfecc*i*on of all spirituall dutyes, & exercise them in the degree wherevnto they are come.

10   *Culpeper to Hartlib, n.d. [September 1641–June 1642?].*   *(13/348–9)*

Mr Hartlib

I hope you will not fayle vpon the deliuery of this inclosed to receiue 10[1], with which (I am very sorry) I cowlde not furnishe you before, but the extreame deadnes of the times muste excuse it; I showlde be glad to vnderstande of your receipte of it by the poste;[14]

My not receiuinge my rents makes me ly closer in the Cowntry then otherwise I showlde; but necessity will shortly command me to be in London, & then I shall be glad to conferre with you at large about Chelsey Colledge;[15] my harty wishes to this busines neyther doe nor shall lessen, thowgh I knowe not what it is that stuns my hopes; I pray

[14] According to the surviving fragments of Hartlib's accounts, Culpeper had subscribed regular monthly amounts in support of his philanthropic endeavours during 1641. £5 was received on 13 April (23/2/12B), a further £5 on 11 May (23/12/3B), and £10 on 14 May (23/10A).

[15] Chelsea College was founded in 1607 as a divinity college. Its provost and 19 fellows were endowed through the bequest of Matthew Sutcliffe, Dean of Exeter. During his visit to England, Comenius attempted to gather the support of various MPs for the establishment of a Universal College, modelled (perhaps) on 'Solomon's House', the research institution of Bacon's *New Atlantis*. Chelsea College was considered as a possible location for such a foundation, which was to be re-endowed with 12 fellows. For Comenius' recollections of Culpeper's involvement, see **Introduction**, p. 126. A later, better known, suggestion for reforming Chelsea College was published by John Dury in his *Reformed Spiritual Husbandman* (1652), Wing D2885. He proposed to convert it into a college for international protestant correspondence – see Young, pp. 43, 54–5; *The Diary and Correspondence of John Worthington*, ed. James Crossley, *Chetham Society*, Vol. 13 (Manchester, 1847), pp. 69–75; GI, pp. 49, 71; HDC, p. 361; M. Purver, *The Royal Society: Concept and Creation* (1967), pp. 214–15.

Commende me moste affectionately to Mr Dury & Mr Commenius, I
reste

[*PS.*] I pray sende your letters by one Will: Heyden the Lenham
Carrier whoe lies allsoe at Billingsgate & by whome you receiue this
for he comes close by the place where I nowe am which the other
dothe not

1642

11   *Culpeper to Hartlib, 5 January [1641/2].   (13/350)*

Mr Hartlib;
         The strange newes from London,[1] makes me heartily desire to heare from you by any firste occasion; But that noe letters may miscarry I pray vse to repeate in euery nexte letter, when & by whome you sente the laste; These Cowncells doe certeinly springe from another spirit, then any of the former, & tende more strongly to a turne of the tyde; & yf these men doe not stande right, I feare that what was good & fitte to be insisted on, will suffer in the company of theire fawltes & errors

12   *Dury to Culpeper, 6 January [1641/2].   ([summary only])[2]*

Culpeper had requested further illustration of the various means by which learning might be reformed and advanced. Dury responds by suggesting a variety of pamphlets and teaching manuals to present an Idea *of the ways forward. Comenius is mostly concerned with the reformation of learning; Dury is more interested in its advancement. Both tasks are complementary.*

13   *Culpeper to Hartlib, 9 January [1641/2?].   (13/334–5 [summary only])*

Culpeper asks for letters to be sent via the Thames carrier to Gravesend for him and sends respects to Dury and Comenius.

---

[1] Culpeper clearly alludes to the arrest of the five members of the House of Commons and one member of the House of Lords on 3 January 1642. Although charged with high treason for their complicity in the Scottish invasion and for declaring war against the king they were escorted back to Westminster on 11 January. See CDPR, pp. 236–37; SRP. ii, 757–58; CSPD (1641–43), p. 236; and J. Forster, *Arrest of Five Members by Charles the First* (1860).
[2] Published by Samuel Hartlib in *A Motion tending to the Publick Good of This Age, and of Posteritie* (1642), Wing D2874, sigs. C4ʳ–D4ʳ. It is edited and republished in part in SHAL, pp. 103–06.

14   *Dury to Culpeper. 13 January 1641/2.   ([summary only])*[3]

Dury speaks of Comenius, Hartlib and himself in 'a knot sharers of one anothers labours'. They work mutually to serve God without respect to private ends. Culpeper must wait upon God's providence in order to be shown to what use God will put his talents. Dury explains that the various treatises by which he proposes to assist the reformation and advancement of learning will only truly work their effects through the influence which they have on individuals' minds and hearts. Other means of providing a 'transient contribution for the elaborating of these Treatises' will undoubtedly assist in the matter. Such means might include benefactions to assist in the foundation of a college. Such benefactions might either be in perpetuity or over a stipulated number of years. Culpeper has been in contact with an individual who might be prepared to assist in such a foundation.

15   *Culpeper to Hartlib, 30 March 1642.   (13/2–3)*

Mr Hartlib

Thanks muste still be the subjecte of my firste lines, for your kinde letter & newes, And nowe I muste confesse to you that the mistaking Mr Commenius his letter to be written (not to you but) to my selfe, was the cause of my error; & that which I fellte was not that Good mans desires which (thowgh in a muche larger proportion) I showlde haue thowght very reasonable but that hee showlde be lefte to write soe muche in his owne behalfe, to me whoe (in that little I am able to doe) shall desire there may not be soe muche priuity betweene vs, as to haue his thanks, & in truthe were I able to doe muche more it showlde be from me as a matter of debte; not of bownty; I hope you haue not trowbled Mr Commenius with any parte of my laste letter, my kindest loue & respectes to him & to Mr Dury from whose best lesure I still liue in hope to receiue some parte of his promise; I intende shortly to be in London, & to bring what I cannot yet receiue, I pray sende me Crompton of the Iurisdiction of Cowrts,[4] & put it to my accownte; I conceiue it will coste about 2ˢ:

yf there be any further discouery of the [perpe*tuus* mot*us*] I desire to heare

---

[3] Published by Hartlib in *A Motion* ... (1642), Wing D2874, sigs. d4ʳ–E1ᵛ. It is edited and republished in full in SHAL, pp. 106–10.

[4] Richard Crompton, *L'authoritie et jurisdiction des courts de la roygne: nouelment collect & compose* (1594), STC 6050; another edition (1637), STC 6051.

16   *Culpeper to Hartlib, 5 April [1642].   (13/4⁻5)*

Mr Hartleb;
        your laste letter saue one, gaue me greate assurance of Mr
[Commen*ius*] his [Per*petuum* Mob*ile*] not onely in the theory but in the
practise; His firste deliuery of himselfe in it was allsoe suche as raised
some expectation, but suche (as with me) dothe (I assure you) yelde
noe prejudice;⁵ I pray commende me moste kindely to him;
        I am of late fallen vpon Platoes woorkes⁶ whome I finde (accordinge
to Acontius testimony of him) full of examples of methode but for
wante of an Analyticall key I am (towards the ende I propose to my
selfe) lame in the readinge him; When you see Mr Dury tell him soe
much & commend me moste affectionately to him, to whome (yf I be
not in London myselfe) I will write by the nexte; You once mentioned
to me a kinde of pumpe of the Moravian Knights⁷ the excellency
whereof (as (I thinke) yourselfe tolde me) consisted in that which is
called the shooe or plogge which hath leather nayld about it; I showlde
be very glad (yf I might) to knowe the reason of it; For I will nowe
attempte somethinge upon the Per*petuus* Mot*us* on my owne strenghte
I showlde be glad to receiue the the [*sic*] booke I mentioned laste

---

⁵ Culpeper is probably referring to a now lost manuscript treatise on the perpetuum
mobile, penned by Comenius under the pseudonym of Johannes Nicomeus. At this time,
several figures amongst Hartlib's acquaintance were exploring the possibilities of perpetual
motion. In his correspondence with Hartlib, the German alchemist Johann Morian first
mentioned perpetual motion on 7 March 1639 (37/10). Although eventually critical of
Comenius's ideas on the subject (see Moriaen to Hartlib, 10 February 1642, 37/102), he
attempted to build a model based on Comemius's principles (3 July 1642, 37/110). As late
as 1657 he was still commenting on the Comenian treatise (30 November 1657, 42/2/26).
See HDC, p. 444. See also *Monatshefte der Comenius-Gesellschaft* (Berlin and Munster, 1892
etc.), v. 245; vi. 65; J. Kvačala, *Korrespondence Jana Amosa Komenského* (Prague, 1897), 245–
46; Jan Kúmpera, *Jan Amos Komenský* (Ostrava, 1992), pp. 219–29; also A. W. Ord-Hume,
Perpetual Motion: The History of an Obsession (1977).
⁶ Jacobus Acontius (Giacomo Aconcio) (1492–1520?) was an Italian diplomat, logician
and inventor who devised a well-known analytical method. Culpeper is referring either
to Acontius's *Iacobo Acontius Tridentini de Methodo. hoc est de recta investigandarum tradendarumque
scientiarum ratione* (Basel, 1558) or to his *Satanae Strategemata. Libri Octo* (Basel, 1565). On
Acontius, see Paulo Rossi, *Giacomo Aconzio* (Milan, 1952) and C. D. O'Malley, *Jacopo
Aconzio* (Rome, 1955).
⁷ Culpeper is here referring to the proposed inventions of the exiled John Christopher
De Bergh, Lord of Wahanzig in Moravia. Hartlib promoted a number of De Bergh's
designs, including a pump which is described in a Latin memorandum in 8/63/1A–2B
with the attached letter to obtain a patent for it (8/63/10A–11B). John Pym considered
employing it in 1639 to drain some flooded mines in which he had an interest. (65/17A–
B – undated memorandum but evidently in Pym's hand and related to his letter of 14
November 1639 to Hartlib (31/3/11A–12B)). Although Culpeper's prime interest in the
pump was evidently its congruence with the idea of perpetual motion, he was no doubt
also attracted to its possibilities for use on his own lands at Appledore on the Romney
marshes which were subject to periodic flooding.

weeke, & one of Mr [Comenius] Janua linguarum of the laste edition[8]
And thus with my beste wishes to you I reste

17 *Culpeper to Hartlib, 13 April [1642].   (13/6-7)*

Mr Hartlib;
        I pray let alone the bookes, because my selfe intend shortly to
be in London;
        The times are intruthe muche distracted, but I am sorry Mr
Commenius hathe & dothe finde soe little contente heere;[9]
        I understand not what you write concerninge Mr Dury yf the place
you mention be with the Lady Mary[10] beyond sea, his resolution then
(as I remember) is changed since I sawe you; yf heere in Englande, I
conceiue then (rebus sic stantibus) it will be noe right to him or his
wishes, all things nowe passinge by the parliamente; But Mr Dury
vnderstands himselfe; I pray presente my beste respectes vnto him; For
the man I haue formerly mentioned that hathe 18000.[l] to bestowe, hee
liues within 7: miles of London, but I may perhaps haue shortly an
occasion to speake with him, thowgh the grownde of a fowndation
which (I am confidente will not faile, is the parliamente, bribed by the
laste & leaste parte of correspondence; but this way muste haue its
owne time, & is not like to moue it selfe yf not relyed on or disserted[11]
        my mony will be ready by the firste I am ashamed to mention it soe
often; I rest

18 *Culpeper to Hartlib, 19 April [1642].   (13/332-3)*

Mr Hartlib;
        My intendance about the taxinge of the laste granted subsidies
hinders my presente resolution for [London] & the slowe cominge in of

---

[8] Culpeper is probably referring to the recent English edition of 1641 (Wing C5511).

[9] The imminent outbreak of civil war in 1642 led Comenius to doubt the possibilities
for universal reformation in England in the immediate future. After some debate, he
accepted an invitation to Sweden from the wealthy Dutch patron, Louis de Geer, and
left England in July 1642 - HDC, pp. 364-66.

[10] Princess Mary, the daughter of Charles I, was betrothed to William of Orange in
1641 and moved to take up residence in The Hague in the spring of 1642. Dury secured
a post as chaplain to her through the good offices of the Prince Elector Palatine, who
apparently interceded with King Charles on his behalf. Dury was appointed on 7 April
1642 and left for The Hague sometime in May - HDC, pp. 225-26.

[11] Culpeper believed that Parliamentary support was essential if the proposed plans for
the advancement of learning, particularly a reformed Chelsea College, were to succeed -
SHAL, p. 36.

monies from my tennants defers your receipte of that which you shall not fayle of nexte weeke;

I muste acknowledge that mr Dury hathe & is likely still to thinke more of what may conduce to those good endes to which he hathe deuoted himselfe then others perhaps doe; & vpon this grownde my ignorance muste subscribe; thowgh I am confidente yf he had continued heere,[12] hee cowlde better haue sollicited his owne busines; & (mr Commenius beinge gone) his occasions & desires wowlde haue beene (at leaste) as plentifully & (I hope) as freely supplyed as elsewhere; & I heartily wishe that in these jealous times, his acceptance of this (all circumstances of it considered) doe not elsewhere (more or lesse) prejudice firste his person & by it his good & juste ends; Hauinge sayde thus muche, my conclusion muste be in this as in all other actions; God knowes what is beste & will bringe that beste to passe in his beste time & way; & yf the thinge & time be beste this meanes will proue soe too

My kinde loue & respecte to Mr Dury & Mr [Commenius]; I reste euer

19   *Culpeper to Hartlib, 13 July [1642].   (13/336–7)*

Mr Hartlib;

I haue intended this longe time to bee in London; but my occasions heere, & little hope of successe in my desires there (by reason of the publique distractions) haue hetherto detained me; & in truthe the goinge away of those 2: good men[13] hathe & dothe yet muche weaken that springe & strenght of resolution that was in me, not but that (me thinkes) I see the same beauty in the woorke, but not the same possibility of the ende; & without possibility of that; all action & motion ceases; When I was in London, Mr [Commenius] was resolued to leaue vs, & then it was euen your opinion, that the presente contribution wowlde haue giuen an ingenuous & plenty full supporte to Mr Duries person, with some ouerplus for his negotiations; till it might please God to raise larger meanes of which I then did not dowbte; & of what aduantage a cowrse of suche tyes & continuall attendance cowlde be to him, I professe I vnderstande not (but perhaps it is my weakenes); I intende to be in London sometime within this fortnight; & shall be glad in the meane time to heare from you of Mr

---

[12] Dury had decided to take up the appointment at The Hague and arrived there by 30 May – HDC. p. 226.

[13] Comenius left England on 21 June and arrived in Amsterdam on 26 June – HDC, pp. 365–66.

Dury & Mr Commenius, for (in truthe) I loue & honore them & those excellente endes they propose to themselues, & (truly) shall valewe myselfe by nothinge more, then in that it may please God to giue me a harte & the honor of contributinge my myte towards them;

I haue heere inclosed sente you Mr Duries laste papers concerninge the generall methode of meditation, in the conclusion whereof you will finde 3: particulars promised by him;[14] which lasste parte yf you will transcribe & sende him from me; I shall be very happy (at his leasure) to receiue an answere to them; I remaine

[PS.] I pray returne the inclosed for I very muche valewe it

20   *Culpeper to Hartlib (with enclosures), n.d. [July–August 1642].   (13/327–31)*

Mr Hartlib;

I pray returne my kindeste respectes to Mr Dury, whoe (concerninge our Churche differences) bringes (I hope) an oliue branche with him, at leaste amonge suche as stande all heartily ingaged againste the common enimy; beinge vnited in one God, one Christe, one Faythe, one hope & differinge in suche thinges onely as (by Mr Duryes great & fundamentall rule of spirituall pacification) owght not (amonge suche as holde sufficient fundamentalls) to interrupte that vnity of the spirite which owght to be helde in the bond of peace; For my owne parte I can (concerninge the Ecclesiasticall differences on the [Parl*iament*] side) say with th' Apostle; All things are lawfull,[15] thowgh in all I still holde a better and a woorse, but I am as confidente all thinges are not expediente because (as in the nexte verse) thowgh lawfull they edifye not but by that Dominion ouer a weake brothers fayth which Saint Paule disclaimes they hazarde the destruction of him I acknowledge that (to preuente false pretence of conscience) there restes in euery assembly of Christian professors a duty of not soe muche as eatinge with one whoe (being called a brother) liues yet inordinately, & I conceiue the Ciuill swoorde ordained to cut of suche whoe (thowgh for conscience sake) shall robbe or murder theire neyghbor; This onely I wishe that (where the Ciuill peace is not broken, nor the spirituall peace (as in thinges not fundamentall) owght not to be broken) there

[14] John Dury, His discourse about his method of meditation' – see below, **Appendix, 197**. Although undated, the discourse was probably extracted from a letter to Culpeper and should be assigned to the middle of 1642. The discourse is listed by George Turnbull in his 'Writings by John Dury' – HDC, p. 309.
[15] 1 Corinthians 10:23 – 'All things are lawful for me, but all things are not expedient: all things are lawful for me, but all things edify not.'

may be a tender regard had to tender (thowgh weake & erroneous) consciences

Thowgh yet vnknowne I pray presente my seruice to Her[16] whose vertues as they haue gained suche an interest in Mr Dury soe muste they (by that intereste & His choyce) haue an influence on those that knowe & loue him.

I wowlde gladly knowe in what pointe the Parliament goes the pitche of my desires

Your 2. packets the laste friday related not to the laste weeke saue in the moderate [Intelligencer][17] & I assure you that (these dogge dayes) newes is a Commodity that will not keepe colde, Pray pardon my freedome

[Enclosures in scribal hand:][18]
An Extract of a Letter

Wold to God all men could bee perswaded to use that moderation which you expresse it is a Lamentable thing that were the Highest principles are of knowledge there is least practise even ther where selfe deny all is acknowledged to bee a duty theire is litle complyance in Charity: what I shall bee able to doe by way of entreaty and perswasion, I know not; but soe long as my time shall bee here I hope I shall not bee driven out of the way of moderation nor ever here after. I have not had yet time to deale with the heads of partyes therefor I can feele noe [judgm*ent*] of the [differen*ce MS edge*] nor have I seen the point of debate as it is in print but shortly I hope to sattisifie [my*self*] in this mater & then shall doe as the Lord shall direct mee and towards yourselfe shall bee at all times reddie to give a more particular account of all my proceedings and intentions that you may assured that I am and will remaine (in hearty praying to God for your happines) and in deed expressing it as time shall offer the occasion) att all tymes.

[following extract heavily edited by another, possibly Hartlib's, hand]
An Extract of a Letter.

I every day grow stronger for an Vniversall Liberty of Conscience <*alt:* nor> can I all together agree with Mr Dury that either in a particular congregation, or a synodycall Goverm*ent* of severall Ch*urch*es their need any eithbond[19] as not to [part] upon occasion<*alts:* ,> or such Cariage

---

[16] Elizabeth of Bohemia, who had appointed Dury chaplain to Princess Mary at the Hague in March 1642 – HDC, p. 225.

[17] *The Moderate Intelligencer* is not identified for this year in N&S.

[18] The following three extracts have every appearance of being copied out of Culpeper's letters by Hartlib for passing on to Dury. They were clearly attached to the preceeding letter amongst the papers and they are on the subject of the discussion referred to in it.

[19] corrected from 'eithbound' – i.e. 'gentle constraint' [?].

of [things] by Vote as should becom*me* a pressure upon ~~on~~ weake
Consciences wi*th* w*h*ich (though weake and Erroneous) we are taught
by the Scriptures to beare, & in Truth if it be sadly weighed, that the
dictates of the Conscience are not (like those of our Reason or will)
submittible at our owne pleasures, to an outward power beinge that
part of the inward man which God doth peculiiarly claime to himself
it might <*alt:* invite all Christians to> vindicate[*H alters from* invited]
one anothers Conscines from Errors by powerfull compullsion of Gods
word<*H:* ,> butt not by owtward punishments to Compell *th*em to *th*at
w*h*ich is not in their owne power, but must be (by our owne Confessions)
though a truth in it<*H:-*selfe> yett a sin*ne* [*H alters from* sine] in *th*em.
And though every mans particular zeale to his owne Fanci's hath
~~allmost~~ <*H:* swallowed ~~the~~> those 2 best of Christian Vertues and true
bagges of Christianity Charity and Humility, yett Naturall <*H:* Reason>
The rules of com*m*on Civility and *the* Lex Talionis[20] might fully teach
us to be *th*at <*H:* to> others w*h*ich we could wish others towards Vs.
The Table is turned & I dare boldly say *th*at there is not a sect now
among us. That if ~~the~~ *th*e*i*e may not tyranize over all the other ~~none~~
<*H:* nine> would not thinke *th*eir Truth (w*h*atsoe ever in it selfe) fit to
be tollerated, & how (but from an ~~outward~~ <*H:* insolent> over-valewing
our owne thoughts can any of us deny *th*at Preiviledge to others w*h*ich
we claime from others as Iust.

Another Extract of a Letter

I am sorry to see *th*at in matters of Conscience, you send mee to
Authority; my reason & will are myne owne though not to Consent
yett to be submitted by me to Authority; but *th*e Conscience is Gods
peculiar, w*h*ich to offend (though Erroneous) is a sinne, & if a sinne in
me to doe it I <*H:* can>not Conceave it (else in *th*em, *th*at by any kind
or degree of Persecution) tempt or force me. The Bishops upon a
Consciencious sight of Errors fore-sooke Romes Authority, wee now
Vpon the like grounds have outed[*altered from* routed] the Bishops,
ag*ain*st whom *th*e greattest Objection was *th*at w*h*ich wee now allow not
others to make & *th*at unpartiall, free unmuzled Tryall of truth w*h*ich
wee thought unjustly denyed Vs from the Bishops, we now as unjustly
and Bishop-like deny to others. Truth among those *th*at can understand
and aprehend it, hath a subduing power bejoyn'd *th*e whippe, & in
those *th*at understand, not *th*e whippe may perhaps breed a submission,
butt not possibly *th*at Consent, knowledge & Faith wi*th*out w*h*ich Actions
most conformable to Truth, are yet in Vs but sin. I reade in *th*e Scriptures
many[*altered from* may] excellent Rules of bearing not offending, not
Iudging, not putting a stumbling blocke in *th*e way of those for whome

---

[20] i.e. the law of retribution as applied in the Roman lawcodes.

(though perhaps weake and eroneous) christ dyed and I read Timotthy 2. 2. 24 [*H:* that wee should bee gentle][21] to teach patient in meknes instructing ever *the*m *tha*t oppose *the*m*selves* nay farther. I finde generally in *the* word of God *tha*t *the* followers of Truth must suffer persecution; but for their persecution of others or whipping of Men into *the* Truth, neithr Precept in Scripture nor ~~precept~~ <*H:* Exampel> any where else but att Rome) I pray pardon this digression in w*hi*ch I am (if erroneous) yett unpartiall in *wh*at concerns me, not being neither Brownist nor Anabapt*ist* but wishing a being amoung us, those, who joyne with us in one Christian and one Common Liberty.

21   *Culpeper to Hartlib, n.d. [1642?].   (13/355–6)*[22]

Mr Hartlib,

I haue spoken with th'elder Sr [He*nry*] Vane[23], and to Mr Pimme;[24] to eyther or bothe of which yf you goe in my name, you will finde them somewhat prepared in the busines; Mr Pimmes answere was that the party was an ecclesiastique & therefore by the late acte not soe fitte to be imployed in secular affaires, this he spake not as an objection with himselfe, but what perhaps others might make; my reply was that the negotiation of Ecclesiasticall peace wowlde (besides the introduction if made to politicke vnion) afforde such farther oportunity to the agente as showld bee thowght vsefull; In this manner I lefte it & by this you will knowe where to beginne & which way to driue your arguments; my feares still make me wishe that Mr Dury's presente cowrse wronge not his cause; They were my firste feares & (I confesse I cannot yet change them; I am too morrow for the Cowntry where I shall be glad to heare from you sometimes; & yf you sende me the Chorus on the times & all the [K*ings*] & parliaments declarations I shall be glad of them; I rest

---

[21] 2 Timothy 2:24 – 'And the servant of the Lord must not strive; but be gentle unto all men, apt to teach, patient'.

[22] The dating of this letter is based principally on the slender reference to Culpeper's doubts about Dury's 'presente cowrse', which is taken to mean his departure for The Hague, doubts already echoed in **18** (19 April [1642]).

[23] Sir Henry Vane (1594–1655) – DNB.

[24] John Pym (1584–1643) – DNB.

1643

Culpeper to Hartlib, 5 April [1643]. *(13/299–300)*

Mr Hartlib;

my occasions will keepe mee from London, yet this fortnight which time (I hope) will be the longeste; In the meane while I haue heere inclosed that letter of Mr Duries (as I conceiue) which you desired;[1] yf I haue missed I haue noe other of that kinde; my thowghts are not yet changed concerninge that good man, whome I still heartily wishe in England, bothe from my former knowledge & presente consideration of the place;[2] from the latter whereof (except Mr Dury cowlde serue subordinate endes) & temporall relations more then he proposes to himselfe) my opinion still is he will venture to leese[3] there where it concernes him to keepe beste holde, I meane the parliamente & his frinds in it whose consente to his being there may perhaps be for wante of a better present answere to his proposalls[4]

A correspondency amonge the Protestant Churches & states[5] were neuer more necessary & that Courte neuer more vnfit to be the seate & nurse to suche a busines;[6] It sauors too muche of the Potentates,[7] some one of whom may perhaps by fits haue a generall approbation of Mr Duries woorke, but after hauinge dwellt awhile vpon it; they cannot but see that right order in the Churche & an aduancemente of religion & knowledge (the likely effectes of this Correspondency), as they haue, soe they still will, caste out the Ecclesiasticall & at the same time shake the Ciuill-Babylon; For certeinly they whoe dare play the Bereans in

---

[1] Not identified.

[2] i.e. The Hague, where the court of Elizabeth of Bohemia then resided. Culpeper had visited the exiled Palatine court himself before the Civil War – see **Introduction**, p. 117.

[3] Loosen.

[4] With the Assembly summoned to Westminster in June to draw up a religious settlement, this was an apparently auspicious moment for Dury's presence – Batten, pp. 96–7.

[5] See Samuel Hartlib, *A Faithfull and Seasonable Advice, or, The Necessity of a Correspondencie for the Advancement of the Protestant Cause* (1643), Wing H986 Thomason, E.87 (14), given by Hartlib to George Thomason, 6 Feb. 1642[/3].

[6] It is unclear whether Culpeper refers to the court of Charles I or that of Elizabeth.

[7] A term redolent of arbitrary government, current among courtiers and churchmen at this time – see also *The Autobiography and Correspondence of Sir Symonds D'Ewes in the Reigns of James I and Charles I*, ed. J. O. Halliwell, 2 vols (1845), ii. 132.

the concernements of theire soules,[8] will not be longe fooled in the lesser, this made the Bishops soe muche for Sabboth recreations & the [King] nowe soe muche for [Bishops].[9] For thowgh it be not right noe [Bishop] noe [King] yet it may be possibly true noe [Bishop] noe suche kinde of [King];[10] For as the Ecclesiasticke & Ciuill Babylon haue growne soe will they fall together, but not by the Potentates whoe muste lamente her, but by the Peoples & nations, whoe will bury her in as muche darkenes as she hathe formerly kepte them; I pray in your nexte presente my beste affections to Mr Dury; whose answer to the laste parte of his letter concerning Methode I doe earnestly desire from him; I reste

23   *Culpeper to Hartlib, 9 April [1643].   (13/301–2)*

Mr Hartlib,

I pray lett me heare from you by this bearer what wee are to expecte concerninge the treaty whether it be off & the Committee returned or what continuance of it,[11] A copy of the Citty remonstrance or petition, & what proceedinge it hathe had;[12] Howe (as your laste intelligence sayes) the [King] yf joined with the [Queen] will be 30 or 40000[l] stronge,[13] when as the partes accordinge to former intelligence make not halfe the number & yf the [King] be soe stronge howe he will be opposed; What particulars the towne affordes of Sir [William] Waller & whether he be slaine or hurte as the newes goes heare;[14] & what other newes the towne affords; I longe for Mr Prinnes seconde

---

[8] Acts 17: 10–13.

[9] Conservative-minded bishops had supported the King's edict enforcing Sunday and holiday recreations, which was greeted with dismay by Puritan reformers – see David Underdown, *Revel, Riot and Rebellion* (Oxford, 1985), ch. 3.

[10] 'Noe Bishop noe King' – King James's outburst at the Hampton Court Conference. The power of bishops, and the appropriate relationship of temporal and spiritual authority, were currently subjects of intense debate. A Bill for the abolition of Episcopacy had been accepted by Parliament in January 1642 – Gardiner, i. 84.

[11] Articles of cessation had been presented to the King on 1 March 1643, to which he replied on 6 March – Gardiner, i. 95–6.

[12] The petition from the Common Council of the City of London on 11 March 1643 for the formation of an association of the kind originally proposed by Pym in October 1642 – Gardiner, i. 39, 99.

[13] The Queen returned to England from the Low Countries towards the middle of February and set up headquarters at York – Clarendon, ii. 467–68.

[14] Sir William Waller (1597?-1668), Parliamentary General and a supporter of Hartlib, Dury and Comenius. At this time he was conducting a successful campaign in Wales and the Marches – DNB; HDC.

booke;[15] & the [King's] negatiue in parliamente wowlde be more
sowndly handled, for Quis sit Iudex[16] is the vniversall question bothe
in Eccesiasticall & Ciuill gouernemente I reste In haste

24 *Culpeper to Hartlib, n.d. [late May-9 June 1643].* *(13/309–10)*

Mr Hartlib;
        There are many persons in this Cownty whoe wowlde nowe
willingly make a voluntary contribution to the Parliamente & pay all
presente & future assessementes[17] but can by noe meanes be browght
to take the oathe or Couenante which is allready passed the Parliamente
men[18] & will (as is generally conceiued) come into the Cowntry; This
bearer is sente on purpose to London that by your kindenes I may be
able to giue them some certaine answere whereon they may rely
whether all refusers though contrib*utors* be [delinq*uents*];[19] I pray be
very inquisitiue concerninge it that I may giue eyther noe answere or
suche as may not faile; for I wowlde not willingly misse where I am
soe muche relied on I conceiue that any Parliament man will be able
to resolue you but (yf you cannot otherwise satisfy your selfe I pray
(rather then faile) resorte to Mr Pimme; my [Lord] of Essex late aduance
muste needes (by this time haue made some newes I pray afford in a
line or two:[20] by this bearer, or what else the towne affoords; That
which rayses this question in these that are ready to contribute is that
eyther in a late ordinance of directions to the Deputy Lieutenants in
generall, or in a particular one to those of Kente there is a line towards
the latter ende which (relatinge to this oathe or Couenante) seemes to
put them, into the Condition of delinquency that shall refuse to take
it; I pray once a againe doe your beste to giue me a true light in the
busines & dispatche the bearer by the tyde on tuesday morninge:

Sunday
night

[15] The prolific pamphleteer William Prynne (1600–1669). Culpeper was anticipating his
important constitutional work, commissioned by Parliament in defence of its soveraignty,
The Fourth Part of the Soveraigne Power of Parliaments (1643), Wing P3962. See DNB and
William Lamont, *Marginal Prynne* (1963), ch. 5.
        [16] 'Who should be the judge'.
        [17] Parliament passed ordinances for weekly assessments 24 February 1643 and 7 May
1643 – F&R, i. 85–100, 145–55.
        [18] The Solemn League and Covenant was passed by Parliament on 9 June 1643 – F&
R, i. 175–76.
        [19] According to the ordinances of 4 March and 3 May 1643 those who refused to pay
contributions were branded delinquents – F&R, i. 100, 139–41.
        [20] Robert Devereux, third Earl of Essex (1591–1646), had taken Reading on 27 April
and was marching on the King's stronghold of Oxford by 10 June – DNB; Gardiner, i.
129, 150.

25   *Culpeper to Hartlib, 13 June [1643].   (13/303–4 [summary only])*

Culpeper has arranged for the purchase and transport of small-arms through Hartlib from Mr Newton in Bishopsgate Street.

26   *Culpeper to Hartlib, 16 June [1643].   (13/307–8)*

Mr Hartlib,
        Euery day is like to bringe foorthe some greate change which makes me desirous to heare from you on munday, vpon which day I will not faile to sende to the Swanne in Grauesende & will appointe the messenger to pay 6:ᵈ to the Waterman that bringes any thinge from you; which you may superscribe vpon the letter that it may passe the safer
        I pray doe me the kindenes that this letter may be deliuered & an answere to it sente to your house & by you returned on Munday nexte
        I haue seene the ordinance for the assembly of divines and am sorry not to finde Mr Dury his name amonge them;²¹ For to the Couenante lately made for the vnitinge of ourselues & to another which I hope shortly to see for the stronger vnion of the 2: [Kingd*oms*] in theire [Com*mon*] intereste of Religion & liberty; a Confession of Faythe wowlde be necessary to beget a better vnion & correspondency between all the reformed Churches & States, against the Ciuill & Eclesiasticall Babylon which God will certeinly bringe to judgemente; And besides the good seruice which (I conceiue) mr Dury might doe at this assembly, it wowlde be a good occasion taken to retire himselfe from that barren imployment;²² & Mr [Pym*me*] (yf but moued) cowlde not be wantinge to it; I wishe you heartily well & reste

27   *Culpeper to Hartlib, 21 June [1643].   (13/305–6)*

Mr Hartlib;
        I haue disposed the 10:ˡ (which the armorer showld haue had) another way; therefore synce he was soe strayght laced he shall nowe stay a while;

---

²¹ The Westminster Assembly, created by a Commons resolution of 12 June 1643 to settle questions of church government and liturgy. Dury was not initially a delegate to the Assembly. See Batten, pp. 97–8; and HDC, p. 237.
²² Dury remained chaplain to the princess Mary at The Hague until May 1644 – HDC, pp. 236–40.

Yf it be possible get Mr Dury into the assembly;[23] & yf you see Mr [Pim*me*] presente my seruice to him & assure him from me the Couenante wowld passe currante yf it were put on euen in these partes, some fewe onely may demurre a while vpon it, but my opinion is, it showlde beginne in the more well affected shires; & a Couenante personall between the 2: nations will ere longe be as necessary; that soe the well affected in bothe nations beinge vnited by Couenant firste with themselues & then with one another; our strenght & our enimies may be fully knowen; I rest in haste

28   *Culpeper to Hartlib, 14 August [1643].   (13/338–9)*[24]

Mr Hartlib;

I heere returne you the papers mentioned in your laste by the poste; Mr Duries conclusion in his discowrse with Dr Riuet,[25] that the [publi*que*] consente of Diuines, showlde (as of necessity) be confirmed by parliament (yf Mr Dury intende soe) I can noe way consente to; whome my religion; reason; & the municipall lawes of my Cowntry haue tawght that noe ty whether diuine or humane can be imposed eyther vpon any one man or any one nation which is Vnum Collectiuum without his or theire consente or approbation & that voluntary & free, for I cannot but allowe a nation that liberty which our Churche allowes to euery priuate man; firste to searche & heare, but then to choose for it selfe; But perhaps I mistake Mr Dury; yf I doe not I dare say he will finde himselfe mistaken; I pray in your nexte commende me very kindely to that good man & once againe put him in minde from me of his promise, for I showlde be glad to receiue somethinge in that kinde from him, beinge that which I haue soe muche hunted for in others but laste & cheefly in him

I showlde be glad to heare from you oftener then once a weeke; & yf you send by the tyde on munday night or be times on tuesday morninge to the Horne in Grauesende I will not fayle to sende one euery tuesday for them & hope ere longe to be out of your debte for all disbursementes; I reste in haste

[23] Dury was appointed to the Westminster Assembly by a Commons resolution of 28 June 1643 – Batten, pp. 97–8.

[24] The dating of this letter is reasonably secure. The 13 August was a Sunday in 1643.

[25] Dury refers to his discourse with André Rivet and responds explicitly to Culpeper's criticism in an undated letter to Hartlib (2/9/17A-18B) which Turnbull dates to early September 1642 but which must be a year later – HDC, p. 231.

[*another hand*:]
This letter should haue beene sent on sunday the 13:th but fayled by
accidente

29   *Culpeper to Hartlib, n.d. [Autumn 1643?].   (13/319–20 [summary only])*

*Culpeper has received the money which Hartlib has sent him and is most grateful.
He is 'muche trowbled' by his personal affairs and can offer no further comment on
the Perpetual Motion. He is more optimistic of the recent direction of public events.
He would like to see the king's cavalry shadowed by a force of Parliamentarian
cavalry which should be raised quickly and despatched to the north. The king will
not be able to confront this force but will have to hinder it by way of a diversion
and then withdraw towards the west and Wales. '& truly methinkes I looke vpon
the [King] as vpon a enemy vanquished towards eueninge, whoe yf not vigorously
pursewed is like to shelter himselfe in the night of the yeere'. Meanwhile the
Parliamentarian advantage should be put to good purpose and the harvest used to
fill all its garrisons. He has been formerly criticised by 'some of the other side' for
advocating the ploughing up of cornfields to deny Royalists the advantage of the
harvest. He now proposes merely that the harvest be 'layed in at right places & that
the malignants may haue the publicke faythe for their corne & the [Parlia*ment]
the use of it'.

30   *Culpeper to Hartlib, 4 October 1643.   (13/10–11)*

Mr Hartlib,
       Cowlde I haue fownde a fittinge messenger, I had sente on
Munday to London, for some suche grownds as might stop the currante
of ill newes in these parts concerning the laste fight & especially
concerning Sir [W*illiam*] Waller whoe is reported here to be beaten;[26]
Vpon the whole matter of what I heare from you and else where, I
cannot but feare that God will not honor soe muche malice & falsenes
as is amonge vs, with victory, & besides I cannot see in the grownds of
reason, how the wayes yet taken can ende this dispute with the [K*ing's*]
Caualry, which can choose when and where to fight, & will (by toppinge
the [Parl*iaments*] horse) be able at all times to distresse the whole army
in victuall; which thowgh able to giue battle yet by the slownes of the
Infantery can neyther hinder the spoylinge of the Cowntry, nor once
distresse the enimy but when (as the other day) [hims*elf*] choses to fight;
You mentioned within this fortnight the generality of a probable way

---

[26] A reference to the loss of Reading to the Royalists on 3 October 1643 – Gardiner,
i, 238.

of treaty (heeretofore layde aside but lately againe by the Skots Commissioners taken vp) which might giue an end to these vnhappy differences;[27] I wowld be very glad to see a platforme of it or (at leaste) to knowe the generall grownds of what all good men soe heartily wishe

You mentioned allsoe an arms made vpon snowe hill of sinewes and silke; I pray inquire the price of a backe & brest; & what it may be affoorded for by the foote square

But that which I moste especially wishe for, & in which Mr Lee[28] on Ludgate hill can directe you were a full information concerning the leatherne ordnance,[29] & (yf it might be, & that the price were not ouer greate) that I might haue one of them for my mony; I haue tried wooden gunnes & finde it will doe, but not without too muche yron and consequently wayght; & I cannot but conceiue that the materialls that binde the brasse Cilinder in leather gunnes beinge applied to woode, the laste wowlde be as stronge and soe muche better as it will not heate thowgh often shot in; Yf (by your helpe) I cowlde in this receiue some light, I wowld immediately perfecte an engine that may perhaps fit our presente warres; my paper-s done; I rest

31   *Culpeper to Hartlib (with enclosure), 22 November 1643.   (13/12–14)*

Mr Hartlib;

I lefte the towne vnsettled in the certeinty of Sir [W*illiam*] Wallers condition[30] or the Scottes beinge come in, I pray together which your wonted kinde intelligence let let me receiue what the towne affords of these 2: particulars;

Mr Felton[31] pretended not to be ready & my occasions called me away; Yf he haue that which is truly vsefull, & can get it otherwise

---

[27] The treaty was signed by the Commissioners at Edinburgh on 29 November, but not ratified till 3 January 1643/4 – CSPD 1641–43, pp. 502; 505; LJ, vi. 364–6.

[28] Captain Lee, 'a hatter vpon Ludgate hill' (**62**, 5 January 1645).

[29] Light leather guns had been used successfully by the Swedish army in the Thirty Year War, and the idea was imported to Britain by gunners who had served with the Swedes. A version was patented by the Scottish gunner James Wemyss (1610?-1667), who set out with his guns from London to join Waller on 3 October. The guns had little effect and were shortly captured. See DNB; P. Young and R. Holmes, *The English Civil War* (1974), pp. 161, 187; C.H. Firth, *Cromwell's Army* (1962), pp. 147–48, 156; *The True Informer* 28 Oct. – 4 Nov. (1643), N&S 629.07, Thomason, E.74. (21).

[30] Waller, having tried and failed to take Basing House, was troubled by massive desertions and by an increasing powerful royalist force – see Young and Holmes, pp. 159–72.

[31] Timothy Raylor, 'Providence and Technology in the English Civil War: Edmond Felton and his Engine', *Renaissance Studies*, 7 (1993), 338–414; also 'New Light on Milton and Hartlib', *Milton Quarterly*, 27 (1993), 19–29.

recommended I shall haue my end that haue noe other ambition eyther in any vsefull invention or the recommendation of it then that it may not be buried in a napkin

Th' inclosed paper is out of Baptista Porta;[32] Yf Mr Feltons invention be grownded vpon the same or like grownds;[33] he shall haue his desires to be the firste practiser of it yf otherwise & that it shall be thowght vsefull, let him vse it thowgh discouered by me but my selfe in this last case will not be restrained from vsing my owne yf I thinke good;

[*enclosure:*]

Poterimus fumo oculos occæcare quod in ciuitatum insultibus et congressibus hostium valde proficere potest; Sed primo considerandus est ventus vt terga nostrorum feriat et in vultibus inimicorum fumum deferat; Conficiantur modioli sicut laternæ, capacitatis qua in os tormenti ænei [subintre*n*t], repleantur puluere euforbij, piperis, calcis viuæ, cineris sarmentorum, et arsenici sublimati; et in cauum tormenti ænei immittantur post pyrium puluerem; vi pulueris rumpentur modiolj papyracei prædicti et fumus pulueris si oculos hostium tetigerit, adæo infestabit vt abjectis armis vix saluti oculorum consulere possint.[34]

The thinge may be muche improued & (yf imployed in the way & nature of morter granadoes against soe small a circuit as Basinge house) wowlde (noe quæstion) haue smoked them out the fume; (yf not allready) may with a small addition be made deadly to the braines

32 *Culpeper to Hartlib, 29 November 1643. (13/15–16 [summary only])*

Culpeper is sorry to have missed last week's letter and blames the carrier. He longs to know whether the Scots will come in for this will release troops in the North to assist Sir William Waller in Hampshire. Kent is for the Parliament but the troops are not hardened nor the county prepared to bear the proportions of assessment to

---

[32] Giovanni Battista della Porta, *Magia naturalis libri viginti*, (Naples, 1589; Frankfurt, 1597), p. 484.

[33] Felton's invention was a mobile structure designed to protect infantry during artillery bombardment.

[34] '*Blind your eyes with the smoke*. This may much profit, when enemies come to storm a City. But first we must consider the wind, that it may be on the backs of our men, and may carry the smoke into the faces of our enemies. Let there be measures made like lanthorns, so wide that they with Power of Euphorbium, Pepper, quick Lime, Vine-Ashes, and Arsnick sublimate; and put them into the hollow of it, after the Gunpowder for by the force of the fire, will these paper-frames break; and the smoke of the Powder, if it come at the eyes of the enemies, will so trouble them, that casting away their weapons, they can hardly save their eyes.' (Translation from *Natural Magick by John Baptista Porta* (1658), Wing P2982, p. 302).

sustain them. He leaves Hartlib to vent these thoughts where they might do some good.

33   *Culpeper to Hartlib, 3 December 1643.   (13/17–18 [summary only])*

Culpeper wants news of the Scots. He is sorry that Felton's engine is not much advanced and fears that he hugs it to himself. Culpeper's word should be sufficient for him.

34   *Culpeper to Hartlib, 5 December [1643].   (13/19–20)*

Mr Hartlyb

I thanke you for your late newes, I pray afforde me some by this bearer, especially what you haue from Hollande, (where I heare the Prince of Aurange is (for his life) fled to Breda)[35] & what certeine intentions there are on the Parliaments side of a league with the States & howe likely to be entertained on the States, & particularly (I pray) in what manner & forwardnes the Scots beginne to appere in this busines, & howe true that is of one gone from them to the [K*ing*]; For yf these things be true, the change of Cowncells in France (vpon the Cardinalls deathe)[36] will (by the Spanishe party there) soe indeauor to vnite the Catholiques all ouer Christendome, as will not onely necessitate but hasten these beginninge of vnion amonge the Protestants & then the vniversal question will be between Protestancy and liberty on the one side & Popery & tiranny on the other; for certeinly Babylon or confusion muste fall as well in Ciuill as Ecclesiasticall gouermente when in bothe (by a dayly greater shining forthe of truthe into the harte of all nations) Reuel: 19: c: 17: & 18: v: shall be fulfilld[37]

35   *Culpeper to Hartlib, 5 December 1643.   (13/21 [summary only])*

Culpeper wants weekly news by the Monday tide until the Scots come in. The Kentish soldiery needs to be hardened to service and there is no apparent reason why some of the Essex cavalry cannot be spared for Sir William Waller's army.

---

[35] William II of Nassau. For the background to his disputes with the estates of Holland see P. Geyl, *Orange and Stuart* (1969), ch. 1.

[36] Cardinal Richelieu had died on 4 December 1642 [N⁵].

[37] Revelation 19: 17–18: 'And I saw an angel standing in the sun; and he cried with a loud voice, saying to all the fowls that fly in the midst of heaven, Come and gather yourselves together unto the supper of the great God'.

36   *Culpeper to Hartlib, 20 December 1643.   (13/22–3)*

Mr Hartlib

I muche feare the pressures that will befall the [Parliam*ent*] by
this longe delay of the Scottes; but suche certeinly were theire intentions
whoe haue all this while retarded theire cominge;[38] Yf they were once
come in; especially yf in the way lately [me*n*tioned] (i) 13000: to
NewCastle 4000: to Hull & the other 4000 to Sir [W*illiam*] Brereton;[39]
my [L*ord*] of Manchester might very well be spared to fall backe
sowthewarde, for the defence of those Cownties for and out of which
his army is raysed & maintained; & yf there were a stronger recreut of
strenght sent down to Glocester [Col*onel*] Massy[40] (as it appeares to me)
wowlde necessitate Hoptons returne into the Weste, & a little, timely
thus implied wowlde goe a greate way;

For this Cownty, It is true wee are nowe farre in better case of
defence then 5: monthes since, But yet our traine bandes are not right,
nor shall wee bee in right posture till the 4: Cownties haue a standinge
auxiliary army of 4000: musketiers & 1000 horse, the musketiers to
carie sixe foote firre trunchions spiked at bothe ends in steade of restes[41]

Thus might 2000 pikemen (beinge the nowe ordinary proportion
allowed to 4000: musketiers) be spared, together with theire officers &
yf these 4000: reduced into 20: Companies & vnder 2: Colonells onely,
were leade on by a Generall, like Lesley[42] in the Scots firste expedition,
not too wise nor greate to be cowncelled, our affaires wowld goe better
on then they haue lately done, & yet (by the abatemente of a 3:ᵈ parte
of the common sowldier & 2/5 partes of the officers) wowlde coste little
more then halfe the charge; especially yf the officers were onely to
joine with a Clarke in euery Regimente in an attestation of the number
of their soldiers but another (vpon it) to pay them Then will the
[Capt*ain*] be as eager for a continuall recreut of their Companies as

---

[38] The Scots did not enter England until January 1644 – Gardiner, i. p. 294.

[39] Sir William Brereton (1604–1661) was a parliamentary commander operating successfully in Cheshire and the Midlands – DNB; cf John Morrill, 'Sir William Brereton
and England's Wars of Religion', *Journal of British Studies*, 24 (1985), 311–32.

[40] Colonel Edward Massey (1619?–1674?), governor of Gloucester, successfully withstood
a royalist siege there in the summer of 1643, during which a version of Felton's engine
of war was employed by the attackers – DNB.

[41] Current military practice dictated that an infantry company should comprise two-
thirds musketeers and, for their defence, one-third pikemen; Young and Holmes, p. 46.
Culpeper's suggestion that musketeers should carry their own version of a pike addresses
the problem of how to defend musketeers cheaply. This was the difficulty which underlay
both Culpeper's interest in light armour and Felton's engine: it was not resolved until
the invention of the bayonet towards the end of the century; Firth, pp. 91–2.

[42] Alexander Leslie, Earl of Leven (1580?–1661), commander of the Scottish forces in
the First Bishops' War – DNB.

they are nowe (for theyr owne priuate gaines) dangerously carelesse & yf [Colonel] Wemmes,[43] Mr Felton, or my selfe, haue or can happen vpon a lyght & usefull brestwoorke,[44] I cannot conceiue but this army (thowgh not greate) may eyther ly vpon the frontiers of the fowre Cownties or (yf occasion require) issue into the weste & be able to passe or stande throwgh or againste all the strengh of the [King's] Caualry; To this ende, I haue lately made a newe tryall of wooden ordinance, & nowe my bindinge holdes but the bricke[45] flyes out which happens (as I conceiue) by the ruggednes of the inside beinge not trily bored; A brasse Cilinder was Mr Feltons invention & therefore not to be vsed without his leaue which yf he affoorde, I wowlde withall knowe howe it may be fastened, for I am alltogether to seeke; To returne to this Cownty; 10ˡ per Cent: vpon the lands of this Cowntie will rayse 52000ˡ per [annum] which [summe] (raysed without pinchinge the landelorde) wowlde plentifully discharge our proportionable rate of 4000: foote & 1000 horse, & this army once ~~an~~ on the winge, the trained bands might retire many of them to the plowgh handle & all to the Cownties peace, & yet ready (yf necessity heereafter require) for the service they nowe doe, & all this (yf my aerithmaticke faile me not) with lesse charge to the Cownty, consideringe the dowble pay the trained bands man (whether hired or seruinge for himselfe) spends to what wowld serue the Common sowldier And what I haue nowe written concerninge my owne Cownty will in euery particular be (I conceiue) very fitly applyed to the London meridiane where (I am sure) the merchante will second me, in the wayes of paiment whoe (where they can auoyde it) admitte not the same seruante to bwy & pay; I rest

[added in a different hand:]
Wee shall goe away at 6 of the clok at [night]

37 *Culpeper to Hartlib, 20 December 1643. (13/24 [summary only])*

A one sentence letter requesting Hartlib to search for and send any ordinances concerning the sequestration of college lands.

---

[43] James Wemyss (1610?-1667), master gunner of England and general of the artillery in Scotland – see above, p. 179, note 29.

[44] A small defensive fieldwork.

[45] 'Breech' – i.e. the tail end of the cannon – OED.

38   *Culpeper to Hartlib (with enclosure), 27 December 1643.   (13/25–7)*

Mr Harblib;
        Englande before Scotlande – thowgh vnder the Scottishe seale, seemes to me noe woonder or objection againste the truthe of a Commission issued by Porter an Englishman,[46] whoe eyther in a customary wante of heede, or perhaps wittingly in a loue & regarde to his owne nation might soe displace them
        And nowe me thinkes I see a sufficiente abundance of matter to giue a liuely representation of our [King] to posterity; And yf the moste pertinent matters of Lawe, reason, & of Facte (which ly dispersed eyther in the declarations of bothe sides or in the pamphlets of the standers by) were by way of Quæres concentrated into the narrowe roome of a printed sheete of paper, it wowlde become a yet more irresistible lyght & might perhaps woorke on suche on the other side whose religious and reasonable consciences are not seared;[47] I know my selfe insufficient for it but yf some more able pen doe not happen vpon it, my desires to have it done may perhaps inforce my owne weakenes to vndertake it –
        (*I vnderstande not the clause of vnlordinge the* [Parliamentary] *Lords yf the knowne lawes wowld permitte, I pray inlarge vpon it*)
        I finde that moste of those whoe from theire education in a kinde of Ciuill Popery apprehende a greate fawlte & danger to resiste the [King] as they calle it, apprehende neyther in not assistinge him, & wowlde I am confidente many of them not onely be contente by way of satisfaction to the [Parliament] but desirous (for the more colorable injoyinge their ease & quiet & sparinge their purse) soe to ingage themselues by some oathe as may binde them to what their owne dispositions leade them to; I haue heere inclosed suche a forme as beinge taken wowlde secure the takers from beinge tempted, & beinge refused wowlde discouer suche whoe wowlde, yf oportunity serued be active againste the [Parliament] & giue a full & an vnanswerable reason to secure them; I wowld not haue suche a couenante tendred till the 2: former had distingwished & ingaged the actiue; & whether then it wowlde be seasonable I make it not a Proposition but suche a question concerninge which (when you haue aduised with others), I showlde be glad to haue your opinion, as allsoe whether when the Scotts are come in), a golden bridge by way of pardon wowlde not be seasonable from the [Parliament] to suche [Gentlemen] whoe without any invitations ab externo, were

[46] Perhaps a reference to Endymion Porter (1587–1649) – DNB.
[47] Culpeper here advocates the compilation of an epitome, similar to those promoted by Dury to promote ecclesiastical agreement as a means of resolving political disputes.

vnawares ingaged at Yorke before the Principall Parties to & in this
busines shewed themselues & when they were in seuerall kindes
proclaimed againste, suche a pardon wowlde extricate them that were
thus cowght & leaue the reste in theire more true colors when these
were extracted, whoe in all the discowrse I meete with are the beste
argumente that side hathe; I had more to say but not time

[*enclosure:*]
That neyther myselfe nor any other by my procuremente or incowragemente or with my priuity or consente shall eyther in person,
mony, cowncell, intelligence or any other way be assistinge to any
forces or cowncells raysed & taken againste or without the consente
and authority of bothe houses of Parliament[48]

39 *Culpeper to Hartlib, n.d. [1643]. 13/312–3*

Mr Hartlib;
        I see your kindenes esteemes more of my thowghts then they
can deserue; But I am of this opinion that yf 2: or 3: honeste men
(hauinge (vpon any subjecte what soeuer) firste communicated the helpe
of theire collections & thowghts to one another) wowld afterwards make
(eache of them) a seconde essay there might be from these seconde
thowghts a short & yet plaine & full resulte be drawne; Thus by the
waye of Quæres might a convincinge extracte of matters of reason
Lawe & Facte be made vpon these times out of the Pamphlets bothe
sides (I praye sende me another Bookers allmanacke)
        Thus might a Committee of Merchants & suche other rationall
assistants as might be joyned to them presente suche a resulte of
theire firste & seconde thowghts as wowlde leaue the treasure of the
[K*ing*dome] lesse subjecte to oppression in the Collection or [frawde
<*H: fraude*>] in the issuinge of it, bothe which I finde too muche taken
vp to the [Parl*iament's*] preiudice; In a woorde thus might excellente
results be made not onely concerning the treasure & militia & other
(as I may call them) subordinate businesses but euen concerning the
very wayes of Cowncell & that euen in the heade itselfe of which the
perfidious disswetude of [Parliam*ent*] hathe not onely hindred that
aduance in which the modernes ages haue giuen to all other artes &
sciences & to this allsoe in some other free Cowntries, but hathe allsoe
obliterated the beawty of that firste Coalition (excellente for these times)
which owr ancestors made & wee muste nowe restore, which in a

---

[48] This proposed oath is similar to that eventually adopted for use against delinquents
in 1644.

woorde is but this, that (all Ius diuinum or immutability being seuered from humane ordinances & reappropriated to the diuine) the peoples of this age & all future (by the same kinde of representatiue body (call it [Parliament] or whate else you will) by which our ancestors firste made the Gouernment) may (accordinge to the Common lawe & 2 statutes make an annuall Visitation howe bothe the supreme & inferior magistrates performe their duties This beinge done; Babylon were fallen. But howe will then the [Kings] of the earthe etcæt stande afarre of & cry Alas, Alas, that great Citty when Popery & illegall Prærogatiue, Tiranny Ciuill & Eclesiasticall shall fall

Yf the Scots be come; An humble petition from bothe nations; & a pardon from the Parliamen (with exemption of Popery, Prelacy, & the Spanishe faction) wowlde be seasonable & wowlde perhaps shake the allready distracted cowncells at Oxforde & howe soeuer proue an vnanswerable future witnes against them, & the Spanish faction wowlde be a proper & sufficient subject for the [Parliament] to take liuery & sesin of theire priuiledges

40 *Culpeper to Hartlib (with enclosure), n.d. [1643–44]. (13/314–16)*

Mr Hartlib;

I am scarce out of one trowble but I am fallen into another before, I was trowbled with the lettinge a greate parte of my estate, nowe all is questioned; About 3: yeeres synce, (beinge deade in the opinion of all about me) I did (vpon my Father's desire) put my whole estate into his hands vpon his promise to resettle it yf I recouered; which when contrary to all expectation did come to passe by Gods mercy to me, my Father (onely because I adhered to the [Parliament]) did (contrary to his owne promise & my filiall confidence) resolue to keepe my estate thowgh formerly settled vpon marriage & 3000¹. portion with my Wife & was soe longe ere he cowld be browght to any kinde of resettlement & as what he did was within the time of delinquency; And to this may be added that the vnanswerable consideration of marriage was (by my [Father's] peremptory appointemente) lefte out of the deedes & another put in which in a legall way might somewhat accuse thence of frawdulency; & this I was forced to take & be glad I cowlde get it; I hope by the equity of my cause & my faythe & constancy to my Cowntry I shall not finally suffer, thowgh I feare it will coste me muche trowble

By the Couenant nowe to be taken wee are to indeauor the extirpation of Popery & Prelacy, whereof the laste hathe a being by & in the Lawe, thowgh theire power gone, the firste vpon certeine conditions tolerated thowgh not allowed publi*que* exercise thus haue bothe a being by & in the lawe to which all priuate persons what soeuer by the Lawes of God & man muste yelde actiue or passiue obedience; The woorde indeauor is by the Assembly interpreted Lawfull indeauors nowe yf I cowld be assured that that were the mind of the 2: howses & that I might take it with that interpretation I cowlde not onely in obedience but with cheerefullnes take it for yf they depended on my castinge voyce in [Parl*iament*] there showld not be such a thinge as eyther of them in Englande; but as a priuate man my whole duty (I conceiue) is eyther to doe or suffer by the lawe not to resiste or assiste againste it, or to indeauor the destruction of any parte of the Lawe but by Lawe & Lawfull meanes & indeauors, I pray informe your selfe & helpe me yf you can; for I am willinge to be satisfied; & (yf I cannot) must suffer

[enclosure in scribal hand:]
By [*the*] Couenant We are to Endeauour [*the*] Extirpation of Popery & Prelacy. The first of which hath no being in [*the*] Law, because all Publike Exercise is forbidden, & not any priuate tollerated, & all Papists euen as Papists (being Convicted Recusants) are vnder diuers penaltyes, which are Intended by [*the*] Law to be meanes of Extirpation of Popery: though hitherto there are no Lawes of Extremity against [*the*m]. The latter indeed (though their coerciue power be gone) hath yet a being in [*the*] Law, vntill it be by Law remoued. [*4 lines deleted*] But for all that We may Lawfully Endeuour to Extirpate both [*the*] One & [*the*] Other. That is in such Lawfull wayes as become each mans place & calling; for .3. reasons. 1. because Popery is vndoubtedly, & Prelacy (sc: such as ours is) may be proued contrary to [*the*] word of GOD. 2. bec*ause* both [*the*] One & [*the*] Other (though in a diuerse degree,) haue beene experimentally found to be preiudiciall, not only to [*the*] true Religion & Power of Godlinesse; but also to [*the*] Peace & Tranquillity of [*the*] State & Com*m*onwealth. 3. because it is part of [*the*] birthright of euery free=Subiect of England, to endeuour (in Parliament time) by Petitions & all Other Sober & orderly wayes, [*the*] Alteration of any Law or Lawes which he conceiues preiudiciall to [*the*] publike good, & so fitte to be altered. He [*then, that*] would not Suffer any such thing as either Popery or Prelacy in England, if they depended on his casting Voice in Parliament, is certainly conuinced of so much Preiudiciall Euill in either of [*the*m, *that*] I am verily perswaded, he not only may but ought to Endeuour (as a foresayd) their Extirpation, & accordingly with Cheerefullnesse to take [*the*] Couenant in [*that*] Respect; And needs dreame of no Other Suffering or Resistance, but with reference to [*the*] Party now in Armes against [*the*] Parliament,

Who endeuour to make euery man Suffer as a Slaue [that] will not Act
with [them]; & against whom there is no Other Helpe vnder heauen
but Resistance since they will yeeld no Obedience at all to Lawes or
Lawmakers, but according to their owne Lawes.

1644

Mr Hartlib;

I haue receiued your letter of 10:ᵇᵉʳ 28:ᵗʰ; Of the dispersed matters of lawe and facte which I wowlde (from the seuerall late pamphlets wherein they ly dispersed) contracte in to a small roome I will nowe giue you a taste;

To beginne with lawe; 1: Whether the lawe be not the onely rule as well to the [King's Prerogative] as to the [subject's] liberty; 2: Whether the Iudiciall judgemente of the legally constituted Cowrts be not the onely bindinge rule to which all parties are to submitte for theire knowledge of or their obedience to the lawe 3: Whether a Iudiciall declaration of lawe in any inferior Cowrte of Iustice (thowgh perhaps erroneous, as in the case of Ship mony)¹ be not (by all parties that acknowledge themselues subiecte to the Lawe) to be submitted to till legally reuersed by judgement of the same or some superior legally constituted Cowrte; 4: Whether this greate truste & power of dispensinge lawe & justice be reposed in the Iudges as eyther infallible or incorruptible & not rather grownded (as in all Voluntary arbitrements) vpon these 2: principles 1: Generall consente 2: Vt sit Finis litium;² 5: Whether the judgement of any priuate man or inferior Cowrte concerninge the knowne Lawes be admittible againste the judiciall judge of a superior or the Supreme Cowrte; 6: Whether the [King's] beste and onely true and bindinge title to the Crowne & the legall appurtenances belonginge to it be not the Lawe; 7: Whether the histories & practise of the former and presente ages doe make it purely impossible for the [King's] to assume more then theire dues 8: Whether a good and consciencious subiecte or the whole subject maye not (without breache of the lawes of God or of that allegiance which (by and according to the lawes of the lande onely) they owe to the [King]) bringe any case of dowbte or difficulty (concerninge theire owne right or Cæsars due) to the Cowrts of Iustice 9: Whether the [King] in recipienda justicia (from the Cowrts

---

¹ In one of the crucial legal disputes of the period, the House of Commons overturned on 12 December 1640 the Exchequer's decision on *Rex v. Hampden 1638* (which had cemented the legality of the ship money levy) – see A. A. M. Gill, 'Ship Money during the personal rule of Charles I: politics, ideology and the law', (Ph.D. Thesis, University of Sheffield, 1991), chs. 1, 2 and 4.

² 'That there should be an end to litigation'.

of Iustice) be not minor aut vt minor subditorum;[3] 10: Whether (this
principle beinge true) the [King] hathe any more right then the meaneste
subjecte of the [Kingdome] (or the whole [Kingdome] in the case of
shipmony), to appeale from any superior Cowrte, especially the supreme
eyther to his owne (beinge presumed ignorant of the lawe) or the legally
superseded judgement of an inferior Cowrt or judges nowe with him;
10: Whether hathe the [King] any more right then the meanest subjecte,
to call them noe Cowrte & a company of ambitious, schismaticall,
factious men to rayse armes against them to protect delinquents &
traitors from them et cæt 11: Whether the Parliamentary judgement &
declaratiue acte of Parliamente in confirmation of it passed in the 11:
of [Richard] 2:[d] (Whereby the Causinge the [King] 1: to beare & rayse
his standard againste the parliament 2: to ride with armed men throwgh
the Cownties of the [Kingdome] to the terror of his good subiects, 3:
to invite ouer forraine forces et cæt were adjudged & declared hygh
treason & the agents accordingly excecuted)[4] doe not stande truly
vnrepealed & a very pertinent presidente for what may happen; Thus
muche for a taste in matters of lawe which I haue ex tempore set
downe as they presente themselues to me; The matters of facte showld
be nothinge else but simples axiomes drawne out by the rule of Analisis[5]
out of the [King's] letter from Madrid to the Pope; bothe the articles
of marriag and other suche vndeniable euidences;[6] & proposed (like
Mr Duryes wayes of negociations) in the modeste way of suche Quæries
as by the rules of humane proof & demonstration can receiue but one
answere; & for those whoe like the Romane Chatholikes can beleeue
or not beleeue what they liste, & in matters of lawe or facte can (by a

---

[3] 'Whether the [King] when in receipt of justice be not inferior or as one of his meaner
subjects'.

[4] Culpeper refers to the Appellant triumph and supsequent repression of 1388–89.
Parliament had impeached Richard II's chancellor (Michael de la Pole) and established
a commission to oversee the king's activities. When Richard declared this an act of
treason, his opponents responded by rallying parliament to outlaw and execute some of
his closest associates. Richard was forced to submit to his opponents – the 'appellants'.
On 3 May 1389 Richard declared that, at the age of twenty-two, he would rule as an
independent monarch. See R. H. Jones, *The Royal Policy of Richard II, Absolutism in the later
Middle Ages* (Oxford, 1968), pp. 47–65; A. Tuck, *Richard II and the English Nobility* (1973),
pp. 121–38.

[5] Dury had outlined the importance of textual analysis ('Analyticall meditation') in
educational terms in *A Motion Tending to the Publick Good of This Age, And of Posteritie* (1642),
Wing D2874, sig. D1[v]. The concern for 'right method' amongst Hartlib and his associates
is stressed in S. Clucas, 'In search of "The True Logick": methodological eclecticism
among the "Baconian reformers"' in UR, ch. 2.

[6] While seeking the hand of the Infanta in Madrid in 1623, Charles had written several
conciliatory letters to the Pope – see *The Letters, Speeches and Proclamations of Charles I*, ed.
Sir Charles Petrie (1935), p. 15. Their disclosure caused much outcry. A copy of one of
them appears amongst Hartlib's papers (43/1).

Romish finall resolution of theire faythe into theire will) bringe all home to theire owne priuate judgements as to an invincible castle, I must referre them to the God of order, whoe (for owr sinnes) may yet a while but cannot finally suffer them; my paper is done; Be faythfull in giuinge me your judgemente You will doe me a speciall kindenes in inforrminge me by this returne whether a house nexte to the Feathers & not farre from the Churche in Common garden⁷ inhabited (within these 6: months) by one Mr Dauy a painter be not yet disposed of the owner liues ouer the way; name me not & yf you can possibly, I pray doe it

Ian 3d 43:   Bookers almanacke/⁸   :CC:

42 *Culpeper to Hartlib, 9 January 1643/4. [Note: Hartlib annotations]*
(13/28–9)

Mr Hartlib;
        Congregationall Churches & a residence of the power of personall excommunication in them, seemes to me the expressed sence of the literall woords of the Scripture; But for Classicall, Prouinciall, Nationall or more Generall Churches; & a power residinge in them (by the way eyther of excommunication (as in the Presbiterian) or non communication as in the other) to reduce a whole Congregationall Churche from its obstinate & contumacious error; These or some of them may perhaps may be deduced out of the Scriptures but to me they seeme noe where expressed, but rather perhaps involued in the Generality of some textes, as: Let all things be done decently et cæt:⁹ And; Let him be to thee as a heathen and a publican;¹⁰ And yf these things which bothe sides nowe contende for showlde finally proue at beste but deductions, or perhaps but humane thowgh fittinge ordinances I cannot conceiue what power eyther side hathe of imposinge on the other but since the lay man & Ciuill power who certeinly haue as good right of [consentinge] to the discipline as the doctrine of the Churche is on bothe sides submitted to, I cannot but hope for suche a composinge

⁷ Covent Garden.
⁸ The astrologer John Booker (1603–67). Culpeper probably refers to Booker's *1643* Almanac (Wing A1330). See Bernard Capp, *English Almanacs 1500–1800: Astrology and the Popular Press* (New York, 1979).
⁹ 1 Corinthians 14:40 – 'Let all things be done decently and in order'.
¹⁰ Matthew 18:17 – 'And if he shall neglect to hear them, tell it unto the church: but if he neglect to hear the church, let him be unto thee as an heathen man and a publican'.

of all differences as the [<X>] Common enimy will little joy in my
sorrowe & trowble for the present condition of 12: [<H: Queen of
Bohemia>] is proportionable to that relation I bothe had & still haue
towards 23: [<H: her>] & hers,[11] & the faythe I beare to 19: [<H:
[Elector?] Palatine>] will render my thowghts very benigne to 28:
[<H: the interests>] of 19 [<H: Prince Elector?>], especially beinge
ready 27: [<H: to stirre?>] I conceiue moreouer that the thinge (yf
done & well receiued on all sides) will bothe tell well abroade for
the aduantage of 15: [<H: Parliament>] & may probably proue soe
to 16: [<H: Prince Elector>]; But whether it will not rayse a kinde
of juste jealousy in 13: [<H: King Charles>] & whether the hyght of
suche thowghts then raysed is like to woorke for the better or for
the woorse by way eyther of feare or despaire, I muste ingenuously
professe my selfe not sufficiente for these things; of this I reste
assured that whatsoeuer the true intentions of 12: [<H: Queen of
Bohemia>] 15: [<H: Parliament>] & 16: [<H: Prince Elector>] be, the
thinge will seeme 22 [<H: otherwy's?>] to 13: [<H: King Charles>];
Nor doe I see any pure necessity of the thinge proposed excepte
the intentions of 15: [<H: Parliament>] 12: [<Queen of Bohemia>] &
16: [<Prince Elector>] be the same with the jealousies that are like
to rise in 13. [<King Charles>][12] But what is fittinge & necessary
may (as it seemes to me) be as well done thinges standinge as they
doe; Yf the intentions should be, not suche as are afore mentioned
but suche a vse & shewe onely of them as may conduce to 21:
[<H: Peace>] a serious consideration wowlde then be had whether
(the present condition & innate disposition of 13: [King] considered)
suche colors may proue (yf not a necessary yet) a probable way to
that ende; Yf these 2: laste points were maturely discussed & resolued
on I cowld then readily conclude (29: [<H: comon consent>] of 15:
[Parliament] & 20: [scotland] without which I conceiue nowe nothinge
to be done) what to cowncell in this business By what I haue
written you may take a taste of my thowghts concerning your firste
Quære Yf I may vnderstande what resolution is inclined to & can
consente to the grownds I shall then giue my faythefull answere
and assistance to your 2: & 3: Quæres & yf the resolution be not
suddenly taken, I muste (of necessity) be sometimes nexte weeke in
London & shall be glad to discusse the whole busines with you
more fully then can be done at this distance; [<X>]

---

[11] Culpeper had been awarded an annuity of £400 per annum for a period of thirty-
five years for his services to Elizabeth of Bohemia since the early 1630s – *Calendar of
Treasury Books i (1660–1667)*, ed. William A. Shaw (1904), p. 445.
[12] A cryptic allusion to the plan, advanced by John Pym and his associates, to depose
Charles I in favour of his nephew, Charles Louis the Prince Elector Palatine – Caroline
Hibbard, *Charles I and the Popish Plot* (Chapel Hill, 1983), pp. 151, 177, 207–08.

Yf (accordinge to the newes heere) Arundell be rendered vp;[13] The settlinge of [*word blotted*] a constante auxiliary army of 5: or 6000: horse & foote (eyther for defence or (yf occasion invite) or offence into the weste) will be (I hope) our nexte consideration in these late associated cownties; I doe muche joy in the vnexpected change of this Cownty, & the strenght of it, but those that liue in the woorste parts can see muche yet to be done which doth not appeare to strangers & (for a generall rule of reformation appliable (I feare) to this Cownty as well as to other places) I muste still beate vpon this one stringe that till (marchantlike) wee seuer bothe our Cowncellers and Actors) from fingringe of mony, till the 4: offices of Cowncellinge, Actinge, Payinge & Recordinge or Bookinge be vnited in our actions & seuered in the persons; wee shall but feede the barren woombe which cries still Giue Giue, but returnes noe frwite; & thus shall wee (like Salomons foole) Giue our strenght to the Cruell, in whome Peace wowlde argue as greate a folly as false musters et cæt: dothe knauery #.

I pray sende me Meades Clauis Apociliptica,[14] newes concerning the house; howe Mr Dury dothe when he comes, where hee is; I wante his way of Analisis; my paper is done

[*Hartlib adds date:* 9 Ian. 1643/4.]

43   *Culpeper to Hartlib, 24 January 1643[4].   (13/30–1)*

Mr Hartlib;
          neyther the seale nor superscription of your laste weekes packet was that which it vses to be, & your wonted kindenes of written intelligence & parte of the printed beinge missinge did adde to my feares of some interveninge accidente to what you sente, I shall be glad to vnderstande the contrary
My [L*ords*] Goringe & Digbies letters of the [pretend*ed* par*liament*] are but the flashinges out of the Oxford Cowncells from the pens of particular men thowgh newely imployed;[15] but a parliamente at Oxforde

[13] Waller took Arundel Castle from Hopton on 6 January, and subsequently retired to winter quarters – Gardiner, i. 254.

[14] Joseph Mede, *Clavis Apocalyptica* (Cambridge, 1627), STC 17766; Culpeper is no doubt requesting the new English translation by Richard More, *The Key of Revelation* (1643), Wing M1600.

[15] The King had summoned a 'parliament' of his supporters to Oxford on 22 December 1643 in response to the invasion of the Scots – Gardiner, i. p. 219; SRP, ii. 987–89. Supporters of the Westminster parliament dismissed the gathering as illegal. Hartlib's papers contain a squib on the subject, written in Hartlib's hand (50/17).

speaks the [K*ing's*] Cowncells in plaine Englishe; but I professe that thowgh I can looke into them, I can not yet see any thinge throwgh them but ruine somewhere 2: Parl: 2: seales 2: 13: what not; I tremble at it; but I cannot but hope allso that those magicians & sorcerers will remember that thowgh their predecessors in Egipte turned their rodds into serpents yet Arons eate vp theirs & thowgh their miracles were enowght to hardens Pharaohs hearte that he wowlde not let the children of Israell goe yet that God browght them out with a mighty hande et cæt;[16] The God of mercy soe directe the [K*ing's*] harte that he may yet knowe, euen in this his day the things that belonge to his owne & his [K*ing*domes] peace

The Faylinge of that reporte of Newcastles beinge taken[17] giues occasion to the willinge (at leaste to speake confidently yf not to beeleeue, that the Scots neyther are nor intende to come in at all, & yf it serued for noe other ende then to please their owne humor I professe I showlde giue them leaue to injoy theire portion of a shorte & false joy by hugginge themselues in it especially some of them whoe are my frinds & therefore suche to whome I cowlde yet wishe a better grownded contente, but I finde that these reportes and beleefes doe (especially in these partes) woorke bothe extensiuely & intensiuely, & therefor by this returne shall desire suche information from you concerning it, as may inable to stopt suche reports

Aboue halfe my estate is (in these deade times) turned into my hands, which hinders my presente journey to London, & will (I feare) much straiten me

I pray giue me Credit for a quire of the largeste & fineste paper of about 18:^{d} the quire

Ian 24th 43:

[*marginal addition:*]
Whether Plimowth be taken or releiued[18]

---

[16] Exodus 7:10–14.

[17] William Cavendish, Marquis of Newcastle, the royalist commander in the north, was at this date hard-pressed by the Scots and forced to retreat with his forces from around Newcastle.

[18] Hopton's new army had threatened to take Plymouth towards the end of November 1642. The town had resisted, however, and continued to hold out against Charles's attempts to capture it. See Gardiner, i. 71, 139, 195; ii. 32.

44 *Culpeper to Sir John Culpeper, 12 February 1643/4. (13/32–3)[19] [Unsigned copy letter enclosed with* **45**]

Sir

Small meanes proove sometimes powerfull, especially if rightly aimed & placed; & who can tell, whether my pen may not proove so now? However, I have a Common Interest in the Subject, of which, and (if I miscount not my wealth) a speciall friendly interest in the person, to whom I now write. By either, or both of these, or what else yourselfe know more powerfull, let mee begge of you, let mee conjure you, to looke sadly & considerately about you in this remaining point of time, before things come to that fatall bivium, beyond which a meeting is impossible, & (from that precipice, upon which our following miseries are like to moove) all receeding will growe to either side more difficult, dangerous & dishonourable, then yet it is, I shall not enter into any particular way of reasoning with you, least I either leave, what I begin, imperfect, or multiplie my few intended lines into more then a Letter: But shall only take the Liberty to remember you of the Trust reposed in you by your Country, whose Service, though truely convertible, with the Office & the Judiciall, hath not yet (if you please to informe yourselfe) either prooved or beene soe accepted in relation to the Person, or Extrajudiciall commands of the King.[20] I cannot but remember you also of the Friends, & number of them, which you carry with you. I cannot but againe conjure you by that Sacred Person, whose thoughts (if hee should herafter proove to bee misled a thing not impossible). may then perhaps joyne with the Law, in turning upon them, who have beene either Commissively or Omissively to blame, to him; And neither here doe I speake without presidents. I must not forget yourselfe, who (without courtship I can assure you) held a full consideration in what I nowe doe. And to all this I may without Vanity tell you, that you are at the best, but upon an even wager, & if you know, I speake within compasse, I pray, put that also into the ballance. Once more, for Gods sake, make not your selfe a partaker of the Sinnes, & dangers of such men, whose ills cannot bee safe, but by attemting greater. And from a Mardecayes heart to my Religion, my Country & my friend, I shall conclude with his Counsell to Hester, the 4. 13. 14 & Moses Example, Hebr. 11. 25. 26.[21] Pray pardon this

---

[19] For Sir John Culpeper, see **Introduction**, p. 118, 121. By the time of the royalist Parliament at Oxford, Sir John Culpeper had made enemies at court but was still held in high regard by the king. His peerage apparently the reward for his services during the siege of Oxford in the following year.

[20] Sir John Culpeper was Master of the Rolls – DNB s.n. John Colepeper.

[21] Esther 4:13–14 – 'Then Mordecai commanded to answer Esther, Think not with thyself that thou shalt escape in the king's house, more than all the Jews. For if thou

Puritanisme; That the King, & the Nobility & Gentry about Him (exceptis excipiendis) may yet even in this their day knowe those things, which belong to their owne & the Kingdomes Peace, hath beene & shall bee the prayers & wishes of His Faithfull Subject, &

   Your etc.

45 *Culpeper to Hartlib (with enclosure), 13 February 1643/4. (13/34‑5 [summary only])*

[Note: enclosure: 13/32]

Culpeper mentions difficulties with the delivery of a packet by the former carrier and recommends the Ashford carrier instead. He asks for news of the landing of the Irish in Scotland and what strength the Scots have left behind for their domestic defence. He asks Hartlib to seal the enclosed letter and have it delivered to Thomas Pattison, a servant to Thomas Culpeper who lodges at the house of Sir Robert Rich in Chancery Lane.

46 *Culpeper to Hartlib, 21 February 1643[4]. (13/36‑7 [summary only])*

Culpeper expresses fears for the neglect of the [cipher: Queen of Bohemia?]. The position of his own estates now seems close to being settled 'thowgh with some losse'. As soon as this occurs, he hopes to return to London in order to 'discharge both my debtes and former promise' to Hartlib. He hopes that the intervention of the Scots to the North will release Parliamentary troops for Gloucester and the South West.

47 *Culpeper to Hartlib, n.d. [February 1644?]. (13/296‑7)*

Mr Hartlib,
   I shall once againe change my Carrier because I seldome receiue your packet in suche due time as I may by one Champion the Ashforde carrier to whome (lyinge about Bilingsgate) I pray sende your letters, he leaues London on thursday night as the others did & you may (yf oportunity invite you) sende by him againe on munday night;

altogether holdest thy peace at this time, then shall there enlargement and deliverance arise to the Jews from another place; but thou and thy father's house shall be destroyed: and who knoweth whether thou art come to the kingdom for such a time as this?'. Hebrews 11:25–6 – 'Choosing rather to suffer affliction with the people of God, than to enjoy the pleasures of sin for a season; esteeming the reproach of Christ greater riches than the treasures in Egypt: for he had respect unto the recompence of the reward.'

I expected that Dr Stewarte showlde appeare for Episcopacy, for I euer knewe him a very pontificall man; but that the [King] cannot change that Gouernement without perjury hathe too muche a smacke of the Et cæt: oathe which (it showld seeme he thinkes) hathe beene by the [Bishops] heeretofore (for theire preseruation at a dead lifte) soe riuetted into the [King's] oathe as himselfe & his associates wowld haue lately done for the subjecte; & in truthe to them that haue compared the anciente & moderne oathes of our [Kings] it is very plain that (to gratify one another) the [King] & Peeres consented on the leauinge out quas vulgus eligerit, (very bugbeare woorde) & then (that that the oathe might gaine in quantity what it had loste in wayght, there are inserted seuerall lines of suche stuffe concerninge the Bishops as (euen at that time when the [Bishops'] votes were taken away) it made some of my acquaintance thinke that the [King] cowlde not passe that acte without danger of perjury, but the yce was then broke & the same reason holdes now; But truly there will be noe right regulatinge of these negatiues, thes corner stones of Babylon, but by takinge them away & restoringe the People to theire primitiue liberty of disposinge of themselues by theire representatiue without askinge leaue of a 100: selfe interessed men; And let but the Commons of [England] stand to theire representatiue; & the question be but made by what title these negatiues holde, they muste eyther yelde the swite, or finde a legall judge that will confirme their right; Thus without a judge they cannot make good their right, & yf they once acknowledge a judge they yelde themselues to be neyther the supreme nor yet a peece of the supreme nor further authoratiue then allowed of the judgement of the true supreme I meane the representatiue

I showlde be glad there cowlde be a way fownde to accommodate the militia, for the swoorde beinge settled will settle all the reste, I pray yf you may giue me a taste of it in your nexte, for I muche more desire it then beeleue it possible,

In an Independents answere to A: S: pag: 27: which you sente me laste weeke;[22] I finde a moste pestilente doctrine of the peoples denying actiue or passiue obedience to the Ciuill Magistrat vpon a supposition of a remote possibility of the magistrates abusinge their power to the ruine of a people in case they had not that helpe lefte them, I am soe farre an Independant as I hope this pamphletter muste not be taken to answere for vs all; I heartily wish the Independants will sticke close to this principle; Eyther to doe or to suffer or to be gone but vpon noe condition or a occasion to resiste the established power; And truly yf elections to Parliamente were (accordinge to the Commonlawe of the [Kingdome] & two declaratory statutes made in Ed: 3: time of the

---

[22] This has not been identified.

Common Lawe) reduced to be annuall, the omnipotency of power placed & intrusted in the representatiue wowlde be fearefull onely to the abuses committed in any the hygher or lower partes of the gouernemente established, but not at all dangerous to the people, whose miseryes as then (suppose the woorste) cowlde not liue aboue a yeere but by theire owne consente, & (in truthe) when our representatiue hathe done its woorke (in freeing the gouernemente from the incroachments of conquestes & tiranny), it selfe wowlde be allsoe soe farre reduced as to be able to doe all thinges but not make it selfe perpetuall for (as I sayd before) annuall election becomes the peoples higheste security as well againstee the [Representat*iue*] it selfe, as againste the abuse of any parte of the gouurnement established by it

    I pray once againe giue me a taste of the way of accommodation concerning the militia

48   *Culpeper to Hartlib, 20 March 1643/4.* *(13/38–9)*

Mr Hartlib

    I am heartily sorry I yet trespasse on you but I hope it will not (nowe) be longe that I shall pay bothe my debte & promise; I am glad to see thinges are carried with that secrecy that the Dutch: [Amb*assadors*] are gone back before you knewe they had opened themselues;[23] Yf once the [K*ing*] doe but acknowledge the [Parl*iament*] the same thowghts & motiues which (nowe) yeldes in that will manifestly promise more & the Oxforde cowncells yf they but begin will quickly mowlder to nothing especially yf (popery & prelacy beinge rooted out, delinquency accordinge to the degrees of it), punnished, & Cowrte dependency (by the 19: Propositions) lessened) there be; not onely a frequente election[24] & (as theire actions shall discouer them) a change of the persons in the Cowncell of State, but some suche Venetian ballatinge way[25] vsed bothe in the choyce of them & by them in theire Cowncells as may free bothe theire elections in the [Parl*iament*] & the actions which proceede from

---

[23] The Dutch had offered to mediate between the king and parliament. The king's intermittent attempts to establish a Dutch alliance caused the Parliamentarians great concern – Gardiner, i. 328–9.

[24] The call for frequent parliaments was regularly voiced by parliamentary thinkers. Culpeper's thoughts on the subject predate the proposals for annual or biennial elections advanced by the Levellers in 1648. See Pauline Croft, 'Annual Parliaments and the Long Parliament', *Bulletin of the Institute of Historical Research*, 59 (1986), pp. 155–87; *The Leveller Tracts, 1647–1653*, ed. W. Haller and G. Davies (New York, 1944), p. 112; *Leveller Manifestoes of the Puritan Revolution*, ed. Don M. Wolfe (New York, 1943), pp. 317–18.

[25] The consitution of Venice, with its complex system of balloting, designed to curb private interest, was much admired by republican thinkers of this period – Q. Skinner, *The Foundations of Modern Political Thought*, 2 vols (Cambridge, 1978), i. 141.

themselues, from those ordinary corruptions which rise from feare, ambition, & (which to me seemes the baseste) a lazy, not yeldinge, but castinge oneselfe into contribution to [an*oth*ers] judgemente, &, that from suche an earthy sluggishe spirit as (vnder the honorable name of humility) makes them more slaues then nature euer intended them; & (thowgh the thowghts be yet too rathe),[26] the places from & by which our [Parli*aments*] are chosen & the wayes of election may perhaps deserue consideration

I rest

49 *Culpeper to Hartlib, 27 March 1644.* *(13/40–1)*

Mr Hartlib;

I haue time onely to claime your promise concerning the prophecy, in your laste

Yf you cowlde by this returne sende me a pennyworthe of Isin-geglasse[27] that I may by the sample knowe it you shall oblige me

You did not (in Mr Duryes memoriall of Mr Fermins engine) set downe the figure of that which beinge applied at the bricke[28] wowlde wowld cure all recoylinge;[29] I pray (yf you can possibly) make a circumstantiall description of it

I shall longe allsoe for your riddle; in which I will thus far essay to preuente you;

By runninge brestwoorkes, halfe the sowldiers (1) the pikemen & consequently their pay, victuall & apparell may be saued; by lesseninge the number of officers there may be allmoste or alltogether a thirde parte: of the other halfe saued; & this which I haue sayde amowntes to fowre sixte partes but howe to saue the fifte I am to seeke ~~wo~~ & wowld be very glad to learne; for thowgh these thinges will not (I feare) be taken notice of in this storme, yet (yf ingenuous & vsefull) they will by degrees come into play;[30]

---

[26] Eager, vehement.

[27] This substance was obtained from various sources, notably the swim bladders of fish, for use as finings in the brewing of beer and in the manufacture of glue.

[28] Breech.

[29] John Dury's account of 'an Engin of warre', designed by a Frenchman named Fermin and consisting of an armoured 'cariadge of 2 peeces of Canon', survives amongst Hartlib's papers (67/2/1A-3B). The engine is remarkably similar to that of Edmund Felton. The surviving copy of Dury's account omits the diagram requested by Culpeper.

[30] Culpeper here replies to the dubious claim made by Felton in his printed tract *Engins Invented to save much Blood and Moneyes* (1644), Wing F660, that his engine will save 5/6ths of an army's pay by obviating the need for pikemen to defend the musketeers (p. 2). The typical regiment comprised 1/3 rather than 1/2 pikemen, as Felton claims – see Young and Holmes, pp. 46–7. Hartlib was involved in the editing and distributing of this tract.

In this malignante place wee haue muche distressed the Scottes; giuen a blowe to Sir [William] Waller, taken Pymowthe by a stratageme, & wee make the [King] to thriue in euery place; Your cordiall muste helpe me; I am very sorry the Scots returne home in to Scotlande, but of euills better they then the Irishe; Oh I feare this late Oxforde vote[31] hath bannished all hopes of peace or other issue then bloode to bothe sides & certaine ruine to one Your et cet.

50   *Culpeper to Hartlib, 4 April 1644.   (13/42–3 [summary only])*

Culpeper has been given back word on the settlement of his estates but promises Hartlib the first monies he receives. As to Felton, it seems that, like most melancholy men, he converses too much with his own thoughts and forgets that he has to do business and that it is not always possible to have both profit and honour. For himself, Culpeper wants neither. However, Felton should not be dropped for that might be regretted later.

51   *Culpeper to Hartlib, 10 April 1644.   (13/44–5)*

Mr Hartlib;
          I haue sente you what you writte for concerning Chelsey Colledge;[32] & till I can receiue some rentes, I haue sente you heerewith inclosed 5^l which (in truthe) I was forced to borrowe for mony goes very harde with me; I pray let let this stay vp your minde till I can some way or other prouide the reste, which shall be with the firste I can, & I hope it will not be longe;
     I pray let the other inclosed be deliuered accordinge to the directions; & let me earnestly intreate you to informe me by this returne 1: Whether there be not an order of the Assembly that the Common prayer showlde bee vsed till another Directory of Woorship showlde be settled, as I heare it was one of their firste; 2: Whether it be not euery Sunday vsed in [Saint] Margarets Church: [Westminster] before the Parliament; 3: Whether there be any kinde of order from the 2: houses againste the vse of it: 4: Whethere be any example in whome the vse of it hathe been eyther punnished or made soe muche as an objection

---

[31] The Oxford 'Parliament' passed a motion declaring the Westminster Parliament to be traitors on 26 January 1644 – Clarendon, iii. 308.

[32] Culpeper had already been involved in the proposed reform of Chelsea College as an instrument for the advancement of learning in 1641–2 – see **10** ([September 1641 – June 1642?]) and **17** (13 April [1642]).

I pray take a little paynes to informe your punctually in these particulars;

I haue inclosed 8:ˢ more with which I pray bwy me a payre of silke kneetops as neere as you can to this color in some hosiers shop; at the nexte belowe Ludgate on the right hande I sometimes vse to bwy, & they knowe my size; I bowght my laste for that price; I pray let me not fayle of them by this returne for I muche wante them; You will excuse this trowble in

52 *Culpeper to Hartlib, 24 April 1644.   (13/46 [summary only])*

The silk kneetops are not the right size, substance or colour. Culpeper asks Hartlib to buy a colour that is easier to find and apologises for the trouble he is causing.

53 *Culpeper to Hartlib, 6 May 1644.   (13/48 [summary only])*

The carrier brings Hartlib £10, raised with great difficulty, to honour (in part) Culpeper's debts to him.

54 *Culpeper to Hartlib, 16 May 1644.   (13/49–50)*

Mr Hartlib;

I am exceedinge well pleased with the propositions[33] and especially with the laste parte concerninge the strengh of the [Kingdome] without the subseruiency of which to the [Parliament] & Cowrts of justice all good lawes haue beene & will bee but so many catchfooles & cheates; as good noe Lawe, as noe Cowrte, as good noe Cowrte as noe excecutiue power, when judgemente is giuen; but yf to the Lawe & Cowrts wee can joine the Militia & the purse, our [King's] may perhaps be heereafter induced to beleeue theire great Cowncell to be as wise as the wiseman did him that had the command of 10: Legions; & till then (as the author of the grande Case pag: the 6: & 7:)[34] wee shall but be grownde to duste between 2: heades eyther of which may obstructe justice at pleasure but cannot open & make it vigorous & this (saythe that excellente author) is woorse then an absolute Monarchy, & in truthe as for this reason the [Parliament] wowlde be restored againste the [King's] pretences, soe will it (in time) deserue a seconde consideration of resstoringe (that firste Parente of all Gouernement) the howse of

---

[33] Gardiner, i. 342–3.
[34] *The Grand Case of England* (1642), Wing G1487. Thomason, E.88 (27).

Commons to its vigour againste the [Lords], but in this the furtheste
my weake judgement dares resolue in this diluculum[35] of these Primitiue
times of Ciuill Protestancy is the vnitinge of the 2: howses, which yf it
cowlde be effected in this excellente time of oportunity by a petition
from the Citty to the house of Commons & a motion from it to the
Lords that the desertinge members of that house showlde (accordinge
to example of the house of Commons) be made (for the present)
vncapable, I cannot but hope that when Lesley is a little neerer, the
howse of Commons & Cowncell of state (& if then allsoe the Citty
come in for its parte it will be the better) may preuayle with the major
parte of these fewe in the house of [Lords] (for the avoydinge of future
distractions in theire Cowncells) to joyne & vote with the Commons in
one house, & yf to this be jojned the consideration that moste of the
Peerage of Englande holde theire honors not in Fee simple or generall
Intaile but in speciall intaile to the heires males onely of theire body; I
cannot but see that yf (by the 18:[th] proposition) the [Parliament] preuente
the makinge of more, these that nowe are (partly by treason present &
future, & partly by exinction in case any line fayle) may in an age or
lesse be reduced to a lesser number & then the small remainder (as in
the Low cowntries) antiquated as inconsiderable.

My paper is done; when you haue read it I pray burne it as that
which (thowgh it muste & will be done) better fitts to the nexte age, &
(whensoeuer) better done then written

55   *Culpeper to Hartlib, 14 August 1644.   (13/51 [summary only])*

*Culpeper comments on a printed broadsheet about a fuel made of straw and mortar
but the quantities are too indefinite as to be able to be experimented with. He asks
Hartlib to send on all he knows. In return, Culpeper will forward an excellent
medicine for the stone provided by an Empirick.*

56   *Culpeper to Hartlib, 6 November 1644.   (13/54)*

Mr Hartlib;
         I [replied *not MS torn*] vpon the answere to my extractes, because
(like an assembly man) he makes many positions & as fewe proofes;
With the same faculty I vnderstande thinges meerely rationall, with the
same (I confesse) raysed by faythe doe I apprehende thinges spirituall,
but that I may (without sinninge) submitte (where I cannot consente)
in the firste but cannot in the laste, an ordinary vnderstandinge not

---

[35] i.e. dawn.

disposed to carpe about woords may conceiue; To the vnjuste judgement of a legall judge in a controuersy about my estate I not onely may without sinne but ought vpon payne of sinne to submitte but to renownce eyther Christianity, or any suche parte of it as my conscience (though perhaps erroneous) thinkes necessary, this I cannot without sinninge againste my conscience & he that by compulsion will teache my eares that good manners & justice which himselfe denies will (to me) proue himselfe the most vnmannerly of the two; I pray send me my owne letters & yf I can answer __ in folly, not accordinge to it, I will;

 pray sent Mr Plats papers[36]

57 *Culpeper to Hartlib, 13 November 1644. (13/52–3)*

Mr Hartlib;
 The preludes & interludes of Mr Plats booke[37] being lefte out, what deserues to be preserued wowlde goe into a narrowe roome; I wowlde gladly see some of his greate booke[38] (soe muche mentioned) & (as wee agreed) suche other experiments as haue not beene heeretofore published by him

I cannot but stande amazed howe the answerer to the extractes (soe lowe a while since & not yet fully vp in the saddle) can soe soone yet thinke of teaching his brethren good manners, The answere to Mr Prinne[39] is (as yourselfe say) very home to the pointe, but (I assure you) holdes nothinge which may not be fownd thowgh dispersed yet fully expressed in the other independents writings; I may perhaps write more of this subjecte nexte weeke; I haue all moste loste my time

58 *Culpeper to Hartlib, 20 November 1644. (13/55–6)*

Mr Hartlib,
 The more I consider Mr Plats former bookes, & his writinges

---

[36] Gabriel Plattes had sent Hartlib a copy of *The Profitable Intelligencer* (Wing P2414) in May 1644, asking him to arrange for its publication; C. Webster, *Utopian planning and the puritan revolution. Gabriel Plattes, Samuel Hartlib, and 'Macaria'*, Wellcome Unit for the History of Medicine, Oxford, Research Publications Number 11 (Oxford, 1979), p. 58.

[37] Gabriel Plattes, *The Profitable Intelligencer* (1644), Wing P2414; Webster, *Utopian Planning*, pp. 58–9.

[38] Plattes's great unpublished (and perhaps unfinished) work, 'Arts Mistress, or the Treasure House of Nature Unlocked' – Webster, *Utopian Planning*, p. 58.

[39] *The Fallacies of Mr W. Prynne* (Oxford [London], 1644). See Lamont, *Marginal Prynne*, ch. 5.

you laste sente me; the more heartily I still wishe that none of his thowghts (not yet published) showld be loste, & therefore yf you withdraw him from his other imploimentes to a reCollection & orderinge of them, you will (I conceiue) muche advance the publicke, & thowgh this present age haue soe muche reuerence to our owne or ancestors wisdome as euery thinge (in churche or state or any other kinde) yf newe to vs (thowgh not in itselfe or the principles of scripture or reason) findes as yet a difficulte passage in mens thowghts; yet from the three yeeres liberty which men haue taken of ransackinge & touzinge those starched vp & vnjointed postures whereine our ancestors lefte vs like soe many images without motion but from without) I cannot but conceiue wee shall by degrees (hauinge firste freede ourselues from a slauishe reuerence of some fewe men or bookes) try euery spirit & that as well in rationall as spirituall thinges; & yf wee can once redeeme ourselues into this liberty, I am very confidente that Mr Plats thowghts (thowgh they lye a while under grownde) will yet then (like corne that dothe soe) afforde the better harueste, & truly yf Mr Plattes ende or hopes are to liue to the harueste of his woorkes, hee is like to finde himselfe deceiued; our resolution must be to plante to posterity thowgh our selues may not perhaps hope to injoy any other part or frwite of the action then to haue done it; yf I may heare from you that Mr Platte is in hande with his recollection I will sende you what I promised, but I pray (since wee aime at preseruation only & not to prepare for the presse) let not this time be spent in transcribinge eyther moralities which thowgh at another time good are yet for the presente imper- tinente, nor yet thinges allready eyther published or soe written as (thowgh priuate) they cannot be loste; All that I wowlde wishe preserued out of that booke of Mr Plattes which you sente me[40] will be written in 2: leaues or 3: at moste; you shall when you will haue it backe againe, & (yf I might) I cowld wishe to see his greate booke[41] as it nowe standes

For the publique I haue noe hope (to speake as a man) but in our geud brethren the Scottes, & from what is paste, it is not probable that God will honor our nation (soe base & false to our owne profession) with its owne preseruation, but will himselfe be honord in the accomplishinge of the woorke by a nation whoe thowgh weaker are yet more sincere; I haue not beene well this laste weeke, I will sometime heereafter giue a reply to the answers

---

[40] *The Profitable Intelligencer* – see **57** (13 November 1644).
[41] 'Arts Mistress' – ibid.

59 *Culpeper to Hartlib, 18 December 1644.   (13/57-8)*

Mr Hartlib,

     I haue not beene lately sicke, but so trowbled about my small liuelyhoode, as that from 500ˡ per annum I am reduced to under 50:ˡ per annum & thus am I become soe farre from beinge able to helpe my frinds as I am my selfe in greate straits; These my late trowbles haue me silente synce I cowlde not giue you that answere I desired; & this hathe allsoe taken of my thowghts from giuinge a reply to the answere of my letters;

     The [Parl*iament*] beinge in it selfe the supreme judicatory & nowe acknowledged by the [K*ing*] it wowld be nowe a contradiction to finde another earthly supreme, to limit or set bowndes to its power, for yf a supreme Iudicatory shall take conusance of any thinge whoe shall judge againste the conusance it assumes, a superior there is not, for then were it not supreme; & for an inferior to judge the supreme, is bothe in Lawe and reason as greate a contradiction; Yf then this supreme shall judge eyther concerning the Crowne it selfe as it hathe often done, or againste the negatiue voyce what earthly legall power can recall the judgemente, & from this grownde I haue longe thowght that the supreme power & legislatiue power are inseparable; for the judgemente of the supreme Cowrte becoms a lawe till repealed, & this made the [K*ing's*] cowncell say that in hauinge the judgemente of the checquer chamber[42] they had as good as a Lawe, it beinge resolued there showld be noe [Parl*iament*]

     And truly this alone yf truly wayghed wowlde disperse the knowne Lawes of priuate fancy as they are tawght at Oxford for howe are the Lawes legally & bindingly knowne but in the Cowrts,[43] whose judgements are the standards of legall truthe

     The Commons vote concerning offices,[44] hath this in it more then is

---

[42] A further reference to the judgement given in the Exchequer Chamber on the case of *Rex v Hampden*, concerning the legality of ship money – see **41** (3 January 1643).

[43] An attack on the royalist belief that the law was an expression of kingly power, the king being himself a living law, or *lex loquens*. Culpeper may have read a number of contemporary pamphlets on the relationship between law and prerogative, including Samuel Rutherford, *Lex Rex: the Law and the Prince, A dispute for the just prerogative of King and People, In which a full answer is given to Sacro Sancta Regum Majestas by Jo. Maxwell* (7 October 1644), Wing R2386 Thomason, E.11 (5); and also *Prerogative Anatomized; an examination of the professions whereby she hath attempted to preferre herself above the Parliament* (4 December 1644), Wing P3219 Thomason, E.20 (4).

[44] The vote at the end of the debate of 9 December on the motion, later known as the self-denying ordinance, 'That during the time of this war no member of either House shall have or execute any office or command, military or civil, granted or conferred by both or either of the Houses of Parliament, or any authority derived from both or either of the Houses' – Gardiner, ii. 90.

eyther mawted or at leaste spoken of (viz) That it dothe exclude all the
nobility, & (by the sympathy that euery kinde hathe to its kinde) is like
to deuolue the power of the Commons of Englande into its naturall
place the howse of Commons. I cowld speake muche of it but I
haue giuen a [*Question*] to your thowghts, I conceiue it of little lesse
consequence to the [Lords] howse then the acte of continuance to the
[K*ing*][45]

I cannot tell howe to aske the continuance of your kindenes excepte
I were better able to deserue it

The intelligencer & Scoute are the onely journalls I desire,[46] & suche
other choyce bookes onely as wowlde be bowght thowgh by a poore
man

60   *Culpeper to Hartlib, n.d. [Autumn 1644?].   (13/317–8)*[47]

Mr Hartlib

I am not more sorry for the differences betw*een* the 2: howses
then glad to see that naturall mother of all Gouernemente, the howse
of Commons, to begin to claime theire owne; & for preuention of
these & suche like differences it were heartily to be wished that there
were (as at firste) but one house,[48] & the birthright of the Peerage to
vote in it wowlde be a sufficient share, & a greater inheritance then
cowlde be allot*ed* to any 100: men at the firste naturall coalition, when
(among the equall sonnes of Adam) naturall abilities might per chance
deserue personall honor but not haereditary power &, yf I may vse the
dictates of my owne reason, I cannot conceiue that our ancestors in
the firste coalition eyther wowld or cowlde binde not onely themselues
but all posterity, by an immutable humane lawe, w*hich* is a contradiction
in nature & reason, to one or more fooles or weake men that might be
borne 500 or 1000 yeeres after; Successiue monarchy circumscribed
by Cowncells [Ecclesiast*icall*] Iudiciall: & politique; electiue by and
accowntable to the arbitrary power of the representatiue body was
that truthe from whence by conqueste, perjury, & oppression wee are

---

[45] The *Act Against a Forcible Dissolution of the Parliament*, passed in 1641, had declared that
the present Parliament could not be dissolved without the consent of its members (i.e.
could not be dissolved at the monarch's pleasure).

[46] *The Kingdomes weekly intelligencer* (Jan.1643 – Oct.1649), N&S 214.001 – 214.332, and
Parliament Scout (Jun.1643 – Jan.1645), N&S 485.01 – 485.84.

[47] This letter is difficult to date with precision. The reference to the possible seizure of
Newcastle, however, probably relates to its siege and subsequent capture on 19 October
1644. The remainder of the letter is not inconsistent with an approximate ascription to
Autumn 1644.

[48] A proposal to unite the two Houses emerged in public debate in January 1645 – see
Gardiner, ii. 106.

strayed & to which at the fall of Temporall Babylon we shall returne; For Babylon (as mr Dury) is quid vniuersall & signifies confusion as well in Temporall as spirituall things & soe (I am confidente) will the fall of it bee; For why else showlde our Temporall Popes cry Alas, Alas;

I am glad like resolutions concerninge the summons are changed the motion onely speakes enowgh what (yf necessity require must & will finally be done;

Popery hathe toleration & prelacy yet a beinge by lawe but the assemblies explications of lawfull indeauors beinge allowed I haue taken it

Since my late reviewe of mr Duryes papers I cannot but passionately complaine of my wante of his way of Analisis, of which did I not finde his promise vnder his owne hand I showld feare my selfe be be vnwoorthy of it

Yf Newcastle were taken I showlde hope well of a Treaty; Yf any Good come from Hollande it muste proceede from theire Prouinciall Cowncells not from their Generall States, which thowgh electiue haue too muche in them of the Potentate; It is the People or middle rancke muste doe it in all places; I pray continue your kindenes by the carrier

1645

61 *Culpeper to Hartlib, 4 January 1644/5.* *(13/59–60)*

Mr Hartlib;

I am moste sadly sorry not for Mr Plattes deathe but his losse &
manner of it;[1] this 20ˢ which the bearer hathe for you hathe stayed in
my handes this monethe (as other monies haue done) onely for an
oportunity of beinge returned, For thowgh my presente pressures be
very greate yet what I had promised was noe more my owne, my
wishes are that it may nowe be implyed as farre as it will goe in the
preseruinge of his children I meane his bookes & ingenuities which yf
you looke after in time may (I conceiue) fall into your handes & by
your care be improued to the publiqꝰe good & his honor, I pray be
not wantinge in it & what farther assistance my lowe condition can
giue you shall not wante; His engine for settinge corne & dunge may
(very likely) be yet bowght for mony at his woorkemans;[2] I conceiue
theire will be better wayes fownde out, but for the presente I heartily
wishe to haue one of his partly to preserue it, partly to try it & partly
to vse it as a step to further thowghts;

I pray send me Mr Feltons booke in print concerninge his engine,[3] &
in a line, what newes the towne affords, by this bearer

62 *Culpeper to Hartlib, 5 January 1644/5.* *(13/61)*

Mr Hartlib

You shall receiue a letter from me by another oportunity that
goes this [morn*ing*] towards London; The bearer heerof will tell you
where his [M*aste*r], Mr Oxinden[4] lodges, I pray (vpon receipte of this)
repayre to [Capt*ain*] Lee a hatter vpon Ludgate hill & desire him from
me & in my behalfe to goe with you to Mr Oxinden, & to him to

---

[1] Plattes died 'in the street for want of food' according to Cressy Dymock; *Legacy*, pp.
183–84; Webster, p. 34.
[2] Plattes's engine, a seed-drill, was first publicised in 1639 and remained of considerable
interest to agricultural reformers; Webster, p. 50. For its development by others see **65**
(21 January 1644/5).
[3] Edmund Felton, *Engins Invented to save much Blood and Moneyes* (1644), Wing F660.
[4] Henry Oxinden of Dene in Kent, eldest son of Sir James Oxinden; he was much
involved in the county organisation of Kent for the Parliament.

testify my sendinge in fowre horses for the [Parl*iament's*] seruice, [hims*elf*] beinge the person that did me the kindenes to see them deliuered in; It may perhaps be of concernemente to me; & Mr Oxinden is one of our Deputy Lieutennants; I pray remember my kinde loue to Capt Lee: & (in your nexte) giue me accownte of this busines

63   *Culpeper to Hartlib, 14 January 1644/5.   (13/62–3 [summary only])*

  Culpeper hopes that Hartlib has received his letter via Mr Oxinden. He again urges Hartlib to pursue the receipt of the four horses with Captain Lee.

64   *Culpeper to Hartlib, n.d. [mid-January 1645?].   (13/64 [summary only])*

Further particulars in respect of Captain Lee and the receipt of the four horses.

65   *Culpeper to Hartlib, 21 January 1644/5. (13/65–8)*

Mr Hartlib;
  I am moste heartily sorry the grande vote is caste out by the Lords,[5] But am as confidente the House of Commons (that true and onely representatiue of the People) muste & will finally insiste vpon theire owne rights & theires whome they represente; & I cannot but conceiue (from the concurrence euen of strangers thowghts which (by a secret prouidence) I obserue to rise in this towzinge[6] age) that men are like (by a reassuminge theire owne judgementes from the vassilage of former ages) to caste of all blinde reuerence of suche pretended powers as (beinge eyther questioned or denied) cannot proue themselues grownded vpon publike consente, or yf they doe, it muste be (as at Oxford) by the knowne lawes of mens priuate fancies or (as it is like to be nowe or heereafter elsewhere) by a plea of longe continuance of what yf once but questioned will be fownde to stande on as sandy a fowndation of justice & truth as theirs at Oxforde, & truly yf men wowlde but rowze themselues out of the muddines of custome & conformity to what we finde in the worlde, & wowlde but aske & reason with themselues concerning what we see, there wowld (as well in the Politickes as in Diuinity and naturall philosophy) appeare an absolute necessity that supremacy muste dwell in vnity, & that vnity

---

[5] On 13 January, the House of Lords voted with only four votes to the contrary to reject the Self-Denying Ordinance – Gardiner, ii. 118.
 [6] 'Dissolving'.

soe composed and ordered as that vpon all occasions it may be able to actuate its power by doinge somethinge; & not (as nowe) by longe protractinge thinges of greate consequence till the losse of occasion & leauinge the greateste (from priuate intereste) without decision; In your weekely intelligence of the 7th of marche, it appeares that (vpon the Lords deniall to passe the oathe of secrecy to be taken by the Committee for the safety of the [K*ing*dome]) Mr Rous[7] was from the Commons commanded (according to your owne words there) to let the [L*ords*] knowe in plaine termes that they had taken too muche vpon them to giue a downe right negatiue to their vote, & to tell them further in the name of the house of Commons and of the Commons of England that yf they retarded theire concurrence, they wowld take suche a cowrse as was answerable to the trust committed to them by the whole [K*ing*dome]. The successe was then good & the right of speakinge or doing soe is (at leaste) as good nowe as then; but to driue the nayle to the heade, yf by a conscientious man it showlde (& why may it not) be asked whether these negatiues of [K*ing*] & [L*ords*] were firste fownded by consente or (yf they were, yet) whether they were (by that consente) made indefesible & irreuocable thowgh fownde prejudiciall to the publike; yf it showld be asked by what Lawe the [K*ing*] had power to make a Lorde, a creature not knowe in this world till about the time of the conqueste, in a worde yf this one question Quid juris were applyed to a 100 suche excresences the firste answere (I knowe) wowlde be Knowne Lawes or olde mowldy customes

But yf it be againe questioned or perhaps denied that the Knowne Lawes of priuate fancy or a mouldy custome cannot destroy that higheste right of a people to dispose of themselues, bothe the rights & pleas muste then be eyther browght before some judge (a thinge nowe soe muche *auoyeded*) or wowlde be yf the people knewe theire right & wowlde stande to those whome they haue trusted) by degrees cast [*Hartlib adds:* cast] by and haste be forgotten

To my former thowghts concerninge the Militia I cannot adde except I cowlde remember what they were; I shall therefore for the presente touche [*Hartlib adds:* touche] vpon suche heads as come in my minde; I conceiue that all Lieutennantes may (as they are by the Spaniarde) be layde aside; All Companies raysed to 200: and all regimentes to 2000: I neuer consented to [Col*onel*] Weemmes[8] brestwoorkes nor yet to Mr Feltons thowgh lygther, because bothe are too heauy for 2: men vpon the place or for one horse vpon the marche but I am still

---

[7] Francis Rous (1579–1659) was John Pym's half-brother and MP for Truro in the Long Parliament. At this time, Dury regarded him as a potential patron of Hartlib and wrote to him, urging him to be the worthy successor to Pym, not only 'in temporal but rather in spiritual purchases' by recommending Hartlib to Parliament – DNB and HDC, p. 27.

[8] James Wemyss (1610?-1667), see **30** (4 October 1643) and **36** (20 December 1643).

confidente that a turnepike vpon 4 small wheeles between 6: & 7: foote longe wowlde in it selfe be very lyght & might (by small pykes) be armed againste the pressure of horse, which hathe beene hetherto the [Kings] greate aduantage; And 2 or 300 of these might be made soe muche more seruiceable then soe many thowsandes pikes as they doe at once become bothe a reste for the musket & suche a defence againste the pressure of horse as dothe not yet not withstandinge (like the pyke) hinder the continuall vse & play of the gunne, & yf to this were added the differencing of the ranckes soe as the firste 2: showlde haue eyther longe gunnes or musket arrowes, the nexte three rankes, ordinary muskets & bullets & the laste 2: or 3: rankes be furnished with a kinde of lyght blunderbus, I cannot conceiue but a regimente or brigadoe of suche men wowlde be furnished for all occasions, & might marche euen in a Campania as free from the inroade of horse as they wowlde doe in an inclosed cowntry, & might in an inclosed Cowntry soe stop vp all hygh wayes, bridges or other passages as wowlde render horse alltogether vselesse; I shall not say of what vse the leatherne ordinance (a thinge of noe vse for battery) might *yet haue haue been* yf mixed with these & charged with musket or pistol bullets; because I haue not hearde of [Colonel] Weems since he was taken; But those thinges (because newe) I expecte not showld yet be taken vp but may perhaps in another halfe age when they haue layen a while buried in mens thowghts for wee are not yet enowgh freed from a blinde reuerencinge of whatsoeuer hathe beene soe as to caste it presently off when we finde a better;

That which I doe more heartily & strongly wishe is in the firste place that all officers might for the presente receiue onely a third or halfe of theire pay & runne a hazarde with the state for the reste; Then wowld the officers on this side be as thirsty as those on the [King's] side of all occasions to ende the warre whereas nowe the continuance of the warre are theire beste advantage & they cannot meritte in the endinge of it but to their owne ruine.

I wishe in the seconde place that noe officer whatsoeuer showlde pay his sowldiers, but that to the payment bothe of the Commanders & soldiers there be 2: sortes of men assigned, one to joine with the [Captain] or (in his absence) with the [Lieutennant] or Ancient in takinge the true number of the souldiers & distributinge a continually changeable leaden coine to them & another (according to the numbers set downe vnder the Captaines & this officers handes together with the patternes of leade to pay the sowldiery & to receiue theire leaden coine, Thus is the officers greate ende of false musters taken away; thus is the treasurer meerely passiue in in his disbursementes, & yf to what I haue sayde there were added a recruitinge regiment or nursery out of which the seuerall regimentes might be weekely supplied, in the roome of the deade sicke or wownded thus wowld the regiments be kept continually whole & fitte for seruice, & the sicke & wownded when concentrated into one body wowlde be the better prouided for; Of this diuidinge all actions of concernmente into parts & committinge euery parte to seuerall persons; none hathe better experience then the great merchante whoe by this & suche other methodes and order are inabled to suche undertakinges as w*i*thout suche rules wowld proue dangerous yf not destructiue; & truly the metaphysicall reason of what I write concerninge the treasury of an army hathe a transcendency throwgh all other trustes & accownts of mony, & the generall rule is this; To deuide euery publike concernemente into as many partes as it will beare & euery parte (like soe many keyes of a treasury) to be committed to to severall persons; of honor; not indigente for it is a temptation; & suche as showlde be bownde to the publike by oathe or bonde, or bothe; For example I haue proposed to some in this Cownty that there might be one kinde of man to hunte or discouer matters of sequestration whether reall or personall; another to let or sell them, a thirde to collecte the mony, a fowrth (as a treasurer) to keepe it; The firste terrier or discouerer to presente his discoueries to a Committee or subcomittee; what is fownd sequestrable to be there recorded, with as many circumstances as the discouery affords; from hence a commande to issue to the seconde kinde of officer to sell or lett; his worke beinge done, returned & recorded; directions then to issue to a third sorte to collecte & deliuer to an vnder or Hygh Treasurer accordinge to the meritte of the thinge; Yf this or sume suche order wer taken, the presente publike officers (many of them hungry indigente men) wowld not soe inriche themselues to the losse & dishonor of the publique, & giue aduantage to those spirites whoe (from the light that euery day increases) not beinge able to argue againste the legall authority of the Cowrtes & supremacy of [Parl*iament*], are yet continually markinge and snarlinge at the injustice, a thinge which thowgh it cannot be purely auoyded as longe as we liue heere vpon the earthe, wowlde yet be taken into serious condideration to preuente suche aduantages as may be & are made use of againste the [Parl*iament*] from this principle that mens mindes are not yet soe generally & strongly inured to submitte to the Courts of Iustice, not onely because they are juste but because (thowgh perhaps vnjuste) they are yet legall, a thinge which I heartily wishe were more pressed vpon mens consciences out of the pulpits, for this strongly settled euery man wowlde haue a ready answere within himselfe to the infirmities imputed to the [Parl*iament*] whether true or imaginary.

There are many small yet necessary circumstances pertinent to what I haue written, which I cannot nowe delineate especially since (in what I haue written) I goe alone therefore may easily erre, but yf you shall

finde any thinge entertained I shall (according to my weakenes) be
ready to giue suche farther accownte as shall be desired

I am very glad you haue fownde a seconde Mr Plattes, & cowlde
wishe (yf not vnreasonable) to haue a module of his way of settinge
corne.[9] I haue a farme this yeere turned into my hands & wowlde
willingly make some aduantage of that inconuenience by makinge
seuerall tryalls, yf eyther in Mr Plattes bookes or elsewhere you can
informe your selfe clothinge corne with a riche Composte I wowlde
willingly be a learner;[10]

But that which my present thowghts moste runne vpon is that
exuberancy of the spirite of nature which I finde (by analogy that
excellente way of inlarginge knowledge) to answere in all pointes to the
Spirite of grace; Our Diuines holde a man to be then in a right way
of saluation when euen our sinnes become soe many occasions of our
greater faythe & puryfyinge our selues by the spirit of Grace; There is
a spirit in nature as there is in grace, There is allsoe in nature that
which answeres analogically to synne;[11] Sinne as it is the greateste
enemy to the Spirit of Grace soe is it allsoe the onely subjecte on which
the Spirite of Grace workes whileste we liue heere, were sinne wholy
caste out wee showld injoy that blessed sabbathe & reste which the
pure Angells & [Saints] doe in heauen but that our life heere might be
a continuall woorke of purifiyinge our selues God hathe suffered sinne
(like the Philistins) to dwell within vs; And truly thus is it in nature
whose spirite yf wee desire to exalte to a greater purity and purifyinge
power it muste bee by keepinge her in continuall combate with her
enemy C'est (saythe an excellente author I haue) vne chose necessaire
d'entremesler ces feces grossieres (analogicall to sinne) a la substance
subtile; Car ou il n'y a que purete il n'y peut auoyr d'action parce que

[9] A reference to Cressy Dymock, the agricultural inventor and enthusiastic cor-
respondent of Hartlib. He claimed to have perfected Gabriel Plattes's invention for
setting corn, mentioned by Culpeper in **61** (4 January 1644/5); see also *Legacy*, pp. 183,
189. Dymock presented the device as a form of perpetual motion machine: Cressy
Dymock, *An Invention of Engines of Motion lately brought to perfection* (1651), Wing D2971. On
Dymock see GI and HDC passim; G. E. Fussell, *The Old English Farming Books: From
Fitzherbert to Tull, 1523–1730* (1947), pp. 44–47.

[10] For the interest in chemical fertilisers sustained by Hartlib and his associates, see
GI, pp. 377–80; [Cressy Dymock], *A Discovery for Division or Setting out of Land* (1653), Wing
H985, pp. 12–[25]('12')]; cf. Gabriel Plattes, 'Mercurius Lætificans', in *Legacy*, pp. 173–
216.

[11] This was a familiar trope of Christian alchemy, expounded at length in one of
Culpeper's favourite chemical works, Jacques de Nuysement, *Traittez de l'harmonie et
constitution générale du vray sel . . .* (Paris, 1621), a little-known French text with a
Hermetic/Paracelsian bias. An English translation by Robert Turner of a Latin version
of Nuysement's work was published in 1657, testifying to contemporary English interest
in the work: *Sal, Lumen, & Spiritus Mundi Philosophici* (1657), Wing N1469. On Nuysement,
see John Ferguson, *Bibliotheca Chemica*, 2 vols (reprinted, London, 1954), ii. 147–8.

rien ne peut agir sans patient;[12] Hoc quid sit (saythe another author) multi quærunt paucissimi inveniunt;[13] A thirde writes thus: [Postquam summus] artifex videret malum ad bonum, quod crearat, accessisse voluit sua bonitate (marke) hujusmodj malitium reprimere non supprimere donec illi placitum foret, malo mox subdens bonum; vti quod conaretur malum exequi per corruptionem; non ex suo conatu sed ex frenatione sui conatus (marke) in bonum, hoc est in generationem transiret;[14] doe you not thinke me mad, It hath pleased God to lay me alltogether aside in this stirringe age & these are the entertainments of my retired life

You once tolde me of one that was excellente in furnaces & generally in regulatinge fire;[15] it is a thinge I muste be acquainted with for bothe in grace & nature thowgh the inwarde motions be the principall; yet the owtwarde adjumants[16] are not to be neglected; & somethinge I shall resolue to try hauinge nowe (after 20 yeeres solitary medidation) fixed my thowghts soe as fully answers & is still confirmed by all I reade, I pray let me haue a woorde from you what helpe I may there expecte & for what, muche (you knowe) is not (at the presente) in my power;

I thanke you for your good opinion and wishes of my beinge in the [Parliament] but truly I am apte to thinke that God hathe ordered thinges better for me, (I am sure) more for my ease, for thowgh I holde the [Parliament's] actions legall & bindinge yet there haue beene and are many to the justice of which I cannot consente; To binde men (by couenante) note onely to keepe but to maintain the lawes, & afterwards to suffer euere priuate spirit to take them away & that none muste soe muche as dare to complaine, this seems to me a pressure upon the consciences of them that loue them & an aduantage giuen to them that are againste them, & suche as truly I haue not yet heard solued; for this & suche kinde of malignancies I bothe am layed aside & suffer, &

---

[12] Nuysement, *Traittez*, pp. 165–66. 'It was therefore necessary, that the subtle substance should be mixed with the gross dregs: for where nothing but purity is, there is no action; because there can be no action, where there is no patient'; *Sal, Lumen* . . . , p. 132. (Clucas, p. 154).

[13] 'It shall be thus: many shall seek and few shall find' – the author has not been identified but the implicit reference is to Luke 13:24.

[14] 'What this may be (saythe another author) many seek but very few find. A thirde writes thus: After the Supreme Creator saw that evil had been added to the good which he had created, he resolved in his goodness (marke) not to abolish it, but to keep wickedness of this kind in check for as long as he saw fit, thereupon subjecting good to evil; in order that what evil might attempt through corruption might be transformed into good, that is, into procreation, not through his [its.?] endeavour but through the restraint of his [its.?] endeavours.'

[15] The German chemist Johann Rudolf Glauber (1604–70) – DSB; Clucas, pp. 150–54; Partington, ii. 343–47; *Great Chemists*, ed. E. Farber (New York, 1961), pp. 115–34.

[16] 'Helps'.

God will be done in it; Yf offences muste needes come I had muche rather suffer then doe them

I haue allmost filled my seconde sheete of paper with suche stuffe as the cowntry & my retired thowghts afforde; In what you eyther approue or disallow I pray let me haue your judgement for nothinge is more harde then to take a right lyghte of a man selfe;

I euery day more & more finde Mr Duryes Analyticall rule of dwellinge & insistinge vpon propositions & woords to be an excellente way for drawinge out, the soule, the spirite & life of a wise writer & to gaine from him (as the Frenche say) une ame de mesme, & truly (to passe by Mr Duries voluntary ingagements to my selfe concerning that excellente talente) I will be bolde to say that yf the world showld loose it by his deathe, he will be thowght to haue buried it & the fawlte soe muche the greater as the talente is now excellente; You will perhaps say I presse home but truly I knowe not howe he will auoyde or answere it my paper is done;

66 *Culpeper to Hartlib, 28 January 1644/5.   (13/69–70)*

Mr Hartlib;

I haue sente you the papers you writte for, & heartily wishe you wowlde indeauor that noe other parte of Mr Plattes bookes be loste;

I very muche approue of your publike thowghts concerninge beggars & schooles for the firste the execution of some lawes allready made for woorke howses is the beste my thowghts yet reache to, & of suche woorkhouses wee may haue excellent patternes from the Lowe Cowntries;[17] For schooles the beste my thowghts can yet suggeste is the hauinge in euery parishe of the [Kingdome] a man that in the churche showlde reade the Scriptures, & in the woorke dayes showlde teache the youthe euery one accordinge to their Capacities & be answerable (to ouerseers) for theire education of this his little cure, as the pastor is for those which are growen vp, & yf in Cowntry parishes which haue a latitude of dirty wayes there were by the publike order taken for places where children might be (at reasonable rates) well & wholesomely borded & looked to it wowld contribute more to the busines then you will (at firste) be aware of; These schoolemasters wowlde be initiated in the wayes of teachinge & sente abroade into the [Kingdome] from suche seminaries & nurseryes as Mr Commenius hathe formerly pro-

---

[17] This is perhaps a reference to an early draft of Hartlib's tract on poor relief and workhouses, *The Parliaments Reformation* (1646), Wing H995A; repr. SHAL., pp. 111–19. For Hartlib's involvement in the promotion of such matters, see GI, esp. pp. 360–69.

posed;[18] & in that shoppe wowlde the compendious wayes of teachinge
be continually (amonge other more excellente matters) be aduanced;
Another consideration wowld be the hauinge of more free schooles
more schollers places in the Vniuersities, & bothe these & all fellowships
limitted to the children of the poore & a certeine number of yeeres
appointed for theire continuance in them that soe more may receiue
the benefit & none (as nowe) suffered to liue a monkishe life to the
prejudice of the publike by buryinge his owne talente & hinderinge of
others; These are my presente extemporary thowghts I pray giue me a
taste of your waye

67   *Culpeper to Hartlib, 4 February 1644/5.   (13/71–2 [summary only])*

*Culpeper sends the following instructions to accompany a box which he is forwarding
to Hartlib. Hartlib is to contact Mr Boyer, a linen draper in Cheapside, who has
a counterpart indenture to one which Culpeper sends to accompany the box. Hartlib
is also to locate Culpeper's brother-in-law, [William] Cage. If Cage is in London,
Hartlib is to inform him that, when he has assembled the two indentures, he has
instructions to hand the box over to him. If Cage is not in London, then Hartlib
will find Boyer ready to give him another box which he is to keep with the first until
he receives further instructions.*

68   *Culpeper to Hartlib, 6 February 1644/5.   (13/73–4 [summary only])*

*Culpeper sends further instructions to Hartlib in respect of the box which he has
recently despatched. Cage is not in London. Mr Boyer now has instructions to open
the box which has arrived with Hartlib and to dispose of its contents on Culpeper's
behalf.*

69   *Culpeper to Hartlib, 11 February 1644/5.   (13/75–6 [summary only])*

*Further instructions for the disposal of the contents of the box which Culpeper had
despatched. Culpeper laments his poverty.*

70   *Culpeper to Hartlib, 7 March 1644/5.   (13/77 [summary only])*

*Culpeper is much in debt. He asks Hartlib to discover what kind of relief would
be available to him, given his encumbered estates, from the fiscal exactions established*

---

[18] Jan Amos Comenius, *A Reformation of Schooles* (1642), Wing C5529.

by two ordinances. He is referring to the ordinance of 2 February 1644, raising money for the Scots' army, and the New Model Ordinance of 17 February, levying for the forces of Sir Thomas Fairfax.

71 *Culpeper to Hartlib, 18 March 1644/5. (13/78–9)*

Mr Hartlib;

I hope for noe good answere concerning the Militia, especially by the States Ambassadors, but yf it proue true that they haue mediated to the [King] for it it will proue an unanswerable objection in the Lowe Cowntries yf the [King] & lords (the [Prince] & State [General]) doe but in any kinde appeare for us wee may finally assure ourselues that the Commons (I meane the States Prouinciall) will (as lately for the [Queen] of Sweden) declare for the Parliament thowgh perhaps againste the wishes of the Hoghen moghens; And truly the States Prouinciall reassuminge or rather (I may say) theire vsinge theire innate affirmatiue power (when the [Prince] & Generall States fayle in good proposalls) is a principall wante I haue formerly obserued in that Gouernmente & showlde (for the good of that State & the good example to others) joy to heare it (vpon some occasionall conteste) bothe assumed & yelded; For in truthe the Ciuill Babylon in all states will neuer be soe justly & naturally reduced into order, as by restoringe the supremacy to that body which (from time to time) is immediately chosen by the people; were yf (after a full information of all the inferior wheeles) it selfe be but reduced (according to the Common Lawe & two declaratory Statutes)[19] to an annuall election the State cannot be but safer,[20] when once a yeere the [Parliament] can cure all the inferiour partes & the People themselues (by a newe election) the errors of the Parliament & till the nations of the earthe can thus render themselues free from all selfe interessed negatiues there will be but a slowe motion towards the happines of a nation whether in religion or liberty;

I haue sente you a note of the horses entered for me by [Captain] Lee with the names of them whoe registred them, I pray when your occasions call you towards Ludgate deliuer it to [Captain] Lee & (from me) desire him that by his meanes I may haue a certificate from the

[19] The two statutes for annual Parliaments passed under Edward III: *4 Edward III c 14*; *36 Edward III c 10*.

[20] Annual parliaments had become, by this date, cherished by 'honest radicals' as a vehicle for controlling royal prerogative and guaranteeing the virtue of the state. See, for example, 'A dialogue between Phileuteros or a parliament man, and Philopolites a lover of his country: or reasons to induce an annual parliament', BL MS Harl. 305, fols 255–73; also *The Short Parliament (1640): The Diary of Sir Thomas Aston*, ed. Judith D. Maltby (1988), pp. 10, 12, 58, 59.

officers & himselfe of concerning my deliueringe in suche geldinges; It may perhaps concern me; I pray remember me very kindly to him

I exceedingly like your projecte of settinge the poore on woorke & wowlde be glad to receiue some perticulars of it;

I pray afford me a woorde what you haue farther done concerning Mr Plats papers & especially his greate booke; for I Valewe my intereste in his woorkes;

I wowld gladly heare of Mr Dury, where he is, what he dothe, & what answere he makes to my often formed desires & the publike intereste in his Analisis;

I hope shortly to be in London, my trowbles beinge somewhat settled

72   *Culpeper to Hartlib, 26 March 1645.   (13/80)*

Mr Hartlib;

          I longe to heare of Mr Dury & some accownte (yf you can of Mr Commenius; I feare they haue bothe loste these 3: yeeres which in suche excellente aymes is too muche; I pray in a woorde let me understande what other Mr Plattes you meane & of what subjecte, for (thowgh of a meane condition) there haue been honeste & rationall men of that name;[21] Giue me a hinte (yf you can) of the materialls on which the poore might be set on woorke which I conceiue muste haue this property as to be in them selues very cheape & common & yet suche as after the woorke added to them will fully pay the charge; I shall be heartily glad of your chimicall bookes; For I am confidente I see a truthe but hauinge walked alone these twenty yeeres I haue reade the slower motion, & knowe not whether I shall come to the ende.

73   *Culpeper to Hartlib, 1 April 1645.   (13/81 [summary only])*

Culpeper cannot yet come to London as he would wish. He requests information as to whether any of the Oxford colleges have had their lands sequestered and, if so, by what ordinance of Parliament. If they have, he requests a copy of the ordinance.

74   *Culpeper to Hartlib, 5 April 1645.   (13/82–3 [summary only])*

Culpeper asks for an account of various items of business he had asked Hartlib to conduct in London. Accompanying the letter is a small barrel with £5 in it as a

---

[21] Culpeper is alluding to Sir Hugh Plats (1552–1611?), author of *The Jewell House of Art and Nature* (1594), STC 19991.

contribution 'from the very lowe condition of one whoe supplies in parte his own necessities by borrowinge'.

75   *Culpeper to Hartlib, 16 April 1645.   (13/84-5)*

Mr Hartlib;

I very muche consente to Mr Brandons booke of the little vse of Colonells & [Lieut*enant* Colo*nells*] in an army & not lesse to the greate charge & greater distractions they make in an army;[22] I am allsoe very muche taken with Mr Bellamyes speeche to the Mayor & Aldermen concerninge theire negatiues (more then conjunctiue) againste the eyther sittinge or actinge of the Common Cowncell,[23] And I cannot but heartily wisshe & (from the juncture of occurrences) hope to see those thowghts more vniversally apprehended & applied & that wee may, not in London, But Englande be restored to that anciente & (by nature) inherente priuiledge of hauinge (from time to time) suche lawes quas vulgus eligerit or (as the more anciente othe in Frenche taken by [Edw*ard*] the 2:ᵈ & 3:ᵈ hathe it more fully and vndeniably que la Communaute de vostre Royaume aura esleu where the Frenche Aoriste takes away all difference in opinion whether eligerit be the preterperfecte or future tence;[24] And yf the intereste of the Commons of Englande in theire representatiue & the impossibility that eyther [K*ing*] or Lorde can make good theire claime (yf but conscienciously questioned) but from a precedente authority of the People, yf this I say were but a little digested in the mindes of men, it wowlde be easily fownde that these hygheste claimes (yf legall) muste be (bothe for their firste beinge & continuance) fownded vpon the authority and grante of that rep-resentatiue in which the People terminated theire firste efluxe or emanation of politicall power & as by this representatiue the people (for themselues) at firste made the gouernmente soe may they by it decide the claimes of eache parte, resolue the reuocablenes or irrevocablenes of the whole gouernemente & by suche lawes que la Communaute aura often make suche changes as time shall discouer to be fittinge; I write not what I wowlde haue the Commons house to doe, for I heartily

[22] John Brandon, *The Reformed Army* (4 April 1645), Thomason, E.276 (14).

[23] John Bellamy, *A Plea for the Commonalty of London; Or a Vindication of their Rights in the Choice of City Officers; and also in the making of By-Laws* (24 February 1645). This publication caused an immediate outcry in London and was answered by *Bellarmius Enervatus*, to which Bellamy replied with *Lysimachus Enervatus* in July – Thomason, E.1174 (3); 281 (3); 1179 (3).

[24] Culpeper refers here to the intense contemporary debate over the meaning of the King's coronation oath. The dispute centred around whether the Latin text 'quas vulgus elegerit' meant those laws which the people shall determine in the future, a meaning more clearly carried in the French text 'que la Communaute de vostre Royaume *aura* esleu'.

wishe that the Peerage of Englande may (like those in Scotlande) vse
that truste they claime, for theire goode for & from whome they
receiued whatsoeuer they holde as legall, & it is my hearty prayers for
the [King] that he wowlde doe the like, but if otherwise, et cæt.

The passages between the [King] & Popishe Hierarchy of Poland of
the on side & the Protestants of the other I am muche more taken with
them then with the two former & truly I cannot but hope that as these
ouertures of a rotten peace haue proceeded from Valerius Magnus &
other suche Emissaries of Rome,[25] soe the Protestante Churches beinge
(by Mr Duries vigilance & care)[26] forewarned of these deuices may be
the more stirred vp to a spirituall vnion & correspondency in things of
soe common & hygh concernemente, towardes which I apprehende
many occurrences which in this juncture of publike affaires, are (by
Gods prouidence) like to proue vsefull,; I knowe my owne weakenesses &
vnwoorthinesses to serue in soe good a cause but yf you cowld nowe
or heereafter aduise me wherein my very small talente might be vsefull
towardes it, my wishes & prayers are & shall be that God will please
to inlarge my hearte & fit it thowgh but for some meane parte in soe
good a woorke;

I longe to heare of Mr Dury & yf it were possible to see him, I pray
when you write to him presente my faythfull & affectionate loue vnto
him, & o howe happy showld I be to receiue his promise concerninge
his way of Analisis;[27] I muche desire an answere of my laste letter I
inclosed to you for Mr [Boman] & yf I migh see what you haue of Mr
Plattes writings I heere faythfully promise you to returne them safe; I
pray afforde me a woorde concerning the subjecte of the other Mr
Plattes book[28]

I reste euer

[*Hartlib:*]
W
qu
quar It is so that

---

[25] Valerius Magnus was a Capuchin monk living in Prague. He was an opponent of
the Jesuits and an adviser to King Vladislav IV of Poland, much trusted for diplomatic
purposes by Emperors Ferdinand II and II. He also became an adviser to King Vladislav
IV of Poland – see *The Catholic Encyclopaedia* (ed. Charles G. Herbermann, 15 vols, 1907–
1912), ix. 537.

[26] A reference to Dury's Parliamentary petition of 1642 on the subject of the necessity
of 'a correspondence in spirituall matters betwixt all Protestant Churches' and his
subsequent pamphlet: *Certaine Considerations, Shewing the Necessity of a Correspondencie in
Spirituall Matters betwixt all Protestant Churches* (1642), Wing D2839.

[27] At this date, Dury was minister to the Merchant Adventurers in Rotterdam. He
would return to England in August 1645.

[28] Hugh Plats (1552–1611?) – see **72** (26 March 1645).

76   *Culpeper to Hartlib, 6 May 1645.   (13/86-7)*

Mr Hartlib;

Your packet sente allmoste a fortnight since I receiued laste Saterday night; of this weeke I receiued none; To preuente all future miscarriages I haue appointed one Champion a carrier of Ashforde to carry my letters; whoe lodges about Bilingsgate & leaues [London] constantly on thursday night; but keepes himselfe more punctually to the eueninge tyde as hauinge farther to goe the nexte day, But in truthe I feare I put you to too muche trowble, & more then my very strayght fortunes are able to thanke you for, besides that (by what accidente I knowe not) seuerall of your late packets haue come antiquated to my handes;

I am moste heartily glad to vnderstande of Mr Duryes happy marriage,[29] & showlde be ambitious (yf in Englande) to be knowen to that subjecte whom his judgement hath fownde *moste susceptible of the beste motions, moste apprehensiue of the cheefeste aymes, & moste generously actiue & resolute to set forwarde the fitteste meanes & wayes leading to ___ those aymes of publique ædification which were* the principall thowgh not onely growndes of *the couenante of theire spirituall frindship*; I thanke you for the 2: treaties concerning Scripturall Analisis; one of them I had before & haue therefore returned it to you; For the other I finde it corresponde with the reste which I haue seene & all of them to promise & relate to somewhat more perfecte which Mr Dury is pleased to invite his frindes to expecte from him, when he showlde obtaine a freedome from those distractions which haue formerly but will not nowe I hope futurely incompasse him; For my owne intereste of wishes in that busines, I am I feare noe competente judge howe farre I may deserue any further share in it, then suche generalls as (without farther particular treaties) may rayse but cannot satisfy an appetite, but howsoeuer it be I cannot butt still wishe that neyther the expectation raysed concerninge Scripturall Analisis & the admirable consequences of it in the vnion of Christians & conversion of Heathens be frustrated, nor yet Mr Dury suffer eyther as a proposer of a thinge beyonde or aboue his reache or as a burier of soe precious a talente yf the worlde might haue had, & showld happen to loose it by his deathe; What I write is from a settled resolution (after a longe turmoyle of thoughts) that there is noe humane possibility of raisinge a communion of Saintes out of this presente Chaos of opinions but by pressinge a Scripturall necessity of charity &

---

[29] Dury married Dorothy Moore, a cousin by marriage to Katherine, Lady Ranelagh, sister to Robert Boyle. The marriage took place in February 1645 (Dorothy Moore indicated her consent to the proposition in her letter to Lady Ranelagh of 11/21 February 1645 (3/2/95A and B); Dury writes of his recent marriage in his letter to Hartlib of 2 March 1645 (3/2/98A and B)).

communion amonge those who soe holde the fowndation, as they may
(all vnsober & furiously zealous thowghts caste aside) hope well of one
anothers saluation & why, (yf there be any consolation in Christe, any
comforte of loue, any fellowship of the Spirit, any bowells & mercies)
<philipp: 2: 1: 3:>[30] suche as sufficiently holde the fowndation &
nothinge destructiue of it, showlde not be like minded hauinge the
same loue till it shall please God (by the spirit of prophecy to reveale
the reste) I cannot see; I pray in your nexte to Mr Dury name me as
one whoe congratulate his marriage & wishe him all happines in it; I
haue returned you Mr Plats papers between which & his pouerty &
[manner] of deathe there seemes to me some contradictions, That the
tryalls of the truthe of what he propownds is & owght to be cheape in
that I like & consente to him; For I am confidente that he whoe knowes
how to restore to the Spirite of Nature its naturall motion in leade or
any other imperfecte mettall he may be able (by the same kinde of
apposition & adaptation of naturall agents & patientes) to highten any
minerall subjecte to that exuberancy of life & spirite which nature by
herselfe cannot reache vnto Quia (saythe Dionisius Zachary) A actiones
eius sunt continuæ,[31] Et (in another place) hæc est ratio cur videamus
naturam illud (Aurum) in melius vltra non transmutare;[32] But to
descende to things more sensible & of presente concernemente;

It is generally taken notice of that the Cownties under the [Parliament]
doe lay out themselues very freely for the [Parliament's] seruice & yet
notwithstandinge it nowe costes this Cownty allmoste as muche to
defende it selfe againste our owne troopes that come back vpon vs as
wowlde pay their arreares; I assure you this giues a juste occasion of
complainte to those that haue been ready to seeke one & leaues euen
suche of the [Parliament] side very muche vnsatisfied as haue not yet
learned with patience to submitte where they cannot consente or
approue, & silences suche others as wowlde gladly at all times be able
to answere for their justice as well as their authority; And truly till the
seeinge & witnessinge onely of the paimente of the Common sowldier
(not the paimente it selfe) be lefte to the commanders the state will be
cousened, the Cownties consumed, the sowldiers still ready to turne
backe vpon us & the commanders bribed to continue the Warre

I pray in your nexte eyther satisfy my sad hearte in this particular
or yf I speake truthe, spreade it (yf you can) into suche handes as may

---

[30] Philippians 2:1 – 'If there be therefore any consolation in Christ, if any comfort of
love, if any fellowship of the Spirit, if any bowels and mercies'.

[31] Dionysius Zacharius [Zachary], 'Opusculum Philosophiae Naturalis Mettalorum' in
Theatrum Chemicum, ed. Lazarus Zetzner, (orig. edition IV vols., Strasbourg, 1613) (enlarged
edition, VI vols, Strasbourg, 1659–1661), i. 729 (in the enlarged edition).

[32] Ibid, i. 733, 'Et haec est ratio cur sit perfectius omnibus aliis metallis, tum quo
videamus naturam illud in melius ultra non transmutare.'

make vse of it, I can conceiue nothinge of more aduantage honor for the [Parl*iament*] than the juste painge of those whoe muste venter their liues, & yf (towards soe goode a woorke), all moste halfe the idle commanders wee cashiered & suche persons & number onely, lefte as were fitteste to aduise what they are to aske there wowld be lesse cheatinge & more action

I cannot certeinly say when I shall come to London excepte you cowlde giue me a Q. wherein I cowlde be seruiceable to any good ende for truly my presente condition is soe suncke & depressed as I haue scarse a good rise lefte vpon which to put my selfe forwarde towardes any good eyther for the publike or my selfe; But God dothe all for the beste; You mentioned Mr Plattes greate booke; I wowld (yf I might) very willingly see it; I pray sende me the price of Cottons Concordance,[33] I conceiue it very usefull, but howe muche more vsefull a concordance of things wowlde be, I cannot expresse, I meane of prayer, faythe repentance et cæt together with the subdiuidinge considerations of them; O howe wowlde it enable euery priuate person to teache himself & to rayse his owne affections from the woorde of light & life; Thus haue I giuen you a taste of my solitary entertainements; my paper is done & (I conceiue) your selfe (by this time) wearied with my impertinences; I reste

[*PS.*] Synce the concludinge my letter I haue resolued to take a review of Mr Platts booke

77 *Culpeper to Hartlib, 20 May 1645.* *(13/88-9)*

Mr Hartlib;

I [rec*eived*] your 2: packets th'other weeke & your single one the laste; For my goinge to London, my lowe condition wowlde (I conceiue) haue kepte me from it, For thowgh (after 2: or 23: yeeres acquaintance with Chimistry) I haue nowe at laste attained to my first resolution in that study (i) of being satisfyed within my selfe & my owne reason concerning that which (Pontan saythe) is not de materia,[34] & which others thowgh improperly to deceiue the readers) call the agente, beinge indeede & in itselfe (thowgh a correlatiue cause of action and motion & that which did at firste & dothe still excite the Spirite of the Lorde to moue in & vpon the waters) yet rather a patiente, & therefore onely

---

[33] Clement Cotton published several biblical concordances in the period 1622-1638; see STC 5842-46.7.

[34] Joannis Pontani, 'epistola, in qua lapide, quem Philosophorum vocant, agitur' in *Theatrum Chemicum* (1659-1661 edition), iii. 734-36.

deseruinge the name of an agente because that true agente or spirit of the worlde (infused into the creature) cannot moue or actuate it selfe but vpon it; thowgh I say I haue that in my thowghts concerning this subjecte which (after 23: yeeres) wowld put many others vpon action or tryall yet I knowe not what depressed & sluggishe spirit wowlde haue kepte me at home; But I shall nowe (vpon your invitation) resolue to see London about the middle or latter ende of nexte weeke; In the meane time let me tell you that this day seauennight I had (by strange accidente) tendred to my viewe suche a Chymicall woorke of Mr Plattes & as you haue noe way mentioned, & suche a further offer of another paper (vpon certeine conditions) as showld treate of the firste agente; Vpon a viewe of the firste I fownde it to be a translation onely of somethinge out of a book called Miracula Chymica,[35] which thowgh perhaps true, yet withoute the firste agent or Key migh well (as it showlde seeme it was resolued) be printed by Mr Plattes, I am promised (yf I shall desire it) the sight the other but it muste be on suche conditions as for the presente are difficulte to me, I pray let me vnderstande howe this comes about & whether I may (from you or by your meanes) expecte the sight of any suche paper, I am very confidente I showlde be able (vpon sight) to giue a neere judgemente on it, & withall (yf true) receiue some aduantage in the particular passages, such aduantage I meane as hathe coste euen those that haue knowen the truth in generall, some time & practise; I reste

78   *Culpeper to Hartlib, 13 June 1645. (13/90–1)*

Mr Hartlib;
      hauinge occasion to sende backe my seruante to London I cannot but desire to receiue a line from you, what effecte the late motions in the house of Commons haue wrowght;[36]
      I am confidente that the hochepot of Royallists, & of the Englishe & Skottishe Aristocracy (I meane the nobility & presbitery) are like to set hande vpon the Independente whoe as he hathe joyned with the other two against the swellinge of Monarchy soe are they vpon the same reason againste the Aristocraticall negatiue or of any suche Churche Gouernmente as shall eyther be imposed on vs by another nation or soe settled as not to leaue a Doore open for suche future reformation as God shall invite vs to; In this contest as the Lords house are like to make a party, soe theire rights are like to be the plea of the reste; For

---

[35] Bernardus Trevisanus, 'De Chemico Miraculo', Ibid., iii. 683–709.
[36] Culpeper probably refers to the motion, agreed by the House of Commons on 10 June, to appoint Cromwell as Lieutenant-General – Gardiner, ii. 238.

the Scotts haue but the plea of a contracte but not that we showld be in all things mowlded by them, The presbitery is hardly in actu, but the Lords negatiue vnder which the reste will shewe themselues will not be soe rightly vnderstood or digested; There is something in projecte in this Cownty, by way of petition that (at leaste during these times of danger) there may be a joining againste the Common enimy & all priuate opinions & contestes layde aside, & truly, though a profeste toleration of all kinds lookes not well to many yet persecution of fellowe Christians for things nether necessary nor hurtfull to the Ciuill state looke worse & to more; for euery one doeth & may truly looke vpon it as that which may fall to his share

I am in haste & reste

79   *Culpeper to Hartlib, 2 July 1645. (13/92–3 [summary only])*

If the civil war were over, Culpeper would much approve of Hartlib's paper on the conversion of the Indians[37] and it is a good sign that, in the midst of 'this fire' there is leisure for such thoughts. Culpeper offers some thoughts on how to keep the Royalist cavalry closely confined in order to leave the Parliamentarian infantry free to undertake a siege. He would still welcome an opportunity to look at Plat's 'great booke'[38] when it is returned to Hartlib.

80   *Culpeper to Hartlib, 17 July 1645 (enclosing list of Helmont's medical writings). (13/94–8)*

Mr Hartlib;
    The reason you hearde not from me the laste weeke, was an vnexpected interveninge occasion as I was puttinge pen to paper

I cannot yet giue you accownte eyther of my owne or Mr Bartines[39] [Perpetuus Motus] but shall very shortly of bothe; In this time of my owne lowe Condition & the absence of those frinds which showlde haue beene my strenght, I finde suche a generall assaulte on all hands vpon our small estate as that it too muche robbes me of my quiet & reposed thowghts

I doe very muche approue of your endeauors concerninge the Excise

[37] 'Memorandum for the Conversion of the Indians' – 3 March 1644 (40/4/1A–2B).
[38] See **57** (13 November 1644).
[39] Barton was an inventor whom Hartlib hoped would stay in England and join his Office of Address – GI, p. 68. According to **97** ([November 1645?]), Barton was at the 'signe of the boule in the bell ally ouer againste the middle Temple gate'; he is probably the Mr Bartne who is reported in 1648 as living at Sittingborne – see **150** (15 March 1648).

in which yf (discarding our many officers that liue vpon it) wee wowlde (accordinge to the Hollande practise mentioned in the Citty Alarme)[40] farme out the seuerall particulars bothe of things & places (vpon very gainfull conditions at firste), & for but shorte terms the state wowlde quickly come to knowe the true valewe of its owne, especially yf the farmers of the seuerall excises were (by ordinance) bownde to deliuer (upon oathe) true accownte what they showld make of theire farme; And yf some fewe places in a Cownty were (as by accidente) kepte in the [Parliament's] hands & executed (as nowe) by officers there wowlde (by compareinge one time with another & one place with another) muche more truthe discouered;[41] And truly were the Excise well settled the [Parliament] would not (as laste weeke) be necessitated (for 200001) to resorte to an Ordinance,[42] which too muche discouers theire owne nakednes joyes their enimies & grieues their frinds

For your busines of your Worke houses & the education of chyldren,[43] It is of suche vaste & future concernemente as in truthe I cannot looke throwgh it but shall take vpon mee the fooles priuiledge of makinge more dowbtes then perhaps a wise man may answere, 1: Whether your Grante of priuiledge owght (as your demande imports) be for euer where (I am confidente) the growndes is not like to endure for a age which time (fewe consider) what change (towards purity) it is like to bringe into the worlde but to let this passe; 2: The strenght vpon which you vndertake soe vaste a woorke is saltepeeter,[44] which yf vented onely in gunpowder will not (I conceiue) euen duringe these vnnaturall warres muche lesse in times of peace & yet muche lesse when the instrumente of warre shall be beaten into ploweshares) become a grownde woorke

[40] *The City Alarum of the Weeke of our Miscarriages Whereunto is annexed a Treatise of the Excise* (7 July 1645), Thomason, E.292 (12).

[41] For the administration of the excise in this period see M. J. Braddick, *Parliamentary taxation in seventeenth-century England: local administration and response*, Royal Historical Society Studies in History, 70 (Woodbridge, 1994), ch. 4.

[42] The Parliamentary Ordinance of 1 July for raising £20,000 for 'the reducing of Oxford' – F&R, i. pp. 723–25.

[43] Culpeper refers to *The Parliaments Reformation* (1646), Wing H995A, Hartlib's tract on poor relief and workhouses. See also 'The proposal for employment of poor immigrants to the city', undated, 53/13/1A–2B; also the scribal copy of the petition concerning maintenance of the poor, undated, 53/2/35A–38A.

[44] Saltpetre (potassium nitrate) was the important constituent element in gunpowder. Its powerful medicinal possibilities and potential as a fertiliser were also highly regarded by Hartlib and his associates. The shortage of saltpetre was exacerbated by a ban on its exportation to England imposed by various European states. The Parliamentary ordinance of 23 October 1643 licensed saltpetre-men to search for and commandeer the necessary supplies throughout the kingdom – F&R, i. 320. This was renewed on 3 April 1644 under Parliamentary scrutiny for a period of two years and again on 7 February 1646 – F&R, i. 418–20; 828–30. Hartlib estimated in 1645 that the state paid £90 per ton for saltpetre, of which £20 went to the ill-regarded saltpetre-men (53/26/1A–B).

for soe many hospitalles & woorke houses; but yf for the vente of your
salte peeter you doe (with mr Plattes) squinte vpon the improuemente
of landes I then question whether (in case the projecte holdes) you doe
not yet interfaire with the Frenchemans proposition you lately mentioned to me[45] 3: For your estimate of the corne in the pidgeons crop,
I doe (vpon my owne experience) affirme that in steade of your 1000:
little lesse then 4000 cleuells of corne will fill a pinte, which (yf true)
takes away 3/4: of your æstimate of what pidgeons eatte, & for what
they leake out it seems to me suche an [indiuiduum] vagum as cannot
be set downe eyther by number or measure, but what I nowe write is
not againste the worke or for pidgeonhouses (for I heartily wishe the
one perfected & the other pulled downe) but that suche small matters
(yf elsewhere examined & fownde not to holde) may not (as too ofte)
prejudice the maine[46] 4: Yf this projecte (by those whoe haue more
throwghly considered it) be indeede of that vaste profit, why is not the
Colledge of spirituall & rationall correspondency thowght of which (not
to disparage this) is of a more sublime nature & yf once (thowgh but
in a small module) set on foote, wowlde deriue its metaphyisicall
influence bothe on this & all other inferiour ingenuities, But to leaue
this busines leaste I seeme againste that which I soe muche like

    I am exceeding glad Mr Dury is cominge ouer & cannot but hope
he will by Gods blessinge proue an angell of peace to this poore
distracted Churche,[47] & (thowgh some late passages of his make me
sometimes affrayde) I cannot yet finally thinke that he can be for theire
persecutinge one another in the leaste kinde whoe (holdinge the same
sufficiente fundamentalls & nothinge to ouerthrowe them) not onely
may but owght (vpon the maine growndewoorke of his pacificall

---

[45] Culpeper refers to Pierre Le Pruvost, a French protestant who, with Hugh l'Amy,
was encouraged by John Dury to present Hartlib and his associates in 1645 with ambitious
proposals for English economic revival through colonising and associated endeavours.
Several copies of the proposition are in the archive and although they differ slightly from
one another all subscribe to a system of economic improvement which was most fully
delineated in a French copy at 12/93A–98B. The proposition was later presented to
Parliament and English translations are at 12/04, 12/89, and 55/10. See also GI, pp.
371–2; 375–6. The family background of Le Pruvost remains, despite research in the
Bibliothèque de l'histoire du protestantisme français and the Bibliothèque Nationale,
Paris, entirely obscure. Hugues L'Amy, sieur de Mohum may be connected to the family
of merchants and pastors of that name from the area around Dieppe.

[46] Culpeper is commenting on Hartlib's proposal to assist the poor by employing them
in the digging and carting of saltpetre from pigeon-lofts, the abolition of useless pigeon-
lofts, and the distribution of revenues saved by the more efficient production of saltpetre
to hospitals and almshouses in parishes throughout the kingdom – 53/26/7A–B.

[47] Dury resigned his pastorate in Rotterdam and returned to London during August
1645 – Batten, p. 104. Turnbull suggests that Dury was thinking of coming to England
as early as 25 July/5 August 1645 – HDC, p. 249. On 12 August 1645 Dury appeared at
the Westminster Assembly of Divines for the first time – HDC, p. 250.

negotiations) to imbrace one another as spirituall brethren but by noe meanes to call in & stirre vp the ciuill swoorde againste one another in which the Scottish presbitery differs (as I conceiue) but in persons from Popery & Episcopacy & in which (I yet hope) wee shall leaue our geud Brethren;

On saterday laste I mentioned Bisterfeild[48] to the [Prince] Elector whoe allready holdes correspondency with him, but thinkes him (I perceiue) a man of more learninge then prudence; For Helmont I haue heere inclosed a note of suche promisinge heads of treatises to which (in seuerall places of his booke[49] I had of you) he referres his reader; He names allsoe the heades of many receiptes which to me seeme to haue an excellency, not onely for the endes for which he mentions them but (beinge applied by the analogie of reason) for more sublime endes; which indeed seemes to me the scope of his whole booke viz: in a subordination to common endes to giue a touche onely, to the worlde of suche conceptions as (yf exalted by the reader to their proper hyght) haue more excellente vses of themselues; Thus (as I told you) in the way to the cure of the stone he directes the readers vnderstandinge to the searche of an vniversall dissoluente which (saythe he) when fownde væ confusioni; Thus in his tracte of feauers[50] he confirmes my former thowghts howe the naturall spirits in all naturall bodies doe (by and accordinge to an occasionall & externall matter) receiue within themselues the impression eyther of an alteratiue or feuerishe & vnnaturall excitation & (by these naturall or vnnaturall excitations) causes that vicissitude of perfection & ruine, generation & corruption which wee may obserue in the inferiour region, where the spirite of the worlde or that spiritus domini (qui ferebatur super aquarum os incubauit aquis)[51] thus excitated eyther in the vniversall body or the specificall or indiuiduall seedes cause a continuall circular motion in the generation & corruption of thinges;

---

[48] Johann Heinrich Bisterfeld was the former pupil and (eventually) the son-in-law of the German encyclopaedist and professor at the Herborn Academy, Johann Heinrich Alsted. Bisterfeld's treatise on logic circulated among Hartlib's acquaintances. At this date he was reportedly 'one of the Prince [of Translyvania's] Cabinet Councel' – see the extract from the letter of John Rulice, Amsterdam, 12/22 February 1644 in 43/21A–22B.

[49] Johan Baptista van Helmont (1579–1644). Only four of van Helmont's works had been published by the time of his death in December 1644 (Partington, ii. 213). These were: *De Magnetica Vulnerum Naturalis et Legitima Curatione* (Paris, 1621); *Supplementum de Spadanis Fontibus* (Liège, 1624); *Febrium Doctrina Inaudita* (Antwerp, 1642); *Opuscula Medica Inaudita* (Cologne, 1644). Hartlib had evidently lent him his copy of the last of these. See generally Walter Pagel, *Johan Baptista van Helmont: Reformer of Science and Medicine* (Cambridge, 1982).

[50] 'Tractus de febribus' in *Febrium Doctrina Inaudita*. Reprinted in *Ortus medicinæ* (Amsterdam, 1648), pp. 11–12 etc.

[51] Helmont, *Opuscula* (Amsterdam, 1644), p. 22 ('De Lithiari').

And truly I cannot but conceiue it probable that [Monsieur] Hel-
monts sonne might (as acquaintance growes) be dealte with all for some
of these secrettes, & yf they were demanded at firste for those ordinary
endes for which his Father proposes them he wowld perhaps be the
lesse shye; I am very confidente his Father hathe lefte him suche
excellente thinges, whereof neyther himselfe nor his sonne knowes yet
the hygheste vse;[52] & the like saythe Helmont of Paracelsus himselfe, &
the like may perhaps be sayde of Mr Carmikill the Scotts [Gentleman][53]
you mentioned to me, whoe wowlde allsoe be dealte withall to open
him selfe to some honeste men; For God (accordinge to his good will &
pleasure) giue some excellente gifte to one the right vse of it another
that none may finde perfection in themselues & all may glorify him the
giuer all;

I feare I haue loste my time & the carier gone

  1 - Initia physica
  2 - De latice Vrinæ
  3 - De Hydrope
  4 - De Venætione [scientiarum]
  5 - De morbis
  6 - Quod calor non digerat in sensitiuis
  7 - Quod in herbis et lapidibus est magna Virtus
  8 - De Spasmo
  9 - De Splæno
  10 - Quod hominum perturbationes in præcordijs circa os stomachi
fabricantur[54]

81 *Culpeper to Hartlib, 22 July 1645. (13/99–100)*

[Note: incomplete]

For your designe of Woorke & Alme houses[55] I thinke it a blessed
woorke, but that other concerning the excise I looke vpon it rather to

---

[52] His surviving manuscripts passed mainly to his son, Francis Mercurius van Helmont
(1614–1699), who himself studied and practised medicine and chemistry. See *Ortus medicinæ*,
preface; Partington, ii. 242–3.

[53] Sir James, Lord Carmichael (1578?–1672). His medical and chemical interests are
several times alluded to by Hartlib. He had been resident in London in the early 1640s
but it was through Hartlib that Culpeper knew about him.

[54] These have mostly been identified as part of the published corpus of Helmont's
writings by the time of his death. They correspond to components of the *Ortus medicinæ*
as follows: 1. 'Causae et initia naturalium' p. 33. 3. 'Ignotus hydrops' p. 508. 4. 'Venatio
scentiarum' p. 20. 5. 'Tractus de morbis' p. 529.

[55] See **80** (17 July 1645).

quenche our presente fire & will therefore (I conceiue) deserue your presente thowghts & indeauors, for yf rightly imbursed & disbursed it will woorke miracles; I showlde be glad to heare of your proceedings in them bothe as allsoe of your saltepeeter business; I am glad you vndertake for Mr Dury as for a man totally for peace not at all for persecution; For his Scripturall Analisis I haue some reasons of late to thinke that he muste (like planters) looke to the future, & this I apprehende from those Herculean pillars which men make to themselues by confininge posibility. to theire narrowe vnderstandinge & truly I finde it farre more difficulte to reduce a man from this ouerweeninge to soe muche sobriety as to giue but an orderly audience, then hauinge gained but soe little) afterwardes to convince the person; But I cannot inlarge my selfe heere

Sir [William] Waller had lefte this Cownty before I receiued your letter, nor in truthe haue I muche intereste in him

I concurre with Mr Dury in his opinion howe muche you are like to deserue from the [Prince] Elector & what I nowe write I shall take occasion to say bothe to others & to the [Prince] Elector himselfe, But (to be free with you in what I showlde be glad to be mistaken) I finde him not ballasted for that greate woorke that may one day perhaps be caste vpon him excepte to fill the chaire & carry the name of busines, be sufficiente which, of successiue princes (in my opinion (I confesse) longe agoe) hathe beene cownted the beste vse; & in these thowghts I hold successiue monarchy the beste of gouernments

I hope I haue nowe cured you of your cowrteships & compliments & that you will for your owne sake invite me noe more to the trowblesome interruption of your better thowghts to which (hauing thus punnished you with your owne wishes) I leaue you & reste

82   *Culpeper to Hartlib, 6 August 1645. (13/101–2)*

Mr Hartlib;

        by your laste letter and packet on friday was seuen-night you lefte me in the midste of the [Parliament's] good successes) somewhat sad & fearefull in that (as you then writte) the Englishe were not soe jouiall (those are youre woordes) as I conceiued them; This your generall expression corfirmed those former feares I haue had of a nationall difference & truly if our geud Brethren (throwgh the aristo-craticall intereste they haue in our presente State & Churche) doe presse too rigidly theire patterne for the subordination of the Ciuill power to the Ecclesiasticall, & for noe liberty of Conscience, I cannot but feare wee shall not longe keepe that Vnion which the Common enimy wowlde joy to see broken;[56] I pray afford me in a woord what showlde nowe interrupte our joyes & hopes; I muste ende

83 *Culpeper to Hartlib, 1 September 1645. (13/103–4)*

Mr Hartlib;

I thanke you for you packet thowgh (I assure you it hathe made me very sad but God will be moste glorified when meanes fayle, especially if wee still looke to him, & I am confidente that the meanes the [King] vses will finally preuayle for vs, after that our Faythe & patience hathe been sufficiently tryed

The fillinge of the house makes me wishe my selfe of it, but my owne disabilities & wante of meanes cooles me yf you thinke me faythfull & knowe where soe to recommende me I shall leaue it to your kindenes[57]

My seruice & thanckes to Mr Dury for his letter which I will answere by the nexte

84 *Culpeper to Hartlib, 17 September 1645. (13/105–6)*

Mr Hartlib

I thancke you kindly that you remember your Frinde & yf it be beste I wishe you may preuayle; The purginge of our greate Committees bothe in their persons & continuance & the better settlinge of the revenewe et cæt will be fittinge woorkes for a filled house

I am sorry for the occasion of the Scottes leauinge vs,[58] but I cannot but hope that God hathe (in it) good towards vs, For in truthe their influence on our Cowncells wowlde haue ballanced their assistance; I cannot but hope wee shall goe further then they haue done in the arraignemente of persecution, & not soe farre in leauinge still the Ciuill sworde at the Churchemans disposinge; The better parte of Ius Regum[59] dothe (methinkes) very hansomely decide the busines by giuinge the minister of the woorde a narratiue & declaratiue power onely but not

---

[56] Anglo-Scottish relations were in turmoil during the summer of 1645 – Gardiner, ii. 285–86, 339–40, 368–69.

[57] Culpeper refers to the exclusions of Royalist members of the House of Commons which were made at this time, amongst whom was his distant cousin and brother-in-law John Culpeper, one of the county MPs for Kent – CJ, iv. 272.

[58] On 13 September 1645 the English Parliament was informed that the Scots' forces had to withdraw because of the threats posed to the Covenanters by Montrose. See *Divers Papers Presented*, Thomason, E.307 (4.), p. 11; CJ, iv. 273.

[59] Henry Parker, *Jus Regum Or, a Vindication* (1645), Wing P404.

in the leaste kinde authoratatiue & to the Ciuill magistrate the whole
coerciue; Thus may the [King] equally with the meaneste be subjecte
to the ministery of the Woorde, & the minister of the woorde (in thinges
Ciuill) equally subjecte to the magistrates coerciue power;

I pray giue me a hinte what Sir our nexte military motions are like
to be; I cannot see howe without 2: armies wee can followe our intereste
in the Weste & Wales at once;

My kinde respectes to Mr Dury, I reste in haste

85   *Culpeper to Hartlib, 30 September 1645. (13/107–8)*

Mr Hartlib;

Your intelligence of the 25th was very welcome, Yf the [King]
his Lords & Gentlemen beginne to shatter I shall hope that the
beginners will invite others to followe;[60] & yet cannot but feare that the
[King] for his owne sinnes and ours, is like to ende this warre (after
more gwilte of our bloode) in his owne ruine;

Oh: what an addition to all our late victories were the Queenes
teares for Essex to confirme vs in our newe module? what an exaltation
were they bothe of Essex in his kinde & of braue Fairfaxe, Cromwell &
Scippon in theire waye, truly were I in my [Lord] of Essex case those
teares wowlde be soe many daggers to my hearte

Yf the intention of a peace be reall[61] which (thowgh from my Brother
because nowe a courtier)[62] I feare, I cannot but hope that the wisdome
of the [Parliament] will not (after this expence of bloode & treasure)
leaue vs after 7: yeeres to a like newe conteste about the sworde it
beinge that which muste assure to us and ours the conditions nowe to
be made;[63] When these warres beganne the successe was dowbtfull, the
true authority of Parliamente not knowen, the bloode & treasure of
this [Kingdome] not layed out, in all which regards, suche an acco-
modation as might (in likelyhood) proue a stop to farther liberty
deserued perhaps a consideration; But nowe that bothe nations and
houses are better vnited the true authority of Parliaments better &

---

[60] The Royalist cause was in disarray – Clarendon, iv. 42–128.

[61] Peace proposals were being proposed by the Scots to the King, and also from the
English Presbyterians to the King – Gardiner, ii. 337–56.

[62] Sir John Culpeper, Cheney's distant cousin and brother-in-law, was master of the
rolls to Charles I. In September 1645, far from supporting any peace initiative, he was
proposing a bold military offensive to secure London for the Royalists – Gardiner, ii.
341.

[63] In the Newcastle Propositions, the period of time during which the authority over
the militia would, following the conclusion of a peace, be vested in the hands of
Parliament was 20 years; but this was evidently the subject of negotiation over the
summer of 1645.

more generally vnderstood; our victorious armies in faythfull handes, & the ende of the Warre (by Gods blessinge) within our viewe I cannot but hope that the wisdome of [Parliament] will not (by takinge onely 7: yeeres in the Militia) bothe acknowlled a kinde of title to the [King] that shall soe settle it & continue woorkinge thowghts & hopes in Him & his party when he shall knowe that after seauen yeeres he may reassume his pretences Yf I cowlde once see the swoorde (by the [Kings] acknowledgemente) vnited in a perpetuity to the Iudiciall authority & publike liberty then might the Cowrts & subjecte say to the [King] Arma tenenti, omnia dat qui justa negat; Till the militia be legally settled in the [Parliament] wee haue noe holde at all in our liberty wee are but tenants at will, & till the swoorde be settled in a perpetuity to us, wee haue (at beste) but a lease in the reste of our temporall happiness which wee are to holde by it

Doe but settle the swoorde, & the assemblinge of [Parliament] theire continuance to sit, theire power to acte, the woords (quas vulgus eligerit) in the [King's] oathe and all other difficulties about the Prærogatiue will be easily decided, wee shall not neede to fight vpon a grammaticall question whether Eligerit be the preter perfecte or future tence,[64] Yf wee haue the Cowrts to judge the Lawe, the sworde to obey & defende the Iudge, & a [King] & Cowrtiers subjecte to bothe, it will be as muche reformation as can be expected in the inferior wheeles; I scribble the more vpon this pointe because I am in greate paine concerning it; I pray (yf you consente) infuse it into some [Parliament] men;

86   *Culpeper to Hartlib, n.d. [Autumn 1645]. (13/292–3)*[65]

Mr Hartlib;

when I was laste in London, you tolde me as I remember of one whoe had a water which (by washinge the face onely) cured the resorte of humor to the eyes; I pray yf for loue or mony there may be some of it procured let me knowe on munday night nexte by the Ashforde carrier whoe (as I formerly informed you) lodges about Bilingsgate; I pray excuse this liberty it beinge for an especiall frinde

One of Mr Prouoste[66] his secrets was a way to keepe fishe for transportation but whether deade or aliue I did not (when you tolde me) aske the question; yf his invention bee to keepe them deade, the

---

[64] See **75** (16 April 1645).

[65] The dating of this letter to Autumn 1645 is conjectural and depends on its being, on internal grounds, closely antecedent to **88** (n.d. [late Autumn/December 1645?]), whose dating is discussed below.

[66] For Le Pruvost, see **80** (17 July 1645) above. For his claims for the better dressing and preserving of fish, see 12/9A–B and the proposed ordinance: 12/181A.

metaphysicke of the invention may perhaps serue to many other very profitable endes bothe of profit and curiosity & truly the arte of preseruation of thinges is a pointe not sufficiently studied or heeded for (besides many other vses) I am confidente wee might (for very many suche summer frwites which will not keepe the ordinary way) turne winter into summer; Sir Hugh Plats cowlde 40: yeeres synce keepe hartychockes rownde the yeere and cherries till neere Michaelmas;[67] bothe these inventions & (which is more) the reason of them is perished (for owght I knowe) with the awthor; But yf Mr Prouste intende to keepe his fishe aliue; I pray then shewe him what my Frenche Companion saythe: Quelques vns ont dit que l'eau douce seule, ne nourrist ny ne produitt rien qu'on voit du contraire, en de cailloux, des coquilles, et des poissons mesmes qui croissent au milieu des eaux; Et de fait mettez des petits caillouz ou poyssons dans quelque phiolle, et de l'eau dessus, la renouuellant tous les jurs, et au bout de quelque temps vouz les trouuerez tellement. accrouz qu'ils ne pourroient sortir ou ils estoient entre:[68] my papers done your etcet

87   *Dury to Culpeper n.d. [Autumn 1645]. (55/10/11–14)*[69]

To Sir Cheny Culpeper

Sir I thanke you for your kinde Remembrance of me in your letters to Mr Hartlib, and praise God for the zeale wherewith he hath endued you to further all good workes tending to his glory in the Publick Reformation of Church and commonwealth. Happy would this people bee, if all that are in place had the same publick and pious inclinations, with affectons soe enlarged, and a spirit noe lesse capable of universall Aimes then yours is. That which you write in one of yours to him Concerning the times and seasons of a full Reformation and Restitution of the church and common wealth under Christ, I leave unto God, the thing I long & hope for; as that which is promised; and would bee faine found fitt to partake of it whensoever it shall bee in any measure therefore I labour to present myselfe unto him without partiallitie[70] in all things to bee found a vessel of Honour purged from earthlinesse and fitted for every good use and I rejoyce to see you walke in the

---

[67] This is alluded to in Hugh Plats, *The Jewel House of Art and Nature* (1594), pp. 1–6.

[68] Nuysement, pp. 54–5; 65.

[69] This letter must, on internal grounds, precede **88**. It is apparently written at an early stage of the preparations for the discussion of Le Pruvost's scheme before the Committee of Petitions of Parliament in or around September 1645.

[70] Dury's vision of himself was as a 'peacemaker without partiality' – see Anthony Milton, ' "The Unchanged Peacemaker"? John Dury and the politics of irenicism in England, 1628–1643' in UR, p. 95.

same way: Let us as fellow Souldiers strengthen on anothers hands by prayers and faithful incouragments unto every good worke blessed are they that sow upon all waters; by waters I understand people and occasons and sciences, by sowing I understand the bestowing of endeavours which may fructifie for good: hee that soweth unto his flesh, shall reape corruption from it; saith the Apostle; Gall. 6–8. 9. 10. but hee that soweth unto the spirit shall of the spirit reap life everlasting; hereupon wee are exhorted not to be weary in well-doing because wee shall reap in due time if wee faint not. therefore patience and resolution to waite Gods time is requisite: but our endeavour must bee as wee have opportunity (saith the Apostle) to doe good unto all men: and especially to those of the household of faith.[71] Now the household of faith is not soe narrow as many men make it, and though it were never soe narrow yet all men are here recommended to us. That aime then and dispositon of spirit, which maketh most universally servicable to others is our best qualification in these times: and when wee are bid sow our seed in the morning [Eccl. 11. 6[72]] and not withhold our hand in the Evning, because wee know not whither shall prosper whether this or that, or both. I conceave that constancie or dilligence is recommended to us in this resolution with a purpose to resign ourselves up to God by depending upon his providence for a blessing, and not trusting to much to our owne prudencie to doe thinges sometime at an adventure; cheifly when wee see that noe harme can come on that which wee attempt; and that there may bee a possibility of some good event. I like your good simplicity and that of Mr Hartlibs extreamly in this kind; but it is not given to all men to become fooles in this way, that they may be truly wise, nor is it fit to adwenture without spirituall discretion, the prudence of the serpent is not whollie useles to a Christian only it must not take away the simplicitie of the Dove. Your advice concerning Mr Pruvost (a man truly of a Public spirit, and a good christian) that hee should desire a patent for 14 yeares which you proposed unto me when you was here and since have mentioned in your Letters to Mr Hartlib I never thought good to offer unto him, because I could not imagine it proffitable either to him or two his worke or proportionable in any measure to the aime which he hath in his propositions and contrivances. for, if hee should seek a patent

1. then his worke would seeme a project indeed and a kind of Monopolie in Trade, which hee whollie is averse from

2. Hee is a stranger and his complices are all strangers as I suppose,

---

[71] Galatians, 6:10 – 'As we have therefore opportunity, let us do good unto all men, especially unto them who are of the household of faith'.

[72] Eccles, 11:6 – 'In the morning sow the seed, and in the evening withold not thine hand: for thou knowest not whether shall prosper, either this or that, or whether they both shall be alike good'.

now for such as are not acquainted here to come amongst the Natives
to drive a trade by vertue of a patent which others understand not to
bee beneficiall to the public: would bee very difficult and if hee could
subsist in doing that which he doth offer, yet there would bee soe much
oppositon of Envie & jeallousie against him; that hardly should be
ever able to proceed.

3. A patent will not reach his aime of a Plantation without which his
worke and designe is imperfect.

4. His Complices who will furnish money & meanes to sett all afoot
will not trust as (I suppose) the securitie of a patent to venture their
money here: if hee should dye; or his patent affter a yeare or two
reversed, what should become of their money. For these and other like
causes I never did speake to him of a Patent but cheifly because I did
see that the man doth understand himself, in his worke, as I conceive
the nature of it is, namely, that it canot bee done but by a State, whose
interest must bee engaged in it to carry it on; and that for him and his
complices none other securitie will serve to draw them on to venture
their substance in this kind, but the Authoritie of the State itself, to
owne the advancement of the designe as that wherin itselfe is principally
concerned; nor can any thing give them true securitie but the maintaining of that order by which all the worke is to bee effectuall. nor
can any authority Inferiour to that off the Common interest of the
State, maintaine the order of soe large a commerce as will be set up
by his propositions. Therfore a Patent will bee a thing wholly unprofit-
able to him: his patent must bee an ordinance, which the State
should make for the Regulating of its owne proffit, to arise from his
undertakings; wherin the Common idle poore people of all sorts will
bee sette a worke by Land and Sea, which will be sette aworke by
Land and Sea, which will be infinitly beneficiall to particulars when all
the idle hands shall bee set a worke not only to maintaine particulars
but to uphold the Public and bring a benefitt to it, wheras now they
are a charge and burden to wast and Consume the Substance of it; &
studie wicked Practises how to wrong it, and their neighbours for a
subsistencie, whence strife and a confussion doth arise, and many
judgments are multiplied upon us. Soe that not only in the way of
Policy; but in respect of Christianitie his worke will bee usefull to the
State, for now multitudes of People, that are without rule in a manner
desperate, and wilde under noe goverment shall bee reduced to certain
employments and brought under Inspectors, who may bee directed
how to teach them, and order their wayes in their callinges to
the attainment of Knowledge and the Exercise of Temperance of
Righteousnes and Godliness: When all vaines of a State are full of
blood and of good spirits, and all the members sound and sett a worke
upon their proper objects, then a State is in case to flourish: but if it

bee full of obstructions in some parts, soe that they receive noe nutriment, and can performe noe actions for the good of others members; then it must needs fall into diseases and languish. Besides this advantage of Employing the poore and idle people, who bring many distempers to the body of a State, because they cannot walke Reglarly and profitably, there is another speciall benffit which I conceave will redound from this enterprise, if the State will Regulat the way of it, which is this, that they shall not only open a way for their owne subjects, to improove their estates and employ their stockes to better advantage for themselves and the public then hitherto they have done: (by which meanes the subjects become as it were the Factors, and the State by a prudentiall addresse is the Principall tradere, and doth manage all their meanes with equalitie for their good) but the stokes and Estates of Forrainers will be drawn in, to increase the Trade and make it beneficiall to the Public. The greater a stock is, the more proffit it doth yeeld; if then merchants are [<soe>] desirous to get other mens stockes into their handes to trade withhall upon reasonable considerations, noe doubt a wise State will not refuse the offer of Forraigne stockes to increase by their industrie its owne Commerce. If the Complices of Mr Pruvost doe bring into England their substance and settle a Trade with the Comodities which they procure unto this Nation, they not only bring an increase of Revenue to the Kingdome but they ingage the Affections of Forrainers to procure the good of this State, and to prevent the inconveniences which may fall to it by Reason of their interest which they have in it: soe that in effect they have as many Agents abroad in Forraigne parts as they have men whose stockes are joyned to the Public way of their trade: I remember that one of the Policies of the Chancellor of Sweden was to seeke out men that had good stockes to engage them in the Trade of Sweden; and by this meanes the Trade is come to great perfection in comparison of what it was beffore; but I am out of my element now; therefore I will not proceed further then my aime doth warrant me, which is to recommend the matter to your Public zeale & to suggest unto you such considerations, as come into my mind, for which the designe should bee entertained for the good of many; that the confusion and distraction which wee lye under may in some measure, if God will, by lawfull endeavours redressed; and that the wordly trades and employments of his people may be subbordinate unto the Kingdome of Christ and become Holinesse unto the Lord when the way thereof shall be advanced to the Public good without partialitie. I know your conceptions are generous in this kind; the Lord grant them good successe. Pray for me that I may have time and grace to intend matters of a more spirituall nature for whose sake I reflect upon these as possibly helpfull thereunto by Gods blessing.

88 *Culpeper to Hartlib, n.d. [Late Autumn/December 1645?]. (13/279–83)*[73]

Mr Hartlib;

   I doe and shall wonderfully joy that by the meanes mentioned in your letter or by any other; there may bee a Colledge begunne without suche publique assistance; as (at the beste) will bothe, moue very slowly on, & (in the ende of its motion) is like to set vp suche Herculean pillars, & ne plus vltra-s[74] as (thowgh good) will yet proue a straitininge to those motions, discoueries, & improuementes, as are potentially in all well principled indeauors, and are (by Gods blessinge) like to emerge from ours; For thowgh I consente with Mr Dury, that wee showld seeke to regulate euen our firste thowghts,[75] yet I cannot but thinke, that the issues of our thowghts and indeauors, as well as the firste preparations of our hearts, are from the Lorde, & wee can as little knowe where they are likely to ende (yf closely followed on in humility & the feare of God) as howe they rose within vs, beinge like the winde, which blowethe when & where it listethe & yet wee knowe not whence it comethe nor whether it goethe; The beginnings and endings of thinges are from God & by vs vnserchable, our part in them and duty concerning them is, wheresoeuer (by Gods prouidence) wee meete them in theire via or fluxu; there to indeauor an improuemente of them as of soe many talents intrusted to our care, still leauinge th'issue of all to God, from whose hande wee firste receiued them; but to take the leuell of things by a lower pararell of reason; It seems very difficulte to me to conceiue largely inought of the issues, which the complications of ingenuities, mannaged & improued by ingenuous persons, may produce; there is not the meaneste spirit (that dothe but stirre vp the gifte of God in it selfe) to whome God giues not some excellency which Hee denies to others & this; that the sight of our

---

[73] The dating of this letter to the Autumn of 1645 is conjectural. However, Le Pruvost's proposal was presented before the Committee of Petitions of Parliament, meeting in the Exchequer Chamber, in September 1645 (55/10/1–24). Hartlib drew up a preliminary version of the venture and probably sent a copy of it to Culpeper since the surviving example of it has 'Sir Ch. [Cul*peper*]' inscribed on the top of it (53/31/1A–5A). So Culpeper's involvement in Le Pruvost's proposal, of which he had some knowledge from July 1645, may have strengthened from around September 1645. Worsley's proposition for saltpetre production is also to be assigned to the months between September and December 1645. Dury had arrived back from Rotterdam in August 1645 and it was thanks to his contacts that Le Pruvost was encouraged to present his petition to Parliament. Various efforts were made upon his return to secure a lectureship or living for him. Charles Webster dates the letter tentatively to 'Autumn and probably December'; UR, p. 216.

[74] 'Ne plus ultra' was the ascription on the mythical Pillars of Hercules. The frontispiece to Francis Bacon's *Great Instuaration* (1620), depicted a ship sailing through a set of pillars with the inscription: 'Plus ultra'.

[75] See **Appendix 197** for Dury's rational basis for scriptural analysis.

wants may keepe vs humble within our selues and towards our God, and our mutuall supplies may beget that mutuall loue which he [commands] to be in his; To come yet neerer to the saltepeeter invention,[76] I cannot but beleeue, that yf some fewe of those spirits whoe (for wante of complicatinge theire thowghts), are nowe soe farre from inlarginge themselues, that they are rather like single sparks buried in deepe ashes & there like to extingwishe, yf suche spirits (I say) cowlde (by the opportunity of suche a colledge as is proposed) complicate theire owne thowghts & suche of other men, as (by opportunity diligente searche & sometimes mony) might be contentrated, there might be a vse made of this way of multiplyinge saltepeeter to an end farre aboue it selfe; For yf saltepeeter be not that very spirit it selfe of the worlde, yet I am confidente from the harmony of chymicall writers that the ayre is that by which the spirite of the worlde begets & manifestes itselfe; & from hence it is that Calid the Iewe a greate phylosopher sayth that the minera-s of things haue theire rootes in the ayre & their heads or top in the earthe;[77] His meaninge is that that nowrishemente which is (from the earth) drawne & specified by euery indiuiduall seede of nature, is by the earthe it selfe firste drawne from the aire; but excepte your thowghts were some what initiated in these subjects I may perhaps be pertinente to the thing but not to the person.

My opinion still is that Monsieur Prouoste were beste to take a patente of priuiledge for 14: yeeres to his owne vse[78] for in truthe this indowmente of the publique, muste (to those moste of men whoe haue not the like publique spirits), seeme eyther folly or knauery, & yf soe, I dare maintaine it to be beste prudence to deale with & expecte from euery man according to his principles, thus doe we make vse of the elements, not by changinge theire natures but by soe adapting theire seuerall motions as may beste fit our endes, This is the way by which wee were (in our creation) lords of the creatures, & this is the way by which wee may be Lords of mens spirits, by consideringe & expectinge from euery man accordinge to his principles and center, for mens spirits may be sayde to haue a center as all other things haue, & this center being once discouered, wee muste not expecte that water showld goe vpwards or the ayre downwards but apply to eache suche a mill or other engine as beste fits eyther;

I cannot describe the engines whereby to plowe growndes, but I

---

[76] Culpeper refers to Worsley's saltpetre project, described in GI, pp. 378–80. Worsley's proposition for a chemical method for its composition is based on his treatise 'De Nitro quaedam' in 39/1/16A–20B. For Benjamin Worsley's career, see Charles Webster, 'Benjamin Worsley' in UR, ch. 11.

[77] Cited by Nuysement, ch. 6 (p. 38 of the English edition) from which chapter Culpeper draws all the following passage.

[78] See the comments of John Dury in **87** (n.d. [Autumn 1645]).

haue heere inclosed an extemporary essay to which vpon a recollection
I cowlde adde yet more; but my opinion is that yf [Monsieur] Prouost
his inuention stande vpon those legs, men will (by passinge by his
materialls & yet vsinge the analogy of his principles) frustrate his
hopes; & this judgemente doe I giue allsoe of Mr Wheelers engine, for
yf it be implied where ordinary engines can worke the difference then
will be, onely in the firste charge in the settinge vp of the woorke;
which in any greate vndertakinge dothe noe way ballance the busines;
For example; towards the improuemente of a 1000 acres of lande by
draininge or floodinge, the difference of 100 1 or 500 1 will not soe
farre ballance the whole business, as to put of one & to put on th'other;
I showld be glad to haue a viewe of Palissy's booke yf it may be without
inconuenience to you & doe heere promise to returne it safe to your
hands, as I shall your latin [manuscript] the nexte weeke;[79] I showlde
cownte it a greate happines that my present lowe condition were suche
as that I cowlde but subsiste in London, that I might be acquainted
with Mr Worsly; his Frinde you mention; & suche other noble spirits
as the towne affoords; & truly from the consideration what a braue
center and stage London is, I rather wishe Mr Dury placed somewhere
in the Citty, where (yf the saltepeeter busines or any other speede well)
hee may improue his more vniuersall thowghts, then to be (in a manner)
buried in a Hamshire liuinge, where his pretious time and giftes will
be (in effecte) caste away vpon a particular congregation whereof one
halfe will not vnderstande him: I cannot but think that Mr Dury or
some frinde can Englishe to you my late Frenche extractes;[80] & I
therefore the rather sente them, that I myght haue eyther your owne
or some of your frinds judgemente on them; for yf I cowlde finde any
that cowlde adde to me in that Chymicall subjecte, I showlde be happy
in his conversation; I cannot but thinke that Mr Dury-s way of searche
of truthe wowld (yf I were master of it) muche aduantage me in this
particular subjecte & some others on which my thowghts woorke, &
truly he that standes alone, as I haue longe done, hathe neede of good
rules for the directions of this thowghts;

You answered me not concerning mr Bartens lodginge; I loue to
loose noe holde I once haue gotten; nor concerning the water for the
eyes, in which I desire not to be ouer trowblesome

I hope I haue nowe tired you with my impertinencies, my Conclusion

---

[79] Probably Bernard Palissy, *Le moyen de devenir riche ou la manière véritable par laquelle tous
les hommes de France pourront apprendre à multiplier et à augmenter leurs trésors et possessions* (new
edition: Paris, 1636). Hartlib's copy may well have been that sent by Mersenne to
Theodore Haack – see *Correspondance du P. Marin Mersenne*, ed. Cornelis de Waard, XVI
vols (Paris, 1945–86), viii. 636; 684. Copies of these letters are to be found amongst
Hartlib's papers: 18/2/3A–4B.

[80] Possibly extracts from Nuysement, *Traittez* – see **65** (21 January 1645).

muste be that yf my letter I writte this morninge be any way trowblesome
to you, your owne liberty shall be the beste kindenes to

[PS.] my deuoyrs to Couent garden

The inconveniencies which I haue obserued in our ordinary husbandry of corne is partly in the corne, partly in the grownde
The errors in the corne :1: firste in not hauing the strongeste of the
seede, for thowgh all that is sowen comes vp; yet from obseruation I
can demonstrate that not aboue an ayght or tenthe parte beares frwites
to haruest 2: for wante of a true depthe, some seede beinge buried &
some other lyinge eyther aboue grownde or soe shallowe as eyther not
to beare or not to continue for wante of roote 3: for wante of a true
distance when many seedes lie in one whole or (at the beste) in one
small furrowe & more then 3/4 of the remaininge grownde is eyther
alltogether vnpeopled, or (by reason of its hardnes) is like the beaten
hygh way vnfit to receiue seede; in moste corne fields I haue obserued
that the corne grewe onely in the furrowes; that between euery 2:
furrowes there might be made one yf not 2 furrowes more, in which yf
that surplusage of corne were rightly placed which (beinge all in one
furrowe) hindred one another; it wowlde then happen that eache graine
hauinge its gauellkinde[81] proportion of grownde wowlde not onely come
to goode but beinge stronge in it selfe & hauinge its juste depthe and
distance wowlde beare that proportion which in nature might be
expected from it
The errors in the grownde are 1: that all the lande is not plowed but
a kinde of bancke or whele lande of 7: or 8: inches bredthe lefte
betweene euery furrowe; 2: the wante of some kinde of quintessenciall
dunge to be eyther comfited on the seed or sowne after it, Saltpeeter
yf not too deare wowld I conceiue [beste?]; There are some other
errors which for the presente I cannot recollecte; To remedy these
inconveniences :1: I wowlde by often castinge gaine the heauieste and
greateste graines as being those that fly fartheste 2: eyther by Mr Plats
inventions, or by one whoe had a patente for it 14: since, or by
[monsieur] Prouosts direction, or (which I cownte as good as any) by
saltepeeter, yf wee can make inowght, I wowlde soe comfite and clothe
the corne as eache graine showld carry to its place its owne dunge 3:
The lande beinge firste, twice or thrice crosse plowed with the ordinary
plowe I wowld afterwards with deepe stronge harrowes mellowe &
breake the grownd & lastely I wowlde (by an engine which I can beste
describe by a patterne and discowrse) make deep narrowe furrowes 3:

---

[81] The name given to the particular land-tenure system prevalent in Kent involving
male partible inheritance.

or 4: inches asunder into which the graines (firste comfited) beinge (by another invention harde to be conceiued but by viewe) dropped at an equall depthe and distance into mellowe earthe I cannot conceiue why why wee may not expecte Isacks increase Gen: 26: 12:[82] or suche increase as Sir Hugh Plats mentions:[83] more then 30: quarters of an acre or at leaste suche an increase as will beate out the ordinary dull way.

I am straitned bothe in paper and time the fittinge of a right kinde of seede to euery kinde of grownde is a part of husandry woorth consideration the closing of the grownde againe after it is sowne dothe very much aduance the kerning

89   *Culpeper to Hartlib, n.d. (13/286–7)*

[Note: cf. 9/1/153 – Dury's method of analysis Rom. 12]

Mr Hartlib;
        I haue heere inclosed Mr Woorsteley-s letter, to whome I pray presente my affectionate and faythfull seruice; I shall exceedingly joy that (yf the publique showlde interuene); the colledge yet showlde be, in or about London; but shall joy yet muche more, yf it shall please God to rayse a meanes amonge ourselues; for I reste vpon this fowndation, that the wayes of goodnes and seruice of God knowne euen to the beste of vs, will finally proue (at beste) but like the dawning of the day to that farther discouery with which it may please god to blesse vs yf with an humble feare, and as in his sight wee directe all our indeauors, & truly there is nothinge I feare soe muche as the making our presente thowghts, Herculean pillars & ne plus vltra-s to our indeauors, & that wee showlde not be as ready to lay holde on what it may please God further to discouer, as to imbrace what He hathe discouerd of his Will; & this the [Publique] is not like to doe, witnesse theire reformations, which (beinge performed accordinge to the beste strenght of the presente age) haue become suche restraints & snares to the future as in [King's Edward's] dayes wee fownde the latin & in this we nowe finde our Englishe masse to be Yf Mr Dury hathe not yet had time to converse analytically with my impertinences, I pray yet let me vnderstande howe he smatters it in generall; I will

[82] 'Then Isaac sowed in that land, and received in the same year an hundred-fold: and the Lord blessed him.'
[83] For Culpeper's familiarity with the works of Sir Hugh Platt see **72** (26 March 1645), **75** (16 April 1645), **86** (n.d. Autumn 1645).

adde onely thus muche that the separation mentioned in my laste to be made by Nature; is not of matter but onely of qualities; for the rule of ordinary phylosophy is true in Chymistry, Omnis actio est inter qualitates[84]; & therefore Pontan saythe[85] – ; He that separates anythinge from the matter as thinking it necessary knowethe nothinge at all in philosophy; for that which is superfluous, vncleane, filthy, fæculente & in summe, the whole substance of the subject is perfected into a fixte spirituall body by meanes of our fire; thus [farre *MS torn*] & by this and many other authors it appears that our ignis non de materia – our ignis contra naturam, our sulphur externum, our fæces impures et grossieres, are not separated, but transmuted onely

I heartily thanke you for mr Duryes Analysis of Rom: 12th[86] but (yf it be lawfull to play the Berean) I pray presente (from me) to his consideration, whether the first woord For in the 4: [verse][87] makes not that & the nexte verse to be a kinde of precedente proposition to the 3: [verse] as yf he showlde say Because we beinge many are one body in Christe & members one of another therefore let noe one member thinke more hyghly (not in generall onely as Mr Dury conceiues without relation to any particular objecte but) of himselfe (as the English translaton hathe it) & that in relation to the reste of the members; my papers done; Our carrier I beleeue goes not this [Week? *MS edge*] I pray sende your letters by the Ashford or Lenham carrier both ly at Billingsgate

90   *Culpeper to Hartlib, n.d. [Autumn 1645]. (13/294–5)*

Mr Hartlib

I did hope and desire to spare the writinge of this letter, but my necessary occasions will hinder me till nexte weeke In the meane time I haue returned mr Woorsteley-s-Propositions[88] which I finde in all (saue that firste of Saltepeeter) to runne parallell with those of Monsieur Pruuoste [~~both~~] of bothe which I am now fully satisfied by Mr Dury-s letter that they cannot be demanded and advanced excepte the intereste as well as the authority of a State be ingaged in it; I shall

[84] 'All action is between qualities'.

[85] Giovanni Pontano [Pontanus] (1426–1503). The passage has not been identified from amongst Pontanus' considerable published writings.

[86] A copy of this example of Dury's method of scriptural analysis is to be found at 9/1/153.

[87] Romans 12:4 – 'For as we have many members in one body, and all members have not the same office'.

[88] Probably Worsley's memorandum 'Proffits humbly presented to this Kingdome' – published in GI, pp. 539–546 (NB: this is from 15/2/61 and not 15/2/23 as stated).

not inlarge muche vpon this subjecte; but cannot doe lesse then tell
you that yf it please God to rowze the mindes of men in other nations
as He hathe done in Hollande, [Sweden *MS edge*] & may doe in this
The effecte will be (when euery nation shall play the beste of theire
owne games) that wee shall all singe the 67: Psalme: Let all the worlde
o God et cæt – Then shall the earthe increase And truly, that (by the
increase of the frwits of the earthe & bannishing that Auri sacra fames)
men may come to liue accordinge to the simplicity of the Patriarchs in
the olde worlde as it is the prayers of all good men soe I muste confesse
it is my hopes, whoe seeke as muche as I can to inlarge my thowghts
that as I doe or showld wishe that God might be glorified throwghout
the whole worlde, so I might towards (not this family, Cownty, Nation,
but) whole mankinde & indeauor the propugation of those meanes that
might effecte that ende, & this I eyther apprehend to be Mr Woorstleys
finall aime or doe by this together with my faythfull and humble seruice
recommende it to him; I pray (yf I may) let me haue a copy of the
inclosed I cannot but againe desire you to rectify Mr Worsteleyes
thowghts of me: I haue beene wittingly contented to let your loue &
kindenes goe on in flatteringe & couseninge it selfe concerninge me
seeinge that thowgh in it selfe it made me not better yet in the
consequence of good acquaintance, it gaue me a rise to better myselfe
but I nowe feare it hathe not formerly done me soe muche right with
your loue as it may prejudice me with mr Woorsteleys judgement which
thowgh well seasoned by your relations, muste yet exercise it selfe on
me as (I see) it dothe on other things, & will then finde (none can more
consciously speake it) nothinge answerable to his expectation; I pray
before I see his face lett me by this returne vnderstande of you; from
what grownde it is that a judgemente soe well able to mannage its
owne issues, showlde goe out of it selfe or (which is more) showlde
vente it selfe into the bosome of soe muche weakness; You packet
concerninge Mr Barten & the eyewater is certeinly miscarried, for I
receiued noe express concerninge eyther of them till your laste I cannot
but take notice of the extensiuenes of that colledge you haue in your
mind & muste returne you your thowghts with this addition that yf
wee can but free our mindes from necessary worldly cares & set them
vpon suche vniversall objectes as leade moste to Gods glory, in our
nayghbors good wee shall by Gods blessinge discouer suche a sea of
ingenuities, as yf He blesse vs not yet more in the choyce and vse then
in the findinge of them, our vnderstandinges may reade in them beyond
sobriety; & loose themselues, & truly, for the applyinge euery ingenuity
to its proper endes, & to finde for euery ende its proper meanes, & to
multiply the complications & immeations of euery thowght or thinge
that shall from time to time emerge, I knowe noe better engine (vnder
Gods blessinge) then Mr Harrisons waye of Index in the extensiue vse

whereof my rawe thowghts can sooner loose themselues then comprehend it[89]

I perceiue by what you writte of Mr Sadler & what I heare from
elsewhere that Independency, is for the presente in very lowe condition,
at which I am noe way startled; but am confidente that for soe muche
as of it, as is for liberty of conscience & againste persecution it will
prevayle, & for that other parte of congregatinge churches & theire
strickenes in them, I neuer shall make any difference betweene an
imperiall, nationall, prouinciall, prebiteriall parochiall or congregationall Pope; bindinge & persecutinge the conscience, is that which
I shall obserue wheresoeuer I finde it in any of them, & shall holde it
for Anti Christian thowgh it transforme it selfe into an angell of lyght
The carrier goes a daye sooner then he uses & I knewe not of it till it
was late this afternoone & therefore shall not haue time to thancke Mr
Dury for his letter but muste doe it next weeke by woorde of mowthe;
In the meane time, his thowghts on the partes of my laste letters
wowlde be an especiall fauor; in which thwgh taken out of seuerall
authors there is yet suche a sympathy & stronge lyght as I haue not
met with in 20: yeeres readinge in any one author, but doe nowe euery
day finde that which is within my viewe, to haue a centrall relation to
the Differente kindes in which euery seuerall author writes; for there is
in them all (thowgh seemingly differente) yet but one true meaninge,
of which Dionisius Zachary writes thus; Contra predictas omnes oper-
ationes (quas antea videram), concludens ad vnam tandem resoluissem
talemque reperissem, quæ conueniret cum omnibus libris the summe
of all is to put nature againe & againe & againe into motion, but
because, of creatures the moste excellent cannot moue, eyther it selfe
or within itselfe, wee muste therefore drawe nature from its center of
repose, for euery thing being drawne from its center falls naturally ito
motion: Your etcet: CC

91   *Culpeper to Hartlib, n.d. [before 22 October 1645]. (13/298 [summary
only])*

[Note: written in black lead]

*Culpeper gives instructions for Hartlib's son to receiue a box from the woman where
he last lodged in London and arranges for its transhipment to him.*

---

[89] Thomas Harrison was a poor London school-master whose method of indexing,
using transferable slips of paper, much excited Hartlib. See S. Clucas 'In search of "The
True Logick"' in UR, pp. 65–6.

92 *(13/113 [summary only])*

Receipt (written in Hartlib's hand) for £20 from Culpeper, 21 October 1645, to be remitted to Mr William Freake (i.e. Freke) in Holland.

93   *Culpeper to Hartlib, 22 October 1645. (13/114)*

Mr Hartlib

my largenes to Mr Sadler[90] will make me the shorter to you; I pray (yf vpon readinge you like th'inclosed) seale & deliver it with the booke & my seruice

I cannot yet appointe nearer then Rochester to meete Mr Wheelers[91] frinde but you shall heare more of that heereafter, perhaps on friday

I sente you a letter by the waterman, written in the bote with blacke leade;[92] I pray let me knowe whether you receiued it

My services to Couent Garden

94   *Culpeper to Hartlib, 31 October 1645. (13/115–16)*

[Note: enclosure: see 13/119]

Mr Hartlib;

I knowe not howe to invite Mr Worsley to my house, because my entertainemente is soe meane, otherwise, I wowlde say he showld be wellcome to my pouerty

From parrallellinge what I haue receiued from [yourself] & Sir

[90] John Sadler (1615–1674). Culpeper sent a copy of some (possibly chemical) work to Sadler; he replied, forwarding a copy of a treatise in return, on 30 October 1645 (46/9/1A) – it is not clear to whom the letter is addressed but it would appear to be Culpeper. Along with Culpeper and Dury he would become a trustee for the projected 'Office of Address' in 1646 – DNB; GI, p. 72.

[91] William Wheeler, the drainage engineer, projector and inventor – see GI, pp. 372–74. He was in the Netherlands from 1638 onwards and patroned by Sir William Boswell in the promotion of his snail-wheel drainage mill. The progressive souring of his relationships with Boswell's servants (amongst whom Culpeper's neighbour, Sir Robert Honywood, figures prominently), and, eventually, Boswell himself, during his residence in the Netherlands is outlined in *Mr William Wheelers Case from his own Relation* (Jan.18 1649) Wing P408 Thomason, E.25 (8).

[92] **91** (n.d. [before 22 October 1645]).

Robert Hoonywood[93] concerning   Mr Wheeler my opinion is that
neyther his vnderstandinge nor will is too muche to be relied on, nor
wowlde I wishe that Mr Worsley venter muche more leaste he be put
eyther to loose or to suche cowrses in his owne defence as others
pretende (after kindenes shewed) to haue beene inforced to I knowe
my selfe not naturally jealous, but I haue moste times obserued that
dislocations or disproportions as well in the minde as in the body doe
woorke more or lesse on the reste of the parts

I haue not time to copy out this rowgh drawght of my present
thowghts & therefore (after perusall) returne it in your nexte packet;
I am in it (I conceiue) juste to Mr Wheeler, & yet soe as for the
publique in the firste place & for particular vse (not liberty as Mr
Wheeler hathe too contracte with others) when the [publique] is
serued, there is a power in others; The firste monyes that wowlde
be venturd wowlde be firste in a module, & then (yf that be
approued) in a searche of the truthe & validity of the Patente &
such a superstructure of legall settlementes as shall be agreed on, &
without this there may (as formerly) arise future disputes & noe rule
eyther to preuente or resolue them,[94] I showld be glad to knowe
yours & Mr Woorsleyes thowghts of this inclosed & what other
proposalls you make that eache may contribute his thowghts to the
publique good intended

I pray giue me at touche of Mr Sadler, & howe Mr Dury speedes
my humble seruice to the Lades,[95] I hope I shall not be pressed this
monthe or 6: weekes for that golde with my beste wishes I reste

[PS.] your forgot my silke

[93] Sir Robert Honywood, a neighbour of Culpeper's and a relative of Sir Thomas
Honywood (1586–1666), had, like Culpeper, also served at the court of the exiled queen
of Bohemia. It was through Thomas's influence that Sir Robert would be appointed to
the Council of State in 1659. In 1650 Sir Robert would serve with Culpeper on the
Council of Trade.

[94] In *A description of the famous kingdome of Macaria* (1641), Wing P2409A, Plattes urged
the state to remunerate inventors. Culpeper believed that the principle should 'bee to
aduance the publicke aime' – see **95** (5 November 1645). He proposed a system in which
inventors should voluntarily surrender their invention to a committee which would direct
the implementation of the design – see 'Culpeper's Comments on Wheeler's Patent',
13/119.

[95] Probably a reference to Dury's wife, Dorothy Moore, and to Katherine, Lady
Ranelagh.

95   *Culpeper to Hartlib, 5 November 1645. (13/117–18)*

Mr Hartlib

Your last on friday gaue me hope of hearinge from you yesterday againe

My inclosed paper laste weeke contained but my suddaine thowghts; but our scope I conceiue muste bee to aduance the publicke aime that is amonge vs;[96] but whether by puttinge it in the firste or seconde place, it will deserue seconde thowghts; there muste be disbursements more or lesse in the beginninge & (thowgh neuer soe muche assurance yet till tryed) some hazarde in those disbursement & howe farre he or those that vndergoe that disbursemente & hazarde may deserue the recompence of a concurrente vse of the invention in a priuate vndertakinge I shall leaue to better judgements; This allsoe deserues to be considered that without some firste particular good examples, the vse of the invention is not like to sell well to others eyther for pubike or priuate advantage; I propose what comes into my thowghts & showlde be glad to receiue yours;

I pray let your sonne call at the Apothecaryes in Bishopgatesstreete for an answere to my laste weekes inclosed & that I may receiue eyther letters or theire answere; It somewhat concerns me,

This paper is not (I conceiue) of the beste of ordinary paper I pray yf there be better lett me receiue halfe a reame thowgh at a bigger price

& Yf you can sende me a bottle of that inke you mentioned & the receipte for the future you shall oblige[97]

[PS.] My seruice to Couent garden

96   *Culpeper to Hartlib, 12 November 1645. (13/121–2)*

Mr Hartlib,

Yf my firste proposalls fayled it was because I proportioned them to what I haue receiued from you of Mr Woorsley, but nowe that (by Mr Woorsleys letter to you) I perceiue that our resolutions and expectatons muste be framed and proportioned to Mr [Wheeler's]

---

[96] Culpeper here addresses a central problem for Hartlib and his associates as they became more involved in the environment of innovation around the 'projectors' with whom they had become more associated. How was individual initiative, skill and investment to be rewarded whilst, at the same time, maintaining the primacy and importance of the public weal? See SHAL, pp. 39–40; GI, p. 370.

[97] This may refer to the printer's ink, whose blackness and permanency Culpeper evaluates in 71/2/3A–B.

disposition et cæt, my proposalls in the future (yf I make any) shall bee in that relatiue proportion as may render them moderate and reasonable; That I did desire and was promised a module,[98] & that I did frame to myselfe some more particular vses of it then drainage of mershes, or fennes all this is true; but that I designed what was anothers, to any speciall vse of momente, in tis there was a mistake; I shall be ready (yf my weakenes be thowght necessary) to vse it in the examination of the module and of the particular profitable vses that may bee made of it, & to this effecte (thowgh my presente condition be very lowe) I doe heereby submitte to a journy to London when your & Mr Worsleyes desires shall summon me, but wishe it may be, when thinges are soe prepared as I may make a quicke returne to my petty Cowntry occassions; I pray presente my seruice to Mr Worsley & thanke him for his good opinion of which I can pretende to noe parte, but a desire of Faythe and Truthe to God an man & euen that compassed about with too many infirmities

I am heartily sorry you feare our losse of Mr Dury for (thowgh God be all sufficiente) yet I cannot but looke on him as a singular instrumente of Churche peace;[99] my seruice to him & to those excellente Women;

I haue some reason to thinke that there is a greater distance between Sir [Robert] Hoonywoode & myselfe the 30: or 40: miles haue formerly made, Yf hee be not too gwilty wee shall close againe, yf he bee I know not whether I shall seeke it Amicus Plato, Amicus Socrates, magis et cæt:

There are two bookes I muche desire to converse with; the firste is the latine manuscripte you lente me when I was in London the other is Mr Plates booke,[100] yf they be not intended suddenly for the presse I cowld wishe (for the enefit of theire conversation) to be at the charge of a transcripte of them

Mr Sadlers letter hathe a greate deale too muche of the ciuill & somewhat too little of what I expected; I shall nowe stande still a whyle & let former passages fermente, with moste dispositions, a cominge carriage taste more or lesse of the fullsome; when by your obseruinge of him I vnderstande that myne hathe not bin soe, I shall (with an eye to the ende for which I firste sowght him) continue our traffique

I pray (as you shall haue oportunity) inform your selfe of the charge on which a schollar may be with Mr Milton; that (yf I haue occasion) I may satisfy suche with whome (till he be more knowne) that con-

---

[98] i.e. 'model'.

[99] Turnbull suggests that Culpeper may be referring to the possibility of Dury's appointment, on 3 February 1645/6, as one of three ministers to preach and officiate at Winchester — HDC, pp. 252–53.

[100] See **56** (6 November 1644).

sideration is like to waygh, There are some good sprincklings in his (as I conceiue it to be) letter of Educaton,[101] but (vnder fauor I conceiue) there is not descendinge enowght into particulars, but rather a generall notion of what experience onely can perfecte;

I greeue that there is not some meanes amonge vs to releeue Mr Harrson[102] & that in charity bothe to himselfe & the worlde I muche feare the losse of his ingenuity

I haue not paper inowght to inlarge my selfe what improuemente there mighte be made by a right adaptation of very many things that are caste away in London especially, & all the greate townes in the Kingdome; Mr Plattes hathe giuen excellent hints concerninge it, & by analogy of reason muche might be added to him; but I muste conclude with my paper & remaine

[PS.] My seruice to Mr Sadler yf you see him

97   *Culpeper to Hartlib, n.d. [November 1645?]. (13/277–8)*

[Note: for dating, see 13/117, 13/123]

Mr Hartlib;

There is at the signe of the boule in bell ally ouer against the middle Temple gate one Mr Bartne (as I am infomed) whoe (as I formerly tolde you) pretendes to haue perpetuall motion, I heard of this his blinde lodginge sometime after my laste returne from London; & forgotte (in my laste letters) to intreate you to inquire onely whether he doe (as I heare) lodge there, that soe (as opportunity shall invite) I may renewe my acquaintance with him; you may (by some messenger) haue it asked whether hee lodge there & the messenger get off without seeinge him by pretendinge that hee will come by and by to the lodginge againe; I pray (yf you can) giue me an accownte of it by this returne; I haue begun with this because I will be sure to forget it noe more

I am glad to finde (by your letter) a confluence of good opportunities concerninge Mr Dury & doe (from an additionall partiality of my owne intereste) wishe that that of [Saint] Crosse or the Sauoy may speede allthowgh (I knowe not from what genius in my selfe) I doe (from my former knowledge of the agente you rely on in it) feare the successe; but howesoeuer I consider that these desires and indeauors are our waytings & knockings at the doore of Gods prouidence to Whose good

[101] John Milton, *Of Education* ([1644]), Wing M2132.
[102] See **90** (n.d. [Autumn 1645]).

will and time wee muste leaue the euente, with this assurance that yf (as David) wee are not (by Him) desgned to bwld the Temple our desires are yet accepted & wee may perhaps be honored soe muche as to prepare some materialls

Yf the latin MS be immediately intended for the presse I shall with the better patience expecte, allthowgh (I assure you) my desires of conversinge with the booke cowlde make me (yf it lay idle by you) wishe for a reuiewe,[103]

I canot but put you in minde of the printinge of Helmontes other woorkes; His paracelsian Alba heste[104] is a thinge admirable, of which I cannot perswade my selfe but I haue fownde some taste in a Frenche author,[105] whoe hauinge at large named both the subjecte ex quo & the preparation concludes in these woordes (viz) Elle est de grande vertu a la dissolution de l'or mesme, ne portante tousjours aucun danger auec elle, estante extraicte d'une substance si familiere au corps humaine; And what better can agree with that of Helmont pag: 118: de Febrib:[106] Quicquid preclara ejusmodi arcana attingunt sordium, dissoluunt secumque rapiunt, sicque medentur febribu et morbis chronicis [plærisque]: the forgoinge page is woorthe the readinge; My meaninge was not to adde muche to Mr Plattes materialls but to inlarge the vse of them; for example, I cannot but thinke & haue done, soe a good while that mr Ioiners[107] invention concerning Salteper was an may (yf fownde) proue but a lainge together & an acceleration by arte of that which mr Platte aduises to leaue to the operation of nature onely, in eury particular vaulte throwgh out the citty; I haue neyther time nor roome to inlarge

I like a liberty lecture very well; but there is muche that might be lectured vpon the greate wheele, which wowld neyther fit the times till all lesser wheels be mended nor yet swite to the humor of the [Parliament] & he that come to neere the horses heeles may perhaps haue his teethe beaten out; I shall (accordinge to my weakenes) joine concering Mr Harison; I feare Mr Prouoste wil not aduance till he pretend good to himselfe; [publique] spirits passe for fooles or knaues, I thancke your for the paper, & the yncke & receipte which I hope to receiue;

---

[103] This is probably the same Latin manuscript to which Culpeper refers in **96** (12 November 1645).

[104] Helmont, *Opuscula medica inaudita* (1644), sig *2 'explicatio aliquot verborum artis' provides a definition of the 'liquor alkahest Paracelsi'.

[105] Nuysement, Part II, ch. 4, p. 182 (of the English edition).

[106] Helmont, 'Tractatus de febribus' in *Opuscula* (1644), p. 118 (last page).

[107] Francis Joyner was a speculative projector who, together with Sir William Luckin and William Hyde had formed a partnership which offered to form a 'Corporation of Saltpeeter-makers' which would take up the production and supply of saltpetre in the kingdom – see the draft bill (undated) in 71/11/2A.

[PS.] my [seruice] to couent garden

98   *Culpeper to Hartlib, 2 November 1645. (13/123–4)*

Mr Hartlib;

I muste firste thanke you for your latin M:S: which I will not fayle to returne accordinge to your desires; I cannot gwesse what concurrente prouidence, that which I mentioned concerning the London aultes hathe met with; but I am still confident that yf it were not a greate parte of Mr Ioiner invention there might yet be a mighty returne made from it; And f I cowlde finde 2: or 3: poore creatures fitte for th'imploymente, I wowlde venter 10: or 20:1 in gatheringe together the shreds of leather & wollen clothe, hay seede, etcæt from suche places where (till their vse be knowne) they may be had for askinge and as (vpon tryall) I showlde finde a returne, soe I wowlde proceede;

I shall be glad you haue fownd Mr Bartnes lodginge, thowg he will (perhaps) keepe me at distance

I am heartily glad Mr Dury beginnes to be looked on, & am nowe very confidente that (yf called) he will remember that as the learnedste Cowncells haue & may erre, soe on the other side truthe it selfe obeyed without faythe becomes a sinne againste Christe in the imposer & not lesse then perishinge and destruction in him that obeyes;[108] but when your latin M:S: shall haue beene duly wayghed, it will set the Ciuill & Ecclesiasticall magistrates bothe agreed, by makinge a difference between diuine truthe, & the ordinances of man obtruded in the roome & with the authority of diuine truthe; I pray remember my seruice to Mr Dury & the Ladies, & remembringe him of notionatinge his essay vpon Mr Webbe[109] or [exemplifyinge] [Acontius's] de Methodo; & yf for the presente you cowlde let me see his essay on Mr Webbe it wowld be a fauor

In your discowrse with Sir [William Waller] you forgotte a cor-respondency for humane learninge & ingenuity;[110] I concurre in all the reste, & wishe wee may be soe happy in Kente

---

[108] A further reference to Dury's possible appointment to a living at Winchester.

[109] Joseph Webbe, catholic physician and teacher, with interests in linguistics and universal language – HDC, p. 302.

[110] Hartlib had proposed to Sir William Waller a complete reformation of the educational and welfare provisions of Hampshire. In 'S. W. Wallers Colledge at Winchester or Plantation of Hampshire' (47/9/33A–B) the changes included the establishment of a new workhouse at Winchester, the foundation of parochial schools in every parish in the county, a complete overhaul of Winchester school and the foundation of a new Academy/University there. The latter was to include departments for learned correspondency, practical divinity and experimental philosophy. A complementary paper (47/9/1A) sketches in those who would be its first scholars as well as its foundation professors (Dury for divinity, Pell for mathematics and Worsley for 'experimentory

This inclosed loste its passage laste friday I pray afforde it your answere; You see I knowe noe bownds but my paper

99 *Culpeper to Hartlib, December 1645. (13/109–12)*

Mr Hartlib;

I feare that th'impertinencies of my laste letter did soe trie your patience as that you accownted sylence the fauourableste answere you cowlde giue them; I confesse my thowghts haue (of late) become like an ouer charginge burden to my spirite bothe in theire multitude and sometimes in their wayght, especially my olde Chymicall companions, which haue hawnted me nowe more then these 20: yeeres, which (yf I durst truste a weake judgemente) are such as (according to that signe of true knowledge mentioned by many writers) in which all the greateste phylosophers seeme to agree, beeinge wholy pitched vpon that onely secret which all of them doe professe neuer to call by its proper name, the effecte and vertue whereof is to put nature into a newe motion as often as the artiste will; this cannot nature doc (sayth one awthor) quia actiones ejus sunt continuæ, (saythe Frier Bacon)[111] quia sibi non contradict; This secret of secrets some philosophers call (but improperly) the agente, not that it acts but because it excitates the true agente into action; a seconde calls it ignis non de materia; a third, ignis contra [naturam]; a fowrthe sulphur [externum] with this note vpon it, hoc quid sit, multi quærunt, paucissimi inueniunt, my Frenche companion[112] calls it fæces impures and (in the same pae) impurites, of which he thus writes, Il faut entremesler ces fæces grossieres a la substance subtile,[113] and his reason next followinge is; Car ou il n'y a que purete il n'y peut auoyr d'action, & with this dothe another latin author harmonize (in the plaineste woords that haue any where read) where speakinge firste of natures hauing separated those fæces grossieres in her generation of golde, he followes on on in these woordes Et hæc est ratio quod videamus naturam illud (aurum scilicet) in melius vltra non transmutare;[114] & with this againe agrees my Frenche companion, where speakinge of the true agente in nature that Spirit of the Lorde that (in the beginninge) moued

philosophy'). This thorough reformation would be funded from the sequestrations of catholic property in the county, the revenues of the deans and bishops of Winchester, the tithes of the diocese, the followships of the former school and additional contributions from the local gentry. The appointment of Dury to a Winchester living was presumably seen as part of this development.

[111] Roger Bacon (1214?–1494).
[112] Nuysement, pp. 165–6.
[113] Ibid., pp. 32–3.
[114] Zacharius, *Opusculum* in *Theatrum chemicum*, i. 733.

in and vpon the waters he writes thus [Puisque] son naturell est d'agir
et que son action et indeficiente, il faut qu'il agisse sur [quelque] chose
et que mesme cette chose ne lui manque jamais; In all that I haue
quoted it may be obserued that it is the incommunicable property of
God to moue himselfe or to giue a beginninge and firste rise to those
motions or actions which are eyther ad intus or ad extra, but the
creature (on the contrary) cannot moue eyther it selfe, or in or vpon it
selfe, but euen the accomplishmente of that naturall luste & desire
(giuen by God to euery creature) of multiplyinge and exaltinge it selfe,
muste & is still actuated in some thinge which (thowgh of one kinde
with the agent) is yet (as the woman to man) bothe without and belowe
it, But howe is it that knowinge my fawlte I still offend with more
impertinencies, but thowgh suche shewe them yet (I pray) to Mr Dury
I dare truste his charity; & intreate him that hauinge firste whayghed
and compared the quotations (for assure him, that (yf I vnderstande
any thinge in this busines) euery worde that is quoted, carries spirit &
life & in it) he will (as vpon Mr Webbs thowghts) make a shorte essay, &
thowgh the discouery of my owne weakenes happen to proue th'issue
yet I shall gaine bothe by the discouery & more by the meanes by
bothe which I shall knowe yf nothinge else yet my owne ignorance

In Mr Worsteleyes letter to you I obserue not soe muche his erroneous
thowghts of me as I doe those more gwilty, because more knowinge
influences of yours, from whence his proceede, I shall allwayes rejoyce
in conversinge with the spirits of good men & I can truly say that I
often rejoyce in that hower in which (by a meere ocasionall readinge
of Dr Gaudens sermon) Gods prouidence browght me to your acquaintance, & hathe synce & dothe still by it bringe me to the acquaintance
of others;[115] But for Gods sake let vs all (whose heartes it shall please
Him to vnite in Himselfe) be rather wachemen one for and ouer
another & forgettinge or (yf possible) not knowinge (I am sure) not
valewinge, our selues by what wee are let vs stirre vp one another, to
presse forward, to the marke that is set before us & with patience
humility, a cheerefullnes to runne that race that endes in an exceedinge
wayght of glory, & forgettinge still what is paste & behinde let vs still
joy in raisinge one another to what we yet are not; I pray presente my

<hr />

[115] Gauden's sermon of 29 November 1640, preached at St Margaret's Westminster,
was ordered to be printed by the House of Commons early in 1641. See *The Love of Truth
and Peace. A sermon before the House of Commons by John Gauden* (1641), Thomason, E.204 (10).
It was in this sermon that Gauden recommended in an aside: 'the noble endeavours of
two great and publique spirits, who have laboured much for truth and peace, I mean
Commenius and Duraeus, both famous for their learning, piety and integrity, and not
unknowne, I am sure, by the fame of their works, to many of this honourable, pious and
learned Assembly' (pp. 40–1). Gauden went on to give Hartlib's address in London as
the place to contact Dury and Comenius (p. 43).

seruice to Mr Woorsteley; and yf after 10: dayes (duringe which time I am somewhat ingaged) my weaknesses shall (vpon his second thowghts, firste rectified by you) be thowghte (by him) seruiceable in the saltpeeter woorke I shall heartily wishe and pray that it will please God soe to directe vs all as that wee may (by his helpinge grace and in his feare) lay some suche fowndation as (by his prouidence) may rise and grow into suche a lyght in the hearts of posterity as that Gods truthe and glory may be more knowne and affected then yet it is

In the meane time I pray afforde me your wonted kinde intelligence; For the transscript concerning the [Perpetuus Motus] I dare not giue that judgemente of the man to which my thowghts (as he [himself] sawe they wowlde) somewhat incline, Hee is Mr Woorstleys frind, But this I assure you that his wante of 20:1 cannot be more suddeine, then so suddeine a procuringe of it is difficulte to my presente lowe condition; I muste thancke you for your receipte for the eyes & showlde alsoe for that water you mentioned because [yourself] know the proofe of it; I haue returned your latin [Manu Script] I pray thinke not amisse that you had it noe sooner, the printed copy makes me (thowgh gwilty) glad, and yf I had one or two more, I wowlde (by lendinge them out in fittinge places) begin to infuse that to which (I am confidente) wee muste at laste come;

You writte me not woorde whether you had hearde of Mr [Bartnes?]

Once againe I pray characterise me aright to Mr Worstley, for in truthe your former character will wronge him, myselfe and finally your owne judgemente; That which I hartily wishe in myselfe were more selfe deniall & that I might be fownde woorthy to serue God & more able in myselfe to render vp myselfe to him in all thinges, but towardes this happiness I finde lesse then nothinge in my selfe and all my hope is that God is all sufficiente & dothe vse to glorify himselfe in the greateste weakenes; vpon this grownde none can make better right or claime to his blessings but that which (towardes this happines) I shall wishe and expecte from my frindes is (as I sayde) theire joy and indeauor to make me better, rather then in what I am, or (perhaps) but seeme to bee, for whoe can knowe the deceitfulnes of the heartes soe muche as of his owne [self]; The God of heauen discouer it to vs all, and make vs bothe be what wee seeme, and seeme nothinge but what wee truly are or desire to bee

I feare Mr Prouostes goinge from among vs without beinge hearde; I pray sende sende me Mr Dury-s growndes why a patente of priuiledge for 14: yeeres were not better than to giue out re infecta, Yf his propositions approue themselues in that time, the state can (at the ende of the terme) assume it to itselfe and goe on where the vndertakers leaue off: & truly yf others had my faithe concerning the change that will be in the worlde before 59: they wowld not muche seeke for a

perpetuity in any thinge but heauen; Paracelsus (whoe died in the yeere
41: of the laste Century or age) speakinge (in his libro tincturæ physicæ[116]
what things were like to happen before or about the 58: yeere of this
currente Century or age, Quinquagessimo octauo anno; ipsius theoriam
fore in flore ait, quo tempore omns ei sint adhæsuri – ita vt in vulgus
passim et infimam plebem ipsius theoria abeat et probetur – nunc
(meaninge his owne age) ita fert tepus, vt scortationi incumbatur,
tantisper, donec tertia pars mundi occidetur gladio, altera asumpta
peste, tertia vix residua; Tunc in locum suum [atque] in [integram] res
restituetur; sed prout nunc sese res [habent], fieri id nequit; [Etiam]
ordines interire necesse est et penitus e mundo tolli, aliâs fieri identidem
nequit;[117] These lines, and some suche others (as others can beare me
witnes) I reade and marked before these times which nowe (from a
rationall prophecy which an obseruinge man may make from a newe
spirit which is lately rouzed in the worlde) causes some woonder in me
at that propheticall spirit which the author had more then 100 yeeres
since; But to returne, I pray let me knowe why a priuiledge patente
were not better then nothinge

My papers done my deuoirs to Couent garden

---

[116] Bombast von Hohenheim [Paracelsus], *Archidoxorum Aureoli Ph. Theophrasti Paracelsi de
secretis naturae mysteriis libri desem … His accesserunt libri De tinctura physicorum*. (Basileae, 1570).
BL 1507/1820.(2). See also Walter Pagel, 'The Paracelsian Elias Artista and the Alchemical
Tradition', *Medizinhistorisches Journal*, 16 (1981), 6–19.

[117] 'in the fifty-eighth year; he says his theory will blossom and then everyone will
adhere to it – so that his theory might spread through the common people at large and
the lower orders and be proved – now (meaninge his own age) such are the times, that
it is brought down to the level of whoredom, all the while until the third part of the
world is slain by the sword, a third taken off by the plague and a third scarce remaining;
then the state will be restored to its proper position and made whole; but in present
circumstances that cannot come about; Even the orders must perish and be altogether
removed from the world, otherwise time and time again it may fail to come to pass.'

1646

Mr Hartlib
        my indisposition of body & the tedious weather for trauell
wowlde (contrary to my desires) haue kepte me from London till I had
somewhat recouered my selfe, but I yesterday receiued a ticket from
the Committee of arreares sittinge in Weauers hall,[1] for the loane of
suche a summe of mony as I neyther haue of my owne, nor knowe
where to borrowe one fowrthe of it; This will not onely occasion but
necessitate my beinge in London on saturday or munday nexte, thowgh
net to pay (for I haue it not) yet to shewe juste cause of nonpaymente;
I pray in the meane time (yf you can) informe yourselfe from some one
or other of the Committee of Weauers hall (whoe are all Citizens) from
what grownde or information this ticket was sente me & whether to
them or to the Committee mentioned in this inclosed ordinance or to
what other place I muste apply my selfe for redresse; I moste heartily
wishe that for the [Parl*iament*] in my owne sake I were soe able; but
the presente burden of my owne & my Fathers debtes (lyinge nowe
actually vpon me) beinge truly wayghed & considered I can make it
good (yf nothinge will serue but the discoueringe of my owne nakednes –
a matter of very greate prejudice) that my presente poore & lowe
condition dothe (for the presente put me truly & really out of the
compasse of this ordinance, but the discouery of this my present
condition I wowlde (yf I cowlde) auoyde, as that which yf knowne
hathe heeretofore ruined many & may nowe doe me; & that you may
see a proportion between my condition & my woords; I doe for my
selfe [W*ife*] & [child*ren*] keepe but 2: mayds & not soe muche as a man;
this was not my former condition but I thanke God that as He hathe
taken away my wealthe Frinds & other wordly comfortes, He hathe in
lieu of them giuen me greater comforts & a minde that wantes lesse,
but this kinde of wealthe will not satisfy weauers hall;
        I pray thincke of me in this busines for yf I be any way pressed in
it I muste (for owght I knowe) goe to prison
        I thancke you for your two m:s
        The one is of Mr Commenius as I suppose by the stile & manner;[2]

---

[1] CSPD (1645–47), p. 119.
[2] Turnbull suggests that Culpeper refers here to Comenius's *Pansophiae Diatyposis*
(Danzig, 1645) – HDC, p. 371.

He calls lowde for attention & hathe (methinckes) too many sowndings or prodromusses before he enters the stage

The other (I professe) is excellente in euery parte; Webbs parte[3] is excellente, Mr Dury-s huntinge of him more excellente & the notion-atinge of his owne thowghts wowld contayne a super excellency; & why by Webbs invention (applied to thinges, & of thinges the beste, the scriptures) may not a man learn to vtter his thowghts (whether to God in prayer, to man in propecyinge, & to himselfe in himnes psalmes & spirituall songs) in that holy & heauenly langwage, & oh: the conse-quences of it; afford me a line on friday, & (yf it be not too muche) somethinge from Mr Dury on my letters

101 *Culpeper to Hartlib, 11 February 1645/6. (8/31/4–8)*

[*Note: includes diagram; partial copy at 71/1*]
Mr Hartlib;

I did not write the laste weeke because I was hardly settled after my returne nor had I any thinge woorthe your readinge;

Concerning printinge I can but write what I haue allready spoken; onely I haue sent you suche letters glued together, as were caste by, by a printer & browght me the morning I lefte the towne, by which (yf I mistake not) you may see howe all the auxiliaries of langwage (viz the 4: laste parts of speeche the, cases, moodes, tences & persons) may be reduced into woords, which (with the blanckes annexed to them) will one with another proue to be as muche as 4: letters, & by consequence (as I suppose) the positor may (for soe much as those auxiliaries amownte vnto, which (yf marked), will proue to be allmoste or alltogether one halfe of the whole woork) sett 4: to 1: the ordinary way, & soe three ayght partes of the time & coste is saued, or 7s-6d- in the pownde; & this without the trowble or coste of any newe kinde of materialls, yf this of glue or any other holde goode; The 4: partes of speeche wowlde be placed in a dictionary or subalphabetary way, of the moodes, tenses & persons I am not yet resolud but it is visible that by that joininge of them, which other woordes will not admitte, the [positor.? *blot/deletion*] shall (seldome set lesse then 6: & many times 10: 11: or 12: letters at once; To what I haue written I may adde that yf by a dictionary or other meanes) the beginnings & terminations of woordes were put into a subalphabetary way, I cannot but thincke that (in lieu of three ayght partes) there might be a full halfe or rather more saued

---

[3] The grammarian Joseph Webbe who had invented a method for analysing language as well as an artificial language – see DNB and S. Clucas, 'In search of "The True Logick"', in UR, pp. 55, 72.

in time and coste; I gaue you a hinte howe with a hundred characters
(& those small & easy) all things in the worlde might be written or (I
will nowe say) printed, which or some suche like yf (like Mr Commenius
his vniuersall langwage) made vniversally currante;[4] might (as those
characters which serue 6: seuerall nations in the bottome of the
Leuante)[5] [serue.²] as a meanes of conversation betweene all the nations
of the worlde, & wowld not be more vniuersall then easy to the positors
hande when euery small character showld signify never lesse then a
woorde, sometimes two or three; But this is too ayery for the presente
occasion as beinge impossible (thowgh not in it selfe) yet rebus sic
stantibus[6] <you promised me that [ere.²] this you wowlde communicate
to me a way of short writing[7] I pray remember your promise>

I am hartily glad that Mr Dury is prouided for,[8] but cannot but tell
you, I showlde be as sorry he showlde make it his journyes ende, I
make noe question but there may be some fownde whoe (vpon that
aduantage which (I knowe) Mr Dury valewes not) may admitte of a
change for a parsonage or (which is better) lecture in London; I shall
(from the emergentes of this weeke) take an occasion to write to Sir
Rob. Hooniwoode <this longe letter puts of this till nexte weeke> that
(by his Brothers[9] intereste in [Parliament]) there may be noe other
conditions concerninge the sworde or militia saue to haue it acknowledged to be legally & wholy in the [Parliament]; for I dare vndertake
to maintaine it that in settlinge the militia in the [Parliament] for 7:
yeeres the [King] gaines more then he giues; When my hand is in vpon
this occasion, & that other concerninge [liberty.²] of conscience I shall
(from the laste) take occasion to inlarge my selfe concerning Mr Duryes
beinge set aparte to his proper taske, as that which will at once
bothe shewe the AntiChristianisme of persecution; & (by [those.²])
fundamentalls with which he hath passed throwgh all the Euangelicalls
Churches) euidence bothe the way & the necessity of the vnity of the

---

[4] On Comenius' schemes for universal language, developed in the mid-1640s and more
fully expressed in print later, see James Knowlson, *Universal Language Schemes in England
and France* (Toronto, 1975); M. Blekastad, *Comenius. Versuch eines Umrisses von Leben, Werk
und Schicksal des Jan Amos Komensky* (Oslo, 1969), pp. 422; 685–89.

[5] i.e. Arabic.

[6] 'as things stand'.

[7] i.e. 'short-hand'. Hartlib had been particularly interested in developing an efficient
short-hand for taking down and distributing sermons. In a letter of 2 February 1640, he
comments on the subject: 'Cartes [Descartes] I heere is very busy in it in the Low
Countryes; Torellus & de la Maire in ffrance Champagnola in England & Mr Johnson
in Ireland. But this latter is preferred before all the rest as having studied this subject
these many yeares over & over . . . ' (7/43A).

[8] Dury was appointed by Parliament the tutor to the royal children Prince Henry,
Princess Elizabeth and, later, Prince James. In addition, he was, at about this time, finally
appointed to the ministry at Winchester – Batten, pp. 113–14.

[9] See **94** (31 October 1645).

spirite in the bonde of peace to be helde in these Churches

I still gaine by your kinde thowghts of me thowgh I muste tell you, that in your character to Mr [Winche.?] of me you wronge your selfe & may doe me; I haue lente my [Contarenus] De Republica Veneta[10] to a frinde from whose hands I shortly expecte it & then I will sende you suche excerpta as I haue allready promised allsoe to some [Parliament] men amonge whome the Venetian way of elections to places & of votinge in places of truste beginnes to be enquired after; In the mean time I showlde be very glad yf you cowld hearken out some oportunity by which I might sende for suche politicall boxes & other deuises as I wowlde giue a noate of; for you cannot imagine howe truly (in thinges of this nature) the sence is like to equall yf not to out goe discowrse & reason; I pray once againe, be intentive to finde some oportunity howe I may (for my mony) haue those Venetian knackes __ __ __

To my Fathers treatise of vsury[11] I shall nowe adde those extemporary thowghts of my owne which you hearde me speake; Of mony there are 3: imploimentes, trade, lande, vsury, of these 3: the firste onely, is commendable of the other two, bothe are idle drones, but the laste not onely idle but of suche a pernicious vermine nature as it subsistes wholy vpon the prejudice of the other two; Nowe that Commonwealth is moste likely to floorishe, where diligence onely is rewarded; idlenes discowraged; & all vermine caste out; which laste beinge done, I meane the vsurer bannished; the hygh valewe of lande [*marginal addition in another hand:* charmidor.?] (beinge then at 40: or 50 yeeres purchase) wowlde discourage the seconde idle man; (whoe (at the rate lande nowe goes) liues idely vpon his landes) when he showld see his nayghbors 500:l (by the helpe of his industry) to yeeld him 50: or 60l per annum to liue on; and himselfe at the same time (throwgh his idlenes) showlde liue poorely & beggerly (in respecte of the other) vpon 10:l per annum as he muste doe, from the same summe of 500l; Yf vsury were taken away or browght to a very lowe rate, then wowlde those trades which [now.?] cannot paye vsury & diligence, be reassumed, then allsoe were it easier & cheaper to the priuate man to dowble or treble the yeerely valewe of his lande, then to purchase soe muche lande of his neyghbor; & by thus dowblinge or treblinge the rente of the lande there wowlde be in a manner soe many newe acres of lande gained to the common wealthe,

Againste what I haue written there is an objection that the lande thus raised in the valewe of its fee simple wowlde increase the presente

[10] Gasparo Contarini, *The common-wealth and gouernment of Venice*, Tr. out of Latin by L. Lewkerior, 1599. *De Republica Venetorum libri quinque* (Lugd: Batavorum [Leiden], 1626).

[11] [Sir Thomas Culpeper], *A tract against usurie. Presented to the high court of Parliament* (1621) STC 6108. See the **Introduction**, p. 116.

landed mens wealthe, & make the like estates invincible & impossible
to the diligence of others, & truly for this objection I can finde noe
other answere, then to wishe that (at the time of takinge away of vsury)
wee wowld complicate with it another lawe, which God gaue the Iewes;
viz of the Fathers diuidinge his wealthe more equally amonge his
children;[12] for by this naturall distribution of wealthe, euery priuate
man wowlde haue soe muche mony and lande, as not to neede to
borrow or bwy, & none soe muche as to lende or sell; & certeinly it is
from this reason that in Hollande (where the more equall diuision of
wealthe makes fewer bothe borrowers & lenders) mony hathe formerly
gone (with out restrainte) at 6:[l] per Cent*um*; There is yet a second
objection what those families showld doe, to which there nowe belonges
neyther lande, nor soe muche as any other kinde of wealthe to beginne
with There was a prouision made by God amonge the Iewes against
this objection, by making euery tribe & euery family in eache tribe
owner of lande & that not to be mortgaged or solde from the family
but till the nexte Iubile, but in this nation rebus sic stantibus, I knowe
for the presente noe better accommodation then that the orphans mony
may be suffered to be lente; & these poore onely suffered (at reasonable
rates) to borrowe it; & thus might 2: objections (heere to fore made
againste the callinge downe of vsury) receiue one answere, yf this
wowlde not serue, newe plantations wowlde, especially yf ordered by
mr Pruuostes principles; but he not fully answeringe these objections
hathe made me wishe that vsury were, (not wholy taken away but) soe
leuelled with what it is at in other Cowntryes that the same trades &
diligence (which joy & thriue elsewhere) might haue the like subsistence
heere; & certeinly the lesse custome eyther from the [K*ing*] or vsurer
lies vpon the merchante or trader the better is all kinde of trade like
to flowrishe; Yf our reuerente assembly[13] wowlde (in steade of raginge
againste theire bretheren) turne theire malice againste this vermine
vsury; & presse the religious objection againste it, I dare say they might
finde more in the Scripture concerning this subject then of that
ecclesiasticall power on which theire mindes runne soe muche; I hope
I haue written enowght to trouble thowgh not to satisfy you on this
subjecte

I shall be glad to heare of mr Woorseleyes proceedings & moste of
all of his accorde whithe Ioyners [M*atters*?]; My seruice I pray to him

I pray enter acquaintance with your Adlinge hill man, & informe
yourselfe of his coates of what stuffe & howe heauy, of his charriots, &
whethere any engine in the easy drawght; & by what engine 2: men

---

[12] Culpeper's views here reflect the particular Kentish custom of gavelkind, which
favoured male, partible inheritance.

[13] i.e. The Westminster Assembly.

can water 30: acres a day, & what else he pretends to, his booke seemes rather an invitation then a discouery;[14]

I pray God make vs truly thanckefull for his blessinges; Wee heare little of our [goud.?] bretheren & truly I expecte little & I pray God Little proue all,

I doe not remember that you euer sente me any description of an academy, nor doe I remember that name of Sir [Francis] Kennaston nor can I finde any suche booke amonge those [many.?] of yours to which I can readily resorte, soe that I beleeue you mistake[15]

I haue other letters to write & muste breake of with my faythfulleste wishes to yours: Mrs Dury & all yours

[*Hartlib writes:* Sir Cheney Culpepers Real [*overwritten* not.?] Characters.]

[*Culpeper:*]
Lines to be printed crosse as these are
[*diagram: two grids with numbering at the top and dots within squares*] [not.? *faintly written below diagram*]
Thus euery seuerall character may (accordinge to the 80: seuerall places in which it may be placed betweene euery two crosse lines) signify soe many seuerall thinges; for heere thinges onely & not letters are intended to be written.

All the auxiliaries of langwage as the [*number.? deleted*] 4: laste partes of speeche; the [cases.?] of nownes; the moodes, tenses, & persons of verbes which (yf put together & considered) makes the greater parte of what is spoken or written; showld be expressed eache of them by certeine characters in certeine places, thus in the nownes one, in the actiues 2: in the passiues 3: / it hathe beene / woords wowlde be expressed

To lessen the necessary number of places and characters all analogies wowlde be put together as Lyght & knowledge by the same character & place & the choyce to be lefte to the vnderstandinge; soe allsoe all [Synonimas.?] to be put together as lamente, bewayle, bemoane, weepe, greeue, & to be lefte to the criticisme of the reader; Thus allsoe all contradictions & inconsistencies may be bothe written with the same character & place as to curse and to blesse; light & darknes, etcæt; And

[14] 'Captain' John Shaw (1620–1680) had just published his treatise *Brief discoveries of divers excellent wayes ... manuring* (1646), Wing S45B. This edition was published under the author's initials; two further editions of 1650 and 1657 were subsequently issued under the name J. Sha[w] (Wing S3020A and S3021).

[15] Francis Kynaston, *The Constitutions of the Musaeum Minervae* (London, 1636), STC 15099. Kynaston established his 'Musaeum Minervae' in Bedford Street, Covent Garden. See G. H. Turnbull, 'Samuel Hartlib's connection with Sir Francis Kynaston's "Musaeum Minervae"', *Notes and Queries*, 197 (1952), 33–37.

these laste propositions wowlde, not onely facilitate the way of writinge with fewe carracters, but wowlde (as I conceiue) rayse in the vnderstanding a right orderly knowledge of thinges according to theire relations

This way of writinge will (yf compared) be fownde to take vp noe more roome then the ordinary way

It may be obserued that in the squares aboue I [haue? MS torn] made no vse of the corners of the squares, which (beinge made vse of) will giue [20?] places more to euery character I haue reade that 6: seuerall Easterne kingdomes doe converse with one another by the meanes of one [common] way of writinge which eache nation reades into its owne langwage, & it is not vnlike to the figures & prickesonge in which moste of the nations [wee? MS torn] knowe, convey to eache other theire numbring or musicall thowghts; In that way of writinge there are neere or alltogether 10000 characters which number muste render the busines difficulte eyther to write or muche more to printe, but in this there be but a 100:, & their seuerall significations accordinge to theire seuerall places beinge ordered by certein rules & rationall grownds, the applyinge of eache character to it proper place & signification will be made easy to the memory or (I may as properly say) to the judgement; In this allsoe the writinge of inconsistencies by the same Character & place will make that little aboue halfe the number of Characters or places, will be necessary, & the writinge all [synonimas?] & analogies allsoe by one character & place will againe very muche lessen the woorke, & will after a little custome be reade with ease & profit to the vnderstandinge

102 *Culpeper to Hartlib, 17 February 1645/6. (13/127–8)*

Mr Hartlib;

After I once perceiued that Mr Wheelers modules were not in Englande, I did not open my selfe to Sir [Robert] Hoonywood or to Sir [Edward] Partheridge & soe muche I pray presente to Mr Worsely together with my seruice;[16] I thancke you for the Saltepeeter Acte[17] but cannot thinke the drawght of it wourthe 500l per annum & am confidente that (yf Mr Woorsely make vse of it) somethinge in it will deserue amendemente; In the meane time let not Mr Woorsely be too confidente of goinge without the Wooman leaste he bringe himselfe to

---

[16] For the disputes in the Netherlands between Wheeler and his opponents, who included Robert Honywood, see **94** (31 October 1645).

[17] 'An Ordinance enabling Saltpeter-men to make Gun-powder' (7 February 1646) – F&R, i. 828–30.

an ill after game;[18] I shall very muche approue of your office yf I may see in mens thowghts a readines to make vse of it, & yet euen then, I showlde dare say that there wowlde be wanting suche a stocke of forreine relation, intelligence & ingenuities to set vp with as (yf your selfe) I knowe yet none besides your selfe that haue it; & when I see in the generalitie of mens dispositions an analogicall Irishe humor which nothinge but an acte of [parl*iament*] can breake from drawinge by the horses tayle, it makes me feare howe your office will proue, but it is harde for me to looke throwgh thinges at this distance[19]

I wishe I were riche enowght to make a journey to London to see Shawe[20] his inventions for thowgh (I am confidente) 2: mens wateringe 30: acres a day will not holde, yet I haue learn'd of you not to vnderualewe a whole man for one disproportion, but hauinge hearde and (as well as I can) weyghed all thinges to holde faste what I finde good in any, allowinge them (in theire errors) the same charity by which myselfe muste stande, I heartily wishe for the description of his plowe his seed barrowe and his composte barrowe & what they wowlde coste, because my thowghts haue runne [mu*che*] vpon this subjecte, & yf I cowld please my judgemente in some suche invention, I wowlde vse it in my barly season this springe; The Scottishe [Parl*iament's*] congratulation to the Citty, without any addresse at the same time to the 2: Houses is a busines of hygh consequence & soe resented by all whome I heare speake of it,[21] but howe soeuer; things will holde well till the [K*ing*] be yet lower, but I feare that finally theire aristocraticall and our democraticall intereste are like to shocke & yf our geud Brethren shall impose theire judgemente on vs eyther in what they thincke beste policy or what they conceiue accordinge to the woorde of God I shall make noe difference between a [K*ing*] & a Scotte; I haue been a moste hearty Scottsman, (none beyonde me); but truly I nowe

[18] This somewhat obscure reference almost certainly refers to claims made by the mistress of Francis Joyner to have a share in the profits from the saltpetre venture by virtue of an invention which she will divulge upon payment of a sum – see 'A Coppie of the Propositions of Ioyner's Mistresse' in 71/11/13B.

[19] Culpeper approved of Hartlib's proposed 'Office of Address' although he was concerned about the possiblity of opposition to it from monopolists and presbyterians – see SHAL, p. 44.

[20] Culpeper's enquiry about the realism of Shaw's claims is answered in 'Shaw's Invention for manuring and improving the land' (6 May 1646) – 67/21/1A-2B.

[21] London and the Scots drew closer together as the English Parliament became divided between Presbyterian and the Independent factions. The City authorities continued to be enthusiastic in their support both for the Covenant and for a Presbyterian settlement, renewing the Covenant on 14 January 1646 – see the two published sermons entitled *The Great Danger of Covenant refusing and Covenant breaking* (by Edmund Calamy), Thomason, E.327 (6); and *Religious Covenanting Directed* (by Simeon Ash), Thomason, E.327 (5). London's petition against religious toleration was published on 16 January 1646 and the Scots sent congratulations directly to the city for its fidelity in the service of God. Gardiner, iii. 28.

feare them; I haue againe looked for musæum mineruæ[22] but cannot finde it & from the title do gwesse it impossible to haue seene & forgotte it

Mr Harrisons invention[23] will be moste excellently complicated with your office yf once settled, & yf once in full motion, it were impossible to mannage it without such an index & to this I am confidente Mr Dury will consente, to whome & those Ladies I pray presente my seruice; & were it not too muche I heartily wishe he wowld giue me an hower or two of his analiticall thowghts vpon my Chymicall quotations, Oh that I cowld but sometimes injoy an hower with him about his Analisis in which I see enowgh to rayse but not enowgh to satisfy my desires

Remember to finde out Dr Webbe[24] yf he be in the London prisons

I pray yf you see Mr Shawe aske him of his coates, what his extraordinaries are in drawinge mappes of lande & what other inventions he hathe, particularly about improuemente of barreine lande[25]

---

103 *Culpeper to Hartlib, 24 February 1645/6. (13/138–9)*

Mr Hartlib

I am sorry you finde soe lowe apprehensions of your hygh aymes; I vnderstande not whoe you meane by the greate man that slyghted them & there are soo many greate men with with narrowe spirits, as (in truthe) you had neede to name him; And the finall resolution you muste settle in your minde vpon these & the like accidentes is, that (after faythfull desires & indeauors in the seruice of God) your rewarde belongs as muche to them as to a successfull issue; & that God in his owne beste time will accomplish what is beste for his owne glory thus may you allways be ready preste when God shall call & (in the meane time) possesse your sowle with patience I haue nowe my Contarenus[26] returnd to me & shall ere longe presente you with a noate of such venetian knacks as I desire; but I shall wish to sende for them by suche meanes as they may be finally myne for my mony

I pray let noe discowragementes diverte you from Shawe; besides

---

[22] See **101** (11 February 1646).

[23] Harrison, apparently a London schoolmaster, had developed a system of indexing which was much commended by Hartlib.

[24] For Joseph Webbe, see **100** (12 January 1646).

[25] Shaw's reply is located in 67/21/1A-2B. In 1649 Culpeper commissioned William Tampon to draw the earliest known map of the Leeds Castle estate (Kent County Record Office, U825P6).

[26] See above, **101** (11 February 1646) and note.

my rationall & experimentall obseruation, I doe of late religiously
condiscend to things & men of lowe degree, at leaste soe farre as to
examine & knowe them

Mr Dury muste finally settle himselfe in a London Lecture, It is a
braue Center for all kindes of correspondency, & a stage where (by
makinge his abilities knowne) he may doe beste right to his aymes;
Wee seldome looke for riche stuffes in shops that are scituated in some
by corner out of the way

Yf the greate booke[27] you sente me laste, had in it but some smartnes,
I showld haue gained euen from an aduersary, & showld not (as I nowe
doe) repine at the price, of which I can finde noe returne but to spende
it by peecemeale in a house of office, but truly his arguments are noe
other then suche as too many of our pulpit men of these times doe
vsually make, but yf the presbyteriall locke vpon the presse were
remoued, & that laudable primitiue custome Cor: 1: 14[28] stored to our
Congragations these men wowlde be kepte within better compasse or
made ashamed of theire quicquid in buccam venerit[29]

The Conjunction of the Aristocraticall party both of Church & State
in bothe [Kingdomes] is (as your selfe knowe) noe newe thinge to my
feares; & in opposition of this the [House] of Commons intereste will
be liberty of Conscience; I haue related to me, the contents of a very
late petition from London, & of a very late demandinge letter from the
[Parliament] of Skotland, I earnestly intreate you that I may not fayle
of bothe, for yf my reputed malignancy hinderd me not I will drawe &
indeauor suche a petitioninge remonstrance from Kent to the Howse
of Commons as may perhaps somewhat abate these rantapike proceedings of our aristocraticall party: my papers done:

[PS.] Inter alia in [Edwards] his booke[30] I obserue Fol: 53: (what I
formerly feared) what disaduantage & objection Lillburne proues to his
party; & howe the other side (for wante of true strenght) take aduantage
(like the Duc:) of the weaker vessells

[27] This doubtless refers to Thomas Edwards, *Gangraena: or a Catalogue* (1646), Wing
E228–230.

[28] I Corinthians 14: esp. 26–7 – 'How is it then, brethren? When ye come together,
every one of you hath a psalm, hath a doctrine, hath a tongue, hath a revelation, hath
an interpretation, Let all things be done unto edifying. If any man speak in an unknown
tongue, let it be by two, or at the most be three, and that by course; and let one
interpret'.

[29] 'speaking the first thing that comes into their heads' (Cicero).

[30] See note 27 above; the passage cited (p. 53) refers to the Leveller, John Lilburne and
the pamphlets produced at the time of his imprisonment.

104   *Culpeper to Hartlib, (enclosing petition written in scribal hand), 26 February 1645/6.   (13/133–5)*

Mr Hartlib:

You might see (by my letter on Wednesday laste) that my blood was stirred at the apprehended effectes which I haue (you knowe) formerly, & doe nowe (more then euer) feare from our Aristocracicall conjuncture; I haue heere inclosed a Petition, which (or the like) I heartily wishe may be sente from our generall meeting (which will be nexte weeke), to the [H*ouse*] of Commons, I wowlde desire you to shewe it to Mr Robinson[31] & that by him it may be convayed to the sight of Mr Peeters[32] (yf knowne to him) whoe is well knowen to our Committee & may aduance suche a seruice more then such a malignante as I yet passe for;

The hyght of the storme wee are vndergoinge calls vpon Mr Dury, yf not for a sydinge yet for a timely publishinge his principles of peace,[33] & I pray (when you presente my service to him & those good Woomen) tell him I am one of those, whoe hope that hee will not be longe silente, I wowlde be glad to heare of Mr Shawe; & I pray let me haue your owne & Mr Robinsons opinion on this petition by Champion the Ashford carrier on munday night; I intende it well but haue not a judgemente aboue & vpon my owne actions I reste

[*PS.*] I pray returne this copy

[*enclosure in scribal hand, with alterations made by Hartlib:*]

The Humble Petition etc. etc.

Humbly sheweth that yo*ur* Petitioners have (with much greefe of heart) behelde and felt the miseries brought upon these 3 Kingd*oms* by the knowne Lawes and interpretations of the private and extrajudiciall opinions of the [K*ing*] and those seducing evill counsellors about him obtruded on the People without and against the judiciall [Iudgm*ents*] of the highest judicatories.

That from a sight your Petitioners have had off a demaunding Letter from the [Parll*iament* of Scotl*and*] and off a lithe lesse then a

---

[31] Henry Robinson (c1605–c1664) – DNB; cf W. K. Jordan, *Men of Substance* (Chicago, 1942).

[32] Hugh Peters (1598–1660) – DNB.

[33] Culpeper is perhaps suggesting here that Dury republish his *A Memoriall Concerning Peace Ecclesiasticall Amongst Protestants* (1641), Wing D2872.

demaunding Petition from the Citty of London[34] both grounded (as your Petitioners humly conceiv) upon the like extrajudiciall interpretations from whence our former miseries have followed your [Petitioners] can not but justly feare such a new fountaine of distractions amoung us, as may render us both weake within ourselves and a scorne (if not finally allso a prey) to the enemies of our Peace.

That your Petitioner humbly conceive the People of this Kingdome of [England] to be subject to noe Prerogative Power or law whatsoever or Interpretation of either, that can not approve and derive it selfe from our owne consent first given and setled (in our names, right and behooffe) by this our [Honourable] representative by the judiciall votes off which only (as your [Petitioners] humbly conceive) the People of this nation have ever (both at and from the begining of this Goverment) and doe [*Hartlib inserts:* still] submitt and bind [themselves] to such politicall acts under, which they accompt [themselves] legally and politically bounde.

That our hopes and humbly desires (from the premised considerations) now, are, that [you.?] our [Honourable] Representative will (in their owne and the Peoples right maintaine this hyghest fundamentall priveledge against the intervening of all Extranationall or extrajudiciall opinions or interpretations whatsoever.

And wee doe further protest that our zeall for our God our Countrie and for our Covenant and promises, though no lesse (wee hope then that off some others) shall not yet make us soe bold, as not (with that meekenes quietnes of Spirit and respect due to this first immediate and supreame efflux from the People from which all other Legall effluences have recieved their secondary beings) to waite patiently for your results without either precipitating them by our owne pressing and directing petitions, or in deavouring to obtrude the extrajudiciall fancies of one County (which though a parte is but a parte) upon the wholle Nation.

And that as wee have hetherto cheerfuly obeyed all your commands for the redeeming of your and our owne highest preiveledges from the extrajudiciall opinions of the [King] and those seducing evill

---

[34] This refers to *A Letter of the Minister of the City of London, presented to the Assembly of Divines, against Toleration*, Thomason, E.314 (8), and to *Several Letters from the Parliament and General Assembly of the Kirk of Scotland to the Houses of Parliament of England, the Lord Mayor and Common Council of London and the Assembly of Divines*, Thomason, E. 344.(12). Both of these were published in January 1646 as part of the controvesy on religious toleration and the proposed Presbyterian church settlement.

counsellors about him soe shall wee with the last remainder of our
blood and fortunes maintaine them in your legall & supreame
authoritie) against all others whatsoever that shall make the like
atempt of ravishing of them from us.

And shall humbly and heartily pray to God that hee will please soe
to establish your hearts and direct your counsells and our obedience
to them as that these our present miseries and distractions may (both
in Church and State) ende in a terrour to the disturbers of our
peace; and in the joy off all such as are Lovers of their God, their
Country and off one another in Truth and Peace

105   *Culpeper to Hartlib, 4 March 1645/6.   (13/136–7)*

Mr Hartlib
      My expectation till this [mor*n*ing] of your answere to my letter
on friday laste, will make this the shorter
      Your resolution to persiste in your office of addresse showes me your
life of Faythe, & howe in this (as in the reste of your life) you wrastle
not onely without but againste hope,[35] & truly it is that excellent temper
to which the sowle showlde be browght in the seruice of God, euer to
labor with those materialls which God affoords & to leaue the successe
to him & I cannot but hope that God will yet rayse some meanes
towards soe good a woorke, in which howesoeuer your will & indeauors
will haue theire Crowne & rewarde
      I cannot imagine what showlde make our merchants soe coueteous
of Mr Dury, a man whome (I am confidente) they vnderstande not,
but I cannot conceiue any possibility of theire gettinge theire will & (yf
all proue right) bothe they and all other monopolizinge Corporations
of Merchantes, may perhaps finde (ere longe) imployemente inought to
defende theire paste incroachements vpon the liberty of the subjectes &
truly the monopoly of trade will proue as greate a greeuance (when
rightly vnderstoode) as any in this kingdome whatsoeuer, nexte vnto
that monopoly of Power which the [Ki*ng*] claimes; & beleue it, nowe
wee are pullinge downe of suche monopolies wee shall starte a greate
many which yet ly hid in the bushes but the greate monopoly muste
firste downe; & then the monopoly of trade the monopoly of Equity,
(a thinge which nowe begins to be lookt into), & the monopoly of

---

[35] Culpeper was responsible for some cautious negotiations to promote Hartlib's 'Office
of Address' amongst various members of the Long Parliament. He encounted opposition
but was able to secure the support of the Independents Robert Andrews, Francis Rous,
and Oliver Cromwell – SHAL, p. 44.

matters of conscience & scripture (a very notable monopoly), all these &
many more wee shall haue in chace & what one hownde misses another
will happen in the sente of & thus will Babilon tumble, tumble, tumble
tumble[36]

I was on munday at the Committee[37] & yf I misse not my ayme you
shall erelonge heare of a petition from Kente againste all Exta-nationall,
Extra-judiciall & sub-judiciall obrasions vpon that Representatiue in
which you will finde the People of this nation will finally concentrate &
settle, & accownte all prerogatiues powers Lawes ordinances & interpretations of them spurious which are not acknowledged by that immediate & supreme effluxe of the people

A presbitery or any other Gouernmente without compulsion or
persecution, noe man (I conceiue) will be againste; And for the Peace
you mention I am confidente that they that moste desire it cannot, and
dare not owne a lesse returne (from all the blood & treasure that hathe
beene spente) then the swoorde, & that (I am as confidente) the [King]
will neuer grante, for it is all, besides I finde somethinge in me that
makes me confidente that the stones of Babylon muste be layde lower, &
that wee shall see the 14: of the [Corinthians][38] restored & the supreme
Ciuill magistrate freed of that hatefull office of beinge hangman to a
fewe men that call themselues the churche:

I knowe not what you meane by the Commissioners concerning
Newarke I showlde be glad to heare it to be vpon surrender but feare
it,

I cannot nowe answer Mr Worsly; I will onely propose my sudden
thowghts :1: that the 50l per annum bee not proposed simply till profit
arise but with this addition allsoe or till the woorke shall happen to be
quitte, & for the former may make a perpetuity thowgh the thinge
showlde fayle, which I thinke is not intended; 2: that the hundreds of
powndes to be deposited or payde, be with this condition yf suche
discoueries as her receipte shall make beyonde what Mr Woorsly
allready knowes be made vse of by him, for it is possible that the
receipte may adde very little or perhaps nothinge that is materiall to
Mr Woorslyes knowledge & then Mr Woorsly will but purchase his
owne at a deare rate; Had onely a parte of the gaines beene demanded
I showlde not haue thowght of these conditions but onely to haue
joined bothe knowledges together, but accordinge to the venture
proposed, there owght (I conceiue) to be more warines; And to satisfy
the Wooman whether her receipte make an addition of knowledge to

---

[36] GI, p. 77.
[37] i.e. The 'Committee of Kent', meeting by this date in Maidstone – see Alan Everitt,
The Community of Kent and the Great Rebellion, 1640–60 (Leicester, 1966), ch. 5, esp. p. 131.
[38] 1 Corinthians: 14.

Mr Woorsly or noe, I conceiue that Mr Woorsly may when he receiues her receipte with one hand put into her hand a collection of his thowghts in another paper & thus herselfe may be fully & vnavoydably satisfied[39]

I pray looke after Mr Shawe; I cannot inlarge my selfe on Edwards booke but vpon your invitation haue returned it[40]

There is one Grassewinckle a Dutcheman that hathe lately written in [quarto] of the Venetian Gouernemente, the booke is in Latin & may perhaps be had in Pauls churchyard,[41] I pray yf you can finde it sende it me by this returne

[*PS.*] My deuoyrs I pray to Walsingham house

106 *Culpeper to Hartlib, 11 March 1645/6.* *(13/140–1)*

Mr Hartlib;
    I haue receiued backe my petition, which (not withstandinge your supposed difficulties) will (within this little while) proue seasonable; & this will come to passe by the [K*ing*'s] action, whoe (rather then parte with (that leaste that can be demanded) the sword) will holde vp this warre till [hims*elf*] be ruined,[42] & the democraticall growinge spirite (for the presente not soe stronge) haue taken such roote in this Nation as (vpon the same reason & grownde) to question the Lord & Presbiter as [thems*elves*] haue firste done the [K*ing*] & Bish*ops* & thus will euery generation thruste out the other; & as wee come neerer the center of Spirituall & Ciuill truthe soe will the motion be quicker & the stay (in any one place or kinde of gouernemente) will be shorter[43]

    I pray inlarge [yours*elf*] concerning the Knight that muste be named & produced for I am at the firste of it

---

[39] A further reference to the mistress of Francis Joyner who wanted to receive £50 per annum 'till there be profit arising', in addition to the initial down-payment, in return for her discovery of an invention or intelligence relative to the saltpetre venture – see 71/11/13B and **102** (17 February 1646).

[40] See letter **103** (24 February 1645/6).

[41] Dirk Graswinkel, *T.I.F. Graswinckelii Dissertatio de Jure Praecedentiae inter Serenissimam Venetam Rempublicam et Serenissimae Sabaudiae Ducem; opposita dissertationi jussu Serenissimi Sabaudiae Ducis evulgatae* (Lugduni Batavorum [Leiden], 1644), BL 596.a.35.

[42] Charles I had been reluctant to accede to the Newcastle Propositions, which had assigned the control of the militia to Parliament for a period of 20 years after the conclusion of a peace. He eventually offered in negotiations a maximum period of 10 years – see C. Carlton, *Charles I: the Personal Monarch* (1983), pp. 310–15; *Letters, Speeches and Proclamations of King Charles I*, ed. C. Petrie (1968), pp. 172–75.

[43] SHAL, p. 41; GI, p. 6.

I haue sente you backe Roberts his booke,[44] hauinge had it these 5̶:
5: yeares, by me; Hee writes very rationally; But all that he writes will
come to nothinge excepte the Monopoly of trade be layed open; To
answere all objections & to trace out a way how trade showlde be
regulated it is too longe, but when the greate Monopoly is taken away
wee shall haue leasure for the reste

For Graswinckel I haue not seen the booke, yf I cowld see them
bothe vpon a price, I will returne eyther mony for them; or one or
bothe; & such consideration for the sight of them (yf I bwy none) as
you shall agree for

Your letter from Newe England tell me where wee may be happy yf
wee cannot be soe in Old Englande, but I hope the beste

The Oxforde cowncells which you mention of lettinge the Independents bringe all to confusion is but a handsome Presbiterian
expression; I wowlde those at Oxforde had noe better resultes towards
theire endes, & hope that finally they will not;[45] forraine ayde beinge
like a drawght of colde water in a deadly feauer, the patiente may feele
halfe a quarter of an howers remission, till the feauer returne more
deadly

My papers done; I pray let me heare of Shawe; your office of
addresse complicated with Mr Harrisons Index, will hardly let me
sleepe; I professe I apprehend greate things of them

107   *Culpeper to Hartlib, 14 April 1646.*   *(13/142‑3)*

Mr Hartlib;

I conjectured seuerall [th*ing*s] laste weeke & you doe not in your
laste letter soe pointe vpon any of them as that I can gwesse what
was actinge in the [Parl*iament*] & Citty; but I am still of opinion
(notwithstandinge your former hopes) that these warres are not at an
ende; I showld be gladde to heare the grownde of your newe fears in
that kinde as allsoe what discouery, or effectes since, the examination
of the L*o*rd Mayor hathe produced; I doe not finde Londons laste
warninge[46] amonge the bookes you haue sente, & yf it be not too
dangerous for you to sende I showlde be glad to see it

I shall be glad to heare of Excetter & Barnstables surrender, that

---

[44] Lewis Roberts published two books. This is either his *The Merchants mappe of Commerce*
(1638), STC 21094; or *The Treasure of traffike* (1641), Wing R1602.

[45] A reference to the efforts of the Queen to negotiate with the Scots and communicate
the results to the Royalists at Oxford through her agent, William Murray, who had been
arrested as he passed through Canterbury on 5 February. He was interrogated on the
orders of the Parliament – Gardiner, iii. 69–70.

[46] *The Last Warning to all the Inhabitants of London* [1645], Thomason, E.328 (24).

our armies might come eastwarde, in relation to an newe enimy[47]

I heartily wishe well to Mr Woorsleyes negotiations & doe hope for some newes of it, my seruice I pray to him

You mention the paper concerninge the fewell, as inclosed but it showlde seeme you forgot it for I fownde it not in the packet

Mr Duries consolatory cowncell is very good, but yf God haue prouided for him in that degree you haue formerly mentioned, I cannot but assure my selfe that his comforts toward you will be suche as that those weaker faythes (which depende vpon your care) may be able to liue by them; Truly my condition is (for the presente) very lowe, & such as I cowlde complaine of, yf I knewe to whome; but God will I hope turne all to my great advantage,

A Lectureship in London; I assure my selfe (bothe in respecte of its owne nature; of the place, & of Mr Duries bothe callinge & disposition of minde) is farre more proper then a pastorall charge & to these considerations I may adde the assurance I haue of an aristocraticall warre; in which I conceiue that these cownties which haue hetherto beene preserued, are like to be concerned, our sinnes are as great; & (to speake in mans reason) this Cownty, lies moste open to forreine invasion; These considerations make me wishe that (synce I am layde by alltogether as vseless heere) some good occasion wowlde call me to London, But what God shall appointe, I shall indeauor & wishe to accownte it beste, thowgh eyther inglorious (as my presente condition is) or perhaps (as it may happen) bitter,

108   *Culpeper to Hartlib, 30 April 1646.   (13/144-5)*

Mr Hartlib;

There are 4: sorts of presente pretenders vpon that supreme [effluxe?] of power from the People which is terminated in the house of Commons, The [King] in the sworde or militia, the Locuste in that AntiChristian thinge which is commonly named Gouernemente Ecclesiasticall; our geud Brethren by theire Extranationall interpretation of our Couenantes & treaties; & a certaine sorte of priuate spirite in this [Kingdome] whose known Lawes heeretofore, & whose knowne meaninge of our Couenants & articles nowe hathe & will prolonge our miseries; To these 4: hathe the House of Commons giuen suche due admonition in their laste excellente declaration as that (notwithstandinge your former confidences to the contrary) I cannot conceiue that my petition wowlde beene soe vnseasonable as you supposed it; & that as

---

[47] Exeter had surrendered on 13 April, whilst Barnstaple held out till 20 April – Gardiner, iii. 92.

wee are reducinge the Ciuill Gouernmente from personall judgemente, soe shall wee at the same time caste of that Ecclesiasticall AntiCristian tiranny, to which the Romane Emperor firste, & afterwards the 10: Kings haue haue for the 12: or 1300 yeeres giuen vp theire power; The firste AntiChristian rise, was of the Elders ouer their flockes the seconde of themselues one ouer another the thirde was of that whole hierarchy ouer the Conscience of the Supreme ciuill magistrate Constantine; which once gained; & by it the Ciuill sworde, AntyChriste sowght not from that time soe muche to cousin as force the conscience; Nowe as these vsurpers of supreme Power haue beene those whoe yelded vp these theire false powers to the beaste, & did at once bothe make & become slaues, soe I cannot but hope & joy to see howe that true effluxe of supreme power hauinge firste freed the people from there Ciuill & Ecclesiasticall Babilons, will afterwards restore Christe to his Spirituall & the People to its Ciuill supremacy; You may perhaps woonder from whence these prophetique fancies flowe, & truly yf you doe, I cannot giue you a particular accownte, my thowghts beinge guided rather by a contellation of obseruations, then by any one or fewe particular reasons that deserue a name; I cannot but admire the the woonderfull prouidence of God that in bothe the rise & fall of AntiChriste, eache followinge generation showlde punnishe the wickednes of the former; The primitiue Christians lazines in spirituall concernements, was punnished in the tiranny of theire shepeards, whoe at once, ingrossed bothe dominion & prophecyinge; This tiranny of the elders was punnished by that thinge wee call a Bishop; whilste tiranny thus crepte into the Churche the Emperors were not lesse tirannous in the State, & theire tiranny (in Constantine the firste Christian Emperor) was againe punished by the tiranny of that mungrell synce called Ecclesiasticall; The supreme Ciuill power thus inslaued in the Emperors, hathe (since the dissolution of the Empire) continued soe in the 10: Kings & thus did the [King] & Bishops loose bothe of them theire vsurped powers to the pope & thus stands the poore ignorante People inslaued to that thinge they calle theire cleargy, the cleargy (by cannonicall obedience, a woord not to be fownde in the Concordance) to the Bishops, to whome allsoe the Ciuill magistrate yelded vp himselfe, & all these to the pope; this imperiall AntyChriste was (throwgh Gods prouidence) pulled downe heere 80: yeeres synce & the spoyle diuided between the [King] & Bishopps; They hauinge fullfilled the Cowncell of God vpon the pope; are themselues bothe of them lately called to accownt by a kinde of Aritocracy in Churche & state; & these againe (Babilon beinge nowe in the precipice of her fall), are (in a quicker motion) called to accownte againe by another generation which thowgh standinge somewhat neereer the truer intereste of the People, hath yet that kinde of dominion in it which was at firste vsurped ouer the People by those whoe are bid to be examples to, not lords ouer Gods heritage; & truly this laste diuell as it had its firste rise in the lazines & voluntary blindenes of the people, soe (throwgh Gods blessinge) is it not like to be caste out but by rowzing all Christians to that noblenes of spirit for which the Bereans were commended; you see rather then nothing I will write fancy

The carrier (I feare) is gone

109   *Culpeper to Hartlib, April 1646.   (13/146)*

Mr Hartlib;

I perceiue by your letter & from elswhere, that the Presbitery carries not away all things soe clearely as you imagined they wowlde; Truly the firste beginninge of AntiChriste tooke roote in the supreme magistrates conscience, & till suche time as the Supreme Magistrate in all States, doe againe free theire consciences from ecclesiasticall tiranny vnder what notion soeuer, & leaue Christe to injoy his spirituall kingdome in the heartes of theire subjects; those our Locustes whether Papall, Epispopall, Presbiteriall et cæt, will neuer leaue stinginge theire fellowe seruants; & beatinge them eyther by the Ecclesiasticall power intrusted to them, or (where that cannot be obtained) by makinge the Ciuill magistrate theire Ho*noura*ble hangemen; & for the maintenance of this Sir Johns jus diuinum,[48] are our Scots & Englishe Aristocraticall interestes, like to joyne in a seconde warre; notwithstandinge all your hopes of peace; & you will finde that (thowgh the [K*ing*] come in) wee shall yet to it againe, after 2: or 3: monethes time, for the gatheringe of cloudes; July or Auguste are not like to be soe cleare as the time of the yeare wowld make it, The Egiptians wowlde haue vs leaue somethinge behinde, to invite our returne; but wee must not leaue one hoofe; neyther in Churche nor State

I haue returned Graswinckle hauinge fownde nothinge in him for my turne; I pray thowgh with some losse returne him[49]

I will in large my selfe heereafter concerninge the balletinge boxes, but I muste tell you that besides them there be other Venetian knackes to be looked after[50]

Some frinds of myne are stirring mainely to get in to the House, but

---

[48] *Qvestions Propounded to the Assembly of Divines By the House of Commons, ... Touching the Point of JUS DIVINUM in the Matter of Church-Government* (22 April 1646), Wing 2692 Thomason, E.335 (11). The preface states that "...all persons guilty of Notorious and Scandalous Offences shall be suspended from the Sacrament of the Lords Supper..." (sigs. A2^{r-v}).

[49] See **105** (4 March 1645/6).

[50] See **101** (11 February 1645/6).

I rather beleeue that God hathe not appointed me to that seruice, nor
can I tell (vnlesse you in large your selfe) of what vse I may be to the
office of addresse; soe lowe is my condition and in suche a precipice of
decay

I feare the carriers gone

[*PS.*] I pray (yf you can possibly finde it) sende me this weeke a Paper
printed neere 2: yeares since concerning compowndinge a fewell of
seacole & other materialls[51]

I very muche desire it

110 *Comenius to Culpeper, Sir Nicholas Stoughton and Hezekiah Woodward,
24 May 1646.   (7/74/1–2)*

[copy: in a scribal hand]

> Vota, & Observantiam!

Generosi, Nobilissimi, Præclari Viri, Domini & fautores honorandi.

Non oblivio Vestri fecit, ut silentio erga Vos uterer toto hoc triennio, &
qvod excurrit: sed turbatæ apud Vos & nos res (Possum alioqvi securè
Vatis illud usurpare: Si obliviscar tui Ierusalem, obliviscatur sui dextera
mea! Cordi enim meo inscripti estis, unde pro Vobis ad Deum meum
perpetua sunt, eruntq*ue* dum vivam, vota) Turbas dixi, Vestras & meas.
Vestræ in conspectu mundi sunt, fatigantq*ue* non Vos duntaxat, sed &
alibi bonos, Vestri et aliorum afflictorum causa ad Deum ingemiscentes.
Meas dum nomino, difficultates intelligo proprias, laborumq*ue* (ad qvos
continuandos Vos qvoq*ue* eum alijs Vestra contulistis desideria &
stimulos) impedimenta varia. Ipsa negotij moles serio aggressu demum
patuit: ut nisi roborasset, adhucq*ue* roboraret, is, cujus virtus in nostra
infirmitate perficitur, toties desperandum fuisset profectò. Confusionum
enim, qvibus res Scholastica undique oppletur (& qvid non?) detegit se
undiq*ue* magis magisq*ue* teterrimum chaos, sordesq*ue* tantæ, ut his
Augeæ stabulis vix ullus Hercules sufficere videatur: & nos tantuli rem
tantam audemus? Accesserunt aliæ remoræ, imprimis ab hostilibus
machinamentis adversus horum locorum Ecclesias, qvæ me quoq*ue*
involverunt: ut itinerationibus, variarumq*ue* rerum (mihi tantisper
parergarum) lectionibus, & scriptionibus (qvarum qvædam jam qvoq*ue*
in luce sunt) bona illius trienij pars, si non major, mihi efffluxerit. Sed
ab his jam respirare datum est, gratiâ Dei (qvanqvam novum qvendam

---

[51] This is probably referring to Richard Gesling's single sheet, *Artificial fire or Coal for
Rich and Poore ... an excellent new invention by Mr. R. G. ... (late deceased,) ...* (1644), Wing
G623.

turbinem minitari videntur): in expurgandis verò Augeæ (Scholarum) stabulis fortassè non deerit consilium Herculanam imitandi industriam: qvi cùm ad expurgandum è Bubili 3000 boum per annos 30 congestum fimum ab Augea Rege conductus esset, Alpheum fluvium ei immisit, sordes*que* qvas particulatim egerere infiniti laboris fuisset, nullo propemodum negotio eluit. Ad eundem planè modum qvicqvid ad repurgandum Scholarum errores hactenus tentatum est particulariter (à nobis etiam ipsis) sine notabili usu fuit: non autem erit, si fluvium qvendam *Alpheum* solerter im*m*ittendi invenerimus consilium. Ille autem fluvius Alpheus, quid est?[52] *Alpha* Græcis primæ literæ nomen est: sed sumitur pro omni primo in suo genere. Interpretabimur ergò Principia sciendi nobis divinitùs data: qvibus, purè fluentibus, non potest non inesse lux & ordo, ad emovendum tenebras & confusionem vim habens inevitabilem, si modò fontes rectè aperire, in alveum unum corrivare, collectis*que* inqvinamentis nostris aptè immittere, noverimus. Sed qvomodo hûc delapsus sum! Hoc unum dicere volui Vobis Patronis & fautoribus meis, non ignavo otio nobis transire tempus, etiamsi ultrà terminos latere videamur: nè Vos vel pristinæ in me poeniteat benevolentiæ, vel à promovendo operæ subtrahendæ manus subeat consilium. Non diu jam verbis lactabimus spes vestras :res sequetur, cum Deo: modò nobis nè subtrahantur qvorum sociâ egemus operâ. Inter qvos cùm sit Georgius Ritschelius, apud Vos nunc agens & egens, necessitates ipsius Vestræ iterùm pietati commendatus volui.[53] Revocare enim ipsum cogito, ut post absoluta (Dei ope) Didactica, grandius illud opus, Pansophicum, adoriamur, & qvid ibi qvo*que* jam tandem per tenuitatem nostram effectui dare volet Dei nostri benignitas experiamur. Rogo itaq*ue* per pium illum Vestrum gloriam Dei quâ datu[r pro] movendi ardorem, nè pium hunc, et ad illa per qvæ gloria Dei promoveri posset piè ardentem, Virum, derelictum esse à necessarijs patiamini. Qvâ possit aut opus habeat, re juvari, prudentia Vestra disqviret facilè: nec ignorare sinet apertus amici nostri communis, Hartlibij, candor. Satis autem ea de re, nè pietati Vestræ diffidere videar.

De publicis nihil est qvod scribam: nisi forsan ut rebus Vestris, post tam tristia nubila serenitatem promittentibus, gratuler; nostris verò ad

---

[52] This allusion was picked up again by Comenius in a further letter of encouragement to his friends in England (possibly addressed to Theodore Haack's cousin, Friedrich Schloer) of 15/25 May 1646 (7/73/5A).

[53] George Ritschel (1616–1683) was a Bohemian who took up refuge in England in the 1640s – DNB. It is quite likely that Ritschel received some material assistance from Cheney Culpeper and Nicholas Stoughton in response to Comenius' request. He dedicated his *Contemplationes Metaphysicae ex Natura Rerum et Rectæ Rationis lumine deductæ* (Oxford, 1648), Wing R1543, to them as 'Amplissimis, Generosissimis . . . Faventissimis Patronis'.

universalem interitum sese disponentibus, ingemiscam. Vos castigavit ut filios pater, nè extra disciplinam essetis, cujus participes sunt omnes: sed virgam amovere jam velle videtur, qvia emendabiles fuistis. Nobis, (in Germania) plaga incutitur super plagam, atque id qvidem tanto tempore, ut reliqviæ tantùm superesse videamur, atque illæ ipsæ tamen hactenùs inemendabiles. Obduruimus enim jàm, & obbrutuimus, ad plagas: ideò nos spiritus vertiginis agit, ut nec Deo nec nobis invicem reconciliari possimus. Hinc & pacis tractatus irriti, omnesque meliorum spes hactenùs fallaces. Interim à tergo imminet nominis Christiani hostis, augenturque terrores. O Deus miserere nostri! In summa, aut interitus rerum, aut restitutio qvædam solemnis, præ foribus esse videtur: ad qvam qvicqvid hactenus vidimus, & videmus, præludia tantùm fuerunt, & præparamenta. Beatus qvi emendat vias suas, ut dignus reperiatur videre opera Dei!

Huic æterno miseratori nostro commendo Vos sanctæ animæ, sicut & me cum Ritschelio meo sancto amori Vestro.[54]

Dabam 24 Maji, 1646.

> Nobilissimæ & Clarissimæ Dignitati Vestræ
> sincerè officijs & ad Deum votis
> addictus

[*Comenius' hand:*]

> Comenius (qui per viam binam
> hæc mittens, priorem epistolam manu
> suâ scripsit; hanc manu alienâ
> transscriptam suâ subscribit)

[*Translation*]

> Good wishes and respects.

Noble, renowned and excellent men, respected patrons and supporters.

It was not through forgetfulness of you that I kept silence toward you throughout the whole of these three years and beyond, but because of the disorders in your affairs and mine. (I can at all events safely employ this saying of the Prophet: If I forget thee, O Jerusalem, let my right hand be forgetful of itself). For you are inscribed upon my heart, whose supplications to my God on your behalf are continual, and will be so for as long as I live. I spoke of your disorders and mine. Yours are before the eyes of the world, and weary not just you, but also good

---

[54] Comenius continued to hold Culpeper in high respect. In a letter of 9 September 1654 to Hartlib he referred to him in glowing terms: 'Qui si literatus et sapiens fuerit, cum quo de Pansophiae adornandae editione agi possit, tanto melius: (Qualis cordatus Vir, D. Geneus Kulpeper, si vivit, et non ad maiora adhibitus, etc.)' – J. Kvačala, *Korrespondence J.A. Komenského*, 2 vols. (Prague, 1897–1902), i. 191.

people elsewhere who sigh and groan to God over your afflictions and those of others. While I call them my troubles, I realise that they are personal difficulties, various impediments to my labours (for the continuation of which you also with others have conveyed your wishes and encouragements). The very mass of business is at last open to serious attack, so that if he whose strength is made perfect in our infirmity had not strengthened us and continued to strengthen us to this day, we would have without doubt been so many times brought to despair. For the horrible chaos of the confusions by which the schools are overspread on every side (and how may it not be!) everywhere discovers itself more and more, together with such a quantity of dirt and filth, that scarcely any Hercules may seem equal to these Augean stables; and are we puny creatures to attempt so great a work? Other delays have come about, above all from the hostile designs against the churches of this region, and they have also involved me: so that the best part of these three years, if not more, has slipped away for me in travelling, reading various things (an incidental labour all the time for me) and writing them (some of which have already been published). But it is now given me, by the grace of God, to have a respite from these things (although they seem to threaten some new whirlwind): but in cleaning out the stables of Augeas (the Schools) perhaps there will not be wanting a plan for imitating the application of Hercules: who, when he was hired by King Augeas to clear out from the cattle shed the dung of three thousand oxen accumulated over thirty years, directed into it the river Alpheus and washed out with almost no effort the filth which it would have been an infinite labour to carry out a little at a time. And clearly in the same way, anything that has been attempted so far on an individual basis (even by ourselves) for reforming the errors of the Schools has been without notable success: but it will not be so if we find a plan for cunningly sending in some river Alpheus. But what is that river Alpheus? Alpha is for the Greeks the name of the first letter; but it is taken for every leading thing of its kind. We shall therefore set forth the divinely given first principles of knowledge; and in them, as they purely flow, there cannot fail to be light and order for removing darkness and confusion, having irresistible strength, if only we have found the way to open the fountains aright, to make them flow into one channel and to skilfully direct them into our collected defilements. But how have I been brought to this state! This alone I have wanted to say to you my patrons and supporters, that the time is not passing by for us in idle leisure, even though we may appear to be unduly aloof. May you not regret your first benevolence toward me or conceive any intention of withdrawing your helping hand from the promotion of the work. We will not for much longer now just foster your hopes: action will follow, with God; provided that those men whose friendly services we require are not removed from us. As George Ritschelius is among them, now living in want in your country, I have desired his needs to be again commended to your goodwill. For I think of recalling him, so that when, with God's help, the Didactica is completed, we may set about that greater work, the Pansophia, and may in this also learn what the loving-kindness of our God may now at last decide to accomplish through our slender talents. And so I ask through that godly ardor of yours for promoting the glory of God by whatever means is given, that you do not suffer this good man, whose holy aspiration is to those things through which the glory of God may be advanced, to be deprived of his necessities. Your discretion will easily ascertain how, or what may be needed, to help him; and the well-known kindliness of our common friend Hartlib will not allow of any uncertainty concerning this. Enough, however, on this matter, lest I seem to mistrust your good nature.

On public matters there is nothing for me to write, unless perhaps I may rejoice in the affairs of your country, giving promise of peace and calm after such ill-omened clouds; but let me bewail our own affairs, which are on the path to universal ruin. The Father has chastened you as sons, lest you should stray from his teaching, in which all men have their part: but he now seems to wish to take away the rod since you have been open to correction. For us (in Germany) blow falls upon blow, and that indeed for such a long time that we seem to survive merely as remnants, and such remnants which nevertheless are so far not subject to amendment. For we are now grown obdurate and insensitive to the blows: and a troubled spirit so affects us that we are able to be reconciled neither to God nor to one another. For this reason peace treaties are unratified and all our hopes of better things are so far belied. Meanwhile from the rear we are threatened by a foe who bears the name of Christian, and our terrors are multiplied./ O God have mercy upon us! To sum up, either the end of all things or else a solemn restitution seems to be at our gates; and everything that we have seen so far and continue to see, was merely a prelude and preparation for it. Blessed is he who amends his ways, and is found worthy to see the works of God!

To this our eternal fount of mercy I commend you, dear godly souls, as likewise I commend myself and Ritschelius my friend to your godly love. Given on the 24th. May 1646

III   *Culpeper to Hartlib, 1 October 1646.   (13/147–8)*

Mr Hartlib;

I returned you Mr Commenius his letter because I cowlde not

meet with Mr Stawton[55] as (I hope) I shall sometime heereafter

You write me woorde that Oxforde rentes muste be tendred at Oxforde & that there are seuerall treasuries appointed, but whether you meane the treasuries of the seuerall Colledges or other treasuries lately appointed by [Parl*iament*] in this you leaue me alltogether vnresolued; I pray afforde me a line concerninge it by this returne, for it muche concernes me

The powder for women in chyldebed is to be bowght at one Mr Thomas, an apothecary in Woodstreete, for 5d a doze, I haue not yet the receipte but hope to get it

The Receipte of the Aqua admirabilis (soe it is called) I haue heere inclosed, but my selfe adde to it a proportion of Gascoygnes powder (which is in the pharmacopja Londinensj & soe it becomes a cordiall not onely reuiuinge, but good againste all infection, the powder & water may be kepte seuerall, or mixed as occasion shall require

I haue allsoe inclosed Mr Duries paper of the Library keeper[56]

I hope Mr Gurdaine[57] hathe deliuered you my papers concerninge Mr Pruuoseste busines, yf not, I pray demande & sende them me; I haue noe leaste hope of that busines till Mr Pruuoste be better informed in what concernes his wishes;

I pray by your intereste at Amsterdame procure me one of Mr Glauberus his bookes nowe in the presse; & a transcript of soe muche of his booke to be printed heereafter as concernes the ouen;[58] The brewinge & boylinge in Woodden vessells was Sir Hugh Plattes invention in his booke printed in the yeare: 1594 beinge 52: yeers agoe;[59] It is too longe nowe to discowrse to you my thowghts & resolutions taken concerninge it; I am very confidente I can make it but shall be glad to receiue the pratise of it from another, I showld be glad to see allsoe his booke de auro potabili[60]

The newes of my [L*ord*] of Ormonde (yf true) is greate & good

---

[55] See **110** (24 May 1646) from Comenius.

[56] The original letters were sent from Dury to Hartlib on 18 and 25 August 1646 (3/3/27 and 3/3/30). The copy extracts, to which Culpeper is probably referring, are at 1/15/1A-4B and 47/14/1A-8B. This paper was published as *The Reformed Librarie-Keeper* (1650), Wing D2882.

[57] The physician Aaron Gurdan, at this date attached to the Savoy Hospital in the city of London – GI, pp. 296–97.

[58] J. R. Glauber, *Furni novi philosophici oder Beschreibung einer Newerfundenen Destillirkunst* (Amsterdam, 1646–1649). Culpeper wanted transcripts of the chapters on furnace (i.e. stills) construction contained in the four unpublished parts (which were subsequently printed in 1647–49). Hartlib had a manuscript copy of Glauber's treatise entitled 'Delineatio singularis cuiusdam recensque inventi furni philosophici distillatorii' from 1643 (16/8/1A-4B); Clucas, p. 151.

[59] Hugh Platt, 'A vessell of Wood, to brew or boile in' – in *The Jewell House of Art and Nature* (1594), STC 19991, sigs. ²I3^{v}-²I4^{r}.

[60] J. R. Glauber, *De Auri Tinctura, sive Auro Potabili Vero* (Amsterdam, 1646).

I pray send me woorde the names of Commoners whose landes are
to be solde & particularly whether Sir John Culpeper be one[61]

With my affectionate wishes to you I reste

[*Hartlib writes:*]

1—[d] french Author

2—[d] Harrison et Kendrick

3—[d] [S*ir* W*illiam* W*aller*] [*two words illegible*]

112   *Culpeper to Hartlib, n.d.*   *(13/311)*

Mr Hartlib

I cannot performe my promise this weeke you shall not fayle
by the nexte, of the drinke & receipte

[*PS.*] The bookes lately set foorthe the good example of Hollande &
my owne reason on bothe makes me incline to liberty of Conscience,
I can without sinne submitte my reason & will to authority, but
conscience is not my owne & therefore not disposable by me, nor can
there be a humane judge of the heart or when it is obstinacy and when
not; yf mr Duryes way can conuince it is well, yf not, charity commands
all to beleeue them ingenuous thowgh erroneous & in that case to bear
with theire errors

113   *Culpeper to Hartlib, 14 October 1646.*   *(13/149–50)*

Mr Hartlib;

I shall not be in towne this weeke as I intended; by reason that
my [Fath*er's*] busines is not yet ripe

I shall much desire to see a taste of your [off*ice*] of addresse, &
towards it I heere sende you the balsome you desired as allsoe a drincke
for the stone;[62] vnder the authors owne hande, whoe grewe riche by
sellinge it by 6s 8d the bottle, beinge little more then a pinte My
mother purchased the Receipte many yeeres synce; & the olde man
beinge nowe deade I may (by the contracte) publishe; it woorks
diuretically & by comfortinge the stomacke, where a firste ill digestion
is that which causes moste illnesses; I haue knowne it very sucessfully
giuen but not soe proper for childing woomen

I pray particularize conceringe the seruante you mention; my [W*ife*]

---

[61] Sir John Culpeper had served as county MP for Kent until he was excluded in
January 1643 – DNB s.n. John Colepeper; CJ, iii. 374.

[62] Hartlib had suffered from the stone since 1642 – HDC, pp. 21–2.

is a good deale ingaged to one heere in the Cowntry & inclines (from an apprehension that the warres are not yet at an ende) to one of a lesse hyght then shee firste proposed; Shee that is nowe in her eye is of the better kinde of chambermaydes; I wowlde gladly knowe, what qualities yours pretends to; my seruice I pray & thanckes to Mrs Hartlib

I muste againe earnestly desire you that Mr Rous[63] may be asked what may be done (without offence to the [Parl*iament*]) in the paymente of Colledge rentes, & that I may not fayle of an answere from you this weeke, for my time is nowe very shorte

With my beste wishes to you I reste

[*PS.*] My seruice I pray to Mr Woorsely; I haue loste my time concerninge some businesses to write of & truly I am alltogether vnsettled more then euer

[*PPS.*] returne me the stone drincke receipte; I haue noe more

114   *Culpeper to Hartlib, 21 October 1646.   (13/151–2)*

Mr Hartlib

I earnestly expected to heare from you by the Ashforde carrier yesterday, concerning my Oxforde busines & in truthe it very muche trowbles me howe to carry my selfe in it

I shall by the nexte sende you the vertues bothe of the powder & bulsome & shall be very glad of your receipte for the stone; as allsoe of the ouen you formerly mentioned, I pray indeauor to giue me an accownte of it

I doe a greate deale hearken after the fowntaines in Germany, for my eldeste girle,[64] whoe is lame of one side by a paralyticall humor; & truly yf (by your meanes) I cowlde heare of any perticuler person soe affected, that had beene cured, I wowlde certainly sende her thether; I pray inquire yf you can whether the water of any of the seuerall fowntaines can be transported; the booke mentions one that can not; I am heartily sorry, you are againe at soe lowe an ebbe, I professe my selfe am as yet in a very helpeless condition, & howe God will dispose of me I know not

I shall not be in towne till my [Fath*ers*] busines be ripe, whoe neglectes his owne busines & hinders me in myne

I cannot imagine what Mr Harrison showlde meane, but my thowghts

---

[63] Francis Rous, MP for Truro. Like Culpeper, Rous had been at the Middle Temple – DNB.

[64] Elizabeth (1640– [post] 1682). She married Christopher Miles.

still hyghten concerning the vniversall vse of his ingenuous invention, &
will (when I am able) assiste it

One thinge you forgotte in your mayde seruante & that is whether
shee cowld (yf occasion required at any time) set her hand to the
makinge of a pye, or suche other quelques choses as woomen knowe
howe to name better then I can; But what doe I trowble my selfe with
these thowghts? whoe for owght I knowe, am not like to haue where-
withall to keepe but these 2: maydes wee nowe haue & truly I sadly
nowe apprehende what (you knowe I haue formerly feared; I shall
loose my time

I reste in haste

115   *Culpeper to Hartlib, 29 October 1646.   (13/153–4)*

Mr Hartlib;

my desires that my chyldren showlde be better followed in
theire learninge then they haue lately beene made me inquisitiue for a
well qualified seruante, but truly when I consider the approachinge
times, & my owne vnhappy condition in a Father whose actions driue
wholy to my prejudice, it takes away that contente & joy which I myght
take in the Fortunes which God & nature had caste vpon me, & will
make me to retire againe to the thowghts of my late priuate & poore
condition & this is the issue of my thowghts concerninge the seruante
you mention

I am sorry you finde suche discowragements in your [*Office*] of
addresse; but I pray howesoeuer, acquaint your selfe with the wayes &
meanes whereby the [M*aster*] of Addresse in Paris gained soe muche
as to haue his office looked after,[65] for (men not louinge to goe out of
theire ordinary way) the greate difficulty which I apprehende in the
busines is howe to put the wheele into motion, & I can not but hope
that (yf that pointe were well studied) God will yet (somewhere amonge
vs) rayse some helpe towards it I extremely longe to heare howe Mr
Woorsly speedes with the Oxforde Schollar; & I am sure he can tell
you what my thowght & propositions to him haue beene concerninge
that very way, & truly what I haue conceiued is from my Chymicall
philosophy; The Poste (I feare is gone

[65] Théophraste Renaudot's Parisian *Bureau d'adresse* served as a model for Hartlib's
'Office of Address' – GI, pp. 68–9, 375; H. M. Solomon, *Public Welfare, Science and
Propaganda in Seventeenth Century France: The Innovation of Theophraste Renaudot* (Princeton,
1975) – see also **125** (9 April 1647).

116 *Culpeper to Hartlib, 4 November 1646.   (13/155–6)*

Mr Hartlib;

My [domestiq*ue*] affaires doe howerly rise into suche a storme as (I feare) my anchor, & cable will hardly holde, but that I shall be forced to committe my selfe to the sea, I meane some place beyonde sea, whether my [Fath*ers*] debtes & bitternes will driue me; besides thowsands for which I stoode before ingaged w*i*th him; I haue (synce his returne into these partes of England) payed & secured allmoste 1500l for him; after a patiente expectation of noe more then an acceptance of my indeauours, & a returne; juste to me, & honorable & conscientious in himselfe in the paymente of his debtes, nowe I haue freed him I can finde noe other hopes but that I muste pay all, or ly for it, yf he can auoyde it; my presente thowghts can directe me to noe other sanctuary than a transmarine, which cowrse I beleeue I shall suddenly take; for in truthe these vaste pressures, added to my owne, will sinck me into some dungeon or other, & my estate which showlde supporte me & pay my Creditors will be swallowed vp for wante of care & order;[66] Some of my frindes (that haue thowght me faythfull to my Cowntry) haue sometimes formerly wished me of the [Parl*iament*] I muste confesse I nowe looke on it as a way wherein I hope I showld not be vnfaythfull & might gaine oportunity to make a more orderly retreicte from these my presente pressures then eyther a prison or a place beyonde sea wowlde afforde me I pray thincke of it for me, I muste away to some busines

117 *Culpeper to Hartlib, 11 November 1646.   (13/157–8)*

Mr Hartlib

my condition, I laste writte you of, still continues, without any other change, then some suche generall promises, as wherein I haue fownde my former expectations frustrated, & yf I nowe againe (as I haue formerly to my disaduantage) rely on them, it will be from this grownd that they are somewhat more solemly made, & besides, I cannot but say, that my wishes for a good ende, make me hope, euen againste hope, & againste suche growndes & principles of judgemente, vpon other mens actions, as haue seldome fayled me

I beleeue it will not be longe ere I be in London; in the meane time I shall be glad to heare from you; I pray particularly marke howe my letters come to your hands, whether vnbroken vp, & sealed (as vsually)

---

[66] The Parliamentary Committee for Compounding set the fine for Sir Thomas Culpeper's delinquency on 4 November 1646 at £1,318 – see **Introduction**, p. 120.

with the snagge with her house vpon her heade; an embleme fitting
my presente condition; I pray sende me a sicknes byll, & onely say
whether the mayde seruante haue yet disposed of herselfe; You were
euer confidente of our geud brethren; I pray let me nowe knowe your
minde, & whether a judgemente, vpon persons or bodies politique, by
their intereste, be not a kinde of infallible way of prophecy, & suche as
cannot fayle but in a selfe denyinge Christian, (I am sure) not in a
wise, poore, & valiante nation of the Scottes; I meane wordly wise; for
truly the oppression (by force) of Christian truthe & liberty, & suche as
harmelesly stande for it, meerely because it will hinder that domineeringe power in themselues, which themselues (soe lately) haue soe
justly hated & suppressed in others is indeed the wisdome of the world,
but suche foolishnes in the eyes of God, as (I am confidente) he now
lawghs to scorne; my papers done: your et cet:

118   *Culpeper to Hartlib, n.d. [1646?].*   *(13/284−5)*

Mr Hartlib,
       I giue you very many thanckes for Mr Duryes essay concerning
the office of addresse,[67] wherein I muste ingenuously confesse the plot
to be well layed, but whether Oxforde be the beste place for that part
of it which concerns spirituall things I am yet to seeke;[68] That parte of
it which is called Accommodation[69] is indeede very vsefull, but this I
assure you that olde Mr Chute Father to Chute the Lawyer,[70] did for
many yeeres attempte to set this office on woorke in matters of
bargaines & sales but cowlde make nothinge of it, because men wowlde
not in (suche concernements open themselues thowgh to theire owne
advantage, & I cannot but adde to this the Irishe humor, of keepinge
theire olde barbarous custome of plowinge by horses tayles, & (for a
visible & wofull example in this Kingdome), all the Royalistes are
alltogether fownded on that Roman Catholik principle of doinge as
theire Fathers did, euen to a continuance in grosse degree of slauery;

---

[67] John Dury, *Considerations tending to the Happy Accomplishment of Englands Reformation in
Church and State* (1647), Wing H981.
  [68] Culpeper refers to Dury's suggestion that Oxford was the most appropriate location
for the 'Agent for Communications'. After discussion with members of the circle it was
decided that London would be its more suitable location − Dury, *Considerations tending to
the Happy Accomplishment of Englands Reformation in Church and State* (1647), Wing H981, p.
53, GI, pp. 70−72, 374−75; see also **129** (22 July [1647?]).
  [69] The 'Office of Address' was to function in two separate sections. The 'Office of
Address for Accommodations' would serve as an agency for labour exchange, whilst the
'Office of Address for Communications' was designed to promote research and innovation − GI, pp. 69−70.
  [70] Challoner Chute, father to Challoner Chute Junior − DNB.

all this notwithstandinge, my opinion is that those, whose spirits God hathe raysed out of this mudde of Custome, muste indeauor (at the leaste) to improue theire talents towards others

In the other office the objection I make is that theire will wante a stocke of ingenuityes, at leaste to beginne with; for men that are of rationall principles onely will not forgoe their commodities of ingenuity but by way of barter, I confesse the spirituall parte will be vphelde gratis when they are once fownde, by suche who will readily spende themselues & be spente for the glory of their Creator, without expectinge any other ende or reward; & this makes me thincke that eyther there showld be 3: parts of the office or (at least) that the care of rationalll ingenuities showlde be annexed to that parte which you call the office of Accommodation for thowgh the materialls be of somewhat a more refined nature, yet the exchange and merchandiz of it is & will be between mechanique disposition, whoe make them selues the onely Center of what & to proue this howe many ingenuities ar loste & buried because Selfe cannot be aduanced, Looke vpon Dr Webbe & Mr Wheeler;

A concentration of all publique ingenuities is indeede possible & will be of admirable vse, & the complications of the same inventions will beget newe

I pray by this bearers returne to morrowe let me (yf you can) knowe the mayds qualifications

I haue sente my [mich*aelmas*] rente to Oxforde, the question I haue made hathe beene onely concerning the 3: yeers arreares, of which yf Mr Rous be come to towne I pray giue me a line, for I am yet vnsatisfied

1647

119 *Culpeper to Hartlib, 28 January 1646/7.* *(13/161–2)*

Mr Hartlib;

I pray intreate mrs Hartlib to knowe of the mayde whether shee be prouided; yf shee be, the busines is at an end; yf otherwise, my Wife will (vpon her owne conditions) take 3: monthes tryall of her, & (yf shee appointes her time) will sende for her[1]

Her beste passage to Grauesende will be (euery day in the weeke) by water, which my [W*ife*] will discharge, & sende a man to bringe her from thence, yf shee be not prouided, & resolue what day (the nexte weeke) shee will be there,

I wowlde gladly heare what impression I lefte behind me, thowgh (in my owne judgemente) I hope little;

My deuoyrs to all the good compa*n*y

120 *Culpeper to Hartlib, 3 February 1646/7.* *(13/163–4)*

Mr Hartlib;

I haue scarce time to tell you my feares that mr Dury will not be able to boygh vp againste the prejudice of opinion, which you mention to be againste his person;[2] I knowe an equall carriage between two Contrary parties dothe sometimes doe well; & yet sometimes againe (betweene parties soe insenced) it leaues a man loste to bothe, & this I feare for mr Dury; I haue written, but whether it be as it showlde, I muste leaue to your judgement,

My occasions will necessitate me shortly to London, but truly, you muste spare your Cowrtships or vse them where they are bothe more deserued & wanted

I pray returne my thanckes for the Hierogliphickes, in which (in truthe) he hathe giuen a very good essay;[3] I haue not time; otherwise

---

[1] See **123** (23 February [1647]).

[2] The suspicion in which Dury was increasingly held at the Westminster Assembly in 1647, partly as a result of his irenicist tendencies, was doubtless behind Culpeper's concern – HDC, p. 259; Batten, p. 110.

[3] Culpeper probably refers to Francis Lodowyck, *A Common Writing* (1647), Wing L2814, which Hartlib published and which Culpeper commented on further in letter **124** (1 March 1646/7).

I will shortly sende you my thowghts for him concerninge merchants accownts vpon this condition that hee will adde his judgemente & ingenuity to them

my seruice [to.?] to Westminster

[*PS.*] sende me Mr Duryes answer yf you haue time

121 *Culpeper to Hartlib, 16 February 1646/7.   (13/165–6)*

Mr Hartlib;

I had sente laste weeke for the mayde, had not my seruante fallen soe sicke as to leaue me alltogether destitute of fittinge meanes; I am nowe forced to make vse of suche as are lefte, I meane the Carrier, whome I haue appointed to conducte her hether yf shee will come

Sometime between the beginninge & middle of nexte weeke I muste be in London; In the meane time I showld be glad (before I shee [Cap*tain*] Westroes face) to haue his solemne answere to my letter & therefore I pray (yf you can) let some oportunity invite him to it; Yf (without tellinge him of my resolution for London) you inquired of his receipte of my letter, & expreste from me a desire of his answere; it might perhaps drawe a fewe lines from him; I pray (yf you can) informe me howe our Kentishe busines is concluded between our Committee & Sir I: Sydeley;[4] I pray remember Mr Dury of his promise to me concerning Pruuostes busines, the office of addresse, & Logicke his thowghts allsoe concerning Dr Gibbons[5] wowlde be a fauor; With my affectionat wishes to you I reste

[*PS.*] My deuoyrs to Westminster

122 *Thomas Westrow.? to Culpeper, 20 February 1646/7.   (13/129–30)*

Sir/

I am extreamly ashaimed that I haue giuen you noe manner of

[4] Sir John Sedley, appointed deputy lieutenant for Kent by the House of Lords in April 1642 – T. P. S. Woods, *Prelude to Civil War 1642* (Salisbury, 1980), pp. 65–6. He was an active participant in the political affairs of Kent – Everitt, *Kent*, pp. 70–74, 80–82, 149–51.

[5] Nicholas Gibbon the younger. Culpeper had probably been sent by Hartlib his 'Medium ad componendas controversias ecclesiae Christianae oblatum a Doctore Gibbono; quod jam approbatum a certis aliquot e Synodo selectis Arbitris, et publico consulto ordinatum ab illustrissimis Regni Paribus, solum adhuc assensum manet Illustris Domus Communium' (20/11/47–48). Gibbon wrote further on this subject and published a broadsheet: *A Summe or Body of Divinitie Real* (1651), Wing G656 – HDC, p. 258.

accoumpt of both your letters all this while The first with Mr Dureys
enclosed I thought to haue talked to you aboute in the country but
being prevented of such a meeting by the vncomfortable wether going
and my haste returning, and meeting your tother of the 10th instante
att my coming to towne on thursday night last I am glad to take this
first leasure to cry your mercy and will thinke of conveying itt to your
hands as well as I can afterwarde../ For the businesse I communicated
the summ of it to severall honest men but founde none so apte to
harken as Crumwell who indeed did rather speake on't to me then I
to him and principally I presume to take an occation to speake of
yourselfe and to shewe what impression those discourses you had with
him had lefte in him but wee had not time to make any great matter
of itt only concluded that wee neede not bee affrayde of itt but shewe
our selues free to't when itt comes in to the howse but that which
seemes to stick with those honest men that I haue offerd itt to is the ill
successe that all such kinde of conferrances haue had hitherto that the
more spirituall men communicate of their principles to formall carnall
men the more antipathy and opposition hathe itt begotten and therefore
they can hardly thinke that if wee should get any such to bee imploy'd
itt would hardly bee worth our labour and then on the tother side if
the Parliament should sende ouer men of their owne way they would
rather make itt an agreement of nations then churches and so rivitt in
that principle of the swoorde and outwarde forse in spirituall matters
so much the harder but that which is the maine and cooles me allso is
that the spiritt of malignity prevailes so farr that wee are by noe meanes
like to haue opportunity to think of doing any thinge that way before
wee bee vtterly routed and [*letters deleted*] [therefore rather hope for] a
deliuerance to rise of out of such a persecution muche sooner and fuller
then wee could possibly expecte itt from the consequence of any
such foundation that could bee layd by the mutuall forbearance of
Evangelicall churches in matters as differente as those among ourselues
here./ I haue not now time enough to state to you the condition of our
affayes I presume you haue hearde that wee only keepe vpp a body of
horse but the maine knack is the Changing the hande for so itt is
intended Coll: [Greicers.?] to bee cheife and all the reste after that rate
[Lyle.?] Cald back from Ireland and [Hoby.?] or Waller or Stapleton in
his roome and this is not much doubted since the late recruite from
Cornwall and and Wales and so all the rest after that rate till wee haue
mauld the Skismaticks and all that haue been too forwarde in this
businesse that so wee may tame the people for euer meddling or stirring
for a Parliament againe then shall King, Kirke and every domineeringe
interest flourish 'till they fall out amonge themselues againe that so ther
may bee a way for the diliuerance of Gods people for that must come
and every stone of Babell you know must downe and since wee would

not bee actiue 'tis necessary wee should bee passiue since wee would not bee engaged by all those tokens which God sente by his people to owne them and ease them of their yoakes wee shall bee maide to see itt at last by deare bought experience and bee ashaimed and confounded for our envy att them but enuffe of this melancoly story till I see you who am

Your very affectionate seruant

123 *Culpeper to Hartlib, 23 February [1647].   (13/131–2)*

Mr Hartlib;

Together with your letter (by the Carrier laste weeke) I receiued an accownte that my Father wowlde bee in the Cowntry, as too day or on thursday & that he wowlde haue me stay for him heere; This is the occasion of my not beinge in London till some time nexte weeke

The mayde will (I hope) finally giue contente, yf shee can receiue it; Shee hathe (by her discowrse) liued in marchantes, & Cowrtiers seruices, bothe which kinde of men (eyther from theire humor or Callinge) doe laye themselues forthe muche more then the Cowntry [gentlemen]; especially humbled (as wee are) by these times; That which wee thancke God for, seemes (I perceiue) small in her eyes, which I impute, not to her minde, but to her former places of life; where euery thinge hathe beene (by her relation) more magnificente, then eyther dothe agree with my presente fortune or will heereafter with my humor, but of this more vpon better acquaintance, for the presente, I conceiue her cheery, plyante yet, & (in relation to her charge) of suche disposition as I like

Truly I neuer apprehended howe my Lord Lysle was designed for Irelande;[6] nor can I nowe apprehende, any grownde for suche a change, as your letter mentions; yf it rise out of the [House of Commons] I shall be apte to thincke that Intereste carries it on; for I neuer conceiued the man of that raysed spirite as to be eminently eyther good or ill

I am sorry for the [Kings] carriage towards our Commissioners,[7] thowgh truly it agrees with my expectation, & driues on to those concernements of monarchy and liberty of Conscience, & (in a woorde) to that downefall of Ciuill & Ecclesiasticall Babilon as I still looke for

---

[6] Philip Sidney, Viscount Lisle, the eldest son of the Earl of Leicester (1619–1698). He was sent to Ireland as Lieutenant-General under Ormonde after the outbreak of the Irish Rebellion. The English Parliament made him Lord-Lieutenant on 9 April 1646, but he did not leave for Ireland until February 1647 – DNB.

[7] Charles I was under the guardianship of the Commissioners of the English Parliament. On 10 February a letter from one of the commissioners was read in the House of Commons reporting the king as saying that, if he waited six months, things would be in such confusion that he would obtain his ends without difficulty – Gardiner, iii. 215.

I am moste heartily sorry for Mr Duryes thowght of returne to his graue, but I hope (by Gods blessinge) for a quicke ressurection; I pray remember him from me of his promises mentioned in my laste; that (in his absence yf wee muste loose him) we may be doinge; thowgh perhaps wee shall not see the corne come vp

I haue done somethinge lately according to Mr Woorslyes laste directions, & shall (ere it be longe) doe more

My humble deuoyrs to that Excellent Lady at [Westm*inster*] to Mr & Mrs Dury & to Mr Woorsly; Yf [Capt*ain*] Westro[8] be in towne, I pray inuite him to giue me an answer; Remember me in the ouen for boylinge, bakinge et cæt

[*PS.*] My [W*ife's*] & my owne kindeste respectes to Mrs Hartlib: I pray

124   *Culpeper to Hartlib, 1 March 1646/7.   (13/167–8)*

[Note: enclosure referred to may be 13/129]

Mr Hartlib;
          my Fath*er* came not home till the latter ende of laste weeke, & hauinge seuerall busines of difficulty to treate w*i*th him, I am yet constrained to stay till nexte weeke

I thanke Mr Woorsly for his care of me in pointe of a seruante & shall speake further with him of it when I come to towne

I heere inclose [Capt*ain*] Westroes letter, that you may see (by it), howe hee & Cromewell conceiue of a forreine correspondency;[9] where it stickes with others; & howe their beinge (at the presente) ouerborne & indeauored (as he conceiues) to be rwined, keepes them from putting themselues forthe, in a [publi*que*] way, I knowe howe farre this is from a right ordered spirite, but those that can play a good game well, are often at a losse, in an ill game I shall (when I come to London) speake with them bothe; & make it good vpon them by strenght of reason howe juste & necessary it is to serue our God & our Cowntry thowgh w*i*thout the rewarde of sucsesse, thowgh truly I haue still a super confidence that God will finally breake those linsy woolsy packinges vp

[8] Thomas Westrow, MP for Hythe and a friend of Sir Cheney Culpeper, with whom he served on the Kent Committee. Culpeper hoped to utilize Westrow's parliamentary position to promote foreign correspondence through John Dury and Hartlib's 'Office of Address' – GI, p. 73; SHAL, p. 26; see **124** (1 March 1646/7).

[9] Culpeper counted on support in the Long Parliament from the Independent MPs Robert Andrews, Francis Rous and Thomas Westrow. On 20 February Westrow wrote to Culpeper reporting the support of Oliver Cromwell for the 'Office of Address' – SHAL, p. 45. See **122** (20 Feb 1646/7).

of thinges, which our ecclesiasticall & ciuill Aristocracies muste make for theire owne defence, & that the stone (nowe in full motion) will not ly still, till it come to the bottome of the hill.

I haue perused Mr Duryes letter to me, & doe especially approue of that rule for the dissentinge brethren, which he takes out of Phil: 3: 6:,[10] soe that his meaninge be, that (after all essayes of accorde), one side make not themselues judges, bothe of the dissentinge partie & of the subjecte of dissente; but leaue it to the good time, when God will reueale it allsoe, rememberinge on all sides that excellente grownde of humility that wee knowe but in parte, & that other excellente rule of charity; By bearinge with one another to fullfill the Royall lawe of Christe;[11]

There is onely one thinge in his letter which (I conceiue) I rather vnderstand not then disallowe; He speakes of a rule by which the dissentinge Brethren showlde walke; Yf by it he meane a rule of holdinge the vnity of the spirite in the bonde of peace, notwithstandinge some differences, I fully agree; but yf (as some other of our assembly men) he expectes a declaration of an vnchangeable rule they wowlde walke by among themselues & in theire owne wayes I can noe way agree to it, as beinge destructiue to that liberty which they desire to maintaine againste, not onely others errores, but euen their owne allsoe, whensoeuer God shall reueale them, & truly these Herculean pillers of infallibility this jurare in verba, (euen) propria, is one greatest proppe of Babell, which the spirituall Sampsons muste pull downe.

I very muche rejoyce at God's Prouidence in the likelyhode of Mr Dury his beinge called to [Saint] Ieames[12] & concerning the fitness of it, my thowghts cannot adde to those of that Excellente Lady to whome I pray presente my humble seruice[13]

Mr Woorslyes expediente concerninge Mr Pruuoste busines, still stickes with me; you name a Custome in Flanders, (I conceiue you meane an vsuall and ordinary way of voluntary contracte between parties) this is goode; From this voluntary Custome in Flanders you grownde a Lawe in Englande (you knowe me an Independente) this Lawe is not soe goode, for (yf a lawe) it leaues as little liberty for an man to dispose of his owne, as the former proposition did

---

[10] Philippians 3:6 – 'Concerning zeal, persecuting the church; touching the righteousness which is in the law, blameless'.

[11] Dury wrote a letter to Oliver St John on 31 March 1646 in which he discussed the differences between the dissenting members of the assembly and their brethren (3/3/7). There is a copy of this letter amongst Hartlib's papers to which Culpeper may refer (3/3/8).

[12] Dury had been invited in 1646 to educate the younger children of the king at St James's Palace – Batten, p. 113.

[13] Katherine, Lady Ranelagh?

I will giue an answere to Mr [Frederick] Lodowicke[14] when I come
to towne; Meane time I will (in generall) vente a conceite I haue met
with, which is; that all things might be hieroglyphically written with the
9: numericall figures & the :o:; The firste 10: figures to make the 10:
genera generalissima or predicamentes, as the figure 1: showld signify
substantia, et cæt; I am confidente it may be done in an irrationall
way, as (ad placitum imponeatis), to haue 100: stand for a horse, 101:
for a dogge et cæt; but that which I smatter in it, is to make it rationall
after the hauing set downe the firste ten figures, & those allsoe to be
soe a newe framed as to runne in to one another better then our
ordinary figures doe, but more of this nexte weeke: my papers done.

125   *Culpeper to Hartlib, 9 April 1647 (sent with 4 books).*   *(13/171–2)*

Mr Hartlib;
        I haue heerewith returned you, the 2: Frenche pamphlets
concerning the office of addresse,[15] your laste manuscripte, & the
forreine tracte, De tolerantia stabilienda;[16] I pray fauor me soe muche
as to convaygh this inclosed to Mr Westroe; my deuoyrs to the good
Company at [Saint] Ieames
        At Mr Duryes returne, I pray remember him of his promises to me;
Shewe him Dr Gibbons paper,[17] & returne it to me (with Mr Duries
opinion vpon it) by the nexte that I may be ready for Dr Gibbons
when wee meete
        I heartily wishe that [Monsieur] Pruuoste were dealte withall, to
quitte his laste proposition, yf that were done I cannot but thincke that
(vpon seconde thowghts) it wowlde be better entertained, & truly since
Mr Pruuoste ayme is to doe good, the circumstances showlde not
discowrage him; my beste wishes attende you

[14] Francis Lodowyck, author of *A Common Writing* (1647), Wing L2814, which was
published by Samuel Hartlib – see letter **120** (3 February 1646/7).
[15] Arnold Boate wrote to Hartlib from Paris on 16/26 July 1648, promising to send
further copies of Renaudot's treatise of his *Bureau d'Adresse* and reported that he had
already forwarded to Hartlib all the material printed on the subject that he could find.
Culpeper may therefore be refering to two French pamphlets which had been sent to
Hartlib by Boate. They were probably *L'vsage et commoditez des Bureaux d'Adresse dans les
Provinces* (n.p., 1639) and *Inventaire des addresses dv bvreau de rencontre . . .* (Paris, 1630). The
former is not listed amongst the works by Renaudot cited in Solomon, *Public Welfare pp.
239–51.*
[16] Godefroy Hotton, *Gotthofr. Hottonis de Christiana inter Europæos Evanglicos concordia, sive
tolerantia in charitate stabilienda tractatus, nudam . . . majoris operis delineationem exhibens. Editio
secunda . . . emendatior* (Amstelaedami, 1647), BL 847.h.20.
[17] See letter **121** (16 February 1646/7).

126   *Culpeper to Hartlib, 14 April 1647.   (13/175)*

Mr Hartlib
    I shall very muche desire to heare from [Capt*ain*] Westroe in answer to my letter; yf your occasions call you to [Westm*inster*] you wowlde oblige me to give him the oportunity; you wowlde oblige me, allsoe with Mr Duryes booke of Churche Gouernemente,[18] I beginne to despayre of his other promises; my devoyrs to all that good company; I reste in haste

127   *Culpeper to Hartlib, 21 April 1647.   (13/176–7)*

Mr Hartlib;
    I pray returne my thancks to Mr Dury for his booke, the preface whereof I holde to be very seasonable for these times, & that which the sober independente cannot objecte againste, for soe longe as Paules plantinge, & Apollos wateringe may receiue theire increase from God & not from the Ciuill Magistrates sworde, this primitiue way may beget (perhaps) fewer, but (certeinly) truer Christians
    As for the Churche module it selfe, I cannot but consente to the generall proposition that There muste be assemblies of Saintes, It is plaine to me howe muche, a number of excellente spirits embodied (whether in rationall or spirituall things) will excell the same persons, standings single in theire severall darke corners, I knowe allsoe & am perswaded, that all the giftes of God, to particular men, (whether, bestiall, rationall, or spirituall) are not (by the intentions of the Giuer) terminable in the stewarde, but by him to be improued towards others; but truly whether these embodyinge of persons, whether congregationall or (as Mr Dury is pleased to call it) Classicall, (a woord not fownde in the Concordance) owght not to be purely voluntary without any other coercion to that Spirituall Kingdome then by the spirituall Swoorde or swoorde of the Spirite, I muste leaue to Mr Duryes thowghts as allsoe whether (in spirituall matters) they that take the other swoorde are not like to perishe by it, & yf soe, then whether our presente reuerente, Aristocratycall, clergy at [Westm*inster*] that forsakinge the example of that Author & finisher of owr faythe, (in his meekenes, lowlines of minde, blessinge & prayinge for his enimies, not beinge hearde in the streetes et cæt) & ridinge in the same manner, vpon the same poore Ciuill jade, vpon which theire predecessors haue done are like to rayse in mens hearts any other then the same kinde of linsy woolsy religion, which wee haue inioyed the 42: monthes, euen euer synce the Ciuill

---

[18] John Dury, *A Model of Church Government* (1647), Wing D2873.

beaste hath beene prieste-ridden; And heere, let not Mr Dury (in excuse of them that are nowe in the saddle) say that the goode tame beaste (not knowing perhaps a better condition or duty) comes of himselfe to the blocke or for politicke endes (suche as are mentioned in the Popes nuntio)[19] will (like the Elephante) take the Clergy with his snowte, & sette him vpon his owne backe; For yf our spirituall gwides be fully perswaded in theire owne hartes that Christs [Kingdome] is not of this worlde, & that sinners may be made the woorste of mere Hypocrites, but not possibly Christians by the Ciuill sworde, I conceiue it wowld be then their duty not eyther to get vp or be set vp in the saddle, but rather to giue the poore beaste better & more spirituall nurtriture; But what doe I trowble you with this, I hope Mr Dury is not in the leaste kinde the objecte of these lines, that onely which I wishe is that Hee and some other learned men wowlde elaborate the magistrates interest in Christe spirituall [Kingdome] but I confesse there is prudence to be vsed in the carryinge of it on; my humble seruice to all that good Company

I showlde be glad to knowe what Mr Worsly hathe done concerninge the younge man; my seruice (I pray) to him

Yf you can heare any thinge of Ragnell I pray afforde me a woorde of it; & yf you can invite a letter from Mr Westro, you will oblige

[*PS.*] I haue not time to inlarge vpon the paper you sente me

128   *Culpeper to Hartlib, 26 April 1647.   (13/178–9)*

Mr Hartlib

I am nowe returned from the Bathe, & showlde be glad to receiue your wonted kindenes on friday; allthowgh I intende suddenly to be in towne

I conceiue the Citty is not alltogether vpon or towards those hygh conditions as when you laste writte to me, nor yet the Scottes, soe neere our borders, thowgh I question not our breakinge & that by it wee shall become a scorne & by woorde to our enimies, nor doe I thincke that our Monarchicall or Aristocraticall benefactors (thowgh they vapor muche) will fare muche better then our presente; I reste in haste

---

[19] D. T., *The Popes Nuntioes* (1643), Wing T4B.

129 *Culpeper to Hartlib, 22 July [1647?]. (13/258–9)*[20]

Mr Hartlib

I haue not till nowe had time to write vnto you & muste nowe be shorte for the poste is (I feare) gone

I am still of opinion that 200[1]. (when payd) is goode to your Creditors, but little to you & yours; & that Oxforde may be (for wante of a better cowrse) a place to giue you a bare subsistence, & that for life onely, but takes you from that stage which is most proper for that [publi*que*] trade of ingenuity, which you desire to put into motion,[21] & will finally proue farre be lowe your aymes, which are to order men, not books, I cowlde heartily wishe your noble Frinds wowlde finde you & mr Dury some London imploymente & subsistence & I am confidente (yf the imploymente be but suche as wowlde leaue you some what free in your times) you wowld make a better returne then yf buried in Oxforde

But more of this nexte weeke when I shall be in London

I pray inquire earnestly & sende me woorde by this carrier whether rentes may be sente yet to Oxforde, & whether leases may be re newed, & whether Dr Sheldon[22] of All soules be remoued

[*PS.*] my affectionate seruice to mr Woorsely, to whome I pray say that I shall accommodate him with all materialls to his desire

130 *Culpeper to Hartlib, [5?] August 1647. (13/182–3)*

Mr Hartlib

I haue not yet corrected Glawberus, & finde it takes me vp more time then I expected; I doe it vpon your desires, & vpon confidence that (vpon perusall) you will correcte my errours, I very

[20] The dating of this letter is in no great doubt. Although the reference to Gilbert Sheldon would suggest the year 1648, the letter does not sit well with the other surviving correspondence for July 1648 and the allusion to the possibility of a place at Oxford for the Office of Address makes 1647 almost equally possible. On 31 March 1647, Sir William Waller had proposed to Parliament, and it had been accepted, that Hartlib be given a sum of £300 in recognition of his services and that 'settling you in a way of future subsistence is recommended to the Committee for the University of Oxford' – see Arthur Annesley to Hartlib, 1 April 1647 (66/3/1A-2B).

[21] Dury had proposed the Bodleian Library at Oxford as the possible center for the 'Office of Address of Communication' in *Considerations tending to the Happy Accomplishment of Englands Reformation in Church and State* (1647), Wing H981, p. 53.

[22] Gilbert Sheldon (1598–1677) – DNB. He was ejected from the Wardenship of All Souls College, Oxford, on 30 March 1648, and on the 12 April he was placed in custody, having refused to surrender his lodgings.

muche longe for Glauberus his ouens or other ingenuities, & am confidente I shall vnderstande the vse of them[23]

I cannot but differ from our Frinds at [Saint] Ieames, concerning my power to doe any thinge yf I were in the army; I muste confesse I muste heartily wishe that there were a perfecte reunion between the 2: parties, beinge assured within my selfe that the [King] will otherwise come to noe reason, but (in the ende) preuayle on bothe; I conceiue allso that the Independente (beinge for the presente) vpon the fore horse) showlde offer peace to the other party & suche fayre conditions as may stande with the beinge of eache party, This wowlde vnite the 2: nations the 2: houses & the 2 parties in eache house, & wowlde cause greefe, feare, & tremblinge in none but suche as deserue to feele them, & (in truth) cannot be made capable of reason or justice; but when (by our vnion, & suche better propositions (from that union) for the good of the People then eache party seuered are like to eyther demand or procure) they are frighted into them, Truly it greeues my sowle that they whoe haue noe other strenght then our diuisions, showlde haue theire spirits soe hyghtened by our folly; But I muste yet deale very freely with you, that (thowgh I wishe this vnion, in respecte of the third party), yet when I consider howe the presbiterian party haue had it severall times in theire power to haue ended this warre, & that the other party hathe not as yet loste one oportunity which God did put into theire hande, when I consider (when our game was at a stande) what fayre intimations (of a harmelesse liberty of conscience) was made to the Independente, & when (by Gods blessinge vpon his faythfull indeauors) hee had done that which the other party eyther cowlde or (which is woorse) wowlde not, howe vnkindly (I had allmoste [said]) vnjustly & falsly he was dealte with all, euen in his wages which he had earned with his bloode, & lastly when I consider that what the Independente hathe done lately, hathe beene (thowgh not alltogether justifiable yet) in defence of that subsistence, which bothe (by promise & in prudence) was due from the presbiterian party; I say when I consider all this & seuerall other suche circumstances I cannot but (in this vnion) wishe that the presbiterian, (in the dispute concerninge the swoorde – as likely a theme of contradiction between these 2: parties as it hathe beene between the [King & Parliament]) wowlde not expecte to haue that truste of which the other is possesste, & (by former experience) cannot for sake, & (at the same time) leaue himselfe soe muche as a little assurance of a future beinge; this pointe of the swoorde beinge settled, I wishe that the [Independent] showld in all thinges else yelde to the [Presbiterian] & yf the [Parliament] (when it is reunited) holde the same growndes towards the [King] it will not be amisse; my conclusion

---

[23] See **149** (11 March 1647[?8]) and Clucas, p. 151.

is that theire hands whoe haue shewed themselues moste implacable, showlde be bownde, & that they that haue the swoorde showld be truly the seekers of peace; my papers done

131   *Culpeper to Hartlib, 11 August 1647.   (13/173–4)*

Mr Hartlib;
    I thancke for your 2: letters & am very glad this laste storme is soe well passed ouer for the presente, thowgh (my opinion is) wee are to expecte a storme from the northe & (yf the [King] be not accorded with, of which I apprehende but little hopes) from the northe weste weste & southe, I meane from Irelande, our owne weste, & France; I wowlde be glad to knowe by your nexte whoe of the other side are taken, & whoe are gone (as is heere reported) to Scotlande, & particularly howe the [King] standes, whome (from some of his owne party) I finde fixedly resolued to doe nothinge, but onely to stand still & see the two other parties play theire game, & in the conclusion to helpe the weakeste, vpon condition that they will declare absolutely for him, & this when their owne game is loste; Howe well his Cowncell will woorke wee haue late experience in the presbiterian, whoe in a despayre of his owne game wowlde haue called in the [King]; but the [King's] time was not yet nor will be till bothe th'other parties haue weakened one another soe as the conqueror is but weake, & the other soe muche onely weaker as to be beaten, then yf the [King] come in he will easily swallowe firste one party & then the other, & truly I cannot see howe (in ordinary prouidence) this can be auoyded, in the way things nowe are, I pray God the wise men on both sides may well way this, I am very confidente that the [King] (from the presente diuisions) will nowe doe nothinge
    I heartily wishe for Glawberus his ouens to disstill in seuerall sorts with & to brewe will & wowlde be at the charges yf they might be had for mony, & am confidente I cowlde vnderstande them, but cowlde howeuer knowe the better howe to aske questions
    With my beste affections to you I rest

132   *Culpeper to Hartlib, August 1647.   (13/184–5)*

Mr Hartlib:
    I thancke you for your letter & newes, & for the transcripte of Glauberus, but showld be yet more glad to see his seuerall ouens, made by himselfe, especially that to brewe et cæt with; & shall not thincke

muche of the charges of makinge & transportinge them, soe as they be done, accordinge to the best modules[24]

I very hyghly approue the expediente you mention concerninge our poore Prince Palatine, & truly (nexte to the liberty & happines of theire owne nation) I knowe nothinge which wowlde be greater glory to them whoe nowe sit at the sterne, or that wowlde, more manifeste their affections bothe to our Religion & our neereste bloode;[25] But howe, 30: ships will be procured & (which is more) with suche secrecy, as is requisite to suche an action; of this I despaire, when I consider what vaste summes haue beene, & yet are collected vpon this [Kingdome] & that yet (all this notwithstandinge) the Army muste ly vpon free quarter; When I see the accownts of the [Kingdome] more exactly & justly mannaged I shall hope for a better issue in what concernes vs bothe at home and abroade, but I feare eache party is more ambitious of the power then of the honor to be reformers of theire Cowntries oppression; I pray God make me a false prophet

I haue heere addressed you by this inclosed to Mr Westroe, but leaue it you your discretion whether you will deliuer or ~~se~~ returne it; I knowe him very Faythfull but howe powerfull to promote this busines I dowbte

With my affectionate wishes to you I reste

Aug wednesday 47:

[PS.] My deuoyrs I pray to [Saint] Ieames.

133   *Culpeper to Hartlib, 7 September 1647.   (13/186–7)*

Mr Hartlib;
        I haue not yet gone halfe throwgh with Glawberus, & truly I finde it a greater busines to translate it out of Englishe then it wowlde haue beene out of Dutche yf I had vnderstoode that langwage; I hope to sende it to you nexte weeke[26]

I am sorry I can see none of Glauberus his ingenuities, or (at leaste)

---

[24] Culpeper had at last received the copy of Glauber's *Furni Novi* concerning ovens which he had requested – see letters **111** (1 October 1646) and **130** ([5?] August 1647).

[25] Charles Louis, Prince Elector Palatine, had been in frequent contact with Cromwell earlier in 1647 with a view to organising an expeditionary force to Germany. The force was to be based on the New Model army and was to have as its objective the assertion of the rights of worship of Calvinists in Germany, rights which were apparently being negotiated away among the plenipotentiaries meeting at Münster.

[26] Culpeper's difficulties in making sense of Glauber's arcane Latin continued until the end of October – see **137** (20 October 1647).

pastboarde or wooden modules of them which (I am confidente) myght be (uery easily)) made; Truly the obstructions I finde stille in my owne little affayres, & the gloomynes that approches in the publique, puts me vpon the thowght of selfe preseruation, & (for the presente) drownes all other,

Mr Andrewes hathe not yet beene in these partes; when he comes, hee shall be wellcome, bothe in your right & in his owne, but truly my lowe condition pretends to noe more then the pure necessities of nature, & I wishe more then hope that, soe muche onely may continue

I heartily wishe I cowlde giue you comforte concerninge the office of Addresse, but truly the nowe preuaylinge goes (& is like yet farther to goe) soe hygh that they will leaue many honeste men behynde them; this I speake, not any way to excuse the other party whoe (by theire carriage, in these laste 15 monethes) haue layde the growndwoorke of our miseryes, whyleste (without contentinge eyther the [King's] party, the Independente, or easinge the Kindome all which they had in theire power to doe) they sowght a domineerynge power for themselues, & nowe (rather then fayle of a reuenge) will call in the [King's] party the Scotts, the Frenche, & the Deuill & all, Flectere si nequeo[27] _____

God be mercifull to the sinnes of this poore nation, & turne his heauy judgements from vs, & sende vse more truthe & charity amonge our selues; The Scots are vpon theire marche, Inchyquin[28] joyned with the Scots in Irelande againste the [Parliament's] forces there; this retards the sendinge of other force thether; The Independente party subdiuided amonge themselues; The army desperately diuided, & (which is woorste of all) euery party delight in nothinge but conqueste, & that not by loue & forbearinge & the Royall Lawe of Chryste, but by the swoorde; & truly, euen those that haue the honesteste hartes, are yet to seeke what to wishe for; & yf what you write be true, that the Scotts haue made a peace with the [King] the other two parties are not to be reconciled; & truly I perceiue from elsewhere that it is not vnlikely

I am called away, I pray pardon this melancholy, which is occasioned from newes which I haue from too good hands

With my beste wishes to you I rest

134 *Culpeper to Hartlib, 15 September 1647. (13/188–91)*

Mr Hartlib;
    You laste was writte & sente away on thursday betimes in the

---

[27] Virgil, *Aeneid*, VII, 312 ('flectere si nequeo superos, Acheronta movebo') i.e. 'If I cannot influence the gods above I will stir up Hell'.
[28] Murrough O'Brien, first Earl of Inchiquin (1614–1674) – DNB.

eveninge, & (the Carrier goinge (laste weeke) by lande by reason of the
greate wynde) you receiued not my letter till eyther late on thursday
night or perhaps not till friday morning; & this I shall take for granted
till I heare (by this returne) the contrary from you; My [Wife] is muche
perplexed for the losse of her receipte bookes, I pray doe me the
kindenes that (yf eyther yourselfe or Mr Woorsly haue them) I may not
fayle of them by this returne, me thinckes I doe remember that one of
you had them againe from me after your firste returne of them, but
cannot be confidente yf you asserte the contrary; My [Wife] dothe
muche valewe them

Concerning the priuiledge of the [House of Commons] in matter of
mony, thus muche (before this [Parliament]) was euer insisted on, that
all firste motion of raysinge mony showlde proceede from them; & they
haue complayned of a breache of priuiledge when the [Lords] haue but
soe muche as named the woorde mony;[29] But for that sole power (you
mention) of raysinge & payinge, it muste & (I [conceiue]) may be feched
from suche a hygher principle as will giue them sole power not onely
to rayse mony but (in case of suche questions as haue lately risen to
the shakinge of our triple fowndation) to judge of suche prerogatiues &
priuiledges as the [King] & [Lords] eyther haue noe right to or muste
acknowledge themselues to haue receiued from the Peoples consente;
And synce the People, neyther, haue vsed, nor (in truthe) can, expresse
themselues but by suche a representatiue as wee vsually call the
[House] of Commons, (thowgh perhaps, somewhat varied in some more
equitable principles in the points of election, vote et cæt)[30] it muste
therefore necessary followe that the [King] & [Lords] muste haue
receiued, & muste still holde, those rights & priuiledges they clayme,
eyther by the swoorde, & in that case, yf the Spaniarde come in vpon
ayghty ayght wee may (yf wee can) driue him out upon 89::[31] or by a

---

[29] The Petition of Right (1628) had declared all loans, aids and benevolences raised
without consent of Parliament to be illegal. During the Short Parliament of April-May
1640 the House of Lords requested the House of Commons to grant supply to the King
before securing the redress of grievances; but this had been resented as a breach of the
privileges of the lower house.

[30] This is the first occasion when Culpeper reflects the debates about franchise reform
current in 1647 during the Leveller agitations. See A. Woolrych, *Soldiers and Statesmen*
(Oxford, 1987).

[31] Culpeper here responds to a series of questions, relevant to contemporary political
debate, from Lady Ranelagh and forwarded to him by Hartlib – 26/13/1–2. They
included:

– 'Whether if the Spaniards had come in by the Sword in [15]80. And the People of
this Land should have sworne Obedience and Fidelitie unto them whilest they had
the power, the people could honestly have by force beaten them out in 89 . . . ?

– 'Whether the Oaths of Allegence and Supremacie taken by the People of this Land,
have not put it out of their power to doe those things by their representative the
Parliament without the Assent of the King, which they might before those oaths

Lawe made by the immediate representatiue of the People, & then Eius est interpretari cujus est condere; Those withe whome I haue lately had frequente dispute in this uery point, seeinge themselues gone in the forementioned wayes of raysinge a right to the [King] & [Lords] haue therefore & doe still indeauor to set vp a third way which they call prescription[32] that soe, where they cannot maintaine theire positions by the lyght of truthe & reason they may yet loose theire opponents in that darke & bottomeles pit where noe rationall meanes of huntinge & serchinge the truthe can be vsed; Vpon this grownde they allowe the Grande Signior[33] a full right to be absolute [Lord] of all his subjectes liues, & to be heyre & excecutor to all theire landes & goods; Vpon this grownde they allowe our nayghbor Christian Turcke (I meane the Frenche [King])[34] vpon 180: yeers prescription, (a little before that time the [Parliament] of France set Tutors ouer one of the wisest of theire [Kings]) to sende the Ianizaries of his garde for any mans goods or life, & truly soe zealous are they in the maintaininge of this invention; as I beleeue that many on that side, the good honeste husbands as well as theire wiues wowlde be very well contented, that (for the melioratinge of the race of theire family) his [Majesty] wowlde vse his right of prescription, in bestowinge what he can spare of his royall bloode vpon theire wiues, & thus wee showlde haue greate store of Princes; nowe

according to the Law of nature have donne justly?'

– 'Whether according to the Fundamentalls of this Kingdome the two Houses of Parliament have power to declare the Law without appeale, without the King joyne with them to make a Declaration of the Law indisputable points by an Act of Parliament?'

– 'Whether upon any Occasion the two Houses have power to make a Law binding to the People without the Royall assent, and whether they bee to judge of the occasion?'

– 'Whether that Clause of the oath formerly administered to the Kings of England whereby they are bound as well to make such Law's as the People shall desire In Parliament as to keepe those made, ever remitted by any act of the People or only neglected thorough the Corruption of Our Kings and those that should have administered it, which not having beene administered to this King?

– 'Whether the People can justly clayme it [*the authority remitted to a king*] from him?'

– 'And lastly; Whether indeed both Houses may Legally levy mony and sequester the Estates of their Opposers, as they have done during this Warr, without and against the Kings Consent or whether that fast power confest by the Law's of this Land to belong to their Parliaments, doe not belong to them only as the Parliaments consist of the 3 States, and so as the King is a part of them and Ioynes with them having power by Interposing his Negative voyce to keepe them from Proceeding without Him?'.

[32] Prescriptive right – or the 'uninterrupted use or possession from time immemorial, or for a fixed period by law as giving a title or right acquired by virtue of such use or possession: sometimes called positive prescription.' – OED.

[33] i.e. The Grand Duke of Muscovy, where (according to seventeenth-century perceptions) all his subjects were 'kholops' (or slaves) to the Tsar.

[34] The Kings of France had the title Most Christian King as well as a long-standing alliance with the Turks.

to bringe them backe againe out this dark dungeon of theire owne
invention, the beste way that I haue fownde (& suche as haue proued
sufficiente) to consider the nature of that thinge which wee call
prescription; & in what cases it operates; And accordinge to that little
skill I haue in the Lawe (for there can be noe suche thinge thinge in
nature) prescription is a right which a man claimes to some thinge
which can belonge to noe particular man by the Lawe of nature, &
this plea is that the thing he claimes is suche as can appropriately
belonge to noe man by the Lawe of nature, & that himselfe & his
Ancestors haue beene soe longe posseste of it as that noe memory of
man or record can shewe the contrary; Vpon this grownde I hold it to
be Lawe, that where any man is possessed of a peece of lande & noe
memory or recorde can ~~see~~ shewe that any other, was euer posseste
of it, this man is (not by nature but by prescription) the true owner of
it & yf a nayghbour or the nayghborhoode, prescribe to a way throwgh
this lande, the plea will holde goode excepte the other which hathe the
lande can (by good euidence) proue that at suche at time & not before
the way began to be vsed, & the grownde of the Lawe is that what
title prescription giues one to the Lande it giues the other to the way
throwgh the Lande, & neyther the lande nor the way beinge suche
thinges as were (by the Lawe of God or nature) appropriated to any
indiuiduall person or persons, there may be a title made to them by
prescription; Hauinge (I conceiued) cleared this pointe that prescription
(in the nature & firste humane constitution of it) was not invented &
set vp with intente that it showlde stande & operate againste any Lawe,
muche lesse againste firste & hygeste of all Lawes, the Lawe of nature;
it muste nowe necessary followe that, (in case eyther where there hathe
beene an interruption of the possession, or where the thinge in question
is suche as belongs (by the Lawe of nature) equally to all the sonnes of
Adam) there cannot be a title made by prescription; I shall (for the
presente) waue that of interruption of possession thowgh (I conceiue)
that our records of Edw*ard* & Richard the seconde cannot be denied,
nor were the then [Parl*iament*] other then suche as from which we
holde to this day, as good[35] (I meane as stronge) lawes as any wee haue
By the way I shall onely obserue that suche [Parl*iaments*] as deposed
[K*ing*s] cowlde allsoe at the same time make good Lawes; But to returne
to my game; Yf prescription (as hathe beene shewed) cannot stande
againste the Lawe of nature, wee muste then returne to the Lawe
Positiue, I meane that Lawe to which (in all politicall coalitions) euery

---

[35] There was a dispute about the role of Parliament during the process leading to the
depositions of Edward II and Richard II. Some of the important statutes taken as
guarantors of the subject's liberty and the privileges of Parliament dated from those
reigns.

indiuiduall person, eyther mediately or immediately, dothe or showlde
giue his consente; The case then standing thus, that euery man is wholy
free by nature, & soe noe right to this his freedome but by his owne
consente; It muste necessary followe that (euery Indiuiduall man beinge
(by nature) put into the possession of this his naturall freedome) yf
nowe any man will lay claime to this his nayghbors liberty, it will
concerne him to shewe & proue that Lawe or consente by which he
claimes; & synce this Lawe & consente was cowlde not be made but
by the other, the interpretation of it & dispencinge of justice by it muste
of necessity belonge to that other vpon that rule Eius est condere et
cæt; And thus haue I browght the Peoples judgemente to be, as the
begginning soe the finall determination of all politicall questions; And
yf nowe it be asked what power the [King] hathe to make a Lorde or
what title eyther haue to a negatiue (in raysinge of mony or et cæt)
ouer 10000000 of people; it may truly be answered that the people &
theire Ancestors, (as sonnes of Adam) were (by nature) free from eyther
[King] or [Lord] (nature made noe suche creatures) & that this theire
naturall inherente liberty cowld not be taken & cannot be claimed from
them but by theire owne consente; And yf therefore the [King & Lords]
will continue theire claime to these negatiues they muste not onely
proue this consente of the People, but it muste be done before them
that made the Lawe, For still the rule holdes Eius este condere etcæt;
And by this or some like principles will the fowles of the Ayre be called
to that feaste where the Fleshe of [Kings] & nobles shall be the foode[36]
    The carrier (I feare) is gone, my humble seruice to that braue Lady
you mention & the reste of the good Company

[*PS.*] I haue not time to reade it ouer pardon my scribblinge, & let me
knowe where I haue fayled that I may inlarge further

135   *Culpeper to Hartlib, 22 September 1647.*   *(13/192–3)*

Mr Hartlib;
        I yesterday met with Mr Andrews[37] accidentally at a nayghbors
house & receiued from him your letter dated the 1: of september by his
owne relation his intention was towards my house but was prevented
by me by that accidentall meetinge, Hee intendes this day (yf not

---

[36] Revelation 19:17–18 – 'And I saw an angel standing in the sun; and he cried with a
loud voice to all the fowls that fly in the midst of heaven, Come and gather yourselves
together into the supper of the great God; That ye may eat the flesh of kings, and the
flesh of captains, . . .'. This takes place during the great struggle against the armies of
the Beast.
    [37] See **149** (11 March 1647[?8]).

hindred by the raine) to be in London; where my selfe muste be some time time nexte weeke yf not before

I shall be glad yf what I writte laste weeke, may haue giuen my Lady any satisfaction in her question; The strenght of what I writte is 1: That prescription (that greate bull warke of the Royallistes) cannot ly or be pleaded to take away that of which euery sonne of Adam is a proprietor & possessor by the Lawe of nature, I meane, an exemption from politicall power; Since that prescription is pleadable, onely in suche things in which noe body can claime a propriety by any kinde of Lawe; 2: Prescription not holdinge, there remaines noe title againste the Lawe of nature but by that Lawe which wee call positiue or politicall; 3: This lawe muste be made by the parties mediate or immediate consente, For what Lawe the swoorde make, cannot be maintained but onely by the swoorde; 4: This consente muste be free & voluntary, for consente; & to be forced is a contradiction; A bonde signed by one imprisoned or threatned to be killed may (by our common Lawe) be avoyded by the party when he is out of prison; & (which is yet muche more) a wooman, imprisoned by a rascall, & there rauished 100 times, nay, married by a forced consente, can (when shee is free) auoyde the marriage, for non concubitus, sed consensus, facit matrimonium 5: Yf my owne free consente be pleaded to take away from me that which is vndeniably myne by the Lawe of nature, in this case it lyes not vpon me to proue that title which none can deny, but on him whoe claimes that in which I am (by the vndeniable Lawe of nature), intitled & possessed; 6: What cannot be proued to be passed away by my owne consente, remaines still myne by that firste & hygheste of Lawes the Lawe of nature; 7: This question & the euidence concerninge it muste be browght before some competente Iudge, which (in the firste place) cannot be eyther the party himselfe that pretends or claimes; (for none (by eyther the Lawe of reason or of this Lande) can be admitted judge in his owne Cause); or any other chosen by him alone, for suche anone is (bothe in reason & Lawe) adjudged all one as himselfe; & then it muste necessarily followe that eyther there will be noe judge fownde, & soe noe judgemente, or decision, & soe the right pretended will proue a jus siccum that is (at beste) a right without meanes to proue or recouer it, or else, he muste be resorted to for Judge whoe was the Lawemaker, that is the very People, & thus is another of the hygheste maximes of our Lawe & of reason preserued in it strenght, Eius est judicare cujus est condere; From these premises, yf the [King] or Lords, showlde claime suche priuiledges, prerogatiues royalties, (call them what you will) as that the People cowlde not beare them, & (vpon the oppression) showld question or deny them; in this case (prescription not holdinge againste the hyghest & moste euidente Lawe the Lawe of nature) the [King & Lords] muste eyther proue theire

Rule to be by the peoples consente, & that consente to be free, & this not before themselues, whoe cowlde not giue that consente, or make that Lawe but before that onely and truly competente judge, in whome onely the power & right of consentinge is naturally & essentially inherente or (yf they fayle in any one of the precedent conditions) they muste (for owght I cowlde yet euer heare from any one to the contrary) goe without what they pretende to; & thus haue I proued the People (in all politicall creations) to be (with reuerence may I speake it) like God in the creation of the worlde; in whome (as the creatures in God) all our politicall creatures (be they as proude as Lucifer) muste acknowledge themselues to liue & moue & haue their continuall beinge, excepte (like Lucifer) they will deserue to be caste out of the politicall heauen; a thinge which is shortly (I beleeue) to come to passe, when the Fowles of the Ayre shall be called to the Supper of the greate God,[38] & shall feede on noe lesse daintyes, then the Fleshe of [Kings] et caet, & that the time comes, when there shall be a newe politicall heauen & a newe earthe,[39] this makes me wishe & pray that all good men wowlde goe forthe (in theire seuerall opotunities) & helpe the [Lord] againste the mighty, which will proue our owne happines as muche as it is our duty

I pray shewe these my thowghts to mr [Dury] & let me knowe whether he can finde a weake lincke in the deduction I haue made; The carrier (I feare) is gone

136   *Culpeper to Hartlib, 13 October 1647.*   *(13/194–5)*

Mr Hartlib

I cannot this weeke inlarge my selfe to Mr Woorsly, by reason of the hasteninge away of the Carrier, I pray excuse it to him

I hope that bothe your selfe & Mr Dury haue written effectually to mons: Pruuoste to knowe whether he will (yf invited) turne his face this way, & whether he will quitte that resolution of takinge mens estates & disposinge of them without theire consente; A state neuer yet acted suche a thinge synce the worlde began, & I am confident this [Parliament] (after soe many pressures & noe satisfactory accownte) will not thincke themselues in case to doe it; & in truthe, yf soe much good be like to be effected, to euery particular man in his owne priuate concernements, euery body will see that there will be noe neede of constraincte – An

---

[38] See **134** (15 September 1647).
[39] Revelation 21:1 – 'And I saw a new heaven and a new earth: for the first heaven and the first earth were passed away; and there was no more sea.'

inseperable companion of moste former monopolies[40] I shall returne [*the*] mony for mye boorder the nexte weeke

I reste in haste

137 *Culpeper to Hartlib, 20 October 1647.   (13/196–7)*

Mr Hartlib,

I haue not yet fully corrected the ill translation of Glauberus; but (in the readinge of him) am soe muche taken, with very many of his ingenuities, that (yf Mr Worsly will take soe muche trowble vpon him,) as (in the trade of soe muche ingenuity & knowledge) to become the Factor, & to goe ouer to Glauberus, & to purchase his ingenuities of him), I shall willingly become a marchante venturer in the busines, & shall be glad to finde others to that number, as that the voyage may be vnder taken;[41] I thancke you for your laste weekes letter; The ordinance for the arreares in the Citty & cowntry relates (I beleeue) to that person whome I addressed to mr Peeters[42] with whome (yf he be reall in Pruuosts busines) I may perhaps joine againe;

[*PS.*] I pray get an essay from Mr Dury concerning Mr Pruuostes proposalls & get him to write speedily to Mr Pruuoste & to presse him to a returne & not to adhere to the laste particular, which (yf juste & rationall) will yet (to this age) appeare the very essence of a monopoly & soe muche woorse as it is in irreuorocable hands

138 *Culpeper to Hartlib, 27 October 1647.   (13/198–9)*

Mr Hartlib;

I haue heere sente you 6:[l] 10[s] for halfe a yeares diet for the

[40] Culpeper refers to that part of the Le Pruvost/l'Amy proposal which was to establish a state-sponsored American colony. Objections to the proposal arose from the land-tenure system based on leases directly from the state. Le Pruvost himself was stringently opposed to monopolies but Culpeper feared that his proposals would entail an eventual return to authoritarian monopoly. See GI, p. 371–72.

[41] Culpeper was evidently working through a draft translation of Glauber's *Furni Novi* into English. In early 1647, 'probably late February' (Charles Webster in UR, p. 223), Benjamin Worsley left England for the Netherlands. Culpeper here clearly ventured (despite his later protestations) to assist Worsley financially if he would undertake a visit to Glauber and purchase one of his furnaces. The trip would not achieve what Culpeper had anticipated – see **169** (1 November 1648) below.

[42] Hugh Peters [var: Peter], (1598–1660) – DNB.

schollar with you,[43] & 30:[5] more for the bookes, which I still wishe may not be multiplied from the stationer; one or two of the Corantoes[44] & some of the moste especiall bookes is that which I desire; I feare I shall not be able to continue to the scholler, & therefore leaste he proue burdensome to you, I wishe, that you wowlde (in time) dispose him some other way; I pray preuente all future dedications of bookes to me, for truly I am not lesse ambitious then woorthy of those honors[45]

You will doe me the kindenes to presente my affectionate seruice to Mr Woorsly & that Mr Wheeler may (by him) knowe, that I shall not deale for his mare

Margaret Cooper returned laste friday from London, and (after a more filthy vexatious carriage towards her Mrs then I can describe) is returned againe thether, hauinge (it showlde seeme) bargained with one Mrs Colier a merchants wife; & (by her owne relation) a secret Papiste, & truly (by her beades, discowrse, & other symtones) wee judge her affected that way; Her course is not muche materiall to vs, thowgh (in truthe) her breaking away with out any warninge, her raylinge (in the fowleste manner), at the seruice & at her Mrs, her indeauoring to tempte the reste of the seruants to a suddaine partinge allsoe, & (as wee vnderstande synce shee is gone) her late spoylinge of good meate, out of a scorne and pride eyther of learninge to doe any thinge or that it showlde be done better by any body else; these particulars (I say) & seuerall others, are suche as (I thancke God) wee haue beene formerly acquainted with

I shall be glad to heare of mr Woorslyes treaty; With my beste wishes to you

[PS.] I pray write me woorde whether the boxe be sealed as my letter is, for the carrier vses to open things

---

[43] In his petition to Charles II Hartlib wrote that he had given support 'to the godly ministers and scholars who were driven in those days out of the Palatinate and other Protestant churches then laid waste . . .' – HDC, p. 3. The scholar in question is probably Adolphus Speed, who lodged with, and was supported by, Hartlib at this time. The hypothesis is strengthened by further references to promises made to Speed by Culpeper in **141** (10 November 1647) and **142** (17 November 1647).

[44] News-books.

[45] This is presumably a reference to the forthcoming publication by George Ritschel, *Contemplationes Metaphysicæ ex Natura Rerum et Rectæ Rationis lumine deductæ* (Oxford, 1648), Wing R1543, with its dedication to Culpeper and Nicholas Stoughton – see **110** (24 May 1646) from Comenius.

139 *Culpeper to Hartlib, n.d. [September/October 1647? – or 8?].* *(13/321–2)*[46]

Mr Hartlib,

you gaue me noe answere what copies you had taken of the Receiptes in my Wifes booke, & in this consisted my principall hope, & I cannot but hope that your desire of them was not eyther for nothinge or in Courtship

The Quommodo of Mr Petis ingenuities is very valuable, especially that of which helps soe muche in quotations or Common places, but where to finde an adequate recompence is the difficulty

Synce Mr Woorsly was pleased to ingage me, towards Sir [Rob*ert*] Hooniwood,[47] I did conceiue, that soe muche knowledge (what reception he fownd) that I might haue [p*ai*d] my personall dues to him, had not beene vnfittinge; but nothinge againste conscience, I pray doe not you nowe occasion any suche thing; I haue sente you suche Polyshe oates as I haue, but the beste of them are suche as come euery springe from that Cowntry

I cannot possibly finde that paper of Glawberus, I conceiue it but halfe a sheete for which I muche craue your pardon[48]

I am sorry for noe better grownd between the Scots & vs, but my hope is that the juste God will not blesse theire indeauors, whoe (rather then affoorde the harmelesse instruments of their Victories & happines a bare beinge) will ioine w*i*th the Wiche of Endor,[49] & really breake that Couenante which others haue, not taken, & yet, better kepte, & whether the breache of the Couenante will not in them that haue taken it be accownted vncircumcision, & circumcision in others whoe thowgh hauinge taken haue yet kepte it I shall leaue to the judgemente of the Righteous God, my papers done, I cowlde otherwise inlarge vpon this subiecte, & giue them the ly whoe can impudently asserte that [the.?

---

[46] The dating of this letter is more than usually problematic. From the references to Petty and Worsley, it would appear to be datable to no earlier than the Autumn of 1647; but his wife's recipe-book, which was reported as lost on 15 September 1647 (**137**, above) must have been found – and some elements of the letter would fit better in the late summer of 1648.

[47] See **94** (31 October 1645).

[48] Culpeper had presumably given up hope of completing his corrections of the translation of Glauber and had returned the transcript (bar half a sheet) to Hartlib. This translation was doubtless put to good use by John French, however, whom Hartlib approached to complete the work. It appeared as *A description of new Philosophical Furnaces, or A new Art of Distilling, divided into five parts* (1651), Wing G846, Thomason, E.649 (3). In his preface, French says that the second and largest part of the treatise was 'in private hands already translated into English by a learned German' [Hartlib?] – sig. A4[r]. Cf GI, p. 387; Clucas, p. 152.

[49] Shakespeare, *Macbeth*.

MS torn] negatiue & swoord belongs to the Princes in all [K*ing*domes] yet knowe they ly in their owne

[*sent* 'with a handfull of Polishe oates']

140   *Culpeper to Hartlib, 3 November 1647.   (13/200–1)*

Mr Hartlib

I haue little time or matter to write; I shall be glad to heare howe Mr Woorsly aduances in his businesses; I haue not yet finished my accowntes; & (till that busines be done) cannot set my thowghts to any thing else; you shall then, not fayle of Glauberus;

Mr Duryes Essaye vpon the office of Addresse dothe very muche please me;[50] I heartily wishe he wowlde inlarge himselfe (in that manner) vpon Pruuostes proposition that soe (where he comes not) his frinds may yet be bothe themselues better satisfied & better able to satisfy others; I reste in haste

141   *Culpeper to Hartlib, 10 November 1647.   (13/202–3)*

Mr Hartlib

I haue heere returned Mr Woorsleyes letter concerning the Intereste of the People, of which I still holde the same opinion, that hee hathe moste excellently described the Intereste, but not soe strongly proued the Peoples title to it as to dazle (thowgh not converte) those birdes of darkenes whose greatest shelter & refuge is to loose themselues & those whome they argue with, in the darcke corners of of prescription & custome, as thowgh that custome of doinge wronge, (even in the face of the originall Lawe of nature) did not soe muche increase the wronge as create a right ___

My other businesses haue distracted me from Glauberus, but I to be nowe suddenly free, and at leasure to perfecte that woorke;

I am sorry the mechanicall Glawberus whome you mention,[51] muste live still eyther in or vpon the precipice of dristresse; In truthe there is a prouidence which euery man owes to himselfe, in carryinge on his expences in that proportion at one time, as that his purse may holde out to the ende, & this is beste done by proportioninge a mans expences to his presente condition; & a resolution not to rayse his expences till

---

[50] John Dury, *Considerations tending to the Happy Accomplishment of Englands Reformation in Church and State* (1647), Wing H981.

[51] It is not clear to whom Culpeper refers.

it hathe pleased God to blesse & increase his stocke; & yf our mechanicall
Glawberus (as you call him) haue not this faculty of his owne, my
opinion is that he muste eyther admitte it from his frindes or (in one
woorde) not expecte theire assistance; His pretences are (I confesse)
ingenuous, but mixed with greate elations concerning himselfe, & not
without disproportions bothe in the judicious part in applyinge them, &
somewhat in his relatinges & stories of them & himselfe; But your rule
is goode, to passe by the woorste of euery man soe as the infirmities
hinder not the vse of what good is him; & in purswance of this your
good rule, I shall (for some small time) allowe towardes his diet &
lodginge 10:ˢ the weeke, & this I shall doe for a relaxation of all our
presente thowghts concerning him; my busines will holde me yet these
10: or 12: dayes & then (I belieue) j: shall be in London, & yf vpon
further discowrse with him I can finde that hee will proue any way
settled in his vaine humors, & that I can any way imploy his ingenuitie
in any way of aduantage he shall (yf he will) goe downe with me; in
the meane time 10:ˢ a weeke will not let him that which is necessary, &
yf you giue me credit for it I will repay you

I feare wee have loste Pruuoste, & doe very muche grieue for it,[52] I
pray yet, doe your beste, & yf wee cannot get the men, let vs (by your
intelligence, from those parts) indeauor to get a history of manner of
his husbandry, in agriculture & pasturage; yf wee haue not (by your
meanes) a perfecte knowledge of the whole busines wee shall yet gaine
enowght to rayse bothe our abilities & desires to a further inquiry

Yf Dr Ducket cowld (by mr Dawson) be dealte withall to discover
howe trees planted in pasture growndes might be preserued from the
brutte & rubbinge of cattell it wowld mightily increase all kinde of
plantations throwghout the [Kingdome], I pray yf he be not gone let
him be tried[53]

I shall set downe my thowghts concerning [parliamentary] power
assoone as I shall be at leasure, for in truthe I knowe nothinge of
hygher concernemente to this and all-other nations

The promise you claime from me concerninge your scholler, I deny
not,[54] but I muste withall remember you that it was made with this
restriction to be continued or discontinued accordinge as my condition
(in these totteringe times) showlde proue, & there was yet one other
condition more, that what I did might be made a leadinge case to
some others of our acquaintance whoe (as well as myselfe) doe bothe
knowe & approue the thinge & by this token I pray presente my

[52] GI, p. 372.
[53] See **143** (22 December 1647), **146** (12 January 1647[?8]).
[54] See **138** (27 October 1647).

humble seruice to that excellente Lady,[55] & remember her from me of her answere from her Brother Mr Boyle;[56] I pray tell Mr Dury allsoe that I hope he will allowe his free contribution to soe good a woorke, That these helpes & suche others as you shall thincke of may be gained, I offer yf these others will come in) to allowe (towards the maintaininge of one clearke) 20:[l] per annum, & shall, (as God shall blesse me) be ready to increase it, till wee can invite the [publiqu*e*] to take notice of its owne intereste in the busines[57]

I will make good your promise to mr Speede,[58] but you knowe it was promised for a time onely, that it might be seene of what vse he wowlde proue in what he pretends to; I pray let him searche where I may haue (for my mony) suche blacke younge tame rabbets as will breede nexte summer; I haue a quarter of an acre of grownde walled in, yf that cowlde be malde fitte to keepe & feede them in for breedinge & soe from hence to turne them in to an open warren I might perhaps make a tryall of it, I am not willing to trowble myselfe with clappers; but onely with makinge a berry

my paper is done & (I feare) the carrier gone

142 *Culpeper to Hartlib, 17 November 1647.* *(13/ 204–5)*

Mr Hartlib

one [principall *MS torn*] condition of what was to come from me, which I proposed & you (in your laste accepted was yf my owne fortune showld stande; Synce laste friday, I understand (from London) that my late hopes of a good conclusion, in that busines, wherein I haue suffered soe muche from my neereste frindes, are are againe vanished & my selfe lefte in somewhat a woorse condition, by hauinge relied vpon them; yf it please God to rayse me againe I shall continue my intentions towardes your selfe & others, yf otherwise I muste prepare myselfe (as well as I can) for what the concurrence of imminente publique storme with my probable condition in it is like to bringe upon me; I shall not

[55] Katherine, Lady Ranelagh, Robert Boyle's eldest sister.

[56] Robert Boyle (1627–1691) – DSB, DNB.

[57] Culpeper evidently put his proposal directly to Robert Boyle and it elicited a wry endorsement from him: 'However, I am more than resolved to continue in this kind of folly, to serve the good of many; and worthy Sir *Cheney* professes himself to be one that will join with me in running this race: for in his last he used these very words unto me – 'I offer, if others of our acquaintance will come, and according as my condition in these tottering times shall prove, to allow, towards the maintaining of one clerk, the sum of *2ol. per ann.* and shall (as God shall bless me) be ready to increase it, till we can invite the public to take notice of its own interesting in the business.' (Boyle to Hartlib, 16 Nov. 1647, in Birch, *The works...Boyle*, vi. 76).

[58] Adolphus Speed – DNB and **139** (27 October 1647).

be in London till I may firste vnderstande that there is a possibility
that I may make a better returne of my indeauors & expences then I
have done this laste yeere; yf the woorste newes come, God I hope will
prepare me for it, & directe me in some suche cowrse as is fitteste for
me, in that extremity wherein I shall be plunged

What I haue written, (together with my service to Mr Woorsly) muste
be my presente answere to his laste letter; What you haue (from my
desires) ingaged your selfe for or to Mr Speede, till this time, I muste
see [paid]

I pray afford me a particular howe the cardes stande shuffled, &
your sense is vpon it, that I may take some timely resolution;

With my beste to you I remaine

143   *Culpeper to Hartlib, 22 December 1647.*   *(13/206–7)*

Mr Hartlib

I pray returne my thanckes to Mr Dawson; His invention of a
bryer & a rubbinge poste is vsuall in these parts in lieu of the other
parte, the garbadge of a rabbit or any other thing of that kinde steeped
in water & squirted upon the trees, is a receipt which I haue formerly
learned elsewhere, but in all these thinges there must be a continuall
reiterated diligence[59]

The Ioyners rubbinge of armes & legges for an ague, is very woorthe
hearkeninge after[60]

I very muche admire Mr Petits faculties in writing & printinge &
heartily wishe that hee were incowraged by some publique recompence
to make them publique; That of his 3: characters allsoe is admirable,
but (to me) moste of all the improuemente he hathe added to Harrisons
invention, but what profit is it? yea what griefe is it to knowe the
quoddity onely, of these & many other inventions, but to be without
any hope of the Quommodo of them?

I shall (at my returne to London), bringe the warminge pestle with
me, I pray excuse my forgetfullnes

I am glad the Army & Citty are againe composed,[61] & showlde be
yet more glad to to see a perfecte vnion between the 2: nations & the
2: Parliamentarian parties in this nation withou which, wee shall bothe

---

[59] See **146** (12 January 1647[?8]).

[60] 'Stroking' for the relief of illness was one aspect of curative physic which interested
Hartlib and his associates. See the *Ephemerides* for 1643 (30/4/88A-B) and 60/4/7B where
stroking was recommended for the cure of toothache and the stone.

[61] Relations between the Army and the City of London continued to be strained during
the autumn and early winter of 1647; Woolrych, *Soldiers and Statesmen*, pp. 198–99, 200–
03.

misse of that ende which our vnion onely can gaine from the [King] eyther by consente or force, & shall become a scorne & pray to those, whose hearts & tongwes (from our folly, not at all from theire owne strenght) are very hygh, but God onely can bringe this to passe, & will yf (for owr sinnes) Hee haue not yet a controuersy againste this Lande, & truly, nothinge makes me feare this more then that I see in the Presbiterian & Scottified party, suche wante of truthe & any leaste tendernes towards those by whome God hathe blessed them with victory, and of true wisdome to themselues, as (rather then to affoorde theire harmelesse Frinds a harmelesse vse of the liberty of theire consciences, – a priviledge which theire very enimies wowlde affoorde them) to joine with the common Enimy, whoe (yf he preuayle) may perhaps (as the Emperor wowlde doe the foolishe Lutherans in Germany) devoure them laste

Synce you had my [Wife's] 2: bookes of receiptes I cannot finde them; Yf your selfe or Mr Woorsly haue them not, I feare they are loste, & yf they be loste, my [Wife] is fully resolued that that vntowarde wenche hathe stollen them as shee hathe done severall other bookes

I pray doe me the kindenes to searche diligently at yourselfe & mr Woorsly for them, & in case the bookes be absolutely loste, my laste hopes are that you have copied them out, I pray ease my hearte, for my [Wife] muche wantes them & accuses my acte of carryinge them to London I feare the Carrier is gone; With my best wishes to you I reste

144 *Culpeper to Hartlib, n.d. [c.March 1647?].* *(13/290–1)*[62]

Mr Hartlib;

This inclosed was sente too late laste weeke & soe returned to my handes, I nowe sende it that (yf you thincke good) you may deliuer this to Mr Westroe, but (by a letter from him laste Friday) I suppose he is like to be in this Cownty

I am glad that there is an indeauor of an accorde between the [presbyterians] & [Independents], for truly it is all the game that remaines to that deuided parliamentary party, & all the growndes of hope that the [King] & his party, may be reduced to reason; I heartily wishe that neyther [independent] nor [presbyterian] wowld thincke that eyther of them can finally preuayle againste eache other yf the [King] & his party

---

[62] This letter is difficult to date with any degree of precision. The reference to Captain Westrow suggests, however, that it might belong to the period in March 1647 when Culpeper was actively soliciting Westrow's support and the rest of its brief contents tends to support this hypothesis.

(as they will certeinly doe) joine with the weakeste; I am one, that holde the Aristocraticall tiranny in Churche & state (as it is in Scotlande) to be as bad as that in France; but they are not yet soe settled in the Saddle nor pretende soe strongly as the [King] & [Bishops *MS edge*] & therefore I heartily wishe they may be borne with in the way as the meanes of a greater discouery & liberty & therefore I heartily wishe that the [presb*yterians*] might haue theire gouernemente allowed, & liberty to the [Independ*ents*], thus the [presb*yterians*] showlde haue the honor to be owned by the State, & the Independente that liberty of searchinge & prouinge all things, which wowlde (in the ende) prevayle; I feare I shall againe fall shorte of the Carrier, I wishe you heartily well; & with my deuoyrs to [Snt] Ieames & thanckes to you for your laste newes, I reste

1648

145 *Culpeper to Hartlib, 5 January 1647/8.   (13/208)*

Mr Hartlib

I haue onely time to tell you that I wante time to answere your laste longe letter

I am a hearty Wellwisher to Mr Petit, Mr Robinson; & My [Lord] Gorings ingenuities[1] but feare the Presbiterian Popery, (I meane that persecutinge Spirite which they haue pulled downe in others that themselues myght get in the saddle), will make some other woorke for our thowghts; what meanes (otherwise) the Scottes insisting vpon suche rights for the [King] in Englande (where they haue noe conusance), as themselues allowe not in Scotlande,[2] with what impudente face can they say that all [Kings] have that intereste in the swoorde which they knowe he hathe not with them, These grosse lyes in the face of theire owne knowledge God may for our synnes suffer, but will not (I hope) finally blesse

The carrier (I feare) is gone

I pray giue me an accownte what wee doe heere in Kente[3] ___ for seriously wee neyther know nor can gesse; onely wee are sure our lords ar wise

146 *Culpeper to Hartlib, 12 January 1647[?8].   (13/159–60)*

Mr Hartlib;

I hope my apprehensions of the presente affayres, cannot hinder me from a right conceiuinge of suche thinges as you shall write; truly my wishes are noe other then that the Scotte & Presbiterian, wowlde

[1] i.e. William Petty (1623–1687) – DNB, DSB; Henry Robinson – see **104** (26 February 1646); and George Goring, Earl of Norwich (1583?-1663) – DNB. Goring had been a leading monopolist and was renowned for his mechanical contrivances in court entertainments. He had returned to England from the royalist court in late 1647 and would lead the Kentish rebellion in 1648. See the following letter for the context to this particular allusion.

[2] Charles had signed 'The Engagement between the King and the Scots' on 26 December 1647 – CDPR, pp. 347–53; Gardiner, iv. 39–41.

[3] On Christmas Day 1647 there had been a riot at Canterbury which was the first overt sign of the unrest which culminated in the rebellion in the county in 1648 – Everitt, *Kent*, pp. 231–34; Gardiner, iv. 45.

haue allowed to others, what they heeretofore thowght reasonable & due from others, & that (for th'ingrossinge that very tyrany to them selues which they formerly condemned, in others) they wowlde not haue made a rente with those their Brethren, by whoses indeauors & Gods speciall blessinge on them, they might haue injoyed those victoryes & the effects of them for which they publikely thanked God thowgh at the same time they hated the instruments; nowe that passions are stirred vp, God onely knowes what will be the euente;

Mr Dausons[4] windinge of brambles about trees is practised in 100: places within 4: miles of this house & whashinge of trees with water wherein the garbage of a rabbit hathe beene put (which I holde to stande vpon the same reason; as lime & dogges dung) was written & directed in that receipte which I had transcribed laste springe; This beinge the truthe I hope againe that Mr Dauson will not be angry yf I accownte not his directions newe; I doe thancke him howeuer for them

The carier is gone

147 *Culpeper to Hartlib, 18 January 1647[?8].*   *(13/180–1)*[5]

Mr Hartlib;

I am exceedingly taken with Mr Petit[6] & Mr Wheelers proposalls, but when I consider that they cannot parte with them without some rewarde, & that noe priuate purse can, and the [publique] will not giue it, I can not but feare that the ingenuities will dy with the men; thowgh truly (I conceiue) they showlde not bury those talents which they haue receiued from God, that by them they might profit many;

For an accommodation in this pointe, I cowlde heartily wishe that

---

[4] 'Mr Dawson' was an arborist to whom Hartlib had despatched the query from Culpeper 'how trees planted in a pasture grounds might be preserved from the brushe and rubbing of cattel' (51/150). Dawson's reply was to counsel the use of 'dogge dunge, and lyme steeped in water, wash the body of the tree, and with a squirt cast the water vpon the end bowes of any fruite trees'. In Hartlib's *Ephemerides* of 1651, he noted a manuscript of Dawson on tree planting, then in Worsley's possession and 'worth the publishing' (28/2/2B). In 1659 John Beale planned to publish a work on forestry to be entitled 'The True Interest of the Commonwealth of England'. This was to include a memorandum between Culpeper and Dawson on protecting young trees from damage by cattle – GI, p. 481; HDC, p. 107; 51/82–92 and 8/26/1; also see **141** (10 November 1647) and **143** (22 December 1647).

[5] This letter carries the date 1647, but Culpeper generally indicates a double year-date for the period from January to March and this letter does not. It may therefore, in fact, belong to this, the following year; internal evidence for its dating does not decide the issue.

[6] William Petty see **145** (5 January 1647/8).

the [Parliament] (in this their time of seekinge the Peoples loue) wowlde appointe a Committee for the examininge & rewardinge of Ingenuities & purchasinge them for publike vse[7]

This power haue the Hogen mogens in Hollande,[8] & by this power haue they at one time (to my knowledge) purchased 4: ingenuities from one Dowglas a Scottes man for 2000:[l], besides many others, which lie in theire treasury of ingenuities, and this they doe, thowgh they make noe presente, & perhaps noe future vse of them, for theire scope is, as muche for preseruation, & rewarde of ingenuity, as for the presente vse of it;

To this Committee, your [office] of Address wowld be excellently subseruiente,[9] in tendring suche ingenuities as (thowgh not to be had without rewarde) are yet worthy theire conusance; That smalleste amonge Mr Wheelers proposalls, (viz of keepinge meate a longe time) is of greate vse, & may (noe question) be farther applied, & truly wowlde the publique purchase it I wowlde willingly pay more then my share, & wowlde make noe question, soe farre to inlarge the vse of it, as to returne muche conveniency & some profit; snowe or saltepeeter are the 2: thinge which I haue thowght of for this ende, of preseruinge of thinges from putrifaction, & (for wante of better meanes) I intende to try the extente of theire power, but yf by those, or any other meanes, the preseruinge of things cowlde be fownde, it wowlde make a greate & sudden change in the better & cheaper prouidinge, & more seasonable spendinge, of what (in the ordinary cowrse) is subjecte to change;

Of Mr Petits way of representinge not of the quotations, but of the very woords quoted, out of all awthors, & that in intuita, there is greate vse to be made, & a farre larger application then euer he is like to dreame of, but what doe I Tantalize my selfe with the thowght of these thinges which ly not within my reache, & where knowledge of the quoddity, serues but to shewe howe happy I may, but shall never, bee?

I shall be in towne ere longe, thowgh I knowe nothinge wherein my weakenes can serue the publique in this greate juncture of affayres; The sworde is all, & but one, & they that haue it not, will not thincke them selues safe, in beinge at the mercy of others, eyther for their happines, or tenets; The [King]; nay all [Kings], haue & doe abuse it, The Presbiterian hathe shewed, that (yf he haue power) hee will let none liue neere him, or soe muche as vnder him, & the truthe is they are

---

[7] Culpeper here returns to a subject which he had already touched on in **94** (31 October 1645) and **95** (5 November 1645).

[8] i.e. the town regents in the Dutch Republic.

[9] The plan for an agency to sponsor innovation was fundamental to the Office of Address – GI, p. 370. The 'Office of Address for Communications' aimed to establish registers of patents, an idea which had already been advocated by, amongst others, Gabriel Plattes in his 'College of Experience' – GI, p. 69.

but Bishops cut into lesser sippets as the Pope was formerly cut into Bishops; The creation of fundamentalls, or (at leaste) compellinge all men (by the Ciuill sworde) to obey theire mocke fundamentalls, This was the fundamentall Popery in the Bishop of Rome, afterwards in the Bishops, & dwells stronger nowe in the Presbiter, till this fundamentall of Popery be taken away & that the dispensers of the Gospell become rather sufferers, then makers of others to suffer, wee shall neuer returne to that primitiue meekenes & lowlines of minde which was in Christe & his Apostles

I am growen muche in loue with my Lord Herber de Veritate;[10] I thincke you tolde me of a booke which he gaue to the [Prince] Elector, which (notwithstandinge the ill you heare of it) I pray (yf you can) be a meanes that I may see it

148   *Culpeper to Hartlib, 25 January 1647[?8].   (8/31/1–3)*[11]

[*diagram*]

Mr Hartlib;

I cannot be in towne this weeke, nor from the towne the nexte,; I shall (for the presente) onely tell you, that I am very confidente (from those seuerall touches which you haue giuen me of Mr Petits ingenuity),[12]

---

[10] [Edward] Herbert, [Earl] of Cherbury, *De Veritate* ([Paris], 1624). Culpeper had most probably access to the third edition, the first to be published in England, of 1645 (Wing H1501).

[11] As with **147** (18 January 1647[?8]), this letter also carries no double year-date and it is possible that it should be dated to this, the following year.

[12] In 1647, Petty patented the design for his double-writing invention, or pantograph. In essence, the device was a pantograph equipped with two or more quills with continuous ink-feed. The first prototype machine was produced by William Petty and tested before nine witnesses on 22 December 1647 (71/7/3A). The witnesses watched Petty transcribe the first chapter of St Paul to the Hebrews with it. The chapter had doubtless been chosen because it was not very long, and perhaps also because it contained the significant verse (v.6): 'That the communication of thy faith may become effectual by the acknowledging of every good thing which is in you in Jesus Christ'. In 1648 his *Declaration concerning the newly invented art of double writing* (1648), Wing P1917 Thomason, E.437 (23), was published. In the pamphlet Petty defended his design patent from its critics and expounded its potential advantages. A manuscript copy of this pamphlet is to be found amongst Hartlib's papers at 71/7/1–6. The device was seen as a potentially valuable means to cut the costs of using scriveners. The innovation was intensively developed by William Petty. With the help of Henry Morris, he presented a lengthy 'Remonstrance', dated to 22 August 1649, before the Council of State. In this document, in return for £1,500, he promised to divulge all the secrets of the 'Double-Writing' invention to the state – PRO SP 18 vol. II, fols 156–159. It was later taken up by the London instrument-maker Ralph Greatrakes; but the difficulties in securing a steady ink supply and robust, accurate joints to the pantograph led to its eventual abandonment.

that bothe his multiple writinge & his printinge is to be done by by that instrumente which (you knowe) I firste learned out of a booke which you lente me & had afterwardes made by your nayghbor, I meane the parralellogramme instrumente; The inlarginge or lesseninge of any mappe is this laste weeke tryed by it; & there hathe beene suche an essay of multiple writinge with it as (from what is tried & what I reade in your letters) the whole thinge is plaine to me, I fully see the way of writinge sixe coppies with one motion, & I apprehende more then a possibility of writinge yet more; I say againe, I will not be certaine that it is his way, but I cannot be more confidente then I am that it will proue a way bothe easy & certaine; The chiefe addition which Mr Petit hathe made to it is, some kinde of brasse pen not alltogether vnlike the ruling pen but somewhat otherwise made, which (being filled will inke will continue writinge a longe time without a recreute & this is the advantage by which the copies will be writte in a shorter time then another that resortes often to the ynke horne will write one coppy; & to proue that they are some suche pennes, yf you viewe the copies you will (I beleeue) finde all the strokes of one bignes; The right placinge of these pennes by screwes or otherwise & of the papers vnder them, a very little practise will discouer;

Towardes makinge this instrumente fitte for printinge there must be added to th'invention, of [suche?] a grownde of waxe & resin mixed with Ceruse or red leade et cet according to the color that shall be accownted beste; suche a grownde I say, as is used for Etchinge, that soe the a sharpe pointe woorkinge throwgh it to the mettall may leaue the letters fitt to be firste eaten by Aquafortis & then the plate thus eaten, will afterwarde printe 30: or 40: or more copies; The greateste difficulty, which yet I soone fownde, was howe to make the Par-alellogramme write backwarde, that soe it mighte (like the ordinarie printeries) printe the wright way & it is done thus

b [*two adjoining diamond shapes*] r

a

Let the fixed center of the paralellogramme be in the middle of :a: & then yf the hande write letters [forwa*rde? MS torn*] at :r: the very same kinde of hande & letters will be written backwarde at :b: & that in a greater or lesse proportion accordinge as the paralellogramme is ordered; There is yet (I consceiue) another way then by etchinge, when the letters shall be defended & the reste of the plate onely, soe a eaten, as that the letters shall not be like the hallowenesses in etchinge, but stande out like the letters of an ordinary printery, of this laste I am not soe sure, but a greate deale confidente; The instrumente is very applicable to manye other endes; I conceiue (by carrijnge the hande ouer a glasse or vpon the backside of a parchement in a darcke roome) that one that can but (with a [blunte? *MS torn*] pointe) runne ouer or

vpon the lineamentes or strokes that are before him, shall be able (more
then the firste inventer, (mentioned in your booke) promised) to make
an exacte picture of any thinge & yet see, neyther the thinge nor his
owne woorke; I haue spente my paper & time vpon this Subjecte;

Yf it were not too muche I cowlde wishe Mr Wheeler wowlde gratify
you with his way of keepinge [fleshe.? *altered*], which being to be done
onely by an intence colde & drines, might be applied not onely to the
preseruation of many other thinges, but (which I moste valewe it for)
to hygh conclusions in philosophy, I meane Chimistry, & that not in
the ordinary way of distillation, but in that hidden & inwarde motion
which nature makes within herselfe; but I am out of my way Yf you
aske Mr Pettit whether his printinge will not be onely, like written
hande & not like the printinge character, you will (by it) see whether I
haue hit right

postscript
I haue missed, in not takinge the right center of the rule or par-
allellogramme; but let not cause you to diffide, for as I haue fownde
my error, soe (yf I had time), I am confidente, I cowlde nowe set downe
the right way; but this is shewed better by ocular demonstration then
by discowrse or writinge, & more of this when I see you
                    [*squiggles*] b [*diagram*] r [*squiggles*]
                                   a
suppose a: to be fixed; & then whatsoeuer you write right forwarde
[with.?] :r: will be written backe warde (& soe to be reade vpon the
other side of the paper) by :b:; & will (by that meanes) printe forwarde &
the right way, eyther by etchinge or perhaps by [the.? *MS edge*] other
way

149   *Culpeper to Hartlib, 11 March 1647[?8].   (13/169–70)*[13]

Mr Hartlib
        I was very sorry I cowlde not see you before I wente, & more
yet that I had neyther your bookes nor papers for Mr Westroe; You
might haue rested assured that in soe good & [publi*que*] a woorke, the
[publi*que*] promoter of it, wowlde not haue beene forgotten by eyther
of vs.
        Yf my Fortunes settle I shall willingly make my selfe bothe an

---

[13] As with letters **147** (18 January 1647[?8]) and **148** (25 January 1647[?8]), this letter
carries only the single year-date and it is possible that it should be assigned to this, the
succeeding year. The reference to the incomplete Glauber treatise, on which Culpeper
was working through later 1647, would make more sense if written in 1648.

example & a sollicitor in the behalfe of the office of Addresse, & I make noe question but Mr Westroe will be (by me) drawne in to become a merchant venturer; I met with Mr Andrewes[14] after I sawe you whoe allsoe (thowgh not soe all aygremente as you conceiue him) is like allsoe to come in to vs;

I receiued Mr Woorslyes letter, & perceiue hee is otherwise opinioned of Wheelers enimies at the Hagwe[15]

Truly my experience assures me that weakenes & falsenes seldome goe asunder; & my opinion is (I wishe I be deceiued) that yf mr Wheelers abilities answere expectation, yet his intentions & professions will not; I shall by the nexte returne an answer to Mr Woorsly, & another (accordinge to Mr Worsleyes desire) to Sir [Robert] Hoonywoode, whoe, with Sir [William] Boswell[16] (yf Wheeler were what he is not) might yet be made seruiceable to the aduance of those water engines,[17] but (yf I mistake not there will proue to be (notwithstandinge Mr Worslyes ingenuity & indeauor) suche a shortwitted craftines, jealousy, & insta-bility, as that men of reason & sobriety will not bwild vpon him, I still wishe I proue a false prophet

Yf Mr Pettit will not perfecte the translation of Glawberus, which I was about, I pray sende it to me, & I will finishe it.[18]

With my beste wishes I reste

[PS.] I pray conveygh this inclosed to Mr Westroe & (yf he will sende) conueygh his answere

---

[14] Robert Andrews, MP for Weobley, Herefordshire.

[15] Benjamin Worsley left for the Netherlands in c.February 1647 – see Webster, 'Benjamin Worsley', in UR, p. 223. In *Mr. William Wheelers Case from his Own Relation* (1644/5), Wing P408, Wheeler gives an autobiographical account of the time he spent at The Hague where "…[i]n all places…[he] had quarrels urged upon" him (sig. A3ʳ). He was attacked by the Prince of Orange's guards (sig. A2ʳ), and believed that Robert Honywood and William Boswell were instrumental in excluding him from the Queen's court in order to advance claims to his engineering innovations (sigs A3ʳ – A4ᵛ) and the resulting profits.

[16] Sir William Boswell (d.1649) was English Resident at The Hague from August 1632. He financed Wheeler's operations – DNB; GI, p. 372.

[17] In particular, Wheeler's snail wheel drainage mill, for which he had been granted an English patent in 1642 – GI, pp. 372–73.

[18] Culpeper had evidently received a copy of Glauber's *De Auri Tinctura, sive Auro Potabili Vero* (Amsterdam, 1646) which he had requested from Hartlib in **111** (1 October 1646) above. He had worked on a translation but was apparently hoping to pass the task on to William Petty – see **130** (5 August 1647), **132** (August 1647), **133** (7 September 1647), **137** (20 October 1647) and Clucas, p. 151.

150 *Culpeper to Hartlib, 15 March 1647/8. (13/209–11)*

Mr Hartlib:

In the firste place, I haue returned Mr Woorsly-s letters, in which I see, muche come to passe, of what I apprehended, concerninge mr Wheeler,[19] whose ingeuities (throwgh his owne inwarde weakenes, & his jealousy of others) will (I feare) be finally buried with him; & till euery particular person, be wrowght on by Gods Spirite, to knowe, & to acknowledge, that the talentes he hathe receiued, (of what kinde so-euer) are not giuen, but entrusted onely; not to spende, but to improue; not to our owne onely, but to others good till this (I say) be woorckte into the Spirites of men, the diuell will hinder the worlde, of a greate parte of the happines, which it might injoy; of that abundance which more communication of ingenuities wowld produce, & of that inno-cence, which abundance of all thinges wowld bringe into the worlde, when all showlde haue enowght, and all beyonde that, wowlde proue a burden, & little or noe advantage, & suche an effecte doe I prophecy to my selfe, concerninge Mr Pruuostes propositions

I am heartily glad mr Rous[20] hathe vnder taken to propose somethinge on your behalfe & am confidente (with you) that yf that once were passed, your office of addresse wowlde not stay longe after; Of your motion concerninge it, my opinion is, that it is well, onely the penalty to be imposed on them whoe (beinge serued) discharge not the Registers, muste be limited, & not lefte, to an arbritary decision & 24: howers may (in some cases) be too shorte a time

I shall be very glad of Dr Chyldes acquaintance,[21] For the Elixir,[22] I conceiue it to be but an exuberancy which the spirite of nature, hathe gained, by its excercise & combate, with its enimy, within its owne body; what this enimy, this Ignis contra naturam, this Ignise non de materia, this sulphur externum these Feces grossieres, This Agens which (as Dionisius Zachary[23] saythe) non est par materialis compositj, & yet

[19] See **94** (31 October 1645).

[20] Francis Rous (1579–1659). See **113** (14 October 1646).

[21] Robert Child (c.1613–1654) was an agricultural reformer who was educated at Cambridge before receiving an MD in 1638 after studying at the Universities of Leiden and Padua. At some time between 1638 and 1641 he left for New England, but by May 1641 he was back in England. He moved to France, went back to New England, and only returned to England in 1647. Child was the author of the 'Large Letter' in Hartlib's *Legacy*, pp. 1–96. See G. H. Turnbull, 'Robert Child', *Colonial Society of Massachusetts Publications*, 38 (1959), 21–53; G. L. Kitteredge, 'Dr Robert Child, the remonstrant. Alchemy in early New England', ibid., 21 (1919), 1–146; GI, pp. 66–7.

[22] In alchemy the elixir was a preparation used to change metals into gold. It was sometimes identified with the 'philosopher's stone' – OED.

[23] Zacharius in *Chemicum Theatricum*, i. 733. For Dionysius Zachary (1510–1556), see 'The Autobiography of Denis Zachaire. An Account of an Alchemist's Life in the Sixteenth Century', *Isis*, 8 (1926), 287–99.

(in its beinge separated by the Spirite of Nature) deserues rather to be called a patiente then an agente; what (I say) this agente is, by which nature, or the spirite of nature, is put into motion, in all those circulations which wee see nature to make & by the reiterated apposition of which, the true Artiste may put nature into those reiterated motions which nature cannot giue her selfe, quia actiones eius sunt continuæ,[24] & (by those reiterated motions & circulations) cause that exuberancy aboue mentioned, what this thinge is & the true vse & mixtion of it, which is made (saythe an author) modo quidem enarrabilj, this wowlde I, (yf I might) learne from Dr Chylde, yf he be indeede a Dr in this Arte; For Nature, or the Spirite of nature beinge (eyther by this or some other way) put into motion dothe (by herselfe) all the reste; by the predominancy of moysture apposed, shee passes from september (throwgh the darke gloomy winter) to the springe, & this, with as little helpe of an owtwarde sunne, as wee vse to haue in that darcke night time of the yeere, From Aries (by the helpe (nowe) of the sunne) shee passes throwgh those Aprill showers & may dewes which (in the Autumnall maturation followinge) become Aer congelatus in terrulis nostris; I pray (yf Dr Chylde be one that will inlarge himselfe), invite his opinion upon these thowghts, For vpon something in this kinde, Standes my little phylosophy

I haue noe booke of Plattes, called Adams arte reuiued;[25] but (bownde vp with other of his treatises) I haue his arte of settinge of corne,[26] which you may commande

I thancke you for your promise concerninge mr Boyles & mr Woorsly, which I can as little expecte as I can yet deserue it

Dr Chyldes frinds projecte, of keepinge water in a continuall warmthe, wowlde (yf true) proue admirable, for very many vses, & particularly for the woorke aboue mentioned I meane betweene the springe & the Autumne, & truly (from the dayly experience of my owne narrowenes) I dare not confine any possibility to my vnderstandinge

I conceiue your story of the Turner[27] not improbable, but rather, that the [Perpetual motion] will be one of the Phylosophers stones, of this, or the very nexte adjoininge age, as allsoe that Linea visibilis, by which, frinds (distante 100: miles or more) may converse, in a minute,

---

[24] Zacharius, *Chemicum Theatricum*, i. p. 729.

[25] Although this work is not listed in Wing or the STC it was cited by Robert Child in his 'Large Letter', published by Hartlib in his *Legacy*, p. 6.

[26] Hugh Plats, *The New and Admirable Arte of Setting Corne* (1600), STC 19993.

[27] Probably the optical lens-grinder and instrument-maker, Richard Reeves, who was working from Kingston-upon-Thames at around this time, and who had impressed Hartlib with the ambitious claims that he made for his telescopes – see A.D.C. Simpson, 'Richard Reeve – the 'English Campani' – and the origins of the London telescope-making tradition', *Vistas in Astronomy*, xxviii (1985), 357–65.

or (as nuntius Inanimatus proposes) what one frinde deliuers at London, at 12: shall be knowen at Bristoe[28] (by the other) before 12: an excellent appurtenante to your office of [Address][29]

My acquaintance that pretended to the [Perpetual motion] is one mr Bartne[30] & lives (yf not very lately deade) at Sittingburne about 6: or 7: miles hence

I heartily wishe the agreemente of the 2: nations, & am confidente it will be,[31] yf, what Aristocracy sees approching towardes itselfe allsoe, rayses not in it a lookinge backe to suche a degree of monarchycall power, as might serue (by joyninge) to vpholde bothe, yf God were not against it; This, & this onely, makes me feare wee shall finally clashe; For (me thincks) I see howe the Lords, in joininge to pull downe the [King], as the Bishops in pullinge downe the Pope, & the Presbiterian in outinge the Bishops, doe nowe finde themselves all deceiued, not foreseeinge that them selues alsoe are but Babylon – cut into sippits & soe, onely the better fitted, for that time, when the fowles of the ayre shall be called to supper, & you knowe, our meate muste be cut & fitted (by euery one, for the mowthe) Before wee can chewe & swallowe it, & truly, this quarteringe of the Popes in Bishops, & Iointinge of the Bishops into Presbiters, in that which wee call Ecclesiasticall, & of the Emperor into [Kings], & of [Kings] into the nobility & noblesse in the Civill Gouermente, it is, but a fittinge them, firste for the spitt, & then for the trencher, thence to the mouthe & soe to the guttes, & from thence, you knowe what will become of all these our benefactors; Amen;

I pray let me know what became of my Letter to Mr Westroe

I showld be very happy yf you cowlde (by this returne) let me know Dr Chylde his sence vpon the touches I have giuen concerninge the Elixir

Nowe (I hope) I am vpon euen termes withe you; & soe muche more as to have wearied you with my impertinences but they are suche as the Cowntry affoords, you are vpon the vantage grownde, & therefore yf you haue a full return in quantity it muste wante in wayght

---

[28] i.e. Bristol.

[29] In which work, entitled 'Nuntius Inanimatus', Culpeper had found this reference is unclear and his memory on the matter failed him on a later occasion. In *Ephemerides*, 1656, Hartlib notes: 'Dee vndertooke to give intelligence what 12 a clock things done at London they should know it before 12 at Bristol. But wither this is expressed in Nuncius Inanimatus of Dees or Bishop Goodwin or Dr Wilkins Nuncius Inanimatus Sir Cheney Culpeper could not tell' – 29/5/101B.

[30] See **80** (17 July 1645).

[31] Culpeper's confidence on this point was to prove misplaced. On 11 April 1648, the Scottish Parliament voted to abandon the treaty between the two kingdoms – Gardiner, iv. 111.

151 *Culpeper to Hartlib, 22 March 1647/8.   (13/212)*

Mr Hartlib

I thancke you for your large letter, vpon the partes of which I cannot nowe particularize havinge allsmoste slipte my time

I still feare that Wheelers folly will drowne all his ingenuities

I showlde be glad by your nexte to know the grownde of Acontius beinge called in I feare it is for that 3: or 4: leaves concerninge prophesyinge, which our spirituall wickednesses will not aknowledge to be the commandementes of God[32]

I am heartily sorrowe mr Rows waytes for the sollicitor[33] whoe (I feare) will not come in to your ayde

I feare our Armies heere will as little agree with the Aristocraticall Intereste in Scotlande as with monarchicall in Englande & our tryumphant sayntes, not beinge them selues true to their owne principles, & declarations, of a free, frequente, & equall representatiue, I feare they will not proue the persons whoe shall haue the honor to restore peace & truthe to this nation, but after hauinge (John like) shewed & boasted of theire zeale for the [Lord] of Hostes, & browght Anty Christe neerer to a Haste, in them selues, they will prove a good dishe for the fowles of the Ayre[34]

I pray convey this to Chamcell*or* Roe[35]

152 *Culpeper to Hartlib, 29 March 1648.   (13/213–14)*

Mr Hartlib

I am sorry for what you write concerning [your] feares from Scottlande,[36] beinge but what I haue from elsewhere, & [your*self*] knowe my former feares from the Scottishe Aristocraticall Intereste bothe in

---

[32] On 24 February 1648, an English translation of Acontius's *Satanae Strategemata* (Basel, 1565) had been published. A member of the Assembly complained about a passage in the book and a committee was appointed to consider the work. The translation – *Satans Stratagems* (1648), Wing A443 – was prefaced by commendations from John Goodwin and John Dury. The passage to which Culpeper refers is on pp. 124–130 (sigs. R2ᵛ-S1ᵛ). See HDC, pp. 261, 312; also *The Diary and Correspondence of John Worthington*, ed. James Crossley, Chetham Society, vol 36 (1855), 143–46; *Minutes of the Sessions of the Westminster Assembly*, eds. A. F. Mitchell and J. Struthers (Edinburgh, 1874), p. 505 (28 February 1648); Batten, pp. 110–11.

[33] Oliver St John (1598?-1673) – DNB.

[34] See **134** (15 September 1647).

[35] Sir Thomas Roe had died in 1644.

[36] Hartlib's fear that the Scots Parliament were about to break the treaty uniting the two kingdoms or demand the establishment of a presbyterian church settlement in England proved to be correct on 11 April – Gardiner, iv. 115.

Churche & State whoe hauinge (for theire owne endes of greatnes &
power) joined in pullinge downe the Power of Monarchy & Episcopacy,
doe begin to finde themselues to be parte allsoe of that Babilonishe
rubbishe which muste downe, & (that theire fowndation, (bothe of
power & strenght of reason) beinge taken away) the superstructed
skreene, is like to fall into a tumblinge motion, soe as theire care nowe
muste bee (yf they can soe ballance the wheele) to take soe muche of
eache of theire incensed enimies as that (yf possible) the wheele may
stande in equilibrio, whilste them selues lie vpon the toppe, for I dare
say that (as the case nowe standes) neyther monarchy nor Democratie
will joine with them, but with this reserued resolution within them
selues, to eate them laste; yet beinge the spawne of Monarchy they are
like to followe theire naturall inclination in joininge & (perhaps) fallinge
with it, & then this [Parliament] which is yet kept up in the spirits of
men, (not for theire owne sakes) may perhaps, (yf they doe not
voluntarily make themselues instrumentall in the intereste of true
[publique] liberty) finde a newe generation presse harde vpon theire
heeles as they doe nowe vpon Aristocracy, & that lately on Monarchy
I knowe nothinge of the Bathe you mention but showlde be glad from
you to vnderstand further of it when your intelligence can furnishe you
from Denmarcke, I hould it likely & woorthe lookinge after;[37] A sheete
boyled in sacke or muscadine & clapte about one that had the plagwe
markes hathe (by reporte that hathe come to me seuerall wayes) &
continued that life which is (ordinarily) accownted desperate, & I holde
this sheete thus soaked, to be but a kinde of bathe, I am sorry for Mr
Sadlers mistake concerning the 1000^l;[38] I am not soe muche deceiud in
your mistake as I was in your former letter & hope very little from the
[publique]

[37] Hartlib had forwarded to Culpeper the description which he had received from
John Dury of the 'Bathes of the King of Denmark' – 8/32/1A. 'There was a box made
of fine wood wherein hee would sit conveniently naked, which did shut very close upon
him to enclose his Body, soe that his Head only did stand in the aire: the opning was
before with a doore to goe in to sit upon a seat: and above to shutte under his chin
about his necke'. Steam was then pumped through the box and the resulting sauna was
particularly commended for sobering up after prolonged heavy drinking. Culpeper clearly
followed the matter up because a reference in Hartlib's *Ephemerides*, datable to June/July
1648, refers to 'A Chirgeon in Wood street not far from Goldsmith hall . . . being an old
acquaintance of Sir Cheny's hath such a sweating or bathing Chaire as Mr Worsly and
Mr Dury describe' – 31/22/18B.
[38] John Sadler (1615–1674) – DNB. He was a considerable supporter of Hartlib and his
enterprises and secured him some of his pensions from the Parliament. See also **93** (22
October 1645). This may refer in some way to the scheme of Mr Sadler's 'for transacting
the exportation of a certain wondrous vnknown rich commodity' from Asia through
Muscovy which apparently promised to raise £2,000 and in pursuit of which John Sadler
left for the Netherlands in the summer of 1648 – *Ephemerides* (1648), 31/22/14A; 15A.

[*Hartlib adds:* Note that the People in the House according to the Patients order hee hauing paid the price of it should have buried that sheet. But they desirous of the benefit kept it wherby that whole Family was in fected and most of them dyed.]

The Lillburnistes time is not yet, they will but wronge theire owne ende, a with drawinge & reseruinge theire strenght may doe well whilste the other rubbishe pulls downe one another;

I am sorry Acontius is soe ill relished (but wonder not at it,) & am as glad that Mr Dury, is by this or any occasion rouzed, I confesse that waytinge vpon oportunities is good, but I allsoe conceiue that sometimes a wise & zealous man will make more oportunities then he findes & truly Mr Dury can neuer bestryde a better cause & author[39]

My Quære (yf I were in towne) concerninge Mr Flemminge engine[40] wowlde be, whether one man or horse to doe as muche as a 100: muste not haue a hundredfolde the time, yf soe, his engine is noe woonder, for in the statique, time & power are the ballance of eache other, but for one man or horse (in the same time) to doe as muche as 100; had beene woorthe the [Parle*ment*] lookinge after; for it wowld mightily lessen the vse of drawght cattell, & truly I conceiue a conjunction of the equipendium, sway wheele, & endeles screwe, will in the same time, muche improue the same power,

I conceiue Dr Gibbons hathe somethinge worthe markinge but I conceiue allsoe that he see muche more in himselfe then the world can yet apprehende. This I obserue to arise in the spirits of men the Scripture must be the rule of our faythe & life, not as it is a dead letter with out us, but as wee finde somethinge within vs that answeres to it; This something is by Mr Dury raysed by an Analisis, Dr Gibbons dothe it by substernements as he calls it; our Churche by the Spirit of God, but howe farre or muche of these or any of these are within our reache or power, that soe wee may neyther neglecte our duty on the one side nor (on the other) rely on suche strenght as wee haue not, this (I confesse) to me is the greateste difficulty[41]

I haue formerly seene Pruuostes laste letter & truly by my former apprehensions & what you laste write I can apprehende noe neerer & more quieste way of pullinge downe & remouinge all the Babilonishe rubbishe, then by suche a plenty of Gods good creatures, as that (all hauinge enowght), superfluity may be a care & burden, not an aduantage

[39] See the preceeding letter.

[40] This is not mentioned elsewhere amongst Hartlib's surviving papers.

[41] For Nicholas Gibbons, see **121** (16 February 1646/7). In his *Ephemerides* of 1648, Hartlib recorded that 'Dr Gibbon affirmed to mee that his divinity-designe was nothing else but the perfecting or performing of one grand desideratum of the Lord Verulam in Divinity' – 31/22/3B.

of honor or pleasure; God hathe better disposed of me then to be of the [Parl*iament*] where I showlde (perhaps) haue pleased none & leasst of all my selfe[42]

I haue noe hope from the publike concerning your office of Addresse,[43] & I feare when priuate intereste shall be sollicited, that it will come but slowly on, I shall nowe ere longe be in towne & then will speake what is fitting to Mr Westroe, but cannot doe it soe well by letter, I conceiue he hathe bothe your bookes

I am extremely sorry for Mr Woorsly whome (to deale freely with you) I muste judge somewhat erroneous, that wowlde not see him selfe well bottomed before hee vndertooke his [jour*n*y],[44] For my selfe I still continue in my late condition, & alltogether vncerteine howe thinges will goe with me

Yf Dr Chylde pleas to spende his judgement on my philosophy, I be gladd to receiue it

153   *Culpeper to Hartlib, 5 April 1648.   (13/215–6)*

Mr Hartlib,

I finde Mr Woorsly, very intentiue in frawghtinge himselfe with riche ladinge, I heartily wishe him good speede, & shall be still glad (yf he continue in the same minde & that my affayres settle) to venter a share; I am still every day more intentiue on the nature & vse of colde, in which the experimente mentioned in your laste, is a very pretty one, yf hee meete with more in that nature hee shall muche oblige me by them – For the menstruu*m* vniversale or Carmihills Altaheste,[45] I muste acknowledge them to be very greate secrettes, But Pontan[46] saythe thus of himselfe – Erraui ducenties super veram materiam; my opinion is, that the vniversall matters is in all places & thinges, but the extraction of it, the adaptation of it, & (which I conceiue farre yet more difficulte) the reiterated puttinge of nature into a fittinge motion, these are the particulars wherein a true phylosoper excells; For non producit seipsam

---

[42] The letter from Le Pruvost to which Culpeper refers is probably that dated 5 January 1648 in Latin (12/22A-B) which presents a luminescent prospectus of progress in return for Parliamentary support for the scheme. By the end of March 1648, no further progress had been made, however, on securing Parliamentary backing for the ambitious project.

[43] Culpeper's scepticism towards any degree of public (i.e. Parliamentary) support for the Office of Address was to prove entirely justifiable – see G. H. Turnbull, *Samuel Hartlib; a sketch of his life and his relations to J.A. Comenius* (1920), pp. 48–9.

[44] Benjamin Worsley had undertaken an extended research trip to the Netherlands from which he would return in 1650 – see Webster 'Benjamin Worsley', in UR, pp. 219–20.

[45] For Sir James, Lord Carmichael, see **80** (17 July 1645).

[46] For Giovanni Pontano, see **89** (n.d.). The passage comes from his treatise *De ignis*.

non monet seipsam, & therefore saythe Zengiuode[47] (speakinge of that heavenly fire which descendes from aboue & dwells in the sublunary bodies), Hoc elementu*m* est omnium quietissimu*m*, ac simile currui, cu*m* trahitur currit, cum non trahitur, stat quiete; Inest omnibus rebus imperceptibiliter & in another place, Ignis est quietissimum elementun, quod motu excitatur, quam excitationen nouerunt viri philosophi; & in the same page, In omni operatione, natura habet excitare ignem, qui a Creatore occulte, in Centrum cujus libet rei inclusus est, talis excitatio fit per velle naturæ, aliquando per naturam sagacis artificis; naturam disponentis,[48] – but what doe I trowble you with these impertinencies; The histericall receipte you sente me a weeke since is mislayed, I pray afforde me another; Dr Chylde is not perhaps of a communicatiue disposition, yf it be soe, I pray trowble him noe farther

I am sorry for that suddeine resolution or rather reuolution of affaires which you feare, but truly thus it muste happen when suche as haue got into the saddle, by pretendinge publiq*ue* Intereste, doe nowe turne all to theire priuate, but the stone is rollinge, & (I am confidente) will not ly still any where but in the peoples true Intereste of an equall, frequente, & powerfull Parliamente, where newe Lawes & (yf necessity or the Peoples will incline that way) newe Gouernments may be orderly settled, & (in case (as nowe) of any question or difference) the olde ones (from time to time) acknowledged; For a politicall creature to receiue its beinge, & yet (Luciferianlike) to holde it from itselfe without any future acknowledgement of its creater, was that which firste made that thinge wee call the Deuill, & caste him out of heauen without possibility of returne; & this woord heauen hathe a politicall sence in the reuelation

I feare I haue loste my time

---

[47] On Michael Sendivogius [Sedziwoj] (1566–1636/46), an alchemical authority much cited by Culpeper, see Partington, ii. 426–29; DSB; Clucas, pp. 154–56. His principal work, of which Culpeper had a Latin copy, was the *Novum Lumen Chymicum* (Paris, 1608; Cologne, 1614 etc). This passage appears in his supplementary work, the *Novi luminis chemici*, his treatise 'De sulphure' *Musæum Hermeticum reformatum* (Frankfurt, 1678), p. 615.

[48] 'This element is the most quiescent of all, and like a cart, it runs when it is drawn and stands at rest when it is not drawn; it is in all things, though not perceptible; & in another place, Fire is the most quiescent element and it is kindled by motion and that kindling is known to the philosophers; & in the same page, In all its workings nature has to kindle that fire which has been put in secret by the Creator at the centre of each and every thing. Such kindling is done at nature's will, at times through the nature of the wise Creator, who disposes of nature itself'. The passage is taken from p. 618 of the treatise 'De sulphure' in *Musæum Hermeticum*.

154   *Culpeper to [Benjamin Worsley?], 9 May 1648.   (13/217–220)*

[copy in the hand of one of Hartlib's scribes with Hartlib's interlinear corrections]

Sir

I thanke you for the favour of your Last of the 27. [April]/7. May. in answere of mine of march the 8th. my rejoinder to the point of cold is, That it is necessary not only for the preservinge of thinges and concentringe of Spirits, but that it hath a great influence upon the generation and mutliplication of that vniversall Spirit of Nature. Il ne faut pas penser (saith the Author of Traitte du Sell) que le Soleil coeleste eschauffe seul la terre, Car nous voyons qu'en l'hyver, alors que le Soleil est plus esloygné de nous que le dedans d'icelle est plus chaud, qu'au plus ardant de l'este, à cause de la chaleur reprimée par le froideur de l'ayre qui l'environne de sorte que le metaux ne laissent a se cuire et peut on dire qui c'est alors que se fayt leur plus grande cuisson;[49] You see I take you by this for a French man; Cold of itself workes nothing, but meetinge with the Spirits of nature when it is motion, it advance (as I conceive putrefaction in the beginninge of the worke and (according to the words above) it doth (by an antiperistesis) seeme afterwards to make a continuall exuberant increase of the Spirits of nature; and that wee may yet further Know that God hath made cold (as all other thinges) for some vse, wee may observe that the raines, dewes or other vapours, which arise from the earth are returne upon the earth againe by the cold region of the ayre; so that though it bee the Centrall Sunne or Spirits of nature which raises with it moysture out of the earth, yet it is by the cold region quod hic aer mutetur in aquam multo subtiliorem quam fuit prima as Zendivoge directes.[50] But what doe I trouble you with my lene melancholly thoughts, when you live at the fountaines. I thanke you for Dr. Kuffler's wife's experiments, especially concerning harty chocks, for which you prescribe sand and a little salt mix't together in a vessell, and set in a very coole but not moist roome.[51] Now what proportion the Salt must beare to the Sand; whether to bee mixed per minima with the Sand, whether the Hartichocks must be buried or how ~~s~~ deepe set ~~downe~~ in the sand,

---

[49] Nuysement, *Traittez*, pp. 108–9 [trans: 'It should not be thought . . . that the celestial Sun alone warms the earth, For we see that in winter, when the Sun is furthest from us that its core is hotter than in the warmest periods of summer because of the heat retained by the cold air which surrounds it – with the result that the metals remain hot and, one may say that it is at that time that they reach their highest temperature'].

[50] Sendivogius, *Novum Lumen Chymicum* in *Musæum Hermeticum*, p. 576.

[51] On Johann Siebert Küffeler and his family, see GI, pp. 388–89. His wife was a sister of Cornelis Drebbel. By this date, they were living in the Netherlands close by Johann Rudolf Glauber.

whether the Vessell must be closed like a barrell; to the sequeres and what else may give light to the experiment, I desire your favourable answer, as also in the Keepinge of cherries and other fruits, whether they may touch one another in the glasse.

Concerning the exaltation of the Spirits of Nature my meaning is that toward that exaltation there is necessary not only a Solution of the body or of bodies but there must afterwards bee such an excitation of the Spirit of nature as that it may (as in the beginning) moove in and upon the waters, and truly if Carmihil and Glauberus and such other great refined witts looke not as well at the excitation of the Spirit of Nature (as by an vniversall dissolvent or menstruum) at the freeinge it of from that compact drie imprisonement, which (in all seedes) it receives in its maturation; they will bee finally found but to flatter themselves, Ignis est quietissimum elementum (saith Zengivode) nisi excitetur quam excitationem noverunt viri Philosophi.[52] Now this excitation and the meanes of it, though sparingly mentioned in the bookes; may yet be picked out; All Authors agree that Natura non movet or producit seipsam, and therefore to cause a motion and production of her, they doe (under some notions) direct the adjoininge of something, and this thing (what ever it bee, one author calls Sulphur externum another Agens; Raimund Lully; Ignis contra naturam; Traitté du Sell fæces grossieres;[53] Ill fut necessaire (saith that Author) d'entremesler ces feces grossieres a la substance subtile, car ou il n'y que pureté il n'y peut avoir d'action parce que rien ne peut ager sans patient. And a few lines after, Or la nature qui est in continuell action pour separer le pur d'avecque l'impur, a la conservation de l'essence et accroissement de la vie a pour son unique Subject cette mattiere entremeslee d'impurites. Pontanus calls it Ignis non de materia for want of which fire (as I conceive) erravi ducenties (saith he) super veram materiam, now what this Sulphur externum, this Agent (which by its beeing separated in the End of the worke deserves the name of a patient) this Ignis contra naturam, these feces grossieres or impurités, this Ignis non de materia, is. This is my question, which if Glauberus either cannot or will not understand; I say againe that you may expect other pretty or vsefull experiments from him; but he will proove to seeke in the greater worke.[54]

I have (this afternoone) had some discourse with Dr. Childe who (I perceive) is confident both from Carmihil and also from his owne Knowledge of the Paracelsian Altaheste, I hold it a precious secrett,

[52] Sendivogius, p. 618.

[53] Nuysement, pp. 165–6.

[54] For Worsley's activities during his stay in the Netherlands, see Webster, 'Benjamin Worsley', in UR, pp. 224–25.

but yet to be no more then the Key and that after the solution [<*H:*
of the body there must bee another solution,>] or rather dissolution of
the Elements, and this by some way of fermentation nor is this
fermentation to bee procured without the apposition of something to
the Spirit of nature, even as barme or yeast is added to worke, to make
it worke; And now that I am upon the working of beere, I will make
to you one observation in the workinge of beere which is that Cold in
the winter hinders it and that as the tunne is kept warme or left to the
cold of the Season, so is it possible to moderate the workinge of nature,
and this agrees with what Nicholas Flammell saith (viz.) that when the
2. dragons have seized upon one another they never cease from
fightinge if the cold hinder them not) till they bee all on a gore blood,
and till that in the end they have killed one another, and out of these
putrified carcases arises our puissant King;[55] I pray yf from my scriblinge
you now apprehend me try whether Glauberus can and will give an
Answer what this Canaanite is that exercises our spirits of Nature,
and what that is in Nature, which like sinne to a gracious soule,
serves to encrease repentance and all the other graces for thus (by the
mercifull and wise God) doe the sinnes worke where the Spirit of
grace hath taken roote, & thus if my Philosophy faile not) doth
something in nature (analogicall to sinn) worke upon the Spirit of
nature.

If as Mr. Hartlibs tells me Mr. Wheeler bee againe at your devotion,
his way of keepinge flesh 3. or 4. moneths might bee applyed to
Hartichokes or any other fruite of the earth I writte to Sir. Rob*ert*
[Honywood] when I writt last to you but (which I marveille at) have
received no answere

I am altogether yet unsetled in my condition if it proove otherwise
with me, I shall according to my former propositions) bee ready to
adventure a share, if yourselfe continue in the same mind with my
Affectionat wishes I rest

155   *Culpeper to Hartlib, 24 June 1648.   (13/221–2 [summary only])*

*Culpeper requests from Hartlib a remedy for deafness which he had once told him
about.*

[55] *Nicholas Flammel, his exposition of the hieroglyphicall figures* . . . (translated by 'Eirenæus
Orandus') (1624), pp. 68–9.

156   *Culpeper to Hartlib, 6 July 1648.   (13/225–6)*

Mr Hartlib

I haue heere lefte you suche booke & papers as remaine with me of yours

I haue turned downe some leaues in the booke of receiptes, which I heartily wishe might be copied out[56]

I pray presente my devoyrs to [Saint] Iames & excuse me that I have not wayted on them

Yf you may procure me the fauor of the sight of that little treatise concerninge clouer grasse from mr Boyles to whome I pray my humble seruice[57]

My kindest respectes to mr Petite, I pray quicken the ripeninge of his thowghts of the [Agric*ultural*] engine;[58] & let him knowe, I haue taken order with you concerning the charge of it, which I will (vpon your intelligence what it is like to be) take order for

With my beste to you I reste

The Receipte=booke

Mr Dimocke[59]

Mr Petit upon Mr Dimocke[60]

Renaudot

Of deafenes

157   *Culpeper to Benjamin Worsley, n.d.   (13/223–224)*

[copy in the hand of one of Hartlib's scribes with Hartlib's occasional alterations]

<*H:* Ex lit. Sir [Cheney] [Culpeper] to Mr Worsley>

The touch you give from Mr Morian concerning Saltpeter, rayses my Chymicall thoughts, and wishes that you would give me leave to

---

[56] His wife's recipe-book.

[57] For the treatise on clovergrass 15/5/26; cf a letter defending its agricultural use in 26/87/1A-4B.

[58] William Petty was becoming interested in the problem of setting corn by means of a seed-drill. Hartlib recorded in the *Ephemerides* for 1648 that: 'He [*Petty*] hathe also scanned and corrected Plats his Calculations about the encrease in Corne. The benefit of this new kind of Agriculture will bee 1. for saving so much in that which is otherwise sowen. 2. in getting of that lesser quantity so much the more of increase.' – 31/22/31B. Petty remained to be convinced. Later that same year, Hartlib recorded: 'Of setting Corne Petty thus writes – I see no great reason why the setting of Corne although it might bee done in perfection should doe any thing more then save seed. Wherfore I should bee glad to bee assured for what end wee trouble ou'r braines' – 31/22/22A.

[59] i.e. Cressy Dymock, who was also developing a machine for setting corn – see GI, pp. 226 and n, 365–66, 473.

[60] This is probably 'An abstract of Mr Demmocks Husbandry-Designe' which is in Petty's hand amongst Hartlib's papers – 62/50/17A-18B.

recommend too Chymicall Queries to you search in these your travels,[61] The first is the exilation of the Spirit of Nature againe and againe into a reitard motion as offten as the Phillosophers pleases for motus generat calorem, Calur movet aquam Aquæ motus causat aerem Aer est omnium viventiu*m* vita sayth Sengijod;[62] but were the question now asked what dose causare motum; In this ponite are the philosophers very Sparinge. Pontan calls it. Ignis non de materia, Another sulphur externum Traitte de Sel call it Faeces grossieres Another author tells us that it is not pars materialis composti, Another tells us of an agente w*h*ich yet (in *th*e seperation which the Spirit of nature makes of it deserves rather the name of a patient, for to be seperated is to bee passive. The second Quere is concerning the intention of cold which (I am confident) will prove more available towards putrefaction in our Chymical confections, and towards the multiplying of *th*e spirit of nature in them then a totall application of hearte, not but that I acknowledge alsoe a spring and an autumne as well in our little world as in the great but my desire is that if wee desire to see a fruitfull summer, wee must passe through the winter quarters, for if wee looke into nature wee shall find winter to be a naturall cause of the fruitfullnes in Summer, I pray (yf you meet w*i*th any thinge concerning these to points) afford your frind aline, and at some time of recreation from more serious thoughts try what relish Mr Morian & Mr Glauberus have of these or such thoughts ·//·

158   *Culpeper to Hartlib, 12 July 1648.   (13/227–8)*

Mr Hartlib;
        I haue onely time to desire that (by your meanes) Mr Petis may put his ingenuity on woorke in makinge that engine for Agriculture;[63] I finde that 3: ynches is better then 4: between the furrowes & in respecte of stones, it will be necessary that the furrowe makers stande one behind another as in the margente

.   .   .   .

.   .   .   .

.   .   .   .

---

[61] Johann Moriaen (?1591– post January 1662) had been born in Nuremberg and, having served as pastor to the reformed church in Cologne (1619–27), had taken up residence in Amsterdam, where he was visited by Worsley who assisted his investigations into saltpetre and metallurgy. See John Young, 'Godly Intelligence: intellectual contact between England and the Netherlands (1638–1662). A study of the correspondence of Johann Moriaen' (Unpublished PhD Thesis, University of Sheffield, 1995).

[62] i.e. Michael Sendivogius [Michal Sedziwoj].

[63] See **156** (6 July 1648).

& soe muste the cornes allsoe, lye; 66: graines from one funnell sowes a rodde in lenght; 2800 graines or there aboutes sowes 45 roddes or perches, beinge the bredthe of moste fieldes with vs; & 2800 graines, is (accordinge to Mr Petis accownte) but 1/7 above 1/4 of a pownd of wheate, soe that one funnell neede holde little aboue a quarter of a pinte; my owne thowghts woorcke allsoe vpon some other way, & I wowlde very willingly, yf I cowlde finde seuerall wayes, or at leaste some one good way, of puttinge the corne into the grownde, at a more euen distance, & depthe,

I pray intreate the fauor from mr Boyles of the treatise of clouer-seede, & (yf you can) sende it by this returne[64]

With my affectionate wishes I reste

[PS.] Afforde me a little newes & if you see [Westminster] I pray aske Mr Westroe from me whether he will write a line; my service to him

159   *Culpeper to Hartlib, 19 July 1648.   (13/229–30)*

Mr Hartlib

I haue heere returned to Mr Pettit bothe his owne letter & an answere to it,[65] I pray fauor me soe [muche] as to convaygh it to him; The worlde (I conceiue) is quicke, I pray afforde me some newes, howe the [parl*liament*] parties agree (I hears they doe) whether what you writt of Lamberte be true, what meanes wee prouide, to face the Scottes;[66] & to keepe all quiet in these & the Weste & norweste partes of the [King*dome*], & what else (you conceiue) may satisfy a longinge minde

The [Kings] party (I perceiue) set up theire reste & hopes, of gaininge Hamilton by maryinge the Prince to his dawghter, & of gaininge the other party in Scotlande in grantinge (what they haue soe earnestly sowght for, & wee (you may remember) haue refused) a vnion of the nations, which yf (by the [Kings] partyes condiscension) it showlde prove necessary vpon future emergentes, I conceiue a vnion of Par-

[64] Ibid.

[65] Possibly a reference to *The Advice of W.P. to Mr Samuel Hartlib for the Advancement of Some Particular Parts of Learning* (1648), Wing P1914, which Hartlib published in 1648. If so, then Culpeper may be the author of the undated and unascribed commentary on it, entitled 'A Remonstrance of the feasibility of the Designes described by W. P. in his Advice to Mr. Samuel Hartlib, concerning the Advancement of Learning and Arts' – 53/36/1A-2B. The remonstrance welcomes Petty's proposals. Although vast sums would be needed to complete the task outlined by Petty, this should not prevent a modest start being made upon some institutional foundations.

[66] John Lambert (1619–1683) had been sent to the north in the expectation of a Scottish invasion. On 8 July the Scots army marched into England led by James Hamilton, first Duke of Hamilton – Gardiner, iv. p. 165.

liaments muche the beste & as I hate negatiues in the supreme cowncell
of a nation (a true Babylonishe intrusion) soe muche more betweene 2:
nations; for seriously all negatiues serue but to retarde & (sometimes)
to hinder greate common concernementes & to let nothinge passe but
that very little that can fitte to seuerall Interests destructiue of one
another; The carrier will be gone

[*PS.*] I pray scatter these hopes of the [K*ings*] party amonge your
frindes; I conceiue it true

Remember mr Boyles treatise

160   *Culpeper to Hartlib, 25 July 1648.   (13/231⁻2)*

Mr Hartlib
            I writte to you on Sunday laste, but haue as yet receiued noe
answere, I pray in your nexte let me vnderstande whether it came to
your handes
I cannot judge of the vse of the glasses which mr Worsley mentions
because I haue noe knowledge of them; but shall be glad to be
acquainted with Fromentill about some other glasses,[67] which I haue
in my thowghts
I pray in your nexte let me vnderstande concerninge what mr
Woorsly wowlde heare from me; To that pointe of mony my laste
answer was,[68] That what I vndertooke was conditionall, That my estate
was as yet vnsettled; That (assoone as my businesses drew to some
periode which (I hope) will be nowe ere longe), I wowlde (yf he admitted
of it) performed what I promised, I am confident he hathe receiued
this letter, & I vnderstande from yourselfe that hee is (for the presente)
otherwise supplied, & my wishes are that Mr Woorlsly wowlde make
himselfe mr of all Glawberus his furnaces, & particularly of his ouen
to boyle with; For Mr Wheeler, I finde that Mr Woorsly his ingenuous
disposition hath formerly & lately obliged him, but I am still of opinion
that an indiscrete man once cosened, is like to haue a continuall feare

---

[67] A. Fromentil, a Dutch optical instrument-maker and lens-grinder. Culpeper refers
to the letter from Worsley dated 22 June 1658 [NS?] in which he describes his meeting
with Fromentil and the comparisons he undertook between his products and other
microscopes. Fromentil was apparently open about his research into improving the
optical quality of his lenses – 42/1/1A.
    [68] Benjamin Worsley had apparently taken Culpeper's offer in **137** (20 October 1647)
at its face value. In that letter, Culpeper offered to 'become a marchante venturer in the
busines' and, in partnership with others, to underwrite the costs of his research trip to
the Netherlands. See also **152** (29 March 1648)

grafted in him; & for my parte as I cowlde not desire to cozen him, soe neyther will I deceiue my selfe, in valewinge what lyes buried in another mans bosome

The Cittyes indeauor to remoue Scippon[69] will not succeede, nor yet that other of gettinge the [Parl*iament*] againe into their owne power, & soe of giuinge Lawe to the [K*ing*dome]; And thowgh you doe not, yet I can from elsewhere vnderstande that the true [Presbit*erian*] & the honeste Independente doe close very neere, I confesse that the cownterfeit [presb*iterian*] & the [Cromwell*ian*] are very farre asunder yet, but I hope the one will be espied & the other somewhat rectified in his bottomlesse principles; I see the Lo*r*ds beginne nowe to moue to their proper center, Let them goe, I hope there may be an expediente fownde as well heere as in the Lowecowntryes to doe our busines w*i*thout them, or a leaste by takinge in those onely whoe continue honeste; That of the shippes is the greateste blowe, & suche as I cannot yet see throwgh; my kinde loue & respectes to Mr Petty to whome I haue not leasure to write, I showlde be glad to heare what he will thincke of finishinge the engine,[70] & that he hathe fownde an expedient for stony lande,

[*PS.*] I pray when you visit [Westm*inster*] nexte conuaygh this inclosed

161   *Culpeper to Hartlib, 2 August 1648.   (13/233⁻4)*

Mr Hartlib

I am very glad of your interpretation of the passage in Mr Woorsly his letter & shall not I assure you be the more backwarde towards his desires, in case my owne affayres once settle

I shall (accordinge to Mr Pettys his judgemente) let Shawe alone till wee haue tryed his experimente, but showlde (yf I might) be glad to receiue a touche of the growndes & wayes he goes vpon, & I heartily wishe that the engine might be dispatched, because I sowe very early beinge nowe ready yf I had corne, & showlde be glad (yf it beare but any probability in it) to make seuerall tryalls of it seuerall grownds this wheate season

I pray write me woorde whence (you conceiue) Colchester showlde

---

[69] Philip Skippon (d. 1660) - DNB. He was appointed commander-in-chief of the London militia at the outbreak of the second civil war on 18 May 1648. When he was commissioned by the House of Commons to raise a regiment of horse to forestall a royalist rising, there was much disquiet amongst presbyterian elements in the City of London and in Parliament.

[70] i.e. the 'corn engine' or machine for sowing seed.

be releeued,[71] where the Prince & Fleete is,[72] whether our ships & the marriners are yet in noe better condition, where Cromwell is,[73] howe farre Hamilton advances,[74] & what opposition is made, & what else this tossinge time affoords, the time I feare is paste

162 *Culpeper to Hartlib, 9 August 1648. (13/235–6)*

Sir

I haue scarce time to intreate your fauor to addresse this to mr Boys,[75] & (yf he takes notice to you of it) to take notice & to informe me howe he likes my cowncell concerninge more vniversall Interestes & principles, & not narrowinge a mans sowle to any one man or party

I haue writte to him allsoe concerninge Winchelsey,[76] I cannot in large on it; Yf you come not downe this weeke, I pray afford a woorde by the poste, yf you doe come downe, I wowlde be glade to meete you in your passage

163 *Culpeper to Hartlib, 16 August 1648. (13/237–8)*

Mr Hartlib,

your letter laste weeke (by my false superscription) wente to Mr Westroe; (I hope) & not to Mr Boys; I reste confidente that (by this) my error is (vpon the deliuery of the letter) discouered & the letters exchanged between you, In that laste weekes letter to you i did (vpon some passages in your former letters from mr Petty) desire that hee wowlde take his owne liberty, eyther of goinge on to perfecte the Engine for Agriculture; or of quittinge the further thowghts of it, I doe nowe againe (vpon your laste weekes letter) reiterate the same thowghts, yet still soe, as that (in what is eyther paste or to come), I may bear

---

[71] Colchester was held under seige by the army of Lord Fairfax and surrendered in late August – CSPD (1648–9), p. 260; Gardiner, iv. 153, 198, 201–02.

[72] The Prince of Wales was expected to sail from the Netherlands where he had been joined by some of the ships which had mutinied at The Downs – B. Capp, *Cromwell's Navy; The Fleet and the English Revolution 1648–1660* (Oxford, 1989), pp. 32–5. For the mutiny see **160** (25 July 1648).

[73] Cromwell and his forces had been in Wales and were currently in the West Riding of Yorkshire – *The Writings and Speeches of Oliver Cromwell*, ed. W. C. Abbott, 4 vols (Cambridge, Mass., 1939–47), i. 609–28.

[74] Hamilton's army had crossed the border and moved into Lancashire – CSPD (1648–9), p. 192; Abbott, *Speeches of ... Cromwell* i. 630–32.

[75] John Boys, MP for the county of Kent.

[76] Culpeper may have been hoping to succeed Henry Oxinden as MP for Winchelsea. Oxinden was eventually secluded at Pride's Purge.

the whole charge, & mr Petty to be at noe other expence then of his time & thowghts, which (whether the thinge proue or noe) I shall holde more valuable then a little mony; & therefore muste (after all) still remaine his debter for his kindenes; I writte allsoe in my laste, that yf Mr Petty wente forwarde with it I showlde (vpon your intimation) take order for suche proportion of mony as shall be farther wantinge, & this I am still ready (vpon your summons) to doe; As for the consequences of the engine, in case it proue, I am stil moste confidente of them; & shall therefore (as I haue formerly expressed my selfe) not spare my purse yf Mr Petty shall thincke goode to contribute his thowghts, yet still soe as to leaue him to his liberty, in case it coste him more then, he accowntes the thinge woorthe; yf the Scottes, Northerne, & Essex affayres ende well; I shall not feare but the Citty will at laste returne towards theire former Intereste; And yf the Citty be once righted, the Reformadoes[77] will not continue soe trowble some, & the marriners (by the Citties ingagemente of them in the behalfe of trade) will be reduced, thowgh I holde this laste, of the marriners, to be the woorst busines that haue befallen the [Parl*iament*], & yet not incurable, yf the parliamenteeres, can (according to [S*ain*t] Paule) thowgh of differente judgementes, holde the vnity of the Spirite in the bonde of peace; I dare say that the charity of men, of differente judgementes (in bearing with one another) is the hygheste pointe of Christianity between man & man, – The greateste of them is Charity;[78] But I dare withall say, that it is allsoe beste prudence, & that it was by that one rule cheefely (of bearing with one another thowgh of differente judgemente) that our nayghbor prouinces, haue succeeded soe well againste theire Tirante; And, it is true that the [K*ing*] of Spaine[79] had his natiue [K*ing*dome], still entire, & the treasure of the Indies to boote, againste a fewe & contemptible prouinces, but yf the [Parl*iament*] wowld study theire true Intereste of vnion, by the vnitinge or accommodatinge of all Interests, the Intereste of the 2: Nations in a [Parl*iamentary*] vnion, eache nation sendinge delegates to the [Parl*iament*] according to theire contribution towards [publi*que*] charges; the Intereste of Religions or opinions within the nation by a harmelesse liberty granted to all suche, as shall cordially joine in the true Nationall Intereste but aboue all the Intereste of the People in a power of consultinge & establishinge (from time to time) theire owne happines, by the major parte of a frequente, powerfull, & freely chosene Representatiue, yf these Interestes (I say) were helde forthe, it wowld strike a greater coldenes to the hearts of the Common

[77] Disbanded soldiers, who petitioned the Lords in June 1648 about arrears of pay and neglect by the Parliament – LJ, x. 301, 347, 351; CSPD (1648–9), pp. 248–49.
[78] 1 Corinthians 13:13.
[79] i.e. Philip II of Spain.

enimy, then Cromwells swoorde, I pray (yf Mr Boyles be come to towne) remember me concerning the treatise of the clouer seede

I am glad (as I write in my laste) for what is (probably) like to happen to mr Woorsly & Morian, but yet I conceiue that thowghe the Menstruum vniversale be gained, there remaines yet the greateste difficulty, of puttinge it in to motion, & I apprehende that that woorke consiste not in any one matter, but in a way of puttinge nature into motion in any matter For calor et siccitus (saythe Treuisan)[80] sunte in excitatione sua sulphure; – Quum excitationem (saythe Zengiuode)[81] nouerante viri philosophi; Naturall heate is sulphur indeede, but it muste be vnderstoode in its excitation; Farewell:

164   *Culpeper to Hartlib, 23 August 1648.   (13/239–40)*

Mr Hartlib,

I hope you haue (by this) or will receiue your miscarried letter from mr Boys or mr Westroe; I haue giuen [Col*onel*] Blunte[82] directions to you; yf he visite you, I pray vse him kindly, & (as from my desires) presente him with the office of Addresse; When I come to London, I shall be admitted to the sight of his ingenuities, & haue my choyce of them -

In answere to mr Demmockes proposition[83] 1: 160: acres of plowed lande is more than I knowe in any one mans hande in this Cowntry; 2: For an incerteine gaine & vpon a projecte, there muste be 30:[l] cleare spente in Instruments, be sides the hazarde of a newe way, vpon which (thowgh a man may try a little, yet) none will be induced to hazarde his whole yeeres croppe, beinge the producte not onely of his lande but of his stocke & paynes; 3: the recompence proposed amowntes not

---

[80] Bernhardus, Count of Trevigo [Trevisanus], (1406–1490) – Ferguson, *Bibliotheca Chemica*, i. 100–105.

[81] [M. Sendivogius], *Novum Lumen Chymicum e naturae fonte et manuali experientia depromptum in duas partes divisum . . .* (1628), p. 158.

[82] Colonel Blunt was an agricultural inventor who lived not far from Blackheath. Hartlib was not entirely convinced of the altruism behind his endeavours: '. . .hee is all for himself and not the Publick' – *Ephemerides* (1649) – 31/22/39B.

[83] Much of Dymock's proposal was contained in his letter to Hartlib of 15 August 1648 – 62/50/1A-B. He proposed to conduct a controlled experiment of the success of his new methods of arable cultivation. Three parcels of land, each over 20 acres would be chosen close by the farm chosen for the experiment. These three parcels would be sown with identical grain in the usual way and their yield compared with that obtained on the experimental farm where Dymock's methods would be applied for a season. Dymock stipulated that the farm in question had to be a minimum of 160 acres and that Dymock would be allowed to keep half the difference in the yield as the reward for conducting the experiment, the remainder being left to the farmer who would conduct the experiment and invest in the new machinery.

to soe muche as the Instrumentes (yf I vnderstande you aright) but onely the halfe of that gaine which very fewe will soe farre beleeue, as to manifeste theire faythe by theire woorkes

These are the presente objections I make

Of mr Petty you will see my minde by this inclosed, which I pray seale & deliuer to him

I am extraordinarily taken with your Experimentall essay concerninge our Lawes,[84] & wishe there might be a concentration of mens thowghts on that subjecte, I conceiue you doe very well to searche him out

I see the [House] of Lords holde the [House] of Commons hands whilste the Citty buffets them;[85] but those brattes of Babylon muste be dashed againste the stones

I still joy at the hopes to see our Frenche Turcke bayted, & doe nowe hope (by your laste letter) that the [Parliament] of Paris hathe passed the Rubicon,[86]

I tolde you in a former letter that my Woade man, in stead of teachinge me his arte hathe cheated me of my mony, & this (truly) is the beste accownte I can giue

I heartily wishe for mr Dury-s booke; my deuoyrs to those frinds when you see them

The treatis of the clouer grasse seede

With my beste wishe I reste

165　*Culpeper to Hartlib, 30 August 1648.　(13/241–2)*

Mr Hartlib,

　　I am very glad monsieur Pruuoste lookes backe towards

[84] The pamphlet Culpeper here refers to is probably *An Experimental Essay Touching the Reformation of the Lawes of England* (17 August 1648), Wing Thomason, E3880 E.549 (20), which Hartlib was clearly sufficiently interested in to enquire further of its author. Sir Balthazar Gerbier, writing from Paris on 24 October 1648 [NS], had evidently read it too: 'I have seene the printed Essay touching the reformation of the Lawes of England' – 10/2/19A.

[85] Culpeper refers to the compromise agreement between the House of Lords and the House of Commons on the question of negotiations with the king, agreed on 1 August, and the presbyterian dissension within the City of London, evident in a petition to the Commons asking for the liberation of the king and an immediate cease-fire – Gardiner, iv. pp. 172–73.

[86] Culpeper refers to the terms drawn up by the Chambre St Louis of the *parlement* of Paris in July 1648. The Rubicon for the Fronde would, in reality, be the Day of Barricades, 26–28 August 1648 [NS].

Englande;[87] my wishes are that (by your nexte letters) you wowlde desire him to renownce his resolutions of puttinge the [Parl*iament*] vpon that hygheste of Impositions of disposinge of euery priuate mans lande, thowgh to the priuate mans goode, The former monsters (in the [K*ings*] time) haue (by cominge still vnder that notion) made it moste hatefull to this nation; This I write not, in relation to any thowghts of my owne but what (I am confidente) the thowghts of others will bee; Yf this knotte were cleared, I showlde indeauor & hope to procure an honorable call for them, & suche an one as might ende (I hope) in theire contente & the happines of this nation

Mr Petty (in his laste) resolues to finishe his Engine of Agriculture, but directes me not, what mony I showlde sende him, I pray let me knowe by the poste & he shall not fayle by the very nexte; I am nowe goinge to sowe my Season, & therefore wishe it done that I might nowe trie it, & yf (when it is done) mr Petty continue his desire of seeinge it goe, he shall be very wellcome to me, & I shall when he will send a horse for him to Grauesend

The engine (when once perfected) may be shipped vpon a milton Hoygh[88] belonginge to one Vsher, or yf he be absente, one mr Tomkinson a corne seller at Queene Lyne will (in my behalfe) directe the shippinge of it

My beste respectes to Mr Petty; My service to mr Boyle, & remember his booke of Clouer seede

166   *Copy letters, John Dury to Culpeper & Culpeper to Dury, 25 September 1648.   (12/23–26)*

Sir cheny:
I Conceive that the difficultie which my Lady Ranalaugh did propose unto me concerning Mounsieur Pruvosts ordinance which should be

---

[87] Hartlib had evidently reported to Culpeper the contents of Pierre Le Pruvost's letter to him of 11 August 1648. In it, Le Pruvost explained that his attempt to interest the Duke of Brandenburg in his schemes for economic regeneration had completely failed: 'Il semble quil veult tenir nos gens et come ses vilageois en Esclauage Et continuer sa nourriture de sanglier par miliers [. . .] a la destruction de son pays Tout son peuple est pour nous mais son grand veneur[s] auec deux ou trois fauoris le tiennent en leurs mains comme nostre Cardinal [*Richelieu*] tenoyt Loys 13me'. Le Pruvost looked to Sir William Waller as the leading instrument to press the case for his scheme before the English Parliament – 7/119/1A-B.

[88] i.e. a hoy, or small coastal sloop, from the small harbour on the Thames estuary at Milton.

past in the Houses to in vite him againe hither may be thus removed.[89]
Let the Trustees who shall bee appointed to Regulat matters by his
advice; bee limited and instructed not to alter the fundamentall way of
trading in staple comodities which this nation doth send abroad to
other countries; [&.?] this clause may bee inserted as a Proviso in the
Ordinance it selfe; but as for all other comodities which are brought
in hither from other Countryes which some particular men doe engrosse
for privat advantage; or other commodities which are scarse, and in
the handes only of some few, who keep the markets at a deare rate; as
Fish, which might bee a staple commoditie of this nation farre more
iustly & easily then it is of Holland (who take all their fish on our coasts
for want of Industrie in us) I say all such commodities which now are
not staple but may become such; by his contrivance of multiplying the
same and selling the overplus abroad as the Hollanders doe againe I
say that all such commodities now not staple amongst us, which he
can make staple; if he encreaseth the quantity of them soe, as to make
us furnish our neighbours with them, wheras now we are forced to buy
them from them: whatsoever hee shall alter in the way of Trade about
them must not bee counted a fundamentall alteration, or if it bee, it
must bee allowed and counted a change for the better for if now the
most part of the handes and stockes of the Kingdome are either
altogether Idle and useles, or not improoved to what they may be if he
shew a way to set them all a worke and make them [<H: more>]
profitable; will not this bee an alteration for the better? & what although
even in the most staple Commodities of this kingdome as Cloath Tinne
and Leade &c. there should be an alteration in the way of Trading but
evidently for the better what prejudice could this bee? therefore I
conceive that the staple commodities which are now setled into Corporations for trade throughout the Kingdome may bee excepted
expresly in the ordinance; and that the Trade with which the Trustees
by Mounsieur Pruvost his advice should medle, should bee only of
Commodities which are not now staple but by his industrie may bee
made such; either by the improovment of Fishing or by the foundation
of the Plantation and improovment of Husbandrie this is one way to
prevent this objection. another way may bee this, to oblige Mounsieur
Pruvost to deale in the presence of the Trustees, with all those that
pretend to an interest or a right to any trade; to give them iust
satisfaction that they may not complaine of any wrong done unto
them & that hee may make it appeare that all the profit which they

---

[89] Dury was once more a key figure in the efforts to attract Pierre Le Pruvost to come
to England again. He translated his letter of 11 August 1648 and was involved in various
efforts to persuade individual members of Parliament to lend their support to the
proposed Parliamentary ordinance to invite him to return – 7/119/3A-B.

can hope for in a setled and just way, shall bee secured unto them only that without their least damage, nay with their greater benefit then ordinarily, they can expect, the public (which is now prejudiced by their way of trading) may be advantaged also. which was that which he offered to the fish Merchants; & would have hadde a conference before the Gentelmen that were committed upon his buisnes which the chief merchands that have monopolized that trade but he could never come to any meeting with them about it for they would accept of noe offers nor did the Comittee call for any of them to conferre with Mounsieur Pruvost about the buisnes; but if the Trustees bee ordered by the Houses to heare and judge of such debates as these for the ordering of Trade in all commodities which are not staple; then I supose there can bee noe cause of any such jealousie as is conceived by what I heard from yow by my Ladyes report. I wish I could have seene yow whiles I was at London and conferred with yow about this and other matters the Lord direct yow in all yowr wayes

Mr Dury

I give yow very many thanks for your letter which (by it 2 expedientes but especially by the last) hath given me ample sattisfaction & in truth if Mounsieur Prvvost can demonstrate how the Merchants may gaine more (in proportion to what they venture) upon the staple Commodities of this Kingdome managed as Mounsieur Pruvost would direct then the subtilest of them doe the ordinary way, and with all that the rest of the Kingdome (though monyed men only and not Merchants might yet doe the like, I can see noe better reason, why those Monopolists, should [deire.?], or the State suffer that (even in staple Commodities) there might not be a change for the best. But now this Answer leads me to another Question which I made to my Lady,[90] as that which transcends or passes through all his severall propositions, The Question is this. How the certainty per centum which is disigned to the private adventurer, and the surplusage which is designed to the [parliament] will be secured to them, at least till time and experience have raysed a good opinion of what is proposed, For (I conceive) it can not bee expected that at the begining, & before the buisnes be fully experimented, that either the publique or Privat will leave a certeine or setled way, for a new and vnexperimented one, though perhaps hold forth upon rationall grounds; my owne thought made the first Quere concerning the private person both for the principall and yearly proffit, and this afternoone a Parl: man made the second as thinking it vnlikly that the Public would forgoe their customes and other Impostes for a

---

[90] Katherine, Lady Ranelagh?

remaynder after 20 lb per centum, that was the summe I proposed to the Privat Adventurer.

The answere I made to myselfe and the [parliament] man, was that I conceived that they who proposed the buisnes would let their owne stocke bee a securitie to both, as farre as it would goe, This expedient I proposed, till yow could [<*H?:* hold>] forth a better. This I am confident of that (without some security at the begining) reason (be it never soe strong) will hardly draw mony out of mens coffers. I pray afford me an answer (at your convenience to these last Queries.

167   *Culpeper to Hartlib, 4 October 1648.   (13/243)*

Mr Hartlib

I pray fauor me soe muche as to conveygh this inclose to my Lady Hraunalage[91] & (yf she please to write an answer) to sende it to me this returne

I perceiue that I am to expecte from mr Petty that (yf I will not submitte to his conditions of an after proposition) he will indeauor to showlder me out of my owne designe; Yf his demandes had beene at firste proposed, I had eyther subbmitted to them, or (without trowblinge mr Petty), haue reserued my owne designe to my owne thowghts; Nowe, I haue opened the designe & my thowghts concerninge it, I haue disbursed my monyes & am ready upon reasonable conditions to disburse more, & claime but my share in that which was wholy myne; but (it showld seeme) is not enowght, except I take suche conditions as are imposed;

I am sorry mr Petty fayles soe muche towards me, & am confidente he will little aduance his owne endes by these wayes

168   *Culpeper to Hartlib, 11 October 1648.   (13/244-5)*

Sir

I haue onely time to tell you that I cannot inlarge; Since you sente not my letter to my Lady Harawnalagh[92] laste thursday, I wishe, it had not gone, for my Wife (very Wooman like) is changed in her presente resolutions concerninge a London life; my humble seruice to that noble company; I am sorry I cannot agree to but muste suffer from mr Petty,

For the inclosed paper all that I can say is that I haue soe little good

[91] Ibid.
[92] Ibid.

fortune in the company of these ingenuous men that I shall not ouer fondly, shut vp with any more, where my plaine meaninge proues ill matched; I reste

169   *Culpeper to Hartlib, 1 November 1648.   (13/246–7)*

Mr Hartlib;

I haue beene at home this laste fortnight, but (to confesse the truthe) Mr Petty his late carriage, & and that [Mons*ieur*] Glauberus is like to turne a Wheeler, hathe bred in me a resolution, not to trowble my thowghts any farther with these kinde of people, & in truthe, the peece of ingenuity mentioned in your laste, muste haue rarer qualities then I can yet apprehende, to give a change to these my thowghts

Wee heartily longe heere for the issue of the treaty;[93] howe the army stande; & what consequentiall hopes or feares are conceiued from bothe; A true vniversall intereste helde out by the [Parl*iament*]; passed by the [K*ing*], & consented vpon by the whole People by a mutuall ingagemente, were the onely way to restore this poore distracted [K*ing*dome]; But this Intereste muste be suche & soe vniversall, as neyther [K*ing*] nor [Parl*iament*] wowlde like; & (in truthe) I finde that in Ciuill gouernmente as well as in religion, there are seuerall sortes of benefactors that obtrude them selues vncalled for, but that vnum necessarium of mens saluation in one or the peoples good in the other is the thinge leaste regarded; These in theire way are of the sorte of those ingenuous men in the firste parte of my letter moste of whose ingenuity consistes in other mens purses and theire owne interestes;

I shall be in towne some time next weeke meanwhile afford the newe of the weeke to [Your affectionate friend etc]

---

[93] The negotiations for the Treaty of Newport began in September 1648 – Gardiner, iv. 214.

1649

Culpeper to Hartlib, 31 January 1648[?9]. (*13/248–9*)

Mr Hartlib,

the Holingburne carrier goes not this weeke soe that (yf you will oblige me with newes in this Crisis of time), you will sende your letters to Billingsgate for the Ashforde or Lenham carrier with directions to be lefte for me at Leedes parcke gate;

I receiued a packette from you on saterday was seuen night but but nothinge in writinge

I muste perfecte mr Dimocks papers[1] to you when I come to London, which (I thincke will be shortly

By way of shorte answere to your paper, I shall (without consideringe the circumstances of this present [Parl*iament*]) say of a [Parl*iament*] in Generall, that it was that firste ordinance of man in this [K*ing*dome] by which all others were made it is that ordinance which cannot change those super or preparliamentary constitutions which were (at firste) made by the People concerninge [its*elf*], for suche pre or superparliamentary ordinances muste be acknowledged excepte like the hogges wee will eate the acornes & not consider the tree, nowe what was & must neede be settled by a superparliamentary power cannot be eyther changed by a Parliamentary eyther concession or interpretation, & yf nowe it be a question whoe makes up the [Parl*iament*] or what the [Parl*iament*] can doe, the answere muste be that in respecte of the [Parl*iament*] none can be judges but they that made it, but in respect of all priuate persons or inferiour magistracies constituted by [Parl*iament*], the [Parl*iament*] it selfe is the proper judge, thus the rule holdes true Eius est interpretare cuius fait condere;[2] They that made the [Parl*iament*] can tell it what power they gaue it & what they reserued; The [Parl*iament*] can tell all inferior magistracyes what power they gaue them & what they reserued, nor can any inferior question the superior way of proceedings

[*PS.*] The [K*ing*] is noe partie to but a parte of the gouernment; The People cannot be called a party, but a body consultinge its owne good

---

[1] Culpeper had returned some of Dymock's work to Hartlib with **156** (6 July 1648) and provided some comments on it in **164** (23 August 1648). He is probably referring to a list of queries on Dymock's ideas for agricultural innovation to which Dymock wrote replies in a letter to Hartlib of 11 June 1649 – 64/14/1–3.

[2] 'It is for the founder to give the interpretation'.

171   *Culpeper to Hartlib, 28 February 1648/9.   (13/250–1)*

Mr Hartlib,

    I muste deferre my opinion of your breade & booke[3] till my cominge to London, which muste be suddenly; & in the meane time, onely in generall say, that the parte of Christians in this worlde is to rule & ouercome by example & sufferinge, & that the Lyon will then, & not before lye downe with the Lambe, not when the Lambe growes powerfull (for that will neuer be) but when the Lyon growews ingenuous & (keepinge onely the name) ceases to haue the nature of a Lyon, this God can doe; & (thowgh it be marueylous in our eyes), he is moste likely to bringe it to passe when all the world (as nowe) are become Lyons in deuowringe one another; & this I conceiue Hee will doe by woorkinge vpon the hearts of Lyons by the example of the harmles innocente Lambe; & thus will Gods glory be seene in bringinge peace, order & harmony out of Warre, confusion, & discorde, & in the Lambes victory vpon the Lyon by turning not destroyinge him, & that by its example of Christian patience & suffering; not by warre & bloode, & yf I cowlde see some some of these signes, & I showlde looke vpon them as the sygnes of the cominge of the Sonne of Man the seconde time,[4] but soe longe as our Apostles, whether Papall, Episcopall, Presbiteriall, Independent et cæt convert men by the Ciuill; not the Spirituall Sworde, & (leauinge theire cheefe duty of watchinge) apply themselues, onely to a weekely taske of Science, falsely soe called, I haue little hope to see the signe of the Sonne of man, I pray bwy & reade a little pamphlet of one Salmon a member or the army & shewe it the noble Lady:[5]

[*PS.*] I pray let me heare from you on fryday

172   *Culpeper to Hartlib, 4 April 1649.   (13/252)*

Mr Hartlib;

    are discourses (when wee meete) are soe various, as that I remember not soe muche as the subjecte wee were vpon, when wee

---

[3] Probably Hartlib's *Londons Charitie* . . . , (1649), Wing H992.

[4] On Culpeper's millenarianism, see GI, pp. 6, 77, 509.

[5] Joseph Salmon, *A Rout, A Rout; or some part of the Armies Quarters beaten up, by the Day of the Lord stealing upon them*, ([10 February] 1649), Wing S416 Thomason, E.542 (5). Culpeper wants the pamphlet shown to Lady Ranelagh.

met at Sommerset house,[6] but nexte weeke, I shall be in London; & then you may giue me the Q: of our discourse

I misse the two bookes which I lente to mr Woorsly, & (as I remember) he appointed to leaue them with you, I pray (yf you can) give me an accownte of them.

These forreigne agreemente make me apprehende the woorste,[7] nor can there be stronge opposition made by vs, yf not vnited; nor wee vnited, but in the Common Intereste, of Liberty & Iustice; nor that be obtained, soe longe as wee change, the persons onely, not the tyrranny; nor can wee hope to be ridde of tirranny, till men, that knowe howe to conquer others, can afterwards conquer & deny themselues; in the greatnes they haue gotte, nay (yf theire Cowntry call for it) in theire owne safety but, durus este hic sermo; & therefore I thincke that there are more calamities to succeede, & that those that will not woorke by vnion of Interestes, & by justice, will (thowgh with difficulty & bloode) Follow some that haue gone before; For the stone will not leaue rollinge & the woorke of God will aduance, eyther by, or vpon those that intereste themselues in it

173 *Culpeper to Hartlib, 4 July 1649. (13/254–5)*

Mr Hartlib

I pray (by this return) giue me credit for an Antimony cup;[8] & yf you can learne where they are to be had & (where you bwy it) learne the quantity of time & of the liquor in which it owght to infuse, & what other circumstances you finde woorthe knowledge; I pray enquire where I may haue Glauberus his glasses grownde that they may fitte very close, one into another for I finde it the life of his way of distillinge

I fownde (at the glasse house yesterday) a remainder of some of

---

[6] Somerset House on the Strand was the first Renaissance palace in England and had been built for Lord Protector Somerset in 1547–50. In 1625, the house had been given to Henrietta Maria and named Denmark House; but, in 1645, she left for the Netherlands and it was taken over by the Parliamentarians and once more renamed Somerset House. (*The London Encyclopaedia*, eds. B. Weinreb and C. Hibbert (1983), pp. 795–97).

[7] Charles II's acceptance at The Hague of Ormond's invitation to lead the Irish Royalists and, possibly, Montrose's agreement with Denmark for material support of a royalist invasion – Gardiner, *CW*, i. 18–19; 67–68.

[8] In Hartlib's *Ephemerides* for 1649 there are various allusions to Antimony cups – e.g. 28/1/25B. In this case, Culpeper seems to have wanted it for the cure of his horse. Antimony cups were especially developed by German monks in the sixteenth and seventeenth centuries – J. Newton Friend, *Man and the Chemical Elements: from Stone-Age Hearths to the Cyclotron* (1951), pp. 82–87.

Glauberus his distillinge glasse herefore bespoken & lefte by Keffler;[9]
the glasses did not fit into one another, but I was there tolde that a
man that imployed by Keffler (and is synce gone with him) did grinde
them for him; Glawberus himselfe in his firste booke & in his chapter
of vessells, promises to discouer the manner of it in his 3^d or $4:^{th}$ booke,
but those are not yet translated;[10] & yet methinckes some Dutche man
might resorte to that booke & chapter; yf I cowlde be resolued whether
I cowlde be fitted in this pointe, I showld eyther trowble you farther
or (perhaps) come to London my selfe & fitte my selfe with furnaces &
seuerall materialls to be distilled; for truly (vpon second readinge of the
booke, I finde a ready way to more discoueries of nature by owtwarde
fire onely, than hathe beene heeretofore helde forthe by any, but, in
philosophy as well as Christianity, it is the inwarde fire or Spirit, to
which wee owght principally to looke & this inwarde spirite yf excited
into motion, will make life to diffuse from the center to the owtwarde
parts; Oh where wowlde this diuinity & phylosophy ende, this other of
Glauberus is, but to discouer, not to exalte, what wee finde in nature:[11]

174   *Culpeper to Hartlib, 19 July 1649.*   *(13/256–7)*

Mr Hartlib,
    vpon viewe of my Traitte du sel et de feu,[12] I finde my selfe
deceiued & that I haue not the authors Traitte de l'or et de ver[13]; &
nowe am as desirous as yourselfe, to get it, yf it be to be had[14]
    I pray inquire what you can whether the Antimony Cup & the

---

[9] Like Culpeper, Johann Siebert Küffeler also had problems with Glauber's glassware –
Clucas, p. 152; GI, pp. 78, 388–91; J. J. O'Brien, 'Samuel Hartlib's Influence on Robert
Boyle's Scientific Development – Part II, Boyle in Oxford', *Annals of Science*, 21 (1965),
266; C. Webster, SHAL, p. 62; G. H. Turnbull, 'Oliver Cromwell's College at Durham',
Durham Research Review, 3 (1952), 17. For descriptions of Küffeler's distillation procedures
see 39\2\18–20, 37–38, 43–44).

[10] Glauber's instructions on grinding glass stoppers were in the fifth part of the *Furni
novi philosophici oder Beschreibung einer Newerfundener Destillirkunst* (Amsterdam, 1646–49),
published in 1649, pp. 18–32. The English translation, begun by Culpeper, was not
completed and published until 1651.

[11] See Clucas, p. 152.

[12] Blaise de Vigenère, *Traité du feu et du sel* (Paris, 1618). This had been translated by
Edward Stephens and published in 1649 under the title *A discourse of Fire and Salt, discovering
many secret mysteries; as well philosophicall, as theologicall* (1649), Wing B3128.

[13] i.e. 'verre'.

[14] This treatise is referred to in Vigenère, p. 52 (English edition). It is perhaps on
account of a confusion that Hartlib wrote in the *Ephemerides*, 1649: 'Blaise de Vigenere'
Treatises besides of fire and salt Sir Cheney Culpeper said hee hath his 2 others of Gold
and Glasse wherein hee confesseth to bee many excellent things' – 28/1/20B.

Regulus of Antimony be the same;[15] yf (by them that knowe) you finde it soe, I heartily wishe, for a proportion of the Regulus, by the nexte occasion, I shall try it vpon a horse that hathe the Fashions;

I perceiue from Hollande that the Prince will (at his nowe being in France seeke to bringe on another treaty with Scotlande For the [Queen] is sicke & the [Queen] a Presbiterian will bee; & yf they can holde the Scotts, the Irishe, & some forreine nations in one hotchpot, then they will begin to hope;[16] Truly, the [Parliamentary] true Intereste were to mediate the turninge of the three nations into a confederacye like that of the Zwitsers,[17] with reseruation to euery nation; of its owne liberty, particular customes, & way of religion, This way hathe lesse of the nimrode, & standes muche more with justice & prudence; & is muche more like to holde, where euery nation hathe the others to helpe againste all common enimies, & none to oppresse them, & In this is man towardes man moste like to God himselfe

I pray sende your letters heereafter, by one Brackle a carrier of [Ashforde? *MS torn*], you will heare of him about Billingsgate; The letter to be lefte at Leedes parcke gate;

175   *Culpeper to Hartlib, 14 August 1649.*   *(13/260–1)*

Mr Hartlib;
          I shall be in London nexte weeke, & shall be glad to receiue from you suche communications, as you are not willinge to confide to paper;

I pray returne my seruice & thanckes to mr Woorsly, of whose cominge ouer, I am glad to heare, & more yet that I haue a place in his remembrance & good opinion, & (yf I may) shall gladly & thanckefully accepte his searches & translations concerninge Glauber: his ouens, & wayes of distillation; which I woonderfully [approue? *MS edge*] & may perhaps (yf it be not presumtion to say soe) be able to adde some small circumstances to his ingenuitye;[18]

But truly I must still say that this wrackinge of nature, is not the helpe that shee expectes from vs, but onely a puttinge her into reiterated

[15] The term 'regulus' was used by early chemists to refer to the metallic form of antimony, apparently on account of its ready combination with gold. – OED.

[16] In fact, Charles II did not arrive in France until February 1650 – Gardiner, *CW*, i. 194.

[17] Culpeper briefly envisaged the foundation of a British confederation similar to that between the Swiss cantons.

[18] Worsley would not, in fact, return to England from the Netherlands until the close of 1649 – He was evidently in London by 29 January 1650 according to the letter from Henry More to Hartlib in 18/1/25A.

newe motions, & that by suche rationall adaptations as irrationall nature is not capable of; Nature hauinge (in golde) arriued at her ayme, ende, or center, of simple puritye shee there doethe, nay muste set downe, For the wisdome of God in nature is suche as that Natura nihil facit frustra;[19] yf shee haue once attained her ende, shee there keepes an euerlastinge sabbothe; except (by an ingenuous artiste) shee bee (as it were) drawne backe from her center of reste; Now the better to discouer howe nature is put into a newe motion, it were well woorthe our consideration, what are natures endes in all her motions, & (by an vniversall consente of writers) wee shall finde them to be, selfe preseruation, & selfe increase, & this, as by a continuall increase of her owne vigour, soe allsoe by castinge forthe whatsoeuer hathe the nature of enmity againste her

Nowe yf these were her aymes in her firste motions, certeinly then yf wee wowlde haue her moue againe, wee muste giue her the same occasion, Whilste there was somethinge of an impure nature, lay within her dominions, shee continued in motion & action; Hauinge ouercome & caste forthe her enimies shee sits still without any further exaltinge of her selfe Hæc (this very separation or castinge foorthe of all impurity) est ratio quod videamus naturam illud (id est [aurum]) in melius vltra non transmutare, saythe Dionisus Zachary;[20] And this certeinly shews theire greate error, whoe are soe intentiue in theire mannuall purifications where as I dare vndertake to make it good, that without an apposition of impurity (rightly chosen) there can nothinge be done in that woorke & thus farre Pontanus[21] agrees with me that, Hee that separates any thinge from the matter; as thinckinge it necessary, knowes nothinge of the woorke; And truly it is vpon these & the like consideration, (touched very sparingly in the bookes) that I haue insisted, nowe these many yeeres, beinge as confidently assured that these distractions & pullinge of nature to peeces, may perhappes be a meanes of our gettinge those rights which natures containes, in that simple perfection wherein wee finde her in all thinges; but that to exalte nature to the exurebancy which is attributed to the phylosophers stone; there needes onely suche a reincrudation as the seedes of the earthe receiue after theire autumnall ripenes; And yf (insteade of these subtile mannuall operations), wee wowld more obserue the intentions, wayes & actions of nature, wee might (without cumbringe our selues about many thinges) more easily attaine that vnum necessarium,

[19] 'Nature does nothing in vain'.

[20] Possibly citing [Denys Zacaire], *Opuscule tres-excellent de la vraye Philosophie naturelle des metaulx, traictant de l'augmentation & parfection d'iceulx* (Anvers, 1567 and later editions) – but this work was apparently never published in Latin and so Culpeper may be referring to another work attributed to Zacaire.

[21] This reference has not been precisely located.

that beste parte, which is soe muche & soe vniversally desired; I doe be fore I am aware too muche beate vpon this subjecte, as beinge that which I knowe mr Woorslyes ingenuity will finde finally woorthe its obseruation

For Wheeler, my thowghts are not muche changed concerninge him that he hathe excellente thinges, which yet from that weakenes & jealousie that dwell in him, will finally be loste[22]

Yf Pruuoste[23] be at Rotterdam, methinckes it might be noe harde matter to invite him (once againe) hether, & howeuer, I wishe that mr Dury wowlde indeauor to drawe from him some of his eocomicall contriuances, & especially the way howe the wealthe of the riche & the diligence of the poore might without cousenage or oppression be united to the contente of bothe;

I pray let me knowe what you meane by the [prosperity] of the [Parliament's] affayres in Irelande, synce townes are euery day loste or reported to be loste, the royall party thancke God, & [Cromwell] is not yet gone, I pray in large vpon it;[24]

176   *Culpeper to Hartlib, 15 August 1649.   (13/262-3)*

Mr Hartlib,
        my desires yesterday were to knowe what you meante by the prosperous affaires of Irelande; I haue synce vnderstoode of the greate blowe that hathe beene giuen to Ormonde;[25] & truly thowgh I can noe way concurre, with the presente preuaylinge party, excepte I cowlde see somethinge from them, towardes the settlinge of the nation, vpon

[22] See **94** (31 October 1645); **147** (18 January 1647[?8]); **151** (22 March 1647/8).

[23] Pierre le Pruvost had, by this date, retired to Rotterdam and was staying with M. Ancelin at the 'Wyn strate'. Some sense of his disappointment at the lack of success of his endeavours in England is apparent from a brief memorandum of 20 July 1649, explaining that his partner Hugh l'Amy had spent three months in London in 1645 in search of authorisation for their project. He himself had succeeded him some two months later and spent ten months there to no great effect (12/110A-B). As he wrote to John Dury on 10 September 1649: 'on dit que les francois se hastent trop et que les anglois sont trop longtemps a consulter et a s'apprester . . . ' – 12/27A.

[24] By mid-June 1649 the Royalist forces under Ormond were advancing on Dublin but on 26 July the parliamentary forces were reinforced with the arrival of troops from England. Rumours of Cromwell's imminent landing forced Ormond to detatch contingents of his army towards Munster. Being reduced in size, the remainder of his forces suffered defeat at Rathmines on 2 August and as a consequence Cromwell arrived in Ireland on 15 August unopposed – Gardiner, *CW*, i. 102, 106; *A New History of Ireland: iii Early Modern Ireland 1534–1691*, eds. T. W. Moody, F. X. Martin and F. J. Byrne (Oxford, 1976), pp. 336–53.

[25] James Butler, twelfth Earl and first Duke of Ormond, (1610–1688) – DNB. Presumably a reference to his defeat at Rathmines.

the fowndation; of a more equall & frequente representatiue, yet in respecte of those other more inveterated Nimrods I cannot but take my share of joy in the presente victory, as beinge confidente that (yf the royall party be humbled), those whoe are nowe at sterne will be more likely to returne to theire firste purity, or yf not, may yet be more hopefully dealte withall, then those others whoe beside 500: yeeres prescription, doe soe bedawbe their [King] with their sacred anno-intinges, & impertinente aplications of Scriptures, as in truthe it is difficulte to conceiue, howe the poore Cowntryman, (after hauinge beene soe many 100: yeeres conscience bownde towards these sacred & soueraygne peeces of Nimrodisme), showlde dare presume to vse soe muche of that reason which God hathe bestowed on them, as but to peepe into the rotten inside of these gaye, maiesticall, sared holyly annoynted outsides, with which the [Kings] & pristes of these times doe couer their nakednesses; But were the royall party layed lowe, it wowlde not be difficulte to finde the beginninge of the Churche & Civill Aristocracy in Scotlande, & very easy (without goinge to a conjurer) to finde the yeere when this party begun theire raygne, nor will the equity of an equall & frequente representatiue finde soe difficulte passage againste these newe setters vp; as againste those others in whose intereste wrong & oppression, is (by longe continuance) growne into a right, & the names of Gracious maiesty, our soveraygne Lorde, & the Lords annointed, haue taken the nature or (at leaste) the forme of realities in mens mindes ____

I cannot but hope that this blowe giuen to Ormonde will giue the [Parliament] side time, till nexte springe at leaste, to consider what they haue to doe; Yf strenght by sea, increase of trade, & (by Pruuostes or some other like proposition) the ease of the people in matter of taxes were seriously taken into consideration it wowlde more vnite our frinds & daunte our enimies, then our implacable & vnChristian hatred of one another doothe nowe rejoyce & giue them aduantage; Towards these good aymes, I shall (thowgh mony is not in greate plenty with me) be ready to contribute towards the charge of Pruuostes cominge ouer hether, soe that yf nothinge come of it, he shall yet loose onely his time

But yf they were invited, it wowlde be the beste way; And towards it my [Lord Chief] Justice[26] promised me to procure & send you somethinge from the Cowncell of State, And your selfe vndertooke that they showlde be tryed whether a ciuill invitation might not drawe them backe; I pray yf you have occasion to see my [Lord Chief] Iustice, that you wowlde together with my humble seruice presente him with what I write; With my affectionate wishes to you I reste

[26] Oliver St John.

177   *Culpeper to Hartlib, 21 August 1649.   (13/264/5)*

Mr Hartlib;
        I sente these two the laste weeke but they returned to my handes, by the carelesnes of those that showlde haue deliuered them to the carrier; I nowe inclose them to preuente repetition, & with all that you may see I did write

I am nowe put off from cominge to London till a little harueste which I haue be a little ouer, & therefore showlde be glad to receiue from you an intimation or taste of what you haue to say to me, when I shall see you

I take notice of late, of the greate vndertakinge, about drayninge the Fennes in Lyncolneshyre;[27] I pray, doe me the kyndenes to informe your selfe of the woorke whether it be substantially vndertaken, & what confidence there is of a goode returne; yf there were any printed mappes of the woorke I heartily desire one, mr Trencher is like to informe you; I feare the carrier is gone

178   *Culpeper to Hartlib, 29 August 1649.   (13/266–7 [summary only])*

There have been problems with the postal deliveries to Hartlib. His supervision of the harvest keeps him from London.   He asks Hartlib to enquire whether the committee for the management of Westminster School will have any lands to manage or just parsonages. If the former, Culpeper foresees a way of disposing of a difficult lease.

179   *Culpeper to Hartlib, 1 September 1649.   (13/268–9)*

Mr Hartlib,
        as my seruante writte you woorde, I receiued your letter on wednesday morninge laste, & your laste shorte one, yesternight, for bothe which I thancke you

In answere to your firste; I haue not yet made tryall of your Antimony, my horse beinge (before) otherwise cured

I heartily joy, in the reprintinge of Glauberus his bookes, with the

---

[27] 'An Act for drayning the Great Level of the Fens, extending itself into the Counties of Northampton, Norfolk, Suffolk, Lincoln, Cambridge, and Huntingdon, and the Isle of Ely, or some of them' was passed by Parliament on 25 May 1649 – CJ, vi. 219; F&R, ii. 130. Culpeper's interest was no doubt due to his possession of lands in Romney marshes.

additions you mention;[28] thowgh, the excitation; of the inwarde & centrall fire of thinges, which is the heauen dwellinge heare on earthe, & not the anatomizinge of them onely, by an owtwarde heate, is that which I study; hauinge (for a longe time) beene of this opinion, that in phylosophy, as well as in divinity; the principall regarde is to be had to the inwarde motions[29]

I doe not knowe, where it is, that I haue formerly hearde, of the way of makinge wines; I thincke it was from your selfe

I thancke Mr Woorsly for his kinde remembrances, but you vndertake, more for him, towardes me, then I deserue I haue not soe greate opinion of Wheelers inventions, as I haue still little, of his discretion to mannage them.

There is raysed suche a concentration of judgementes concerninge an American plantation, as truly, I am muche joyed, in the assurance of the greate change, it is like to make in Europe; still contributinge to the accomplishemente of the 67: Psalme;[30] it beinge demonstration to me, that (yf a plantation & trade were once nationally vndertaken in suche manner as hathe beene proposed by [mons*ieur*] Pruuoste), the nauigation wowlde be inconsiderable, which wowlde serue, to bringe the quintessences (as I may call them) of America into Europe, & (by this meanes) beate out all ꓥ Europe in their staple commodities, thus (necessarily) bringinge downe the valewe of our landes, in this parte of the worlde, & thus, (bothe in landes & in all the good creatures of God which proceedes from them); there will be a happy leuellinge, when to him that (of the thinges of this worlde) gathers little, there is noe lacke, & that he that gathers neuer soe muche (his nayghbors allsoe, hauinge enowght) hathe (as to the continuance of Babylon) nothinge ouer; I therefore muche rejoyce in Mr Duryes addresses to Pruuoste, nor is my joy without relation towardes Himselfe, in that I finde him noe suche narrowe Presbiterian, but that he can set himselfe, to the woorks of righteousnes & peace, euen in the middste of crooked & peruerse generations; still sowinge good seede, & trustinge God, that yf not nowe, wee shall yet, at the generall harueste, returne againe & bringe our sheaues with vs, restinge assured (in the meane time) that the kingdome of God is not meate & drincke (or thinges of the like nature), which recommende vs not to God, but righteousnes, & peace, &

---

[28] In 1649 the fifth and final part of Glauber's *Furni novi philosophici oder Beschreibung einer Newerfundener Destillirkunst* (Amsterdam, 1646–49) was published. However Culpeper more probably refers to the second edition of *Furni novi philosophici* published in Amsterdam from 1648 to 1650 in three volumes.

[29] As Clucas suggests, Culpeper began to take exception to Glauber's chemistry on philosophical grounds – Clucas, pp. 152–54.

[30] esp. Psalms 67:6 – 'Then shall the earth yield her increase; and God, even our own God, shall bless us'.

joy in the holy Ghoste, & that, in euery difference of opinion (still holdinge the fowndation, thowgh (perhaps) stubbe doe happen to be bwilte vpon it) as well as in euery nation, Hee that fearethe God, & woorkethe righteousnes, is accepted of Him; & that therefore wee showlde not judge one another any more, wee showlde not offende eyther Iewe or Gentiles (worse men (I am sure) wee cannot finde amonge one another) but rather (with [Saint] Pawle) be all thinges to all men, that, by all=meanes, wee might gaine some, walkinge by the same rule & beinge of the same minde in suche things as are reuealed, & (yf there be any thinge else), waytinge with loue & patience till God shall reueale that allsoe, all partyes beinge soe humble in the meane time as to remember that wee see but in parte, wee knowe but in parte; But to goe on

I shall be very happy in receiuinge any light from you concerninge the American plantations, & yf what you mention, may be confided, my seruante may transcribe it & I promise you, it shall be safely returned

I know the Fennes to be a greate busines, yf rightly carried on, but that of which I made a question, in my former letter, was, whether the woorke was soe carried on, as that it were like to continue, for (vpon my knowledge) it may be soe done as presently to decay againe, as it formerly hathe done

I showlde be glad to see the lande taxes taken of,[31] for the Cowntry man is like to judge of right or wronge, by his purse, rather then any other standarde

I muche desire an inlargemente concerninge the bancke you mention, for I apprehend mighty things from it[32]

---

[31] i.e. the monthly assessment on property, imposed as an expedient during the civil war. When the old assessment expired in March 1649, the Rump Parliament imposed a new one of £90,000 per month. See B. Worden, *The Rump Parliament, 1648–1653* (Cambridge, 1974), pp. 167–68.

[32] The allusion is to the proposal for a land bank, made by Henry Robinson in *Briefe Considerations concerning the Advancement of Trade and Navigation* (1649), Wing R1666. It was subsequently taken over and developed by William Potter, one of Hartlib's correspondents. Through the bank, Potter proposed that bills could be issued on the security of the registered land, and that these bills would then be payable at sight to the bearer. He subsequently published his scheme in *The Key of Wealth* (1650), Wing P3034 and then remodelled it in *The Trades-man's Jewel* (1650), Wing P3036. Potter's scheme was criticised in an anonymous essay printed at the end of Dymock's *A Discoverie for Division* (1653), Wing H985, sigs. E1ʳ-F1ʳ. Potter wrote further on a Bank of Lands and Hartlib published one of his essays in the *Legacy*, 'A Bank of Lands ... by Mr. William Potter ... on Improvement of Land', pp. 289–99. In 1649, both Culpeper and Dury had become interested in the operation of public banks through Henry Robinson's proposal – see *Ephemerides*, 1649 – 28/1/26A and 29B. Culpeper himself compared the operation of the banking system of Amsterdam with aspects of the Robinson/Potter proposal – 30/2/15–16.

The merchantes Cowrte is admirable, & the records or Rolles concerninge landes;[33] noe lesse; & yf there were the like allsoe, for bills bondes, et caet concerninge mony, there wowlde be two greate conveniences in it 1: the monied man wowlde be browght to pay to Churche, Poore, & State; 2: Deepely ingaged Debtors might thus be discouered, & soe not too muche credited

I cannot but hope that you will preuayle in your office of addresse & truly it will be a moste vniversall & braue busines, I intende to be in London nexte weeke

180 *Culpeper to Hartlib, 7 November 1649. (13/270–1)*

Mr Hartlib,
        I shall not be in towne till munday, & in the meane time showlde be glad (by your kindnes) to knowe howe the world jogges

I woonderfully joy that the taxes will be taken off, & the Excise relyed on;[34] concerninge which all I can advise is, that it be layed on all thinges that haue the nature of superfluity; <Reuel: 18: 12: 13:>[35] vpon all the marchandise of Babylon, & that it be layde upon nothing that serues for sobriety & necessity; & thus the riche or vayne man onely, shall beare the burden (those onely, whoe are the marchantes & bwyers of the Babilonishe wares), & those whoe are eyther poore, or (yf riche yet) soe sober as to liue to, or neere the necessity of nature, shall goe scot free

I reste in haste

---

[33] Sir Balthazar Gerbier had proposed to Hartlib in the summer of 1649 on his return from Paris the cataloguing and classifying of the Rolls series, as had also been proposed by the *parlement* of Paris. Hartlib suggested the use of Harrison's indexing system – *Ephemerides*, 1649 (28/1/20A-B). However, this, and the other allusions by Culpeper are probably to proposition emanating from Henry Robinson.

[34] The abandonment of the monthly assessment was rumoured through the summer of 1649 by the *Moderate Intelligencer* and other newspapers. The 'Act for the speedy raising and levyiung of Moneys by way of New Impost or Excise' of 14 August 1649 declared 'the Impost of Excise to be the most equal and indifferent levy that can be laid upon the People' – F&R, ii. p. 213.

[35] Revelation 19:12–13 – 'The merchandise of gold, and silver, and precious stones, and of pearls, and fine linen, and purple, and silk, and scarlet, and all thyine wood, and all manner vessels of ivory, and all manner vessels of most precious woods, and of brass, and iron, and marble. And cinnamon, and odours, and ointments, and frankincense, and wine, and oil, and fine flour, and wheat, and beasts, and sheep, and horses, and chariots, and slaves, and souls of men.'

1653–1657

181 *Copy notes on bees from Culpeper/Stirk, in Hartlib's hand, 14 February 1652/3. (55/3 [summary only])*

Culpeper comments on information elicited from George Stirke [Starkey] in New England about using molasses as a substitute for abstracted honey from beehives in order to overwinter the swarms.[1] English molasses were not as good as Barbados molasses because they were mixed with lime. He also provides observations on Starkey's suggestions for when to knock the bees out of the hive, and how to keep the overwintering colony protected.

182 *Culpeper to Hartlib, 18 February 1652/3, copy, with numerous Hartlib emendations. (39/1/5 [summary only])*

Culpeper tells Hartlib that a friend had described to him some twenty years previously an industrial process by which saltpetre was manufactured at Hamburg and then marketed to the Spanish military forces. He urges Hartlib to discover more about it. 'For I am perswaded that God wil goe beyonde the Diuell in his owne Materialls of Destruction, by Changinge the use of them into a blessinge, For that is moste agreeable to his Power & goodnes . . . '.[2]

---

[1] George Stirke [Starkey] (1628?-1680) – DSB, DNB. Starkey arrived in London from New England in November 1650 and met Hartlib for the first time in December. By 1653, Hartlib was actively collecting material for his miscellany of writings on beekeeping, *The Reformed Common-wealth of Bees* (1655), Wing H997. Starkey contributed two letters to the publication, giving information about the natural history of the Bermudas of relevance to apiculture (pp. 15–40). The small collection of Culpeper's surviving letters from the 1650s indicate his developing interest in bee-keeping – see, especially 26/29/49–50, which is a series of queries concerning the experimental bee-hive designed by William Mewe. See Timothy Raylor, 'Samuel Hartlib and the Commonwealth of Bees' in *Culture and Cultivation in early Modern England*, eds. Michael Leslie and Timothy Raylor (Leicester, 1992), ch. 5.

[2] There are numerous undated extracts amongst Hartlib's papers which report the success of the merchants in Hamburg in making and trading in saltpetre – see, e.g. 39/1/25–7.

1654

183   *Culpeper to Hartlib, 25 February 1653/4.   (13/272–3)*

Dr Browne[3] (towardes the profit to be made by bees) proposes two thinges of absolute necessitye (viz) Foode, & conveniente roome; His deficiency (as I apprehende) in the firste of these is that (without naminge any foode, as seuerall [other.?] awthors doe, & particularly Dr Chylde in his letter of Husbandry[4] lately printed by yourselfe) he leaue vs onely to what nature affords bothe for plantes & seasonable time for bees to gather in, & in bothe these particulars (to omitte others) there may be muche helpe giuen to nature; For the fashion of his hiues thowgh I muste commende it as very ingenuous, yet I shall (leauinge others liberty of judgemente & practise) say onely thus muche that the square figure may (vpon consideration) proue the beste in that there may better be placed a till or drawer in the bottome of it, into which (beinge drawne foorthe) there maye (from time to time) be foode layde for any particular hyve *w*ithout any disturbance, to or from the reste of the hyues; wher euery particular hyue, may (yf occasion requires) shutte up & fedd by itselfe (which in the orderinge of bees) may proue (many times of good concernemente[5]

For your other letters, (not to trowble my selfe with those metaphors &

---

[3] Thomas Brown, minister. Brown had told Hartlib of his experiments with bees in September 1652 and his work is mentioned in numerous notes made by Hartlib on beekeeping – *Ephemerides*, 22 September 1652 (28/2/34B; 26/29/43B and 58A). Culpeper is evidently referring to Brown's discourse which was published in *The Reformed Common-wealth of Bees* (1655), Wing H997, pp. 3–8.

[4] Robert Child (ca. 1613–1654) was the author of the 'Large Letter' in Hartlib's *Legacy* – see **150** (15 March 1647/8). The enlarged second edition of the *Legacy* [(1652), Wing H990], had recently been published and included Arnold Boate's 'Annotations upon the Legacie', pp. 103–18, and the anonymous 'Interrogatory relating … to the Husbandry and Natural History of Ireland', pp. [121]-[143] (sigs. R1ʳ-V1ʳ). Culpeper refers here to Child's discussion of beekeeping in his 'Large Letter' (*Legacy* (1652), Wing H990, pp. 46[49]-52).

[5] '*A Querie upon the description of Dr. Brown's new invented Bee-Hive*. Whether the square Figure may not prove the best, in that there may be placed a bill or drawer in the bottome of the Hive, into which (being drawn forth) there may from time to time be food laid for any particular Hive, without any disturbance to or from the rest of the Hives, where every particular Hive may (if occasion require) shut up and feed by it self, which in the ordering of Bees may prove many times of good concernment.' *The Reformed Common-wealth of Bees* (1655), Wing H997, p. 11[9] (sig. C1ʳ).

allegories, which I neyther vnderstande nor am concerned in)[6] I cannot but still heartily wishe, that eyther a modell were to be had accordinge to a true scale, or (which were better) directed to a place in this towne where wee might haue suche a hyue made, as wherein the whole waye of woorkinge of that little creature might be seene;[7] by which wee might (I am confidente) haue vnsophisticated wines of our owne, cheaper & better then from other nations[8]

But yf neyther suche a hyue, nor the module of one can be obtained, a desription yet wowlde be an obligation vpon those whoe study the quiet & good of this Commonwealthe in the aduance of the commonwealth of bees & suche other ingenuities; With my beste affections to you I reste

184 *Copy notes on Worsley's Discourse in Hartlib's hand, Culpeper, 10 July 1654. (39/2/14-17)*

Sir Ch. [Culp*eper*] observations upon
Mr Worsly's discourse[9]

[6] Timothy Raylor suggests that Culpeper's dislike of the elaborate, and potentially divisive, allegorical possibilities of bee-keeping reinforced Hartlib's own evasiveness and helps to explain why he was careful not to include such material in his eventual publication – Raylor, 'Commonwealth of bees', p. 112.

[7] The making of experimental hives to new designs, and incorporating glass observation panels, was an important feature of Hartlib's *The Reformed Common-wealth of Bees* (1655), Wing H997. In an undated note amongst Hartlib's papers there is an enthusiastic list of questions posed by Culpeper about the new hive of William Mewe, which had glass panels in it. Culpeper's first question is: 'A full description of the transparent hyue, in every parte of it; & (yf Mr Mewe haue anye to spare) that he will sende one to London by the Carrier which comes from his partes.' – 26/29/49A-50B. Raylor, 'Commonwealth of bees', pp. 101-05.

[8] Hartlib had sought to promote honey as an alternative to sugar. In his 'Large Letter' in Hartlib's *Legacy* Robert Child suggested that honey could be used to make wines and liquour – *Legacy* (1652), Wing H990, p. 52). Culpeper is echoing this hope which Raylor suggests dates back to the rise of English sugar consumption in the early Renaissance. (Timothy Raylor, 'Commonwealth of bees', p. 100).

[9] By this date, Benjamin Worsley was in Ireland. The 'Discourse' to which Culpeper refers survives only in an undated copy of it made by Cressy Dymock (42/1/26-27B) and which may have itself have been a response to an earlier (unascribed) letter forwarded to him for his comments from Culpeper. The argument in Worsley's 'Discourse' is required to make sense of Culpeper's reply, and to appreciate the vigour of the chemical discussions which were taking place within Hartlib's circle at this time.

Worsley begins with a disquisition on chemical nomenclature, pointing out that the use of terminology was particular imprecise, and particularly when it came to the uses of the term 'mercury'.

Worsley accepts the vegetative principles as applied to the chemical composition of metals: 'there is a participation of the same lyfe blessing vegitative & multiplicative virtue, as was given in the creation to plants & other seeds bearing boddyes'.

That key of putrefying Mettals – to bee found everywhere – and made by nature herselfe.

Q. Whether by the putrefying bee meant the Philosophical Worke, or a Worke of any other hight, then what Nature (in her owne operations without any helpe from Art) vses in all her Metalline and Mineral productions?[10]

Q. Whether a Menstruum of noe further hight or strenght then what nature only gives it, can cause a putrefaction of the Metals or Minerals. I mean such a Putrefaction as Ripley[11] intends when he says.

Thy Water must bee seven times sublimat
Else shal no kindly dissolution bee
Nor putrefying shalt thou now see
Nor liquid pitch nor colors appearing
For lack of fire within thy glasse working.[12]

Worsley further accepts that, at the heart of the chemical composition of metals there was an inward and spiritual mercury, sometimes called 'Sperma or Anima cuius libet Mettali'. When metals putrify or decay, the important constituent changes are within this spiritual mercury. Further, nothing transmutes by itself and it a complex and fundamental transformation involving sulphur in which new substances, 'sol' and 'luna' are formed.

So, when chemists claim to have extracted the 'mercury [*symbol*] currens' from a particular metal, they are deluding themselves if they think they have extracted the 'principium seu prima Materia Metallorum'. In particular, it is mistaken to imagine that Helmont's Alkahest, or universal solvent, can abstract the 'prima material' or 'principium Metallorum'. What he writes may suggest otherwise, but this is the problem of nomenclature and terminology.

The problem for chemists remains a fundamental one; 'noe man knowes or discernes this [symbol: *mercury*] & how to gett itt out of the Metalls vnlesse hee be first filius Artis Because alsoe this [symbol: *mercury*] is not to bee had without a prævious Colliquation, or Philosophicall putrifaction of the body out of which itt is to be extracted, This putrifaction is the great secret for this beeing not to bee made by any such thing as distroyes the crasis of the metall mutch less itts spiritt, or virtue of vegetation'. If ever located, this way will constitute the Menstruum Philosophorum, but it will only be made open to those who are pure of heart.

[10] The fundamental direction of Culpeper's critique is to question the degree to which what he propounded about the nature of the 'sperma' or 'prima materia' in the chemical composition of metals can properly be held to describe the observable properties and behaviour of metals within nature.

[11] George Ripley, Canon of Bridlington (1415–1490) – DNB. A complete edition of his works had appeared most recently from Kassel in 1649: *G. Riplaei … Opera omnia chemica*, ed. L. H. Combachius, (Cassellis, 1649).

[12] 'Thy water must be seauen times sublimate,
Else shall no kindly Dissolution bee,
Nor putrifying shalt thou none see;
Like liquid pitch, nor colours appearing
For lack of fire within the glasse working.'
George Ripley, *The Compound of Alchemy, or the ancient hidden Art Archemie … set forth by R. Rabbards*, (1591), STC 21057, sig. E1[r].

The Merc. of the Phil. is one thing.

The Acetum or Azoth of the [Philosophers] is another thing.[13]

Q. Whether the Merc. of the [Philosophers] (as it stands contra-distinguished from their Azoth) bee any other then the Mercury of Nature.

I doe not meane common mercury which never had or (as some [Philosophers] hold) or hath lost one necessary ingredient of its life and motion: but j meane such Mercury as Nature (being alone without the helpe of Art) vses in her Mineral Operations!

Q. Whether the Azoth Phil. mentioned here to bee of a much more active and potent vertue then the Mercury) bee any other thing then what is 6. 7. 8. 9. or 10. times sublimated by those Wise men of the East to whom the Star appeared, except by Azoth bee meant Flamels[14] black stinking Earth which comes after the winters putrifaction and which (afterwards in the next page) hee advises to bee devided into two Parts for operations (there) after mentioned.

None know's how to prepare the Azoth that discernes not how to handle and fix the Merc. Phil.

Q. Whether the fixing of the Merc. bee not per duplicem ignem?

Q. Whether that fixing bee not in Aurum or æs Phil?

Q. Whether towards the Azoth there bee required (in and from the beginning) more then a six weekes latter Spring immediatly before the darke and yet rainy winter comes on.

Hee who will be capable of discerning either of these must be able to discerne

1. that there is a real vegetative Life in Mettals equal to that in other Bodies.
2. wherein this life principally consists.
3. how to actuat this life, and how to make it a more living life.
4. the tendernes of it. What so destroyed it, as to spoile the Motion of it. What hinders it from a suscipiency of further Life.

Q. Whether all the Requisites to bee discerned here by a true [Phil-osopher] concernes not a certain Life, that ought bee in Mettals and Minerals as in other Bodies or Seedes?

Q. Whether the spoiling of the Motion of this Life, and the re-actuating of Life and Motion spoiled, doe not import a life which (though spoiled) may (toties quoties)[15] be restored to its Motion?

Q. Whether the spoiling Life of its motion can come by any thing then per defectum aut humiditatis or of some such other thing, which

---

[13] Azoth was another term employed by alchemists for the mercurial first principle in all metals. It was also the name given by Paracelsus to his universal remedy.

[14] i.e. Nicholas Flamel – *Nicholas Flammel, his exposition of the heiroglyphicall figures . . .* (1624), pp. 80–1.

[15] 'as occasion demands'.

some [Philosophers] call the Agent which is junctum materiæ. Quia
Natura non producit seipsam. Quercetan. contra Aubert. in Theat.
Chym. Vol.2. p.189. Et Dionis. Zachary in Volum. prim. Theatri
Chy. p.830. et 831.[16]

Q. Whether the principal meanes wherein this fore-mentioned Life of
Mettals and Minerals and the actuating or rather re-actuating) of
it consist's be not a re-apposition (toties quoties) of an humidity
that this life or Spirit of the Lord may have Waters to move in, or
of that fore-mentioned Agent without which. Ignis (saith
Sendivogius) est quietissimum Elementum nec movet nisi excitetur.
Quam Excitationem (saith that Author) noverunt viri Sapientes.[17]

Q. What is meant by the tendernes of the life fore-mentioned, for j
professe that j am here absolutely to seeke.

I shal add two Queries more emergent from my owne thoughts.

1. Q. What that or those things and operations are which Riply
mentions in his Ch. of Putrefaction
To ligge together six weeks let them have etc.
From the ground of their grave not rising that while
Which <NB.?> secret point doth many a one beguile.[18]

And in his Ch. of Sublimation.

Keepe it. – with temperat heate a downe
Full fourty day's till it wax black and brown
For then the Soule beginneth to come forth
From his owne veines. etc. etc.[19]

---

[16] These references are to the 1602 edition of the *Theatrum Chemicum* which appeared
in Ursel in 1602.

[17] Sendivogius, 'De sulphure' in *Musæum Hermeticum* (1678), p. 618.

[18] 'Therefore at the beginning our stone thou take,
 And burie each one in other within their graue,
 Then equally betwixt them a marriage make,
 To ligge together sixe weekes let them haue,
 Their feede conceiued, kindly to nourish and saue,
 From the ground of their graue not rising that while,
 Which secreat point doth many a one beguile.'
Ripley, *The Compound of Alchemy*, sig. F1ʳ.

[19] 'In *Sublimation* first beware of one thing,
 That thou sublime to the top of the vessell:
 For without violence thou shalt it not down bring
 Againe, but there it will abide and dwell,
 So it reioyceth with refrigeration I thee tell,
 Keepe it therefore with temperate heate adowne,
 Full fortie dayes, till it wexe blacke and browne.
 For then the soule beginneth to come out
 From his owne veynes, for all that subtill is
 Will with the spirite ascend withouten doubt,
 Beare in thy minde therefore, and think on this,
 How here eclipsed been thy bodies,

Cor. the .2. 7. 11.[20]

Behold this selfe same thing that yee sorrowed after a godly sort what a clearing of yourself it wrought in you? Yea what indignation? yea what vehement desire? yea what zeale? yea what revenge? etc.

Q. What these words may meane being applied to the Spirit and worke of Nature? and

Whether there bee not in Nature something that answers to Sin in the worke of Grace?/

185   *Culpeper to ?. n.d. [post 16 May 1654] ([summary only])*[21]

Culpeper is disappointed that clover-seed husbandry has been so badly received in Ireland. It is important to consider which components of the experiment with it failed. The three most common difficulties are with elderly seed, the wrong kind of soil and a poorly prepared tilth. The last, albeit less common, reason for crop failure lies in drought. He suggests a renewed experiment, stressing that, from his own and other people's experience, it will 'double and treble the profit or rent of the Land'. *On the other hand, if the crop is mown, it will* 'like Corn, impoverish the ground; so no man can eat his cake, and yet still have it'. *However, he intends to experiment with pasturing some sheep on a clover fields.* 'I have known already the experience of some who have this spring, (before there was any pasture elsewhere) kep 8 Sheep of an acre, which is double the proportion, which the best land in *Rumney Marsh* will bear'.

1655

186   *Copy [extract]: Culpeper to Hartlib, 3 June 1655 (with emendations by Hartlib).   (61/7/11)*

I thanke you heartily for y*our* <Reformed> Comon*wealth* of Bees and Virginian Silkworm: The busines of the Silke Wormes was notable

---

As they doe putrifie subliming more and more
Into water, vntill they be all vp ybore.'
Ripley, *The Compound of Alchemy*, sigs. H3ᵛ-H4ʳ.
[20] 2 Corinthians 7:11 – 'For behold this selfsame thing, that ye sorrowed after a godly sort, what carefulness it wrought in you, yea, what clearing of yourselves, yea, what indignation, yea, what fear, yea, what vehement desire, yea, what zeal, yea, what revenge! In all things ye have approved yourselves to be clear in this matter.'
[21] This letter is printed in the *Legacy*, pp. 248–9. It is possible that the letters printed on pp. 245–6 and 247 may also be from Culpeper.

from the beginning and (by your meanes vnder [God]) it is like to prove of notable consequence to that Plantation and this (j would say if j should not lye) Comonwealth: And truly the most of the rest of the hints are excellent and (if j mistake not) they fall vpon an Age are like to receive and bring forth the fruit of them. And this will proove a kind of besieging of Babilon in its Out-Workes; I meane in outward things by such a plenty of them, that the gatherer of little will have no lacke, and then they who for their exercise of Dominion are called Benefactors, will have nothing over that will deserve the titles of Majesty[*altered from* Majesties] Highness Grace *etc*. Oh that to these Discoveries were added the care of better Education of Children to a greater ingenuity of heart and head. It is a griefe to see, how little men have either of ingenuity in the vse of the Creature, or of honesty in the vse of their talent to a mutual good.

1656

187   *Copy [extract]: Culpeper to Hartlib, 13 October 1656.*   *(70/3/1–2)*

For the Germans fructifying Water, I have yet had noe Experience of it, but doe (:in my owne thoughts:) builde very much vpon the hinte I have taken from it, though (:as you know my manner is in like cases:) I shall not binde my selfe (:empirically:) to the Receipt;[22] Iohn Bate in his Book of the Mysteryes of art & nature, fol: 261. proposes the making of Salt-Peter, by the mosshing of qvick lime with warme water, then vapouring away the Water by the Sunne.[23] This proposition, (:beeing such, as some neighbours of mine have tried, & found to bee true, hath lately caused me first to rest assured, that the excellency of lime, the richest compost (:ordinarily

---

[22] There are various allusions to continental fertilizers amongst Hartlib's surviving papers, many of them based around the nitrogenous elements of saltpetre. This may relate to the entry in the *Ephemerides* for 1658 where Hartlib notes: 'There is a vniversal fructifying Compost of Lime of certain efficacy (for which a great price hath beene given by the Danish Ranzau) deservedly most highly to bee valewed, and by Sir Cheney Culpeper, to bee fully made out . . . ' – 29/7/14A.

[23] '*To make Saltpeter*. Take quick lyme, and pour water upon it, and let it stand six dayes, stirring it once or twice a day: take the cleere of this, and set in the Sunne untill it be wasted, and the Saltpeter will remain in the bottom.' – John Bate, *The Mysteryes of Nature and Art: conteined in foure severall tretises*, 2nd edition (1635), STC 1578, p. 261 (sig. 2L3').

knowne:) qvantity for qvantity, consistes in the Salt-peter that is in
it; In the second place to make a practicall & diligent searche &
observation, what qvantity of Salt-peter a loade of lime will yeelde:
which beeing found, (:I am confident:) will proove not above 1/20
parte of the Loade: And I am confident, that this 1/20 part beeing
improoved, according to the Parisian Experiment mentioned in your
Legacy, printed in the yeare 55. fol:110.[24] will (:at least:) eqvall your
Germans Receipt, & if the [*H. cleanest*], well chosen & soe steeped
could bee sowed at a fitting & just distance & depth: it would (:I
verily beleeve:) occasion our beginning to singe the 67. Psalme: &
(:as I once told you:) wounde the Divell with his owne Engine of
gunpowder.[25]

And this is the best answer, I can for the present give you: but shall
bee glad to learne of others.

1657

188   *Culpeper to Hartlib, 25 June 1657.*   *(13/274)*

Mr Hartlib;
          I thancke you for your husbandry receipte, which I shall trye, &
doubte not but (vpon the reason of it to improue
          I thancke you allsoe for your receipte for the piles; to which I (like
a bolde begger) craue the addition of the other
          I pray oblige me soe muche as to convaygh this inclosed to mr
Sletcher to be inclosed in his nexte packet to Hollande; I am (this
morning) leauinge the towne, & haue noe more time then to tell you
that I am

189   *Culpeper to Hartlib, 27 June 1657.*   *(13/275–6)*

Mr Hartlib,
          I thancke your for your seuerall receipts; I shall try that
concerninge the multiplyinge of corne, & (I veryly beleeue) shall
improue it, by some receipts (in the like kind) which I haue from your
selfe & elsewhere

---

[24] *Legacy*, p. 110.
[25] See **182** (18 February 1652/3).

I showlde (yf it might be obtained) be very happy in a fewe graines from my Lady Hilliarde[26] by meanes of your frinde

I shall allsoe be a bolde switer[27] to you for your other receipte), for the piles[28]

I haue noe more time then to subscribe my selfe

190 *Culpeper to Hartlib, 13 July 1657.* *(42/15/3–4)*

Mr Hartlib,

I giue you many thanckes for your receipte for the pyles; & shall (synce your kindenes hathe promised it) hope for the other allsoe, when it shall come to your handes

I haue heere inclosed sente you what I finde amonge my papers from Dury concerninge, Correspondency, & shall serche further vpon your more particular directions, I pray returne the booke, when you have made use of it,

You will doe me a kindenes to returne me Standishe[29] his booke, which I lente you, when you had an intentions to reprinte it

I have not yet seene Mr Floode[30] but shall doe it as soone as he returnes from London

The newes of your healthe will be allwayes wellcome to

[*PS.*] I pray conveygh the inclosed to Mrs Dury

---

[26] According to a memorandum on Italian grain amongst Hartlib's papers, Lady Hilliard had planted enough grain in her garden at East Florsley in Surrey to sow an acre of land. The only difficulty was apparently 'how to scare away the birds which for the most part devoure it.' ('Memo*randum* on Italian Grain in Scribal Hand', 12 June 1657 – 62/50/13); *Ephemerides*, 1657 – 29/6/14A.

[27] i.e. 'suitor'.

[28] There are several suggested remedies and palliatives for piles, from which Hartlib had long been a sufferer, amongst Hartlib's papers. Those referred to in Hartlib's *Ephemerides* for this year involve red cabbage and boiled cream – 26/6/3A, 10A, 13B. Cf **191** (20 July 1657).

[29] Arthur Standish (fl. 1611–1615), an agricultural author – DNB. Standish's published works were: *The Commons Complaint* (1611) STC 23200.5 (further edtions 1611 and 1612); *New Directions of Experience of the Authour for the Planting of Timber and Firewood* (1613), STC 23204 (further editions 1613, 1614, 1615 and 1616); *A Second Direction, for the Increasing of Wood, and the destroying of vermine* (1613), STC 23206.4, (further editions 1613 and 1614). In 1659 Beale proposed to publish a work on forestry which was to include the memorandum between Culpeper and Dawson on protecting trees from cattle as well as sections of Standish's *The Commons Complaint* (Beale to Hartlib, 22 March 1659, 51/99–101).

[30] In the *Ephemerides* for 1657 Hartlib notes that there was a descendant of the English alchemist Robert Fludde, a Mr Flood 'heire to all Robert de Fluctibus not far from Maidstone [who] hath a MS. of Husbandry which hee promised to give to the Publick by Sir Cheney Culpeper.' – 29/6/13B.

191 *Culpeper to Hartlib, 20 July 1657. (42/15/5–6)*

Mr Hartlib;

I haue (nowe) received your receipte againste the piles,[31] & (with it) those other papers you mention, for bothe which I very heartily thancke you.

In your receipts for the piles, (composed of piece greece, tanners ooze, & sheepes-dunge) there is one passage which I vnderstande not; (viz) *till he bee well*[32] For (yf I misvnderstoode you not), this medicine was intended for ease, but not for a perfecte cure, which (by experience) I finde (yf it haue continued longe) to be dangerous to the life, not lesse then stoppinge of an olde issue; nor knowe I any other meaninge of your woords, [excepte] you meane a cure for the presente & for that time; & this I the rather thincke because, (as I remember) the person from whome you had the receipte, neuer goe without them; I pray answer this by the nexte;

For your papers of the heathe,[33] I haue (allready) brewed some beere with it, but not (yet) druncke of it; But that which giues an alloye to the busines is, what one Sir Edward Partheridge[34] speakes with huge confidence; (viz) that the vse of heathe in steade of beere doeth cause madnes or phrenzy; I pray (in your nexte letters into those severall parts where it is vsed) propose the objection & (yf you can) get an exacte accownte, howe longe they haue vsed it, & what ill effecte (in that or, any other kinde) they finde; For I am very desirous (beinge firste strenghtened against suche [*blot*] objections) to become an example in the constante vse of it, that haue longe belefte that hops were not appropriately designed to the makinge of beere

---

[31] This particular remedy is detailed in an undated fragment which was apparently given to Hartlib by John Dury. He had it from 'Colonel Baxter or Barkestead' – i.e. Sir John Barkstead (d.1662), a goldsmith from London who became a military officer and was one of the regicides. 'For the piles. Take one lb of piece Grease, and boyle it in a Pipkin with one Gallon of Tanners wose in which there must be no Lime, but as it comes from the Oake barke. Let them boile together, untill they come to two quarts, then set it by untill it be Cold, and then take of the Cake of Grease and scrape of the dreggs that you will find on the lowest side of it, then melt it together, and so keep it vntill you make use of it as followeth. Take halfe a lb of sheeps dung very fresh, pick it so that there be no gravell in it, take 4 ounces of the grease aforesaid prepared, beate them well together in a stone Morter, untill they come to a perfect paste. Rolle it up into suppositers . . . '.

[32] Barkstead claimed that his condition was completely cured by the ointment.

[33] Culpeper refers to a discourse on heaths by Thomas Bates. Bates concluded that beer brewed from heath was more advantageous to the body than that brewed with hops. He also dismissed the claim of the 'objection of madnesse', to which Culpeper alludes – 63/3/28. Hartlib also notes the '[objection] against Heath,...whither it will not breed some other diseases it being vsed so long as Hops.' (*Ephemerides*, 1657, 29/6/17A).

[34] For Sir Edward Parteridge, see **Introduction**, p. 117.

The interwouen passages concerninge the recoueringe, & aromatizatinge of beere or other liquors, are soe goode, as that I cannot but claime your kinde promise, as well for suche others, as allsoe for that more singular one yet, which you are promised for the piles; I shall be glad allsoe to knowe, whether the paper I sente you laste weeke concerninge correspondency, be suche as you desire; With my beste wishes to you I reste

192   *Culpeper to Hartlib, 6 September 1657.*   *(42/15–7–8)*

Mr Hartlib;

I am heartily sorry I cannot stay longer to be more acquainted with Mr Dalgarnoe, & with his vniversall Character;[35] I conceiue that (by your frinds[36] & relations at Oxforde) you informe your selfe concerninge bothe his person & what he pretends to; I allready finde by discowrse with others, that it is like (in the vulgar opinion) to be looked vpon as too good to be belefte, & truly I thinck it agrees with the present wayes of God, whoe (to me) seemes (euery daye) coming forthe in suche manner as that the wise of this worlde, will wonder & perishe

I praye (in your nexte lines) giue me bothe your thowghts of him, & to what cowrse you directe him

193   *Culpeper to Hartlib, 15 September 1657.*   *(42/15/9–10)*

[Note: partial copy at 70/3/1]

Sir

the beste thanckes I can returne you for your late communication of many vseful ingenuities is (after experience) to ascertaine you of the reality of them, [*which*] (in my retired waye) I shall (from time to time) indeauor to doe

---

[35] George Dalgarno, (ca.1626–1687) – DNB. Culpeper refers to Dalgarno's *Character universalis . . . A new discovery*, (Oxford, 1657?), Wing D128A.

[36] On 1 May 1658, a printed testimonial was prepared on behalf of George Dalgarno to advertise the potential of his 'universal character'. At its head it carried the recommendation of Richard Love, Lady Margaret Professor of Divinity at the University of Cambridge. A further declaration of support beneath it carried the names of 31 backers, headed by 'the University of Oxford'. The subscribers are a roll-call of Hartlib's associates and it is impossible to conceive that the printed testimonial had not been prepared with his assistance. Amongst the 31 signatories was that of Sir Cheney Culpeper – 49/1/3A-B. For George Dalgarno's 'universal character', see V. Salmon, *The study of language in seventeenth-century England* (Amsterdam, 1979), ch. 9.

The 2: thinges that doe (at the presente) moste affecte my thowghts are, 1: The fertilizinge of barren landes; that lye out of the reache of ordinary amendmente, & that eyther then by quintessencinge or exaltinge of ordinary composte to more then an ordinary richenes, or by suche imbibitions,[37] as wee haue received late information of from Hamborrowe[38] and some from Harderwicke,[39] Paris; & some allsoe from a person nowe residing (thowgh a stranger) among vs;[40] And yf the puttinge of [the? *MS torn*] corne (thus imbibed & fertilized) into the grownde at a certeine & fit distance & depthe cowlde be once (perfectly) made out amonge vs, there wowlde be some aduance made towards the accomplishing of the 67 psalme;[41] For the imbibition of corne, when I consider 1: howe muche the richeste dunge exceedes the woorste; 2: howe muche that beste dunge or composte (by often fallowinge of it) may be exalted; 3: that, of the beste dunge (yf meshed as the brewers doe malte) there is not (truly) aboue one twentieth or thirtieth parte goode, the remainder (when thus meshed) beinge not good eyther for the lande or for the dunghill; I confesse, that I doe not soe muche woonder (as I did at firste) that the imbibinge onely, of corne showlde woorke such feates; but doe rather set my thowghts on woorke, howe (by all manner of wayes) to exalte composte; that soe from thence I may proceed, firste to meshinge of it, & then to the imbibing of corne in, suche a contracted quintessence, as will remaine, when the insipide water is exhaled by the [sunne?] otherwise; & this (I conceiue) muste & will serue, till the arte of fermentation shall haue opened a wyder doore to the stupendious multiplication of all things

For the vniversall character & langwage; to be attained in a weeke; I holde it to be one of the things of nowght, that will bringe to confusion that citty of Confusion which muste fall before our newe Ierusalem will appeare, & the Allelujahs be heard, which followe immediately after the Alas Alas of the [K^s: Capt:] etcet; I praye let me heare further of the person, & what incowragemente he findes; my paper is done, & the Carriers (I feare) passed by;

---

[37] i.e. the soaking of grain in fertilizer prior to its planting.

[38] i.e. Hamburg.

[39] i.e. Harderwijk in the Dutch Republic.

[40] This is almost certainly Mr Bedloe, from the Netherlands, about whom Hartlib had a report in 1653 through a friend of Mr Williams, a gentleman-farmer from Norfolk who was an enthusiast for agricultural improvement. According to the *Ephemerides*, 1653, he 'promiseth to furnish Husbandmen with a Liquor for imbibing of seed-corne wherby the seed being sown in the most barren ground (soe it bee fresh) shal produce as rich a crop, as the same quantity of seed would have done in the best prepared land according to the vsual course of Husbandry' – 28/2/79A.

[41] See also **179** (1 September 1649).

194   *Culpeper to Hartlib, 20 September 1657. (42/15/11–14)*

Sir

    your Communications, as they are pleaseante in themselues, & from the hande from whence I receive them, soe are they, allsoe in this respecte, that manifeste, that God hath given you eyther more healthe & leasure from your paynes, or a minde calme serene & aboue them, I showlde be glad to heare of the firste, but shall (in your behalfe) heartily wishe & pray for the laste, & hope you will doe the like for me in what maye befall me

    I thancke you for your waye of enrichinge barren lande,[42] & (yf it had come sooner) it showlde (within these 2: yeeres) haue saued a good deale of mony in my purse; But (under correction) I am not satisfied, what quantity is meante by a *small quantity of vnslaked lime*,[43] to be sprinckled vpon 2: yards square of turfes; nexte I wowlde gladly knowe the meaning of /*And soe bwild vp your heape*/[44] whether it be meante, the earthe syde to the earthe syde & the grasse syde to the grasse syde, still with lime betweene the grasse; But (truly) the quickest waye to answere all these and all other queres, were to haue resorte to the Quaker vpon his promise, for (to give you my judgemente accordinge to your desires) the thinge is rationall for the breakinge vp of barren grownds; but (vnder correction) I conceiue) farre shorte of what a riche naturall composte maye be exalted to by a vicissitude of continuall fallowing & fermentinge of it for severall yeeres before it be vsed, for (yf (as I have known by experience) the fallowinge of driuen land for 3: or 4: yeeres dothe fully restore it, to a riches beyonde dunge) I cannot beleeue but (yf the practise be begunne upon a richer roote of lyme or pidgeon dung) it will (as honeste Gabriæll Platte[45] intimates) mownte (in a shorte time) to suche a stupendious riches; that a little maye be afforded to be carried seuerall miles, & doe woonders vpon suche barren grownds as (in the ordinary waye) lies not in the reache of the dunge [cororte.?]; And I haue often wished that this experimente were fully tried, & doe beleeue it wowlde, exalte the matter or earthe thus handled beyonde what can (yet) be apprehended, & I dare asserte that ther is noe dunge comparable to what the plowe (thus) makes

    Hauinge (with much pleasure) perused your papers of the vniversall character, & langwage, I shall (a little) tell you my opinion of the firste, for as to the laste, I confesse it alltogether beyonde me

---

[42] 26/70/1a ('Anthony Pierson his universal compost'). Similar Suggestions appear in John Shaw, *Certaine plaine and easie demonstrations of divers easie wayes* (1657), Wing S3021, which Hartlib may have published – ('Title page in scribal hand', 62/21/3).

[43] 26/70/1A.

[44] Ibid.

[45] See **56** (6 November 1644) and **61** (4 January 1645).

Firste (by the 16:^th of [Iune.? *altered*]) he writes (yf I mistake not) onely the Radixes, & expresses all the Auxiliaries (which are 2: thirds of our Langwage) onely by prickes, & thus a pricke onely, signifies, neuer lesse then a woorde; sometimes (perhaps) two or more; To knowe the priority & posteriority of the prickes in readinge, In this (I conceiue) maye be one of the misteries

Nowe supposinge that the Radixes onely be written; the question which I showlde make is whether (to vse Bisterfildes woords in an excerpte you gaue me at the time of our first acquaintance) there be a wisdome & reason in the characters of the Radixes, vsque ad summos apices,[46] soe as that letters in woords, & strokes in characters, & parts of characters, doe truly analogize to elements of things or in things; thus (accordinge to Bisterfild)[47] Or & Vr (yf I remember aright) signify the one light & the other fire in that langwage which Adam vsed when he gaue names to thinges, which (saythe Bisterfild) the presente Iewe vnderstands not; & the rationall difference (saythe Bisterfild) betweene those two names Or & Vr dothe analogize to the difference of the 2: things signified by them; Yf Mr Dalgarnoes Characters be non ad placitum imponentis,[48] but rationally significante vsque at summos apices, my nexte question wowlde be whether it be the same with Adams langwage & (yf not) whether there might not be (a radice) a thirde character framed more easy to the hande & yet as comprehensiue of receiuinge the prickes about it, for the characters (yf I mistake not) seeme to me, not soe easy to the pen as some others maye be; I conceiue that all Synonimes maye be written with one character & eyther lefte to chritisisme, or differenced by some adiuncte; I propose alsoe to Mr Dalgarnoes thowghts whether one line in steade of 2: or 3: which Mr Lodowicke[49] vses) wowlde not (in case the radicall Character be ad placitum imponentis) & might not (by the change of the place onely, ouer, in, or vnder the line) multiply a fewe of the easiest characters into a double, treble, quadruple number of significations, soe one & the same Character might signifie the heauen aboue the line the earthe belowe the line, the ayry region in the line; Thus one character might (in the Politicks) the Parliament (yf we had a free one) the people, & the magistracy in the line, & (by this hinte & the analogy that is in thinges) euery character wowlde have its rationall signification accordinge to the place it was fownde in & not be lesse capable of the attendant prickes about it; But what doe I (like a childe

---

[46] 'down to the last jot'.

[47] See **80** (17 July 1645).

[48] 'not placed according to whim'.

[49] Francis Lodowyck, author of *A Common Writing* (1647), Wing L2814, whom Culpeper had previously mentioned in the letters of **120** (3 February 1646/7) and **124** (1 March 1646/7).

in the woombe) conceite thinge of that worlde I neuer yet sawe or chritisize vpon the Slauonian tongwe of which I vnderstand not one woorde; Truly I wishe I cowlde serue the Publique in the recommendinge of it to some in authority, nor shall I (as my pressures will giue me leave to be in London) be wanting to doe my beste, thowgh (I thincke) you knowe, bothe the presente times & the relation I stande in, to them; Yf I were in London I wowlde accepte of Mr Dalgarnoes indeauors, that (by them) I might be the better able (with all faythe & truthe to him) to recommende it (vpon my owne knowledge) to others, & I haue allsoe two girles[50] whoe (before I hearde of Mr Dalgarno), were very desirous (yf they had beene in towne) to have beene Mr Riches schollers, as beinge the best Mr I cowlde heare of for them,[51] But yf Mr Dalgarnoe will teache them they shall learne of noe other, & yf you dare vndertake for me I will vndertake for them & my selfe (yf wee learne any thinge of him) that wee shall indeauor to doe him what right wee can, but noe leaste prejudice; Sir I shall not take vpon me to valewe the teachinge of that which I holde to be of a pretious & invalewable consequence to the worlde, but I wishe that (yf Mr Dalgarno showlde be pleased to take vs or any of vs into the number of his schollers) I maye (by your fauor & kindenes) knowe the rate he receiues or expectes from others; That beinge knowne, I am confidente, I shall (I am confidente) doe the parte of a juste man, & of a thanckefull man, according to the meritte of the thinge when I shall be better able to judge of it; And yf (this particular being first relolued on) hee shall (till better accommodated) haue leasure to retire hether for a shorte time, hee shall be wellcome, as to the presente, & shall not returne empty towards suche occasions as maye wante the vse of the Presse; I mention not this as to be otherwise taken notice of then as it swites with your judgement for him, & with his owne occasions & desires

I praye thancke Mr Hartlib, when you see him; & Mr Clodius;[52]

Sir (yf I mistake not) you tolde me once of one in Oxfordshire, whoe (by often Fallowing or plowinge a riche plotte of earth) did designe to rayse saltpeeter finally from it; I am sure I haue hearde of some suche history, & (as I remember) it was from yourselfe, & I doe againe professe, that I knowe nor can imagine noe bownde that can be giuen

---

[50] Culpeper refers to his two surviving daughters, Elizabeth and Cecilia.

[51] Jeremiah Rich (d. ca 1660) – DNB. Rich was also responsible for popularizing a short-hand writing which had been originally invented by his uncle, William Cartwright. It was first published in his *Semography, or Short and Swift Writing, being the most easiest, exactest and speediest Method of all others that have beene yet Extant* (1642), Wing C717.

[52] Frederick Clodius, Hartlib's son-in-law. Hartlib's eldest daughter Mary had married Clodius probably in the late summer of 1653 – HDC, p. 8; on Clodius's work as an alchemist see GI, pp. 302 ff.

to the exaltation in riches & strenght, that may be made of earthe soe handled; I cannot allsoe (which I ouerpassed in the firste parte of my letter) but craue leaue to differ from [Coll:] Moncke;[53] for a larger proportion of Lyme then your receipte mentions, does (by dayly experience) agree with our landes in this Cownty And Iohn Bates his experimente (a thinge approued) in his booke printed in quarto, fol: 261:[54] doethe plainly & vndeniably evidence that the riches which the Lyme giues to the earthe is the saltepeeter, which (saythe Bates there) will (by meshinge onely, & euaporatinge) remaine behinde; & truly yf saltpeter doe proue (vpon experience) to be the good, the riches, or strenght which the lime conteines & giues to the earthe, the conse-quences are too many & greate for my wearied hand to discourse nowe vpon, which makes me wishe for Mr Dalgarnoes helpe, that my pen might keepe pace with my minde, which is one excellencie which Mr Dalgarnoe hathe not mentioned in his vniversall character

I pray remember me very affectionately to him

You receiue this by a speciall occasion, & yf (any time vpon tuesdaye) you send an answer to one Mr Jenckins in Ieames streete at the ende of Petty France, it will be with me upon wednesdaye; And yf I maye hear from you of Mr Dalgarnoes conditions & willingnesse to come into Kente, a horse shall meete him at Gravesende; With my affect: wishe to you I reste

195   *Culpeper to Hartlib, 6 October 1657.   (42/15/15–16)*

Sir

I haue beene, soe tossed to and froe, this laste fortnight, & am soe yet, as I haue scarse had leasure to be ciuill, & thanckefull to you for your Communications,

I shall (ere longe) haue occasion to be in London, & shall then vnderstande more in an hower from Mr Dalgarnoe then I can at this distance in a weeke; I shall therefore desire this onely nowe, that (by your kindenes) I may thanck him, with this onely in generall concerninge his invention, that it is very ingenuous; but I beleeve withall that the firste essaye of it will not be perfecte, nor will the perfection of that & many other things that are cominge foorthe into the worlde, arise from any one person or age, & this is juste in God to doe, that euery man (in his owne particular) maye walk humbly, & Hee Himselfe maye have His due of that glory which Hee will giue to none; I doe not see

---

[53] Colonel Monk's success with lime is reported in an undated anonymous mem-orandum on Antony Pierson's universal compost – 26/70/1–2.
[54] See **187** (13 October 1656).

(synce those prickes & pointes are relatiues to the Radixes) howe the antecedentes pricke & pointes can be set downe, till their Radixe be spoken & written & this (I conceiue) will be a greate checke to the pen when the radixes muste firste be set downe, before the precedente auxiliaries, can be represented by theire prickes & pointes, but of this more heere after

A dyall for the 5: sences, is a thinge I comprehende not; but I must walke humbly, & not confine possibility to my narrowe vnderstandinge

Your illnes causes sorrowe, yet not without greate contente that you have bothe leasure & kindenes in the midste of it to remember [your affect*ionate* frind]

196   *Culpeper to Hartlib, 20 October 1657.   (42/15/17–18)*

Mr Hartlib

my sorrowe continues wíth your paines, But the beste wee creatures can doe, is to wishe & pray that God may strenghten you; I neuer heard any thinge from you of the stupendious composte in Gardiners lane,[55] & showld be glad (yf I might) to be acquainted with it, For the generall nature mentioned by Mr Boyle, it will reste as a mistery, till (layinge aside Aristotle & all that rabble) wee (better) vnderstande the motion of the spirit of the Lorde in and vpon the waters; As it was in the beginninge, is nowe, & euer shallbe, whilste this greate stillatory of the Lord shall laste

I showlde be glad to knowe, that Mr Clodius were ready for me

[55] In the *Ephemerides* of 1657 Hartlib wrote of a 'Mris Iackson widdow to Dr Iackson once dwelling in Gardiners lane got from her Husband vpon his death-bed the vniversal compost for enriching of the most barren Ground whatsoever.' – 29/6/21B.

Appendix

197   *John Dury to Culpeper (1642?).   (1/4/9–18)*[1]

Sir

I am very desirous to gratify yow in the virtuous desire which yow have expressed vnto me concerning the Method of Meditation:[2] for I thinke myselfe a debter more to yow therein, then vnto others because your zeale doth leade yow to more vniversall conceptions then others are capable of; if therefore it were Gods will to open a Dore of vtterance vnto me towards yow at this tyme, at least so farre as to initiate yow fully in the way of future conference with me about this matter, I would be exceeding glad not only for your sake, but even for mine owne sake, that I might have a fitt object to worke vpon, & to bring forth the particulars which lye in my mind & which without some good & fitt opportunity I cannot be drawne to elaborate & putt to paper.

I am willing then at this tyme to show yow my conceptions concerning the first Principles of the Method which I thinke euery one should follow that will walke by a Rule in ordering his thoughts for Meditation & consultation. Here yow have the aime of my present discourse with yow, wherein yow may observe distinctly that I presuppose. 1. that a Man is able to order his owne thoughts 2. That the meanes to bring <order> them is a certayne Rule by which he should walke. 3. that this Rule hath certayne Principles of which now I am cheifely to speake. 4 & that the ends or rather the objects towards which the thoughts are to be ordered are the Acts of Meditating & consulting. If any body make these presupposalls disputable or if yow should make a doubt of them I cannot proceede cleerly with yow except I know where his or your scruples doth lye that some principle wherein we can agree may be taken vp to resolve it. But supposing that these things are not so much scrupuled & made disputable as not well & fully vnderstood then

---

[1] This is an undated copy which is headed 'Ext*ract:* Culpeper & Mr Durie aboute the spiritual Analysis'. 'Cheney' has been erased after 'Sir' on the first line and the original was apparently a letter addressed to Culpeper. Its date remains problematic. Turnbull ascribed it to '1641?' (HDC, p. 309). 1642 is more likely – see **14** (13 July [1642]). The Biblical references are accurate and refer to the Authorized King James version. They have not, therefore, been expanded in footnotes.

[2] A fragment of an apparently larger treatment of this subject is also to be found amongst Hartlib's papers in a manuscript treatise of John Dury entitled 'A DISCOURSE Shewing a Method of spirituall meditation in Holy Matters . . . Presented to Sir Will. Waller by I.D.' – 26/4/1A-10B. Turnbull dates this to '1640?' (HDC, p. 309).

before I proceede I must open the same vnto yow. I say then concerning the first that my meaning is not that a Man hath any sure command over himselfe that all the risings of thoughts in his mind should be vnder his power either to prevent thoughtes which he would not have to come in his minde or to laye downe thoughtes rison or to reduce at all tymes into good order the thoughts that cannot be laid downe; this is not my meaning for I know that the preparations of the heart in man & the Answer of the tongue is from the Lord. prov. 16. 1. & that mans goings are of the Lord & that therefore he cannot vnderstand his owne way in respect of the first motions thereof ibid. 20. 24. to which that place of Ierem: 10. 23. is parallel. O Lord I know that the way of man is not in himselfe & it is not in man that walketh to direct his steps. viz the first motions are not from a Man nor can a man by any humane instruction or habituall practise & premeditation attayne to any sure perfection that he shall be able to direct & overrule all his thoughts & the actions which proceede from thence vnto his owne preconceived aimes & ends: for although a mans heart doth device his way, & layeth plots vnto it selfe & maketh many resolucions; yet the Lord is he who directeth a mans steps towards the event thereof. *<left margin:* prov. 16. 9.*>* so that neither the first motions of the mind nor the constant & absolute progresse thereof is in our power: but this I meane when I say that we are able to order our thoughts vizt. that the vnderstanding of a man hath received from God a reflexive faculty to consider of it selfe & its owne actions & of all things belonging vnto the motions thereof; to the end that they may be brought into some regular frame & freed from confusion & vnsetlednes for the prosecution of matters wherevpon the spirit is fully bent & ought to be fixed. This reflexive[*altered*] faculty is given to the nature of all mens vnderstanding but it is not in the power of euery one to make vse of it or to make right use of it. for neither can euery one reflect vpon himselfe & his owne making when it is most expedient; nor when he doth reflect vpon himselfe & vpon the acts of his vnderstanding can he do it all tymes as he ought to do it: but this ability to make vse & to make right vse of the reflexive faculty is a peculiar gift of God & he doth bestow it vpon whomsoever he pleaseth. for as Elihu saith to Iob. there is a spirit in man & the inspiration of the Almighty giveth them vnderstanding: *<left margin:* Iob. 32. 8.*>* so it is certayne that although the faculty of ordering our wayes be in the soule yet except God breath vpon it & make it alive it cannot either act or act any thing aright but it lyeth there as a dead thing without motion whilest a man doth walke at randome in a vaine shew not knowing himselfe what he is doing: or if perhaps he doth take notice of himselfe (as naturally men vse to do) it is rather to flatter himselfe in idle conceipts & imaginations or to follow eagerly some particular plots then to order & regulate his wayes vnto true felicity & subordinate his motion vnto the lawfull ends for which they should be vndertaken. [Thus] I must be vnderstood in the first presupposall aright least I should seeme to attribute too much vnto our owne abilityes in nature & exempt the motions of our heart from Gods imediate working vpon it as if he did leave it wholy to a mans selfe; or as if by any act, method instruction & direction which we can give, any man should be made able to rule all his thoughts so that they should be composed at all tymes to attayne to any object which he should propose vnto himselfe. This must not be thought but my meaning is to be conceived of the ordinary faculty of reflecting vpon our selves how to make vse of it in the feare of God when we find our selves moved to intend good & lawfull matters for our owne & others edification: how then we should frame & compose our meditations & consultations to attayne by Rule vnto the ends for which they are vndertaken & not to proceede as fooles & children do at randome; in the acts where Reason & wisedome should take place is the true object of this discourse & the source of the first supposall.

The second presupposall I thinke hath no difficulty for if a man doth graunt that there is a reflexible faculty in the vnderstanding & that this faculty can act vpon the thoughts & that these thoughts can be ordered & freed from confusion, I do not see how he can make a doubt of this vizt. that the means to order our thoughts should be some Rule or other according to which the understanding should be proceede in working vpon it selfe. And then concerning the third in like [manner] if it be graunted that where order is to be observed thence a Rule may be vsed, it cannot be denied but that in ordering things by Rules, Principles must be observed whence the Rules are to betaken: for seeing by ordering is implyed a setting of things in a presedency and consecution one to another; & by a Rule is meant either the forme & frame or the reason why the precedency and consecution ought to be so & not otherwise. And seing all formes & frames which are rationally composed have a ground in the being & nature of the thing, whence they arise; therefore it cannot be denied but that the Rules by which humane thoughts are to be ordered must have Certaine Principles; which Principles we will now speak of (God Willing) in briefe, that yow may have an overture made vnto yow, either to proceede by your selfe vpon the grounds that shall be afforded vnto yow, or to call vpon me hereafter, & give me cause to open my selfe further in due tyme for your better satisfaction.

Yow have now already vnderstood that by Principles I meane the grounds of Rules by which a man is to walke in his thoughts of Meditation & consultation; the end then to which we drive is to Meditate & consult aright; by meditating I conceive the act of the minde reflecting vpon the nature of any thing to dive into the true properties & vses thereof. By consulting I vnderstand the act of the mind reflecting vpon the Actions which are to be vndertaken or left of or not vndertaken about any thing; to gaine some good end wherevnto they should be directed according as it may be conceived to be or not to be possible or vsefull. from whence yow may gather that the Acts of the mind which are to be regulated (which we call Meditation & consultation) are not now to be considered in respect of the subjects whereupon they are to reflect (which we have called the natures of things & the Actions which may be intended by vs for some good end) but in respect of the Reflection it selfe, that whether we meditate or consult we may have a Rule to order the reflection of our mind, vpon any subject whatsoever. The Rule then which we seeke at this tyme is to be gathered from the nature of the Acts of the minde to set them in their right frame one towards another, & not from the Relation which they may have towards the discovery of any thing in respect of outward objects. yow see then that the Acts of the mind as they have a twofold Relation soe they admitt of a twofold Rule; for as they relate other objects besides themselves they must be made proportionate vnto the ends which the vnderstanding aimeth at in these objects; but as they relate one another they must be ruled & ordered according to their owne inward propertyes & made answerable vnto the end wherefore they ought to reflect one vpon another. where I observe, that to find the Principles whereby these Acts are to be regulated is to discover three things 1. what the Acts of the mind of man are & how they are distinguished? 2. How they stand in relation one to another in their seuerall inward propertyes? 3. What the end of this relation is? & how it must be gayned? for this Relation is the grounds of the Reflection; & the end of that Relation is the first inward Principle of goodnesse & of that well being wherevpon the nature of the soule of Man hath bin framed & constituted; & from which all the well ordered Acts thereof must naturally flow & what soever is not answerable therevnto in the agitation of thoughts & motion of the mind is to be judged irrationall & void of vnderstanding

Now then to lay open the Acts of a mans mind it is not possible except we know what a Man & what his mind is. By a Man we conceive this Creature which we find our selves to be as we are distinguished from all other living & animall things by the frame of our body & of our soule which the scripture saith was made after the image of God which image of god (since we have lost it) is now vnknowne vnto nature: & therefore by the vse of naturall Reason no man can know himselfe truly what he is; because he hath lost the Idea of the image after which he was made. But the scripture having told vs that our body was made of the substance of the earth, & that by the breath of the Lord into our Nostrills we are become a living soule; & that

God made vs thus after his owne image that we should vnder him as his substitutes bearing his image & likenes in this world, have Dominion over all the rest of the Creatures which are therin. I say the scripture having taught vs thus much: we have by this Doctrine a new Principle of knowledge whereby to discerne ourselves what we are & what our mind is & what the end is wherefore it was put in our earthly body, of which things I will not now speake at large; but in a word I will tell yow what according to this scripturall Truth I conceive man & his mind to be. viz. a spirit a soule & a body joyned together in the powers of an eternall Rational & sensuall life whereof the Acts should be answerable one to another according to the predominant or subordinate propertyes; wherein they are all to be answerable vnto the life of god. The acts then of the life of man they are threefold some are sensuall, some are Rationall & some are spirituall. The sensuall arise from the body & its outward or inward sences, the Rationall arise from the facultyes of the Naturall soule in the imagination of the mind, in the memory, in the discerning & judging facultyes & in the will. The spirituall arise from the conscience bearing witnesse of the will of God & of our agreement or disagreement with the same. By which you see what is called the minde of man whose acts we would regulate viz. the living faculty of the spirit dwelling in the Conscience & of the Rationall soule dwelling in the will & vnderstanding. As concerning the sensuall life wherein we differ not from beasts we make it no part of the mind of man although we hold not that man hath more soules then one or that those Acts of the sensuall life are to be neglected & no way brought vnder a Rule: but we affirme both, that the soule is but one & also that these Acts may & might be regulated although we conceive that they belong not properly vnto the life of the mind. Thus then we see what the Acts of the mind of man are & how they are distinguished namely into the Acts of the spirit dwelling in the Conscience & into the Acts of the Rationall soule dwelling in the memorative vnderstanding & willing facultyes to which the whole sensuall life & all the Acts of the inward & outward sences are subordinate.

The Relation wherein these Acts stand one to another in respect of the propertyes of these facultyes whence they proceede is this that the faculty of the spirit in the acts & enditements of the Conscience is supreme & predominant above all the rest: to which the Rationall faculty of the soule in the acts of Memory, vnderstanding & willing is imediately subordinate; & to these the acts of the imaginations & sensuall passions are subservient & submitted. And if this Relation & subordination be altered so that the sensuall should be predominant above the Rationall or the Rationall above the spirituall Acts, then all is out of order & a mans life is either Beastly or Divilish.

The end wherefore this Relation & subordination of the faculties of man was thus appointed & ordered by God; is, that in the right use of these facultyes he should expresse the Image & life of God, wherein he should be able to rule over the rest of the Creatures to bring them to the state of Happines: that Gods glory might appeare as in himselfe so also in euery one of them according to the degree of their perfection. so that to gaine this end for which God hath thus framed the mind of man, the Rule is none other but to observe the true Relation where in God hath sett vs which is 1. that our spirits should be in our Conscience wholy subjected vnto his spirit & dependant from him (who is the father of spirits) in all things so with out his leave and the knowledge of his will by reflecting vpon his word ingrafted in our hearts we should not presume to thinke say or do anything 2. that our Reason should in all things be a servant vnto the enditement of the spirituall word made manifest vnto our Conscience to obey it & to make the truth and goodnesse thereof plaine & evident to our selves & others. 3. that our sensuall motions should be a servant vnto the prescripts of Reason to helpe our rationall facultyes to expresse the will of God & apply it vnto those with whome we have to deale outwardly.

From all which yow may gather (for these are the Principles which I did intend to speake of) much more then I am able at this tyme to vtter: for here yow have a fountayne of Rules, from whence many directions may be taken how to order the Acts of the minde in respect of their mutuall relation one to another for consider that in all things whereof we do thinke except they be merely spirituall & Divine so that they are no wayes subject vnto sence there ought to concurre the Act of Conscience of Reason & of the imaginative faculty which in the inward sence & the head of all the other sensuall facultyes; & seing these Acts should continually concurre in all the minding of outward matters, the Rule is that they must not be confounded nor preposterously brought forth: but that we should first order the Acts of our minde within it selfe before wee proceede to meditate upon any particular Object: For except the conscience bee cleare & at rest in respect of God, the understanding will not perfourme the duetye aright: & if the understanding facultie bee out of order, the senses will not bee well imployed to minister & seeke out evidences or to represent them orderly vnto the Rational abilities. So that to laye the first ground worke of meditation & consultation aright, a man of Iudgement should looke to himselfe, that these three great wheeles of the minde, bee well composed & sette in order one towards another: the Conscience, the Rationatiue abilitie; & the Sensitiue facultie: Lest the Conscience being under guilt, & defilements; bee separat from God, whoe is the Author [*left margin:* Iam 1. 17] of all good gifts, & from whose mouth alone Wisdome doeth proceede. Prov. 2. 6. For God doeth not giue true Wisedome & Understanding, but unto such as come to him to seeke it: Now to come to him, or to seeke wisedome from him without Faith, it is neither possible, nor can any thinge bee receiued at his hand. For without Faith it is impossible to please God. Hebr.11. 6. And hee that is of a doubting & wauering minde, mut not thinke, that hee can receiue any thing of the Lord. Iam. 1. 6, 7. But when the conscience is not cleansed & purified from dead workes, there must needes bee a doubting, & wauering in it, when it commeth before God; & so it will bee found unfitt to receiue Wisedome or direction from him. For God giueth to a man that is good in his sight, wisedome & Knowledge, & Ioye, but to the sinner hee giueth travell. Eccles. 2. 26. nor can Wisedome enter or finde place into an uncleane soule: because it is prepossessed with sinne [*left margin:* Esai.59. 2.] which maketh a sep-aration betwixt God & it. Besides all which; it is to bee considered, that as the feare of the Lord, is the beginning of wisedome; so the Spirit that hath not a dependence upon the word of the Lord, can haue no wisedome; because Ieremie sayth: [*left margin:* Ierem. 8. 9.] That seeing they haue rejected the word of the Lord, what wisedome is in them? There can bee no wisedome where the word of the Lord is not regarded; & this word cannot bee regarded, except the heart bee possessed with his feare: & this cannot bee excepted the Conscience bee sanctified, & cleansed from dead workes. So that wee see the first Principle & preparatiue unto Meditation, must bee the composing of the heart towards God; to sette our selues to thinke of that which is to be thought upon, as in his presence through his feare depending upon his word, & desiring his direction; that not onely with his leaue & permission, but by his order & according to his will wee maye doe all thinges, & thinke all our thoughts. This predisposing of the mind towards God, to reflect first upon him in all our meditations, is like unto the Tuning of an Instrument before a man doeth beginne to playe a piece of good Musick: so by drawing neare to God, with a good conscience, in cleansing it from all superfluitie of naughtinesse & calling upon him by Faith for grace & direction; the strings of the soule are tuned & sette in a good Harmonie, that the spirit of wisedome which proceedeth from him maye playe some harmonious melodicall piece upon the same: which without this tuning of the soule cannot bee done: And this Tuning cannot bee perfourmed, except the conscience bee brought neare unto God, & bee able to looke upon him, that it maye bee inlightned. For by looking to him & comparing it selfe to his will & Livinge word, it receiueth light, first to see & judge itselfe in what estate it is; & then to judge other thinges alsoe: for then it reflecteth upon all thinges (& chiefly upon the inferiour faculties, which are subordinate unto the motions of the Spirit:) with a commanding power: so that they all stoope & yeeld to it, to become answereable unto the Intentions of the spirit, which are conceiued by a good Conscience, to bee aimed at in the worke of meditation & consultation: And lett euery man who desireth to go safe in any businesse of consequence, bee sure that hee neuer fall to worke without this preparatiue: For without it hee may runne himselfe into errours & those very daungerous, & hee cannot possiblely walke by true light & Rules, as longe as the great Maister Rules & principle of light is not made use of, which is the subordination of the Intents & purposes of the heart unto God to sette it in a frame, which maye bee answereable unto his Will. This then is the first maine Principle of true order, to bee settled in the Thoughts to bring the conscience to reflect upon God, & settle itselfe, towards him in the businesse which is to bee minded.

The second maine Principle is, to haue a care to cleare the naturall understanding, from prejudices & forestaled opinions, which are like filmes ouer the eyes of the mind through which it cannot looke soe as to discerne the right shape of thinges, otherwise in themselues sufficiently apparent.

These prejudices arise from a narrownesse & stinting of the thoughts unto thinges too particular. Therefore before wee beginne to meditate or consult, wee should abstract from particulars & state the Question whereof wee are to thinke in generall tearmes; which should comprehend the true nature of particulars. Which being done, the Termes of the Question are to bee considered & examined; that the properties thereof maye bee discouered. To which effect the Acts of Ratiocination should bee obserued & rightly ordered; which are:

1: To discerne distinctly the differences of matters belonging to the tearmes of the Question.

2. To compare those distinct matters together with the thinge enquired after; that from their agreement or disagreement, the judgement maye gather the Resolution of the Question.

3. To applye the Question Generally resolued, unto the particular matter in hand: where the circumstances of the particular are to bee lookt into; to finde how farre they answere or answere not, unto the Generall determination of the Question.

Thus then the Acts of Ratiocination should proceede by degrees: for the maine Principle, whereby they are to bee regulated is this, that the understanding must proceede alwayes from thinges foreknowen, to that which is unknowen; by single notions to proceede unto compounds: which may bee done, either from Generalls, foreknowen, to determine particulars unknowen: or from particulars forknowen, to gather the generall notion wherein they all agree; for both wayes the reasoning facultie should proceede.

First to state the Question which is to bee made the subject of meditation, by summing up the particulars foreknowen; into one Generall head & propertie of their Agreement. Secondly to resolue that

Question into its distinct matters, to discerne the properties thereof. Thirdly to compare those properties with the thing sought after, to see what they will discouer of it in Generall. And lastly to applye that which shall bee discouered in generall to the particular, as it standeth under its circumstances. And to this last Act of Reasoning, which concerneth the circumstances of particular matters, the use of sense doeth concurre to enquire, obserue, discerne & helpe to compare thinges together by their outwardly perceptible Realities, which leade the understanding, to the apprehension of more inward properties.

Now the Principle by which the Acts of sense are to bee regulated is this, that they should bee kept from confused wanderings; & bee made to reflect upon the observation of circumstances, according to the suggestion of Reason in the order by which matters, are to bee compared one with another; for except circumstances bee taken in their right places, the application will not bee cleare, not rightly made. The Imagination then, & the Memorie (which haue receiued the Ideas of circumstances obserued by outward sense) must bee commanded; to make report of the same in that order & for such intents, which reason subordinat unto Conscience shall require to bee done; for the decision of that which is enquired after by waye of meditation & consultation: And if these Principles of order in the Acts of the minde within itselfe bee carefully obserued: I suppose no man can doubt but that the progresse will bee effectuall towards the discouerie of Trueth, in the objects of Meditation, & of goodnesse in the objects of consultation. For all the worke the mind of man is sette upon, is nothing else but Trueth & Goodnesse, to finde the same in Matters & Actions. And because Truth & Goodnesse are complicated together, so that the one is neuer without the other; Therefore they are sought joyntly & neuer found but together. But the instinct of nature leadeth men more to desire Goodnesse then Trueth; for Trueth is sought because it is knowen to be good: but the notion of Goodnesse is different in the capacities of men; & therefore is sought differently according to the apprehensions which men haue of it. For some apprehend nothing to bee good, but what is answereable unto the delight which they take in sensuall objects: others apprehend the goodnesse of Rationall objects: & some are exalted unto Spirituall objects. Whence wee finde three sorts of men in the world: Some (but fewe are such:) seeke before all thinges & in all things, the Goodnesse which proceedeth immediately from God in the Life of the Spirit. Others, who liue in a Rationall & Morall waye, content themselues with the fruits of naturall Knowledge in the workes of their understandinge. And lastly some liue in their sensuall Appetites, as beasts doe. The first sort of men are Citizens of heauen. The second are Rulers of this world; the third are Slaues of the world. These different properties of men; are to be found more or lesse in all the meditations & consultations of men about particular objects. For when the mindes of men runne chiefly upon temporall matters to seeke bodily ease & contentement, unto themselues in all thinges whereof they meditate & consult: they debase the use of their Reason, & pervert it to become a slaue unto lust. And if they rest in a temporall content of thinges not meerly bodily, but somewhat alsoe rationall; To haue power & honnour, & preeminence, to rule ouer others by their understanding, they are in some degree better then others, but yet not truely sette upon that which is good. And therefore none but such as in the Acts of meditation & consultation, raise their thoughts, first to a Spirituall good, which is permanent unto life eternall. And then comprehend under it as subordinat matters thereunto, the objects of Reason & sense: None (I saye) but such order their thoughts aright; And whosoeuer walketh by this Rule hee maye expect, that in seeking the Kingdome of God, other thinges shall bee added unto him, according to the promise of Christ Matth. 6. 33. Now because I labour in the wayes of my calling, & in all the meditations which I use to propose unto others, to drawe mens thoughts unto this Rule, [<*H?:* therefore>] although none doeth contradict the proposalls which I make; yet I finde that they are not much relished: Because most men, euen of this Calling wherein I liue, seeke not truelye that which is Spirituall, but [<*H?:* rather>] that which is temporall, either in a Rationall or sensuall waye: for except they can perceiue a particular present advantage of honour & credit, or of profit to themselues, they neuer care for that which is Spirituall: And this is the cause why I cannot finde a Patron for my worke, because I doe not sette my minde to serue endes & particular interrests, unto which all parties nowadayes are wedded; & can relish nothing but what is subordinat thereunto.

This then is the combate which I haue to fight with the Spirits of men; namely to bring them from their privat aimes to a true generall good, wherein the glorye of God, & the salvation of soules, without any other respects may bee advanced. I haue added this Digression to lette you see, that I neither can, nor will expect promotion for my endeavours, but from such as can & will followe with mee these Principles of Meditation, & Consultation to joyne with mee therein to further the Publick Good, whereat I aime: For except mens aimes concurre, there can bee no reall conjunction of endeavours: And it is not lawfull for mee to leaue my Aime & way of meditation to serue inferiour endes; & seeing they cannot raise their thoughts, to walke with mee by these Rules, I am like to bee, as I am, continuallye deserted: Yet I am not discouraged; for I knowe that my reward is with him, whom I serue: & hee in due tyme is able to open mens [*left margin:* X] eyes, to see that they wearie themselues for vanitie, & wander in the foolishnesse of troublesome counsells; so long as they followe [*left margin:* X] not these grounds of meditation. For all the plotts & perposes of men meerely Rationall, though neuer so plausibley & strongly laid, will vanish when the Kingdome of God draweth neare; which is now at hand, & then nothing, but what is truely Universall & Spirituall shall remaine. If then wee doe not intend to loose our labour, & bee frustrate of our Reward; wee should sowe to the Spirit, by a sound waye of Spirituall Meditation & Consultation in all matters which wee take in hand; That euery purpose wherin wee desire to walke Rationally amongst men, & to applye our senses in a Right course, may bee first considered as in the presence of God conscionablely.

These are the generall Principles of Meditation, & Consultation which a man by the Grace of God is able to make use of, for the ordering of his thoughts in all particular objects: & according to these grounde Rules maye bee giuen, concerning these following matters: whereof I hope I shall gette by me to spreade more at large hereafter.

1. Of Scripturall Interpretation; to shewe the waye both of finding out Analytically the true Litterall, Materiall & Mysticall sense thereof, & of demonstrating & delivering, the same unto others according unto the seuerall Degrees, of their capacitie compositively.

2. Of Humane Speculation to shewe the waye; How men should order their thoughts, to finde out hidden Trueths in naturall thinges; and to propose orderly unto others, that which they haue found.

3. Of Spirituall & Humane consultation: To shewe how in Spirituall matters doubts of conscience, may bee resolued: or thinges belonging to the Edification of others prosecuted & proposed. And how in Humane affaires the wayes of Prudencie, to finde out & followe the best courses of doinge businesses should bee intended:

And you shall neuer bee more willing to putte mee upon these taskes, then I shall bee to elaborate the same, according to the Abilitie which it shall please God, to graunt unto mee with tyme & leisure; which I am desirous to spend upon Your edification, as being the Trueth

Your most affectionat
& faithfull servant in
Christ

Iohn Durye.

198 *John Dury to Culpeper, copy, n.d. [1642?].*   *(39/2/83)*[3]

Mein Herr Cheney, wie ich, was ich von bewuster Correspondenz
gestriges tages zu papier gebracht, heute angesehen; bin ich beynah im
zweifel gewesen, ob ich euch solches schicken solte, oder nicht: in
betrachtung, dz ich keine hieher gehörige absonderliche dinge berühre,
in welchen, (wie ihr zu reden pflegt) eine sache gleichsam mit händen
gefühlet werden kan. Doch gleichwol hielte ichs vor gutt, Euch mit
einer kurtzen beschreibung des jenigen, was ihr von mir zu wiszen
begehrt, nicht lange auffzuhalten. Was die particularia anlangt, so
können dieselbte zu einer andern zeitt gar leichtlich hinzugesetzt
werden. Ich pflege nicht eine materi durch die particularia durch-
zuziehen, sondern viel lieber einen richtigen grund zu legen, ausz
welchem vernünftige leute auf die particularia schlieszen können, wo
sie nur die umbstände und gelegenheit des stats, in welchem sie
leben, in acht nehmen. Vorschläge, die nicht auf allgemeinen und
unwiedersprechlichen warheiten gegründet sind, bestehen nicht lange.
Ists uns aber darumb zu thun, dz wir eine allgemeine verbeszerung
unsers wesens einzuführen, und bey allen und jeden nutzen zuschaffen
gedencken; so müszen wir nothwendig die gründe unserer rathschläge so
tieff legen, wie tieff die maszgebungen der natur hierzu im menschlichen
verstande verborgen liegen; damit also der baw, so darauff gezimmert
werden soll, bisz auff unsere nachkommen unverrückt und unzerfallen
stehen bleibe. Dasz nun die meisten unter uns nicht so ferne sehen,
sondern es nur bey diesem oder jenem proposito, so ihnen zu handen,
und lieblich fürkommt, bewenden laszen; daszelbte soll mich, der ich
den menschen von der erde zum himmel, von einer sich und das seine
allzusehr suchenden vnd liebenden unarth zur werthen gemeinschafft
der Heyligen, und zu einer auf keine eigennützigkeit sehende liebreiche
dienstferttigkeit zu bringen gedencke, nicht darzu bewegen, dz ich
hierinnen ihrer schwachheit folge, sondern vielmehr veranlaszen, ihre
gemüter auffzumuntern, dz sie nebenst mir nach dem warhafften zweck,
wodurch dem gemeinen Besten weidlich auff die füsze gehoffen werden
kan, gerade zulauffen; und ihnen zu erkennen zu geben, welcher gestalt
alle und iede particularia nach einem gewiszen richtscheit abgemeszen,
an ihrem eigenen orth gesetzet, und unter das gemeine beste gestellet
werden solten. Denn so lange wir nicht die materien ausz ihren
eigendlichen ursprungen herausz holen, und solche grundfesten legen,
die durch keine gegensätze können umbgeworffen werden, so werden
wir in dem wercke, deszen wir uns unterfangen, nimmer so fort

---

[3] NB The common German endings which are abbreviated in the manuscript have
been silently expanded in this transcription. The substance of the letter suggests that it
is a covering letter to the preceeding treatise.

kommen, dz uns nicht immer andere eines andern, und vielleicht auch wol beszern, überführen. Deszhalb laszt Euch diese meine auffgesetzte allgemeine gründe nicht all unnötig und wol entbehrlich fürkommen, sondern nembt sie an, als solche regeln, an welchen zu seiner zeit alle particularia geprüfet, und nach welchem sie auch in gehörliche ordnung eingeschräncket werden müszen: dz, wenn von uns gefordert würde, wir solten die ursachen unsers verfahrens dieszfalls auff- und darlegen, wir deszen gründliche warheiten und warhaffte gründe, dawieder kein gewiszenhaffter oder verständiger man etwas auffbringen und einwenden könne, bereit und ferttig in unsern händen haben mögen. Man musz alles von dem, was vorhergeht, anfangen, wil man die menschliche vernunft meistern. Vom förderſten, sag ich, das bekandt ist, müszen wir dahin kommen, dz wir die menschen sehen laszen, was unbekandt ist: und vom Höchsten Gutt dahin, dz wir sie die nutzbarkeit deszen, was ihnen von sich selber heilsam und erspriszlich fürkommt, finden und lieben laszen. Geliebts Euch, diese sache in irgendt einer absonderlichen handlung unserer dreyfaltigen Correspondenz zuver-suchen,[4] so wird sich der gebrauch dieses meines allgemeinen Discurses [augenblicklich] weisen. Können, bey unser zusammenkunft, was die particularia anlangt, weitläufftiger mit einander handeln, und von den unterschiedlichen weisen dieses werck fortzustellen, die man auff ein interim zur hand nehmen könte, nothwendiger unterredung pflegen. Befehl Euch hiermit Gott, und verbleibe

Ewer dienstschuldiger Knecht
und trewer Freund in [Gott]
Iohn Dury.

[*translation*][5]

Sir Cheney, when I looked today at what I had yesterday set down on paper concerning the correspondence you know of, I was close to doubting whether I should send you such matter or not, considering that I touch on no particular subjects pertaining to it in which (to use a phrase of yours) a matter may be rendered virtually tangible.[6] Yet I nonetheless saw good not to leave you long in expectation of a short description of that which you desired to know of me. So far as the particulars are concerned, these may easily be added at another time. It is not my custom to sift every particular of a matter, but rather to establish a true foundation from which reasonable people may deduce

---

[4] This is presumably referring to Dury's correspondence both with Hartlib and Culpeper at this time.

[5] The editors are grateful to John Young for providing this translation.

[6] Lit: 'be virtually felt with the hands'.

the particulars, so long as they but take into account the circumstances and condition of the state they live in. Propositions not grounded in general and incontrovertible truths cannot long be sustained. But if our business is to introduce a general reformation of our being and to consider promoting the good of each and everyone, then we must necessarily lay the foundations of our advice as deeply as the lineaments ordained it by nature are hidden deep in human understanding, so that the edifice to be built upon it may endure unshaken and unfallen for our posterity. [The fact] that most people do not see so far, but satisfy themselves with this or that proposition that seems to them convenient or attractive, does not move me, whose concern it is to bring men from earth to Heaven, from the evil of overmuch seeking and loving of oneself and one's own to the worthy communion of saints and to a charitable willingness to serve that seeks no self-advantage, to follow their weakness in this; far more does it give me occasion to quicken their spirits, that they might fairly rush alongside me toward the true goal by which the common good may most widely be advanced;[7] and to give them to understand in what manner each and every particular, gauged by a certain level,[8] should be set in its proper place and subordinated to the common good. For so long as we do not fetch our materials from their true sources and lay such foundations as can be overthrown by no contradiction, so long shall we be unable to advance so far in the work we have undertaken that others may not constantly charge us with undertaking another, and perhaps even a better. Therefore do not let these general principles of mine that I have set down seem unnecessary and superfluous to you, but take them as such rules against which all particulars must in their time be tested and by which they must be ranged in due order: so that when it is demanded of us that we set forth and expound the reasons for our actions in this matter, we may have fundamental truths and true foundations of them ready and to hand, which no honest or reasonable man may object to or gainsay in any way. To master human reason, one must always begin from what has gone before. From first known principles, I say, we must advance so far that we can bring people to see what is unknown: and from the Highest Good bring them to discover and love the exploitability of that which seems to them intrinsically salutary and fruitful. Should it please you to try this matter in any other particular treatment of our tripartite correspondency, the use of this my general discourse will at once reveal itself. When we meet, we shall be able to treat together at greater length of matters pertaining to the particulars,

---

[7] Lit: 'be helped to its feet'.

[8] 'Certain' retains the ambiguity of 'gewiss' which can mean either 'particular' or 'infallible'. 'Level' is used in the sense of a modern 'spirit level'.

and engage in necessary discussion of the various methods that might in the meantime be employed for the furtherance of this work. I commend you herewith to God and remain

Your willing servant and true friend in God,

John Dury.

INDEX

Note: *This index contains references to names, places and subjects mentioned throughout the text including footnotes (the latter without any specific separate indication). Biblical citations have not been indexed.*

III
THE CROMWELLIAN
DECIMATION TAX OF 1655
THE ASSESSMENT LISTS

Edited with an Introduction by
J. T. Cliffe

CONTENTS

ACKNOWLEDGEMENTS

The transcripts of Crown Copyright material in the Public Record Office are published with the permission of the Controller of Her Majesty's Stationery Office.

ABBREVIATIONS

BL	British Library
C.5,C.6	Public Record Office, Chancery Proceedings, Six Clerks' Series
C.33	Public Record Office, Chancery, Entry Books of Decrees and Orders
CCAM	*Calendar of the Proceedings of the Committee for the Advance of Money*
CCC	*Calendar of the Proceedings of the Committee for Compounding*
CSPDom	*Calendar of State Papers, Domestic*
DNB	*Dictionary of National Biography*
Henning	B.D.Henning (ed.), *The History of Parliament: The House of Commons 1660–1690*, 3 vols (1983)
PRO	Public Record Office
S.P.23	Public Record Office, State Papers Domestic, Committee for Compounding
S.P.28	Public Record Office, State Papers Domestic, Commonwealth Exchequer Papers
S.P.29	Public Record Office, State Papers Domestic, Charles II
Thurloe State Papers	John Thurloe, *A Collection of State Papers of John Thurloe*, 7 vols (1725)
VCH	*Victoria County History*
Wards 5	Public Record Office, Court of Wards, Feodaries' Surveys

INTRODUCTION

The Decimation Lists

The royalist uprising of March 1655 led the Protector to adopt a number of measures aimed at improving internal security, in particular the appointment of major generals, each with responsibility for a particular region;[1] the establishment of a new county militia; and the introduction of an extraordinary or decimation tax which was intended to provide the necessary funding for the militia troops. Unlike the monthly assessment for the support of the regular army the decimation tax was a discriminatory tax in the sense that it was specifically designed as a levy on royalists or suspected royalists. In the event, however, it proved to be one of the most short-lived of taxes. On Christmas day 1656 Major General John Desborough introduced a parliamentary bill for its continuation and in a first reading debate on 7 January declared that

> I believe no man has come under a decimation but such as have either acted or spoken bitterly against the Government, and for their young king, and drank his health. Many have escaped that have done such things. I hope they shall come under decimation..... I think it is too light a tax, a decimation; I would have it higher.

Unimpressed by his advocacy, many MPs took the view that it was an unfair and divisive tax and at the end of January the bill was rejected.[2] This effectively sealed the fate of the decimation tax after a period of operation which had involved the levying of three half-yearly payments.

The most interesting type of document associated with this ephemeral fiscal measure is the county assessment list: that is, a list of the persons taxed together with the sums which they were required to pay. Such lists are valuable for the light they throw on political sympathies as perceived by the major generals and their associates, on the landed income of those singled out as delinquents and on the extent to which the decimation scheme fulfilled its declared objectives. Detailed information of this kind was requested by the Protectorate government for monitoring purposes and subsequently Charles II's Exchequer

---

[1] For a full list of the major generals and their divisions or associations see the Appendix, below pp. 425–8.

[2] Thomas Burton, *Diary of Thomas Burton* (ed. J.T.Rutt) (1828), i, 230–43, 310–21, 369. *The Parliamentary or Constitutional History of England* (1762–3), xxi, 48–55.

officials called for similar returns. At the Public Record Office there is no separate category of decimation papers and it has therefore been necessary to undertake an extensive search with results which suggest that many of the assessment lists submitted may have been destroyed. Among the Commonwealth Exchequer Papers (S.P.28) there are lists for Bedfordshire, Cambridgeshire, Derbyshire, Essex, Hertfordshire, Kent, Rutland and Sussex while a Hampshire list has been found among the Exchequer lay subsidy rolls (E.179).[3] In the case of some counties (Cambridgeshire, Essex, Hertfordshire, Kent and Sussex) there are three lists, one for each half year in the period June 1655 to December 1656. As is well known, the *Thurloe State Papers* contain initial assessment lists for a number of counties[4] : Bedfordshire, Cumberland, Essex, Huntingdonshire, Northamptonshire, Rutland, Suffolk, Sussex and Westmorland. Where appropriate these have been included in the text which has lists for a total of fourteen counties. In addition, there is a section entitled 'Other Counties' which consists of individual assessment figures derived from various sources.

The Decimation Tax Arrangements

The decimation tax was inaugurated in orders 'For securing the Peace of the Commonwealth' which were issued by the Protector and his Council on 21 September 1655.[5] The tax, it was explained, was to be levied on such persons in England and Wales whose estates had been sequestered for delinquency or who had been in arms for the late king against the Long Parliament or for Charles Stuart his son 'or have adhered to, assisted or abetted the Forces raised against the said Parliament'. This was subject to the qualification that the arrangements would apply only to individuals who had an estate of inheritance or a life interest in lands, tenements or hereditaments worth £100 a year or more or who were in possession of a personal estate worth £1500 or more. In the former category the rate of tax was £10 a year for every £100 of annual revenue and in the latter category £100 for every £1500 and *pro rata*. When an individual was financially qualified in both respects the assessment was to cover his personal estate as well as his real estate but there was an element of choice as to the methodology to be followed: in such cases he was to be 'assessed and taxed for the said Fifteen hundred pounds at the rate of Ten pounds per annum also, or after the rate of One hundred pounds for Fifteen hundred pounds, and after those proportions for every greater Sum'. The tax

---

[3] S.P.28/153, 159, 181, 197, part 2, 219, 226, 334, 342, unbound documents. E.179/176/554.

[4] *Thurloe State Papers*, iv, 239, 240, 427–8, 434–6, 511–13, 561–3.

[5] PRO, State Papers Domestic, Commonwealth, S.P.18/c/136.

would be payable in half- yearly instalments, the first on 21 December and the next on 24 June. For anyone refusing to pay the tax or neglecting to pay within twenty days after the appointed day the penalty was sequestration of his real estate.

The orders also made provision for the appointment of a 'competent number' of commissioners in each county who would sometimes be described as commissioners for the security or preservation of the peace of the Commonwealth. So far as their fiscal responsibilities were concerned they were charged with identifying all persons who were liable to be taxed, establishing the value of the real and personal estate which they owned within the county or which had been in their possession on 1 November 1653 and assessing the amount of tax to be laid on each individual. The selection of the commissioners was left to the major generals who were naturally anxious to ensure that they were men who could be relied upon. Some of those appointed were major landowners such as Samuel Dunch in Berkshire, Sir Thomas Honywood and Sir Gobert Barrington in Essex, Richard Norton in Hampshire, Sir Thomas Barnardiston and James Calthorpe in Suffolk and Sir Richard Onslow in Surrey. In the main, however, the commissioners were persons of more modest income and social standing.[6]

The orders of 21 September 1655 offered little detailed guidance and this occasioned some doubt and uncertainty among those who were responsible for their execution. In November the Lincolnshire commissioners informed Secretary Thurloe that while the gentlemen whom they had summoned to appear before them were generally compliant

> they insist upon the allowance of their debts and other engagements upon their estates, by way of defalcation; which the major general acquainted us and signified unto them was intended to be allowed, notwithstanding the orders of his highness and the council and their instructions do not thereunto particularly authorize or direct us.

This issue had in fact already been raised by Major General William Boteler at the request of the Northamptonshire commissioners. In response the government made it clear that no allowance should be made for debts or encumbrances. Writing from Leicester on 24 November Major General Edward Whalley (whose association included Lincolnshire) told Thurloe that he was very glad to have this ruling, adding that it would 'very much shorten our work'. Not surprisingly, those who were being proceeded against took a different view: on 31 December, for example, Sir Edward Hales was complaining that the Kent commissioners had decided to make him pay 'for the entire value

---

[6] *Thurloe State Papers*, iv, 225, 285, 363, 427.   S.P.28/227, letter from the Essex commissioners, 30 January 1656/7 (unbound). *CSPDom, 1655–6*, 8.

of my estate, neither discounting debts, taxes, nor other annuall charges'.[7]

Another point on which clarification was sought concerned the approach to be adopted in the case of landed property which had been sold since November 1653. In his letter of 24 November Whalley reported that he and his commissioners had concluded that they should only tax such estates as were in the possession of the delinquents or of trustees acting on their behalf either on or since the date of the original orders, that is to say 21 September 1655; but that they should also certify what estates were in their possession on 1 November 1653. After considering this question the Council ruled that the assessment should be based on the landed property which had belonged to the delinquent in November 1653 and that the tax should then be levied on the estate which he currently owned.[8]

A substantial amount of property had been sold by the Treason Trustees as a consequence of the legislation enacted in 1651 and 1652 for the disposal of estates forfeited to the Commonwealth for treason.[9] In a letter addressed to the Protector in December 1655 Major General Charles Worsley observed that many Lancashire royalists 'were papist-delinquents, and their estates quite sold by the state, which will make us all much short of what we expected'. Subsequently, in February 1656, Cromwell received a report from the Durham commissioners which revealed a similar state of affairs. They assumed (he was told) that the purchasers of the forfeited estates had been acting as agents on behalf of the original owners who would therefore have regained possession. When such delinquents appeared before them, however, they sought to escape their liabilities by producing fraudulent deeds of conveyance.[10] A number of royalists who appear in the text had been named in one or other of the acts for the sale of forfeited estates. These include Sir Thomas Dacre, Sir Francis Howard, Andrew Huddleston, Sir Richard Musgrave and Sir Edward Radcliffe, all of whom are to be found in the Cumberland decimation list, Rowland Eyre of Hassop in Derbyshire, Richard Thornhill of Kent and Peter Giffard of Staffordshire.[11] The treatment of forfeited estates was a difficult and sensitive issue and the Protectorate government may well have decided that it would be expedient to regard it as a matter for local discretion. In practice much depended on the attitude of the major generals and the

---

[7] *Thurloe State Papers*, iv, 179, 212, 241, 251, 364–5, 411.

[8] *Ibid*, iv, 241. *CSPDom, 1655–6*, 34.

[9] Acts of 16 July 1651, 4 August 1652 and 18 November 1652 (Sir Charles Firth and R.S.Rait (eds.), *The Acts and Ordinances of the Interregnum, 1642–1660* (1911), ii, 520–45, 591–8, 623–52).

[10] *Thurloe State Papers*, iv, 340, 541.

[11] Firth and Rait, *op.cit.*, 521, 541, 591, 624, 635.

commissioners. Some men such as Eyre, Thornhill and Giffard were taxed in the normal way, apparently on the implicit assumption that they had regained possession of their estates. In Cumberland, on the other hand, it was agreed that Dacre, Howard and Musgrave should each pay a 'voluntary' contribution of £10 a year, 'no visible estate appearing', while in Bedfordshire Sir Lewis Dyve, who had been one of the most active royalists in the county, managed to escape decimation altogether.[12]

Surprisingly, the orders of 21 September 1655 make no reference to the possession of property in more than one county despite its obvious relevance to the question of eligibility. This point was belatedly acknowledged in an additional instruction for the county commissioners which was dispatched two months later. In such circumstances, it was explained, the total value of a person's real or personal estate would determine whether he satisfied the financial criteria which had been laid down; if so, the commissioners should only tax him on the property which he owned in their particular county.[13] In effect the new instruction highlighted the potential drawbacks of a tax scheme which was to be operated on a county basis. Not only was there a need for consistency in evaluating an individual's political loyalties when he had lands in two or more counties but it was also important to ensure that the financial criteria were properly applied where there was any element of doubt. The fact that a major general usually had responsibility for a block of counties was clearly helpful in this respect but some royalist landowners had widely scattered estates. While the central government sought to keep in close touch with what was happening at the local level its involvement in individual cases was very largely confined to the consideration of petitions from persons who were attempting to secure exemption from the tax or the provision of guidance in response to requests from the major generals or their commissioners. However, there were a few special cases in which it took the lead and accepted the offer of a once-for-all payment or composition as an alternative to decimation.

Cases Handled Centrally

William Cavendish, Earl of Devonshire, who was seated at Chatsworth in Derbyshire, owned estates in a number of counties. On the eve of the Civil War he had commanded a landed income of some £8000 a year, excluding two large jointures worth £7200 a year in all.[14] In December 1655 the President of the Council sought particulars of the

[12] See pp. 429–30, 432, 433, 442 and 452.
[13] PRO, State Papers Supplementary, S.P.46/xcvii/fo.158.
[14] Lawrence Stone, *The Crisis of the Aristocracy 1558–1641* (1965), 136.

Earl's estates from the major generals concerned. Since, he explained, the Earl owned property in several counties the Protector and his Council had decided to allow him to appear and give bond in Middlesex 'for all'. When Major General Whalley complained about this method of procedure he was assured that there was no intention of exempting him from the decimation tax or of diverting the money which would be received from the militia forces in the counties where his estates were situated.[15] If returns were sent in from Buckinghamshire and Lancashire they do not appear to have survived but the returns from the other counties[16] offer a virtually complete picture of his income:

	annual value		
	£	s	d
Derbyshire	2346	17	9
Huntingdonshire	1568	10	5
Nottinghamshire	596	6	8
Somerset	50	0	0
Staffordshire	252	3	2
Suffolk	1101	15	8
Yorkshire	2175	6	8
	8091	0	4

Eventually it was agreed that the Earl should pay £4000 in full discharge of his fiscal liabilities. Half this sum was allocated to Major General Hezekiah Haynes and the other half to Major General William Boteler for the support of their militia forces. No doubt Major General Whalley felt aggrieved.[17]

Another nobleman allowed to compound was Warwick Lord Mohun who had estates in Devon and Cornwall worth £4000 a year. In June 1656 it was agreed that as he had satisfied the Protector and the Council that he was well affected his voluntary offer of £500 should be accepted and he should be discharged from all proceedings against him by Major General John Desborough and the Devon commissioners.[18] Sir George Pratt, a London merchant who had a country seat at Coleshill in Berkshire, owned property in various counties but this was not the main reason why he was deemed to merit special treatment. Despite the fact that he had recently served as high sheriff of Berkshire the

---

[15] *CSPDom, 1655–6*, 78, 122. *Thurloe State Papers*, iv, 434.

[16] *CSPDom, 1655–6*. 111–12, 122, 124, 160, 234, 242, 247. In 1647 the Buckinghamshire property was said to be worth £400 p.a. (*CCC*, 66).

[17] *CSPDom, 1656–7*, 44, 46, 89, 104. Haynes had responsibility for Suffolk and Boteler for Huntingdonshire.

[18] *CSPDom, 1655–6*, 393. C.33/260/fo.381.

county commissioners took the view that he was liable to be taxed. This led him to submit a petition seeking exemption and in October 1656 the Council decided that Major General William Goffe should interview him with the object of discovering where his sympathies lay. Goffe subsequently reported that Sir George had freely expressed his dislike of the Cavalier party and had assured him of his loyalty to the Protector and his government. As a token of his good faith he made a voluntary contribution of £500, which was allotted to Goffe for his pay as a major general, and in return he was granted an absolute discharge.[19]

The Selection Process

The first task of the county commissioners was to draw up a list of persons who in their judgment were liable to be taxed. Obvious sources of information for this purpose were the compounding papers of royalists who had been involved in one way or another in the Civil Wars and the sequestration accounts which had been maintained by the parliamentary committees in the various counties. In the course of November 1655 Major General Whalley asked for lists of the royalists within his association who had compounded with the committee at Goldsmiths' Hall, together with particulars of their estates; by this means, he told Secretary Thurloe, 'we may have a certain charge against those whose estates and actions we cannot so well discover'.[20] Whether there was a general outflow of information from the records of the Goldsmiths' Hall committee remains unclear, though it may be noted that on 26 November Major General Charles Worsley, whose association consisted of Cheshire, Lancashire and Staffordshire, was reporting that the commissioners were proceeding against all those who had been compounders.[21] In some counties such as Kent and Essex a considerable number of royalists had compounded for their estates with the local parliamentary committee; and in Essex at least they had been obliged to declare any property which they owned in other counties. In Kent, however, the former parliamentary committee refused to allow Major General Kelsey to see their compounding records.[22]

Since the orders of 21 September 1655 specifically referred to the liability of persons whose estates had been sequestered for delinquency it was clearly incumbent on the county commissioners to make full use of the sequestration records. In Essex Thomas Smyth of Hill Hall considered that the commissioners had been too undiscriminating in drawing on this source of information. In March 1656 he related, in a

[19] *CCAM*, 799–800. *CSPDom, 1656–7*, 128, 134, 156.

[20] *Thurloe State Papers*, iv, 156, 185, 211, 212.

[21] *Ibid*, iv, 247.

[22] S.P.23/ccliv/24I. A.M.Everitt, *The Community of Kent and the Great Rebellion 1640–60* (1966), 294.

petition which he submitted to the Protector, that his estate had been unjustly sequestered but he had been discharged after furnishing proof that he was well affected to Parliament. The Essex commissioners, however, had found his name in the sequestration book and since he could not immediately find his discharge he had been forced to make the first payment of his assessment.[23]

According to Clarendon most of the revenue from the decimation tax was derived from

> those who never did, nor ever would have given, the King the least assistance, and were only reputed to be of his party because they had not assisted the rebels with a visible cheerfulness, or in any considerable proportion, and had proposed to themselves to sit still as neuters, and not to be at any charge with reference to either party; or such who sheltered themselves in some of the King's garrisons for their own conveniency.[24]

From the surviving evidence it is clear that, although Clarendon was exaggerating, a substantial minority of the persons taxed had neither compounded for their estates nor suffered the penalty of sequestration; and that while some of them were too young to have been actively engaged in the Civil Wars there were many who had clearly decided that neutrality was the best policy. In a draft letter addressed to the major generals which was submitted for the Council's approval in October 1655 there was a passage indicating that lists of persons who were currently suspected of disloyalty would shortly be distributed to them. In the event this passage was omitted, probably because the major generals had recently forwarded such lists to the central government.[25] Not surprisingly, the decimation lists contain the names of many of the individuals who appear in these intelligence reports, including some who had been arrested on suspicion at the beginning of October.[26]

Occasionally it was thought prudent to seek guidance from the central government on whether a particular individual should be taxed. In November 1655 Major General Boteler asked Secretary Thurloe to let him know whether the Protector considered it appropriate to exempt the estates of two of the major landowners in Bedfordshire, the Earl of

---

[23] *CSPDom, 1655–6*, 210. Smyth had been taxed at the rate of £110 a year.

[24] *The History of the Rebellion and Civil Wars in England. ... by Edward, Earl of Clarendon* (ed. W.D.Murray) (1888), v, 394.

[25] PRO, State Papers Supplementary, S.P.46/xcvii/fols.156–7. The lists supplied by the major generals were collated in three books: BL, Additional MSS 34,011, 34,012 and 34,013.

[26] *CSPDom, 1655*, 367–8. Those arrested who were subsequently required to pay the decimation tax include Sir John Tyrrell, Sir Henry Appleton, Sir Benjamin Ayloffe and Sir William Hicks of Essex, Sir Sackville Glemham and Edward Rookwood of Suffolk, and Samuel Thornton and Thomas Story of Cambridgeshire.

Bedford and Sir Robert Napier of Luton Hoo. Sir Robert's estate, he told him, had been sequestered for three years 'though afterwards (as it is alleadged here) when he saw which way success was like to goe he did for some litle time sitt in the long parliament'. Evidently the Protector came down in favour of exemption since neither man appears in the Bedfordshire decimation lists. On the other hand, the commissioners for Middlesex and Westminster decided in January 1656 to levy the tax on that part of the Earl's estate which fell within their jurisdiction.[27]

Initial reports from the major generals on the number of royalists who were liable to be taxed were often far from encouraging. Bedfordshire, Huntingdonshire and Rutland, it was stressed, were small counties while even in such larger counties as Norfolk and Suffolk there were comparatively few delinquents. Writing from Chichester on 16 November Major General William Goffe told Thurloe that in Sussex so many of the delinquents were dead 'and soe much of their estates sould that I feare the revenew raysed by the taxe in this county will not bee very considerable'. Other major generals also felt it necessary to remind the central government that the estates of many royalist landowners had been sold by the Treason Trustees.[28] What caused particular concern, however, was the constraining effect of the financial qualifications which had been prescribed. In a letter dispatched on 19 November Major General Boteler lamented that there were not many delinquents in Bedfordshire 'whose estates arise so high as to fall under our decimation'. Similarly, Major General Worsley reported that in Cheshire, Lancashire and Staffordshire many persons 'that have been very active against the parliament, and were looked upon to be men of good estates, will hardly be brought within the compase; for one hundred pounds *per annum* is a good estate in these parts'. As a means of rectifying the situation some major generals proposed that the threshold for real estate should be lowered to £50, £40 or even £20 a year and that for personal estate to £500 or even £300.[29]

The following table shows the total number of individuals who were taxed in each of the counties for which assessment lists have survived:[30]

Bedfordshire	19
Cambridgeshire	18

---

[27] *Thurloe State Papers*, iv, 218, 406. Napier's estate in Bedfordshire had been valued at £1796 a year by the sequestrators (BL, Additional MSS 5494, fols.13–14). In 1648 he had been secluded from the Long Parliament as a consequence of Pride's Purge. The Earl of Bedford's brothers Lord John and Lord Edward Russell were both taxed: see pp. 429, 431 below.

[28] *Thurloe State Papers*, iv, 171, 208, 227, 229, 274, 333, 340, 511.

[29] *Ibid*, iv, 218, 224–5, 235, 257, 321, 333, 341, 344–5, 742.

[30] Some men figure in more than one of these totals.

Cumberland	31
Derbyshire	22
Essex	99
Hampshire	37
Hertfordshire	20
Huntingdonshire	5[31]
Kent	91
Northamptonshire	36
Rutland	9
Suffolk	30
Sussex	31
Westmorland	19

As regards other counties it appears that twenty royalists were taxed in Dorset and eleven or twelve in Wiltshire.[32]

A considerable number of wealthy royalists had died before the introduction of the decimation tax. In some cases the son or a younger brother who had inherited the estate found himself taxed as a delinquent but this was by no means a common occurrence: in Sussex, for example, no attempt was made to levy the tax on the estates which had once belonged to such royalist squires as Sir Edward Alford, Sir Edward Bishop, Sir Thomas Bowyer, Sir Thomas Gage of Firle Place and William Gage of Bentley. In the main, and bearing in mind the restrictive nature of the financial criteria, the county commissioners appear to have been reasonably thorough in identifying the royalists of the Civil War period who were still alive, particularly when they were actually resident in the county. There are, however, a few major landowners, men such as Thomas Chicheley of Cambridgeshire, Nicholas Steward of Hampshire and Sir John Harrison of Hertfordshire, whose omission from the decimation lists cannot readily be explained.

In all, there are 65 individuals in the decimation lists who owned property but were not resident in the county concerned. But if this suggests a high degree of efficiency on the part of the commissioners they were certainly not infallible in this respect. Richard Thornhill, for example, was taxed in Kent where he was seated but his Essex property was overlooked; and others who benefited from such lapses include the Earls of Northampton and Thanet, Lord Bergavenny, Sir Wingfield Bodenham of Rutland, Sir Thomas Culpeper of Kent and Dowse Fuller of Hampshire.

---

[31] Only two of these individuals were actually seated in the county.

[32] These included Sir John Strangways, Sir Gerrard Napier and Sir Hugh Wyndham of Dorset and Sir James Thynne of Wiltshire (*Thurloe State Papers*, iv, 324–5, 336–7).

The Proceedings of the Commissioners

During the months of November and December 1655 the major generals and the commissioners held meetings in the county towns and other principal towns and summoned the persons on their lists to appear before them and bring with them particulars of their estates. In some counties those who were singled out in this way were reported to have been compliant; but in others the proceedings were not so smooth. Some great noblemen were in fact distinctly unco-operative. Writing from Northampton on 13 November Major General Boteler informed Thurloe that on appearing before the commissioners the Earl of Northampton had peremptorily refused to give security for the payment of his tax assessment on the grounds that this could make it difficult for him to mortgage property to pay his debts. Other Cavaliers who were present had been encouraged to follow his example but by immediately declaring the Earl a prisoner he had persuaded them to submit.[33] According to a report from Major General Kelsey a meeting which he had held at Kingston in Surrey had been even more fraught with difficulty. The Earl of Southampton, he related, had first declined to bring in a particular of his estate. Although he had relented under pressure he had then refused to give security and many others had joined him in his resistance to the tax. Unfortunately, Kelsey complained, there was no prison at Kingston.[34]

Some men who were summoned categorically denied that they were guilty of disloyalty. In an account of the proceedings in Sussex Major General Goffe wrote that Sir William Morley had consented to be taxed 'but takes it very much to hart that hee should bee still reckoned a malignant, having long been satisfyde of the justice of our cause, and indeed very good men here doe speake well of him, and I beleeve his highnes will bee solicitted about him'.[35] In Leicestershire a number of wealthy gentry, among them Sir Robert Shirley, Sir Erasmus de la Fontaine and George Faunt, were so incensed that they immediately decided to submit a petition to the Protector seeking exemption from the decimation tax.[36] The Kent commissioners, wrote Major General Kelsey, were 'much discourag'd that the chiefest enemys of greatest estates are like to be freed' by making direct approaches to the Protector and his Council. He had heard that Sir George Sondes might already have been exempted although he was 'as great an enemy to the state as any of the rest'; and that the Earl of Thanet and Sir Edward Hales 'are both gone to London, with hopes to get an order to supercede our proceedings'.[37]

[33] *Ibid*, iv, 189.
[34] *Ibid*, iv, 234.
[35] *Ibid*, iv, 208.
[36] *Ibid*, iv, 335.
[37] *Ibid*, iv, 293. In fact all three men were taxed: see p. 443 below.

In a petition which he submitted Sir Charles Egerton described his encounters with the Staffordshire commissioners in some detail. He had first appeared before them in December when they had been unable to tell him what the charge was. At a further session in March 1656 they had asked him many questions but ignored his request for a written statement of the charge. On this occasion, he lamented, 'I was sentenced that at my next Summons I shold bring in particulars of my whole estate: whereupon I feare they will proceed to assess it, and also asperse my good name, who have lost in the Parliament service aboute nine thousand pounds'. In May Major General Worsley informed Thurloe that Sir Charles had been put on trial at Stafford and it had been decided that he should be taxed.[38]

In considering the value of both real and personal estates the commissioners were well aware of the dangers of relying solely on the particulars which the owners were required to provide. On Christmas day 1655 Major General Goffe was writing from Sussex that 'Men do now begin to be very industrious to bringe their estates to be under £100 *per annum*'.[39] Major General Worsley emphasised in correspondence with Secretary Thurloe that he was determined to ensure that the assessments were made on the basis of actual values. In November 1655 he reported that the Cheshire delinquents had supplied particulars of their property and steps were now being taken 'to come to a true account of there severall estats by comparinge that they bring in with what survay we have of ther estates in 1640, and if wee find that deficient wee intend to survay those estates that wee have a doubt of'.[40] In some counties at least the commissioners made use of sequestration accounts or compounding papers (though many who were taxed had neither compounded nor been subject to sequestration). While cases can be found in which there is a close correlation between the valuation on which the assessment was based and the corresponding figures in these earlier records it is clear that the commissioners were conscious of the fact that circumstances could have changed either favourably or otherwise during the intervening years. The Norfolk commissioners, wrote Major General Haynes on 19 November 1655, had virtually finished their work, 'exceeding in their assessing the bookes of sequestration'.[41]

On occasion the commissioners might dispatch one of their officials on a fact-finding mission but it would have been difficult to mount an extensive operation of this kind before the deadline of 21 December 1655 which had been set for the first half-year payments of the tax.

[38] BL, Additional MSS 6689, fo.320. *Thurloe State Papers*, iv, 765. *CSPDom, 1656–7*, 10.
[39] *Thurloe State Papers*, iv, 344.
[40] *Ibid*, iv, 179, 247.
[41] *Ibid*, iv, 216.

When Major General Goffe sent Thurloe a provisional assessment list for Sussex on 24 November he observed that if the estate of Sir William Morley or any other delinquent had been undervalued it was because the commissioners had lacked better information and added that 'wee may go higher when wee have cleare grounds so to doe; wee thought it best to bee doing something for the present, for it will cost very much tyme and charge to come to an exact knowledge of men's estates'. Similarly, Major General Whalley was writing from Lincoln in January 1656 that the tax assessments had been made upon the particulars which the delinquents themselves had brought in but the commissioners were now sending out messengers to inquire into the truth of them.[42] In the surviving decimation lists, however, there are comparatively few adjustments to the original assessment figures and these more often take the form of reductions than increases.

The Yield from the Decimation Tax

From November 1655 onwards some of the major generals forwarded their estimates of the annual yield from the tax within their particular associations: £2000 in Northamptonshire, nearly £500 in Rutland, £600 or £700 in Wiltshire (with a few additions in prospect), £4000 in Lincolnshire, nearly £1500 in Nottinghamshire, £1500 in Sussex, £1000 in Hampshire, £1000 in Berkshire and £5000 in Cheshire, Lancashire and Staffordshire.[43] More precise forecasts of the annual revenue were to be found in the initial assessment lists which were sent in:[44]

| | per annum | | |
	£	s	d
Bedfordshire	668	4	7
Cumberland	532	9	0
Essex	2689	3	4
Huntingdonshire	279	10	0
Northamptonshire	1600	6	0
Rutland	436	8	9
Suffolk	1069	12	0
Sussex	1235	0	0
Westmorland	423	2	0

---

[42] *Ibid*, iv, 239, 434.

[43] *Ibid*, iv, 189, 218, 274, 315, 324–5, 333, 337, 340, 434, 639.

[44] *Ibid*, iv, 240, 427–8, 434–6, 511–13, 561–3. Some major landowners in Northamptonshire, including the Earl of Westmorland and Sir William Farmer, had apparently secured exemption since the receipt of Major General Boteler's provisional estimate of £2000 (*ibid*, iv, 511). The Sussex list was largely restricted to persons residing in the western part of the county.

The following table shows the actual receipts which were recorded by the county treasurers as distinct from the anticipated revenue:[45]

		£	s	d
Bedfordshire:	third half-year	396	10	$0\frac{1}{2}$
Cambridgeshire:	first half-year	185	1	6
	second half-year	162	9	6
	third half-year	124	5	4
Derbyshire:	total receipts	1244	8	$7\frac{1}{2}$
Essex:	first half-year	1346	19	8
	second half-year	1175	19	8
	third half-year	822	17	4
Hampshire:	second & third half-years	1038	5	8
Hertfordshire:	first half-year	402	2	6
	second half-year	353	2	9
	third half-year	337	1	4
Huntingdonshire:	first half-year	31	6	6
	second half-year	14	3	6
Kent:	first half-year	1551	16	2
	second half-year	1277	18	6
	third half-year	1106	9	6
Rutland:	total receipts	575	4	7
Sussex:	first half-year	524	10	0
	second half-year	504	10	0
	third half-year	446	0	10

In some counties at least many royalists were slow to pay their tax assessments despite the fact that the orders of 21 September 1655 empowered the commissioners to apply the penalty of sequestration if there was any significant delay.[46] The first half-year payments were due on 21 December 1655 but in Hertfordshire nothing was received until March 1656 while in Kent the receipts were spread over the period 18 December 1655 to 12 July 1656.[47] On 27 February 1656 the President of the Council sent out a circular letter in which he instructed the major generals to ensure that all arrears of tax were paid in without further delay.[48]

From an early stage there were warnings that the revenue from the decimation tax was going to be insufficient to meet all the expenditure

[45] In the main these figures are drawn from the decimation lists (see below). The Huntingdonshire figures appear in a report forwarded in June 1656 (*CSPDom, 1655–6*, 396).

[46] See p. 409 above.

[47] See the Hertfordshire and Kent lists below.

[48] *CSPDom, 1655–6*, 201.

which it was intended to cover. In February 1656 Major General Goffe told Thurloe that in Sussex and Hampshire the receipts would only amount to half the sum required for the pay of the militia while Major General Boteler reported that within his association (which consisted of Bedfordshire, Huntingdonshire, Northamptonshire and Rutland) there was a shortfall of £1080.[49] The authorised expenditure figures for the county militia of England and Wales are set out in the Appendix. For the year beginning 24 June 1655 the total amounts to £80,067 13s 4d but in June 1656 the Council decided that some retrenchment was necessary and approved a reduced total of £67,010 5s 8d for the second year. A comparison of the estimated or actual receipts for individual counties with the corresponding figures in the Appendix provides confirmation that some major generals, including Goffe and Boteler, were faced with severe financial problems. On the other hand, the estimated receipts for Major General Worsley's counties of Cheshire, Lancashire and Staffordshire (£5000 a year) and for Major General Whalley's counties of Lincolnshire (£4000 a year) and Nottinghamshire (£1500 a year) are considerably in excess of the authorised expenditure figures even before their reduction.

In the case of both Essex and Kent the decimation papers enable us to compare the receipts with the actual expenditure:[50]

		receipts			disbursements		
		£	s	d	£	s	d
Essex:	first half-year	1346	19	8	1534	13	2
	second half-year	1175	19	8	1172	19	0
	third half-year	822	17	4	711	12	0
	total	3345	16	8	3419	4	2
Kent:	first half-year	1551	16	2	2181	11	3
	second half-year	1277	18	6	768	14	7
	third half-year	1106	9	6	1620	12	0
	total	3936	4	2	4570	17	10

The disbursement figures for Essex exclude the sum of £120 which was paid into the Exchequer on 7 February 1662.

[49] *Thurloe State Papers*, iv, 497, 511. Boteler estimated that the receipts within his association would amount to some £2984 a year (*ibid*, iv, 512–13).

[50] S.P.28/153 and 159, unbound decimation papers. (See also S.P.28/110, part 2, fols.248–9, 263 for some documents relating to the pay of the Essex militia). The disbursement figures include the pay of the county treasurers. It has been suggested that in Kent the yield of the tax proved sufficient, with a small margin, to cover the pay of the militia (Everitt, *The Community of Kent*, 294).

Occasionally money was switched from one county to another within the same association. In December 1656 Major General Whalley forwarded a paper certifying that the pay of the Derbyshire militia together with certain other expenses amounted to £1189 13s od for the year ending on 24 June; that the receiver for Derbyshire had paid £433 and the receiver for Lincolnshire £67; and that consequently there remained £689 13s od in arrear. After considering this paper the Council gave order that the receiver for Derbyshire should pay a further £423 7s 5d and the receiver for Leicestershire (another of Whalley's counties) £266 5s 7d.[51]

By June 1656 the government had become so concerned about the failure of the decimation tax to provide sufficient funds for the support of the militia that it was decided that greater centralised control was necessary. In a declaration approved by the Protector on 13 June it was decreed that the Army Committee 'shall have the care, mannageinge and orderinge of the whole businesse of bringing in, receivinge, disposeing and issueing forth of the monies'; that the county treasurers should forward all the money which was raised to the Receivers General (that is, the Treasurers at War) in London and submit copies of their accounts to the Army Committee; and that warrants should be issued by the Army Committee for the payment of the militia forces.[52] All the evidence suggests, however, that the declaration had little practical effect. The accounts of the Treasurers at War contain no reference to decimation money apart from the Earl of Devonshire's contribution; and it is apparent that in counties for which detailed records have survived the money received continued to be held and disbursed locally at the direction of the major generals.[53] In March 1657 the major generals were told that any remaining funds should be distributed fairly with a view to clearing the arrears of pay of the militia but there are indications that this instruction was not always complied with. In October 1658 it was reported that there was £200 of decimation money remaining in the hands of the Suffolk receivers while in January 1659 Captain Thomas Garrett, the former county treasurer for Norfolk, was ordered to pay into the Exchequer the £500 or £600 which was still in his possession.[54]

Far from improving the situation grew worse as the number of persons taxed declined and with it the receipts which came in. The main factor responsible for this trend was the willingness of the Protector

---

[51] S.P.25/lxxvii/554.

[52] S.P.25/lxxvii/902–4.

[53] PRO, Exchequer, Pipe Office, Declared Accounts (rolls), E.371/305, 306, 307. (The references to the Earl of Devonshire's contribution are in E.371/306). S.P.28/153, 159, 197, part 2, 226, 342, unbound decimation papers.

[54] *CSPDom, 1656–7,* 304. *CSPDom, 1658–9,* 169, 239, 244.

and his Council to look favourably on requests for exemption from the tax. Among those who managed to extricate themselves in this way were some of the wealthier landowners, men such as Richard Earl of Dorset, Lord Henry Paulet (a brother of John Marquess of Winchester), Sir Thomas Wiseman and Thomas Smyth of Essex and Sir John Monson, Sir Robert Thorold and Stephen Anderson of Lincolnshire.[55] The case of Sir Thomas Wiseman (who had been taxed at the rate of £120 a year) is particularly well documented. On 13 January 1657 the Council gave direction that his petition should be considered by Major General Haynes and any three of the Essex commissioners who happened to be in London. This led to the submission of a certificate by four of the commissioners in which they expressed the opinion that Sir Thomas was a fit subject for the Protector's favour; and in the light of their advice the Council authorised Haynes and his commissioners to discharge him 'if equitable'. Subsequently, on 30 January, Sir Thomas Honywood and other commissioners issued an order discharging him from all further proceedings and requiring the treasurer, Edward Elliston, to repay the sum of £120 which he had received from him.[56]

The Text

On 4 February 1652 the Rump Parliament passed an act which declared invalid all titles which had been granted by the late king since 4 January 1642.[57] Some of those who compiled the decimation lists were careful to observe the law in this respect but others were not: we find, for example, that Sir William Halton, who had been created a baronet in September 1642, is shown as an esquire in the Cambridge-shire list which is reproduced here while in the Essex list he is allowed his title.[58] In cases where a title has been omitted the point is highlighted in the notes printed below, which because of their number have been placed at the end of the texts (below pp. 453–92).

Generally, the county commissioners preferred to tax real estate rather than personal estate. This is hardly surprising since the value of real estate was much easier to verify. In the case of the Sussex lists it is immediately apparent that all the assessment figures are based on the valuation of landed property while the Suffolk list draws a clear distinction between real and personal estate. In other cases it may

[55] *CSPDom, 1655–6*, 89, 92, 172, 210, 234, 396. *CSPDom, 1656–7*, 249. *CCC*, 1069–70, 1433. For Sir Thomas Wiseman see note 56.

[56] *CSPDom, 1656–7*, 225, 241, 249. S.P.28/227, letter from the Essex commissioners dated 30 January 1656/7 (unbound).

[57] Firth and Rait (eds.), *The Acts and Ordinances of the Interregnum, 1642–1660* (1911), ii, 564–5.

[58] See pp. 431 and 435 below. It is interesting to note, however, that Halton appears as a plain esquire in the Essex list printed in the *Thurloe State Papers* (iv, 435).

reasonably be assumed that the tax was levied on real estate unless there are specific references to the contrary.

While the original spelling has been fully retained the punctuation has been modernised and abbreviations have been extended. In addition, a more austere approach has been adopted to the use of capital letters in accordance with modern practice.

Where exceptionally the original text is defective because of wear and tear the missing portion has been inserted in square brackets provided that it is readily identifiable; otherwise a gap has been left.

In the case of dates which fall between 1 January and 24 March the New Style date has been added.

In both the manuscript lists and the lists printed in the *Thurloe State Papers* there is an unnecessary abundance of noughts. For the sake of clarity this form of presentation has been discarded: for example, '010 00 00' has been changed to '10 0 0'. With the same object in view the roman numerals used in the Hampshire list have been changed to arabic numerals. Finally, the pound sign has been modernised throughout.

APPENDIX
EXPENDITURE ON THE COUNTY MILITIA

The following table shows the approved expenditure on the county militia of England and Wales, (1) for the year beginning 24 June 1655 and (2) for the year beginning 24 June 1656 (S.P.25/lxxvii/861–80 and 884–901). The 'establishment', as it was termed, covers the pay of the major generals, the militia officers and soldiers, and the county treasurers and other civilian staff, together with certain minor items of expenditure.

	(1) per annum			(2) per annum		
	£	s	d	£	s	d
Major General John Lambert's division						
Yorkshire	4288	12	0	3628	12	0
Durham	1189	13	0	917	13	0
To Lambert or Colonel Robert Lilburne his deputy for these counties	666	13	4	666	13	4
Total	6144	18	4	5212	18	4
Northumberland	1189	13	0	917	13	0
Cumberland & Westmorland	1189	13	0	949	13	0
To Lambert or Colonel Charles Howard for these counties	666	13	4	666	13	4
Total	3045	19	4	2533	19	4
Lord Deputy Charles Fleetwood's division						
Hertfordshire	1189	13	0	913	13	0
Oxfordshire	1189	13	0	929	13	0
Buckinghamshire	1189	13	0	913	13	0
To Fleetwood or his deputy Major William Packer for these counties	666	13	4	666	13	4
Total	4235	12	4	3423	12	4

	(1) per annum			(2) per annum		
	£	s	d	£	s	d
Cambridgeshire	1189	13	0	839	13	0
Isle of Ely	869	13	0	757	13	0
Essex	2189	6	0	1809	6	0
Norfolk	3188	19	0	2606	19	0
Suffolk	3188	19	0	2606	19	0
City and County of Norwich	869	13	4	869	13	4
To Fleetwood or Major Hezekiah Haynes for these counties	666	13	4	666	13	4
Total	12,162	16	8	10,156	16	8

Major General John Desborough's division

Cornwall	2189	6	0	1789	6	0
Devon	3188	19	0	2628	19	0
Dorset	1189	13	0	959	13	0
Somerset	2189	6	0	1789	6	0
Wiltshire	2189	6	0	1799	6	0
Gloucestershire	2189	6	0	1757	6	0
To Desborough	666	13	4	666	13	4
Total	13,802	9	4	11,390	9	4

Major General Edward Whalley's division

Derbyshire	1189	13	0	912	13	0
Nottinghamshire	1189	13	0	912	13	0
Warwickshire	1189	13	0	912	13	0
Lincolnshire	2189	6	0	1799	6	0
Leicestershire	1189	13	0	912	13	0
To Whalley	666	13	4	666	13	4
Total	7614	11	4	6116	11	4

	(1) per annum			(2) per annum		
	£	s	d	£	s	d
Major General James Berry's division						
Glamorgan, Brecknock & Radnorshire	1189	13	0	926	13	0
Herefordshire	1189	13	0	927	13	0
Monmouthshire	1189	13	0	894	13	0
Pembrokeshire, Carmarthenshire & Cardiganshire	1189	13	0	926	13	0
Shropshire	1189	13	0	927	13	0
Worcestershire	1189	13	0	927	13	0
Six counties of North Wales	1189	13	0	989	13	0
To Berry	666	13	4	666	13	4
To his deputies	–	–	–	666	13	4
Total	8994	4	4	7853	17	8
Major General William Goffe's division						
Berkshire	1189	13	0	917	13	0
Hampshire	2189	6	0	1779	6	0
Sussex	2189	6	0	1779	6	0
To Goffe	666	13	4	666	13	4
Total	6234	18	4	5142	18	4
Major General Charles Worsley's division						
Cheshire	1189	13	0	939	13	0
Lancashire	1189	13	0	939	13	0
Staffordshire	1189	13	0	912	13	0
To Worsley	666	13	4	666	13	4
Total	4235	12	4	3458	12	4
Major General Thomas Kelsey's division						
Kent	3188	19	0	2648	19	0
Surrey	1189	13	0	889	13	0

*Major General Charles Worsley's division

	(1) per annum			(2) per annum		
	£	s	d	£	s	d
To Kelsey	666	13	4	666	13	4
Total	5045	5	4	4205	5	4

Major General William Boteler's division

	£	s	d	£	s	d
Huntingdonshire	1189	13	0	} 1587	6	0
Rutland	869	13	0			
Northamptonshire	2189	6	0	1769	6	0
Bedfordshire	1189	13	0	904	13	0
To Boteler	666	13	4	666	13	4
Total	6104	18	4	4927	18	4

Major General John Barkstead's division

	£	s	d	£	s	d
Middlesex & City of Westminster	1189	13	0	932	13	0
To Barkstead	666	13	4	666	13	4
Total	1856	6	4	1599	6	4

City of London

	£	s	d	£	s	d
Civil officers	190	0	0	88	0	0

Registrar General

	£	s	d	£	s	d
	400	0	0	400	0	0
Grand total	80,067	12	4	67,010	5	8

*Worsley died shortly before the revised 'establishment' was approved on 24 June 1656 and the name of the major general responsible for Cheshire, Lancashire and Staffordshire was left blank. His successor, who was elected on 18 July, was Colonel Tobias Bridge (*CSPDom, 1656–7*, 28).

THE DECIMATION LISTS

BEDFORDSHIRE

The following list appears in the Thurloe State Papers (iv, 513). It was forwarded to Secretary Thurloe on 7 February 1656. The figures are the amounts of tax payable for a whole year.

	£	s	d
Richard Conquest of Houghton-Conquest, esquire[1]	120	0	0
Sir Thomas Leigh of Laighton-Beuzard[2]	135	0	0
Owen Brest of Rowney in Southill parish, esquire[3]	45	16	0
William Palmer of Hill, esquire[4]	48	19	0
Francis Crawley of Luton, esquire[5]	25	2	0
George Blundell of Cardington, esquire[6]	11	0	0
Sir Lodowick Dier of Collneth, baronet[7]	44	6	10
William Geery of Bushmead, esquire[8]	50	0	0
John Russell of Wooburne, esquire[9]	1	0	0
Edward Russell of the same, esquire[10]	50	0	0
Richard Farmor of Westning, esquire	12	0	0
Mr Fettiplace of Little Barford	13	6	0
Mr Hilsden of Hockley[11]	9	10	0
Richard Taylor of Clopham, esquire[12]	90	0	0
Henry Osburne of Chickson, esquire[13]	10	0	0
Mr Audley of Bigleswade[14]	2	4	9
Sum total	668	4	7

It is interesting to compare the above list with a Bedfordshire list forwarded in January 1657 which has survived among the Commonwealth Exchequer Papers (S.P.28/219, unbound document). In the latter there are a few changes in the persons named and a number of variations in the tax assessments, including some major reductions. Although the document is in a poor condition it has been possible to restore the basic text with the aid of the preceding list.

A true [partic]uler account of all [. . . . sums of money] assessed upon the [ ] within the said countie [of] Bedford upon the [extraordinary] tax for one [half] yeare from the xxiiiith day of June 1656 to the xxvth day of December 1656 (vizt)

	£	s	d
Richard Con[quest] of Houg[hton] Conquest esquire	33	0	0

Sir Thomas [Leigh] of [Leighton Buzzard], knight	67	11	2
Owen Brett esquire for his estate in Southill	22	18	0
William P[almer] of Hill esquire	24	9	6
George [Blund]ell of Car[dington] esquire	10	0	0
Richard Farmor esquire for Westning	6	0	0
Sir Lodowick Deyer of Colmouth baronet	22	3	5
John Russell esquire for Wooburne		10	0
ffrancis Crawley of Lutoon esquire	12	11	0
Henry Osborne esquire for Chyckton	5	0	$0\frac{1}{2}$
Robert Awdley of Bigleswade gentleman	1	2	4
Mr Fettiplace for Litle Barford	6	13	0
Richard Taylor of Clapham esquire	26	16	7
Thomas Hilsden gentleman for Hockley	3	5	0
Humphrey Ionemonge of Ampthill gentleman[15]	5	0	0
William Geery of Bushmead esquire	15	0	0
Mr Berry the elder of Cranfield	1	5	0
	263	5	$0\frac{1}{2}$

Upon the reveiw of the estate of the aforesaid Mr
Berry wee have added the summe of one pound
and five shillinges for this halfe yeare and for the   1   5   0
future Alsoe wee have assessed upon the estate of
Sir Erasmus De La Fonntaine[16] for his estate in
Holme in this countie for this halfe yeare the
summe of £44 and for two halfe yeares in arreare
ending the xxiiiith day of June 1656 the summe
of £88 which said estate hath formerly beene
concealed which in the whole is   132   0   0

The whole summe	396	10	$0\frac{1}{2}$

[*signed by*]
    Edward Cater
    John Cokayne
    William Whitbread
    William Andrewe

CAMBRIDGESHIRE

*The Cambridgeshire assessments are recorded in a note which has been preserved
among the Commonwealth Exchequer Papers (S.P.28/334, unbound document).
This contains three lists, each covering a half year in the period between June 1655
and December 1656, but only the first list is reproduced in full. The document is
endorsed 'Mr Bendish his Accompt of decimations' and 'delivered in 11 Junii 1662'.*

It is clear therefore that it was provided for the information of Charles II's officials.

Six moneths of ye decemation tax, viz from June ye 24th 1655 to the 25d December 55.
Of the said six monethes beeing the first half yeares payment I received as followeth

	£	s	d
James Renolds esquire[17]	3	10	0
Thomas Soames esquire[18]	8	0	0
Colonell John Russell[19]	37	7	0
Colonell William Wyllys[20]	8	10	0
John Picot esquire[21]	12	10	0
Sir William Compton[22]	10	5	0
And more of him for his Lady's estate	10	0	0
John Millicent esquire[23]	10	0	0
Colonell Anthony Hammond[24]	7	10	0
Colonell Samuel Thornton[25]	5	0	0
Mr Robert Turner[26]	4	9	0
Robert Henly esquire[27]	45	8	0
William Hallton esquire[28]	17	2	6
Sir Benjamin Ayloff[29]	2	10	0
William Nevill esquire[30]	1	0	0
Collonell John Fisher[31]	2	0	0
	185	1	6

[*signed at the bottom of the page*]
     Thomas Bendish

The second list, relating to the half year from 25 December 1655 to 24 June 1656, contains sixteen names, one more than in the first list, and records a total sum of £162 9s 6d. Robert Henley's name is omitted and two additional names appear:

	£	s	d
Henry Cooke esquire[32]	13	16	0
Sir John Wake[33] for ys and the other halfe yeare	9	0	0

The third list, relating to the half year from 24 June to 25 December 1656, contains thirteen names and records a total sum of £124 5s 4d. Hammond, Thornton, Halton and Cooke are omitted and a new name is added, that of Thomas Story. In addition, several of the assessments have been increased.

	£	s	d
John Picot esquire	13	3	4
Collonell William Wyllys	10	0	0
Collonell John Russell	39	12	0
Mr Thomas Story[34]	5	6	0

CUMBERLAND

The following list appears in the Thurloe State Papers (iv, 561–2). It was drawn up on 10 January 1656 and forwarded to the Protector on 28 February when it was accompanied by a Westmorland assessment list (see below). In their covering letter the commissioners for Cumberland and Westmorland stressed that 'some have made address for abatement, wherefore this list will be subject to some alteration'. The assessment figures are for a whole year.

	£	s	d
William Layton of Dalemaine, esquire[35]	14	0	0
George Denton of Cardew, esquire[36]	10	0	0
Sir Edward Musgrave, knight and baronet[37]	31	6	0
William Musgrave of Fairbanke, esquire	11	8	0
William Carleton, esquire[38]	10	10	0
John Lamplugh of Lamplugh, esquire[39]	22	0	0
Thomas Pattrickson of Stockhow	10	0	0
John Whelpdale of Penreth, esquire	13	13	0
Joseph Penington of Mulcaster, esquire[40]	52	0	0
Christopher Richmond of Catterlin, esquire	14	0	0
John Senehouse of Seafkaile, esquire[41]	15	0	0
Sir Patricius Curwen, knight and baronet[42]	40	0	0
Sir Francis Howard[43] upon his own offer, and with his own consent, no visible estate appearing	10	0	0
Sir Philip Musgrave, knight,[44] upon his own offer and consent, no visible estate appearing	10	0	0
Sir Thomas Dacre, knight,[45] upon his own offer and consent, no visible estate appearing	10	0	0
Richard Kirkbride, esquire[46]	10	0	0
Richard Crackenthorp, esquire[47]	18	0	0
Thomas Dikes of Wardell, esquire	10	0	0
Thomas Wybergh, esquire[48]	10	0	0
John Irton of Irton, esquire	10	0	0
Robert Fisher of Brackenthwait	15	0	0
Sir Edward Radcliffe, knight and baronet[49]	20	0	0
Anthony Bouch, gentleman[50] for his personal estate	22	0	0
Sir John Penruddocke[51]	4	4	0
Colonel William Huddleston[52]	55	0	0

	£	s	d
Sir George Dalston[53], for his estate in Cumberland	26	8	0
John Aglionby, esquire[54]	10	0	0
Joseph Patrickson, esquire[55]	10	0	0
Christopher Blencow, esquire[56]	12	0	0
William Musgrave of Crookedale, esquire[57]	16	0	0
Andrew Huddleston, esquire[58]	10	0	0
	532	9	0

DERBYSHIRE

A Derbyshire list which has survived among the Commonwealth Exchequer Papers (S.P.28/226, bundle of unbound papers) shows the total amount paid by each individual under the decimation tax arrangements. It can be assumed that in most cases, if not all, this sum represents three half-year payments covering the period June 1655 to December 1656. The list is annotated 'Captain Doughtie's Account, Decimation'. As can be seen from the text the list was submitted in 1663. The document also contains a section on disbursements which is not reproduced here.

Derbyshire. A perticuler of the sums received of the severall persons charged with the decemation tax in the yeares 1655 and 1656, 1657.

	£	s	d
Sir Thomas Milward knight[59]	28	10	0
Rouland Eayre esquire[60]	178	10	$10\frac{1}{2}$
William ffitzherbert esquire[61]	47	2	3
John Lowe esquire[62]	19	10	8
Henry Gilbert esquire[63]	65	13	4
John Milward esquire[64]	95	14	0
Henry Merry esquire[65]	40	9	[ ]
Sir John Harpor knight[66]	289	18	[ ]
Sir Wolstan Dixie knight[67]	13	3	1
William Bullocke esquire[68]	79	17	9
John Shawcrosse esquire[69]	30	15	0
John Lowe gentleman[70]	21	0	0
ffrancis Earle of Shrewsbury[71]	53	11	8
Gervas Pole esquire[72]	15	18	0
ffrancis Leeke esquire[73]	46	1	8
Thomas Gaunt esquire[74]	6	3	$6\frac{1}{2}$
Henry Vernon esquire[75]	35	14	0
William Orme esquire[76]	4	0	0
Thomas Godbehere[77]	16	17	3
Sir Paul Neale[78]	50	12	6

John ffrichvilla esquire[79]	90	5	0
Rouland Eayre gentleman[80]	15	0	0
The totall	1244	8	$7\frac{1}{2}$

This is a perfect and true accompt by mee
[*signed*]   Samuell Doughtye

This sheete of paper containinge the accompt of Mr Samuell Doughty for the taxe of decimation was delivered by him as a true accompt with the ffifteene acquittances or papers thereunto anexed attestinge the same the first day of June one thousand six hundred sixty and three upon his oath before us.

[*signed*]   Hath. Doughtye
                    Richard Lewis

A notable omission from the list is the name of William Earl of Devonshire. This may be attributed to the fact that (as explained in the Introduction) his case had been handled centrally. In January 1656 the Derbyshire commissioners returned the value of his estates in the county as £2346 17s 9d a year (CSPDom., 1655–6, 122)

ESSEX

The Essex assessments are recorded in three notes, each covering a half year in the period between June 1655 and December 1656 (S.P.28/153, unbound documents). These documents were received in Whitehall on 11 June 1662. Only the first list is reproduced in full. There are also details of disbursements which are not printed here.

The accompt of Edward Elliston, treasurer or receyver of the extraordinary tax charged by ye commissioners for the county of Essex for ye halfe yeare ending December ye 21th 1655 with ye Disbursements therof as followeth:

	£	s	d
Sir Henry Clarke[81]	10	0	0
Sir Henry Appleton[82]	8	0	0
Thomas Argoll esquire[83]	8	0	0
Salter Harrys esquire[84]	10	0	0
Sir Humfry Mildmay[85]	22	10	0
Richard Everard esquire[86]	13	0	0
Stephen Smith esquire[87]	25	0	0
Henry Pert esquire[88]	18	0	0
William Abell[89]	6	0	0
John Aylet[90]	5	0	0
Roberte Haynes esquire[91]	5	0	0
Sir William Howard[92]	9	0	0

Thomas Roberts esquire[93]	12	0	0
Sir Beniamyn Ayloffe[94]	25	0	0
Henry Leamon gentleman[95]	5	0	0
John Aylet of Braxted gentleman[96]	12	10	0
Anthony Browne esquire[97]	20	0	0
Robert Drury gentleman[98]	5	0	0
Sir Henry Audly[99]	50	0	0
ye Lady Ann Harrys[100]	10	0	0
Roberte Milborne esquire[101]	7	10	0
James Altham esquire[102]	40	0	0
James Milborne gentleman[103]	7	10	0
Ralph Everard gentleman[104]	7	10	0
Roberte Newport gentleman[105]	5	0	0
Colonel John Mildmay[106]	6	7	0
Thomas Mead of Lofts esquire[107]	21	0	0
John Crush[108]	2	0	0
Richard Luckin esquire[109]	31	17	8
Anthony Maxy esquire[110]	11	0	0
Thomas Mead of ffarnham gentleman[111]	4	15	0
Sir John Lucas[112]	65	0	0
Sir William Halton[113]	16	0	0
George James esquire[114]	7	0	0
Sir Andrew Joyner[115]	12	0	0
John Lyn esquire[116]	10	0	0
Richard Sams esquire[117]	18	0	0
Thomas Thorowgood gentleman[118]	5	0	0
John Barfoote esquire[119]	10	0	0
William Burrows esquire[120]	3	0	0
Sir William Hicks[121]	8	0	0
Thomas Pomfret gentleman[122]	5	10	0
Peeter Alexander gentleman[123]	5	0	0
Henry Nevill esquire[124]	55	0	0
William Glascock esquire[125]	15	0	0
Charls ffitch esquire[126]	21	0	0
James Reynolds esquire[127]	21	10	0
George Walton esquire[128]	9	0	0
John Wright gentleman[129]	6	0	0
Thomas Thompson junior[130]	10	0	0
Thomas Legat esquire[131]	9	0	0
Richard Humfry esquire[132]	20	0	0
Sir John Tirrell[133]	32	10	0
Roberte Audly esquire[134]	6	0	0
Sir Cranmer Harrys[135]	25	0	0
Mr Richard Cooper[136]	4	10	0

Sir Thomas Wiseman[137]	60	0	0
Charls Maynard esquire[138]	10	0	0
Edward Bendloes esquire[139]	20	0	0
Richard Boothby gentleman[140]	7	0	0
Sir Denner Strut[141]	7	0	0
Mundeford Brampston esquire[142]	5	0	0
Gamalaell Capell esquire[143]	20	0	0
Edward Sampford gentleman[144]	5	0	0
Nicholas Searle gentleman[145]	5	0	0
Thomas Luther esquire[146]	25	0	0
John Greene[147]	5	8	0
Edmond Humfryes gentleman[148]	7	0	0
William Dautry esquire[149]	8	5	0
James Silverlock esquire[150]	15	0	0
Captaine Roberte Vesey[151]	7	10	0
James Earle of Carlyle[152]	110	0	0
John Searle gentleman[153]	5	0	0
John Lucas gentleman[154]	5	0	0
Sir Roberte ffen[155]	8	0	0
Sir William Martyn[156]	20	0	0
John Sams gentleman[157]	5	10	0
Roberte Roe esquire[158]	5	0	0
George Coldham gentleman[159]		5	0
Doctor John Johnson[160]	6	0	0
John ffreeze gentleman[161]	5	0	0
John Brasier gentleman[162]	5	10	0
John Aylet[163]	5	8	0
Roberte Turner gentleman[164]	4	0	0
Thomas Baynes[165]	6	0	0
Thomas Tompson senior[166]	5	0	0
Phillip Causton junior[167]	6	6	0
Thomas Trewlove gentleman[168]	6	0	0
Richard Uphill[169]	5	0	0
Rolfe Pettus gentleman[170]	5	0	0
William Ayloffe of Braxted esquire[171]	5	0	0
Sir Richard Mynshall[172]	22	10	0
Thomas Smith esquire[173]	55	0	0
Doctor Hynton[174]	5	0	0
John Fanshaw esquire[175]	5	10	0
ye Earle of Northampton[176]		8	0
William Barnes[177]	6	0	0

The totall somme received for this halfe yeare is wherof to be deducted my owne sallary at 6d in	1346	19	8

ye pound for ye £1346 19s and 8d received as

aforesaid comes to	33	13	6
soe ther remaynes	1313	6	2

[*signed*] Edward Elliston

The second list, relating to the half year ending on 24 June 1656, contains 85 names, as compared with 97 in the preceding list. Those omitted include Sir Andrew Joyner (Jenoure), Sir William Martin, Thomas Luther and Thomas Smith (Smyth). The total amount collected was £1175 19s 8d. In the following cases the assessment was reduced:

	£	s	d
James Reynolds esquire	14	0	0
John Brasier gentleman	5	0	0

The third list, relating to the half year ending on 21 December 1656, contains only 64 names. Those omitted include the Earls of Carlisle and Northampton, Sir William Halton, Sir Thomas Wiseman, Henry Nevill and Edward Bendloes (Benlowes). The total sum collected was £819 16s 8d.

An Essex list which appears in the Thurloe State Papers (iv, 434–6), was submitted by the commissioners on 18 January 1656. In virtually all cases the individual's place of residence is recorded and this information has been drawn on in the preparation of the notes on the manuscript list which has been reproduced above. In this printed list the assessment of Richard Cooper is shown as £4 instead of £4 10s but this may simply be an error of transcription. In comparison with the manuscript list there are three omissions, John Fanshawe, the Earl of Northampton and William Barnes, and two new names, George Sames or Sammes the elder and Henry Owghan. (It has been necessary to edit Sames's name which was rendered as 'Samestheldor'). The following assessment figures are for a half year.

	£	s	d
George Sames the elder of Toleshunt[178]	5	0	0
Henry Owghan of Wodham gentleman[179]	5	0	0

HAMPSHIRE

The following list has been found in the class of Public Record Office documents known as the Exchequer Lay Subsidy Rolls (E.179). It bears the reference E.179/176/554. It is apparent from the wording of the preamble that it is a copy prepared after the Restoration and indeed this is confirmed by a note indicating that it was forwarded by Thomas Muspratt, or received from him, on 22 May 1661.

The document contains details of disbursements which are not reproduced here. As will be seen, the assessment figures are for a whole year. For reasons of clarity arabic numerals have been substituted for Muspratt's roman numerals.

Com. Southampton An accompt of all such monyes as Thomas Muspratt gentleman received of the severall persons hereunder named as treasurer of the county aforesayd (by order and comand of then Major Generall Goffe) for one whole yeare begining the 24th of June 1656 and ending the 25th June 1657 for that illegall tax called decimation (vizt)

	£	s	d
Mr Peter Gillham[180]	10	17	8
Mr George Carew[181]	5	14	0
the Lord Ogle[182]	47	2	0
Edward Norton gentleman[183]	12	0	0
James May esquire[184]	12	0	0
John Ford esquire[185]	16	13	0
Mr Stephen March[186]	10	0	0
Henry Phillpott esquire[187]	12	12	6
Peircy Edgcombe esquire[188]	50	0	0
Mr Lowe[189]	3	0	0
Mr John Weekes[190]	10	0	0
the righ honourable the Earle of Southampton[191]	379	6	0
Lawrence Hide esquire[192]	24	7	6
John Lawkner esquire[193]	18	11	8
Doctor Warner[194]	8	0	0
Edward Cocke esquire[195]	8	16	0
Sir William Kingsmill[196]	19	8	8
the Marquis of Hertford[197]	30	0	0
Douse Suller esquire[198]	50	0	0
Richard Goddard esquire[199]	24	0	0
Sir Thomas Badd[200]	24	8	0
Mr Matthew Cuffand[201]	10	0	0
Mr Golduyer[202]	14	15	6
Mr Richard Compton[203]	36	13	6
Henry Tucker esquire[204]	11	0	0
Nicholas Mason esquire[205]	10	0	0
Mr Edward Leayne[206]	10	0	0
Mr Walter Gifford[207]	15	14	0
Mr William Chamberlaine[208]	10	0	0
George Phillpot esquire[209]	19	9	8
William Barrow esquire[210]	10	0	0
William Poawlett esquire[211]	5	6	0
Sir William Courtney[212]	7	10	0
Henry Foyle esquire[213]	8	0	0
George Pitt esquire[214]	60	0	0
Richard Goldstonn esquire[215]	20	0	0

	£	s	d
Herculas Tarrant[216]	3	0	0
The totall some received as aforesaid is	1038	5	8

HERTFORDSHIRE

The Hertfordshire assessments are set out in a booklet annotated 'Decimation' among the Commonwealth Exchequer Papers (S.P.28/197, part 2, unbound document). The first item is a list recording the total payments of each individual taxed. This is described as 'The accompt of Thomas Cowley, receiver of the tenthes or extraordinary tax in the county of Hertford for one yeare and a halfe endinge the 21th of December 1656'. The total sum collected was £1092 6s 7d. Besides this cumulative table there are three other assessment lists, each relating to a half year between June 1655 and December 1656. The list which appears below covers the first of these half years. The document also contains details of disbursements which are not reproduced here.

Receipts of the tenths or extraordinary tax in the countie of Hertford for 6 moneths endinge the 21th of December 1655, vizt

	£	s	d
Sir John Watts of Tewinge[217] – 22th of March 1655/6	10	0	0
Sir Thomas Hide baronett of Albury[218] – 25th March 1656	110	16	0
James Altham esquire of Latton in Essex[219] for Buckland nere Royston – 26 March 1656	12	10	0
Mr Thomas Meads of [Farnham][220] – 26 March 1656		10	0
Mr Thomas Brande of Stocking Pelham – 28 March 1656	6	5	0
Mr William Cole of Salisbury Park alias Shenley Hall – 28 March 1656	6	0	0
Captain James Silverlocke of Stifford in the county of Essex[221] – 29 March 1656	2	5	0
Sir John Monson knight and baronett[222] for his lands in Wormley – 29 March 1656 [*in the margin*: Burton in Lincolnshire]	2	3	6
Sir Thomas ffanshawe of Ware Park[223], being a moiety of £133 6s 8d for his personall estate – 31 March 1656	66	13	4
Humfrey Shalcrosse of Hatfeild esquire[224] – 12 Aprill 1656	57	1	0
Sir ffrancis Boteller of Tewinge[225] – 12 Aprill 1656	5	0	0

	£	s	d
Sir George Boteller of Tewinge[226] – 12 April 1656	6	13	4
Mr George Price of Eshur in Surrey[227] – 19 Aprill 1656	5	0	0
Mr John Duke of Sheeringe in Essex[228] – 19 Aprill 1656	5	0	0
Raphe Bash of Stansted esquire[229] – 19 Aprill 1656	21	19	6
Captain William Kingsley of Sarratt – 19 Aprill 1656	6	5	0
Doctor Thomas Turner[230] for his estate lyinge in Thundridge – 19 Aprill 1656	5	7	6
Jeremiah Becke esquire[231] for his estate in Cheshunt – 28 Aprill 1656	6	0	0
Sir Thomas ffanshaw of Ware Parke hath paid the 2d moiety of £133 6s 8d for his personall estate – 31 May 1656	66	13	4
	402	2	6

The second list, relating to the half year ending 24 June 1656, contains nineteen names, one more than the preceding list, and records a total sum of £353 2s 9d. Sir Thomas Fanshawe does not appear in the list but there are two additional names, Sir Thomas Williamson and Sir William Howard. The significant changes are as follows:

	£	s	d
Sir ffrancis Boteller knight of Tewinge for his real and personall estate in this county and personall estate att Pidsey Burton in Holdernes in the county of Yorke, received the 3d of July 1656 – the sum of five pounds	5	0	0
George Price esquire of Eshur in Surrey – 11th July 1656 for the estate of Mr Thomas Reydon by George Mason	5	0	0
Raphe Bash esquire of Stansted – 11th July 1656	21	19	6
Raphe Bash esquire of Stansted, by an order of the 14th of Aprill 1656, for 3 monethes due the 24 of June 1656 – received this the 11th day of July 1656	5	5	0
Sir Thomas Williamson[232] 28th June 1656 and 22s more entered belowe, paid by Phillip Dixon	48	0	0
23 August 1656: received of Sir William Howard of Tolsbury in Essex[233] for one whole yeare due 24 June last past	30	0	0

30 August 1656: received of Sir Thomas
  Williamson by the hands of Phillip Dixon 22s
  which with the £48 above written is his full
  due for one whole yeare endinge the 24th of
  June 1656

	£	s	d
	1	2	0

The third list, relating to the half year ending 21 December 1656, contains 20 names and records a total sum of £337 1s 4d. There is one new name, John Keeling, and the list also provides a definitive figure for Ralph Bashe's assessment.

	£	s	d
The 15th of January 1656/7 received of Mr John Keeling of Southill in the county of Bedford[234] for one yeare and a halfe	18	4	6
The 17th of Januarie 1656/7: received of Raphe Bash esquire of Stansted by John Skipwith	32	9	6

HUNTINGDONSHIRE

As assessment list for Huntingdonshire is printed in the Thurloe State Papers (iv, 512). This was forwarded to Secretary Thurloe on 7 February 1656. The assessment figures are for a whole year.

	£	s	d
Molineux Audley of St Ives, gentleman[235]	34	6	0
Sir John Hewett[236]	16	0	0
The Earl of Devonshire[237]	156	17	0
The Earl of Northampton[238]	12	7	0
Stephen Anderson[239]	60	0	0
Sum total	279	10	0

KENT

The Kent assessments are recorded in a booklet which has survived among the Commonwealth Exchequer Papers (S.P.28/159, unbound document). It contains three lists, each relating to a half year in the period between June 1655 and December 1656, but only the first list is set out in full below. There are also details of disbursements which are not reproduced here.

The accompt of the extraordinary taxe assessed by the commissioners in the county of Kent and payable ye xxi th day of December Anno Domini 1655, vizt

	£	s	d
[*received from*]			
William Hugesson esquire[240], 18 December 1655	9	0	6
Captaine Thomas Stanley[241], 20 December 1655	6	15	6
ffrancis Clarke esquire[242], 21 December 1655	16	19	0
Sir John Darrell knight[243], the same day	50	14	6
Mr Edward Darrell[244], the same day	17	1	0
George Newman esquire[245], 21 December 1655	11	6	0
Mr Zouch Brockman[246], 2 do Januarii 1655/6	9	4	4
Mr James Taylor[247], 3 Januarii 1655/6	6	19	6
Mr William Brewer[248], the same day	7	1	0
Mr Henry Ruffin[249], 7 January 1655/6	9	11	0
Sir Anthony Aucher knight[250], the same day	17	19	0
Thomas Gibbon senior[251], the same day	8	3	0
Sir Christopher Harflet knight[252], the same day	12	9	0
Captaine Thomas Courthoppe[253], ye same day	11	3	0
Sir Thomas Palmer knight[254], the same day	21	4	0
Sir Roger Palmer knight[255], the same day	11	7	0
Mr Arnold Braemes[256], the same day	18	0	0
Mr Robert Owre[257], the same day	7	10	0
Mr John Boys[258], the same day	12	13	0
Mr Gibbon Hawker[259], 8 January 1655/6	7	19	4
Captaine Thomas Osborne[260], the same day	5	4	0
Richard Thornehill esquire[261], the same day	63	0	0
Mr Richard Lee[262], 10 January 1655/6	16	18	0
Sir Thomas Colepeper knight[263], ye same day	10	16	0
Thomas Colepeper esquire[264], the same day	21	0	0
Mr Mathew Bunce[265], the same day	12	3	0
Captaine Robert Bargrave[266], the same day	9	10	0
Phillip Warwicke esquire[267], the same day	6	10	0
Doctor John Warner[268], the same day	31	0	0
Sir Thomas Godfrey knight[269], the same day	49	7	0
Mr William Norton[270], the same day	9	15	0
Sir Edward Bathurst knight[271], 10 January 1655/6	11	15	0
Mr James Newman[272], the same day	5	0	0
Mr John Marsham[273], the same day	20	2	0
Mr Henry Pettit[274], the same day	5	15	0
Mr John Smith[275], the same day	5	3	0
Mr Edward Roberts[276], the same day	9	10	0
Mr Thomas Hardres[277], the same day	14	7	0
Sir Nicholas Crispe[278], the same day	26	4	0
Mr Henry Haslin[279], the same day	5	14	0
Mr John Gookin[280], the same day	5	5	0
Mr Thomas Lambarde[281], the same day	27	5	0

Mr Henry Gilburne[282], the same day	8	0	0
Richard Spencer esquire[283], 16 January 1655/6	8	15	0
Mr Thomas Southland[284], the same day	16	17	0
Mr Thomas Lee[285], 22 do January 1655/6	7	13	6
Sir Henry Appleton knight[286], the same day	7	15	[0]
Mr Thomas ffinch[287], 24 January 1655/6	11	0	0
Mr Henry Cooke[288], 25 January 1655/6	20	15	6
Mr George Cooke[289], 28 January 1655/6	12	16	0
Mr George Skynner[290], 31 January 1655/6	5	2	0
Captaine William Meriwether[291], ye same day	5	10	0
John Earle of Thanet[292], 14 ffebruary 1655/6	157	7	6
Mr Thomas Harlackenden[293], 18 ffebruary 1655/6	21	4	0
Mr Anthony Hamond[294], 19 ffebruary 1655/6	12	14	0
Sir Edward Hales baronet[295], 20 ffebruary 1655/6	301	15	0
Sir Robert Poynes[296], the same day	3	18	0
Mr John ffarnaby[297], the same day	5	0	0
Mr Nevill Hall[298], the same day	9	7	6
Mr Thomas Thatcher[299], the same day	5	0	0
Mr Richard Bennett[300], 26 ffebruary 1655/6	4	5	0
John Lord Abergaveny[301], 3 Marcii 1655/6	19	13	0
Mr Thomas Brett[302], 18 Marcii 1655/6	7	10	0
Doctor Thomas Bird[303], the same day	5	0	0
Sir Richard Hardres knight[304], 19 March 1655/6	5	0	0
Mr John Bill[305], the same day	1	10	0
Mr Edward Taylor[306], the same day	5	0	0
Sir George Sonds knight of the bath[307], ye same day	50	0	0
Mr George Swanne[308], 20 Marcii 1655/6	5	0	0
Mr Thomas Gibbon junior[309], the same day	5	0	0
Mr John Struggles[310], the same day	10	0	0
Mr Walter Sabin[311], the same day	5	13	0
Mr William Pix[312], 5 Aprill 1656	15	9	6
Mr Jeremy Gay[313], 7 Aprill 1656	5	0	0
Mr Ralph Philpott[314], 10 Aprill 1656	5	0	0
Sir Allan Zouch knight[315], 30 Aprill 1656	3	0	0
Sir Leonard ffarby knight[316], 7 May 1656	6	13	0
Robert Goodhugh[317], 12 May 1656	5	0	0
Mr Stephen Ginder[318], 13 May 1656	5	0	0
Mr John Best[319], 23 May 1656	5	0	0
Sir James Hales knight[320], the same day	15	0	0
Mr John Greenstreete[321], 3 Junii 1656	5	0	0
Mr Mathew Robbins[322], the same day	5	0	0
Mr John Brett[323], the same day	5	0	0
Mr Henry Thomson[324], the same day	9	1	0

	£	s	d
Dr William Steed[325], 4 Junii 1656	30	8	0
Mr Christopher Hobert[326], the same day	5	0	0
Mr John Woodgreene[327], 28 Junii 1656	7	9	0
Sir Thomas Peyton baronet[328], 8 Julii 1656	26	12	0
Mr Thomas Argall[329], 12 July 1656	5	0	0
Summe totall is	1551	16	2

The second list, relating to the half year ending on 24 June 1656, contains 76 names, as compared with 90 in the preceding list, and records a total sum of £1277 18s 6d. There is one new name, Arnold King; and in addition there are certain other changes which are indicated below. Arabic numerals have been substituted for roman numerals both here and in the third list.

	£	s	d
Mr Arnold King[330], 22 August 1656	7	7	0
Received more of him then for soe much payable 21 December 1655	7	7	0
Received of Mr John Boys the 22th August 1656 besides 30s overpaid 7 January 1655/6	9	13	0
Received of John Earle of Thanet the 10th of September 1656 besides £26 17s 6d overpaid by him the 14th of ffebruary 1655/6 the summe of	103	12	6

The third list, relating to the half year ending on 21 December 1656, contains only 62 names while the total sum collected was £1106 9s 6d. Significant changes are as follows:

	£	s	d
Received of Sir Leonard ffarbey 17 January 1656/7 besides 10s overpaid 7 May 1656 the summe of	5	13	0
Received of John Earle of Thanet 30 Marcii 1657	100	0	0
Received of him more the 20th of Aprill 1657	30	10	0

NORTHAMPTONSHIRE

The following list is printed in the Thurloe State Papers (iv, 511–12). It was forwarded to Secretary Thurloe on 7 February 1656. The assessment figures are for a whole year.

	£	s	d
Edmond Neale of Wollaston, esquire	35	0	0
John Bourne of Ufford, gentleman	10	0	0
Walter Kirkham of Finshead, esquire[331]	10	0	0
Thomas Styles of Walton, gentleman[332]	7	16	0

Robert Kirkham of Finshead, esquire[333]	13	4	0
John Siers of Loddington, esquire[334]	28	10	0
Sir Edward Watson of Stoke-Albany park[335]	17	14	0
Sir Thomas Cave, senior, of Stanford[336]	73	14	0
Richard Kinsman of Broughton, esquire	10	0	0
Henry Howard of Winwick, esquire[337]	110	0	0
Charles Compton of Northampton, esquire[338]	13	0	0
John Atkins of Gretton, gentleman	10	0	0
Captain Thomas Willoughby of Weston-Fanell[339]	10	0	0
Alexander Ekins of Weston-Fanell, gentleman	10	0	0
John Bagshawe of Cullworth, gentleman	7	4	0
Charles Cockayne of Rushton, esquire[340]	120	0	0
The Lady Ann Farmor of Northampton[341]	54	0	0
Thomas Rudd of Higham Ferrers, esquire[342]	40	0	0
Doctor Samuel Hinton at Onley[343]	15	0	0
Sir Justinian Isham of Lamport[344]	87	4	0
Sir Anthony Haslewood of Maidwell[345]	63	10	0
Sir Edward Griffin of Dingley[346]	160	00	0
Jeffrey Palmer of Carleton, esquire[347]	50	0	0
William Warner of Lubnam, esquire[348]	40	0	0
William Stafford of Blatherwick, esquire[349]	75	0	0
Edward Page of Oundle, esquire	23	0	0
Sir Christopher Hatton of Kirby[350]	100	0	0
The Earl of Northampton at Castle Ashby[351]	100	0	0
Sir Richard Winfield at Haslebilck[352]	9	0	0
Mr Hacke of Peterburgh[353]	26	6	0
William Stidolph, esquire at Wittering[354]	45	0	0
Sir Richard Shuckburgh of Farthingstone[355]	10	0	0
Sir Thomas Wilbraham of Charleton[356]	50	0	0
Sir Anthony Morgan of Heyford[357]	81	8	0
John Preston at Cold Ashby[358]	32	16	0
Sir Thomas Pope of Walton[359]	52	0	0
Sum total	1600	6	0

Colonel Cooke pretends Sir Anthony Morgan's estate is in him: if it be allowed so to be, it will take off £81 8s 0d *per annum* out of the said £1600 6s 0d, and then 'twill be *per annum* but £1518 18s 0d.

RUTLAND

The Rutland assessments are recorded in a document annotated 'Mr Woodcocke. Decimation' which has been found among the Commonwealth Exchequer Papers

(S.P.28/342, unbound document). A note at the end of this single sheet of parchment indicates that it was forwarded or delivered in to Charles II's officials on 7 August 1662. The document contains a cumulative list covering the three half years between June 1655 and December 1656. There is also a section on disbursements which is not reproduced here.

The accompt of Peter Woodcocke the elder gentleman for the severall sumes of money received by him in the county of Rutland for decimations comenceing the twenty fowerth of June one thousand sixe hundred fifty and five (vizt).

	£	s	d
[*received from*]			
Baptist Lord Noell, Viscount Cambden[360] for three halfe yeares charge	240	0	0
Wingfeild Bodenham esquire[361] for one yeares charge	17	12	7
Doctor Clement Bretton[362] for three halfe yeares chardge	15	0	0
Richard Bullingham esquire[363] for three halfe yeares chardges	30	0	0
Edward Heath esquire[364] ffor one yeares charge	80	0	0
Sir Thomas Mackworth[365] for three halfe yeares charge	90	0	0
Richard Wingfeild esquire[366] for three halfe yeares charge	64	1	0
Eusibee Pelsant esquire[367] for three halfe yeares charge	38	11	0
	575	4	7

There is also a Rutland list in the Thurloe State Papers (iv, 412). This was forwarded to Secretary Thurloe on 7 February 1656. The annual assessment figures which it contains are in accord with the figures in the preceding list but there is an additional name:

	£	s	d
Arthur Warren of Whisondine, esquire[368]	20	8	2

SUFFOLK

The following lists are printed in the Thurloe State Papers (iv, 427–8). They were forwarded by the Suffolk commissioners to the Protector on 17 January 1656. The 'third head' which is mentioned is that section of the orders of 21 September 1655 which inaugurated the decimation tax.

Suffolk. The humble certificate of the commissioners appointed by his highness and council for securing the peace of the commonwealth within the said county of Suffolk, of the names of all such persons within this county yet come to our knowledge which are comprized in the third head of his highness's orders, and the tax assessed and set upon every one of them according to the said orders and instructions.

	taxed *per annum* £
Edmund Pooley of Bury, esquire[369] for his real estate	25
Robert Gosnall of Oatley, gentleman[370] for his real estate	10
Sackvill Glemham of Glemham, esquire[371] for his real estate	40
Thomas Stanton of Mildenhall, gentleman for his real estate	10
Lawrence Britton of Hadleigh, clerk[372] for his real estate	20
And for his personal estate	300
Edward Rookwood of Euston, esquire[373] for his real estate	30
Edward Warner of Mildenhall, gentleman for his real estate	12
Sir Henry Wood of Bury[374], for his real estate	60
John Hamond of Mettingham, esquire for his real estate	10
Earl of Devonshire[375] for his real estate	110
Sir Daniel de Lyne[376] for his real estate	20
Thomas Jermin of Rushbrooke, esquire[377] for his real estate	35
Dr Edward Aylemere of Claydon[378] for his real estate	13
Benjamin Cutler of Spraughton[379] for his real estate	26
Richard Everard of Hawkendon, gentleman[380] for his real estate	10
Sir Roger Palmer of London, knight[381] for his real estate	48
John Rea of London, gentleman for his real estate	11
Thomas Soame of Westly in Cambridgeshire[382] for his real estate	10
Robert Naunton of Letheringham, esquire[383] for his real estate	45
Henry Cooke of Thurington, esquire[384] for his real estate	150
Henry Lamb of Wetherden, gentleman for his real estate	10
Richard Chapman of Livermore for his real and personal estate	50
Richard Bacon of Culford, esquire[385] for his real estate	15
Henry Wingfield of Crowfield for his real estate	10
Sir William Harvey[386] for his real estate	200
William Castleston of Bury, esquire[387] for personal estate	100
Thomas Roberts of Little Braxted in Essex, esquire[388] for real estate	7
Sir John Cotton of Cambridgeshire[389] for his real estate	50

Sir Henry Audley of Barton, knight[390] for his real estate	24
Mr Robert Vesey of Ipswich for real estate	8
17 January 1655/6 total taxed	1469

The names and estates of such as are under value, comprised in the third head.

	real estate £	personal estate £
Dr Cross of Saxham[391]	60	
Robert Shepherd of Stanton, clerk[392]	50	
Jasper Brydon of Fornham, gentleman		200
Richard Martin of Melford, gentleman[393]	50	
John Clarke of Bury, gentleman	8	
Thomas Strutt of Hundon, gentleman	30	
Francis Cheney of Eye, gentleman	22	300
Arthur Denny of Thrandiston, gentleman[394]	30	
James Webb of Mildenhall, yeoman	8	
Mr Gordon of Broome, clerk[395]	20	
Dr Martin of Thurington[396]		20
Thomas Allyn of Laystoff, gentleman[397]	30	
Thomas Townsend of Woolpit, gentleman	20	10
Robert Sharp of Bury, gentleman	18	100
Baptist May[398], son of Lady May of Bury, no estate at present		
Charles May, son of the said Lady May		20
Thomas Langley of Eye, gentleman	50	
Thomas Crane of Beccles, gentleman		40
Edward Rogers of Hoxne, gentleman	20	
Sir Frederick Cornwallis[399]		100
Captain Taylor of Ipswich[400]		100
George Gage of Wingrave esquire[401], a voluntary contribution of	80	
John Woodward of Bury, gentleman	20	100
William Johnson of Thurlo Parva, gentleman[402]	20	50
James Portus of Tudenham, clerk[403]	18	70
George Patridge of Creating, gentleman[404]	10	50
17 January 1655/6		

SUSSEX

The Sussex assessments are recorded in a booklet which has survived among the Commonwealth Exchequer Papers (S.P.28/181, unbound document). This is annotated 'Sussex. The accompt of Thomas Collins of the monyes receaved in the three westerne rapes of the countye of Sussex, upon the extraordinary, otherwise called the decimation, taxe, by the Protector beginning in the yeere 1655'. Sussex had six rapes or administrative divisions and the three western rapes were Chichester, Arundel and Bramber (though one of the individuals listed, John Ashburnham of Ashburnham, was in fact seated in Hastings rape). Writing to Secretary Thurloe on 7 November 1655 Major General William Goffe told him that it had been decided to begin the decimation proceedings at Chichester, mainly on the grounds that 'theare are very few malignants that will come within our reach' in the eastern parts of the county (Thurloe State Papers, iv, 161). The document contains three assessment lists, each relating to a half year in the period between June 1655 and December 1656. Only the first list is reproduced in full. There are also details of disbursements which are not printed here.

Sussex. The accompt of Thomas Collins of the monyes by him receaved for the use of Oliver Lord Protector by vertue of an order of the said Protector and his Councill of the 21th of September 1655 by way of an extraordinary taxe upon the particuler persons hereunder named, assessed by the then commissioners for securing the peace of the Commonwealth in the county of Sussex made to bee payable the xxith of December 1655, as followeth

[received from]	£	s	d
Robert Anderson esquire[405], his estate being valued at £200 per annum	10	0	0
Mr Richard Bridger[406], valued at £300 per annum	15	0	0
Brune Bickley gentleman[407], at £100 per annum	5	0	0
Thomas May esquire[408], valued at £400 per annum	20	0	0
John Lewkner esquire[409], at £700 per annum	35	0	0
George Gunter esquire[410], at £100 per annum	5	0	0
Walter Buckland esquire[411], at £50 per annum	2	10	0
William Ryshton gentleman[412], at £100 per annum	5	0	0
Robert Exton gentleman[413], at £100 per annum	5	0	0
Sir William Morley knight[414], at £1500 per annum	75	0	0
Henry Byshopp esquire[415], at £200 per annum	10	0	0
Thomas Kempe esquire[416], at £140 per annum	7	0	0
Sir Garret Kempe knight[417], at £1000 per annum	50	0	0
William Sandham esquire[418], at £100 per annum	5	0	0
Thomas Payne gentleman[419], at £150 per annum	7	10	0
Richard Tayler gentleman[420], at £200 per annum	10	0	0

Peregrine Palmer esquire[421], at £600 per annum	30	0	0
John Covert esquire[422], at £300 per annum	15	0	0
Mr Humfrey Byshop[423], at £100 per annum	5	0	0
Sarah Coxe widdow[424], at £100 per annum	5	0	0
Richard Lord Viscount Lumley[425], his estate being valued at £1200 per annum	60	0	0
John Carryll esquire[426], at £1600 per annum	80	0	0
John Ashbornham esquire[427], at £850 per annum	42	10	0
Pierce Edgcombe esquire[428], at £200 per annum	10	0	0
Robert Edsawe gentleman[429], at £200 per annum	10	0	0
sum total	524	10	0

[*signed*]

Thomas Collins

The second list, relating to the half year ending on 24 June 1656, contains 24 names, one less than in the preceding list and records a total sum of £504 10s od. The only change of substance is the omission of Thomas May.

The third list, relating to the half year ending on 21 December 1656, contains 21 names and records a total sum of £446 0s 10d. Walter Buckland, Henry Bishop, William Sandham and Robert Edsawe are omitted and there is one additional name, William Garway. The significant changes are as follows:

	£	s	d
William Garway esquire[430], at £570 per annum	28	10	0
reduced – John Carryll esquire, at £1050 per annum	52	10	0
reduced – John Ashbornham esquire, at £210 16s 8d per annum	10	10	10

A Sussex list which appears in the Thurloe State Papers (iv, 239, 240) contains 24 names. This is a preliminary list which was forwarded by Major General William Goffe on 24 November 1655. There are five additional names which do not figure in any of the manuscript lists. (It should be stressed that the inclusion of these persons does not reflect any widening of the geographical coverage since they were all resident in the western part of the county). The additional particulars are set out below, together with certain other variations.

	value of the estate per annum	taxed per annum
	£	£
Mr Coldham of Stedham[431]	150	15
Sir Edward Ford of Hartin[432]	700	70
Mr Caroll of Hartin[433]	2500	250

Mrs Dooble of Midhurst[434]	700	70
William Goble of Graffen[435]	100	10
Mr Walter Buckland of Tratton	200	20
John Ashborne (sic) of Ashbornham	800	80
Mr John Weston of Rothey[436]	200	20

WESTMORLAND

The following list is printed in the Thurloe State Papers (iv, 562–3). It was forwarded to the Protector on 28 February 1656 together with the Cumberland list. The assessment figures are for a whole year.

	£	s	d
Christopher Dudley, esquire[437]	25	0	0
John Dalston of Acronbanke, esquire[438]	30	0	0
Colonell Lowther[439]	10	0	0
Thomas Wilson of Hensham[440]	50	0	0
Richard Brathwait of Burneside, esquire[441]	20	0	0
Nicholas Fisher of Stainebanke-greene	12	10	0
George Middleton of Leighton, esquire[442]	10	0	0
Thomas Preston of Holker[443]	15	0	0
John Philipson of Calgath[444]	10	0	0
Sir Thomas Sandforth[445]	20	0	0
Thomas Strickland of Siher[446]	16	2	0
Sir George Dalston[447] for his estate in Westmorland	22	0	0
Bryan Tayler[448]	20	0	0
James Bellingham[449]	25	0	0
Anthony Duckatt[450]	27	10	0
Robert Hilton[451]	20	0	0
Sir John Lowther[452]	75	0	0
Henry Wilson[453]	10	0	0
James Moore[454]	5	0	0
	423	2	0

OTHER COUNTIES

The following assessment figures are drawn from various sources, including private estate papers. Details are given in the notes.

	taxed per annum		
	£	s	d
Cheshire			
George Warburton of Arley[455]	100	0	0

Cornwall
John Tredenham of Philleigh[456]   60   0   0
Lancashire
William Farington the elder of Worden[457]   20   0   0
Middlesex
William Earl of Bedford[458]   300   0   0
Norfolk
Thomas Knyvett of Ashwellthorpe[459]   80   0   0
Northumberland
Arthur Gray[460]   10   0   0
Sir Edward Radcliffe of Dilston[461]   50   0   0
William Strother of Kirknewton[462]   23   0   0
Staffordshire
Peter Giffard of Chillington Hall[463]   100   0   0
Worcestershire
Thomas Lord Coventry[464]   400   0   0
Yorkshire
Brian Cooke of Doncaster[465]   100   0   0
Thomas Crompton of Great Driffield[466]   32   0   0
William Earl of Devonshire[467]   217   10   8
Michael Warton of Beverley Park[468]   224   12   8
Sir George Wentworth of Woolley[469]   71   10   0

NOTES

The following notes contain many references to the royalist composition papers (Public Record Office, State Papers Domestic, Committee for Compounding, S.P.23). When submitting a particular of his estate a would-be compounder was required to declare what it had been worth on the eve of the war before the general decline in the revenue from landed property. The figures which have been drawn from this source take account of any subsequent additions or other amendments to the original particular. When out-rents (for example, fee farm and leasehold rents) are separately identified these have been deducted but no adjustment has been made for annuities, rent-charges or loan interest which were payable out of the estate.

There are also references to a 'Royal Oak list'. This list was drawn up shortly after the Restoration when the possibility was being considered of introducing a new order of knighthood, the knights of the Royal Oak, as a means of rewarding Charles II's supporters. It is printed in Thomas Wotton's *The English Baronetage* (1741) iv, 363–80 under the title 'A list of Persons Names who were fit and qualified to be made Knights of the Royal Oak, with the Value of their Estates, Anno Dom.1660'. It is also reproduced in John Burke, *A Genealogical and Heraldic History of The Commoners of Great Britain and Ireland* (1833–8) i, 688–94, though here the Derbyshire section has been inadvertently omitted.

Bedfordshire

1 Richard Conquest (1597-c.1670) was a former royalist colonel and a suspected papist. He had compounded for property valued at £549 p.a. In 1651 it had been claimed that his estate was worth £1400 p.a. but it was soon heavily encumbered. In 1668 he mortgaged lands worth £800 p.a. (*CCAM*, 1191–4. *CCC*, 1821. S.P.23/ccv/631, 633–5. C.33/215/fo./672; 217/fo.407; 218/fo.677; 227/fols.670–1; and 273/fo.491).

2 According to their compounding papers Thomas Lord Leigh of Stoneleigh, Warwickshire (1595–1672) and his son Sir Thomas of Hamstall Ridware, Staffordshire (1616–1662) had estates in various counties worth some £3400 p.a. In Bedfordshire they held a long lease of the manor of Leighton Buzzard from the dean and canons of Windsor. In July 1656 Sir Thomas sought exemption from

the decimation tax. (*CCC*, 1134–6. S.P.23/ccxxxvi/777,779,799. *CSPDom, 1656–7*, 45)

3 Owen Brett (c.1598–1658) was the son of Sir John Brett of Edmonton, Middlesex. Royalist compounder: £460 p.a. (all in Bedfordshire). (*CCAM*, 1317–18. S.P.23/ccxxi/87).

4 This was Sir William Palmer (d.1683) of Hill in Old Warden who had been knighted in 1642. Royalist compounder: £490 p.a. (S.P.23/lvi/fols.309–10).

5 Francis Crawley (d.1683), a barrister, was the son and heir of Sir Francis Crawley (1584–1649) who had been one of the Justices of the Common Pleas. Sir Francis had compounded for an estate valued at £464 p.a. in possession and £30 p.a. in reversion. Royal Oak list: (Francis Crawley) £1000 p.a. (*DNB* (Sir Francis Crawley). *CCAM*, 746. *CCC*, 1562. S.P.23/cxciv/419, 423–4).

6 It had been reported that George Blundell (1621–1688) had £300 p.a. in Bedfordshire and £150 p.a. in Cambridgeshire (though he does not appear in the Cambridgeshire decimation lists). Royal Oak list: £1200 p.a. He was knighted in 1661. (*CCAM*, 1148. *CCC*, 1688).

7 Sir Ludowick Dyer (1605–1669) livd mainly at Colworth, though he had another seat at Great Haughton in Huntingdonshire. Royalist compounder: £900 p.a. in possession and £500 p.a. in reversion. He was not apparently taxed in Huntingdonshire. (*CCAM*, 1235. S.P.23/clxxiii/325).

8 William Gery (c.1612–1659) of Bushmead in Eaton Socon had compounded for property valued at £300 p.a. He left an estate in Bedfordshire worth between £600 and £700 p.a. which was seriously encumbered. (*CCC*, 1680–1. S.P.23/cxcix/251, 257. C.5/523/145).

9 For Lord John Russell see under Cambridgeshire.

10 Lord Edward Russell had an annuity of £500 out of the estate of his brother William Earl of Bedford who was seated at Woburn. In December 1655 he sought exemption from the decimation tax, claiming that he was no enemy to the government, and in February 1656 he was granted a discharge. (BL, Additional MSS 5494, fo.9. *CCC*, 846).

11 Thomas Hillersden of Stoke Hammond in Buckinghamshire had compounded for property valued at £130 p.a., including £80 p.a. at Hockliffe in Bedfordshire. (S.P.23/clxxiv/41, 45, 55,57).

12 Richard Taylor of Clapham (1620–1667) had compounded for an estate in reversion valued at £450 p.a. Besides his Bedfordshire property he owned the manor of Foxton in Cambridgeshire which was sold after his death for £1800. Royal Oak list: £1000 p.a. In 1660 he was said to have been imprisoned several times for his

loyalty. (*CCAM*, 958. *CCC*, 1275. C.33/241/fo.675 and 243/fo.114. S.P.29/xi/141).

13 Henry Osborne (1619–1675), a former royalist colonel, was a younger son of Sir Peter Osborne of Chicksands Priory who had compounded for delinquency. He was knighted in 1673. (S.P.23/ccxvi/625–7)

14 Robert Audley of Biggleswade (and formerly of Northill) had compounded for an estate valued at £83 p.a. in possession and £50 p.a. in reversion. Most of the property was in Lincolnshire. (S.P.23/clxxiii/99. *CCC*, 931)

15 Humphrey Iremonger, an attorney, had been sequestered but had been discharged on appeal. According to the Bedfordshire sequestration accounts he had property at Stanbridge worth £72 p.a. in 1642. In 1651 it had been alleged that he was a Catholic. (*CCAM*, 1231. BL, Additional MSS 5494, fo.9. *CCC*, 2716).

16 Sir Erasmus de la Fontaine (d.1671), who was seated at Kirby Bellars in Leicestershire, had been fined £1000 for delinquency. His Leicestershire estate appears to have been worth between £300 and £400 p.a. He was one of several Leicestershire gentry who sought exemption from the decimation tax. (*CCC*, 3021–2. *Thurloe State Papers*, iv, 335).

Cambridgeshire

17 For James Reynolds see under Essex.

18 This was Thomas Soame of Westley Waterless who also appears in the Suffolk list.

19 Lord John Russell (c.1620–1687), a younger brother of William Earl of Bedford, was of Covent Garden, London and Shingay, Cambridgeshire. He had been an MP in the Long Parliament until disabled in 1644. Royalist compounder: £795 p.a. in possession and £241 p.a. in reversion. (*CCAM*, 710. *CCC*, 1208–9. S.P.23/lvi/fols.194–5).

20 Colonel William Willys (c.1615–1676) was a younger brother of Sir Thomas Willys of Fen Ditton. Despite his plea that he had deserted the king's forces he had been required to compound. (*CCC*, 1564).

21 This was John Pigott of Abington juxta Shingay. Royalist compounder: £203 p.a. in possession and £130 p.a. in reversion. (S.P.23/clxxiii/193).

22 Sir William Compton, a younger brother of James Earl of Northampton, had compounded for an estate at Erith in Kent but had subsequently been forced to sell it. The Comptons had property at Fen Drayton in Cambridgeshire. (S.P.23/ccxi/9, 15. J.J.Wilkinson, *History of Erith* (1879), 37. *VCH, Cambridgeshire*, ix, 293)

23 John Millicent of Barham Hall in Linton had compounded for an estate valued at £6 p.a. in possession and £200 p.a. in reversion. Royal Oak list: £700 p.a. (*CCC*, 1598).

24 This was probably Anthony Hammond of St Albans Court in Nonington, Kent. See under Kent.

25 Samuel Thornton of Soham had compounded for an estate valued at £250 p.a. (S.P.23/lvi/fo.340).

26 Of Westley Waterless.

27 Robert Henley (1591–1656) of the Middle Temple and Henley House in Somerset had been one of the Six Clerks in Chancery and Master of the King's Bench Office. He had been fined £9000 for delinquency. In December 1655 the Cambridge commissioners reported that they had been informed that he had £3000 p.a. in the county and the Isle of Ely and that they intended to tax him at the rate of £300 p.a. unless he met their demand for a particular of his estate. At his death he left property in various counties worth £4000 p.a. which descended to his sons Sir Robert Henley of the Grange and Sir Andrew Henley of Bramshill, both in Hampshire. (*CCAM*, 272. *CCC*, 927. *Thurloe State Papers*, iv, 350. Thomas Wotton, *The English Baronets* (1727), ii, 71. C.33/205/fo.405).

28 This was Sir William Halton of Little Sampford in Essex. See under Essex.

29 For Sir Benjamin Ayloffe see under Essex.

30 This was probably the son and heir of Henry Nevill who was taxed in Essex.

31 In 1649 it had been reported that John Fisher of Wisbeach had property in Norfolk worth £80 p.a. (*CCAM*, 808).

32 This was apparently Henry Coke of Thorington in Suffolk. See under Suffolk.

33 Sir John Wake (d. *circa* 1660) was seated at Piddington in Northamptonshire but does not appear in the surviving assessment list for that county. Royalist compounder: £469 p.a. In 1652 it had been alleged that he was a Catholic. Wake was heavily indebted and died in the King's Bench prison but the family fortunes were eventually restored. (*CCC*, 1589–90. S.P.23/ccxxxvi/699. *CCAM*, 539. *CSPDom, 1660–1*, 240).

34 Thomas Story of Chesterton had compounded for an estate valued at £214 p.a. Royal Oak list: £800 p.a. (S.P.23/lvi/fo.136).

Cumberland

35 William Layton had compounded for property valued at £64 p.a. (S.P.23/clxxiii/237).

36 George Denton had compounded for an estate valued at £80 p.a. (second composition). (S.P.23/ccxxvii/783).

37 Sir Edward Musgrave of Hayton Castle (c.1621–1673) is said to
have sold over £2000 p.a. of his patrimony as a consequence of
his involvement in the Civil Wars. Royalist compounder: £430
p.a. (second composition). (J.Nicolson and R.Burn, *The History and
Antiquities of Westmorland and Cumberland* (1777), ii, 155.
S.P.23/ccxxvii/779).

38 This was Sir William Carleton of Carleton Hall who had been
knighted in the first Civil War. He had compounded for his estate
with the Newcastle committee. (*CCC*, 2982).

39 John Lamplugh, a former royalist colonel, had compounded twice
for his estate: (1) £230 p.a., (2) £120 p.a. Royal Oak list: £1000
p.a. (S.P.23/ccxxiv/165 and ccxxvii/767).

40 Joseph Pennington of Muncaster (d.1659) also owned property in
Lancashire. Royal Oak list: (his son William) £1000 p.a. (*CCC*,
2767. BL, Additional MSS 24,121, fo.157).

41 This was John Senhouse of Seascale Hall who also had an estate
in Lancashire. Royal Oak list: (his son Wrightington) £600 p.a.
(*CCC*, 1703–4).

42 Sir Patricius Curwen of Workington (c.1602–1664) had been a
member of the Long Parliament until disabled in 1643. In 1645
the county committee had reported that his Cumberland estate
was not worth more than £500 p.a. In 1660 the estate revenue
amounted to £679 p.a. (S.P.23/clxxix/598. C.B.Phillips, 'The
Royalist Composition Papers and the Landed Income of the
Gentry: A Note of Warning from Cumbria', *Northern History*, xiii
(1977), 165).

43 Sir Francis Howard of Corby Castle (1588–1660) was a younger
son of Lord William Howard of Naworth. He had property in
Cumberland, Durham and Westmorland which had been sequestered for his recusancy and delinquency and subsequently sold by
the Treason Trustees. Royal Oak list: (his son Francis) £1500 p.a.
The son is said to have had an estate worth £2000 p.a. (*CCC*, 232,
2588. Nicolson and Burn, *op.cit.*, ii, 336–7).

44 Sir Philip Musgrave (1608–1678) was of Hartley, Westmorland and
Edenhall, Cumberland. He had been a member of the Long
Parliament until disabled in 1643 and had served as commander
in chief of the royalist forces in these two counties. His sequestered
estates had been sold by the Treason Trustees to representatives
of the family. Royal Oak list: (his son Christopher) £1000 p.a.
(*CCC*, 2308).

45 Sir Thomas Dacre of Lanercost had also had his estate sold by
the Treason Trustees. (*CCC*, 1727).

46 Of Ellerton.

47 Richard Crackenthorpe (d.1661) was seated at Newbiggin, near

Appleby, in Westmorland but does not appear in the surviving assessment list for that county. Royal Oak list: (his son Christopher) £600 p.a.

48 Thomas Wybergh was of St Bees in Cumberland and Clifton in Westmorland. He and his late father had compounded for an estate valued at £200 p.a. (*CCC*, 2436).

49 Sir Edward Radcliffe (1589–1663) was seated at Dilston in Northumberland. His estates in Cumberland, Northumberland and Yorkshire had been sequestered for his recusancy and delinquency and some of the property had been sold by the Treason Trustees. In 1672 his son Sir Francis had an estate revenue amounting to over £6000 p.a. See also under Other Counties. (*CCC*, 2589–90. *Archaeologia Aeliana*, New Series, i (1857), 98).

50 Of Cockermouth.

51 This was apparently John Penruddock (1619–1655), the son of Sir John Penruddock (1591–1648) of Compton Chamberlayne in Wiltshire, who had recently been executed for his part in the royalist uprising which bears his name. According to their compounding papers they had estates worth £740 p.a. Their ancestors had lived at Arkleby in Cumberland. (S.P.23/lv/fo.66 and lvi/fo.327).

52 This was Sir William Huddleston of Millom Castle (d.1669) who had been knighted during the first Civil War. He had property in Cumberland, Yorkshire and Oxfordshire worth £1700 p.a. Compounding particulars: £651 p.a. in possession and £180 p.a. in reversion. (*CCC*, 1699. C.33/307/fols.159–60. S.P.23/ccii/83).

53 Sir George Dalston of Dalston (c.1580–1657) and his son Sir William (1614–1683) had both been members of the Long Parliament until disabled. They had estates in various counties which were valued in their compounding papers at £1281 p.a. (including £497 p.a. in Cumberland and Westmorland). Their estate revenue, however, may have been as high as £3000 p.a. See also under Westmorland. (S.P.23/cxcii/509,510,517,519–21,527,528,533–7,539,543. M.F.Keeler, *The Long Parliament, 1640–1641* (1954), 151).

54 Of Carlisle.

55 Of Carswellhowe.

56 Of Blencow.

57 William Musgrave of Crookdyke had recently inherited the estate of his grandfather Sir William Musgrave who had compounded with the Newcastle committee. (*CCC*, 1556–7).

58 Andrew Huddleston of Hutton John had been sequestered for recusancy and delinquency and in 1653 his estate had been sold by the Treason Trustees. (*CCC*, 2226–8).

Derbyshire

59 Sir Thomas Milward (1572–1658), who had formerly been Chief Justice of Chester, was seated at Eaton Dovedale. Royalist compounder: £388 p.a. (S.P.23/ccviii/879).

60 Rowland Eyre of Hassop was a convicted recusant and a former royalist colonel. Besides his Derbyshire estate, which was worth over £1400 p.a., he had property in Leicestershire and Staffordshire. His estates had recently been sold by the Treason Trustees but in 1662 he was described as a man of £3000 p.a. (*CCC*, 2319–21. S.P.28/209A, Derbyshire sequestration accounts (unbound). S.P.29/lxvi/35).

61 This was William FitzHerbert of Tissington (c.1629–1697). During his compounding proceedings the Derbyshire committee had put the value of his estate at £537 p.a. Royal Oak list: £1000 p.a. (S.P.23/cxcix/685).

62 This was probably John Lowe of Alderwasley who had succeeded his father in 1653. (*CCC*, 2008).

63 Henry Gilbert of Locko (1598–1657) had compounded for an estate valued at £395 p.a. in possession and £69 p.a. in reversion. (S.P.23/clxxiii/260).

64 John Milward (1599–1670) was seated at Snitterton Hall in the parish of Darley. In 1645 the Derbyshire committee had certified that his estate was worth £624 p.a. in possession (Derbyshire) and £110 p.a. in reversion (Staffordshire). At his death he left property in these counties worth £1100 p.a. (S.P.23/clxxiv/591, 601, 605–6. C.33/265/fo.385).

65 Henry Merry of Barton Park was the son and successor of Sir Henry Merry, a convicted recusant. Royalist compounder: £697 p.a. (including £486 p.a. in Derbyshire). (S.P.23/clxxxviii/832, 833, 838, 851, 856, 858).

66 Sir John Harpur (d.1677), who was seated at Swarkeston, had compounded for an estate valued at £1407 p.a. in possession (including £1107 p.a. in Derbyshire) and £1875 p.a. in reversion. (S.P.23/clxxiv/683, 684, 694–7).

67 Sir Wolstan Dixie (1603–1682) was seated at Market Bosworth in Leicestershire. According to his compounding papers the family had an estate worth £991 p.a. in possession (including £80 p.a. in Derbyshire) and £460 p.a. in reversion. His son Sir Beaumont had an income of £2000 p.a. on succeeding to the estate. (S.P.23/ccxii/551–2, 556–9. C.33/297/fo.363).

68 William Bullock of Norton had inherited the family estate in 1650 following the deaths of his two elder brothers. It had been valued in John Bullock's compounding papers at £750 p.a. (Derbyshire

and Nottinghamshire). Royal Oak list: £1000 p.a. (*CCC*, 1132–3. S.P.23/ccxxx/79, 82).

69 John Shalcross of Shalcross Hall in Taxal had compounded for an estate valued at £200 p.a. in possession and £50 p.a. in reversion. (S.P.23/clxxiii/197).

70 This was probably John Lowe of Hasland Hall, near Chesterfield, who died in 1657. Royalist compounder: £66 p.a. The family was a cadet branch of the Lowes of Alderwasley (note 62 above). (*CCAM*, 1071. *CCC*, 960. S.P.23/clxxiv/1,5,7).

71 The Talbots, who were seated at Albrighton in Shropshire, had property in a number of counties. Francis Talbot, Earl of Shrewsbury (c.1623–1668) had recently succeeded his father who had been sequestered for recusancy and delinquency. When compounding in 1654 the new Earl had put the value of the estates at £3018 p.a. (including £520 p.a. in Derbyshire). In 1659 he was involved in Sir George Booth's rising. (*CCC*, 1773–7. S.P.23/ccxxxiv/fols.188,189).

72 This was probably Gervase Pole of Spinkhill. The Poles were a Catholic family. During the 1630s it had been reported that their estate was worth £250 p.a. (*Catholic Record Society*, liii (1961), 425).

73 This was Francis Leeke (1627–1679) of the Chantry in Newark, Nottinghamshire who was created a baronet in 1663. Royalist compounder: £587 p.a. in possession and £416 p.a. in reversion. The Derbyshire property was valued at £337 p.a. (S.P.23/ccxxi/909–10).

74 Of Underwood.

75 This was Henry Vernon (d.1659), the son and heir of Sir Edward Vernon of Sudbury (d.1657). In 1662 the Vernon estates, which were located in several counties, were said to be worth £3000 or £4000 p.a. (S.P.29/lxvi/35).

76 William Orme of Longdon, Staffordshire had compounded for property valued at £186 p.a., including £30 p.a. in Derbyshire. (S.P.23/cxcix/289, 301).

77 Of Darley.

78 Sir Paul Neile (1613-c.1686), who was seated at Hutton Bonville in Yorkshire, was the son of Richard Neile, Archbishop of York. Royalist compounder: £1110 p.a. in possession (including £340 p.a. in Derbyshire) and £15 p.a. in reversion. (S.P.23/cxciii/337).

79 John Frescheville of Staveley (1607–1682) had compounded for an estate valued at £735 p.a. in possession (including £635 p.a. in Derbyshire) and £100 p.a. in reversion. The declared value, however, bore little relation to the actual value; in the reign of Charles II the manor of Staveley alone was worth £3500 p.a. In February 1656 he sought exemption from the decimation tax on the grounds that he had been well affected to the government ever

since compounding. In 1665 he was ennobled as Baron Frescheville. (S.P.23/ccviii/489–90. BL, Harleian MSS 6819, fo.5. *CCC*, 1048).

80 Of Bradway in the parish of Norton.

Essex

81 Sir Henry Clarke of Pleshey had compounded for an estate valued at £194 p.a. in possession and £122 p.a. in reversion. (*Commons Journals*, v, 687).

82 Sir Henry Appleton of Great Baddow (d.1670) had compounded for an estate in reversion valued at £302 p.a. According to a contemporary, Richard Symonds, he had an estate worth £400 p.a. in the 1650s. See also under Kent. (S.P.23/clxxiii/147. BL, Harleian MSS 991, fol.25).

83 Thomas Argall of Great Baddow had compounded for an estate valued at £640 p.a. (£390 p.a. in Essex and £250 p.a. in Kent). See also under Kent. (S.P.23/ccx/293, 297–9).

84 Salter Herris of Broomfield was a son of Dame Ann Herris and a half-brother of Sir Cranmer Herris, both of whom appear in this list. He had compounded for his estate with the Essex committee: £132 p.a. in possession and £210 p.a. in reversion after his mother's death. (S.P.23/ccliv/24I. *CCAM*, 1220).

85 Sir Humphrey Mildmay of Danbury had compounded for an estate valued at £695 p.a. (£620 p.a. in Essex and £75 p.a. in Somerset). His son John also appears in the list. (S.P.23/clxxx/810, 811).

86 Of Boreham.

87 Stephen Smith of Blackmore had compounded with the Essex committee for an estate valued at £410 p.a. (S.P.23/ccliv/24I).

88 Of Arnolds in Mountnessing.

89 The Abells had long been seated at West Bergholt but William Abell is described in the list printed in the *Thurloe State Papers* as of Horkesley.

90 Of Kelvedon.

91 Of Copford.

92 Sir William Howard of Tollesbury, who was a younger son of Thomas Earl of Suffolk, had been one of Charles I's courtiers. Royalist compounder: £168 p.a. (all in Essex). See also under Hertfordshire. (S.P.23/clxxx/182, 190).

93 Thomas Roberts of Little Braxted had compounded with the Essex committee for an estate valued at £259 p.a. See also under Suffolk. (S.P.23/ccliv/24I).

94 Sir Benjamin Ayloffe of Great Braxted (1592–1662) and his son William (1618–1675), who also appears in the list, had both sup-

ported the royalist cause. In compounding Sir Benjamin had put the value of his estate at £617 p.a. in possession and £158 p.a. in reversion; it had been alleged, however, that it was worth £1500 p.a. Royal Oak list: Sir William Ayloffe £1000 p.a. See also under Cambridgeshire. (*CCC*, 848–9. S.P.23/clxxiii/179 and ccxi/391, 395, 397, 401, 407).

95 Of Stanway.

96 Of Great Braxted.

97 Of Witham.

98 Of Tendring.

99 Sir Henry Audley (d.1667), who was an alleged papist, was of Berechurch in Essex and Barton Hall in Suffolk. It had been reported that his estate was worth £1360 p.a. At his death he left property in several counties worth £2000 p.a. See also under Suffolk. (BL, Additional MSS 5494, fo.106. *CCC*, 901–2. *CCAM*, 405. C.33/275/fo.69).

100 Dame Ann Herris, who lived at Writtle, was the widow of Sir Arthur Herris of Woodham Mortimer. (*CCC*, 2213–4).

101 Robert Milborne owned the manor of Marks in Great Dunmow. He was probably the father of James Milborne of Great Dunmow who also appears in the list.

102 James Altham of Mark Hall in Latton (1614–c.1675) had compounded for a 'clear estate' of £500 p.a. In 1661 he was made a knight of the Bath. In the reign of Charles II the Essex estate was worth at least £800 p.a. See also under Hertfordshire. (*CCC*, 879. C.33/256/fo.263 and 291/fo.620).

103 See note 101.

104 Of Mashbury.

105 Of Great Chesterford.

106 John Mildmay of Danbury was the son and heir of Sir Humphrey Mildmay: see note 85.

107 Thomas Meade of Wendon Lofts (1620–1678) had been a ward of the Crown. Court of Wards valuation, 1638: £719 p.a. He had compounded with the Essex committee for an estate valued at £970 p.a. (£700 p.a. in Essex and £270 p.a. in Norfolk in right of his wife). (Wards 5/14, feodary's certificate. S.P.23/ccliv/24I).

108 Of Roxwell.

109 Richard Luckyn was of Dives Hall in Chignall. In 1650 it had been reported that he had an estate worth £600 p.a. (*CCAM*, 1220).

110 Anthony Maxey of Bradwell Hall, who was the grandson of Sir Anthony Maxey, had succeeded his father, Greville Maxey, in 1648. He sold some of his property. (Thomas Wright, *The History and Topography of the County of Essex* (1831, 1835), i, 265).

111 See also under Hertfordshire.

112 Sir John Lucas of St John's Colchester (1606–1671) had been created Baron Lucas of Shenfield in 1645. In 1625 his father had left estates in various counties worth £3500 p.a. Royalist compounder: £1753 p.a. (including £1340 p.a. in Essex). (C.33/207/fo.243. S.P.23/cxcv/555, 556, 559, 563, 566).

113 Sir William Halton of Little Sampford (c.1620–1662) appears to have remained neutral during the Civil Wars. In 1659 he had an estate worth £900 p.a.: £400 p.a. in Essex and £500 p.a. in Cambridgeshire. See also under Cambridgeshire where he is shown as William Hallton. (C.33/213/fols.329–30).

114 Of Manuden.

115 This was Sir Andrew Jenoure of Great Dunmow who died c.1692.

116 John Lynn of Little Horkesley had compounded for property valued at £100 p.a. in possession and £345 p.a. in reversion after the death of his father. This included £325 p.a. in Essex. (S.P.23/ccxi/763–4, 769–70).

117 Richard Sames of Little Totham, who was the son of Sir Garrard Sames, had been a ward of the Crown. Court of Wards valuation, 1631: £330 p.a. (Wards 5/14, feodary's certificate).

118 Of Fordham.

119 Of Lambourne.

120 William Burrows of Woodford had compounded with the Essex committee for an estate valued at £820 p.a. in possession and £20 p.a. in reversion (£50 p.a. in Essex and £790 p.a. in Leicestershire). (S.P.23/ccliv/24I).

121 Sir William Hicks (1596–1680) was of Ruckholt, Essex and Beverstone, Gloucestershire. Although he had been appointed a member of the Essex parliamentary committee he had also been a royalist compounder: £800 p.a. (including £160 p.a. in Essex). (S.P.23/ccxxxvi/153).

122 Of Stock.

123 Of Nevendon.

124 Henry Nevill was of Cressing Temple, Essex and Holt, Leicestershire. He and his sons had been ardent royalists. In 1644 it had been reported that he had estates worth £6000 p.a. but he had fallen heavily into debt following their sequestration. To enable him to sell his Essex property it was agreed in June 1656 that the decimation tax with which it was charged should be levied instead on his Leicestershire estate (which was worth £1500 p.a.). Royal Oak list: £2000 p.a. (CCC, 863–4, 3262. C.33/222/fols.563–4; 232/fo.500; and 234/fols.120–1).

125 Of Farnham.

126 In a Chancery suit of 1673 Charles Fitch (or Fytch) of Woodham

Walter was said to have left an estate worth £700 p.a. (C.33/241/fo.752).

127 James Reynolds of Helions Bumpstead also had property at Castle Camps in Cambridgeshire: see the Cambridgeshire list. (*CCC*, 1942).

128 Of Great Burstead.

129 Of Brook Street.

130 Thomas Thompson's father appears later in the list. Both men were of Berden.

131 Of Hornchurch.

132 Richard Humfry or Humphrey of West Hanningfield had compounded with the Essex committee for an estate valued at £472 p.a. (S.P.23/ccliv/24I. *CCAM*, 1220).

133 Sir John Tyrrell (1579–1675) was of Herongate and Springfield Barney. Royalist compounder: £400 p.a. His son John was created a baronet in 1666. (S.P.23/clxxiii/61).

134 Robert Audley of Woodham Ferrers had compounded for an estate valued at £318 p.a. (£242 p.a. in Essex and £76 p.a. in Cambridgeshire). He does not appear in the Cambridgeshire decimation lists. (S.P.23/ccxix/791, 793–5).

135 Sir Cranmer Herris of Woodham Mortimer does not appear to have been actively involved in the Civil Wars. In 1671 he put the value of his estate at £2000 p.a. (C.33/237/fo.602).

136 Richard Cooper of Walthamstow had compounded with the Essex committee for property in Essex and London valued at £260 p.a. (S.P.23/ccliv/24I).

137 Sir Thomas Wiseman of Rivenhall (d.1659), who had recently succeeded his father, also had property in Kent. In January 1657 it was decided that he should be exempted from the tax. (BL, Additional MSS 5494, fo.107. *CSPDom, 1656–7*, 225, 249).

138 Charles Maynard of Walthamstow (d.1665), a former Exchequer official, was a younger brother of William Lord Maynard and the parliamentarian Sir John Maynard. He had served as a royalist colonel. Royal Oak list: £1000 p.a.

139 This was Edward Benlowes of Brent Hall in Finchingfield (1602–1686), a friend and patron of literary figures. According to Richard Symonds, writing about this time, he had an estate worth £1000 or £1200 p.a. Between 1655 and 1657, however, he disposed of all his property and subsequently settled in Oxford. (BL, Harleian MSS 991, fo.16. Thomas Wright, *The History and Topography of the County of Essex* (1831, 1835), i, 662–3 and ii,29).

140 Richard Boothby of Canons Hall, Wanstead had compounded with the Essex committee for an estate valued at £200 p.a. (S.P.23/ccliv/24I).

141 Sir Denner Strutt of Little Warley had compounded for an estate valued at £680 p.a. in possession and £150 p.a. in reversion. At his death in 1661 he left property in Essex, Suffolk and Lincolnshire worth at least £720 p.a. (S.P.23/ccvii/395. C.33/230/fols.407, 423).

142 Mundeford Bramston of Little Baddow (d.1679) was the barrister son of Sir John Bramston, Chief Justice of the King's Bench. In May 1656 he sought exemption from the decimation tax. Knighted in 1661, he served as a Master in Chancery during the years 1660 to 1676. (*CSPDom, 1655–6*, 331).

143 Gamaliel Capel (d.1683) was seated at Abbess Roding. In 1643 it had been reported that his father, Sir Gamaliel, had lands of inheritance worth £400 p.a., together with some church leases, and there is supporting evidence for this in the Essex sequestration accounts. (BL, Egerton MSS 2646, fo.255. S.P.28/218, Essex sequestration papers (unbound)).

144 This was Edward Sandford of Norton Mandeville.

145 Of Widdington.

146 Thomas Luther was seated at Sutton in Stapleford Tawney. Royal Oak list: £1000 p.a.

147 Of Epping.

148 Edmund Humphrey of Layer Marney had compounded locally for an estate valued at £153 p.a. (S.P.23/ccliv/24I).

149 The Dawtreys of Doddinghurst had property in Sussex but they are not represented in the Sussex decimation lists. (*CCAM*, 489).

150 Of Stifford. See also under Hertfordshire.

151 The Veseys or Veaseys were of Wicks Park.

152 James Hay, Earl of Carlisle (c.1612–1660), who was seated at Waltham Abbey, had lived for some years in Barbados. According to his compounding papers he had a total estate revenue of £2600 p.a. (S.P.23/clxxiii/181).

153 Of Epping.

154 Of Lower Breton.

155 Sir Robert Fenn of Aldham and his son Robert had compounded for an estate valued at £525 p.a. (including £180 p.a. in Essex, £120 p.a. in Hertfordshire and £146 p.a. in Suffolk). Both men had been officers of the royal household. (S.P.23/cxcvii/803–6).

156 Sir William Martin or Martyn of Woodford had been a member of the Essex parliamentary committee.

157 John Sames of Little Totham was probably a younger brother of Richard Sames (note 117 above).

158 Robert Roe was a son of Sir William Roe of Higham Hill in Walthamstow who had been a member of the Essex parliamentary committee. (*CCAM*, 480).

159 In view of the modest amount of his assessment it seems likely that George Coldham of Sheering had property elsewhere.
160 Dr John Johnson of Sandon was a physician.
161 Of Great Braxted.
162 Of Colchester.
163 Of Colchester.
164 Of Saffron Walden.
165 Of Radwinter.
166 See note 130 above.
167 Of Great Clacton.
168 Of Dagenham.
169 Of Dagenham.
170 Of Kelvedon Hatch.
171 See note 94 above.
172 Sir Richard Minshull (d.1667), a Catholic, was seated at Bourton in Buckinghamshire. According to one of his compounding particulars he had an estate worth £909 p.a. in possession and £100 in reversion. This included property in Essex which was valued at £406 p.a. (S.P.23/lvi/fo.341).
173 Thomas Smyth of Hill Hall, Theydon Mount (1602–1668) had inherited this estate from his nephew Edward Smyth who had served under Prince Rupert. In March 1656 he sought exemption from the decimation tax, claiming that he had been discharged from sequestration on proof of his good affection. In 1661 he was created a baronet. (*CSPDom, 1655–6*, 210).
174 This was Dr Samuel Hinton (1599–1658) of Lichfield in Staffordshire who had been awarded a doctorate of law at Oxford and had held a fellowship at Trinity College, Cambridge. Royalist compounder: £197 p.a. (including £38 p.a. in Essex and £70 p.a. in Northamptonshire). See also under Northamptonshire. (S.P.23/ccxi/721, 727, 733).
175 John Fanshawe of Parslow, who was a former Duchy of Lancaster official, had compounded for an estate valued at £265 p.a. (including £160 p.a. in Essex). A contemporary, Richard Symonds, put the value of his estate at £300 p.a. (*CCC*, 1300. S.P.23/lvi/fo.219. BL, Harleian MSS 991, fo.7).
176 For the Earl of Northampton see under Northamptonshire.
177 Probably of Saffron Walden. (*CCAM*, 983).
178 This was George Sames of Tolleshunt Major.
179 Of Woodham Walter.

Hampshire

180 This was Peter Gillam of Winchester.

181 Of Hamworthy in Dorset.

182 Sir William Ogle of Michelmarsh (c.1600–1682) had been a member of the Long Parliament until disabled in 1643. In 1645 he had been created Viscount Ogle. Royalist compounder: £28 p.a. For many years he was heavily in debt and largely dependent for his income on the jointure lands which had been settled on his second wife by her previous husband. (S.P.23/lvi/fo.286. G.E.C. (ed.), *The Complete Peerage* (1910–59), x, 39–41).

183 Edward Norton, who had fought on the royalist side, was a younger brother of Richard Norton of Southwick, one of the leading parliamentarians in the county.

184 James May of Coldre was the son and heir of Sir Humphrey May (1573–1630) who had been Chancellor of the Duchy of Lancaster, 1618 to 1629. Royalist compounder: £230 p.a. in possession and £370 p.a. in reversion after the death of his mother (including the Coldre property valued at £120 p.a.). In 1657, following litigation, it was agreed that his mother should make over the Coldre estate to him in lieu of an allowance of £150 p.a. (S.P.23/lvi/fols.34–5. C.33/208/fols.1094–5).

185 John Ford of Eling was a younger brother of Sir Edward Ford of Uppark in East Harting, Sussex (see under Sussex). (*CCAM*, 983. *CCC*, 1688).

186 Stephen March of Newport, Isle of Wight had compounded for property valued at £66 p.a. (S.P.23/ccxx/829, 833. *CCAM*, 1093).

187 Henry Philpott of Thruxton had compounded for an estate valued at £364 p.a. in possession and £232 p.a. in reversion. (S.P.23/clxxiii/143. *CCAM*, 366–7).

188 Pierce Edgcumbe of Mount Edgcumbe, Devon had been a member of the Long Parliament until disabled in 1644. Royalist compounder: £1788 p.a. (including £576 p.a. in Hampshire and the Isle of Wight and £210 p.a. in Sussex). Royal Oak list: £2000 p.a. See also under Sussex. (S.P.23/cxcix/403–5, 433–5, 463, 465).

189 This was presumably Richard Lowe of Harbridge, a royalist compounder, who also had property in Wiltshire. (*CCC*, 1973).

190 John Weeks of Harbridge also had property in Cornwall. (*CCAM*, 989–90).

191 Thomas Wriothesley, Earl of Southampton (1608–1667) was seated at Titchfield. Royalist compounder: £3718 p.a. (including £2721 p.a. in Hampshire). (S.P.23/lvi/fols.288–9 and clxxiii/321).

192 This was Laurence Hyde of Hinton Daubney, a merchant. (*CCC*, 1183).

193 John Lewkenor was seated at West Dean in Sussex. See under Sussex.

194 This was Dr John Warner the former Bishop of Rochester. See under Kent.

195 This was probably Edward Cooke of Crondall.

196 The Kingsmills of Sydmonton had estates in a number of counties. Sir William Kingsmill (1613–1664) had claimed in 1645 that he had always been well affected to Parliament and that he had only £300 p.a. in possession. His mother, who died in 1672, had a substantial jointure out of the estate. At his death he had £800 p.a. in possession; in contrast his son, another Sir William, enjoyed an income of £3000 p.a. (*CCC*, 882–3. S.P.23/ccxxi/761–4, 773, 774. C.33/223/fols.148, 560–1; 235/fols.248, 720; and 293/fo.156).

197 William Seymour, Marquess of Hertford (1587–1660) was seated at Tottenham House in Wiltshire. Royalist compounder: £2851 p.a. in possession and £637 p.a. in reversion. In addition, his son Francis Lord Seymour and grandson Charles Seymour had compounded for lands in possession which were valued at £1963 p.a. (S.P.23/lvi/fols.270–2, 275–6).

198 This was Dowse Fuller of Romsey who had been appointed a member of the Hampshire parliamentary committee. In 1651 his estate had been discharged from sequestration on the grounds that there was no evidence of delinquency. At the time when the decimation tax was levied on him he was £7000 in debt and following his death in 1657 an Essex manor was sold for £5900. (*CCC*, 105, 2807. C.33/209/fo.1028).

199 Richard Goddard of Salisbury, a lawyer, had compounded for an estate valued at £380 p.a. (S.P.23/clxxiii/210).

200 Sir Thomas Badd of Came Bishop in Fareham (d.1683) had compounded for property valued at £340 p.a. (S.P.23/lvi/fo.62).

201 Matthew Cufaude, a recusant, lived at Cufaude near Basingstoke. In January 1654 he had sought to compound for two-thirds of his estate. (*CCC*, 1487–8).

202 This was probably William Goldwyer of Bure in Christchurch.

203 Richard Compton of Bisterne was the son and heir of Sir Henry Compton of Brambletye in Sussex who had compounded for property in various counties which he had valued at £3133 p.a. Some parts of the estate had been settled on his younger sons. Richard Compton was forced to sell a considerable amount of outlying property but in the reign of Charles II he had an estate revenue of £3000 p.a. (S.P.23/ccv/1–3, 5, 9, 21–8. *VCH, Gloucestershire*, vi, 217, 253. *CSPDom, 1660–1*, 446. C.33/316/fo.492).

204 Of Winchester.

205 Of East Worldham.

206 This was Edward Lewin of Christchurch. (*CCAM*, 760. *CCC*, 1089).

207 The Giffards of Chillington Hall in Staffordshire were a Catholic

family. Walter Giffard, who lived at Marston in that county, was the son and heir of Peter Giffard (for whom see under Other Counties). In March 1655 his Hampshire property had been sold by the Treason Trustees. (*CCC*, 3146).

208 William Chamberlaine of Lyndhurst had compounded for his estate as a papist in arms. (*CCC*, 1755–6).

209 George Philpott of Compton was a recusant. In 1651 he had mortgaged the manor of Compton. (*CCC*, 2095).

210 Probably of Bure in Christchurch.

211 William Pawlett of Poultons in Overton had compounded for property valued at £423 p.a. (S.P.23/clxxiv/91).

212 Sir William Courtney, who was a recusant, resided at Bambridge in the parish of Twyford where his wife had a jointure by a former husband. Royalist compounder: £80 p.a. (*CCC*, 1841, 3287. S.P.23/ccx/7, 9, 17, 29).

213 Henry Foyle of Winchester had recently had his estate sold by the Treason Trustees. (*CCC*, 2697–8).

214 George Pitt of Stratfield Saye (1625–1694) had inherited estates in various counties worth £4000 p.a. following the death of his father in 1644. Although he had not been actively involved in the Civil Wars he had chosen to compound but had only declared property worth £1417 p.a. Royal Oak list: £4000 p.a. (C.33/237/fo.518. S.P.23/ccxiv/339–40, 345, 359–60).

215 This was Richard Goldstone of Amport.

216 Of Penton Grafton.

Hertfordshire

217 Sir John Watts of Tewin had compounded for an estate valued at £374 p.a. which he was due to inherit from his father. (S.P.23/ccvii/673, 674).

218 Sir Thomas Hyde(1594–1665) does not appear to have been sequestered. In 1649 it had been alleged that he was a royalist, a depopulating landlord and a simoniacal patron of church livings. At his death he left an estate worth £3000 p.a. (*CCAM*, 1079. C.33/259/fo.403).

219 For James Altham see under Essex.

220 Thomas Meads (or Mead) is described as of Farnham (in Essex) in a subsequent list. He was also taxed in Essex.

221 James Silverlock also appears in the Essex decimation lists.

222 As indicated, Sir John Monson (1599–1683) was seated at Burton in Lincolnshire. Royalist compounder: £2282 p.a. (including £20 p.a. in Hertfordshire). In January 1656 he had sought exemption from the tax assessed on his Lincolnshire property and on 14 March an order had been issued for the discharge of his estate.

(S.P.23/lvi/fols.279–80. *CSPDom, 1656–7*, 249. *CCC*, 1431).

223 Sir Thomas Fanshawe (c.1596–1665) had been a member of the Long Parliament until disabled in 1643. Royalist compounder: estates in Hertfordshire and Essex valued at £1660 p.a. Although he was heavily in debt he was fortunate to be assessed only on his personal estate. In 1661 he was created Viscount Fanshawe. (S.P.23/ccviii/675, 687, 691).

224 Humphrey Shalcrosse was a London scrivener who had grown rich through his moneylending activities. He sought exemption from the decimation tax. In 1656 he bought the Digswell estate (near Hatfield) and made it his family seat. (*CSPDom, 1655–6*, 383. *VCH, Hertfordshire*, iii, 83).

225 Sir Francis Boteler (1612–1690) had served under Strafford in Ireland. In 1647 he had inherited the Hatfield Woodhall estate from William Lord Boteler of Brantfield. (R.Clutterbuck, *The History and Antiquities of the County of Hertford* (1815–27), ii, 345–6).

226 Sir George Boteler or Butler (1583–1657), who was Sir Francis Boteler's uncle, had been a gentleman of the Privy Chamber to Charles I and a close associate of Strafford. He had lived for many years at Ellerton in Yorkshire but was buried at Tewin. Royalist compounder: £422 p.a. (all in Yorkshire). (S.P.23/cxcvi/1).

227 Of Esher.

228 John Duke of Sheering was not taxed in Essex.

229 Ralph Bashe or Baesh of Stanstead Bury had inherited a considerable estate in 1653, though it was encumbered with a rent-charge of 500 marks p.a. which was the subject of litigation. In 1661 he was made a knight of the Bath. Royal Oak list: (his son Edward) £1500 p.a. (C.33/207/fo.1347).

230 Dr Thomas Turner (1591–1672) had been appointed Dean of Canterbury in 1644. See *DNB*.

231 Jeremiah Beck of Castle Acre, Norfolk had compounded for an estate valued at £1380 p.a. in possession and £55 p.a. in reversion. This included property at Cheshunt in Hertfordshire (£120 p.a.) which he held in right of his wife. (S.P.23/ccxx/197, 199, 200, 207–9).

232 Sir Thomas Williamson (1609–1657), who was seated at East Markham in Nottinghamshire, had compounded for an estate valued at £2057 p.a. This was before his marriage to Dionysia Hale who was in possession of the Hertfordshire manor of Lannock. (S.P.23/clxxiii/16. *VCH, Hertfordshire*, iii, 174).

233 For Sir William Howard of Tollesbury see under Essex.

234 John Keeling served as Lord Chief Justice of the King's Bench in the reign of Charles II. In 1662 he was knighted. Although he had a considerable estate at Southill he was not apparently taxed in

Bedfordshire. Royal Oak list: (his son John) £600 p.a.

Huntingdonshire

235 Molineux Audley had inherited the estate of his brother Thomas who had put its value at £219 p.a. when compounding. In 1650 it had been alleged that he had £500 p.a. in land. (S.P.23/lvi/fo.156. *CCAM*, 1250–1).

236 Sir John Hewett of Waresley (c.1598–1657) had property in a number of counties. Royalist compounder: £809 p.a. (including £270 p.a. in Huntingdonshire of which he had been a joint purchaser with his son John). In 1650, however, it had been alleged that he had concealed lands in Hertfordshire worth £400 p.a. (S.P.23/ccxi/449, 450, 453, 454. *CCAM*, 1145).

237 William Cavendish, Earl of Devonshire (1617–1684) was seated at Chatsworth in Derbyshire. See also under Suffolk and Other Counties.

238 For the Earl of Northampton see under Northamptonshire.

239 Stephen Anderson of Manby in Lincolnshire had compounded for an estate valued at £1326 p.a. in possession and £1000 p.a. in reversion (including £600 p.a. in Huntingdonshire). In December 1655 he sought exemption from the decimation tax, claiming that it would ruin him, and an order was issued that proceedings should be suspended until further notice. Eventually he settled at Eyworth, the family seat in Bedfordshire, and in 1660 he was said to have an estate revenue of £3000 p.a. (*CCC*, 1069–70. S.P.23/lvi/fo.6. *CSPDom, 1660–1*, 149).

Kent

240 William Hugessen of Provender in Lynsted had compounded for his estate with the Kent committee (fine £600). In 1660 he was knighted. (*CCC*, 459).

241 Of Hamptons in West Peckham.

242 This was Francis Clerke of Rochester (c.1624–1686), a barrister, who had compounded locally (fine £200). Clerke built up a large estate in Kent and elsewhere and made Ulcombe Place his family seat. In 1660 he was knighted. (*CCC*, 460. C.33/268/fo.823. Henning, ii, 88–9).

243 Sir John Darell was seated at Calehill House in Little Chart.

244 Edward Darell was a younger brother of Sir John Darell.

245 George Newman of Rochester, a former parliamentarian colonel and committeeman, had compounded locally (fine £700). (A.M.Everitt, *The Community of Kent and the Great Rebellion 1640–60* (1966), 216, 284. *CCC*, 460).

246 Zouche Brockman of Cheriton had compounded locally (fine £367). (*CCC*, 458).

247 Of Aylesford.

248 William Brewer was of Ditton. In 1653 his father, Thomas Brewer, who was a recusant, had sought to contract for two-thirds of his estate. (*CCC*, 2455).

249 Henry Ruffin of Eastchurch had compounded locally (fine £300). (*CCC*, 460)

250 Sir Anthony Aucher of Bishopsbourne had compounded locally (fine £700). (*CCC*, 458).

251 Thomas Gibbon of West Cliffe and his son Thomas (who also appears in the list) had compounded locally (fines of £200 and £100 respectively). (*CCC*, 461).

252 Sir Christopher Harfleete of Hackington had compounded locally (fine £250). (*CCC*, 461).

253 Thomas Courthope of Hackington had compounded locally (fine £250). (*CCC*, 461).

254 Sir Thomas Palmer of Wingham (d.1656), who was a baronet, had compounded locally (fine £1000). (*CCC*, 461).

255 Sir Roger Palmer of London, who was a younger brother of Sir Thomas Palmer, had held the office of Cofferer in the household of Charles I. He had been a member of the Long Parliament until disabled in 1644. Royalist compounder:£1809 p.a. This included £278 p.a. in Kent and £300 p.a. in Suffolk (but it had subsequently been alleged that the Suffolk property was worth £500 p.a.). See also under Suffolk. (*CCC*, 1394–6. S.P.23/lvi/fo.237. *CCAM*, 180).

256 Arnold Braemes of Bridge Place (1602–1681) was a Dover merchant of Flemish descent. He had compounded locally (fine £800). In 1660 he was knighted. (*Camden Fifth Series*, i (1993), 40. *CCC*, 457–8. Henning, iii, 707).

257 Of Davington.

258 This was probably Sir John Boys of Bonnington (1607–1664), a royalist commander who had been knighted in 1644. He had compounded for £100 p.a. in possession and £9 p.a. in reversion. During the 1650s he was heavily involved in royalist plots and early in 1655 found himself under arrest. (*DNB*. S.P.23/ccix/491. Everitt, *op.cit.*, 245, 270, 282–4, 286).

259 Gibbon Hawker of Challock had compounded locally (fine £300). (*CCC*, 461).

260 Thomas Osborne of Chilham had compounded for an estate valued at £130 p.a. (S.P.23/lvi/fo.170).

261 Richard Thornhill of Olantighe was the son and heir of Sir Timothy Thornhill (d.1648) who had been a member of the Kent parliamentary committee. Royalist compounder: £1020 p.a. in

possession (£970 p.a. in Kent and £50 p.a. in Essex) and £875 p.a. in reversion (all in Kent). In 1651 his sequestered estate in Kent had been let at £1095 p.a. (S.P.23/cxxii/319 and ccliv/101. *CCC*, 2255-7).

262 Of Great Delce.

263 Sir Thomas Culpeper of Hollingbourne had compounded for property in Kent, Sussex and London which was valued at £1177 p.a. His decimation assessment presumably took account of the fact that £500 p.a. was payable out of the estate to his son Sir Cheyney who had been chairman of the Kent committee which had been set up after the rebellion of 1648. (S.P.23/lvi/fols.191-3 and clxxxviii/63-5, 82, 91-2. Everitt, *op.cit.*, 274, 289).

264 This was probably Thomas Culpeper of Hackington who was deeply involved in royalist plots and had been arrested early in 1655. His father, Sir Thomas (d.1643), had left property worth £800 p.a. but a considerable part of the estate was still in the hands of trustees who had taken on responsibility for paying his debts. In a Chancery suit begun in 1660 Culpeper sought to regain possession of the trust property. (Everitt, *op.cit.*, 283, 304, 306. C.9/34/21. C.33/207/fols.412-3).

265 Of Throwley.

266 Robert Bargrave of Patrixbourne had compounded locally (fine £350). (*CCC*, 460).

267 Philip Warwick (1609-1683), the royalist politician and historian, had been a member of the Long Parliament until disabled in 1644. In his compounding particular he had disclosed that the manor of Frogpoole (Frognal), Chislehurst (worth £200 p.a.) had been mortgaged to him and he had subsequently settled there. About 1647 he had married Dame Joan Boteler, a widow with a jointure of £500 p.a. In 1660 he was knighted. (*DNB*. Henning, iii, 674-7. S.P.23/lvi/307. C.33/240/fo.108 and 283/fo.443).

268 This was Dr John Warner (1581-1666), the former Bishop of Rochester, who had property in several counties. See also under Hampshire for the assessment on his lands in the Isle of Wight. (*DNB. CCAM*, 260-4).

269 Sir Thomas Godfrey of Heppington in Nackington had been a ward of the Crown. Court of Wards valuation, 1625: Kent £973 p.a., Sussex £100 p.a. Sir Thomas had been a member of the Kent parliamentary committee but from 1648 onwards he had been associated with the Cavalier party. In 1650 it had been reported that he had an estate worth £1000 p.a. In August 1656 he sought exemption from the decimation tax. (Wards 5/43, feodary's certificate. *CCC*, 328, 2600).

270 Of Fordwich.

271 Sir Edward Bathurst (c.1603–1674), who was seated at Lechlade in Gloucestershire, had been created a baronet in 1643. Royalist compounder: £516 p.a. in possession and £320 p.a. in reversion (but £153 p.a. issuing out of the estate for ever). In January 1656 he sought exemption from the decimation tax and it was ordered that the proceedings should be suspended until further notice. During the reign of Charles II the Gloucestershire property was worth £1000 p.a. (S.P.23/clxxiii/287. *CCC*, 3267. C.33/257, part 2/fo.337 and 275/fo.751).

272 James Newman of Rochester was a younger brother of George Newman (note 245 above). (*CCC*, 460).

273 John Marsham (1602–1685), who was of Whorn's Place in Cuxton, had been one of the Six Clerks in Chancery until removed from office by the Long Parliament. Royalist compounder: £246 p.a. In 1660 he recovered his office and was made a baronet. His son, another Sir John, had an estate worth £2000 p.a. (S.P.23/clxxiii/203. C.33/305/fols.455–6. Henning, iii, 23–4).

274 Of St John's in Thanet.

275 Of Wickhambreux.

276 Edward Roberts of St Thomas's Hill, Canterbury had compounded locally (fine £300). (*CCC*, 458).

277 Thomas Hardres of Canterbury (1610–1681), a barrister, was a younger brother of Sir Richard Hardres who also appears in the list: see note 309 below. In 1676 he was knighted. (*DNB*. Henning, ii, 490–1).

278 This was Sir Nicholas Crispe (d.1656) of Quex, Birchington. (He should not be confused with Sir Nicholas Crispe of Hammersmith (c.1598–1666) the customs farmer who has an entry in DNB). In 1649 it had been claimed that he and his father had always been well affected to Parliament. In a Chancery suit Sir Nicholas was said to have left property in Kent worth £700 p.a. besides his wife's jointure; in all, £1000 p.a. (*CCC*, 1908. C.33/246/fo.357).

279 Of Meopham.

280 Of Ripple Court.

281 Thomas Lambarde of Westerham had compounded locally (fine £200). (*CCC*, 461).

282 Henry Gilbourne of Bromley had compounded locally (fine £160). (*CCC*, 461).

283 Richard Spencer of Orpington (1593–1661), who was a younger son of Robert Lord Spencer of Wormleighton, had compounded for an estate valued at £398 p.a. (S.P.23/lvi/fo.323).

284 Thomas Southland of Ickham had compounded locally (fine £500). (*CCC*, 461).

285 This was possibly Thomas Lee of London who had married a sister of John Warner, Bishop of Rochester.

286 For Sir Henry Appleton see note 82 above.

287 Of Kingsdown.

288 This was probably Henry Coke of Thorington in Suffolk who had married Margaret Lovelace, the daughter and sole heir of Richard Lovelace of Kingsdown. See under Suffolk.

289 George Cooke of North Cray had compounded locally (fine £150). (*CCC*, 457).

290 Of Monkton.

291 William Merriwether of Shepherdswell had compounded locally (fine £150). (*CCC*, 460).

292 John Tufton, Earl of Thanet (1608–1664), who was seated at Hothfield Place, had a large estate which was considered to be worth £10,000 p.a. This included substantial property in Sussex but he does not appear in the decimation lists for that county. Although he had paid a composition fine of £9000 his support for the royalist cause had been spasmodic and he had sided with Parliament during the Kent insurrection of 1648. In December 1655 he sought exemption from the decimation tax but his request was strongly opposed by Major General Kelsey. (*CCC*, 839–40. *Commons Journals*, iii, 572. BL, Harleian MSS 991, fo.39. *Thurloe State Papers*, iv, 293. Everitt, *op.cit.*, 161, 187, 245, 254–5, 258, 293–4).

293 According to a contemporary, Richard Symonds, the Harlackendens of Bearsted had an estate worth £600 or £700 p.a. (BL, Harleian MSS 991, fo.39).

294 Anthony Hammond of St Alban's Court, Nonington had compounded locally (fine £640). He was one of the most active of the Kent Cavaliers. See also under Cambridgeshire. (*CCC*, 460. Everitt, *op.cit.*, 102, 245, 249, 268).

295 Sir Edward Hales of Tunstall Place (1626-c.1684) was the grandson and successor of Sir Edward Hales (1576–1654) who had been a member of the Long Parliament until disabled in 1648. In 1643 Sir Simonds D'Ewes had noted that the latter was a man of £5000 or £6000 p.a. Sir Edward the grandson had compounded locally (fine £2000). In December 1655 he sought a reduction in his decimation assessment but met with opposition from Major General Kelsey. In the reign of Charles II he sold considerable property. (BL, Harleian MSS 164, fo.356. *CCC*, 461. C.33/239/fo.555 and 249/fo.327. Henning, ii, 465–6).

296 Sir Robert Pointz (d.1665), who was seated at Iron Acton in Gloucestershire, had compounded for an estate valued at £204 p.a. (including £74 p.a. in Kent). In the reign of Charles II the

Gloucestershire property was said to be worth £25,000. (S.P.23/ccx/197, 203. C.33/264/fo.281).

297 John Farnaby of Eythorne was the eldest son of Thomas Farnaby of Great Kippington, Sevenoaks (c.1575–1647) the celebrated schoolmaster and classical scholar. Both men had been zealous royalists and John Farnaby had compounded locally (fine £120). In 1650 it had been reported that the family had an estate worth £500 p.a. but generous provision had been made for his half-brother Francis. (*DNB. CCC*, 460. *CCAM*, 1221).

298 Nevill Hall was the son and heir of Sir William Hall of Kennington (Kent).

299 Of Frinsted.

300 This was possibly Richard Bennett of Kew in Surrey. (*CCC*, 1011).

301 John Neville, Lord Bergavenny (1616–1662), who was a Catholic, seems to have lived mainly at Sherborne in Oxfordshire where his wife had an estate. Royalist compounder: £1053 p.a. in various counties. In 1649 he had also sought to compound for the reversion of an estate in Kent, valued at £500 p.a., which was then in the possession of his mother. This included the family seat at Birling. Although he had property in Suffolk and Sussex he does not appear in the decimation lists for those counties. In the reign of Charles II the estates were worth £5000 p.a. (*CCC*,869–72. S.P.23/ccvi/23–7. C.33/311/fo.282).

302 Thomas Brett of Snave had compounded for an estate valued at £122 p.a. (S.P.23/cci/941,947)

303 Dr Thomas Bird, an ecclesiastical lawyer, had been described as of Coventry when compounding in 1647. (*CCC*, 1594).

304 Sir Richard Hardres (1606–1669), who was seated at Hardres Court in Upper Hardres, had been created a baronet in June 1642. Formerly a member of the Kent parliamentary committee, he had joined the royalists in 1648 and had been forced to compound (fine £400). He was wealthy enough to be able to charge his estates in Kent and Yorkshire with £300 p.a. for his wife's jointure and £120 p.a. for the upbringing of his younger children. (Everitt, *op.cit.*, 146, 154, 243, 244, 249, 250, 264, 267. *CCC*, 459. C.33/247/fo.318).

305 Possibly of Reigate in Surrey.

306 Of Adisham.

307 Sir George Sondes of Lees Court (1599–1677) had compounded for an estate valued at £1625 p.a. in possession and £600 p.a. in reversion (with out-rents amounting to £47 p.a. payable out of the estate). In December 1655 his attempt to secure exemption from the decimation tax led Major General Kelsey to protest that he

was a great enemy of the state. In 1676 he was created Earl of Feversham. At his death he left estates in several counties worth £7000 p.a. (S.P.23/lv/fols.151–3. *CCC*, 867–8. *Thurloe State Papers*, iv, 293. Everitt, *op.cit.*, 122, 226–7. Henning, ii, 456–7. C.33/249/fo.434).

308 Of Eastchurch.

309 See note 251 above.

310 This was John Strughill of Lydd.

311 Probably of Canterbury.

312 Of Hawkhurst.

313 Of Nonington.

314 Possibly of St Lawrence in Thanet (Ramsgate).

315 Sir Allan Zouch, who was a recusant, had property in Kent in right of his wife. In 1648 it had been reported that he had an estate in Norfolk worth £180 p.a. (*CCAM*, 1263–5. *CCC*, 116, 2702–3).

316 Sir Leonard Ferby was of St Paul's Cray.

317 Possibly of Canterbury.

318 Of Benenden.

319 John Best of Canterbury, a lawyer, had compounded locally (fine £226). (*CCC*, 459).

320 Sir James Hales of The Dongeon, ner Canterbury, had compounded locally (fine £350). (*CCC*, 458).

321 Of Borden.

322 Of Faversham.

323 Of Hawkhurst.

324 Henry Thomson of Chatham had compounded locally (fine £140). (*CCC*, 458).

325 Dr William Stede, an ecclesiastical lawyer, was of Stede Hill, Harrietsham. In 1650 it had been reported that he had estates in various counties worth £2000 p.a. (*CCC*, 328, 2614).

326 Christopher Hobart was probably a kinsman of the Hobarts of Blickling in Norfolk.

327 John Woodgreene of Strood had compounded locally (fine £100). (*CCC*, 461).

328 Sir Thomas Peyton of Knowlton (1613–1684) had been a member of the Long Parliament until disabled in 1644. His estate was then considered to be worth £1000 p.a. Subsequently he compounded locally (fine £900). During the 1650s he was one of the leading royalist conspirators in Kent. (*CCC*, 459, 864. S.P.23/clxxiii/180. Everitt, *op.cit.*, 244, 266, 279–81, 285–6, 303, 315).

329 Thomas Argall was of Great Baddow in Essex. See under Essex.

330 In 1650 it had been noted that Arnold King of Bromley had an estate worth £300 p.a. (*CCAM*, 1221).

Northamptonshire

331 Walter Kirkham was the son and heir of Robert Kirkham (note 333). Royal Oak list: £800 p.a.

332 In 1649 it had been reported that Thomas Styles had property in Lincolnshire worth £35 p.a. (*CCC*, 1929).

333 Robert Kirkham of Fineshade Abbey (c.1594–1656), a barrister, had compounded for an estate valued at £722 p.a. (all in Northamptonshire). (S.P.23/clxxxvi/47–50, 54, 71, 72. *CCC*, 1088).

334 John Syers had compounded for an estate valued at £509 p.a. (including £339 p.a. in Northamptonshire). (S.P.23/cciv/745–6, 749–50).

335 Sir Edward Watson (1586–1658) was a younger brother of Sir Lewis Watson of Rockingham who as a reward for his loyalty to the king had been created Lord Rockingham in 1645. Royalist compounder: £126 p.a. (S.P.23/ccv/939, 945, 947, 951, 953).

336 Sir Thomas Cave (d.*circa* 1664) and his son Sir Thomas (1622-c.1671) had both been active royalists, though they had not apparently compounded for their estates. The latter may have been taxed in Leicestershire where they also had considerable property. (*CCAM*, 1048–9).

337 Henry Howard, who was a younger son of Thomas Earl of Berkshire, had served as royalist governor of Malmesbury. He also had property in Lincolnshire. (C.33/255/fo.271).

338 He may be identified as Sir Charles Compton, a younger brother of James Earl of Northampton, who had been knighted in 1643. Royalist compounder (when described as of Grendon): £84 p.a. (S.P.23/ccvii/527. *CCAM*, 1380).

339 This may have been Thomas Willoughby of Olney Park, Buckinghamshire who had a lease of lands at Castle Ashby from the Earl of Northampton. ("Weston-Fanell' should read Weston Favell). (*CCC*, 1247, 2096–7).

340 Charles Cokayne (1602–1661) had been created Viscount Cullen in August 1642. Royalist compounder: £1737 p.a. in possession and £1715 p.a. in reversion. (S.P.23/clxxiii/287. *CCC*, 1383–4).

341 Lady Farmer was the widow of Sir Hatton Farmer (d.1640) and the mother of Sir William Farmer (1621–1661) who had been a royalist colonel. She had reportedly lent Charles I the sum of £1620. Sir William had compounded for an estate valued at £234 p.a. in possession and £788 p.a. in reversion after the death of his mother. (*CCAM*, 998–9. S.P.23/lv/fols.163–4. *CCC*, 1063–4).

342 Thomas Rudd had compounded for property valued at £275 p.a. (S.P.23/lvi/fols.255–6).

343 For Dr Samuel Hinton see note 174.

344 Sir Justinian Isham (1610–1675) had compounded for Leicestershire property in his possession valued at £627 p.a. and Northamptonshire property valued at £614 p.a. in reversion after the death of his father Sir John (1582–1651). According to the Isham family papers, however, the Lamport estate was worth £1000 p.a. while the total revenue from his lands of inheritance amounted to over £1600 p.a. (S.P.23/cxcv/1, 2, 11–13. Mary E.Finch, *The Wealth of Five Northamptonshire Families 1540–1640*, *Northamptonshire Record Society*, xix (1956), 36–7).

345 Sir Anthony Haslewood (1600–1660) had compounded for an estate valued at £1070 p.a. Royal Oak list: (his son William) £3000 p.a. (S.P.23/ccvii/717. *CCC*, 1862).

346 Sir Edward Griffin (c.1605–1681), who was a former courtier, had been a member of the Long Parliament until disabled in 1644. He had compounded for an estate valued at £1205 p.a. (all in Northamptonshire) but it had been alleged that it was actually worth some £1800 p.a. In July 1656 his request for exemption from the decimation tax was referred to Major General Boteler and the Northamptonshire commissioners. (S.P.23/cxcv/605, 607–8. *CCC*, 1206–7).

347 Geoffrey Palmer of East Carlton (c.1598–1670), a barrister, had been a member of the Long Parliament until disabled in 1642. Royalist compounder: £257 p.a. He was created a baronet in 1660, served as Attorney General to Charles II and built up a large estate. At his death he left property in Northamptonshire, Leicestershire and Lincolnshire worth over £2000 p.a. (S.P.23/clxxiii/320. C.33/236/fo.832. C.6/195/97).

348 Of Thorpe Lubenham.

349 William Stafford (1627–1665) had compounded for an estate valued at £1298 p.a. (including £700 p.a. in Northamptonshire). Royal Oak list: £3000 p.a. His son William had an estate in several counties worth £1500 p.a. (S.P.23/ccxvii/105–6, 109, 123–4. C.33/280/fo.88).

350 Sir Christopher Hatton (c.1605–1670) had been a member of the Long Parliament until disabled in 1642. During the years 1643 to 1646 he had been Comptroller of the King's Household and in 1643 had been ennobled as Lord Hatton of Kirby. Royalist compounder: £2236 p.a. in possession and £160 p.a. in reversion (with £130 p.a. issuing out of the estate for ever). For some years he had been living in France and in February 1654 his wife had asked the Protector to allow his estate to be discharged from sequestration, stressing that he was heavily in debt. In 1662 his Northamptonshire property was said to be worth £1370 p.a. (*DNB*.

S.P.23/clxxiii/321. *CCAM*, 1209. *CCC*, 1579–82. BL, Additional MSS 34,222, fo.88).

351 James Compton, Earl of Northampton (1622–1681), whose principal seat was at Castle Ashby, had compounded for estates in various counties which were valued at £5417 p.a. In 1650 he had claimed that his father had left debts amounting to £30,000 and in 1655 he was involved in litigation with some of the creditors. He also appears in the Essex and Huntingdonshire decimation lists but he was not taxed in Bedfordshire or Cambridgeshire, two of the other counties where he had property. (S.P.23/ccxviii/1–3. *CCC*, 1246–51. C.33/205/fols.1515,1516).

352 For Sir Richard Wingfield see the Rutland list where he appears as plain Richard Wingfield, and note 366. His Northamptonshire property was at Haselbech.

353 This was apparently William Hacke of Peterborough. (*CCAM*, 831–2).

354 William Stydolphe of Headley in Surrey had been an Esquire of the Body to both James I and Charles I. Royalist compounder: £893 p.a. (including £520 p.a. in Northamptonshire). At his death in 1659 he left property in several counties worth £1500 p.a. (S.P.23/ccxiv/563, 565, 566, 569, 577. C.33/252/fols.286–7 and 262/fo.169).

355 Sir Richard Shuckburgh (1596–1656), who was seated at Upper Shuckburgh in Warwickshire, had been a member of the Long Parliament until disabled in 1644. He had been accused of delinquency on a number of occasions but had maintained that he had never assisted the royalists. According to Richard Symonds, writing in 1645, he had an estate worth £2000 p.a. (*CCAM*, 1155. *CCC*, 98, 1218. BL, Additional MSS 38,480, fols.1–18, and Harleian MSS 911, fo.36).

356 Sir Thomas Wilbraham of Woodhay, Cheshire (1601–1660) had compounded for an estate valued at £1232 p.a. Royal Oak list: (his son Sir Thomas) £3000 p.a. (S.P.23/clxxiii/93).

357 Sir Anthony Morgan (d.1665) had inherited an estate in Northamptonshire worth £1200 p.a. on the death of his half-brother Thomas who had been killed in action in 1643. Both men were Catholics who had taken up arms for the king. Sir Anthony also had property in Monmouthshire worth at least £300 p.a. In 1654 he had borrowed £3000 in order to clear his estate from sequestration and in return had undertaken to pay £600 p.a. for seven years. (C.33/229/fo.264 and 250/fo.69. *CCC*, 1898–1901).

358 This was probably Sir John Preston of Furness Abbey in Lancashire (c.1642–1663) whose royalist father had been created a baronet in

1644. His mother was Jane Morgan, one of the daughters and coheirs of Thomas Morgan of Heyford Hall (see note 357 above). The Prestons, who were a Catholic family, had property in a number of counties which was worth over £1300 p.a. Royal Oak list: (his brother Thomas) £2000 p.a. (*CCC*, 1898–1904. *CCAM*, 305, 827).

359 Sir Thomas Pope of Wroxton in Oxfordshire (1598–1668) had compounded for an estate in several counties which was valued at £1007 p.a. In April 1656 the deputy Major General for Oxfordshire testified that he had once been imprisoned by the king and was well affected. Following the death of his nephew Thomas Pope, Earl of Downe, in 1660 he succeeded to the title. (S.P.23/cxcviii/492. *CCC*, 1612).

Rutland

360 Baptist Noel, Viscount Campden (1612–1682), who was seated at Exton, had compounded for estates in various counties: £2024 p.a. in possession and £5424 p.a. in reversion. (S.P.23/lvi/fols.53–4).

361 Sir Wingfield Bodenham of Ryhall (who had been knighted in 1642) had been imprisoned for refusing to pay his composition fine but had finally submitted in 1653. His father, Sir Francis, who had died in 1645, had left an estate in Rutland, Huntingdonshire and Norfolk worth £700 p.a. which was charged with a jointure of £300 p.a. for his widow. (*CCC*, 850–2. C.33/209/fo.876).

362 Dr Clement Bretton of Uppingham had formerly been a fellow of Sidney Sussex, Cambridge and rector of Church Langton, Leicestershire. Royalist compounder: £66 p.a. (S.P.23/ccix/223, 231).

363 Richard Bullingham of Ketton had compounded for an estate valued at £163 p.a. (S.P.23/ccii/39, 41).

364 Edward Heath of Cottesmore, a barrister, was the son and heir of Sir Robert Heath (1575–1649) who had been Solicitor General and Lord Chief Justice of the Common Pleas. Royalist compounder: £916 p.a. in possession and £200 p.a. in reversion. In 1661 he was created a knight of the Bath. (*DNB* (Sir Robert Heath). S.P.23/cc/461–2).

365 Sir Thomas Mackworth of Normanton (c.1625–1694) had compounded for an estate valued at £441 p.a. in possession and £310 p.a. in reversion. This included £729 p.a. in Rutland. (S.P.23/cxcvii/859–60, 865–6).

366 This was Sir Richard Wingfield of Tickencote (c.1621–1663) who had been knighted in 1642. Royalist compounder: £427 p.a. in

possession and £180 p.a. in reversion. His son John (1652–1680) had property in Rutland and Northamptonshire worth £600 p.a. See also under Northamptonshire. (S.P.23/clxxiii/106. C.33/268/fo.841).

367 Sir Euseby or Eusebius Pelsant of Cadeby in Leicestershire, who had been Esquire of the Body to Charles I, had received his knighthood in 1645. He may possibly have compounded locally. (*CCC*, 111).

368 Arthur Warren of Whissendine had sold his estate at Simpson in Buckinghamshire since compounding. Besides his property in Rutland he had rent-charges amounting to £360 p.a. out of lands in Nottinghamshire and Staffordshire. In February 1656 it was decided that he should be exempted from the decimation tax. (*CCC*, 937–9. *CCAM*, 658–9).

Suffolk

369 This was probably Sir Edmund Pooley or Poley of Badley who had been knighted in 1646. Royalist compounder: £320 p.a. in possession and £132 in reversion. In 1655 Robert Reyce put the value of his estate at £600 p.a. Royal Oak: £1000 p.a. (S.P.23/cxc/659, 665, 667. BL, Additional MSS 15,520, fo.30).

370 Robert Gosnold of Otley had compounded for an estate valued at £253 p.a. in possession and £133 p.a. in reversion (all in Suffolk). (S.P.23/clxxxvi/872–3).

371 Sir Sackville Glemham of Little Glemham (d.1660) had been knighted in 1646. He was the son and heir of Sir Thomas Glemham (d. *circa* 1649) the royalist commander. In compounding they had valued their estates at £625 p.a. (though Sir Thomas was said to have inherited property worth over £2000 p.a.). For the Glemhams the 1650s represented a further stage in their financial decline. (*DNB* (Sir Thomas Glemham). S.P.23/cc/32, 41. BL, Additional MSS 15,520, fo.121. C.33/223/fols.391–2).

372 Dr Laurence Britton or Bretton had been rector of Hitcham. (*CCAM*, 414–5. A.G.Matthews, *Walker Revised* (1988), 329).

373 Edward Rookwood had compounded for property valued at £268 p.a. In 1651 it had been noted that his debts exceeded the capital value of his estate. (S.P.23/cxcvii/819–20, 823–5. *CCAM*, 1378).

374 Sir Henry Wood (1597–1671) had served in the royal household for many years. Royalist compounder (when described as of Hackney, Middlesex): £270 p.a. in possession and £70 p.a. in reversion. Sir Henry built up an estate (mainly in Suffolk) worth £4000 p.a. and settled at Loudham Park, near Wickham Market. (*CCC*, 2072. S.P.23/ccxiii/423. C.33/265/fo.128; 281/fo.126; and 289/fo.61).

375 For William Earl of Devonshire see also under Huntingdonshire and Other Counties.

376 Sir Daniel Deligne of Harlaxton in Lincolnshire had compounded for an estate valued at £1352 p.a. (including £375 p.a. in Suffolk). (S.P.23/lvi/fols.108–9).

377 Thomas Jermyn, who was the elder brother of Henry Lord Jermyn, had been a Groom of the Bedchamber to the Prince of Wales and a member of the Long Parliament until disabled in 1643. Royalist compounder: £3610 p.a. in various counties. (*CCC*, 1869–70. S.P.23/ccxvii/759).

378 Dr Edward Aylmer was a grandson of John Aylmer, Bishop of London, and the second son of Samuel Aylmer of Akenham Hall who is said to have left him an estate worth £1200 p.a. He had formerly been rector of West Hanningfield in Essex. Royalist compounder: £448 p.a. (all in Suffolk). In December 1656 his widow submitted a request that the tax (which she described as £16 p.a.) should no longer be levied. (BL, Additional MSS 5829, fo.98. S.P.23/lvi/fo.38. *CSPDom, 1656–7*, 189).

379 Of Sproughton.

380 Of Hawkedon.

381 For Sir Roger Palmer see note 255 above.

382 For Thomas Soame see also under Cambridgeshire.

383 Robert Naunton was the nephew of Sir Robert Naunton (1563-1635) who had served as Secretary of State, 1618–23, and Master of the Court of Wards, 1624–35. In 1655 Robert Reyce noted that the estate which he had inherited was said to be worth £800 p.a. (BL, Additional MSS 15,520, fo.106).

384 Henry Coke of Thorington (1591–1661) was a younger son of Sir Edward Coke the celebrated jurist. See also under Cambridgeshire and Kent.

385 The Bacons of Culford were a cadet branch of the Bacon family of Redgrave.

386 Sir William Hervey of Ickworth (d.1660) had married a rich widow, Lady Penelope Gage of Hengrave, who was a recusant. In 1658 his son John acquired an estate worth £1400 p.a. through his marriage to Elizabeth Hervey, daughter of William Lord Hervey, who had a jointure of £800 p.a. settled on her. (*CCC*, 2777. *Historical Manuscripts Commission, Eleventh Report*, Appendix, part ii, 264–5. C.33/255/fo.43).

387 William Castleton was probably a younger son of Sir William Castleton of Bury St Edmunds.

388 For Thomas Roberts see under Essex.

389 Sir John Cotton of Landwade in Cambridgeshire (1615–1689) had compounded for an estate valued at £350 p.a. After compounding

he had married Jane Hinde through whom he had acquired the
Madingley estate near Cambridge. The assessment of £50 p.a.
was presumably levied only on his Suffolk property. Surprisingly,
he does not appear in the Cambridgeshire decimation lists.
(S.P.23/clxxiii/52. *CCAM*, 558. W.A.Copinger, *The Manors of Suffolk*
(1905–11), iv, 158, 160 and v, 268–9).

390 The Barton estate, where Sir Henry had built a 'handsome' house,
is said to have been worth £300 p.a. His principal seat was at
Berechurch in Essex: see under Essex. (BL, Additional MSS 5829,
fo.100).

391 This was Dr John Crofts of Little Saxham who had been rector
of West Stow. In 1660 he was appointed Dean of Norwich.
(A.G.Matthews, *Walker Revised* (1988), 332).

392 Robert Shepherd or Shepard had been rector of Hepworth,
Suffolk. (Matthews, *op.cit.*, 344).

393 The Martins of Long Melford were a wealthy Catholic family. Sir
Roger Martin (c.1586–1657), the head of the family, had been
sequestered for recusancy. (*CCC*, 2794, 3180).

394 Thrandeston.

395 John Gordon of Brome had been rector of Oakley. (Matthews,
op.cit., 336).

396 Dr Edward Martin (d.1662), the former Master of Queens' College,
Cambridge, had been residing for some time with Henry Coke of
Thorington (note 384) who had once been a member of the
college. (*DNB*. Matthews, *op.cit.*, 84–5).

397 Lowestoft.

398 Baptist and Charles May were sons of Sir Humphrey May (1573-
1630) and Dame Judith May. The eldest son, James May, was
taxed in Hampshire: see note 184.

399 Sir Frederick Cornwallis of Brome Hall (1610–1662), a former
courtier, had been a member of the Long Parliament until disabled
in 1642. Royalist compounder: £800 p.a. in Suffolk and Norfolk.
In 1661 he was appointed Treasurer of Charles II's household and
ennobled as Baron Cornwallis of Eye. (*CCC*, 1389–90.
S.P.23/cciv/591, 599).

400 This was possibly Captain John Taylor. (*CSPDom, 1660–1*, 57).

401 'Wingrave' should read Hengrave. When compounding George
Gage had put the value of his estate at £10 p.a. but in 1650 had
volunteered the information that he had married a widow, Dame
Frances Tresham, who had brought with her jointure lands in
Northamptonshire worth £336 p.a. She was one of the daughters
of Lady Penelope Gage of Hengrave. (*CCC*, 2624).

402 Little Thurlow.

403 James Portus had been accused of serving as a chaplain in the

king's army but was apparently able to keep possession of his living of Tuddenham St Martin. (Matthews, *op.cit.*, 341).

404 This was George Pateridge of Creeting St Mary.

Sussex

405 Robert Anderson of Chichester had compounded for an estate valued at £373 p.a. (including £316 p.a. in Sussex). (S.P.23/ccv/575, 577, 586).

406 Richard Bridger of Ashurst had compounded for property valued at £40 p.a. (S.P.23/clxxiii/273).

407 Of Chidham.

408 Thomas May of Rawmere, Mid Lavant (c.1604–1655), who was a nephew of Sir Humphrey May, had been a member of the Long Parliament until disabled in 1642. During his compounding proceedings the Sussex committee had reported that the estate had been worth £500 p.a. before the outbreak of the first Civil War. Royal Oak list: (his brother John) £600 p.a. (S.P.23/clxxvi/201–3, 205, 217, 219, 223).

409 John Lewkenor of West Dean (1624–1669) had compounded for an estate valued at £459 p.a. in possession and £172 p.a. in reversion (all in Sussex). His mother, for her part, had compounded for property valued at £352 p.a. Lewkenor had subsequently acquired half the manor of Steventon in Hampshire through his marriage to an heiress (see under Hampshire). In 1661 he was created a knight of the Bath. (S.P.23/clxxxvi/578, 598, 602 and 604, and ccv/563, 567. *VCH, Hampshire*, iv, 172).

410 George Gunter of Racton had compounded for an estate valued at £254 p.a. in possession (Sussex) and £60 p.a. in reversion (Isle of Wight). (S.P.23/cxcvii/477–80. *CCC*, 1237).

411 Walter Buckland of Trotton, who was a suspected papist, had compounded for an estate valued at £320 p.a. in possession and £62 p.a. in reversion. This included £190 p.a. in Sussex. In the preliminary assessment list which appears later the value of his estate is shown as £200 p.a. Royal Oak list: £900 p.a. (*CCAM*, 1082. S.P.23/ccxii/77, 97–8).

412 In 1645 William Ryshton of Earnley had informed the Committee for Compounding that his estate was let at £137 p.a. (*CCC*, 921).

413 Of Chichester.

414 Sir William Morley of Boxgrove (1606–1658) does not appear to have compounded for his estate. In 1658 it was reported that Sir William Morley, a man of above £3000 p.a., had cut his throat. (O.Ogle, W.H.Bliss and others (eds.), *Calendar of the Clarendon State Papers in the Bodleian Library* (1892–1970), iv, 92).

415 Henry Bishop of Henfield was a younger brother of Sir Edward Bishop of Parham. In December 1655 Major General Goffe told Secretary Thurloe that he also had £200 p.a. at Islington. (*Thurloe State Papers*, iv, 344).

416 Thomas Kempe of Slindon was the second but eldest surviving son of Sir Garret Kempe (note 417). Royalist compounder: £111 p.a. (S.P.23/cxc/537).

417 Sir Garret Kempe of Slindon had compounded for an estate valued at £952 p.a. in possession and £50 p.a. in reversion (all in Sussex). The Kempes were a Catholic family and Sir Garret himself was a Church Papist. (S.P.23/ccxii/273, 277, 287, 291–6, 311–16, 319. *CCC*, 1960–1).

418 Of Chichester.

419 Of Petworth.

420 Richard Taylor of Earnley had compounded for property valued at £182 p.a. At the time of the decimation proceedings he was living at Petworth. (S.P.23/lvi/fo.159).

421 Peregrine Palmer (1605–1684), who was seated at Fairfield in Stogursey, Somerset, had been a soldier of fortune and had served as an officer in the army of Gustavus Adolphus. Royal Oak list: £1500 p.a. Later on in Charles II's reign he had an estate revenue of over £2000 p.a. (Henning, iii, 198–9).

422 John Covert of Slaugham was the nephew and eventual heir of Sir Walter Covert (d.1632) who had left estates worth £3500 p.a. Royalist compounder: £92 p.a. in possession and £3400 p.a. in reversion (including £2500 p.a. which was in the hands of trustees). In July 1656 he sought exemption from the decimation tax. He was knighted in 1660. (C.6/118/31. S.P.23/clxxiii/179. *CSPDom, 1656–7*, 24).

423 Humphrey Bishop was seated at Chilcombe in Dorset. Royal Oak list: £800 p.a.

424 Sarah Cox of Chichester had compounded for an estate valued at £110 p.a. She was the widow of William Cox, a canon and precentor of Chichester cathedral.

425 Richard Viscount Lumley (1589–c.1663) was seated at Stansted, Sussex and Lumley Castle, Durham. Royalist compounder: £1068 p.a. in Sussex and £705 p.a. in Durham. (S.P.23/lvi/fols.183–7).

426 The Carylls of West Harting were one of the leading Catholic families in Sussex. In 1633 Sir John Caryll (1583–1652), a recusant, had a rent-roll amounting to £1779 p.a. According to the compounding papers of his son John (1603–1681) the total estate revenue in the early 1650s was in excess of £2300 p.a. In the preliminary assessment list his estate is shown as £2500 p.a. (BL, Additional MSS 28,242, fols.26–7, 32–3. S.P.23/clxxiv/211, 213–14,

217, 221, 223–4, 233, 249, 251, 254–5, 257–8, 265).

427 John Ashburnham of Ashburnham Place (1603–1671) was a former courtier who engaged in moneylending activities. He had been a member of the Long Parliament until disabled in 1644. Royalist compounder: £360 p.a. In 1654 he had been arrested and imprisoned on a charge of sending money to the exiled king. In December 1655 the Council referred his case to the Major Generals who were responsible for the counties in which his estates were situated. (*DNB*. Henning, i, 552–3. S.P.23/ccvii/117. *Thurloe State Papers*, iv, 354).

428 This was Pierce Edgcumbe of Mount Edgcumbe in Devon who also appears in the Hampshire list: see note 188.

429 Of Chancton in Washington.

430 William Garway was of London and Ford, Sussex. Like his father, Sir Henry Garway, he was a merchant. Royalist compounder: £56 p.a. in possession and £120 p.a. in reversion (all in Sussex, though in 1644 he had property in other counties which was said to be worth £400 p.a). (S.P.23/cxc/814, 824–5. *CCAM*, 350. *CCC*, 1481).

431 William Coldham the elder of Stedham had compounded for property valued at £216 p.a. (but charged with £100 p.a. for his widowed daughter-in-law). (S.P.23/ccii/581, 585, 589).

432 Sir Edward Ford of Uppark in East Harting was the son and heir of Sir William Ford who had compounded for an estate valued at £579 p.a. (S.P.23/clxxiii/128).

433 This was John Caryll of West Harting: see note 426.

434 Margaret Dobell was the widow of Walter Dobell of Streat (d.1640). In 1643 her sequestered property in Lewes rape had been let at £567 p.a. Royal Oak list: (her stepson Walter Dobell) £1000 p.a. (S.P.28/218, Sussex sequestration accounts (unbound)).

435 Graffham.

436 Roffey.

Westmorland

437 Christopher Dudley of Yanwath had compounded for an estate valued at £90 p.a. in possession and £40 p.a. in reversion. (S.P.23/clxxxviii/418, 424).

438 John Dalston of Acornbank, who was the son and heir of Sir Christopher Dalston, had compounded for an estate valued at £176 p.a. in possession and £60 p.a. in reversion. Royal Oak list: £600 p.a. (S.P.23/lvi/fo.201).

439 This was John Lowther, the son and heir of Sir John Lowther (note 452). (*CCAM*, 1444).

440 Thomas Wilson of Haversham Hall had compounded for property

valued at £62 p.a. in possession and £147 p.a. in reversion. (S.P.23/lvi/fols.171–2).

441 Richard Braithwaite (c.1588–1673), who was a minor poet, was of Burneside or Burneshead in the parish of Kendal and Catterick in Yorkshire. Royalist compounder: £488 p.a. (including £188 p.a. in Westmorland). In the late 1650s, however, his estate revenue amounted to at least £1000 p.a. Royal Oak list: (his son Sir Thomas) £1500 p.a. (*DNB.* S.P.23/ccix/845–6, 855–6. C.B.Phillips, 'The Royalist Composition Papers and the Landed Income of the Gentry: A Note of Warning from Cumbria', *Northern History*, xiii (1977), 165–6).

442 This was Sir George Middleton of Leighton in Lancashire (1600–1673) who had been created a baronet in 1642. Royalist compounder: £600 p.a. (including £130 p.a. in Westmorland). (S.P.23/ccvi/767, 769, 773, 779, 793).

443 Thomas Preston of Holker in Lancashire had compounded for an estate valued at £776 p.a. (including £133 p.a. in Westmorland). (*Lancashire and Cheshire Record Series*, lxxii (1916), 88–9).

444 John Philipson of Calgarth was the brother and successor of Christopher Philipson who had compounded for an estate valued at £70 p.a. in possession and £20 p.a. in reversion. (S.P.23/clxxiii/253).

445 Sir Thomas Sandford of Howgill Castle was the son and heir of Sir Richard Sandford who survived him. He had been a member of the Long Parliament until disabled in 1644. (*CCC*, 1460).

446 This was presumably Sir Thomas Strickland (1621–1694), a Catholic, who had been knighted at the battle of Edgehill in 1642. He was the son and heir of Sir Robert Strickland (1600–1670) of Sizergh Castle, Westmorland and Thornton Bridge, Yorkshire. The Strickland estates were reputed to be worth £1000 p.a. but they had been heavily encumbered for many years. According to Sir Thomas's compounding papers the Westmorland property was worth £210 p.a. and the Yorkshire property £457 p.a. (Henning, iii, 504–6. H.Hornyold, *Genealogical Memoirs of the Family of Strickland of Sizergh* (1928), 106, 136–7. S.P.23/clxxviii/471, 475 and 477 and ccxxvii/921).

447 For Sir George Dalston see under Cumberland.

448 Bryan Taylor was of Meathop.

449 This was James Bellingham of Levens Hall (d.1680). He was the son and heir of Alan Bellingham (d.1672) who had inherited estates in a number of counties following the deaths in 1650 of his brother Sir Henry Bellingham and nephew Sir James Bellingham. According to the family's compounding papers these estates were worth £1374 p.a. Royal Oak list (Alan Bellingham): £1500 p.a.

James Bellingham left property worth £3000 p.a. (S.P.23/cxcvii/
423, 427–9, 433, 457 and ccxxx/95, 97, 98. Phillips, *op.cit.*, 166.
C.33/208/fo.99 and 275/fo.947).

450 Anthony Ducket of Grayrigg had compounded for an estate
valued at £197 p.a. Royal Oak list: (his son James) £800 p.a.
(S.P.23/cxi/807, 809).

451 Of Murton.

452 Sir John Lowther of Lowther Castle (1606–1675) had estates in
Westmorland, Cumberland and Yorkshire (but he does not appear
in the Cumberland decimation list). Royalist compounder: £1418
p.a. In 1642, however, his estate revenue had amounted to £2511 p.a.
Royal Oak list: (his son John) £4000 p.a. In 1678 he was said to have
left property worth at least £6000 p.a. (Henning, ii, 768–9. Phillips,
op.cit., 164–5. BL, Claydon House MSS (Letters) (on microfilm), letter
of Philip Lord Wharton dated 11 February 1677/8).

453 Of Underley in the parish of Kirkby Lonsdale.

454 Of Bainsbank, near Barbon.

Other Counties

455 George Warburton (c.1621–1676) had been suspected of delinquency but had managed to avoid sequestration. In January 1656,
however, Major General Worsley told Secretary Thurloe that he
was hoping to prove that he had been in arms for the king and in
March it was reported that he was to be taxed at the rate of £100
p.a. on his Cheshire property. Warburton also had an estate in
Worcestershire. In 1660 he was created a baronet. (*Thurloe State
Papers*, iv, 449–50, 639. *CCAM*, 1178–9).

456 In November 1656 Elizabeth Tredenham, the widow of John
Tredenham, related in a petition to the Council that her husband
had been taxed at the rate of £60 p.a.; that he had sought
exemption; and that the commissioners for Cornwall had recommended that his request should be granted. Royal Oak list: (his
son Joseph) £900 p.a. (*CSPDom, 1656–7*, 167).

457 Among the published papers of the Farington family there is a
receipt dated 17 January 1656/7 which records that William Farington the elder (who died in 1657) had paid £10 for his half-yearly
decimation charge. Royalist compounder: £219 p.a. Farington,
however, had grossly undervalued his estate. Royal Oak list:
(his son William) £1000 p.a. (*Chetham Society*, xxxix (1856), 117.
B.G.Blackwood, *The Lancashire Gentry and the Great Rebellion 1640–60*
(*Chetham Society*, Third Series, xxv) (1978), 119, 120. S.P.23/ccxii/409,
421).

458 William Earl of Bedford (1616–1700) had sat as an MP in the Long

Parliament before succeeding his father in 1641. During the first Civil War he had changed sides twice and had been sequestered, though only for a short period. In January 1656 the Middlesex commissioners informed him that they had assessed him at £300 p.a. for an estate worth £3000 p.a. within the county and the city of Westminster. Although he was seated at Woburn in Bedford-shire he was not apparently taxed in that county. In 1641 the total estate revenue had amounted to £8500 p.a. (*Thurloe State Papers*, iv, 406. Gladys Scott Thomson, *Life in a Noble Household* (1937), 45. *DNB*).

459 Thomas Knyvett (1596–1658) had been imprisoned in March 1643 after the suppression of the Lowestoft rising but had successfully challenged the sequestration proceedings. In December 1655 his steward informed him that the Norfolk commissioners had assessed the value of his estate at £800 p.a. and the decimation charge would therefore be £80 p.a. Knyvett made representations but in April 1656 the commissioners told the Protector that there was no evidence of his good affection to the Parliament's interest and they therefore intended to proceed. (B.Schofield (ed.), *The Knyvett Letters (1620–1644)* (1949), 32–48. BL, Egerton MSS 2717, fo.90. *CSPDom, 1655–6*, 345, 347. *Thurloe State Papers*, iv, 705).

460 This and the next two entries are derived from a bundle of depositions by Northumberland royalists taken in 1662 (S.P.28/351). Arthur Gray, who may be identified as a younger brother of Sir Ralph Gray of Chillingham, was said to have paid £15 in all.

461 Sir Edward Radcliffe testified that his estate in Northumberland had been under sequestration during the years 1646 to 1653 and that his total losses had amounted to at least £16,000. In 1663 his Northumberland estate was valued at £1781 p.a. and that of his son Francis at £1222 p.a. The decimation charge of £50 p.a. may have been assessed only on that part of the estate which had not yet been sold by the Treason Trustees; alter-natively, the commissioners may have accepted the offer of a 'voluntary' contribution. See also under Cumberland. (John Hodgson, *A History of Northumberland* (1827–1858), part 3, volume i, 324, 329–30).

462 William Strother had compounded for an estate valued at £290 p.a. in possession and £165 p.a. in reversion. In 1663 the value of his estate was returned as £510 p.a. (PRO, State Papers Supplementary, S.P.46/civ/fo.119. Hodgson, *op.cit.*, part 3, volume i, 343).

463 Peter Giffard (c.1581–1663) had been sequestered as a papist in arms and his Staffordshire property had been leased out at £800 p.a. According to the family papers the rent-roll of his Staffordshire

estate amounted to £1047 p.a. in 1655 and he was taxed at the rate of £100 p.a. The Giffards also had estates in Warwickshire and Hampshire (see note 207). Royal Oak list: (Walter Giffard) £1500 p.a. (*CCC*, 2711. Staffordshire Record Office, Giffard of Chillington MSS, D590/593, rent book (no pagination).).

464 Thomas Lord Coventry (c.1606–1661), whose father had been Charles I's Lord Keeper, was seated at Croome Court in Worcestershire. He had been suspected of delinquency for some time and had recently been taken into custody. In February 1656 the Worcestershire commissioners reported that it had been decided to tax him at the rate of £400 p.a. on the basis that he had an estate worth £4000 p.a. in the county. (*CCC*, 2892–3. *Thurloe State Papers*, iv, 546).

465 Brian Cooke (1620–1661), a lawyer, had joined with his father in compounding for an estate valued at £1188 p.a. (all in Yorkshire). According to his brother George the decimation tax cost him £150 which suggests that his assessment was £100 p.a. Although the Cookes had sustained heavy financial losses they were able to buy an estate at Wheatley, near Doncaster, which became the family seat. (S.P.23/cxc/561–2, 565–8, 571–2, 589, 591. *CCAM*, 704–8. Joseph Hunter, *South Yorkshire* (1828, 1831), i, 55, 58–9).

466 After the Restoration the government was informed that Thomas Crompton had paid £32 for 'his decimation'. This was presumably the annual charge. Royalist compounder: £360 p.a. in possession and £100 p.a. in reversion (all in Yorkshire). (*CSPDom, 1660–85, Addenda*, 60. S.P.23/ccviii/430, 432, 436, 446).

467 The Yorkshire commissioners forwarded information about the Earl of Devonshire's assessment in January 1656. See also under Huntingdonshire and Suffolk. (*CSPDom, 1655–6*, 124).

468 Michael Warton (1623–1668), whose father had been killed while fighting for the king, succeeded his grandfather, Sir Michael Warton, in October 1655. The latter had compounded for an estate valued at £2821 p.a. (including £2096 p.a. in Yorkshire). Among the estate papers of Michael Warton there is a receipt dated 22 December 1656 which records the payment of £111 16s 4d as his half-yearly decimation charge for the Yorkshire property. (S.P.23/clxxxvii/283, 289, 291, 303, 305, 310. *CCC*, 955–8. Yorkshire Archaeological Society, Archer-Houblon Collection, DD42A/107).

469 Sir George Wentworth of Woolley (c.1600–1660) had been a member of the Long Parliament until disabled in 1642. Royalist compounder: £936 p.a. (all in Yorkshire). Among his estate papers there is a receipt dated 31 December 1655 for the payment of £35 15s od 'for ye tenth parte of his Reall Estate at Woolley and

elsewhere within this County of Yorke'. In view of the date this was clearly for half a year. At his death he left an estate worth some £1200 p.a. (S.P.23/cxcix/117–18, 121, 133, 137, 139, 141, 151. Brotherton Library (University of Leeds), Wentworth of Woolley MSS. The decimation tax receipt has the reference MS.Dep.1946/1/16(4)).